```
PN        Clifton, N. Roy,
1995        1909-
C54
1983      The figure in film
                             71797
```

DATE			

The Figure in Film

N. Roy Clifton
has also written

The City Beyond the Gates
  A Children's Allegory, 1972

Moments in a Journey
  Selected Verse, 1983

The Figure in Film

N. Roy Clifton

An Ontario Film Institute Book

Newark: University of Delaware Press
London and Toronto: Associated University Presses

Associated University Presses, Inc.
4 Cornwall Drive
East Brunswick, N.J. 08816

Associated University Presses Ltd.
25 Sicilian Avenue
London WC1A 2QH, England

Associated University Presses
2133 Royal Windsor Drive
Unit 1
Mississauga, Ontario, Canada L5J 1K5

Library of Congress Cataloging in Publication Data

Clifton, N. Roy, 1909–
    The figure on film.

    Bibliography: p.
    Includes indexes.
    1. Moving-picture plays—History and criticism.
I. Title.
PN1995.C54   1983   791.43′01′5   80-54539
ISBN 0-87413-189-8

Printed in the United States of America

Allusion, simile and metaphor can succeed in the printed and spoken word. . . . The motion picture has no use for them, because it itself is the event. It is too specific and final to accept such aids.

Terry Ramsaye, *A Million and One Nights*

The novel, moreover, makes use of such literary devices as tropes, which have no counterpart in the experience of film.

Roy Paul Madsen, *The Impact of Film*

Contents

Foreword

Authors of books about motion pictures know how difficult it is to describe scenes from motion pictures; not visual happenings, but their meanings and how these meanings are achieved. At times, description seems beyond words! It appears to be so because grammar and vocabulary seem to be lacking. The cinema should not depend upon words to make its meanings clear, which perhaps is only right, and words therefore cannot always be found for cinematic meanings. Those writers who have ventured into the semantics of cinema in an attempt to say what the meanings are have usually been so obscure that most readers have found little to reward them in their search for an understanding of signs and symbols and semiotics, the latter being the presently fashionable term. It is at times frustrating for writers to find that what the director and his camera and the animator with his drawings can accomplish so quickly and easily in visual terms requires pages of print to explain in literary terms. Spottiswoode, who wrote *A Grammar of the Film,* made an important beginning, but, many of the cinema's literary fellow travelers have created a wilderness of abstraction.

In film technique there are hundreds of uses of metaphor, simile, abstractions, recurrences, similarities and differences, subverbal levels, and things in context. Roy Clifton has spent a lifetime studying and analyzing the figure in film, and in this book he has not only described the terms in a logical and well-organized pattern but also illustrated them by bringing to life the scenes from motion pictures that represent the various uses of the figures. He ranges over many kinds of films from different countries, and few readers who are cinema enthusiasts will be able to resist the urge to rediscover the films of their lifetimes and to think anew of the meanings that are a part of their expression. This painstaking and lengthy study teaches so much in a manner that is both fascinating and exciting. Just as it is a constant challenge to filmmakers to devise figures in their films, so is it a challenge for audiences to recognize them. This book should stimulate both artists and audiences into the greater awareness of the depth and range of visual language in the cinema.

Gerald Pratley

Ontario Film Institute
Toronto

Acknowledgments

I must thank the staff of the Ontario Film Institute, not only for allowing me the free use of its excellent reference library, but for the unfailing patience and care with which they responded to all my requests.

I am grateful to the copyright holders, acknowledged beside the stills, for the use of the stills to which their names are attached, and to Christopher Chapman, John Halas, Keith Learner, and Richard Williams for their trouble in supplying stills from their films. I also greatly appreciate the assistance of the National Film Archive Stills Library (London) in finding and obtaining reproductions of something over half of the stills I have used.

Finally, I wish to thank Faber and Faber Ltd, London, and Random House Inc., New York, for permission to quote from "The Express" by Stephen Spender, which appears in *Collected Poems* (Faber) and *Selected Poems* (Random); and to the Canadian Radio-Television Commission for permission to quote from the statement by Ted Kotcheff before the Symposium on Television Violence.

The Figure in Film

Part I

Preliminaries

1

Introduction

1 The Approach

A *trope* is said to be a way of using words that alters the common meaning of the words used, their inwardness, while a *scheme* changes the common way of putting words together, their outer arrangement. But writers have disagreed on the meaning of the terms, and some doubt if the distinction is valid or even valuable,[1] for can any change in arrangement be quite without effect upon the meaning? Especially in the phrase *figures of rhetoric, figure* has been used as including both *trope* and *scheme*.[2] Not only is this convenient; it is a route round a distinction of little value in film.

Many figures copy and refine the ways in which men and women are prone to speak in the grip of strong feeling, with exaggerations, unfinished sentences, like-nesses, repetitions. Those who heard an actor or orator took him to be feeling the emotion, of which the mimicked form was both apt and pleasing in itself.[3] Will the filmic analogues have a like effect? This I leave the reader to answer from his or her experience.

This book, which has grown from an article written over thirty years ago, is an inquiry whether figures can be found in film, and what is their character there.[4] It is necessary to start with the names for established figures; and where analogues to these figures occur, to use the same term for a similar form both in film and litera-ture, is clearly an economy of thought.

On the contrary, to come to such an inquiry with a bag of terms and the theories they presuppose is to risk using the films to justify notions held beforehand, rather than let the films form the notions. I have striven to use the smallest number of technical terms, and those least colored by theory, and in this way to eschew jargon, the sclerosis of critical style.[5] Where I find, however, that clearness is best served by using a term, I admit it with reluctance and say what I take it to mean.

I prefer to write of what I see on the screen, ignoring the technical means that placed it there. If I seem to approach a person or thing, it is no concern of mine that the camera taking the picture may have been carried by a dolly, a crane, a track, or a shoulder. It is immaterial for my purpose, for example, that the shot of the sea from the crashing plane in *Foreign Correspondent* (Alfred Hitchcock; special effects by William Cameron Menzies) was taken from the nose of an airplane, projected onto a paper screen in the studio, and that at the supposed moment of striking the sea, a tankful of water erupted through the screen and onto the fleeing pilots in a model cockpit built in the studio. For me, as a viewer, it is an approaching shot of the sea.

I have circumscribed in the title a narrow suburb of the art of film. Even so, of the thousands of films made, no large part can be seen in the leisure time of a teacher. Of the much smaller number made with more than common imagination, I have seen a larger proportion, but at best the book is based on samples. Since however these are drawn from a number of countries and from nearly fifty years of filmgoing, I hope I have touched on all the important figures to be found in film, and their principal applications.

2   Creative Memory

Logicians, legal counsel, and film critics agree that "The line of demarcation between imagination and memory . . . is sometimes hard to draw,"[6] and that "all observation is fallible, even our own."[7] Jonathan Rosenbaum speaks of "creative memory"[8] and Noël Burch of "my own capacity for making up things after the film is over."[9] The full meaning of a shot is often clear only after it has left the screen, and the meaning we give it reconstructs our memory of what we saw. When on later viewings I have not been able to find a shot in the form in which I remembered it, it has thrown some doubt on all impressions formed on a single viewing. As against this, frames are sometimes lost when breaks are spliced, collectors mutilate, and films are abridged for television with little concern for directors' nuances.

I had often praised a striking down shot of a large city square, overlaid with a texture of moveless umbrellas, except where a line was jolted across it by the flight of an assassin underneath the surface. Yet, on last seeing the film, there was no long down shot, and no more than four umbrellas were jogged, leaving Alfred Hitchcock with a surplus of undue credit *(Foreign Correspondent)*.

In such a book as this, however, creative memory is more forgivable than it may be elsewhere. If what I describe is filmically possible, it still illustrates my point, and may even flatter the director. William Empson remembered a line of Rupert Brooke's as

The keen
Impassioned beauty of a great machine

which much impressed him as a "daring but successful image." Having occasion to look the line up, Empson found that Brooke had written instead "unpassioned," which struck him as "intellectually shoddy," "impassioned" having come from his creative memory.[10] I hope that few cases of this will be found in the present book. The reader can at least be assured that I shall cite from no film I have not seen, without so saying.

3   Intention

Viewers must, in general, assume that what they find in a film is intended by the director.[11] To do otherwise would be a slight, even though the viewer may harbor doubts. Vanderhof hurls a dart across the frame. In the next shot, at the time and place where the dart would have landed, and about the size of the dart, is a cigar in the mouth of A. P. Kirby. It was as if Vanderhof had shut Kirby's mouth up with his dart, and considering what he has had to say of Kirby and his views, it could be taken as a witty carry-over, conveying Vanderhof's irritation. The film as a whole, however, in shooting as well as acting, can only be described as trite as well as stagey (running to the most conventional character stereotypes), and the suspicion arises that this one touch of film was an editorial accident. On principle, nonetheless, it must be considered as an example of substitution, a form of anadiplosis, and credit must be given (*You Can't Take It with You*, Frank Capra).

4 Theatrical and Filmic

What is meant by filmic, as against theatrical? Christian Metz proposed five "circles of specificity," the first including characteristics found in the greatest number of other arts, and the fifth including characteristics nearly unique to film.[12] I have adapted these circles to distinguish only theater:

Common to Theater and Film	i.	*It requires a picture that must be composed.* So does theater, painting, sculpture, photography, comic strips, television.
	ii.	*Its pictures move and are accompanied by sound appropriate to what it shows.* True also of theater and television.
Unique to the Film	iii.	*Its pictures are mechanical reproductions.* So are those of television and photography. This enables the use of such effects as angle, dissolves, negative image, focus, dissociation of sound from source, multiple images, camera movement, and so on.
	iv.	*Its mechanically produced pictures can be edited in any order of succession.* So can those of television. This gives rise to montage.

From this it will appear that theater uses means like the movement and grouping of persons, and dialogue or natural sound; film uses these means as well as changing the viewer (in changing the camera) to various vantage points, distorting the image, adding sound not belonging to the image, and placing any image in succession to any other.

5 Overlap

A figure cannot be treated in isolation from other figures. Antithesis is discussed, not merely in the chapter of that name but also under montage, which can often be antithetical. To treat ellipsis fully, anadiplosis must be considered there, as well as in the chapter devoted entirely to it. This will remind the reader that an image may combine several figures, or be seen as different figures from different viewpoints. To locate all examples of a given figure, the reader should use the index.

6 The Inaccessibility of the Film

It is easy to read a poem again, at once or after digestion: few people sit through two showings of a film. Even in larger cities, a film is unlikely to come back after its first showings; certainly not at a time you wish to see it. Television revives unexpected films, often abridged or with edges cropped, sequences, or even two parts of a carry-over, separated by commercials, which, if the theory of montage is sound, must give some curious twists to a director's intentions, and, at the very least, regular dollops of unscripted suspense. I have seen the soldiers report to Herod that all the children had been killed: "Not one is left alive." But before our fears are allayed by seeing the infant Jesus carried away by his parents along a road lined with crucified rebels, a montage intervenes. I then heard of a pill that puts more pain reliever into the bloodstream, of something that is definitely *not* an aerosol hair spray, of a child who wonders why his mother wears the particular bra she does, and after a welcome reassurance that we would return to *The Greatest Story Ever Told* after these announcements, of a beverage with a thousand natural flavors, of a dried soup that was better than canned soup, and then, after the soup, the infant Jesus among the crucified. With the greatest respect for people's ability to turn off when they don't wish to listen, I must conclude first, that advertisers—on good grounds—assume that most of us do not; secondly, that this is not the ideal exposure for any serious artistic work.

To reread a poem that baffles at first sight can be most rewarding, and as a poet once said to me, a philosopher can surely be allowed to write poems for other philosophers. The likelihood, however, of a film's being seen only once,[13] the high cost of making films and the need for a wide unscholarly circulation to recover the cost deny the philosopher-director the indulgence of obscurity, and impose the discipline of clarity at first sight.[14] Regardless of what further depths may be found by the few who may see it again, if a figure in a film fails to reach its meaning to most of its viewers while they are watching, it may as well not be there.

7 Content

This book is on form, and examples have been chosen, when apt, regardless of content; yet I am clear that form is a tool and only content can justify what it costs a community to make a film. In a practical view, content is a film's effect on the viewer, in reinforcing old ways of acting or shaping new ones, and the worth of the content is what it adds to peace, to the understanding, or tolerance of others, and to the viewer's ability to achieve the highest kind of life of which he is capable. In this view I am not alone; but since the matter is peripheral here, I must merely refer the reader to other sources.[15]

A statement often made and easily refuted, that films have no effect on what we do, continues to paralyze constructive action. The refutation of this view began at least as far back as the Payne Fund Studies in 1933.[16]

The Royal Commission on Violence in the Communications Industry (Ontario 1976) points out how widely violence permeates what is seen on television, and sets out what investigation has established. Seeing violent acts on film and television has been shown to cause expectations of violence, to teach techniques of assault and other crimes, to give rise to violent acts through imitation, to lend prestige to individual criminals, to increase tolerance of violence or insensitivity to it, in ourselves and in others, and to worsen social situations by distorting reality.[17] It has been known for some time that children tend to accept as true what they see on the screen.[18]

The report moreover points out that the theory of catharsis is not considered valid. By this theory, our proneness to violence is satisfied by seeing violence inflicted, and we are less likely to show aggression ourselves. On the contrary, most studies agree that the more violence we see in the media, the more violent our acts become. The report notes too the approval and encouragement of brutal acts implicit in their often going unpunished, and from not showing the consequences in physical pain and lifelong handicaps. The director of research raises the question whether society should be given its choice between antisocial (self-destructive) and prosocial programming.[19]

Barry Wiles reports a case that shows not only how strong an effect a single showing may have but also the kind of change that prosocial films might bring about. Under war conditions, petty theft was rife among children. After the showing of a Children's Film Foundation picture on "stealing by finding," managers of theaters in which it ran complained of their offices becoming lost property rooms.[20]

If it pays advertisers to spend considerable sums to show over and over, on the television screen, people using their products, believing that what the viewers have seen they will imitate, it should occur to a reasonable person that it is even more likely that viewers will do themselves what they see done in the longer screen time given to entertainment films.[21]

There is also what Christian Metz calls the form of the content.[22] Ivor Montagu has written [23] that the pleas of those who make sadistic scenes (or pornographic ones, he could add) are hollow and, very often, hypocritical: "it is no more necessary to depict actual physical images of blood in order to show the callousness of crooks, politicians, and strategists, than it is to show images of copulation in order to study the human torments and complications of love . . . Sometimes, the phenomenon . . . is all the stronger, all the more expressive and poignant, all the more effectively and unforgettably portrayed, when it is not shown at all"—when it is shown, that is to say, by figurative means. There is murder in *Cry the Beloved Country* (Zoltan Korda), yet the film arouses compassion in us, never aggression. There are street-walkers in *Turn the Key Softly* (Jack Lee), but their lack of glamour, not their appeal, impresses us. *Breaking the Sound Barrier* (David Lean) pits man against the physical universe, giving the widest scope to human courage and imagination; it grips us to the end; and yet there is no villain, no malice, no man against man.

It is not merely that many films like *Deadfall* (Bryan Forbes) are much ado about no one of any importance—high-class thieves in this case—about whom we could hardly care less; but others like *Black Moon* (Louis Malle) dehumanize people to emotionless automata, and after seeing them, our own feelings are chilled. Even a film so beautifully made as *Himiko* (Masahiro Shinoda) depicting the assassination, torture, and intertribal slaughter that we are led to believe were daily life in third-century Japan, gouges every ounce of agony out of tattooing around the eyes or drawing fingernails, while awakening in the spectator surprisingly little sympathy for "the martyrdom of man." It merely conditions us to accept more easily the cruelty it vividly pictures.

On the other hand, the most humane of messages will reach but few, if the maker is not fully versed in the means at his command, and is timely in using them. *Not Wanted* (Elmer Clifton), is about a girl with unsympathetic parents who falls in love and is left with an illegitimate child. The film shows what help she found, her placing of the child, and a later happy marriage. The intention could not have been better, but the film was mediocre and unimaginative. Its first run was not well attended, and I have not seen it since.

I once saw on the same day Alfred Hitchcock's *Murder* and Ingmar Bergman's *Winter Light*—important themes in both, the hanging of an innocent woman and a clergyman's loss of belief in God. I wrote on Bergman's form two sentences—it was simple and unobtrusively apt; on Hitchcock's I wrote two pages—his was clever. But Hitchcock never made me feel what it was like to await the day of one's hanging, or the passionate obsession that led Fane to murder or Sir John to prove the innocence of which he was sure. As in *The Birds*, Hitchcock had no concern to understand or explain. But the inner agonies of Bergman's people kept recurring to me, long after *Murder* had left my mind. Hitchcock is like the boy in *The Silence* (Ingmar Bergman), who breaks into a roomful of dwarfs, points his pistol at them, and makes nasty noises, at which they obligingly fall down. To neither the boy nor Hitchcock are people human beings, with concerns, dilemmas, feelings, history or philosphy; to Hitchcock they are not men but chessmen, bits of a composition or montage that intrigue him, merely the digits needed in solving a technical problem.[24]

The Do It Yourself Cartoon Kit (Keith Learner) makes the satiric point that in the motion-picture chase, anything can chase anything else—the structure creates the excitement. The film shows people and vehicles in hot pursuit, then a crowd of matches chasing one that escaped, some straggling and falling, black figures running frantically round a red vase, and some bits of paper trying to catch others (pl. 23). Now, if a director of skill and imagination can hold our interest, no matter what the topic, why is the topic so often murder and maiming, or sex without civility, when we know that the more we see of this, the more it will happen?

The day I am writing this, a film is advertised in these words; "Raping, Burning, Hanging, Shooting, Stomping, Scalping, Whipping." It is hard to believe that twice in the last century, people have been willing to die to preserve the culture that gave us this film.

Form is not enough.

2
The Trope and Its Translation

1 The Trope Is a Human Trait

The men of the Altamira who doomed their prey by painting on cave walls the boar and bison they hunted, the Ojibway who brought pain to an enemy's body by piercing a carving of him, and the Pharaoh who crossed his breast with flail and crook, to show unlettered men that he ruled their crops and flocks were wielding tropes or figures, for these are as old as man. The single stone of the medieval altar was the oneness of Christendom and the five crosses on it, the five wounds of Christ.

We feel pleasure on seeing writing we know on an envelope; we learn of growth and cultivation from a single farm or garden. The mother in *Virgin Spring* (Ingmar Bergman) hugged the dead body of her daughter. The old man in *Diary of a Chambermaid* (Luis Buñuel) went to bed with a pair of ladies' high-buttoned boots. Sucksdorf reveals the Lapps by showing us one old man and a boy, dreaming in springtime *(The Wind in the West)*. We live in figures, and breach our bounds of space-time by the tool of metonymy.

> To name an object is to suppress three quarters of the poem's pleasure . . . to suggest it, that is the dream.[1]

An image or picture is vivid, cogent, and memorable. Writers and orators have always known this; common speech concedes it; it would be strange if directors ignored it. "Why, man, he doth bestride the narrow world Like a Colossus," and here is Caesar, one leg either side the harbor gap, and men in ships tilting their heads to catch his distant disregarding glance. In common speech, word spreads "like a house afire".

Hamlet speaks in the compact metaphor

> O, that this too too solid flesh would melt,
> Thaw and resolve itself into a dew,[2]

as if his flesh were ice. The gangster, too, in metaphor, "rubs out" people as easily as chalk or pencil.

Macbeth's hand would

> The multitudinous seas incarnadine,
> Making the green one red.[3]

23

Deep feelings demand huge hyperboles. So may wit: it was said of a comedian's out-of-tune fiddle, that you could rope a heifer with the slack in his G-string.

Things are made into persons. A cynic poet wrote, "Gold . . . can pocket states, can fetch and carry Kings"; or as we say every day, "Money talks."

2 The Verbal Figure Translated

Consider the translation of "Beaded bubbles winking at the brim" into film. How regular or continuous would bubbles have to be to suggest beads without ceasing to look like bubbles too? How even in size? From what angle should we see them? Down, showing the whole beaded circle? From the side, showing only a few beads through the glass? These problems do not arise in reading. The poet's imagination supplied a beadedness that must have been incomplete in the bubbles he remembered; and our imaginations too, responding to the word, supply in size and regularity, the beadedness needed. The "winking" I believe comes when we move our eye from a vanished bubble to one still whole, thus creating a winking, as if a bubble had burst and returned. The winking is in our perception, and any filmic jugglery cannot capture this. As we read we turn words into sounds and images. The effect is not the same when we are given a finished image instead of words.

It has been tried. At a point in Goofy's adventures "the curtain of night" suddenly drops as if from the flies and begins glittering with stars (*Saludos Amigos*, Walt Disney). "A pretty face comes your way," says the owl in *Bambi* (Walt Disney and David D. Hand). "You are knocked for a loop." He falls backward around the branch one full circle. In *Donald's Dilemma* (Jack King) "The tears welled up in her eyes." The Duck Girl's pupils, as if they were glass bowls, filled half up with green water. When Donald was angry, three ducks bounced in a triple tantrum: he was "beside himself" (*Trombone Trouble*, Walt Disney).

In *Henry Aldrich Gets Glamour*, (Hugh Bennett) a young man pretends at the telephone to ask a movie star to come to a dance with him. Before he can read a fake telegram to explain her nonarrival, she steps off the train and kisses him as if she had known him for years. His fellow-conspirator Dizzy knocks his fists against his forehead in disbelief, and the whole scene begins to swirl past faster and faster—a suggestion of Dizzy's mind being "in a whirl."

Even with serious intent, a secondhand literary likeness seems to us no less hackneyed for being conveyed in images instead of words. In Abel Gance's *La Roue*, as a visitor laughs at the slow climb of the cog wheel car as it climbs a mountain, a snail is superimposed on it—a commonplace of tongue and pen for centuries. The practice of quoting and picturing epigraphs often seems to us forced. The wheel that gives its name to *La Roue* does not come from the trains that are part of the setting; it is the one referred to in epigraphs from Victor Hugo, Rudyard Kipling, and others, "the Great Wheel which does not move without crushing someone." But whether the rotating wagon wheel seen at the start or the several shots of a circle of peasant dancers that bring up the rear of the film add much to the message is open to doubt.

Imperfect translation of a verbal figure can be found in *Distant Thunder* (Satyajit Ray). During a famine that killed five million people, three times we see a shot of yellow clay, whose tenants are two orange butterflies, but not a trace of green. In a context of famine, we think of drought. It was said in a line of dialogue that rice had been shipped to the soldiers fighting in Burma, but while we never see a paddy-field at harvest, showing its abundance or any shipment out of the village, the implication of the barren clay makes a strong impression. Satyajit Ray said in an interview that, while waiting to shoot, he had noticed the butterflies and saw them as an image of nature's indifference to human suffering, "butterflies dancing while men starved."[4] Now, seen from above, their feet were hardly to be noticed, and their wings fluttered little, even less than the normal instability of butterflies' wings. In words a striking antithesis, the image tends to translate in context, not into "dancing butterflies," but "barren harvest."

Film figures must free themselves from the word.

Part II

Figures of Association

Symbol or Significant Object

1 Things with Meanings

Someone crossing a desert passes a skull: we think of death. There are not here the four parts of a simile: *Caesar* dominates the Roman *world* as the *Colossus* bestrode the *harbor-entry* at Rhodes. And yet there is a figure, for the skull has a meaning beyond itself. It is a thing that suggests an idea. It never ceases to be what it is, a skull that lies on the sand; it is diegetic, part of the situation in which the characters are acting; but by having a meaning beyond being part of the setting, it enriches the story. To make the mere things of a story glow with its meanings, this is the work of the symbol. There is more agreement on the meaning of symbol than on that of many terms, but significant object, or things with meanings, are synonyms that may help to anchor the use of the word in this chapter.

2 Analogies in Other Arts

Using the eloquence of things is not new. Imposed by cultures where few could read, it is still to be preferred in film, as more vivid than words. In scene six of *Marriage à la Mode*, Hogarth paints in things the pitiful end of the marriage. There is no carpet, the chair is upset, a jug is lying on the floor, picture frames are black, not gilt, a dog has paws on the table and is eating the pig's head set there, and the dog's ribs are showing. (A pig's head was the cheapest meat a butcher provided.) The husband was nowhere to be seen, and the wife's father was taking the ring from his dying daughter's finger.

In Athol Fugard's play, *Hello and Good-Bye*, Johnny Smit's father had lost a leg and was bedridden. Until his father's death, Johnny had been at his father's call, day and night. After the father's death, Johnny kept running in with "Wilson's Beef and Wine" and on other imaginary errands, to give himself some reason for living. Johnny and his sister, a prostitute, search for their father's money, but all they find is reminders: photographs, an accumulation of unused left shoes, a smock of hers, shoes her mother would not let her wear, a dress—"It smells like mother." Johnny starts walking round on his father's crutches, "It's so easy to walk with crutches." Johnny has never worked; serving his father had given his life meaning. Now, on his father's crutches, he will tell a tale and beg. His need for money, and his need for self-excuse, combine to make Johnny a psychological cripple, of which the crutch is the visible sign.

3 Theatrical Uses

Picture, mime, costume, and situation are common to film and theater. The workers in *Metropolis* (Fritz Lang), one column trudging mechanically out as another enters, bent, keeping step, faceless with eyes on the ground, all wearing the same cap and overalls, are the director's image of industrial man. The jealous Himiko has Takehiko tortured, and kneels beside him, stretches out her arms, and with lithe movements of wrists and fingers, her hands become a quickly twisting wormy mass: "Little creatures have cured him," she says (*Himiko,* Masahito Shinoda). The stern doctrinaire soldier becomes a happy smiling woman, as she nurses her White Russian captive back to health, after they are wrecked on an island. She hears with wonder his stories from books she had never heard of. Bare legs and feet, skirt and loose hair have taken the place of uniform and rifle (*The Forty-First,* G. Chukhrai). A secretary who is discharged puts her hat on and goes; the new one comes and takes hers off (*The Love of Jeanne Ney,* G. W. Pabst). Chris Ford, captain of an oceangoing tug in wartime, unable to find a corkscrew, bangs down on the cork of a bottle, and the wine splashes a red stain on his white shirt. He and his guest laugh; but his wife is struck with doom, as by an omen. Two captains before him she has loved, and both have gone down with their ships (*The Key,* Sir Carol Reed).

4 Words as Objects

On occasion, a printed word may be used as an object. In *Trouble in Paradise* (Ernst Lubitsch), Madame Colet and the Major come out of her box, her purse having been stolen. His eyes are on the ground looking as he follows her through an open door. The door closes to show us the word *Dames.* Its meaning for us is not *Ladies,* nor that this is the women's washroom: it is the Major suddenly discovering where he is. He emerges furtively in haste, and observes one of the maids, glowering severely from a doorway.

5 Uses: Time

Showing the passage of time by a multiplication of cigarette butts, curled in a tray or strewn on the ground, is a common convention (*Blackmail,* by Alfred Hitchcock and a number of others). Thorold Dickinson used umbrellas for a change. Lord Derby arrived at Ten Downing Street to observe Disraeli's umbrella already in the stand. He added his own, and after a dissolve, we see it filled with umbrellas (*The Prime Minister*).

The same can be said of sheets fleeting from calendar pads, as in *City Lights* (Charles Chaplin). There is greater interest in linking the measure of time with how the time was passed. The sheet for June is superimposed on a chunk of rock: a hammer lands on the rock and the sheet falls—and so for July and August (*I Was a Fugitive from a Chain Gang,* Mervyn Leroy). Professor Rath tested the heat of Lola Lola's curling tongs on the calendar sheet for *November 27.* In close-up we see the tongs grasp and pull off *November 29, December 2, December 27,* the year *1925,* and then in larger print *1929* (*The Blue Angel,* Joseph von Sternberg).

The length of time a unit stands for may be left intentionally vague. If the guests drink up the champagne, and the butler must send for more, the loss of the key to the cellar will be discovered, and so will Devlin down there investigating. Hitchcock shows us the bottles in the cooler dwindling down from thirteen to seven, to five, to three (*Notorious*). A measure is established: zero we know is the climax. In *The Hidden Room* (Edward Dmytryk) the unit of measure is a square in a crossword puzzle. As Dr. Riordan waits for his wife to return, he lays his revolver down on a newspaper. His hands push the revolver aside and expose the crossword puzzle. Dissolve to the same scene, paper, hand, and revolver all where they were, but the blanks nearly all filled in.

It is more precise to show change in a thing whose rate of change we know. In *Ecstasy* (Gustave Machaty) we dissolve from a scene in which Eva has blown a bee from off a flower to one with pods and ripe ears of wheat, and we assume a lapse of months.

A tall, slim, gray-dressed visitor, with bifurcated beard, one hand with grip, and the other with an eloquent rolled umbrella, addressed the assembled convicts: "the object of the administration of this prison is not punishment but betterment. . . . We are therefore giving into your possession some small oaks. . . ." His voice continues as the screen shows two small trees beside the prison wall. Dissolve to three more shots of the same scene, the trees larger in each. Then to a circle of prisoners with guard and iron palings in the foreground, and a guard letting Volck through the gate, as the speech ends: "some of you will have left here by the time they reach maturity, and will have returned to the life of decent and honest members of human society" (*Passport to Heaven*, Richard Oswald).

Growth may be conferred on the ungrowing. In *Seven Days to Noon* (John and Roy Boulting) an atomic explosion was threatened in a week's time, if terms were not met. As police pursued their search, every time we saw a clock, its diameter was larger.

The opposite of growth is wear, and this too can measure time. On a closed gate is a mine-owner's notice of lockout; dissolve to the same notice, its writing gray, its edges ragged, and pan down to the men sitting beneath it (*The Stars Look Down*, Sir Carol Reed).

Mere change in style imports the passage of time, but if dates are important, the wise director adds them. A couple is dancing; pan down to legs and feet in a dance of 1911 (printed on the shot). Cut to legs and feet doing a foxtrot, with 1923 superimposed (*The Struggle*, D. W. Griffith).

6 Uses: Place

Odd Man Out is a Greek tragedy in film. Johnny McQueen, weak from months of hiding, insists against the advice of his friends on leading a robbery. His weakness frustrates the robbery and leads to his death. Unity of time and place is emphasized by our seeing and hearing a tall clock tower throughout the film. The clock is seen at the start in up shot as it strikes four. As Dennis climbs on a roof, as the cabby rids himself of the dying Johnny, the clock is there in the distance; as Kathy looks out of Father Tom's window, its face is large across the square. In the streets, at Father Tom's, and in Lukey's studio, its chime is heard. At the end, as Father Tom and Shell walk away from the dead bodies of Johnny and Kathy lying in the snow, the camera pans up to the clockface—it is twelve. Only eight hours have passed. There was no escape—after all the happenings of the day, Johnny was still within a mile of where he had murdered (Sir Carol Reed).

Film can cut from any place to any other, but something more is needed for expressing distance between. The rhythmic fall and rise of wires that sag between poles as seen from railway windows, and the rush of track down frame under the front of an engine suggest movement between (*Passport to Heaven*, Richard Oswald).

7 Uses: Environment and Class

Things quickly establish a social level. Take, for example, Kitty's room in *Scarlet Street* (Fritz Lang). She is lying on a couch, reading the magazine *Love Stories* and wearing a thin wrap with straggles of rabbit fur. She is eating grapes from a bowl that lies on the floor with an ashtray and a pile of magazines, and is spitting the seeds to a sink piled high with dirty dishes. While she talks, she thrusts a stick of gum into her mouth and drops the wrapper on the floor. On one of a row of hooks along a plank nailed on the wall a nightgown hangs; on a table across the room a phonograph plays a closed groove over and over, no one seeming concerned.

The girls in *Going Down the Road* (Don Shebib) wear their hair in curlers to an island picnic. Nearly all the time we see them out, they are eating—potato flakes, cheese sticks, popcorn—and the men's hands are hardly ever without a bottle of beer. All the furniture they have is table, bed, lamp, and television set. Our clothes and other things, and how we keep them, are like a plaster cast of what we are.

Besides the environment we choose or make, there is that which is thrust upon us. Tucker, a sharecropper, has been bold enough to buy a farm. He had overlooked the house, which he finds later is small and one-roomed. We see him shoring up the veranda roof with a piece of four-by-four. We see him catching the rain dripping from the ceiling for drinking water. The December picture on the calendar of warmly clad people riding in a sleigh shivers in the wind that finds the cracks in the wall. As we draw back, we see on the wall a forlorn little girl drawn by a child, and a shelf with three jars of preserves nearly empty, and two paper bags of cornmeal and "Family Flour," the empty tops curled nearly to the bottom. The curtains are clearly made from bags, for the printing did not quite wash out. The walls on two sides are papered with news. Metal plates and cups are laid on the bare table. When the dog was given his share of the trapped opossum, we saw the gaps between the boards of the floor (*The Southerner*, Jean Renoir).

8 Uses: Character

The callousness of Lacombe Lucien (the French country lad who joined the Gestapo) is shown by his killing a yellow bird from a window by slingshot, and by his shooting all the rabbits in sight with his father's gun. When the boy looks in at a door, and sees a fellow officer pushing the head of his village schoolmaster under water, he walks out with no sign of emotion, and a dog lying beside the door yawns. We transfer the yawn to Lucien—just part of the day's routine (*Lacombe Lucien*, Louis Malle).

What does Abel Gance make of Napoleon? He often shows Napoleon alone in the frame: once as a boy, for example, sent outside by his teachers for fighting, another time in Paris seated at a table, listening to the mob in the street, or, in the final sequence, projected on three screens, while the side screens are alive with men in hand-to-hand conflict, only his head seen in the center screen, calm and self-possessed, superimposed on a turning globe of the world. The impression from these and many other shots of Napoleon alone is of a man self-contained, ever weighing people and possibilities, always in command of himself and others (*Napoleon*).

What does Pudovkin make of Kerensky? He puts him on a huge stage, with trumpeters blowing a fanfare (pomposity). He is seen with plump smiling women, who wear kid gloves (ladies' man). We see the clapping of hands (love of applause). A factory owner stands beside him, speaking for him (tool of the capitalists). The stage is adorned with well-dressed people (one of the bourgeoisie) *(The End of Saint Petersburg).*

Characterization may run to caricature, as in Eisenstein's, or perhaps it was Aleksandrov's, go at Kerensky.[1] He is shown marching up a wide staircase, followed by two aides-de-camp a dozen steps behind him. "Minister of the Army," says a title. He goes up a second flight, "Minister of the Navy"; and a third flight, "Prime Minister"; and fourth "Etc., etc." (pl. 13). Intercut with these is a statue holding out a laurel wreath. It is as if Kerensky saw himself constantly rising to stations of greater and greater grandeur. He shakes a Czarist officer's hand at ludicrous length; and members of the attendant bourgeoisie leer approvingly. He hesitates in front of a tall double door. Close-ups of his hands twisting one of his gloves uncertainly alternate with six shots of a peacock, spreading its tail, erecting its head, swirling round, and otherwise prideful. Kerensky and a statue of Napoleon are intercut, both with arms folded in the same way, followed by straight ranks of glasses, decanters, and toy soldiers. It is fairly clear what the director thinks of Kerensky, though the vehemence of the attack defeats its intention, and amuses more than convinces: we are indeed sorry for Kerensky: he could not possibly have been as conceited, we think, as the director made him *(October).*

9   Uses: Inner States

As distinct from character, passing states have been shown in three ways: first, by what a character does with something; second, by how the character responds to something; third, by what a director does with something.

In the first of these, the thing manipulated may stand by metonymy for a person or situation the notion of which is emotionally saturated. After Hans has suffered a heart attack, he and Irmgard make up a quarrel and he plays a record that reminds him of happy times they spent together. Some days later he grows morose and will not eat with the others. He stops the record playing, breaks it, but holds it on his knee *(The Merchant of the Four Seasons,* R. W. Fassbinder).

Margaret Hammond cannot forget her dead husband enough to marry Frank Machin. Coming home from an evening with Frank, her hand strokes the fur of the coat he has given her. She then kneels in front of the grate of her stove, its ashes dead and white. An image of her divided feelings *(This Sporting Life,* Lindsay Anderson).

The thing may have a meaning for us of which the manipulator is unaware. Colonel Nicholson leans over the rail of the bridge he had designed, and his men, British prisoners of war, had built. He speaks, partly to Colonel Saito who stands near him. "I realize sometimes that I am nearer the end than the beginning, and I ask myself . . . whether anything I have done has made any difference." And then his swagger stick, a symbol of command, falls from his hands to the river, strikes the surface, and is lost. It was his lack of doubt as to what his duty was as a commanding officer, and his will to carry it out, that had enabled him to defy Colonel Saito's pressures to do what he felt unconscionable. And now, with his doubts, the stick drops from his hands *(The Bridge on the River Kwai,* David Lean).

On his first morning in Sir William Beeder's flat, Gulley Jimpson rises from bed and wraps himself in an eiderdown, which rises behind his head like the high collar of a bulky chasuble. He advances with stately movement, rises up on a bench, and with ritualistic dignity, draws on the white sacrificial wall the first stroke of his mural, a vertical charcoal line. The artist as the voice of God (*The Horse's Mouth*, Ronald Neame).

In *The Face of Another* (Hiroshi Teshigahara), a man wearing a plastic mask because of severe burns to his face, makes love to his wife after picking her up at a railway station. He calls her a prostitute, and she weeps. "Surely you know I can recognize you by other things than your face." At this, he stops pulling off his plastic mask, the lower half loose over his mouth and jaw, the upper half tight: the grotesque look of a man secure neither of what he was nor what he is.

A ventriloquist's dummy, Hugo, seems to take on an independent life, uttering rude remarks to his master, Maxwell Frere, and expressing a preference for Sylvester Kee, another ventriloquist. Frere takes to drink. At last after "smothering" Hugo, he tramples him to dust. When Kee visits Frere in a mental hospital, Frere, mute since being admitted, now smiles vacantly, and says, in Hugo's voice, "Hello, Sylvester, I've been waiting for you." Two conflicting feelings toward a fellow performer, jealousy and admiration, one of them uncontrollably projected on Hugo Fitch (*Dead of Night*, Alberto Cavalcanti).

The thing may have no significance in itself, but may merely be the handiest means of expression. During Bertha-Marie's affair with Artinelli, she twice opens up the flap of her purse and conceals her face from us (*Variety*, E. A. Dupont). The doctor standing by Margaret's bed says, "She's gone." Machin rises. "No, she's not" he says doggedly, once, and twice, and on a third vehement "No," pounds with his angry fist a spider he sees on the wall (*This Sporting Life*, Lindsay Anderson). Four drivers and the manager watch closely, as a truck is loaded with liquid nitroglycerin. One carrier trips on the gangway, but recovers himself. There is an offscreen sound of breaking glass. The camera pans to Bimba, one of the drivers. He looks down, and the camera follows his glance to show on the ground a broken wineglass, shattered by his clenched fingers (*The Wages of Fear*, Henri-Georges Clouzot).

In the second place, a character may not use a thing, but may, in responding to it, reveal a state of mind. A wardrobe creaks open toward us. We see, as Tony does, in an up oblique shot, a military greatcoat, as if a soldier stood there facing out. It was his new foster father's. Tony backs up, and with tears in his eyes, runs from the house. He had clearly suffered ill-treatment from someone in uniform (*The Divided Heart*, Charles Crichton). In *Miracle in Milan* (Vittorio de Sica), a sullen crowd watches richly clad people arrive in cars at the theater. Toto smiles, puts his bag down, and claps for them. He thinks they are beautiful. For him their clothes are not a symbol of wealth and cause for envy. He is perfectly happy with what little he has, and thus can enjoy the elegance of the rich as much as they themselves.

Third are things that reveal feelings, thoughts or bodily states that characters are unaware of or choose to conceal, or ones a director wishes to draw attention to.

Thoughts and feelings. As Captain Cantrip and Lady Franklin ride in the motorcar, they talk of Rupert Brooke's "Grantchester." We see in the glass partition the chauffeur's back, and reflected on it, her image. During a convalescence, she had found his polite solicitude and sturdy self-confidence a strength to her. She never suspected that he had come to think of marriage with her. The reflected image reminds us that now, as he constantly does, he is thinking of her (*The Hireling*, Alan Bridges).

Pavel has concealed a Jewish girl in his attic, and hears a radio announcement that those "sheltering unregistered persons will be shot." He is standing on a balcony, and hurls his cigarette down on the floor. This is followed by a close-up of a pot boiling on a stove, foam lifting the lid, and pouring down the sides. Pavel enters and takes the lid off his wrath (*Romeo and Juliet and Darkness*, Jiri Weiss).

Whether feet be people or things, directors often use them to tell us moods and personalities. Arrogant, high-flung feet of soldiers parading in Berlin; prisoners' feet in Russia, ill-shod, stamping to keep warm; the feet that climb the brisk steps of success and the feet that falter (*Moscow Strikes Back*, ed. by Slavko Vorkapich; *Rhapsody in Two Languages*, Gordon Sparling). And Volck's, the Captain of Köpenick's, feet: he dresses as a captain, to get, he hopes, the passport the authorities refuse to grant, because he has been in jail. He has requisitioned a squad of ten soldiers, on the strength of his uniform, "on orders from the highest authority." He takes over the town hall, and gives orders to the mayor. Ten pairs of feet enter from the left in high-stepping precision. Then come the two shuffling feet of William Volck, complete with spurs, and bringing up the rear, a dragging sword (*Passport to Heaven*, Richard Oswald).

Abnormal states. Carol Richmond is alone with a sculptor she knows has committed murder. She is keeping a long worktable between them. He is seen in the same frame as a large head, three or four times life-size, with dark hollows for eyes, shallow brow, domed head, sharp chin and nose, and the nape of the neck rising up to the skull without curve. Shrill with fright, she cries, "You're mad, mad, mad." This is also said by the sculptured head, shown three times, deformed, grotesque (*Phantom Lady*, Robert Siodmak).

Marshal Tyler speaks to the dean of Norwalk of a strange client obsessed with a compulsion to murder (it is himself). In an up shot he stares fixedly down as if at the dean. On a table to left of Tyler all we see of a lamp with a dark shade is an oval of light, which, with its dark edge, is a huge white eye magnifying the intensity of Tyler's glare (*Flesh and Fantasy*, Julien Duvivier).

Bodily sickness. The last shot of Susan's disastrous operatic career, thrust upon her by Citizen Kane, is a close-up of a lamp. Its filament suddenly dims out. From this we cut to a foreground silhouette of someone lying on a bed, breathing stertorously. She has taken too many sleeping pills (*Citizen Kane*, Orson Welles). A man and a boy, their upside-down faces glowing green in the dark, give an immediate sense of abnormality. They have eaten tainted fish, begged from restaurants, without boiling it (*Dodeska-Den*, Akira Kurosawa).

These things are all diegetic—the director has found something in the surroundings of his people that serves his purpose of revelation. Fantasy makes the diegetic possibilities almost limitless. In *The Meshes of the Afternoon* (Maya Deren), the leading character takes a key from her mouth. It becomes a knife, which crops up often from then on, lying on a table or on steps, under the sheets of a bed. At last she dies. A key—a means of entry, the answer to a problem—is equated with death.

10 Uses: Situation

A composition of things and people may with great economy give us the meaning of what we see happening (pls. 21, 28).

The captain of an ocean-going tug, liable to be called at any time to salvage a torpedoed ship, tosses and shouts as he sleeps, and a telephone throws its shadow on the wall (*The Key*, Sir Carol Reed). The veil on Clytemnestra's face for concealment, the net around Agamemnon for entrapment, and the steam from his bath for ambush and confusion were used in *Elektra* (Michael Cacoyannis).

The Jackal, an assassin, having heard that the police know the color of his car, stops at a fork in the road: Italy right, Paris left. He pauses. Then he reaches back, pulls over the canvas top of his car, and drives left. A decision—to continue his mission, and hide himself (*The Day of the Jackal*, Fred Zinnemann). The dissolving of two cloth caps and a fur hat into two bowler hats and a top hat signifies the corrupting influence of Paris on Russian communists (*Ninotchka*, Ernst Lubitsch). Dennis flees from Belfast police. As he runs down a street, we see a curtain drawn and a door close (*Odd Man Out*, Sir Carol Reed). A tiny state, preserving medieval ways, essays an invasion of the United States, intending after surrender to claim postwar aid. Images of anachronism are six white arrows embedded in the tire of an American general's jeep, the invading army of twenty secretly crossing the Atlantic in civilian clothing, carrying suit cases and long bows, and the sergeant wearing modern medals over his chain mail (*The Mouse That Roared*, Jack Arnold).

Some symbols nearly epitomize the whole story. As V. S. Pritchett says, they are facts in themselves, steps in the story, and at the same time, symbols, giving a close texture.[2]

Having spent the night with Lola Lola, a singer in cabarets, Professor Rath, a hitherto highly respectable teacher, is late leaving for school. As he bustles down the circular stairs she says, "Aren't you going to say good-bye?" He stops, and all we see above the floor is his head. She stoops to kiss him. We have an irresistible sense of his having, through her whim, shrunk in stature from the man he had been. He loses his students' respect and his teaching post, and becomes her despised appendage (*The Blue Angel*, Joseph von Sternberg).

Sailors from a destroyer board a fishing vessel to subdue a crew protesting over dangerous working conditions. We retreat over a deck strewn with dead bodies, and we hear four offscreen volleys that we know are the end of the leaders. Superimposed on this is the rising sun flag of Japan with a splotch of blood on the fly. Then a shot of the destroyer (government) and the mother ship (capitalist) riding the ocean side by side (*The Crab-Canning Ship*, So Yamamura).

A bank robbery came to grief when the thieves took lodgings at Mrs. Wilberforce's. This led to disagreements. Every attempt at disentangling themselves from her came to nothing. Two incidents suggest this. Twice Professor Marcus had to drag his long muffler from under Mrs. Wilberforce's feet. When the last conspirator was leaving the house, the strap of his cello case caught in the door, and in trying to pull it free, he undid the case, and strewed the porch with bank-notes. All five gathered up the notes, and entered the car for a colloquy on what Mrs. Wilberforce would likely do (*The Lady Killers*, Alexander Mackendrick; pl. 15).

No one who has seen *The Wages of Fear* (Henri-Georges Clouzot) can ever forget the truck of nitroglycerin. From the road we look up at the wide fender, with slanted black and white stripes, and a white patch in the center shouting the word *explosives*. A gaudy constellation of ten lights outlines the profile of the truck against the night, and along the sides, thin streaks of light glimmer down from strange black hoods. No crew could be seen through the glass of the windshield. A ferociously roaring engine insinuates the truck slowly and cautiously toward us. A wheel settles gently into a hole and creeps out again. A high penetrating whine from the siren completes the terrifying image. The truck is a huge ominous monster that at any moment might shatter itself and all aboard it into a million unidentifiable fragments. We see it again as it moves towards Jo, up to his neck in a pool of oil, foot caught in an obstacle he is trying to dislodge. The great black and white fender threatens closer and larger, as underneath the oil the wheels destroy him. The truck is a mechanical monster using and consuming men for its own purpose: it is the "Southern Oil Company," to whom men are an expendible raw material.

The end of an era is concisely caught in shots of white soldiers filing past a black quartermaster, handing in their rifles; a white girl doing a striptease to a black audience, one of whom she invites to take off her pasties; and a white nanny training black children (*Africa Addio*, Jacopetti and Prosperi). What more needs to be said: the thing carries the irony.

11   Uses: Comment

The director's viewpoint, apparent enough in most of the above examples, may be told in things that have the air of being brought in for the purpose, so easily can they be severed without injuring the story.

To soothe Squire Western's rage, his sister says, "Suppose the man Sophia loves is the man you would choose?" Shots of calves and other animals listening intently. "Who is that?" "Mr. Blifil." They are now in the barnyard. We who watch know very well that it certainly is not Mr. Blifil. So it seems do the two roosters and five or so geese, who all nod their heads in a knowing way, as who should say, "Now that *is* news!" (*Tom Jones*, Tony Richardson).

The director of *Glass* (Bert Haanstra) is not an unqualified machine-lover. At a certain point on a conveyor, a pair of pincers seizes a bottle by the neck and lifts it off the belt. When a bottle with a broken neck arrives there, it stays, for the pincers cannot grasp it. Succeeding bottles queue up and fall through an escape-way to the floor in a quickly growing pile of broken glass, the pincers moving precisely to and fro with empty claws.

After the death of Marat, in *Marat-Sade* (Peter Brook), one of the players slyly pours a pail of black paint. Then with a mischievous deprecating expression, he pours white paint from another bucket. Was the dead man bad or was he a saint? Mad or sane? Right or wrong?

12   Uses: Premonition and Reminiscence

Things can suggest events gone or to come. In the tower scene in *Foreign Correspondent* (Alfred Hitchcock), the fall of a man from the top of the tower is hinted at by the fall of a schoolboy's cap seen flitting down to the street below, and by two shots of the empty silent observation platform, as the assassin looks to see if he is unobserved, as if his victim were flung from the tower and he had fled. If the shot had included the assassin, his victim, or both, it would not have had this effect.

When he was young, Johnson had been imprisoned as a runaway apprentice. As president, he has to consider a compromise proposal relating to personal freedom. He takes from a drawer the shackle chiseled from his ankle. We know what he must be thinking (*Tennessee Johnson*, William Dieterle).

When Captain Scott and his wife talked by the sea, they noticed a set of footprints stretching ahead of them, and he said he would like to make the first steps in an unknown country. After our last look at Scott, as he murmurs "Eleven miles," the distance to the next camp he and his men were too weak to attempt, we are shown again the footprints on the sand (*Scott of the Antarctic*, Charles Frend).

An old man stops and looks at a pile of stones and then goes on. They had been intended for a new farmhouse planned by him and his younger son. His elder son, who now owns the farm, prefers to keep the old building. A painful reminder (*Farrebique*, Georges Rouquier).

13   Uses: Abstractions

A concrete thing may express an abstract notion (pls. 40, 41).

A spy, chased by children, upsets a fruit barrow, halfway down a steep flight of steps. The fruit bouncing and careering with him and after him down the steps—things in fast movement—carry the meaning, *speed* (*The Case of the Missing Ape*, James Hill).

In the seventh episode of *Dreams That Money Can Buy* (Hans Richter), each rung of a ladder disappears the moment the climber lifts his foot off it. In this journey no turning back, *irrevocability*.

The *impenetrability* of Citizen Kane's secret comes to us in the No Trespassing sign, from which we pan to the chain-link fence, the ornamental iron gates, to see within them the distant pyramidal castle, with a single lighted window, dark on the dusk. After we (but no one in the film) have learned the secret of "Rosebud," we return to the distant castle, the fence, and the sign (*Citizen Kane*, Orson Welles).

Susan Alexander screams in a tantrum after a bad review of her operatic debut, and refuses to go on the stage again. Her eyes rise to show us that Kane is approaching, and as he reaches her, his black shadow blots out of her face all detail. "You will continue singing," he says to her. This visual obliteration signifies his *dominance* (*Citizen Kane*).

A blind man stands on the street, when Gippo leaves the police station after betraying Frankie. The blind man is seen twice more, the final time to tell of the pound note Gippo had given him. His unblinking stare, though sightless, suggests an *all-seeing power* that will call Gippo to answer for what he did (*The Informer*, John Ford).

A priest says to Ivan the Terrible "The Lord be your Judge." (*Ivan the Terrible*, S. M. Eisenstein). We see four burning candles, and beyond them one eye of a huge icon. We see it several times. Is it a *watching* church, or the *omniscience* of God?

In *Anna Karenina* (Julien Duvivier), a locomotive becomes an image of *destiny*. We never see a human driver, we never see a wheel, it glides without pause. A wide funnel tapers down to a round boiler, as if head and body, with a spreading apron below, its widest part. When first seen, the engine is patched with snow and a round lamp glows on either end of the bar above the apron. An old workman between the tracks with his back to the train turns when it is almost on him. It never slackens pace, and the old man clings weakly to the apron, until he can hold no more, and slips beneath it. At the end when Anna walks toward it, we are looking up at it, a silhouette, its glowing headlight below the funnel and the two apron lights making three white eyes in the dark. We approach Anna in down shot, a passing train flashes light on her face, which then grows white and whiter, before she falls, the engine grown vaguely huge, above and beyond her. It passes over us (pl. 42).

A similar sense of *impersonal retribution* comes from repeated shots of police in *Odd Man Out* (Sir Carol Reed). It is the repetition of the image that has the effect, and its distance. Even the inspector who says most says little that reveals him: he is professional, self-possessed, emotion controlled—part of a process more than a person. A hand enters and pencils a curve around the landward approaches. A policeman's palm rises into the frame. A single constable asks for identification. Pairs of police patrolling in slow step, standing at the corners of streets, stopping cars, asking for identity cards, pursuing, waiting when Dennis breaks out of a streetcar— deliberate, watchful, everywhere, they recur throughout the film as a leitmotiv. At the very end, at the iron pales that bar from the sea and freedom, when Kathleen fires and the police return volley kills her and Johnny, the police are a ring of white lights, headlights and hand lights, along the line where the snowy ground meets the black of the night.

Anthony Asquith gives us an image of *anonymous menace* in *Cottage To Let*. Barrington, an inventor, is sitting looking right beside a projector. An offscreen crash of glass is heard, and a gust of wind ruffles his hair and the coils of film around his neck. He calls out and goes off. The projector, now centered in the frame, continues the steady click of the shutter, the impassive hum of the motor. The steadily turning reel casts a shadow on the wall, light flickers from its lens, disturbing in its broken rhythm. The butler enters, finds the room empty, window broken, curtains flying, and runs past the projector. We now slowly approach its unruffled hum, its dark mystery, and its flashing light, as we hear a second clink of glass. We feel the peril in the nameless gust and shattering glass, in the empty shadowy room, the gleaming chinks of light in the ceaseless black projector and its gunlike threat, secretive and indifferent. An effect of ellipsis, as much in what is not shown as in what we see.

14 Uses: The Abstraction Death

Death is commonly conveyed in metaphor. Things can serve too, but they hover on the edge of metaphor, for the choice of thing may imply what death is like.

"One day the pain went, and he felt very peaceful." A down shot of Bader, face calm; the window in a watery-distorted shot, light fading, darkness gathering. In a door seen from across his bed, two nurses were talking. "Be quiet," says one, "there's a boy dying in there." We hear his voice: "Dying—we'll see." His face, and the darkness, begin to lighten (*Reach for the Sky*, Lewis Gilbert). In *A Man for All Seasons*, (Fred Zinnemann) when Sir Thomas has laid his head on the block, the camera follows the ax as the headsman draws it out from under the straw and raises it high. He pauses, and the ax plunges down and off the screen, which is instantly black. Anastasia lifts a bowl of wine fearfully. We know it is poisoned. The bowl rises up over her mouth, eyes, and head, blotting her out (*Ivan the Terrible*, S. M. Eisenstein). Death is oblivion.

In *Barrier*, an old man in a wheelchair turns left at a crossroads with traffic lights, while others jog on straight ahead (Jerzy Skolimowski). In *Virgin Spring* (Ingmar Bergman), the murdered girl raises her head before she dies, and a small sapling's trunks cast bars across her face, one erasing her eyes, the other her mouth.

Perry, an escaping spy, is mortally wounded at a garden fete, in a tent with a distorting mirror. We see his twisting face in the mirror, softly lit with a spot of light in the center. He sinks and, as he falls, the spot of light rises from off his face. The distortion suggested pain; the migrant spot, the disappearing life (*Cottage to Let*, Anthony Asquith).

Death can be seen too as a thing—like the body—broken or abandoned. Klara, from her invalid's chair, oversees the packing of her china. She calls the servants lazy devils, keeps tapping her cane, shouts, "move, move, move." Jane, a servant, reaching to a top shelf, loses her grip and pieces crash to the floor. There is no tapping, no shouted rebuke. Jane turns to see: Klara is dead (*The Wolf Trap*, Jiri Weiss). The schoolmaster in *He Who Must Die* (Jules Dassin) stands between the refugees and the barricades and implores, "Don't shoot. They too are Greeks." He runs up the steps crying, "Go back, or blood will be shed." A volley rattles out. The crowd, running in panic up the steps, like a rising blind, exposes the white-suited schoolmaster, lying head down, water from a broken pitcher spilling lower and lower down the steps, and a dropped bundle bumping down to the bottom.

Death is often conceived as a person. It is the hooded horseman of the moors in *Run Wild, Run Free* (Richard C. Sarafian), riding up a sloping horizon followed by a pack of dogs, whose death's head we glimpse as he turns briefly toward us. It is a princess in black and her two black cyclists, who roar suddenly up and leave a body on the road (*Orphée*, Jean Cocteau).

In *The Seventh Seal* (Ingmar Bergman), Death, black-gowned and hooded, meets a crusader knight returning home to his country. To gain time in which to satisfy himself that God exists and that life keeps on after death, the knight proposes a game of chess: "So long as I am besting you, I live." Through the film, the knight, and we, are time and again beset by hints of his ineluctable death. The skull mask of a player they meet who personates Death hangs on a tree or perches on a pole. The squire questions an artist who is painting the Dance of Death on a chapel wall. A girl is placed on a ladder to be dropped on the fire as a witch. A woman dead of the plague is despoiled of rings and bangle, and the thief later falls dead from the same cause. An actor who flees the wrath of a blacksmith whose wife he seduced has taken refuge up in a tree. The actor sees the black-robed one sawing the trunk. "But I have a performance tonight!" "Canceled because of the actor's death." The same black-robed figure appears from time to time to the knight as they make their moves on the chess board, until the knight loses heart and misplays. At the end, on a distant horizon, Death leads a line of the knight and his party, each holding to the one in front, in their Dance of Death. A game which Death at last always wins.

What the dead leave behind are the things of death: trousers and coat on a chair, shoes waiting below, and a meal on the table (*Carnet de Bal*, Julien Duvivier); a piano lid closed in an empty concert hall, one row of lights after another surrendering to the gloom (*Appassionata*, Olof Molander). After the smoke had cleared, the foxhole that had housed men we had come to know was only a pit, and on its edge was a human arm, bleeding at the shoulder end—a grisly synecdoche (*The Human Condition*, part 2: *The Road to Eternity*, Masaki Kobayashi). In *Earth* (Aleksandr Dovzhenko), Vasili, who drives the first tractor to come to his kolkhoz comes toward us down a lane. We retreat before him as he starts to dance, and the dust of the lane rises to veil his feet. In a long down shot, he stands where three lanes meet, his ever more rapid feet nearly invisible. At the crack of a shot, the music stops and he falls. A man leaves the undergrowth and runs. The dust settles, leaving the body clear and still. Besides the antithesis between the climax of swiftest movement and the instant stillness, there was death in the drifting away of the last trace of his doings, the dust of the dance.

It may be death as felt by those who are left. Monsieur Verdoux looks out of a window, remarking on Endymion. The woman calls him to her room and he leaves the frame. After a pause, the moonlit vista dissolves to the same scene by day. Verdoux reappears and walks briskly down to the kitchen. He sets at the table two opposite places, and on reflection, takes one away. He has done away with her place, as he has done away with her, but more—her killing had sat so lightly on him that it had even escaped his mind as he laid the table (*Monsieur Verdoux*, Charles Chaplin).

After Iphigenia reaches the summit, there to be offered in sacrifice to Artemis, we glimpse her twice more, distant pale in the white smoke from the sacrificial fires, as if her body were dissolving, as if in some silent other world, as if already a shade (*Iphigenia*, Michael Cacoyannis).

15 Absence

Meaning may come, not merely from things present but from absence of those expected. As Ivan the Terrible looks down a long table, mugs, hands, and arms come from both sides to pledge the toast, but not faces, not the intentions faces hide or show, intentions he neither knew nor trusted (*Ivan the Terrible*, S. M. Eisenstein). In the conformist world of *Fahrenheit 451* (François Truffaut), it was the people who lived in the house without the television aerial whom neighbors avoided. A patient dies on the operating table: the absence of expression on the white masks of surgeons and nurses as eyes looked round at one another said more of shock and bafflement than faces could have done (*Green for Danger*, Sidney Gilliatt).

16 Setting as a Thing with Meaning

The macabre has its conventions. In such films as *Vampyr* (Carl-Theodor Dreyer), there are gouts of dripping candle wax, miasmic mists, doors that open on their own, the skull, the spider, the cobweb, the coffin, the clouded moon, and other like matters. The mood, as much as the story, may be the message.

Blue-gray and white is the world of Ivan, immured in a prison camp in the Soviet North. White for the snow and the quilted coats of the guards; blue-gray for the sleeping huts, the quilted uniforms of the prisoners, the shadows on the snow, and the long arctic night. Even the khaki of the soldiers was grayed, the red star in their caps, and the flame in the stove touched with purple, as if they were chilled by the dismal place (*One Day in the Life of Ivan Denisovitch*, Casper Wrede).

The Third Man (Sir Carol Reed) is mostly set at night, with black shadows and wet cobbles, in wastes of rubble, in vast empty marble halls, in streets, cafés, and amusement park nearly deserted, and in the close vaults of sewers. Anna walks back to her loneliness between rows of pollards dropping their last leaves on a gray day. A twilight world of desolation; its people without hope (pls. 35, 36).

King and Country (Joseph Losey) is largely set in low, small, shadowy rooms, where obstacles like timber props, bunks, boxes, and tables are frequently met, entered by short, narrow alleys, which turn at right angles into others. People are shown close, in half- or full-length shots, and keep their heads down to avoid hitting beams. In these gray and gloomy places, only faces or occasional pools of water seem white. It is a confined cavernous existence—that of a soldier in World War I. Black and white shots of the kaiser inspecting troops, of marching soldiers and battleships place us before the first World War. A woman is singing in a drawing room, and as we see her accompanist, Vera Brittain, whose life is the story, the black and white modulates to colour for the rest of the narrative. We have passed from history to life, to the impassioned concerns of a young woman who lived in those times (*The Testament of Youth* part 1, television, Moira Armstrong).

17 Meaning Suspended—Hyrmos

Although the thing is usually one of whose meaning the audience is possessed, in some cases the thing is shown and the meaning disclosed later, as in the figure hyrmos.

The thing may symbolize a past experience, repressed from consciousness, the quest for whose meaning is the story, as in *Spellbound* (Alfred Hitchcock). It is black lines on a white ground, which for J. B. are always charged with emotion. He may see it as lines on a dressing gown, or as railway tracks, or shadows cast by ridges on a coverlet. By the end an incident repressed in childhood is brought into consciousness. We slide with him down the converging lines of a stone coping to dash his brother to his death on the sharp spikes of an iron paling.

18 Sound

The thing can be a sound.

In *Dangerous Moonlight* (Brian Desmond Hurst), Carol has persuaded her pianist husband, Stefan Radetsky, that he can best serve occupied Poland in raising money by giving concerts. But every time he hears or plays the "Military Polonaise"—the signature tune of Radio Free Warsaw—he feels he should be with his fellow Poles who are risking their lives. At his last concert, the audience clamors for an encore. As he sits at the piano, they are quiet, and he says, "The last music to come from Free Warsaw." He looks up at Carol, where she sits with her father in a box. We approach to her drawn face. She rises and leaves. In the halls and lobby she hears the music still, and in the taxi, she hears it broadcast. Upset, she goes to her father's house, and then to the hotel where she and Stefan are staying. Stefan has gone: Poland has taken him.

19 Symbol and Metaphor

There is a zone in which it is not certain if a figure is a symbol or metaphor: we feel a comparison hovering, but find it hard to define.[3]

When Johnny, wounded, falls from the window of the escaping car in *Odd Man Out* (Sir Carol Reed), and picks himself up and runs, a little white dog jumps down from a set of steps and chases after him. The pursuit of Johnny had started, and ended only eight hours later. The particular dog may bring to some viewers' minds the abstract notion *pursuit*. For others, it may be a kind of proleptic metaphor for all those in the story, who, for one reason or another, were after Johnny.

The youngest Cameron (Southerner) is shot in battle. The youngest Stoneman (Northerner) comes up and raises a ferocious bayonet to give the coup de grâce. He suddenly recognizes his friend, bends down to help, is himself shot and falls. With his last gesture, he places his right arm around the other's body (*Birth of a Nation*, D. W. Griffith). It may be merely a melodramatic ending. It may further suggest the killing of friends and brothers, which the Civil War was, or that friendship is greater than politics, or that all men are brothers, and that war is fratricide. Its meaning is neither precise nor single, but it is clearly intended for more than a private event: it reverberates with meanings beyond itself. It is a symbol: it may be a metaphor.

Closer still perhaps to a metaphor is the indestructible worker in *Arsenal* (Aleksandr Dovzhenko). The ammunition of workers defending a building gives out, and the troops arrive. A worker stands up, defying the troops to shoot. Three soldiers raise their rifles and fire. Still the worker stands. The soldiers cry, "Fall! Fall! Are you wearing armor?" The worker tears opens his shirt, defies them again, and again their fire is powerless. This is not reality: it is hortatory fantasy, or propaganda. The man is a symbol that says the workers can never at last be defeated. He is, by synecdoche, all the workers. If we say that he is to the firing troops what the mass of workers is to the economic and military might of the capitalist establishment, then we have the four elements needed for a metaphor. Symbol, metaphor, or synecdoche—it could be any one.

20 Meaning Conferred by Culture[4]

From what source does a thing gain its meaning for us? To what degree can a director count on our reading it correctly, or giving it any meaning. This a director must carefully calculate.

In making *M*, Fritz Lang was safe in assuming that nearly every viewer would know that a knife might be used for a meal or a murder.

Over how wide an area does an X mean extinction, prohibition? A building is confiscated for housing hidden books. Two planks in the form of an X are nailed across its doors and windows. As Montag walks the railway line to the woods that hides the walking books, two lines of tracks are superimposed in a cross. Does this cross suggest a forbidden road (*Fahrenheit 451*, François Truffaut)?

A director may use a thing that conveys his meaning to those who share a not-widely distributed subculture, if it merely enriches his tale, but not if a viewer needs its message to understand the story clearly and fully.

Some meanings are shared by those who have lived in the same time and place. For those who lived in wartime Britain, a telegram was a symbol of dreaded news (*In Which We Serve*, Noël Coward and David Lean; *Carve Her Name with Pride*, Lewis Gilbert). They would also notice the white, red, and black—the colors of the Nazi flag—worn by the woman speaking on television in *Fahrenheit 451* (François Truffaut). Today, with omnipresent clocks and watches, a puffing factory whistle is no longer an infallible sign that a day's work is over (*The Struggle*, D. W. Griffith).

What allusions in art and literature can a director be sure of? In *The Great Dictator*, Chaplin assumes that we know Rodin's *Thinker*, for Hynkel shows us *The Thinker of Tomorrow*. He leans as before on a pensive left elbow, but the right arm is raised in the Nazi salute. A poet shoots himself. The blood on his brow is followed by a laurel wreath. To those who would see *The Blood of a Poet* (Jean Cocteau), a limited audience, the wreath would likely still be read as an award for artistic excellence. It might not be wise to trust it further.

Some meanings hold only for a class, a country, or a period.

To understand fully the scene in *Hangmen Also Die* (Fritz Lang), where a riot starts in a cinema, the viewer needs to be seized of several meanings not given; that the river on the screen was likely the Moldau, that the music heard was a tone poem depicting the river, that the river was a symbol of Czechoslovakia itself, that the tune was felt both by Czechs and Germans to be a symbol of resistance. The end, in which a quisling Czech stands in front of the beam, printing his black silhouette on the projected countryside, has thus a deeper meaning.

Events that might be trifling to viewers unversed in medieval Japan, like white horses charging round a courtyard or a flight of birds entering a room, must be explained as evil omens (*Throne of Blood*, Akira Kurosawa).

Even within a culture, context alters meanings. In a locked-out mining town, drinking hot water means poverty (*The Stars Look Down*, Sir Carol Reed); for wealthy men with weak stomachs, it could be medical treatment. Stacks of unwashed dishes in *Scarlet Street* (Fritz Lang) are feckless management; in a Park Lane scullery, likely a banquet.

In all cases, the thing chosen must make essential action clear to the intended audience. They must know in *Les Deux Timides* (René Clair) that a white flag is a token of surrender. A cook who has plugged her ears against the sound of fireworks is unaware that people, in the house and out, have opened fire on one another, each believing the other a party of bandits. Placidly unaware of the battle raging around her, the cook shakes a white dust cloth out of a window, which those in the garden take to be submission.

Do notches cut in the mast of a lifeboat mean for everyone the number of days they have sailed? Does a circular mask showing the sea surface, and crossed by two graduated lines at right angles, convey the presence of a submarine to everyone? The director here made sure by cutting in, the first time he used it, the U-boat commander using the eyepiece, just before it. On the other hand, when a sailor waves two half oars with bits of canvas hung from them, even those who have never heard of a semaphore know he is sending a message. The director expects us to know the sound of an airplane, but he has someone tell us that a distant throbbing heard on a calm night is a U-boat recharging its engines (*Western Approaches*, Pat Jackson).

21 Meaning Conferred by Convention

Not to accept conventions would hinder communication; they are concise, they mean the same to most viewers, they enable lesser matters to be disposed of quickly. The fingered speech of Kathakali dancers and the masks of Pantaloon and Columbine are known and read, as words are, and their meaning is instantly taken. A film with every shot using a convention would seem, and some do seem, hackneyed, but used with judgment, conventions must not be scorned.

There are conventions of a culture—dry skulls on desert sand as men pass (*Nine Men*, Harry Watt; *The Back of Beyond*, John Heyer; pl. 1). There are conventions of a medium—that voices heard in a film when the speaker's mouth is closed are internal musings (*Hamlet*, Laurence Olivier; and others); that when a scene goes out of focus, there is loss of consciousness (*Oliver Twist*, David Lean; and others). There are conventions of a particular director that run throughout his films—in Chaplin's films, we have come to accept that a large man with a beard is villainous, pompous, or stupid, or all at once (*The Immigrant*, and many others).

The Houses of Parliament have come to signify arrival in London (*Foreign Correspondent*, Alfred Hitchcock); and the Statue of Liberty, in New York (*The Immigrant*, Charles Chaplin). An ear superimposed, in silent films, was a sign that someone was listening (*Variety*, E. A. Dupont). Circling vultures are commonly seen after battles, especially in deserts, but may be a premonition of death (*Snow White and the Seven Dwarfs*, Walt Disney). The spider signifies deceit: Lizaveta lies awake in bed, and we hear Suvorin's voice, "You are dear to me." We know that he is courting her only as a means of gaining a secret from her aunt. A large spider is climbing its web at the right of the frame (*The Queen of Spades*, Thorold Dickinson). White is for goodness (*Snow White and the Seven Dwarfs*, Walt Disney) and black for villainy (*Throne of Blood*, Akira Kurosawa).

Directors can exploit for surprise a habit of trusting without inquiry all those we meet who are dressed in white, and expecting the worst from those who are bearded and in black: we could remember that in Peking, players dressed in black are honest and brave, and those dressed in white must be carefully watched.

22 Meaning Conferred by Context

The context may give a thing its meaning. In *Colonel Blimp* (Michael Powell and Emeric Pressburger) a stuffed bear in Wynn-Candy's hall holds out a tray, and in a second viewing a visitor places his card on the tray. Later still, a man searching rubble after an air raid uncovers the bear, and we know that its owner's house has been destroyed.

We know that a goblet given by Ivan to his wife is poisoned. How? The boyarina, Euphrosyne Staritzskaya, overhears Ivan saying that he will confiscate the boyars' estates to break their resistance. "You take too great a step, Ivan," she says. She turns and uncovers a goblet, and with shadowed face, shakes a powder into it and then covers the cup with her black cloak. Anastasia, sick in bed, cries for a drink. The boyarina's hand rises above the wall and places the goblet. Her secrecy, her ill will, her garb of black all combine to convince us of evil intentions (*Ivan The Terrible*, S. M. Eisenstein). In the same way Hitchcock has used a cup of coffee *(Notorious)* and a glass of milk *(Suspicion)*.

23 Meaning Conferred by the Narrative

The first image in *The Silent Nephew* (Robert Enrico) is a fat Laughing Buddha. Henri, a boy of ten, runs in and strokes it affectionately. He calls it "old ugly." It is seen again in several incidents. Henri's retarded brother, Joel, is six, cannot speak and still wets his bed, but his parents love him and watch carefully over him. Henri and his parents live in his grandmother's house. She and most of her family are embarrassed by Joel, are unkind to him, and press his parents to send him to a home. The grandmother treasures the Buddha figure, for her husband brought it home from the East, and one of Henri's cousins says that it is what Joel will look like when he is old. After Joel's accidental death, Henri and his parents leave the house. The night before, Henri takes the Laughing Buddha and pushes it out of a window. It was the occasion of a cruel word about Joel, who would now never live to be old, so it too must not survive as an unkind reminder. The sneer on the figure's face perhaps suggested the cold condescension of his grandmother and all his uncle's family toward him and his. The Buddha ties him to them, and breaking it vents his rage towards them and breaks the tie. A complex feeling, not easy to compass fully in words.

The context thus becomes the whole story.

In *High Noon* (Fred Zinnemann), we are shown again and again the empty railway lines converging on the plain, to keep us aware that at twelve o'clock, a train bearing Frank Miller will come along them. It becomes more and more clear that Marshal Kane must face four gunmen quite alone. After his deputy marshal resigns, for example, the next shot is the tracks, and we pan to the three gunmen who wait at the station for Miller.

Two films begin with things, and only when the film is over is their meaning clear. One starts with a room, a black cloth, a chair overturned and leaves of an open book fluttering in the breeze. Pavel, a boy, enters the open door, and he starts when the door behind him slams with a noise like a rifle shot. He picks up a briefcase from the floor and fondles it lovingly, and as he stands with his back to the door, we approach to a close-up. This is the end. He had found Hana when he entered the abandoned flat of a Jewish family, whose guinea pig he had promised to care for. She was Jewish and had hoped for help from them. He had hidden her in the attic, but she had run out and been shot, for she felt that her presence was a threat to those who lived there. Pavel is left with her case, the Latin book they had studied, a black cloth that had covered the window, and the chair she had sat in, which he had brandished when they had heard a knock at the door and had then thrown down (*Romeo and Juliet and Darkness*, Jiri Weiss).

In the Weiss film, the story is a single flashback, and once it begins, we forget the opening things: they are merely a device to pique our curiosity. In *Citizen Kane* (Orson Welles), an editor sends a reporter out to find the meaning of Kane's last word, "Rosebud." After he said this, Kane died and a glass globe fell from his fingers. The reporter asks, in each interview, what the person knows of the enigmatic word, and thus we are kept reminded of it throughout the film. We see Kane as a boy, sleighing in falling snow, before wealth came to his mother and he was sent from home to be educated. As an old man, after his second wife has left him, he enters her bedroom, and heaves in all directions, bags, bedding, tables, shelves, books, pictures, and in doing this, his fingers close on a glass globe and we hear him say "Rosebud." He lifts the globe and looks at the particles in it falling like snow. He forgets his fury, and, holding the globe, walks out of the room with remembering eyes, unaware of a score of watching servants. After his death, we float over acres of possessions, and reach a furnace door, as a workman throws in a wooden sleigh. We approach, and the heat is blistering the paint in which the trade name is lettered, R-O-S-E-B-U-D. His wealth had given Kane the means to insist on his will in all things: the snow and the sleigh were the days before this, the days of lost content. We and the reporter shared the search: we found, he did not. This suspension of meaning to the end is the figure hyrmos.

24 Meaning Conferred by Manipulation

We often reveal what a thing means to us by what we do with it. When Brigadier General Wynn-Candy and his bride moved into their house early in the century, they had a telephone installed. "We'll have a lot of fun with that," he said. Not a serious instrument of living, only a fashionable toy. He hangs his hat on the mouth-piece (*Colonel Blimp*, Michael Powell and Emeric Pressburger).

A mentally retarded girl passes in front of a wide, high mantelpiece flanked by a tall five-branched candelabrum. She pauses to genuflect and cross herself. To her discrimination, it had the likeness of an altar (*Foolish Wives*, Erich von Stroheim).

Use can tell us also something of the culture to which the user belongs. Where the rulers' maxim was, "Keep them busy, keep them happy," and books were considered a source of unhappiness, Montag's wife, uncovering a book, sweeps it off onto the floor, as if it were vermin, whose touch was contamination (*Fahrenheit 451*, François Truffaut). In *War Game* (Peter Watkins), we see an unshaven parson playing *Silent Night* by pushing a record round with his index finger—after an atomic war.

Consider, as a neutral object, a pile of horse dung lying on the street. It was left by the horse drawing a dairy wagon, which had crossed the street as the Fletcher Field Drum Corps approached. The permanent force cadet officer heading the column looked neither to right nor left (nor down), his foot striking square into the pile. The file of cadets behind him divides fastidiously in two, giving the pile of dung a wide berth: the professional and the amateur distinguished, the trained, and the not-specially-wanting-to-be-trained (*The Apprenticeship of Duddy Kravitz*, Ted Kotcheff).

25 Meaning Conferred by Combining Images

Two or more things put together may have a meaning neither would have by itself.

In *Great Expectations* (David Lean) there is a shot from under Pip's coach: large and close the vigorous galloping legs of the horses and the road beyond them rolling swiftly toward us. It conveyed a fine sense of movement. After a few seconds, there was superimposed on this a wide white map of the road that moved slowly down the frame, centering in succession Gravesend, Dartford, Woolwich, Greenwich, and then with London the map stopped moving. To movement has been added "movement on the London road".

After Wynn-Candy's marriage, we move down from his wife's face to her wrist, as he leans toward her from his chair and kisses it. Now follows a series of shots, as of leaves in an album turning from right to left, each with a photograph and a card of invitation superimposed, one in Italian, another dated from a German Club in Tokyo, and so for places around the world. Then a blank page, superimposed on which is a cutting from *The Times*, in which Clive Wynn-Candy thanks his friends for their sympathy in his recent irreparable loss. Then a series of pages turn, all blank. And now, on his blue trophy wall, there appear one at a time, the heads of a moose "Nova Scotia 1935," a polar bear "Labrador 1936," and a red deer "Cairngorms 1938." From this grouping of things, we take the following meanings: his wife and he traveled widely, they were well and internationally connected (their invitations come from select circles), and they form attachments to people and places (those who live in the present only do not keep albums). After his wife's death, the general traveled no more, perhaps did nothing, and after a long interval (the turning blank pages) he did hunt in Canada and at home, going back to a hobby pursued when younger (*Colonel Blimp*, Michael Powell and Emeric Pressburger).

In *M* (Fritz Lang) (German version) a child on her way home from school bounces her ball on an advertising pillar. Not specially significant; but her ball keeps hitting a poster offering a reward of ten thousand marks for a child murderer. This makes her one of the children at risk. A shadow falls on the pillar of a man's hatted head, and a voice is heard, "What a pretty ball." Is this child the next victim? In another scene, Becker, the murderer, comes out from a shop, smiling at the little girl he has beside him. In a close-up his hand brings a knife out of his pocket. He snaps it open. A hidden pursuer starts up alertly. Murderer, child, and knife is the combination. Then there is another close-up of the knife, cutting spiral slits in the skin of an orange. Knife and orange mean something different.

26 Meaning Conferred by Lighting

A director paints with light and with light creates meanings. In three shots the vast plans projected by Ivan the Terrible are suggested by light and shadow. First, Ivan is half-length in the foreground, his arm around an orrery set on a pedestal, his shadow faint and large on a distant wall. Then his head is shown, bottom left, looking right, where the shadow of the orrery, huge on the wall, fills the frame. Lastly, as Ivan rises from his chair and leaves by a low arch, his great shadow quickly catches up and shrinks into Ivan himself (*Ivan the Terrible*, S. M. Eisenstein).

Light has added meaning to faces. We first see a supposed witch in a dark doorway, her bright white face a mysterious glow melting into the blackness in which it floats (*Day of Wrath*, Carl Theodor Dreyer). Madness in *Catherine the Great* (Paul Czinner) showed less in the actor's mime than it did in a dot of light reflected in each of his eyes. A child's face, holding back a secret, is black all but the left eye, as she lurks behind a bedpost (*The Innocents*, Jack Clayton).

Black has a number of meanings.

Nell Bowen falls into the hands of Mr. Sims, the chief apothecary of *Bedlam*, (Mark Robson) and he puts her in with Tom, a patient kept in a cage. Tom, his chains removed, rushes toward us. As he clutches the bars that keep him from us, he is burly, and in silhouette, unknown, inhuman. Sims invites Nell, as a reformer who believes in treating "loonies" gently, to enter the cage. She hesitates, but enters. As Tom turns toward her, the lighting is frontal, molding the face of a dumb, but essentially gentle, certainly tameable, beast. It was a metaphor: to see clearly, to understand, is not to fear.

To test the reliability of Karl Brunner, one of his officers, Gestapo Colonel Henkel remarks, as they look through a glass at women being sterilized, "It is a good thing I didn't tell the American that Anna Muller will soon be a patient here." Brunner, we know, loves Anna. We see the two of them: Karl's face impassive; Henkel's, looking at Karl, but black-shadowed, invisible. As if beyond a one-way mirror, Henkel sees but cannot be seen. What he thinks of Karl we cannot tell, for black tells nothing, and black, by convention, is evil (*Hitler's Children*, Edward Dmytryk). The countess has concluded some sinister convenant with Saint-Germain. She kneels in a church, looks up, and says, "Have mercy on me." In an up shot of a statue of the Virgin, a light goes out, and blackness covers her face: no mercy (*The Queen of Spades*, Thorold Dickinson).

27 Meaning Conferred by Angle

Meaning can be added by angle—the way a director has us look at something (pls. 2, 22). To see a man the other side of a coatrack, one eye on either side of the post, makes his intentions inscrutable. It is a kind of half-mask, and only a full face can tell thoughts. It was Doris's bearded benefactor, whose wife was mentally ill and whose daughter tormented him (*Dreams*, Ingmar Bergman). The boyars plotting against Ivan are shown only in part, as they slink behind thrones or huge crosses, or down out of the frame. They seem to be hiding from us, for something is placed between us and them (*Ivan the Terrible*, S. M. Eisenstein).

Sanders is jealous of Corby, whose sparring partner he is, and when Sanders's girl is mistaken for Corby's wife, Sanders would have punched him. A trainer persuades Sanders to take his feelings out on a punching ball. Hitchcock places his camera, so that Corby's head in the background and the punching ball in the foreground cover the same space, as if Sanders imagined he was punching Corby (*The Ring*). In like manner, when Dr Renault, the villain, is first seen, his head is replaced by a Florence flask, twice head size and featureless, which stands between him and us, giving him the look of an ogre (*Zombies on Broadway*, Gordon Douglas).

A self-absorbed husband is dozing in the bathroom on his wedding night. His bride lies on the bed. We see her flowers on a window sill, and through the pane beyond them, the rainy night. She goes to the window and looks down at the street, where a man and a woman are kissing under an umbrella. Then looking from outside at the rain-splattered window we see the flowers as if they were drenched with tears, which pass by hypallage from the bride's face to the window pane, as nature weeps with her (*Ecstasy*, Gustave Machaty).

28 Meaning Conferred by Distortion

There are many ways of distorting the visual image, some of which are mentioned elsewhere. One case is enough here, where distortion suggests an inner state. Elizabeth's husband gets out of bed, saying he is evil, and bangs his head on the mirror until it cracks and his head bleeds. She sits up in bed, her head narrowed, her shoulders hunched up, her face pinched; a fuzzy line has almost rubbed out her nose and mouth. It is as if, watching her husband, she shrivels. She moves, the camera moves, and we see that the source of distortion is the crack in the mirror, for what we saw was her reflected there (*Kamouraska*, Claude Jutra).

29 Meaning Conferred by Movement

Meaning can be conferred by movement. Nell was invited as one of a party to stay in a haunted house, for the purpose of psychic investigation. The house comes to delight her. She runs into the library and dances, her echoing voice telling us, "I want to stay here." The camera rises along the rail of a circular staircase, keeping it fully in focus, while the background, out of focus, whirls dizzily. A long shot down from the top of the stairs shows her circling below. The swirling movement of the camera suggested her exhilaration, perhaps the sensation of constantly turning as she danced, with the hint of an invisible presence ascending the stairs (*The Haunting*, Robert Wise).

30 Meaning Conferred by Montage

Montage is discussed at greater length below. One example will illustrate that things presented in shots that are part of a set or series will be colored in their meanings by other shots in the set: it is another kind of context.

Cleo has a very sick stomach. A fortune-teller has given hints of suffering to come, and has refused to give the meaning of two cards. Cleo and a friend go to see a comedy. In it a man says good-bye to his girl, who, dressed in white, runs down the stairs. The man puts on dark glasses. The girl's dress is now black, and she falls on the floor unconscious. A black car comes. He buys a wreath. He takes off his glasses to wipe away the tears, and now she is lying dressed in white again. She sits up. The car is also white. "Just these damned glasses," he says. This is an allegory of what happens to Cleo. As the car carrying her and her friend enters a darkened archway, she is telling her friend her fear of cancer and death: she will know for sure when the doctor calls her that night. She sees a mountebank swallowing frogs alive, and is disgusted. An awning with *Bonne Santé* on it strikes her as ironical. The taxi stops by a shop that sells carved African masks, from which she turns with a shudder. At rehearsal, she is offered three songs, from which she picks the most melancholy, "Cri d'Amour." As she sings, the camera moves but keeps behind her an unrelieved ground of black. When the song is over and the camera leaps back, we see that the only black in a white room is a single narrow panel. After trying on hats at a milliner's, Cleo picks a black one. Her mood picks only what matches it, from all that is going on around her. *Bonne Santé*, the mountebank, and the masks are not mementos mori, taken by themselves, but here combined, and for her, they are (*Cleo from Five to Seven*, Agnes Varda).

31   The Visual and the Verbal

If an image is not fully explicit or might carry a meaning other than that intended, or might not be seen as a figure at all, and is thus in some respect imperfect, words may have to complete it.

Barney has served his term on a chain gang; another convict has died. As the wagon bearing the coffin passes Barney, the driver offers him a ride and he climbs on, sitting down on the coffin. It might be thought, "Life on the chain gang has killed, if not his body, at least part of Barney." But that is not the message. One of the convicts watching the wagon says to another, "There's only two ways of getting out of here . . ." (*I Was a Fugitive from a Chain Gang*, Mervyn Leroy).

An elderly woman convict, just released, goes to the butcher to buy meat for her dog, and inquires about rabbit. The butcher pooh-poohs this and insists on selling her stewing beef, and quotes her the price per pound. In close-up, we see the scale left and the butcher's face right, as the moving arm swings full across to stop at one pound, as he says, "eight ounces and that'll be tenpence." We gathered that he knew her "trip to the Riviera" had been a stay in prison, but this antithesis of the seen and the spoken expresses his kindness with great economy (*Turn the Key Softly*, Jack Lee).

32   Matters of Practice

The worst we can say of any significant thing is to doubt its significance.

There is the famous image of *Metropolis* (Fritz Lang), of a man, his legs apart, laboriously moving the three hands of an enormous clocklike face. The image does suggest the hardest physical labor, and under the strain, he collapses. The intended meaning, no doubt, is the pitiless exploitation of the working man by the owner, but the edge is taken off the meaning by two things. First, we have no idea what the machine is for and why the operation is needed at all. Second, all the other equipment suggests an advanced electrical culture (which can even make robots look like living people), so why should so simple an operation need a man to do it?

To make a clock express anything else but the time of day is not easy. It can be done, with powerful effect, when we know the very minute a bomb is going to explode, and every clock face brings us closer to doom (*Sabotage*, Alfred Hitchcock; *Seven Days to Noon*, John and Roy Boulting). In *The Day of the Jackal* (Fred Zinneman), the day of the intended murder was guessed, but not the hour or minute. Clocks open many scenes, intended, no doubt, to express the pressure of time; but a clock is a scale of hours and it was the shrinking fund of days that kept heightening the pressure. The clock, then, instead of creating suspense, often sets us wondering why the director was careful to let us know that the cabinet was meeting at seven, expecting to find out that at that exact time some other related event was also happening, when in fact nothing was. When a scale of any kind is used for suspense, we have to know at what other point on the scale the feared event will happen, to compare with the point at which we are now. The clocks in the film never made the leap from "the time" to "time."

Some films are composed of images, which the mind cannot assemble to form a rational consistent meaning, and this is intentional. *Black Moon* is a film of this kind. The director, Louis Malle, expressed his intentions, in part, as being negative, to avoid logical construction, psychological premisses, the working out of story or character, conventions of the film dream, and, as far as possible, dialogue.[5] I cannot quote his positive purpose, because, as Malle himself said, if he could have put it into words, there would have been no point in making the film; and the film itself, for me, had no meaning at all.

Malle used the unicorn, he said, both as a phallic symbol and one that stands for virginity. I knew that these were possible meanings, but it still added nothing to the meaning of the film. Of the story it is enough to say that Lily's orange car runs over a raccoon. She finds the road blocked by a large gun, and witnesses the killing of a file of women soldiers by a company of male ones. She makes a run across country in her car with shattered windscreen, and enters a seemingly deserted house. Naked children arrive, leading a pig on a leash; a unicorn appears and disappears; a brother and a sister, who are mutes, revive a strangling mother by the sister's giving her suck and a glass of cognac. Lily pursues the unicorn through a gate in the wall, where it seems to have become a pig, on which she trips and falls. She is now beaten by the children, but when she looks up, they are gone. There is a flower that squeaks when she steps on it. Snakes climb out of a drawer she opens. There are doors that open of themselves, rats that chatter loudly on leaving the room, the sister and brother gravely streaking one another's faces with paint, a glass of milk that fills itself up, and other similar things. Brother, sister, and Lily move through most of these events with the least possible trace of expression on their faces.

It seems to me that successful treatments of travels to strange countries have not merely cast off the logic of the world we know: they create a self-consistent logic of a different kind. Dreams, during the dreaming, seem, in all their happenings, perfectly rational. It is the logic of the answers given to Alice by the inhabitants of Wonderland that is devastating. The other world of *Orphée* (Jean Cocteau) conveys a strong sense of order and law. The irrational is what the person using the term cannot explain, and this may apply to me here, but I do have Malle's word that he intended the irrational. We have minds that seek a logical pattern, and a work of art must satisfy both mind and feelings; and even as to feelings, *Black Moon* left me completely cold. If a film neither satisfies my mind nor touches my emotions, if its things have no meanings for me and it runs its full course without a touch of humor, it seems natural to ask, what is the value of the film? Malle must have the final word: it was women and children, he said, who liked the film, not men.

I must end with a thing I think I can fully explain. Charlie Chaplin puts a bottle down to go and rescue the Big Fellow. There is no one else on the jetty, nor is anyone shown removing the bottle, and yet it is not there when Charlie returns. I propose the following meaning for the bottle's absence: the script girl didn't make a note (*The Adventurer*, Charles Chaplin).

Part III

Figures of Likeness

4
Repetition

1 Identity and Likeness

The first figure of likeness to consider is obviously *repetition*, where the likeness, at first sight, seems to be the closest possible, that of identity, but even here exact identity is rare and likeness a better word.

In this figure the meaning intended lies in the repetition, and not in any single showing of the image repeated. When an image is seen again, its meaning will not be the same, by our merely remembering it from before, and by all we have seen on the screen between the two occurrences. The context, in short, cannot have been the same for both viewings, and neither, therefore, can what the image conveys. The director, moreover, will know that an often small or subtle change in an image seen more than once is not only more interesting than mere identity but is a means of emphasizing change. Altering a single element in an image several times repeated, always in the same direction—larger, paler, shabbier—brings out the one characteristic in which the images differ. Repetition, then, as a figure, should perhaps be qualified as rhetorical or significant repetition.[1]

We see the rump of a departing rabbit. We then see Charles Prince raising his gun. He shoots, mutters "Blast!," and lowers the muzzle. The same unhurried rear end of the rabbit, now seen again, has gained in meaning: hunting, we observe, is something Prince was not born to (*Nothing But the Best*, Clive Donner).

It is not necessary to consider here what semiologists call *plurisituationality*, the capacity, that is, of a word or image to express the same generalized meaning in more than one context, as a word like *chair* does in language.[2] First, the film image is of one particular chair; it is not an idea *chair* to which all particular chairs approximate, however much they differ in the use of wood or metal, in period, cloth, or color; it may be a seat, a weapon, or something in the way. Its value depends too on the lighting, framing, and angle used in taking the film image. Generalization has to be reached in film by other means. Second, a figure is a word or image, not only standing for an object but using the object as a means of expressing something beyond itself, and this meaning is rarely quite the same in any two films, apart from a limited number of conventions. Vultures or skulls have a fairly constant significance, but a black-shadowed face may mark a man as either unknown or evil or secret. Third, the meaning conveyed is, as suggested, not quite the same for any two successive showings of the same image.

2 Theatrical Uses

Repetition is one of the oldest figures. It is in the nature of rituals; the plot of *Oedipus the King* is repetition with variation; it still is effective today. After we hear Lady Brocklehurst's conviction that "The fact is. . ." usually begins a lie, each time we hear the words, our curiosity is aroused as to what will come after, and whether Lady Brocklehurst will see through it.[3] When Charles Surface throws down the screen and cries, "Lady Teazle, by all that's wonderful," and Sir Peter follows with "Lady Teazle, by all that's damnable," the change in one word, repetition combined with antithesis, give us a strong dramatic shock.[4]

The film uses repetitions of words as the stage does. In *Heart of a Nation* (Julien Duvivier), we see the poster in 1939 for "Mobilization Générale," and we remember seeing the words before, in 1914. Froment père's peasant father had served in the war of 1870, and as he makes ready to fight in 1914, he repeats his father's words, "We have vineyards, fields, factories . . . We make, they rob." And in 1939, again the words are spoken.

There is a saw in the theater from which it is hard, even in film, to free ourselves. It runs, in one version, "You tell the audience you're going to say something, then you say it, then you tell them you've said it, and if God is good, they'll grasp it." It seems to apply not merely to telling the audience facts they need to know, but in heightening comic situations. In *A Home of Your Own* (Jay Lewis), almost all the incidents come in threes. The prospective owner, for example, goes to inspect his house three times, first to fall on his face in a pool, second, to be almost buried in sand, and third, to be hoisted by a crane. When we see him coming to the house a third time, we thrill with anticipation at the misadventure we are certain is on its way.

Repetition has its more subtle uses. Maria Tura tells a young admirer to come to her dressing room when Joseph, her husband, starts the speech, "To be or not to be." Tura comes downstage to half-length, looks up from the book he is reading, pauses, and says the words. This is cut at once to Slobinski, springing to his feet in the third row of the stalls, and conspicuously upsetting a row of spectators in his hurry to leave. We return to Tura, surprise in his eyes, his voice growing louder up to "outrageous fortune," as if trying to reach the departing airman's ears. Later, Tura comes home to find Slobinski asleep in his bed. He had been parachuted into Poland on a mission and been hidden by Maria without Tura's knowing. After inspecting the intruder, Tura conceals himself beside the bed and begins "To be or not to be," on which the sleeper awakes, pulls on slippers, and walks away (*To Be or Not To Be*, Ernst Lubitsch).

So ingrained is this rule of three that when a pattern occurs twice, we expect it again, and a director perhaps ignores this at his peril. There are two references to climbing in *Carve Her Name with Pride*. Violette hid from her future husband by climbing a tree. As she and an underground worker passed a church in occupied France, she says, "This is the town where I was born. See that tower? I climbed that when I was seven." At this point, I was certain that at some point in her pursuit by the German police we should see her climbing. But no. Lewis Gilbert—presumably because he was filming an historical happening—left it at two.

3 Accumulation

The figure *accumulatio* is repetition, considered as adding strength to the statement repeated.

In *Ecstasy* (Gustave Machaty), there are seven shots of the husband, first of his feet entering a door, then his head and shoulders, from different angles, looking for someone. A prism shot shows him still searching, five like images at once, each slightly varied. The cumulative effect is of a search over a period of time, and with some intensity of purpose.

4 Leitmotiv

The *leitmotiv* is a form of accumulation. In *Mr. Hulot's Holiday* (Jacques Tati), we see an old woman, whose husband walks about six paces behind her, gawking around in all directions but hers. The couple seems to recur countless times. They are always first in the dining-room, continually going out, by day and by night, like an incarnation of the aimless futility of holiday places and their patrons.

Twice we are shown two men, each holding a leg of a body suspended over a parapet. When luminous steam sweeps up from a train entering the tunnel below them, we see the legs in silhouette for a moment, and when the steam clears, the corpse has gone—into an empty wagon on the passing train. Other corpses go the same way, and from here on, a burst of steam above the edge prepares us for another drop in the population (*The Lady Killers*, Alexander Mackendrick).

The Rainbow (Mark Donskoi) depicts the German occupation of a Russian village. Throughout the film there are shots of village or countryside that include hanging corpses, as if death by execution were a circumstance of life.

Some leitmotivs, more than others, deepen in meaning with each successive context. The poster in *The Informer* (John Ford) may be verbalized as a symbol of chance or fate: it is a visual hyphen between the three whose lives it mars. Gippo Nolan strides along in an up shot. He stops at a poster offering a reward of twenty pounds for the capture, dead or alive, of Frankie McPhillip. He taps Frankie's picture with an admiring fist, and, after a furtive look around, rips it from the wall. Gippo walks away, and as he stops to listen to a street singer, the poster blows down the street and tangles in his legs. Next we meet the streetwalker, Katie, whom Gippo loves. A well-dressed man is watching her. Aware of the man, she walks away slowly. The wind blows the poster against her legs, and she stoops to disentangle it. Later a third character enters by way of his legs: field boots walk past a pair of civilian ones. The civilian ones turn to look back. The poster blows along the road and catches on the boots. Hands pick the poster up, and our gaze rises to see Frankie himself looking at his own face on the vagrant poster. Gippo informs the Black-and-Tans, and is going to use the twenty pounds they pay him to send Katie to America; but he falls in with an old crony and before dawn the money is drunk, or given away, or wheedled out of him. Gippo is summoned before Gallagher, the commandant of the Irish Republican Army, and Gallagher places a copy of the poster on the fire, with Frankie's face and the words "Twenty Pounds Reward" facing upwards. We see Gippo's face, impassive, and Gallagher's, as he turns from the fire to Gippo, surmise in his eyes. Mulholland's eyes are on Gippo too; and O'Connor broods as the flames dance on his face. Gippo's eyes turn to the fire—the poster, charred, floats in a draft up the chimney. Like it, Frankie was gone, the money nearly gone, and a breath of vengeance was in the air that even Gippo's whiskey-sodden brain could smell.

Where the leitmotiv is not, as in *The Informer*, an image found in the story itself, but imported from the outside, it calls attention to itself by its unexpectedness and the stimulus to give it a meaning in the story. *Teorema* (Pier Paolo Pasolini) starts by quoting *Exodus* to the effect that the Lord would lead his people out by way of the wilderness. A pan shot follows of a reddish stony desert, without a single plant or person to be seen. After this are shots of factories, hills rising in flat fields of asphalt, without a single plant or person to be seen; so the desert through which the Lord is to lead his people in the story is that symbolized by the factory and parking lot. The mother, daughter, and son of a well-to-do family form a strong attachment for a young man, their guest, because (it is suggested) of the idle lives they lead, and his departure leads to mental disturbance of one kind or another in all three. The servant of the family, also fascinated, is disturbed in a different way: she fasts and levitates. Ten times throughout the narrative, the red stony desert is cut in, often with cloud shadows passing quickly over it, and the film ends in the desert, with someone seen there for the first time. It is the father, who takes off his clothes in a railway station, and in the next shot is walking naked over the desert stones, and in close-up gives an agonized cry. So the film begins, ends, and is interrupted by an image of the barren, unproductive life of the people shown.

It is hardly needful to add that film composers know their Wagner well, and repeats of music linked with persons or situations are common practice. Now and then a change in a situation or the plight of a person is emphasized by a variation in the music. In *Cynara* (King Vidor), for example, when Warlock and Doris are together during the early days of his wife's absence, Irving Berlin's "Blue Skies" is sometimes heard, perhaps as they are punting on the river. As his wife's return chills their relationship, "Blue Skies" may come harsh and loud, in moody minor, or broken and hesitant.

5 Repetition with Development

When an image is repeated with a consistent change in size or order, the meaning conveyed is direction. This is commonly done with printed symbols.

In the first of a series of billposters in *The Ring* (Alfred Hitchcock), One-Round Jack Sanders is in fourth place, at the bottom, and Bob Corby in large letters at the top. In the second poster, Sanders is in fourth place, but in larger type. Then, as people pass a poster in winter clothes, we see him third out of five. In the next one, Corby's manager points him out as being in second place; and at last, in the poster for Royal Albert Hall, the top bout in largest letters is "One-Round Jack Sanders versus Bob Corby."

As a destroyer is about to sink its first submarine, our attention is held by the ping of the Asdic apparatus, and the steadily shrinking figure of the range from nine thousand to two hundred yards (*The Cruel Sea*, Charles Frend).

Less common, but more effective perhaps, is a change in things.

Laurel and Hardy, owners of an electrical equipment shop, are so absorbed by a feud with the grocer beside them, that they pay no attention to a very short man who walks out of the shop with a toaster under his arm. On his next visit the man carries a table lamp and an electric clock. Laurel watches him, curious but unconcerned, as if to say, "Well, he looks as if he knows what he's about." Then it is a standard lamp and a hot plate. The fourth time, as they are putting up a sign, "Will be back soon," the man is going in with a wheelbarrow, looking neither to right nor left, just minding his own business, and as Laurel and Hardy return, they find him wheeling out a washing machine. At the end, they squeeze between their front door and the back of a moving van, and look around mystified at an empty shop (*Tit for Tat*, Charles Rogers).

City for Conquest (Anatol Litvak) portrays three careers in a series of cups. The first night Peggy and Murray met, they won a prize for an exhibition of dancing. At last they become professionals. One sequence contains these elements: to the sound of applause, Peggy and Murray spotlighted on a dancing floor, bowing; a marquee announcing a competition; a prize cup, dancing feet, and one after another, three cups, each taller than the one before it, each inscribed for a different step, Rhumba, Tango, Samba, each with a few bars of music followed by clapping. The final shot, following the largest cup of all, is a shaving mug in close-up, holding a brush. As a hand reaches for the brush, we retreat to show Danny, the truck driver who loves Peggy, shaving in a slum room.

One of the most subtle uses of repetition is found in *Olympiad, Part II* (Leni Riefenstahl). The diving sequence starts with a diver approaching to full length along a diving board. He dives toward us, fills the frame, and we follow his descent to the water—a shot of some length. Then we see several kinds of dive, all the divers' faces seen clearly. They move with military precision. Three times we see spectators, giving their smiling approval. As the sequence passes halfway, there are no spectators, no full-length shots; the approach to the end of the diving board is gradually shortened, until at last we see the diver only from board to water. The angle is up, and the eye soars and sinks with the diver's body. The camera moves away, there is more sky seen, there is a just perceptible slowing of movement. The shots are now nearly all from the diver's left. Preliminaries are now completely gone, and every dive is cut in during flight, giving an unending succession of arcs of movement. A new angle comes in, from above, making more apparent the shrinking in size of the diver's body as he falls. The splash of the water entry now is cut, so it is a continuum of soaring flying figures, in the same curves, hypnotically throbbing. We are looking from the divers' right and up from far away at black bodies against a glowing sky. Movement is still slowed a little to stress its curves, but the tempo is quickened by cutting more and more off the end of the dives, stopping now when the diver reaches diving board level coming down. There is now but a steady pulse of swooping silhouettes, and the tiny figures fly like swallows, as if it were always one person continually soaring and sinking, never falling to earth or water, nothing else to be seen but sky or cloud. So strong was the physiological effect of this developing rhythm that viewers have been heard to say that it took minutes after the film stopped for their heartbeats to slow down to normal.

6 Repetition with Variation

A set of movements, done over and over, unchanged, may bring out the drudgery of daily practice (*The Seventh Veil*, Compton Bennett), but in most cases, repetition with change is both more interesting and truer to life. It must contain a part that stays the same (providing the repetition) and one which alters.

Khymr the peasant buys new shoes and a new suit. He leaves behind him his old boots and leg cloths, but the tailor politely hands them to him. On his way out of the shop Khmyr drops them unobtrusively, but a polite assistant picks them up for him. Thinking himself unobserved, Khmyr puts them down as he enters the revolving doors, but the doorman brings him back and makes sure that he takes them; and so for other tries. The scope here for the best mime is limited, for the changing elements—the way of dropping the boots, and the person who thwarts him—are few (*Happiness*, Aleksandr Medvedev).

To suggest McGinty's voting thirty-seven times, Preston Sturges separated out and repeated several times a single simple detail of the procedure. Three times, for example, we see McGinty greeting the returning officer, "Hello Bill" (the password), on which he is identified as a person known to be dead or absent or sick, as whom he votes. Then the director switches to another briefer synecdoche, McGinty pulling the curtain of the polling booth, repeating it several times; then to another, McGinty running fast up or down steps of a polling station. Each repeated act stood in this way for a vote cast, but by changing the part that stands for the whole procedure, the director holds our interest *(The Great McGinty)*.

As the art lies in the fresh detail invented for each recurrence, the scope for this grows with the number of the variables. In *The Key* (Sir Carol Reed), a salvage tug sails four times to bring back a torpedoed merchantman, and each time it is attacked. On the first occasion, the tug was strafed by airplanes. A submarine some distance off was the second attacker, and the third was a submarine coming out of a mist, quite close. The fourth attack nearly destroyed the tug: the masts fell, flames flared out of the hatch, and several men were injured. As the attack varied, so did the manning of the guns, the navigation, and other incidental details. We saw four "attacks," but few, if any, images more than once.

In *The Key*, things like ships and shells and submarines placed a limit on what could be varied. As the variables grow in kind and number, the constant element becomes harder to define. A growing respect between two men, Yank and the Boatswain, is told sufficiently by showing us their behavior as they work together, plugging the deck, working tied to long ropes in a heavy sea, or tipping a body into the sea at a funeral *(San Demetrio London,* Charles Frend).

One of the subtler uses of repetition is to show the same happening twice, adding details when we see it again, subduing others that had more weight when first we saw them. The same scene begins and ends *Brief Encounter* (David Lean). It is set in a railway buffet. A man and a woman are sitting at a table, not speaking. A second woman comes to the table and exclaims, "Laura, what a lovely surprise!" Laura introduces Dr. Harvey to Dolly Messiter. "He's going out to Africa next week." The doctor and Laura exchange resigned looks as he rises to fetch tea for the visitor. A bell rings; he rises. He takes his coat, presses Laura's shoulder with his left hand, and goes out, not looking back. Dolly moves to where he had sat. Up to here the two versions differ only in small changes of emphasis. When Dr. Harvey tells Dolly, "The sugar is in the spoon," in the first scene we are looking at him, in the second one, the camera never moves from where it was, on Laura; we hear his voice only.

In the opening version, we are now watching Laura, the whistle of an express heard soaring in power as it enters the station. We pan with Dolly as she rises and goes to the counter. As she talks to the manageress, she turns and looks surprised. We look at the table—empty. We look at the door, as Laura enters and leans against it. "I just wanted to see the express go through," she says. A bell rings. Dolly goes to the counter for a glass of brandy and is told that the bar is closed. "But when a woman is sick . . ." she says, and is given the brandy. Laura sips the brandy without relish, and they rise to catch their train.

In the ending version, we approach Laura. Her voice is heard without her lips moving. "I felt he was going out of my life." A whistle is heard and the first puffs of an engine. Her voice continues, "he might not catch the train . . . would come back and pretend he had forgotten something. I prayed for him to do this. . . ." The rising insistence of the approaching express is broken by the double ring of a loud bell. "The express . . . of course it doesn't stop. . . ." Dolly is seen at the distant counter. Dissolve to Laura, the camera slowly tilting her body forty-five degrees to the left. She rises, goes out the door, and rushes to close-up, body still off center. We are looking at the tracks, as the train swoops down from the top of the screen. We see Laura's face in close-up, light flashing rhythmically across it, hair blowing. "I really meant to do it, Fred. . . ." The Rachmaninoff concerto is heard and continues after the train dies away. Her body no longer tilted, Laura turns back to the restaurant. From inside, she opens the door, closes, and leans on it. "I nearly fainted . . ." We retreat from a close-up of her face to find her sitting at home. The last word is said: the concerto, heard on the radio, prolongs the feeling.

To the incident, as a drinker of tea seated at another table might have seen it, the ending adds what it was as Laura felt it. By this time, too, we have been privy to their meetings, once a week and few, and have seen their affection grow. It is as if the director had said to us, "Do you see that man and woman sitting at the table, their silence interrupted by a tactless chatterbox? I will show you that moment's meaning."

7 Change of Context—One Repetition

It should be clear from the above that a single repetition serves a different set of uses from those served by several repetitions.

One repeat may, like a simile, point an analogy (pls. 3, 4).

In *Knight Without Armour* (Jacques Feyder), a line of men stand with backs to a high wall, three with blindfolds. Three soldiers crouch around a machine gun, and one is standing beyond them. Countess Alexandra, presiding in the White Officers' Mess, hears a machine-gun firing, "executing some commissars and other red bandits," she is told. Shortly after, she and the White army flee, the red flag is raised, and the white flag with black eagles is left on a step to be trod on. A Red officer, lounging at a messroom table, tells a waiter to bring him better vodka. We see another line of men along the same wall, three with blindfolds. Three soldiers crouch around a machine gun, the one standing beyond raises his arm and the gun fires a volley. The likeness of the executions hints at a likeness in trial, judgment, and attitudes on both sides.

During the pouring of a brick, Holland picks up on the tip of his umbrella, a speck of gold that had fallen on his toe. That would be worth six shillings, at current prices, he points out severely to the operator. Later on, as he watches Pendlebury, pouring lead into molds of the Eiffel Tower, he picks up with the same umbrella a drop of molten lead. We see in his eye and the port of his head that the two pourings have bred a plan: they will ship the stolen gold as Eiffel Towers (*The Lavender Hill Mob*, Charles Crichton).

A second use of one repeat is to make vivid a lapse of time and a change of situation.

Shortly after World War I, Brigadier-General Wynn-Candy sits at a long table with a very distinguished company, including his friend, Theo Kretschmer-Schuldorff, a German officer just out of prisoner-of-war camp. In November 1939, Kretschmer-Schuldorff, a refugee from Nazi Germany, knows only one person in England and is rescued from the police by Wynn-Candy, who exclaimed that he would vouch for the German "with everything I have, sir." Dissolve to a long shot of the same long table, only the two of them seated, and one servant. Two old men—all that are left of their world (*Colonel Blimp*, Michael Powell and Emeric Pressburger).

In *Oil Lamps* (Jiri Weiss), Stephanie twice walks in the park with Paul. Once, when they are affianced, on a Sunday morning, she is walking with her arm in his, smiling proudly at her soldier, pleased at the townspeople who politely raise their hats or nod, all very elegant but for a sour expression on his face. Outside a shop, he repulses with scorn a fat-bodied halfwit, who salutes him with a mindless grin. Late in the film, now married, they walk in the park again on a Sunday morning, he in uniform as before. He suffers from advanced syphilis. His feet drag and she supports him; he is only partly aware of what is going on. She is ashamed, and looks but covertly at those who pass. They meet the halfwit. Paul returns the other's grin and makes a gesture towards joining him. Stephanie firmly keeps Paul with her, and the halfwit follows. The feet of Paul and the halfwit are both splayed, both drag the ground. For a few seconds, as one is behind the other, we note the resemblance and remember their former meeting.

We are shown a patient, Margaret, buying a blouse at her mother's insistence. It is hard for Margaret to say "no" to anyone. We see her holding three different blouses up in front of her. The salesgirl holds out one with ruffles in front (such as her mother wears), and says it would suit her perfectly. At home, Margaret looks at herself in the glass, the blouse held in front. "I hate this blouse," she says, and bursts into tears. After treatment, we see her shopping again. We approach her, past the salesman's back, as he is speaking. "Dressy, sensible, and the new stylish spring blue." She slowly smiles with a feeling of pleasure, and says, "I'm sorry, but I don't like anything you have shown me. Have you anything else? Can you show me something a little gayer" (*Feeling of Rejection*, Robert Anderson).

Obviously, as in theater, a form of words may recur in an altered context. Verloc, seeing the customary burned cabbage, as usual says to his wife, Stevie's sister, "Why don't we send next door for some lettuce?" It was dangerous for him to forget that Stevie, who was always sent to buy the lettuce, had lately been killed (*Sabotage*, Alfred Hitchcock).

As well as the lapse of time, repetition may tell its nonlapse.

As Orphée moves through a mirror into the land of the dead, the clock is striking 6:00, and a postman is putting a letter through the slot. As Orphée returns through the mirror with two companions, the clock is still striking 6:00, and the postman still dropping the letter. All that happened between the two identical shots was as quick as a thought in the mind, taking "no time at all" (*Orphée*, Jean Cocteau).

A third use of one repeat is in confirming predictions. Grainger, a racing driver, is recovering from an accident. The nurse winds his clock at 9:45, and leaves him reading to soft radio music and the ticking clock. As we approach close to the bed, he looks up, startled, for all the sound has died away to a dead stillness. He looks at the clock—4:15. He rises, goes to the window, and parts the curtains with surprise on a bright summer afternoon and the sound of birds. He sees below a hearse drawn by two black-plumed black horses, with a driver in livery looking straight ahead. As the camera makes a quick approach, the driver looks up to say to us, "Room for one more inside, Sir." Grainger goes back to sit on his bed, leaning his head on his hands. The ticking and the singing rise into awareness, and the clock he looks up at is at 9:50. We approach the night sky through the window. Later, out of hospital, Grainger takes his place at the end of a queue for a bus and asks the man in front for the time: "A quarter past four." A bus stops. Grainger is about to enter, when the conductor turns toward him, and his face is that of the man who drove the hearse. Taken aback, Grainger hesitates. The conductor says, to hasten him, "Room for one more inside, Sir," waits, shrugs, and then rings the bell. In a close-up of Grainger's face he stares, unable to move. The bus recedes. At a cross street, a long truck enters from the left. The bus veers to avoid it and crashes down the embankment (*Dead of Night*, Basil Dearden).

A fourth use of one repeat is seen in *Brief Encounter,* above. Here the very same event is seen again, with another choice of detail and a deeper meaning.

8 Change of Context—Two Repetitions

The effect of the rule of three (two repetitions) is noticeably different. First, it has a sense of completeness: three times nearly tells a story quite by itself.

In *Moscow Nights* (Anthony Asquith), Briokov, a wealthy peasant, is in love with Natacha, and is the means of preventing the execution of Ignatov, whom she loves. Briokov's is a melancholy part. He is shown three times listening to a gypsy orchestra. First, at the party he had arranged for Natacha, it is playing lively music, as he is bustling about in preparation. Second, when, disappointed, he has drunk himself to forgetfulness and is wearily beating time. Third, at the very end, after he has said his last good-bye to Natacha, he sits forlorn and unheeding.

Three rides on a white horse sum up the life of Bishamber Rai, a once wealthy landowner, now poor. First, we see him galloping from a distance and alighting at his large mansion, a debonair young man. Later, he stands watching his son gallop off, never to return. Lastly, his money all spent on a magnificent concert, to which all his neighbors had been invited, Rai is seen galloping away on a sandy shore. In a half-length shot we have seen the desperation and fear on his face: we know he will not come back. The hull of a large wrecked ship is the only thing breaking the level horizon. He gallops toward it. As it looms up, the horse rears and the rider falls. In close-up, Rai's eyes are closed, and blood flows from his mouth (*The Music Room,* Satyajit Ray).

In the second place, two showings may impress an expected pattern, in order that the third may exploit it—the detail of a day's work, a theatrical act, or an office routine. Schoolchildren used to spell and ask you to pronounce, Mac-Intyre, Mac-Namara, Mac-Innis, and then mac-hinery, to trap you into mispronouncing the last.

The second time we see a trapeze act, one performer waves back his two companions from leaping (*Variety,* E. A. Dupont). This is a fairly obvious break in routine; but in most cases, and in any series at all complex, a stronger effect is gained by showing the detail twice as commonly done and then disrupting it.

On the stroke of 8:00 every morning Dr. Rath reaches the high school, books under his arm, and enters the classroom with the same procedure. He tells the students to sit. He draws out of a back pocket a large white handkerchief and blows his nose, observing the class as he does so. Then with equal alertness and confidence, he opens a memorandum book on his desk. This we see twice. The third time, he comes from spending the night at the cabaret, the worse for drink. The clock is eleven minutes past eight. He hesitates at the door, and then enters his classroom. Chalked on the board are two cartoons: one shows him holding a harp and floating in clouds, in the other a pair of woman's legs are tucked under his arm. Lola Lola's name is on the board set as an exercise in writing. He turns to the class and is jeered, and only the headmaster's entrance restores order. The more his daily habits are impressed on our mind, the more of a shock is the anarchy of the third entry (*The Blue Angel,* Joseph von Sternberg).

The third occurrence may shrink to a single detail, a mere synecdoche. The clink of his nickel is very distinct as the bartender passes through the turnstile to the railway platform. Carol's nickel sticks (which draws our attention to it) but it does go in with a like distinct clink. Only the two are on the platform, he distant, she close. We see the converging track and hear an approaching rumble. Both face toward us, her eyes alert as to what the man behind her is doing. He looks to his right, hands restless: the entrance is deserted. He changes his coat from one hand over to the other. He spreads his fingers and leans forward, as if to run toward her back. Along the tracks we see the looming train. We see them both, she leaning forward, as if expectant. We hear, and recognize, the clear clink of a nickel dropped in the turnstile. The bartender looks left. A black woman enters the platform. The train flashes in (*Phantom Lady*, Robert Siodmak).

9 Simultaneous Repetition

The split screen or multiple image presents at one time images normally seen one after another; on three separate screens, as used by Abel Gance; in a splitting of a single screen, as done by Dziga Vertov; or in an assembly of subframes on a wide screen, as used by Christopher Chapman.

A limitation in the use of multiple images lies in these words of M. D. Vernon: "Thus a rough generalization may be made that the total amount which can be attended to at any one moment is constant. If attention is concentrated on a small part of the field, little will be perceived in other parts; if attention is diffused over a larger area, no one part will be very clearly and accurately perceived."[5]

First, we are concerned here with multiple images felt or known to be such. Special effects photography creates a single impression with several images, as, for example, in *Things to Come* (William Cameron Menzies), where one wave of airplanes followed after another (this the top half) over the cliffs of Dover (this the bottom half). The airplanes were models, the cliffs the actual place, and yet we perceived them as a single place and event as a consequence of simultaneous montage. It was, in fact, a use of the split screen with the split hidden.

There is no doubt that a peripheral awareness of several similar events is a different impression—vaguer and more generalized—than a foveal concentration on one. The four, and then nine, subframes of Abel Gance's *Napoleon*, in each of which a pillow fight is raging, while not identical, have common elements of movement, of blows, and the flight of feathers. They may be taken in as a single abstract movement, or examined in one frame, with very little input from the others.

In a like scene, as Ivan's wake is being celebrated, we see in the eight small panes of a window eight various pictures of Ivan as a boy, as if looking in at the wake with different expressions of interest, as, perhaps, when a boy, he had looked in at someone else's wake (*Shadows of our Forgotten Ancestors*, Sergei Parazhdanov).

In *The Man with a Movie Camera* (Dziga Vertov), on either side of a screen split in the center, mirror images of a tram move together to vanish in the center line, or top and bottom halves of the screen may show different shots of city traffic.

Abel Gance's three screens set side by side are another means of depicting multitude. He has put, for example, on either side screen mirror images of a column of troops, coming into sight small in the distance and sweeping offscreen in the foreground, and in the center, nearly full length, the front of a column, four abreast, marching hugely toward us (*Napoleon*).

Christopher Chapman places on a dark screen a number of subframes of differing shapes and sizes. He points out that in *A Place to Stand*, an hour and three-quarters' footage is run in seventeen and a half minutes.[6] We are, he feels, aware of it all, but look at what interests us, a somewhat more optimistic view than Vernon's. It will be obvious, if used for narrative purposes, and assuming that Vernon is correct, that members of an audience might not all look at the same place, and each might find a different story, some perhaps no story at all. If all the subframes are different, and art requires the exclusion of the nonessential, then the only way of ensuring that the viewer does not miss the essential frame is to do away with all the others, and thus preclude the multiple frame as a narrative device.

A Place to Stand, however, is not a story, but a regional survey, and in Christopher Chapman's practice there, the various images presented at the same time, where they are not identical, very often show the same event. It is clearly of no consequence at which of four vertical frames the viewer looks, when each one, side by side, shows a flow of red molten iron. The meaning is the same for each, the several images combining to convey an abundant output. The director sometimes guides our attention by having each of the divers in four subframes plunge in succession from the left.

When the contents of the subframes are sufficiently different, Chapman may limit the choice to two. He will show us in up shot men trimming limbs off a tree, and in the frame beside it, the branches landing on the ground; or on the left side a debate in the legislature, and on its right, but narrower, the visitors' gallery. As a variation, the two outer frames of three may show a burning forest, and the center one an airplane approaching, spraying water. In a sense these count as repetition, for we view the same event wherever we look. As a means of emphasis, all but one of six subframes may leave the screen, and that one at the same time grow larger (pl. 5).

It remains to note some of the possible variations: two rows of four squares each across the screen; a row of four and a long horizontal one above them; three on a diagonal; five, four, or three vertical panels; five in a quincunx; four in a bottom row and a fifth moving from left to right above them. In one, top left, we see the head of a man blowing glass, a furnace of molten glass in the center, and bottom right, the orange tip of molten glass at the end of a blow pipe, suggesting by its angle the end of the pipe seen in the top corner: contrasted in visual pattern, alike in topic. All eight subframes may show us the same caboose of a train slowly vanishing around a curve, each at a different point in time. Of two subframes, one may show a train running off left, and the other a train running off right, diverging in opposite directions, but a like pattern of movement. Six subframes of a hockey game had all the familiar blue cast of the television screen and rounded corners, thus adding to the meaning "hockey," "hockey seen at home on many screens" (pl. 6).

To what degree does the multiplication of images add a figurative meaning that is not present in any one image by itself? Simultaneous images can add a sense of size or quantity, where the content of all the subframes is nearly identical: a great many simultaneous pillow fights, a huge steel industry. As the visual images differ more and more, it is either an abstraction of moving lines or it is no more nor less than an array of small close-ups, with rather less time to absorb the detail than if they were mounted one after another.

Despite its limitations, simultaneous repetition has a place in fiction. In a series of alternating shots, Frémissant, a timid young man, and Garadoux, a bold unscrupulous fellow, both suitors for the same lady, are each seen alone, practicing words, gestures, and blows for use at their next meeting, each facing a different side of the screen. After this, each on one half of the screen, we see Garadoux to the right and Frémissant to the left, each in his own room, knocking down, kicking, and otherwise doing damage to an imaginary opponent, each doing the same act in unison with the other, both together making a single pattern, easily seized as a whole, showing too that the situation has had the same, almost automatic, effect on both men (*Les Deux Timides,* René Clair).

At the end, Frémissant has married the girl. In the last frames of the film, the screen is split into three. The right picture appears first, the rest of the frame remaining black: it is the girl's father, sitting in bed, reading. Then on the left, Garadoux appears, also reading in bed. Last, in the center, Frémissant and his wife are in bed together reading. One at a time, they catch our attention by moving. The father turns his light out, and the frame is black there. Garadoux, in a fury, throws his lamp on the floor. The pair in the center stop reading and look at one another, a little nervous. Frémissant looks toward us, reaches up, and pulls down a blind between us and them. Here, by introducing one at a time, and catching our attention by movement one at a time, the director has successfully avoided a diffusion of attention and has focused the viewer's attention exactly where he wished.

10 Superimposition

Superimposing one image on another, when used for the same purpose as the multiple image, is subject to the same limitations—the vagueness of the whole and the likelihood of concentration on one of the images. It has this advantage: the eye need not move, for both images use the same space.

In *Fahrenheit 451* (François Truffaut), the same man is doing the same thing in both images. Montag is waiting as his wife's blood is changed. He is sitting right, facing right, full length. On the left half of the frame, his head and shoulders are superimposed, head on his hand, leaning, waiting. By repeating the image, slightly varied, the idea *waiting* is reinforced.

11 Uses: Comedy

Recurrence is a staple of comedy. Sullivan, a film director, has dressed as a tramp to gain experience of "suffering." Finding him broke and hungry, a girl in a diner buys him breakfast. No director will give her a part in a film, and she is on her way home. Sullivan, grateful for the meal, says he will drive her home in a car that belongs to a director friend of his. When Sullivan turns up in his own car, she is sure (from his clothes) that he has stolen it. They hear a police siren, and, looking in the rear vision mirror, they see two motorcycle policemen catching up to them. She looks anxiously at Sullivan, who says with great aplomb, "There's absolutely nothing they can do." We dissolve to the two of them, facing us through the bars of adjacent cells. "What did you say?" she says. He repeats in the same firm tone, "There's absolutely nothing they can do." The second time, the situation contradicts the statement, for one thing that "they" can clearly do is put them in jail (*Sullivan's Travels*, Preston Sturges).

Toto, passing the hut of a newly arrived family, is wet by a maid who empties a glass of water behind her without looking. Her mistress threatens to discharge her. Toto the Good says, "You mustn't. It was nothing. I like water." Smiling, he takes up a pail of water and pours it over his head. The mistress smiles; the maid smiles and looks grateful. Toto is later going round a corner, shrinking wet and cold in his clothes, when the maid comes down an alley toward him, again with a pail. She dumps the water in it over his head and skips away with glee down the alley (*Miracle in Milan*, Vittorio de Sica).

An act repeated may amuse us more than if it were seen once. Holland is supposed to have tried to foil the robbery he actually committed. He and his chief enter an office whose door is lettered "Chief Cashier." Three of them come out and march to the door of the Deputy Chairman, and close it behind them. From here four emerge to see the Chairman. They knock, enter, and close the door, and we hear clapping. All with appropriate modesty on Holland's part (*The Lavender Hill Mob*, Charles Crichton).

12 Uses: Memory

Seeing an event again is near to remembering it. Kierkegaard wrote that the two were the same, but in opposite directions: what is recollected is repeated backward, whereas repetition is recollected forward.[7]

Vicky Page has been told that she is to dance the leading role in *The Red Shoes* (Michael Powell and Emeric Pressburger), and Julian Craster that he is to compose the score for it. It is a moment of elation for both; each refers to the ballet as "my ballet." Their backs are to us as they lean over a parapet, and we hear a train shushing-shushing softly through the dusk. The steam rises and covers them. At the end of the film Craster waits at the station and hears the train approach, now busily buzzing a rhythm of three like some great insect. We see Vicky's red-shod feet fleeing down flights of steps. In long shot she mounts the parapet and leaps over. The approaching train, the same parapet, bring back to us—and surely to Craster—the happy moment when both had reached the crest of their careers, and link to it the moment at which his music and her dancing had wrenched them apart and faced her with a choice between her marriage and her dancing beyond her power to make.

13 Uses: Patterns of Experience

In some, perhaps all, lives, a certain kind of event seems to keep on happening, a confirmation, perhaps, of astrology. *O Lucky Man* (Lindsay Anderson) suggests this in an interesting way. It is the story of a young man, Travis, whose faith in his fellow men is slowly undermined by a series of incidents as he looks for work. Some actors play several parts, all of which have a similar character, and we gain the impression that the young man seems to be meeting the same types of people wherever he goes. When he starts as a coffee salesman, and later tries for a part in a film, the same person plays one of his fellow applicants, not as the same man but the same type. His first landlady invited him to bed when he arrived. She wore the same face as the Scottish vicar's wife. He had escaped from a secret war plant, and had collapsed, exhausted, and was about to eat the fruit which decorated the church at Harvest Thanksgiving. "But that's God's food," she said. "You're just a child," she added, and gave him her breast to suck. From looking the same, from being alike in character each time, from the sometimes puzzled glance by Travis, on seeing the same face on a different person, we have a sense of patterns happening over and over.

14 Repetition as an Element of Structure

A story may show a repeated pattern of experience, arising from character or outer circumstances, as it may in prose fiction or on the stage. Twice at a critical moment in *Shoot the Piano Player* (François Truffaut), Edward Saroyan left the woman who loved him and when he came back she was dead. On the first occasion, his wife had confessed that as a condition for his tremendous advance as a concert pianist she had allowed herself to become his impresario's mistress. She hated herself for it. He left the room. In the hall he thought, "I knew I should not leave her at that moment." He turned and ran back. The room was empty, the window open: she had leaped out and killed herself. Later, he and a barmaid with whom he had fallen in love arrive at his brother's farm just as they are about to be attacked by two former accomplices in crime. She and Edward are just ready to go. He leaves her to have a last word with his brothers. She runs to the house to warn the brothers of the gunmen's arrival, and is shot.

In a second way, a film may end as it begins, in a kind of cyclical structure. The same happening starts and ends *Brief Encounter* (David Lean). The impression is stronger where, as in *The Ox-Bow Incident* (William A. Wellman), the visual pattern that starts and ends is also the same. Two men enter a town, riding toward us up a deserted street. A dog walks across in front of them, and we hear an accordion playing "The Red River Valley." At the end, when all is over, the same two men ride on the same empty sloping street out of town. After they pass, the same dog returns across the street, and the music of "The Red River Valley" ends the film.

The most fully cyclical film is perhaps *Dead of Night* (Basil Dearden and others). It starts with a man driving toward us, trees lining the road on either side. He stops in close-up. There is a two-story half-timbered house away from the road. The man shakes his head, starts the car, and drives up to the front door. As the owner introduces his fellow guests, the visitor says he has been there before; he has dreamed of the visit. He describes the next arrival and predicts what will happen, ending with "something terrible after the lights fail." He wants to go, but they press him to stay. Several guests tell stories of unexplainable happenings, the generator does fail, the visitor is left alone with a skeptical psychiatrist, who cannot see because he has dropped his glasses. The visitor strangles the psychiatrist, and after a whirlwind final fugue of people and places from the earlier stories, he is being choked by a ventriloquist's dummy, when he is wakened up at home by a telephone ringing. It is an invitation to go to the country by a stranger, Elliot Foley, to talk about redesigning his house. Then the opening shot again, up the tree-lined road, the stopping, the shaking of the head, the driving up to the door. Is this the dream, or is it the dream's fulfillment? Repeated backward or recollected forward?

In a third way, an event, action, situation, or visual image may recur again and again in the course of a film, which knits it together in a pleasing and compact structure. *Carnet de Bal* (Julien Duvivier), for example, is the story of a woman seeking out each of the partners she had at a ball many years before, curious to see what had become of them. Bridging the episodes is her dance card, on which their names are written (Julien Duvivier).

Several strands of recurrence are intertwined in *The Set-Up* (Robert Wise).

1. The film starts with a street clock at 9:05 P. M., after which we see Stoker Thompson talking to his wife. He is leaving to fight a boxing match across the street in the Paradise City Stadium. At the end of the film Stoker is beaten almost unconscious and his hands broken for not throwing a fight. We retreat to include the same clock at 10:17—his whole life changed in an hour.

2. As we see Stoker at various stages of changing, he looks out of a window toward his hotel room. The last time the light is out. He smiles: his wife is coming to see him fight. One after another, boxers leave the changing room to fight and return, one worried youngster coming back a winner. Gunboat Johnson who has kept telling everyone that Frankie Manila was knocked out twenty-one times, but ended up middle weight champion, returns unconscious.

3. Stoker has given his wife a ticket and would like her to see the bout, but she cannot bring herself to see him knocked out again. She did reach the door of Paradise

City, but a gloating roar of applause drove her away. She walks the street, but is constantly reminded of what is happening in the stadium. A radio set in a shop she passes describes the knockout of Gunboat Johnson. She strolls idly into an arcade, where someone is operating a machine with two puppets boxing, one knocking the other one out.

4. When Stoker looks for a way out of the stadium, by which to elude the gangsters, only the last of three crash doors he tries will open.

5. A boxing bout itself is a repetition with variations. To the doings in the ring, the director has added other goings-on within the stadium, each occurring four or five times:

6. Five times Stoker looks toward the empty seat where he hoped his wife would be.

7. A fat man in the audience is seen eating, each time stuffing something different into his mouth: popcorn, hot dog, ice cream, soft drink, peanuts.

8. Stoker's second and manager, who have taken the bribe to have him throw the fight without telling him, are seen in various degrees of jubilation and fear during the bout.

9. The gangster (who paid the bribe) and his moll (who has a bet) are shown in changing moods as the fight goes on.

10. A companion describes the fight to a vicious blind man.

11. An excitable supporter of Stoker is with her unexcitable husband.

12. Lights recur to mark the numbers of the rounds. The intertwining of these recurrent happenings give the film a ropelike strength, scope for vigorous editing, and the pleasure we find in the return of the known and familiar.

The same strength is found in *Each Day That Comes* (Graham Parker). This film has three strands. First, Stella wakes, and makes ready to leave the small town in which she has grown up—she rises, packs, washes, drinks coffee. In a second strand, eight times or so, we see the people and places she passes as she walks with her suitcase to the station. As we do a daily task for the last time in a house we are leaving, as we walk down a street in a place we have lived in all our lives till then and know we may never see it again, things, places, acts bring past happenings back to mind. These become the third strand: a little girl is seen with two boys; she catches the bouquet at a wedding; an old woman says, "Lovely morning, Stella," and Stella turns and says, "Yes, it is a lovely morning"; "Don't touch me," she says to a boy; she soars in a swing. Each of these scenes recurs more than once; others only once. Her mother dies; "Why don't you marry?" a drunk asks her—"Easy. No one asked me"; "What's going to happen if all the young people leave," says someone. And so Stella's past keeps coming back, and we keep coming back to her last morning rituals and her last walk away from all she has been.

15 Repetition and Other Figures

Since montage is dealt with below, it is merely needful to mention here that some kinds of montage can also be seen as repetition with variation. In *The Plough That Broke the Plains* (Pare Lorentz), the effect of drought in the West is felt in the piling up of shots linked by likenesses:

deserted machinery;
a spider scuttling over cracks in parched ground;
feet walking through *dust;*
up shot of a briskly turning windmill;

lowering clouds of *dust;*
dust swirling up a village street;
dust blowing into a house under a closed sash;
dust blowing along a field;
dust piled on a floor and in a fireplace;
a *dune* piled against the side of a house;
two children shoveling *dust;*
a family leaving with a car and trailer;
a pan across the ribbed face of a field, with only a blade of grass here and there.

Repetition can be antithetical. In *Woodstock* (Michael Wadleigh), a woman singing a song is seen twice, on one side of the frame in orange light, and in blue on the other.

An image in *A Hen in the Wind* (Yasujiro Ozu) would not be a metaphor unless repeated. While her husband is at war, a wife has difficulty in keeping herself and her little son. The husband comes home, and after an estrangement arising from what she was driven to do to pay a medical bill for the child, they are reconciled and resolve to love and trust one another for the child's sake. In the opening scene of two converging walls, two men enter and walk along the right-hand wall away from us. Something white on their backs picks them out from the other working-class passersby. One of the two is holding up a black umbrella. The last shot of the film is the same, except that both are holding up umbrellas. Unless we remember the first scene when we see the last, there is not a metaphor, for either scene by itself is an accident of traffic. Taken together, the first pair is the marriage with one partner absent, the final one is the marriage with both together again. There is also a hint, the umbrella being a cover against rain, that one of the pair in the first scene is unprotected.

In a rather less subtle use, of repeated metonymies, one of two sisters, who have murdered a series of men, tenderly brushes Hoskings's hat, sets it on a shelf in a cupboard, already filled with ranks of men's hats, closes the door, and with it, the case of Hoskings. Like tombstones, the hats preserve the memory of earlier victims and imply by their presence the repetition of the act we have just seen of setting them there (*Arsenic and Old Lace*, Frank Capra).

5
Simile

1 Two Things

The placing together of two different things tends to lead a viewer to think of what they have in common, and thus to emphasize a single characteristic. To use what Eric Partridge calls a "battered simile," if we say a hat sat on is "as flat as a pancake," we are inviting the listener to ignore the size of the hat, its material, decorations, and color, and keep his mind alone on its levelness of surface and shallow depth.[1] The simile here—and this is usual—moves one way: the hat is like a pancake, which is not to say that the pancake is like the hat. The simile may be suppressed, as in this farmer's story:

> I was dancing with a girl the other night, and she kept getting taller and taller.
> "What's the matter?" I said. "You keep going up and up."
> "I've got a wooden leg," she said, "and you keep spinning me round the wrong way."

We all know that "wooden legs" today are not screwed on (I wonder if they ever were) and are made of steel, so besides hyperbole, there is something of fantasy too. But to what is the leg compared? It seems irresistible to me: the three-legged round piano stool that rose or sank on a threaded shaft by turning the seat.

Comparisons may go beyond words. In Caspar David Friedrich's painting, *Two Men Contemplating the Moon* (1819), the roots of a nearly prostrate dying oak are drawn to look like long clawed hands against the moonlit sky, bent at the wrists. In Salvador Dali's painting, *The Woman with a Face of Rose* (1957), the woman's only visible leg appears to be wearing a stocking with a seam down the back. There are, however, rivets on either side of the seam, and in the calf, the seam and leg appear to be splitting open,—as if the leg were shaped from a sheet of metal. When a seventeenth-century artist drew Apollo, known by lyre, by laurel or by rays, topping it by the face and wig of Louis the XIV, he as much as says that in figure and gifts, perhaps that of healing scrofula, Louis is like Apollo.

Just as an artist can draw a thing to look like something else, an actor can use a thing as if it were something else. Pooh-Bah, as he sings his famous trio, brings the curved edge of his fan down on Ko-Ko's neck like the blade of an ax, and Ko-Ko responds as if it were one (*The Mikado*, television, John Seaborne). The Chaplin simile is to use a thing as if it were something else. Mime, indeed, is used in film and theater with equal ease. When the detail is so small that most of the audience would

71

miss it if done on stage, the microscope of the camera lens makes it clear to all. This increases the number of things the film can use for comparisons. How much of Chaplin's horological surgery could be seen, by someone seated halfway back in a theater? Yet all in a cinema can see the can-opener making incision in the back, the telephone receiver used as stethoscope, and the pathological spring deftly removed by tweezers (*The Pawn Shop*, Charles Chaplin).

The manipulation is peculiarly filmic when physically impossible: a coffin creeping fast over the desert, like a furtive malicious beetle, scuttling on some evil errand (*San Simeon del Desierto*, Luis Buñuel); the piano keyboard that Bugs Bunny slides sideways as if it were a typewriter carriage, so as to reach the keys (*Rhapsody Rabbit*, Isadore Freleng).

2   Is a Simile Possible in Film?

Raymond Spottiswoode writes that the film has no way of saying "like," so the *simile* in film is not a possibility.[2] If you compare Aeneas to an oak, by showing the oak, the viewer will merely assume that the tree is part of the scenery, because you cannot say in film, "Aeneas is steadfast, like an oak."

Jean Mitry writes too that in literature, the word "like" is a warning to the reader that Aeneas is part of the story, and the oak is not, but merely describes him.[3] In film, oak and Aeneas are images of equal weight, and film has no means of placing one in special relation to the other.

Both objections leave out of account the working of the viewer's mind, which, given an adequate cue by an actor or director, may add the vinculum that springs the simile. Passing a farm by road, I once saw an old bathtub, partly covered and filled with water for cattle to drink. It was easy to see into the owner's mind: the thing said as plainly as possible, "In size and shape a bathtub is like (and can be used for, made into) a cattle trough." The use to which he put the bath was the outer sign of the word "like" in his mind.

When Chaplin, in *The Fireman*, sets the plates for lunch, the way he holds them and flips them into place, tells us that he is thinking of the plates as playing cards. Object A is used as if it were object B, one seen, the other suggested, as if Chaplin had said in words, "I dealt the plates for lunch," or "I dealt the plates, like cards."

A director too is not without the means to arouse the word "like" in the viewer's mind. We draw back from the vast amphitheater, where a jury is deciding whether or not Peter Carter must leave the earth (as he should have done twenty hours before but for an error). The rings of heads become rings only. A haze clouds the image, which dissolves to a spiral nebula. As well as giving a sense of immensity, as well as telling us where the celestial trial is being held, it is hard not to feel that the director is showing us how an amphitheater is like a nebula (*A Matter of Life and Death*, Michael Powell and Emeric Pressburger).

It is only necessary in logic to point to a single, clear, filmic simile to refute the general proposition that similes are impossible in film. Other types of filmic simile will be examined that may or may not escape the objections of Spottiswoode and others who share his views.[4]

3   Likeness and Difference

It is clear then that in every simile there is present both difference and likeness, and both are a part of its effect. By ignoring differences, we find a simile and may perhaps find an antithesis in the same event, by ignoring likeness.

In *The Lion Has Wings* (Michael Powell, Brian Desmond Hurst, and Adrian Brunel), for example, Hitler, standing on a rostrum, speaking, gesticulating, alternates with shots of bookmakers, hawkers of patent medicines, food vendors, and others, all of whom are bent, for their own gain, on persuading others. Here is an unexpected likeness in persons different in country, prominence, and function. The commentary lies in the likeness and gains force from the difference.

In *The Lady Eve* (Preston Sturges), a passenger boards a liner by tender. This was conveyed by the two vessels' whistling. We see a convulsive spurt of water and hear a desperate, soundless puff before the siren of the tender found its voice. There was a stuttering amazement, a drunken incoordination to these elaborate preliminaries, foiled by the liner's lofty unruffled burst of sounding steam. Here things that are like, in place, in sound, and in function, are unexpectedly contrasted. The commentary lies in the difference and gains force from the likeness.

But it often is not as easy as this to say on which side the commentary lies. To tell us that wars are won as well as by food as they are by munitions, Pare Lorentz *(The Plough That Broke the Plains)* compared the gaits of a tank and a farm tractor. Shots of each are intercut alternately, taken from a similar angle, each peering slowly, for example, over the summit of a slope. The slow heaving advance of the tank to shatter and the tractor to sow were likened in purpose by a likening in pattern and showing them one after another. Lorentz showed the tank and tractor both from ground level coming to the camera. From this angle, the lugs of the tread pouring endlessly over show them both in the way they are most alike, and the greatly different back and top are not seen. But which was the commentary intended: fighting and feeding as two sides of the *same* nation at war, or the *contrary* deeds of growing grain to feed men and firing guns to kill them?

Another case. It is 1919 in Alsace Lorraine; it is underground. In a gallery of a French coal mine, a miner, trapped and exhausted, is tapping on an air pipe. One of the German rescue crew breaks through to where the miner is. In an oxygen mask, as if wearing the wide eyes and the tube-like mouth of an insect, the rescuer has lost humanity, and the mask is German. Dissolve to the war that is just over: French soldiers lying in a field, hurling grenades. The tapping on the pipes continues, quickens, is now a machine gun's rapid staccato. Over a rising knoll, German soldiers advance in gas masks. The miner who tapped, now in uniform, is rigid with terror. A German soldier has reached him, and the two grapple. With his hand under the other's chin, the German thrusts back the Frenchman's head. Now we return to the mine, to see the French miner pulling off the mask of the German rescuer, who with hand under the miner's chin is thrusting back the Frenchman's head. The mask is torn from the German's face; the Frenchman collapses. The rescuer pauses, then quickly strips off the rest of his breathing gear, and begins dragging the unconscious man. He stumbles against a wagon, setting it slowly moving down a gradient. Till his grip relaxes, the rescuer heaves. He falls. The rescued and the rescuer, the Frenchman and the German, lie together, poisoned by the same gas. Faster glides the wagon; at a curve it leaps from the tracks; it crashes (*Kameradschaft*, G. W. Pabst).

There are likenesses in visual pattern: the masks, palms thrusting back a chin, the grapple. There is a change in circumstance—from the tunic of war to the smock of peace, from the mask of the killer to the mask of the rescuer, from gas the ally to gas the foe, from paddock to cross-cut. In each case, the deadly gas of mistrust and violence has threatened the lives of both, and the unhindered car, whatever symbolic load we charge it with, leaps from the tracks to smash. The two men stand for two

nations. It is a comparison that continues to echo deeper meanings, which difference and likeness both combine to create.[5]

4   Abstraction

To create a simile is to choose or abstract from one total event a single characteristic it shares with another. The differences between the events, however great, are ignored. The greater they are, indeed, the more striking the simile becomes.[6]

A dish of ice cream and a barrow of cement are only alike in the shape and texture of their surfaces. Size, container, substance, and use are all different, but a slice of peach and a cherry as the final touch to a serving of cement from a mixer, draws our attention to this one likeness (*Rhapsody in Rivets*, Leon Schlesinger and Isadore Freleng).

Starving men, snatching hope from the farthest reach of resemblance, stew a boot, test its readiness, twirl spaghetti laces, and eat with grimaces of gusto. They cling with desperation to the slender likeness, and refuse to admit the overwhelming difference (*The Gold Rush*, Charles Chaplin).

How abstraction works is clearly seen in *Modern Times* (Charles Chaplin), where the Little Fellow takes a brace and bit, and bores three holes in a cheese, before cutting off a piece for a customer. This implies two kinds of cheese: one with holes and one without, and if a customer orders the kind with holes, you bore them. Whether the two differ in other ways, as crumbly or hard, strong or mild, red or white, veined or mottled or not, made from the milk of cows, ewes, nanny goats or buffaloes, from skim milk or whole, is left out of account.

The director must have an eye for the narrow lune of likeness where things that are highly unlike overlap, and thus abstract a new class of things, defined as having this trait in common. He must also be able to shoot or edit them in such a way as to make this common trait so clearly visible that the word "like" leaps to the viewer's mind.

The rings on convicts' ankles and those on donkeys' noses are threaded both with chains that signify how their keepers view them. Differences of brain, speech, mode of walking, and all the rest are ignored, and the one trait in common, rings and the chain, can hardly fail to impress on the viewer that both are used as animals for labor (*I Was a Fugitive from a Chain Gang*, Mervyn Leroy).

Ignoring all but one characteristic is a basis for comparison in science, in fields as different as those of Adam Smith and Linnaeus.[7] It is also a simplification found in a child, his imagination unhindered by many facts, who makes nothing of finding a bread knife in the teeth of a comb or a steering wheel in a round wooden bowl. Eisenstein finds this in Chaplin.[8] The mind that makes a simile must see things unencrusted by knowledge and attitudes. As in lateral thinking, one must reach in a nonhabitual direction, thrust through the accumulated associations of years, and find a new and unexpected likeness.[9] It is this unexpectedness that gives their charm to children's and Chaplin's similes. To enjoy the longness of spaghetti (unseen when piled on a plate) Chaplin stands on his chair and lets it hang, but cannot tell it apart from streamers hanging down from the ceiling. To consider the difference in texture, flavor, and moisture would spoil an intriguing fancy (*City Lights*, Charles Chaplin). If you can wring water out of clothes, why not out of dishes (*The Pawnshop*, Charles Chaplin)?

By alternating a man panting from fear and jealousy and steam breathing from the cylinders of the railway engine he nearly rammed, the man's emotional disturbance is magnified (*Ecstasy*, Gustave Machaty).

5 Hyperbole and Fantasy

In choosing a likeness to link two things, we may so ignore proportion or substance as to carry us beyond the possible into fantasy. A woman in a Welsh hat and costume sits on a stool, and plucks harp music from the spokes of a pennyfarthing's front wheel, twice her seated height (*Music Academy,* John Halas and Tony Guy; pl. 7). At least spokes and harp strings are both of metal, and a taut bicycle spoke will give a musical note. Hyperbole certainly, but plausible. But when moonbeams are plucked to the pacing of a bass viol, and a cobweb is a rippling harp, we are enchanted by the outrageously impossible: the silent and intangible is now solid and audible (*The Boogie Woogie Man Will Get You,* Walter Lantz and James Culhane). When Vulcan plugs his ears with a pinch of cloud, it becomes a solid without benefit of chemistry (*Trombone Trouble,* Walt Disney). When fish swim out of cupboards, we have done something either to the fish or the air (*The Magician,* Ivan Renc and Pavel Hobl). And when Bongo parts a waterfall by pushing the water to one side, like a curtain, a discontinuous flow is made a solid mesh by a waft of the hand (*Fun and Fancy Free,* Jack Kinney).

Fancy in film has hardly any limits. An intersection of freeways suddenly convolutes itself to a knotty coil of cables (*Diary,* Nedeliko Dragic). In a *Monty Python* installment (television, John Davies), a creature falls to the ground, a lorry goes over it, leaves it buried, and flips a gravestone into place behind it. Hands begin growing out of the grave, followed by arm-stems up to the elbows. A child with a basket stands at the foot of the grave, until all are finished writhing out of the ground. Then with a pair of scissors, she passes along, snips off their hands, and puts them into her basket—like flowers. If you can plant a seed or a slip or a stolon, why not cut people off and plant them too?

Charlie and the Big (gouty-footed) Fellow are imprisoned in a revolving door. Charlie bends to free his cane, which has wedged the door, and his head, which is pinched between the door and jamb. After several Herculean tugs, the door flies free with such power that Charlie is flung up the stairs to the second floor, along a hall and into a room where he spins round and round until stopped by the porter,—like a Roman catapult on a vertical axis (*The Cure,* Charles Chaplin).

In *King Size* (Kaj Pindal; pl. 8), an antismoking film, matches stood, flaming end up, for torches; cigarettes circling the edge of a cake were candles, four cigarettes side by side in the mouth were a musical instrument, a full package, tilted on a stand, lid opened back, was a rocket launcher. Here it was mostly change of size which changed the function. The match torch stood three times the height of a man.

Taking this a step further, Bernard Longpré starts with a simple line, a piece of rope, and makes it a snake, a spring, a stair, a hoop, a swing, and, by adding eyes at the right places, a variety of odd creatures (*Nebule;* pls. 9, 10).

6 Inner State

Where a likeness is presented as one perceived by a character, not by us, it may be a means of letting us know his thoughts or feelings.

Charlie, an escaped convict, wakes up, catches sight of his striped pajamas, looks startled, feels up at the bars above his head on the brass bedstead, still uncertain, and is only reassured when a valet brings his clothing (*The Adventurer,* Charles Chaplin).

Mathieu, driving at night, has run an animal down, stopped, and found blood on the roadside. He worries about it, and goes back the following day to find and shoot the animal. As his wife pours the breakfast coffee, drops fall on the table. We see Mathieu looking, a close-up of the drops, brown on the table, a flash of the drops of blood we saw on the road, and then the table again, the brown drops and his hand withdrawing. The flash (we had seen it before and could recognize it easily) was "as quick as thought" and as sharp as a blow (*Belle*, André Delvaux).

7 Simile Expressed by Manipulation of the Actor

In some of the instances above the comparison is made between a thing as we would use it and the thing as used by a character. When a thing made for one purpose is used for another, we have demonstrated a simile; we are thinking and acting the word "like," even if it never passes our lips (pl. 7). This is not peculiar to film or mime. An Irish uncle said to me once, "Ach, my hair's so thin, you can comb it with a towel," comparing the teeth of a comb to the rather shorter nap of a Turkish towel. Opening a back volume of *Punch* at random, I found the skirt of a curtain lifted over a table "like a tablecloth."[10]

The painter, the wit, and the man of science are adept in finding likenesses missed by the rest of us.[11] The consequence is a kind of double synecdoche—they bring out in two different things a part of each only, the one trait they share in common: the red color in paint and ketchup (*Saps at Sea*, Gordon Douglas), the reflecting shiny surface of a bald head and a mirror (*Safety Last*, Fred Newmeyer and Sam Taylor).

The first source of manipulative similes must be Chaplin. As *Monsieur Verdoux*, he finds a place in the telephone directory with fingers that seem to be counting banknotes: he is seeking the address of another woman to murder for her money. As *The Vagabond*, he lays a checkered shirt on a barrel for tablecloth, shaping the sleeves for napkins, and later tucking one under his neck. As the barber in *The Great Dictator*, he pulls up the headrest of his barber's chair and buffs his fingernails with it, changing its function and its name by what he does with it. After Big Jim, ravenously hungry, has snatched a leg of chicken from Charlie, and is wolfing it fiercely, Charlie timidly strokes the fur of Jim's parka. He is clearly thinking, even if he does not say, "Good doggie" (*The Gold Rush*).

In the wealth of similes in Chaplin's films, some are more elaborated. As a waiter in *Modern Times*, he is taking a duck to a customer, and is swept away by dancers rising from their tables and filling the center of the floor. At last he reaches a carving table, and one of three young men snatches the duck and runs away tucking it under his arm like a football. Charlie intercepts, catches the duck, runs as in a football game, dodging the three opposing players, and leaps onto the carving table and another table beyond it, scoring a touchdown as he crashes to the floor with his customer. As a stage hand in *Behind the Screen*, Charlie dons a helmet and lowers the vizor to keep out the odor of the man to the left, who is biting off lengths from a huge bundle of onion tops. There is a double simile here. Onion odor is like poison gas, and the medieval helmet and visor is like a gas mask.

Manipulations can tell us about the manipulator. Chaplin's manipulations are mostly bright-minded; Laurel and Hardy's mishaps arise from obtuseness or carelessness. In *Dirty Work* (Lloyd French), for example, both are looking at a picture on the wall, as Laurel is shoveling soot into Hardy's pants instead of into the bag he is holding. It is a practical simile, for he is acting as if two things could serve the same purpose, because they are alike in being made of cloth, are open at the top, and stand the same height from the ground. It requires an abnormally long time for what their senses know to penetrate to the brains of both the filler and the filled. We feel that we could never be as leaden-witted, and the more soot we see bagged up in Hardy's trousers, the more superior we feel, and the more amused we are.

Harvey steps back into the shadow, holding his violin case like a tommy gun (*The Lady Killers*, Alexander Mackendrick). Montag, about to burn a trayful of books, places his head through the neck and dons a kind of chasuble. One fireman helps him on with his gauntlets, another places his square window mask over his head, and a flamethrower is handed to him by a third, with deference. Before each stage of the robing, Montag and the fireman faced and paused, each with a sober dedicated mien. The garb was not needed for safety, for others equally close to the fire did not wear it: it marked a high priestly office. The function was a solemn one, of great public significance (*Fahrenheit 451*, François Truffaut).

Filmic manipulations may range from the possible to the highly fanciful. The constable on point duty in *Capriccio* (Ole Askemen), in white gloves and white cap cover, cues the traffic with a white conductor's baton. Mischa Auer has ripped half the trousers (one leg each) off Olsen and Johnson. He takes off both legs of his own, and fronts them defiantly: what can they do to him now? They defeat him with a simile. They snatch the date from a calendar pad, slap the 10 on his back, down his head into the starting position, and fire a pistol. In shorts, vest, and bare legs, he sprints away (*Hellzapoppin*, Harold C. Potter). There is nothing impossible so far. Hands could be dried on a cat, and perhaps a death certificate blotted with a kitten, as Dr. Pratt does in *The Wrong Box* (Bryan Forbes). Plausibility begins to be strained as an end of wool from the Little Fellow's underwear somehow feeds in with the skein he is holding, and a blind girl, as she winds it up in a ball unravels the garment through a space in his waistcoat (*City Lights*, Charles Chaplin). A postman's using the tailgate of a truck as a desk for sorting and canceling his letters as he cycles behind it, is equally unlikely (*Jour de Fête*, Jacques Tati). So is Harold's means of escaping a landlady seeking her arrears of rent. He and his friend hurriedly don their coats, hang them on hooks in the corner of the room, and pull up their legs above the hem, thus becoming or looking like clothes hung on the wall (*Safety Last*, Fred Newmeyer and Sam Taylor). The extreme of improbability is forking a boiling boot as if it were meat or fish (*The Gold Rush*, Charles Chaplin).

8 By Using the Outer Shape

That was the character's telling us how he perceives his world: "To me the tailgate of a truck is like a desk." This the director may also do, and tell us how he perceives the world or his characters. When we see the browning pages of burning books writhing up as in agony, it is almost an allusion to Milton's words, "as good almost kill a man as kill a good book." We feel a life is being destroyed (*Fahrenheit 451*, François Truffaut).[12]

René Clair's comparing a factory to a prison was full and convincing from his making the visual pattern of assembly line and prison workship nearly identical: the width of table, spacing of people, and the angle from which they were shot; the silence both of the factory lunch room and the prison meal; the supervisor behind the seated workers, the guard behind the convicts; the short steps with which both moved; the uniformity of the costume: both pattern and angle corresponded so closely that a viewer could hardly fail to complete the simile (*A Nous la Liberté*).

It is as open to the motion-picture artist as to Friedrich or Dali, to draw flames in such a way that they look like, or gradually become, women and reptiles (*Night on*

Bald Mountain: Fantasia, Wilfred Jackson); or seeds like women in crinolines or cossacks to look like thistles (*Nutcracker Suite: Fantasia,* Samuel Armstrong, pl. 11); or provide a broom with an aura quickly changing in color, as if likening a magical spell to an electrical charge (*The Sorcerer's Apprentice: Fantasia,* James Algar). When Richard Williams changes the spire and apse of a church to a spiked soldier's helmet, the simile brings together war and religion; and by changing the coils of the snake that is wisdom's crest to the spiral of a still with mounting bubbles, he links truth and science (*The Little Island*).

A comparison may occasion surprise or please as decoration; it may also reveal a neglected likeness in structure. If a canoe breaks in the middle, and its two ends rise up and close like the jaws of a shark, it is merely playful; it says little of any value of either shark or boat, and it is not the boat that swallows the man but the sea (*Mr. Hulot's Holiday,* Jacques Tati). If a bull sharpens one horn on the other, pulls them out and throws them like daggers, this goring at a distance brings out the piercing function of horns (*A Bully Romance,* Paul Terry). If, instead of comparing an elephant's trunk to a snake, the two linked by little more than sinuous movement, as in *Dumbo* (Walt Disney), its legs are compared with piers of a bridge, we become aware that both in man and nature a like relation can be found between size, shape, and number of supports and the weight they can carry (*Mites and Monsters,* Donald Alexander).

9 By Allusion

The citing of a passage from an earlier work in a later parallel case is a form of simile. It may in film take the form of a similar composition, and the closer the situations are in meaning, the more effective it is; but it is present only for those who have seen the earlier film.

In *The Seventh Seal* (Ingmar Bergman) the final scene is of Death leading the Knight, his Lady, and his company up a slope to the left, tiny in silhouette on a distant horizon, and the player pointing them out to his wife. In *Night Train* (Jerzy Kawalerowicz), made only two years later, a group of three police and a captured murderer, with one figure following, is seen walking to the right along a ridge, tiny in silhouette on the distant horizon, as the train they left starts off and one passenger points them out to another, suggesting thus that the murderer too was being led to his death.

Music too may suggest a likeness. Having lured away the peasant guarding a granary (a small hut on stilts), speculators bore from underneath to gain the grain. They are so many and so impatient that they all rise up and carry off the granary itself on their shoulders. As the hut walks off, as if on its legs, we hear Moussorgsky's Baba Yaga music from *Pictures at an Exhibition,* an allusion to the Russian fairy story of the hut that walked (*Happiness,* Aleksandr Medvedev).

10 By Inclusion in the Frame

Perhaps the simplest way to arouse the word "like" in the viewer's mind is to place the two like things in the same frame.

A wounded Mongolian boy, a putative descendant of Genghis Khan, is being nursed back to health, captive of an invading army, to be set up as a puppet ruler. He rises, bandaged, from his chair, and before many steps, collapses from weakness, grabs for a table, and upsets an aquarium. As he lies helplessly on the floor, the out-of-water fish squirm and suffocate on the floor beside him. Both he and they are helpless and out of their element (*Storm Over Asia*, V. I. Pudovkin).

McTeague in *Greed* (Erich von Stroheim) keeps canaries. He is a dentist. He kisses Trina when she is under ether, and his canary above him hops excitedly. It accepts a mate when he marries. The two nestle together as McTeague and Trina embrace, and flutter when they quarrel, suggesting thus the primitive level on which Trina and McTeague are living.

When war starts, Passworthy in helmet and brassard says good-bye to his son, who also wears a helmet and bears a drum. Passworthy speaks about "real soldiers," and walks off, holding his suitcase up and beating it like a drum. Then the screen is filled with the huge shadows of soldiers, marching across the screen from lower right. At the bottom of the screen, small, white, and clear, is the boy in the helmet, beating his drum and marching from the left against the flow of the troops, who perhaps, the suggestion is, are grownups playing children's games (*Things to Come*, William Cameron Menzies).

By photographing half the screen at a time and masking the other half, Laurel and Hardy are shown to the right as adults, playing checkers, to the left as children, photographed further off to seem smaller, and playing with blocks on the floor. The blocks must be five inches square but look half the size, the fireplace is twice their height, the bannister the height of their heads, and the furniture in proportion. (Since children's heads are normally bigger than those of adults in relation to their bodies, they look strangely emaciated.) Though one pair was intended as the children of the other, it is hard not to think, seeing them together on the screen, that the adult pair, in many ways, never stopped being children (*Brats*, James Parrott).

11 By Sound

The mere addition of sound may in itself create a likeness.

After an evening of consuming many wines, a man goes into a bathroom, finds an eyecup, lifts it up to his eye as he says, "The Queen," and makes the gesture a toast (*Here We Go Round the Mulberry Bush*, Clive Donner). A thief enters a house, turns the dial of a safe, and the sudden onset of music makes of the safe a radio set (*Dial P for P*, Fritz Freleng). As Mrs. Joe opens her mouth and berates Pip in mime, there is a screech in the brass of the music that underlines the scene, a translation to nonverbal sound of her words and mood (*Great Expectations*, David Lean).

When Watanabe, a timid civil servant who has spent his life avoiding decisions, learns that, having cancer, he has six months to live, he clings to the only person who has shown interest in him, a girl clerk in his office. "This is silly," she says as they sit in a café, "we have nothing to say to one another."

"I have no one else," he says.

Down below their balcony, one of a party of girls brings in a large birthday cake. Suddenly, something his companion says brings him up short. "There is something I can do," he says. "If we don't do something, then nothing will be done."

He rises with decision and leaves. The stair from the balcony starts at an angle, both sides of which are lined with girls, who sing, as he walks down, "Happy Birthday to You." After he has left the frame, a girl enters and walks up—clearly she for whom the song was intended—but not before the director has left a sense that Watanabe is born to a new life (*Ikiru*, Akira Kurosawa).

A director may do the opposite—not give us a musical simile for the image, but images that music arouses in him. "This," he says, "is what the music is like to me."

Three canons are given visual form by Norman McLaren and Grant Munro in *Canon*. First come cubes, each moving along the same path on a checker board, one after the other. In the second version, four stick figures make a series of movements, strides, pivots, circlings-round, and so on, each starting later than its predecessor. In the third, a succession of men and one woman cross a tightrope, each performing the same set of movements as the one before, the woman with variants.

To Leon Schlesinger and Isadore Freleng, the Second Hungarian Rhapsody of Liszt is like the vigorous bustle of a building site.[13] A dog with a lion's mane (the "condogtor"?) mounts the rostrum to applause from the sidewalk superintendents, and follows the score on a blueprint. The building proceeds by floors as a symphony by movements, for at one point, he turns over a page and we read, "Second Floor." To a mounting scale a hod carrier flies up a ladder, and down again as the music falls. A pair of paws above a wall lays a course of bricks along it, one brick to a note. In the seven-note phrase with the heavy beat on the last, two huge men with tiny hammers tap the first six in turn, and a small man with a huge hammer brings down on the seventh. Toward the end, the baton-wielder looks at his watch. It is five minutes to five, and with a last mighty accelerando, the building is topped and the flag is raised on the final note. Then, as a sleepy hammerer leaves for home, he slams the door, and the whole tall pile tumbles down, leaving a wrack behind, just as after the last note of a performance, nothing is left but remembered fragments of what we felt as we listened (*Rhapsody in Rivets*).

The director's program need not be the composer's. There is certainly a primitive sound in *The Rite of Spring*, but Stravinsky's titles "The Youths and Maidens," "Dance of Abduction," and "Mystic Circle of the Adolescents," relate to primitive people. Disney however, has found in the music the world before man. Gray and rose mists drift past until through a gap we see fiery breath blasting through a many-nostriled earth. The fitting of the volcanic explosions to the irregular accents in the music give the illusion that the music has been written to the images, not the reverse. And so through the growth of amoebas, fish, lizards, pterodactyls, and the death of a generation, with such conviction that—more than a mere simile—he has almost persuaded us that his images are a mere tautology for what has already been fully said in the music (*The Rite of Spring: Fantasia*, Bill Roberts and Paul Satterfield).

12   By Movement

The addition of movement, or changing the character of movement, may arouse a resemblance.

The performance by Bugs Bunny of the same Second Hungarian Rhapsody is briefly mentioned above. As his paws play higher and higher notes, on what are for him, huge keys, the keyboard slides to the left, like the carriage of a typewriter, which lets him play the upper notes. When the bell rings, Bugs runs it back with his left paw to its proper place (*Rhapsody Rabbit*, Isadore Freleng).

From outside a building, we see an elevator, but it is rising one square (or window) up and one square over, as if it were climbing stairs. On reaching the square at the extreme left, it runs across that row to the right, and begins rising again, one up and one over, for another flight (*A Hare Grows in Manhattan*, Isadore Freleng).

In *The Fall of the House of Usher* (Roger Corman), the narrator fights his way through a crowd of Madeleine's ancestors, and ends up collapsing by a door and reaching up to the chain and lock that bars it. By the slowing of his movement, and its general character, it is as if he were moving through water or some more viscous liquid that resisted his thrusting muscles and vetoed his will.

13   By Succession or Montage

The simile by succession: here is where the lack of the word "like" in film is felt most strongly, but not to the same degree in each of the following varieties: the nondiegetic, the verbally assisted, the diegetic, and the long series.

Some prior considerations first. A flock of sheep is interposed in shots of jostling people (*Modern Times*, Charles Chaplin). The setting is the city; there are no flocks of sheep within miles, and they can, therefore, form no part of the story or diegesis. Presumably, then, according to the Spottiswoode school, the viewer's response is complete bafflement, or an assumption that a shot has strayed by mistake from another film, or a dogged belief that the director must have had some reason for placing the shot there, perhaps because there really were sheep in that street, for some undisclosed reason, or because (as a few, but certainly not all, may do) they see something in common between a flock of sheep and a crowd of people. So without the word "like" or something like it, it would seem that few could be counted on to find the simile.

In a second example, the four close heads of Councillor Huggins and his three fellow plotters are followed by four black-faced sheep in a market pen. Then we see the auctioneer who is selling them. The four plotters are met on market day, so the sheep are nearby in another part of the market. The viewer should not be baffled nor should he think the editor made a mistake. The sheep, though, do not figure further in the narrative, so there is a question whether they are or are not part of the story, even though they are part of the setting (*South Riding*, Victor Saville).

In both cases, it should be noted, culture may help the viewer find the simile. Likening people in crowds to sheep in flocks, and morally deviant people to black sheep, are both proverbial, so the leap of imagination required is not great. The viewer who remembers the proverbial phrase, who sees the plotters and then the sheep, and suddenly says to himself, "Those fellows are black sheep too" has caught the point.

Now the reason the viewer is able to make this connection is that the sheep come immediately after the plotters. Where two things compared are both in the same frame, the evident intention of the director to include what is there leads us to search for a meaning in what he shows us. If a simile is not completed in the viewer's mind, the story is not hurt, for all the impercipient viewer has lost is a comment made by the director. Where the two things compared come in succession, surely a juxtaposition in time, as well as in space, will lead at least some viewers to supply the "like" intended; and those who do not, still have the story intact, if not enriched. If anyone, in short, supplies the "like" is there not a simile? Is the simile any less there, if any one person fails to find it?

We are prone to link events that are close in time. We note a coincidence, we speak of things that "are more than coincidence." A director can surely count on this, and give it a strong cue. To strengthen this there is in film a now fairly firmly established convention, exploited in various ways, that what is seen in succession is to be read together for meaning. This too a director can count on.

Consider the following examples in the light of these reflections; first, nondiegetic ones. There are opening sculptures of military men and objects, a company of troops marching from the left, and then a double column of school girls, shown from their waists down, walking in step from the right, in black-and-white striped uniforms. This is reinforced later as the principal walks along their lines (with squeaking shoes) to inspect them, and the girls turn, march, and arrange themselves in four rows, with many more shouted commands than seems to be called for by the simple drill, as five teachers move in a file and turn to the front as one. The school is part of, and reflects, a military culture (*Mädchen in Uniform*, Leontine Sagan).

In a second class, the verbally assisted simile, the director states it in words and then shows it in images. A poet says the Little Widow is wearing a coat of stars, and then we see her, down through the glitter of a chandelier (*La Ronde*, Max Ophuls).

To be a member of the Convention, said Victor Hugo, was like being a wave on the ocean. Quoting this, Abel Gance cuts together two trains of events. One shows Napoleon in flight from Corsica. He stands gripping the mast or bends bailing water, as his tiny boat swoops down into the troughs or is hoisted up to the peaks of tumultuous waves. Huge billows charge toward us and cloud the lens. Unsteady horizons lurch from the horizontal. The boat cants at parlous angles, but always closer. These shots were seen turn about with sittings of the National Convention: movement as tumultuous, but now from people jostling, fighting, gesturing, from quick pans, from rocking the camera, and then a frame filled with a honeycomb of human faces, shot looking down from a pendulum, which swings toward us, pauses and swings away again over the crowd, carrying over from shots of Napoleon at sea, the heaving of the waves. Near the end of the sequence both of these are seen superimposed (*Napoleon*).

The third, the diegetic simile, is likely the best: if the simile is not caught, there is no unmeaning residue to confuse the viewer. A White Russian cast ashore on an island contracts a fever. His delirious tossing in bed alternates with the storm that roars from off the Aral Sea. If we link his bodily disturbance to the blast that lashes his hut, the story is enriched; if not the storm can be taken as merely a setting (*The Forty-First*, G. Chukhrai).

In *La Bête Humaine* (Jean Renoir), Jacques waits by the tracks. A train roars by. It is raining heavily. Severine meets him. They walk together to a small hut by the tracks, and the camera falls to their feet as they cross the threshold. It pans then to a water butt below the eaves. The face of the water is exploding from hurtling rains, a tumid core of water from the spout thrusts into the barrel's deeps and over its edge a surge of water weaves wavering cords down the staves. Dissolve to the barrel from the same angle, the water now a calm glass for a clear sky. We pan back to the doorstep. The man's feet slowly come and wait, hers join them. An engine slowly enters a station, softly shining, without a sound, clothed in mystery. One of the two events compared is here implied or suppressed.

The fourth kind, the long series, by mere accumulation of images sets our minds looking for what links them. Citizen Kane's things—animals, paintings, sculptures, buildings, printing presses, gold mines, paper mills and piled-up unopened crates—must have had some common value for him: what was it (*Citizen Kane*, Orson Welles)?

The best example is perhaps from *Colonel Blimp* (Michael Powell and Emeric Pressburger). Clive Wynn-Candy embodies the traditional assumptions of the public-school Englishman. One of these is that war is a form of sport followed by gentlemen, in which prey is hunted under certain customary observances. His aunt invites him to stay with her, saying she has plenty of room for all he could bring home. "How much room!" she says. There is a shot of a wide wall, glowing blue as if on a late afternoon horizon, furniture low on the wall to spread its dimensions. The shadow of Clive enters, and then himself, and he stands, his back to the camera, looking a while at the great wall, which impresses its immensity upon us. The possibilities open to him must then have seemed almost limitless. He turns toward us, walking off left, and the shadow swells large and larger, almost covering all the subdued blue. We hear the crack of a rifle, and on the blank blue wall, in close-up, there appears an animal's head, and underneath a date and a place. The same thing occurs with kob or waterbuck, gorilla, crocodile, and other animals, from various outposts of empire, and at various dates from 1902 to 1914; each time there is a rifle shot, followed by the animal suddenly appearing on the blank blue wall. The last of these enters to a solemn roll of drums, the tip of an elephant's trunk, which widens, as the camera slowly raises its eyes, up to the great skull: Indian Elephant, Bengal, 1914. In a longer shot, the camera pans from the elephant along the wall to a stand, and this time we hear a machine gun. On the stand is a German helmet, with Hun, Flanders, 1918 underneath. Its inclusion in the series, with a label of the same form, preceded also by a burst of gunfire, tells us that the owner of them all had collected the German with motives much the same as he had the others.

14 Simile in Structure: The Part That Is like the Whole

A single incident or image may give us in minature the meaning of the whole story. *The Wages of Fear* (Henri-Georges Clouzot, Charles Yves, and Claude Vanel) starts with four beetles drawn along on strings. As an ice cream cart comes, a shirted but unbreeched boy rises and lets them hang. The film tells about four men who lack the $300 and visa, without which they cannot leave San Miguel. An oil company hires them to drive two truckloads of nitroglycerin. The pay is high and one load arrives, but all die. The image came, however, before we had met the men and could give it meaning, and by then it was forgotten.

The likeness will impress us more when seen in the middle, when the roles of the characters are clear. In *The Go-Between* (Joseph Losey), the boy Leo catches the farmer Ted Burgess out in a cricket match. By then it is fairly clear that it is through the boy, used by them as a messenger, that the affair between Ted and a well-to-do girl will come to grief.

The most effective place for the part that is like the whole is likely the end. At the close of *Blow-Up* (Michelangelo Antonioni), a line of people with clown-painted faces watch two of their number mime a tennis game. Both clowns' eyes and camera follow the imaginary ball. The leading character, a photographer, is standing by himself outside the fence. The girl player, standing at the wire mesh, gestures to where the eyes of all have placed the ball that soared over the fence. The photographer hesitates. Then he mimes a throw, and follows with his eyes its imaginary trajectory. We see him in long shot against the green of the grass, we hear the beat of invisible volleys. Suddenly the photographer is not there either, only the green grass. His photographing girls modeling fashions, fascinating teenagers, halfheartedly trying to solve a crime, flitting around in expensive cars, and buying an airplane propeller on impulse—has it suddenly seemed but gaudy painted people playing with nothings? Has he suddenly doubted if anything about himself was real either? And vanished?

Several figures throughout a film may help to sharpen the edge of its message. A devout and innocent girl causes two men to die: one hung himself in consequence of her chastity, and the other, one of the beggars she had taken off the street, raped her and was killed at the instigation of her cousin Jorge, a consequence of her unpractical charity. The harmful possibilities of innocence are compressed into two similitudes. The camera pans up the rope from the neck of the suicide, and where it is tied to a tree, we see the wooden handles of a skipping rope. A skipping child opens the film, and is later seen skipping under the tree where the body hung. The suicide's son, Jorge, in going over his father's effects, finds a cross, from the side of whose shaft he folds out a knife; the cross becoming a handle for wielding death. Viridiana's change of heart is shown in another similitude. As a postulant nun, she carried with her, and contemplated every night, a crown of thorns. When her asceticism, seen by Jorge as pride, is shaken by encounters with the world, she knocks at his door humbly. He invites her in to play cards with the maid he has taken as his mistress, and she complies without protest. Intercut with this is the child, throwing on a bonfire, among other discarded objects, the crown of thorns, and later pulling it out and watching it burn to ash (*Viridiana*, Luis Buñuel).

15 Intention

Can the viewer find a simile of whose presence in the film the director was unaware? Can there be an unintended simile? In *Pas de Deux* there are two dancers, lit from the side, and thus seen as white outlines. The dancer's image leaps to a new place, but a duplicate image stays behind, and only after a pause follows in the same path to form once more a single figure. There are two of her on the screen at one time, as if (which sometimes actors do) she first imagined the movement, and then her body caught up to her thought. Later a dancer leaps, and a dozen clonal images ripple across the screen, till all have sunk at last into the still, single, and final figure. The aerial image has an elastic feeling, as if a moment in time were stretched and released. When the movement pivots on one end, as when a leg moves, it is like a fan opening and closing. Is Norman McLaren merely plotting the path of a movement, as a line of dots on a map shows the route of a ship? If so, can a simile not consciously intended by the artist be said to be part of the message? Or should we credit an artist no matter what his prime and conscious intention, with whatever any viewer finds in his film? (pl. 12).

In this study it must be assumed that the director intended any figure found, and the effect it has on the viewer (with a single qualification, in the chapter on Metaphor). But if a film is a new collaboration with every separate viewer, this must apply to all responses, however unique. In *Saguenay*, a pair of water drops in close-up swelled before they dropped and looked, for all the world, like a pair of bullfrogs, whether or not Chapman saw them so. At the end of *Marie-Louise* (Leopold Lindtberg), the children evacuated to Switzerland are going home. There is a down shot from the back of the train of the disturbed and blurred space between the rails. It is a symbol of departure, but it can also be seen as the wake of a ship, even though there is no sufficient cue in the film to lead one to think that this was the director's intention.

16 Matters of Practice

A comedian trying too hard to be funny is always painful, and a simile that seems contrived also puts us off. This occurs twice in *City Lights*. Charlie refuses a prof-fered pudding, round, white, and solid with a saw-edged paper doily underneath it.

He changes his mind and turns. Where the pudding had been there is now leaning against his couch, sitting on the floor, a bald-headed man with a very curious saw-edged wreath around his head. Charlie tries to cut a helping of skull. To make it look like a scalp, the pudding was given a hard porous surface—highly unappetizing. On the other hand, the bald man's headdress looked nothing as much as a doily with the center missing. Even in a quick scene the situation is too farfetched for us to enjoy it. In another place, a metal drum stands at the corner of a building. A crusty man on the left has laid on the drum bread and cheese for a sandwich. To the right of the drum, Charlie is washing his face, and the soap is also on the drum. With his head in the basin and eyes closed, his hand gropes, finds the cheese, and, when it won't lather, throws it away. The crusty fellow puts the soap in a sandwich, takes a mouthful, and lets out a bellow. Now cheese is like soap only to the eye, in color, size and shape; but Charlie's eyes were closed, and the crusty fellow is watching something else, so both made their mistake by smell and touch, the two ways in which cheese and soap are easily distinguished.

How far apart can two events be, and still spring a simile in the viewer's mind? In *The Crab-Canning Ship* (So Yamamura), a hook enters down to the corpse of a worker wrapped in sacks with a rope around its waist. The hook is thrust under the rope and the body hoisted up and over the side. We think at once, "Another factor in production," for although it was some time before that we had seen slingfuls of crabs hoisted into the ship, and slingfuls of crates hoisted from the mother ship to a transport, the director had repeated the operation a sufficient number of times that its image was revived when the corpse was hoisted from the deck. Once would not have done it.

Must we always be quite clear about what is being compared? In *City Lights* (Charles Chaplin), Charlie sucks a length of spaghetti with a swooshing sound: very machinelike in sound and mime, but the kind of machine—vacuum cleaner, suction pump, or anteater—no one can tell. It is effective; is it a simile?

Does a simile justify itself, or must it serve the story? We are told in *The Rival World* (Bert Haanstra), that insects eat a third of all our food. We see on the screen, a man with goatee, and a goat with goatee, both eating with vigor, both the same size on the screen, shot from the same angle. It is good for a passing smile, but where is the point?

Our attention is caught in *Fahrenheit 451* (François Truffaut) by a cut from the window of Montag's asbestos suit (as he burns books) to a boy looking through a window, both windows and heads the same size, and then back to Montag. The boy is merely a casual looker-on—the similarity tells us nothing. Was it an accident?

A girl in *Belle* (André Delvaux) kills her dog who is badly injured, because Mathieu, who loves her, cannot bring himself to do it. She then kills a man she lives with who wears a sheepskin coat of the same texture, color, and shagginess as the dog's. We see him lying, with his head and legs barely seen, and blood showing almost as on the dog. She killed the dog because she loved it, and the man because she loved Mathieu more. She shot both dog and man because Mathieu shied from doing it. All that the deaths have in common is the person who brought them about. The director pointedly makes the bodies the same in appearance: it was hard to see how it strengthened the story.

6
Metaphor

1 Metaphor and Simile

Many tropes have a two-headed air to them: of a fingered scarf and the feeling it betrays; of a rusted sword and reverberations of the past it reawakens; of dying hands clutching soil and the attitudes revealed of man and country; of the seen that conveys the unseeable—the clock without hands that means death. How we name the trope in a given case will often follow from the form it is given.[1] This is especially so in film, where the characteristic words "as" or "like" are added in the mind of the viewer and cannot unfailingly signal a simile.

This caveat having been entered, it may be said of the simile that whether the word "like" is used or supplied, it keeps its two members apart, each unchanged by the other, and our attention is drawn to a likeness between them as they are. One morning in the bath, I thought, "The cat is playing dice in the hall." Here I had fused into a single impression my knowledge of the cat's being in the hall, my hearing of a sound and comparing its rattle to that made by dice. It was metaphorical in form. I could have said, "The sound that the cat is making in the hall is like that of a man throwing dice," and made it a simile, by keeping each side of the comparison clearly set apart in meaning from the other. Fanciful gambling cats are not hinted at. When we see the peasant Khymr, head hanging down, asleep on the driver's seat of a water tank, and the horse in the shafts down on its knees, head also drooping, the director is clearly saying, "Like teamster, like horse," we add the word "like" and make it a simile (*Happiness*, Aleksandr Medvedev).

In the *metaphor*, on the other hand, the two members blur into one, the image and the meaning beyond it being taken in at the same moment, as if the image had lost its own identity and could only convey the figurative meaning contrived for it.[2] Indomitable struggle is what we take from a man's advancing slowly and with effort through billowing black smoke (*We From Kronstadt*, E. Dzigan); revolt from an arrow's piercing and snatching from the holder's hand his wand of office (*Robin Hood*, Michael Curtiz); political domination from the map of Norway pounded by a fist (*The Moon Is Down*, Irving Pichel). We could say that the arrow's snatching away the wand of office is like the rebels' taking its holder's power from him, but the image makes both statements at once, and being brief and vivid, much more powerfully. In Priestley's words, a metaphor is a simile contracted to its smallest dimensions.[3] As Coleridge suggests, the figurative meaning shines through the image.[4]

2 The Image and the Gloss

The two parts of a metaphor are thus an image on the screen, and some event or idea compared with it, together giving a visible form to an attitude or comment. The two parts, or extremes, as Winifred Nowottny calls them, may each so interpenetrate the other that their disentangling takes time and concentration.[5] Words are needed—but seemingly hard to come by—through which each of these parts or functions may be clearly distinguished. Those proposed by I. A. Richards are widely used.[6] The event in the narrative with which the metaphor deals he calls the *tenor*, the comparison that carries the comment he calls the *vehicle*. With due deference to Richards, these terms smell a bit too much of the lamp (as overscholarly usages once were described) for popular discussion of the film.

Film consists of arrangements, not of words but of images. The word "horse" is decoded by the mind on its way to the image *horse;* in film there is no word, only image. As far back as the seventeenth century, the word "image" has been used as a synonym for trope, but it is too confusing to admit this meaning in discussing films, so in this book the word is used only for the pattern projected on the screen, black and white or colored. This image is one of the two parts or extremes of a filmic metaphor, so it is simple economy to use the word "image" for it, instead of adding another.

The other part or extreme embodies the resemblance, which adds to the image the director's attitude, or his gloss or comment on it. Of these three, I suggest "gloss." "Gloss" (from the Greek) is a word of explanation inserted in a text, or a comment on, or interpretation of it; and "gloss" (from the German) is a surface luster added to an object. In both cases the original remains, but the gloss has added enrichment. The gloss is also a glass, through which we see the image differently; or a glaze to color an image that could exist without it. All these are ways of saying what a metaphor does, being as it is an image on the screen, enriched by a gloss or glaze added by the director.[7]

When her lodgers realize that Mrs. Wilberforce will certainly confess to the police her nonexistent guilt, and implicate them, they sit glumly around the room. Louis makes the decision: he snaps open his springknife, and throws it at the tabletop, where the point of the knife embeds in close-up. The image is the embedded knife, but the gloss is clear: Mrs. Wilberforce must die (*The Lady Killers*, Alexander Mackendrick).

Three cords run across a table, and over each a man's unsteady hand is holding a knife—that is the image. But the men are dressed as guards, and the cords hold the trapdoor under the Boy's feet, which, if dropped, would hang him. So the hovering knives are impending death—this is the gloss (*Intolerance*, D. W. Griffith).

A valentine on the mantelpiece has "Marry me" written on it. After much thought, Boldwood goes to the mantelpiece and throws the valentine on the fire. As paper and words are slowly consumed, the blue of water fades in on the yellow flames, as if gradually quenched by the following shot of a small pond where sheep are being dipped. It is a double gloss: the burning valentine rejects the marriage, the watered flame (a common convention for passion) slakes the love (*Far from the Madding Crowd*, John Schlesinger).[8]

3 The Viewer Completes the Metaphor

It is clear from these examples that the viewers must make the metaphor:[9] they are given cement and gravel, but they must mix the concrete. They know the situation;

they see the knife, they know what a knife can do: they must fuse these into the gloss intended. The metaphor is there for those who do, but not for others.

So little is sometimes left for us to do, that the metaphor can hardly be missed. In *The Gold Rush* (Charles Chaplin), when Big Jim is delirious with hunger, a man-size chicken takes the Little Fellow's place. For Big Jim at that moment, any living thing was food. Bugs Bunny leaps into the air, comes down spiraling rapidly, stretches into a thin, drill-like shape, burrows rapidly into the ground and vanishes (*The Hare-Brained Hypnotist*, Leon Schlesinger and Isadore Freleng).

On the other hand, when Gatsby is entertaining Daisy, a rich girl who had said, "rich girls don't marry poor boys," he opens up the sliding door of a huge cupboard, and begins taking out neat piles of shirts and throwing them around the room. We see her, head and shoulders, shirts hurtling through the air in various colors above her. We see her holding to her cheek a pink shirt, murmuring, "I've never seen such beautiful shirts before." Then with her back to us, in a circular chair, we see beyond her the opened and emptied cupboards with Gatsby in front of them and around her a litter of scores of colored shirts. Here the shirts are money: they express the careless contempt of the rich man for things he can buy again many times over, things which can be relaundered and restacked—work for which he has all the servants he needs (*The Great Gatsby*, Jack Clayton). This requires a little more from us.

4   Dead or Background Metaphors

We speak of new things by using the words for older ones we think are like them. From *boat* we get *gravy boat* and *stone boat*, one a boat in shape, and the other traversing earth instead of water. When talk leaves things of sense, we reach for metaphor, telling ideas by means of things. *Examine* meant *to weigh*, but scales are not an image that comes to our minds today when we use the word. Fowler calls these "dead metaphors," and by such corpses language lives and grows.[10] *Sift*, he says, is less dead than dormant. We still sift flour; when we sift evidence, there is still such a smell of the kitchen to the word, that if someone were to speak of "leaving no stone unturned to sift the evidence" we should feel that there was something wrong about it. Dead metaphors are also said to recede into the background of the language when only the metaphorical sense is left and the user entirely unaware of the metaphor.[11]

Up and down shots in film are dead metaphors. In using words, we speak of someone's being above us in rank, station, or ability. There is a metaphor here of a scale, with most at the top (of money, weight, or acumen) and least at the bottom. We speak of looking up to, or down at, someone, with again an implied scale on which we place ourselves in relation to others. It is common practice in film to look up at a dominating person and down at his victim (pl. 22).

For example, in *The Yellow Balloon* (J. Lee-Thompson), Len, a criminal, has played on Frankie's sense of guilt for another boy's death to blackmail him into stealing. When the boy tries to escape, Len takes him to an abandoned underground station with intent to kill him. After a chase, the boy falls. A foot slowly moves in beside the boy's arm. He looks around, sees it, and looks up. An up shot from ground level or lower shows Len, half-length, looking down from a towering height with a threatening frown. Our sense of someone greatly exceeding us in strength, able to stop us rising and escaping, still is hardly felt as a metaphor.

Now doors are different. In word and image, to close a door is to make an end. It is a strong image, and if there were fewer doors in film this would be very much a live metaphor; but use deadens, and the door as a metaphor lies asleep till something a director does denies the closing door's finality, and brings it alive.

In *Blithe Spirit* (David Lean), the revenant Elvira and her living husband are slipping into the lovemaking of her mortal days. We see his hand glinting red through her transparency, and wonder how it will be. The camera moves toward the door of the room they are in. It opens. Through the doorway we see them in a mirror, talking. The door closes. "That," the director says, "is all you are going to see." And it is.

It happens otherwise in *The Ipcress File* (Sidney J. Furie). The back of the man at the window feeding the sparrows said, "Close the door." Palmer closed the door on us and we saw the name on the plate. At this point it is natural to assume that we are not to hear what passes between them. But no—we leap at once inside the door, and eavesdrop unhindered. And yet how easy it is for the camera to stay inside as the door is closing, and still see the name on the plate, or the name could be seen on the door before it was opened. By contradicting the metaphor that was dormant in the closing door, the director has brought it alive and made us aware of its meaning.

Eric Rohmer saw the danger of the door. In *Chloe in the Afternoon*, he deftly avoids it. Frédéric knocks and Chloe opens the door. When it is partly closed, and we can see them both still through the gap, Rohmer cuts to inside as the door is closed and avoids exclusion.

Put beside these the door of the lighthouse in *Thunder Rock* (Roy Boulting), which Charleston slams after the airplane has left him. Through a barred gate in the door we see he is leaning against it, shooting the bolt, and then he slams the wicket shut on us. He is closing us, the world, out, to bring back six people, who died there ninety years ago in a shipwreck. After he has met and heard from them, Charleston comes out of the door again, and as we see him against the dawn clouds, he breathes deeply: he cannot, he finds, evade responsibility for the affairs of the world, and when the airplane comes back, he will leave his rock. Here the door is clearly metaphorical, reflecting Charleston's decisions.

In *The Fallen Idol* (Sir Carol Reed), the girl with whom Baines is having an affair walks out of the teashop where they have met. There was no use in their meeting again, she said, under these conditions. She pulls the door shut as she leaves, and the side we see of the sign that hangs there says *Closed*. The closing door does not close the affair, but it expresses in a metaphor her intention of closing it.

We each must make our own list of dead metaphors, for the deadness of a metaphor depends, of course, on how often we have seen it. However complex a metaphor, after many times it shrinks to a simple signal. Our list may include the birds that rise in the sky after death, the flight of a soul (*The Passion of Joan of Arc*, Carl Theodor Dreyer); the windblown sheets of a calendar pad, for the passing of days (*Scarface*, Howard Hawks); the people who seem confined in body or mind, seen through the geometry of gates or fences (*A Yank in Rome*, Luigi Zampa; *No Reason to Stay*, Mort Ransen); the newspapers rolling off presses that stand for the millions who read the news we see printed there (*Citizen Kane*, Orson Welles). Down shots of railway tracks from the fronts of moving engines have had a fascination for many directors: they writhe off to twin themselves, and swing back to one again as if alive, to signify change from place to place, either for those in the story or us the viewers, and for my part, I hope directors never cease to like them (*One Night of Love*, Victor Schertzinger; *Night Mail*, Harry Watt and Basil Wright).

5   Uses Not Specific to Film

The forms of metaphor to be found in film include some that are found in other arts.

In *Marriage à la Mode,* Scene i, the pictures on the wall all show violence—Saint Laurence being grilled alive, Saint Sebastian bound on a tree as a target for archers, Judith carrying the head of Holofernes, and other like events. In the situation itself, two dogs are shown bottom left, chained one to the other and looking away from one another without interest. So, seated above them, are the prospective bride and groom, their elbows together and a band on her sleeve as if a rope tied them, and each looking the opposite way from the other. This would make an excellent filmic figure.

As on the stage, a situation in film may have a sense beyond its immediate incidents. Ivan, a Czech boy of ten, taken from his parents and brought up as a German, has been given by a court back to his Czech mother, and has left his German foster parents with reluctance. It was important, said one of the judges, that Ivan should assume the responsibility of caring for his mother, now that he was the only member left of her family. In the final scene, a conductor comes to their compartment on the train and asks for their tickets. The mother does not understand the German, and brings out her passport. The conductor is impatient. Ivan puts his hand in his mother's purse and finds the tickets. The conductor looks at the tickets and gives them back to the boy, who drops them in his mother's purse. She takes them out and gives them back to him. He puts the tickets in his pocket and looks contentedly out of the window (*The Divided Heart,* Charles Crichton).

6   Metaphors Expressed by Inclusion in the Frame

The possible ways of expressing metaphors can conveniently be referred to as their syntax. The example from Hogarth shows that the choice of what to include in a single frame is a means found both in film and in painting.

Nearly the first shot in *Repulsion* (Roman Polanski), the study of a schizophrenic with a paranoid thrust, is an expressionless masklike face with oval eyecoverings. As we move back from the face, we see it is a woman lying on a table as if dead. Drawing further back, we see Carol, in white smock, seated by the table, holding the woman's hand, quite still. Her working partner comes in, takes the eye coverings off, and she and the woman in the facial pack both ask Carol if she is asleep. As in the Hogarth picture the two dogs reflect the attitudes of the two humans, so here the clay-packed face is as void of expression as Carol's, who, unrelated, withdrawn from the outer world, lives in a soundless unreality.

A mental patient comes downstairs with a razor in his right hand. He is suspected of murder. Dr. Brulov, sitting at his desk, chats to the patient, says he got up to work as he couldn't sleep, is about to have a glass of milk, and invites the patient to join him. As the doctor walks left past the patient and comes back with the milk, the razor-holding hand is at the left, huge in close-up. It is thus kept in our minds, as it is in the doctor's. The doctor pours the milk at his desk and walks back with it. The patient raises the glass with his left hand, for the right still hangs down, holding the razor. He raises the glass to his mouth, his eye on us and the doctor. Then, as with his eyes, through the milk-hazed bottom and above the white flow, we see the doctor. The milk rises up and fills the frame with white, erasing the doctor and the room. The whiting out from the frame of what the patient sees anticipates his later loss of consciousness from drinking the milk, for the doctor tells us afterward that the bromide he added to it was "enough to knock out three horses" (*Spellbound,* Alfred Hitchcock).

7 By Angle

Pastor Erickson, who has doubts about his faith and an inability to feel the afflictions of others, has told Mrs. Persson that her husband had committed suicide, but she declines his offer to have him pray with her. "I must tell my family," she says, and goes in. From outside, we see him looking in through the window, as she stands at the end of the dinner table, the children seated around it. Always looking in from the outside was his affliction (*Winter Light,* Ingmar Bergman).

It is interesting to compare two films using the same angle, and note how the mere angle determines the effect. A Turkish soldier rides into a wide hall, hoofs clattering on the tiles, and at the end of a rope, is the shepherd Manolios, bound. The soldier rides around a pillar and away, leaving Manolios on the floor, his hands tied behind his back, his tether dropped beside him. Manolios had been chosen to play the part of Christ in the Passion Play, and, Christlike, had shown compassion for refugees from a village burned by the Turks. In a long down shot, the wealthy village magnates, who keep in well with the Turkish rulers, close in a circle around Manolios. Panayotaris—Judas in the Passion Play—draws his knife and completes the ring. The time of Manolios was accomplished: there was no escape (*He Who Must Die,* Jules Dassin).

In *Hamlet* (Laurence Olivier), act 5, the king's hand enters the frame in close-up and grasps the crown. He covets it still, even when mortally wounded. In a long down shot, as the king moves uncertainly, clutching the crown to his chest, a guard of halberdiers that ring the place lower their halberds, all pointing to him, like spokes to a hub. He is dying, his crimes exposed, his wife dead before him. The halbert points are the bounds of the ground he rules. He falls and dies.

It is angle that makes the circle; it would not seem such if it were seen from floor level. Only when looking down with an eagle's eye, "The wrinkled sea beneath him crawls." Only when looking up with a fish's eye does the sea skin become a ceiling that seems a floor from above looking down (*Underwater,* Frank Donovan).

8 By Lighting

Shadows are variously used.

A woman is dying in a workhouse. We see the matron seated left frame, and two old crones who help her, squatting between her and the fireplace, which casts a light on them all. We hear a sound from the dying woman's bed in the darkness behind them and a black shadow moves across the high brick mantel above the fire (*Oliver Twist,* David Lean).

Calvero, a clown who has lost his gift of holding an audience, has helped a young dancer recover her confidence. She has danced for the producer and choreographer, and been given a role, and after a few words, they have left the stage. The camera closes in, and we are now aware of the clown seated upstage in the shadow. Someone shouts to turn out the lights. On each of four successive clicks, Calvero's face darkens more and more till only a faint gleam around his eyes tells us he is there. She has reached the Limelight, and he is lost and forgotten in the shadow that houses has-beens (*Limelight,* Charles Chaplin).

9 By Replacement

The gloss may replace the image.

In *The Red Shoes* (Michael Powell and Emeric Pressburger), Victoria Page is being applauded. She is bottom right in a white spotlight; the edge of the stage curves across the frame; the sound of the applause is that of the greenish sea surfing over rocks, which fills the space above the curve where the audience would have been sitting.

Billy Liar's father and mother have been grumbling about his ways, and he has answered them, on the whole, temperately. He is in a corner by a stove making tea. Suddenly he turns, the pan in his hand has become an automatic rifle and he is wearing an American soldier's uniform. The gun blazes and crackles annihilation. He then turns to the corner, back in his own clothes again, and continues with tea (*Billy Liar*, John Schlesinger).

10 By Movement

Movement may be that of people or things, or what appears to be theirs; or it may be clearly our, or the camera's, movement in relation to them.

From outside a fence, a peasant sees through a knothole a kulak seated at a table, his arms resting comfortably on it, and Vareniki cakes rising up from the plate and floating into his mouth. "That's what I call living a czar's life," said the peasant (*Happiness*, Aleksandr Medvedev).

In *Things to Come* (William Cameron Menzies), rumors and unseen forces are suggested by posters and headlines: "EUROPE ARMING," "ALARMING SPEECH," "10,000 PLANES DEMANDED," "WARNING TO EUROPE," "WAR STORM BREWING." We see the words above a holly seller, on walls, on buses, in front of paperboys, and in newspapers. First, on streets with people, then with no people seen, giving a sense of air alive with rumors, and last of all, in an up shot, like the overhead part of a sandwich board, "WAR SCARE" grows and glides toward us, till it shows only the one word "WAR," looming ever larger with ominous momentum.

The train taking Jennifer to London to buy clothes for her coming wedding to Kenway travels left across the screen. Kenway's car keeps pace with the train and they wave. In a long down shot, the road now curves away, sharply. His car turns its back on the train and hastens to bottom right. We feel, before we know, that he has made a decision not to come back to her (*The Rake's Progress*, Sidney Gilliatt).

Andreas, a Bolshevik, waits in the rain for Jeanne, whose family are Czarists. We see a man with a flag leading a file of women, then Jeanne passing by smoking ruins, with sky gray and rain falling, and overall a sense of desolation. The two meet in close shot and embrace. A boat waits at a wharf for passengers. The column of women reaches the two, and the standard-bearer thrusts between them saying, "Don't trust her. She's not our kind." His file of women trudges on between them neither one looking at the other. The last woman passes, but the two still stand apart, awkward, speechless. After a time, she goes, and he makes an impulsive movement forward, but stops. The man with the flag is official doctrine that undercuts feelings and imposes imperatives. Andreas later is sent to Paris, where Jeanne went, and a taxi-driver friend brings her to the park where Andreas waits impatiently. We see his back, as he keeps pace with the taxi, and in between a railing reels past. Sometimes we are he, the railing flitting past in front of us, and Jeanne waving beyond it; sometimes we are she, and he is running along the railing looking at us. At last the railing comes to an end, and he rushes out toward the stopping taxi. As we see the moving railing, we think of the file of moving women, but whatever its gloss, that which kept them apart has come to an end (*The Love of Jeanne Ney*, G. W. Pabst).

A little girl was killed when the bus in which Ackland was bringing her home struck a railway bridge. He is obsessed with his guilt at keeping her late. He rises from bed, goes to the window, and opens it. A train passes with whistle blowing (as he had heard it before the accident). There is a quick approach to his face as he tenses, and a gradual withdrawal as he walks away from the window and little by little relaxes. The sudden approach to close facial detail is like a vivid intense resurgence of the accident. It is almost a blow (*The October Man*, Roy Baker).

In *The Stars Look Down*, the approach is even more of a blow, coming from a greater distance. Davy returns home earlier than expected, sees a light in the upper windows of his house and Joe Garland's car in front. From quite a long shot we pounce in a flash to his face, with an abrupt stop, like a hammer striking its mark (Sir Carol Reed).

11 By Succession or Montage

Eisenstein asserted that any two pieces of film stuck together create a new concept, and this is more certainly so when a director puts them together not by chance but intention.[12]

In the full version of *Greed* (Erich von Stroheim), as a gloss to the narrative, a huge gilded hand is cut in on a black background, and the hand is closing on a naked man and woman held within it.[13] They resist and then collapse.

Here the object that carries the gloss is not to be found in the persons or setting of the story. It may conveniently be called nondiegetic.[14] There are striking examples of these in the work of Eisenstein and Pudovkin.[15]

The interjection of an image, that is not easy to place as part of the story, even with slow cutting, may leave some viewers baffled on first viewing. The subconscious effect is speculative. Current opinion seems to be that the gloss arising from action or setting is more immediately effective, and more artistically satisfying.[16]

Radshaw, in urging better treatment of the workingman, would brandish a saber used to disperse the crowd at Peterloo. In later political life, he abandons pacifism during the war, reduces the "dole" when serving on a budget committee, and is accepted socially by those of the opposite party. At the age of seventy-five, speaking at a banquet, he says he has never allowed personal considerations to dim a torch of principle. As he stops, his mind blank, he turns to the Lord Mayor, and seems to see instead the face of the miners' leader, who scorns him as a renegade. Later, at home, he looks at a picture of the slum street where he was born, takes from a shelf the book he wrote, *Crusade against Poverty*, and remembers voices: his own, "a new heaven and a new earth . . ."; the crowd's, "We want Radshaw"; and, as he looks at his wife's picture, hers, "I believe in you, I always have." He crosses to the mantel and takes the saber from its brackets. After he had made his political name, he had had a sheath made for it. He tugs at the saber with all his strength, but cannot draw it. His valet comes in. "Draw it," says Radshaw, but the valet does no better, "It must have rusted in, it hasn't been drawn for so long." Radshaw is bowed over the sword, almost in tears. "Come on, my Lord, it's time for bed." After the two are out of sight through the door, we pan to his chair and then to the saber on the floor, rusted and undrawn for many years, and so the film ends (*Fame Is the Spur*, Roy Boulting).

12   By Parallel Action

A special kind of succession is the intercutting of two parallel stories, one a gloss on the other. A husband finds out that another man, less crabbed and suppressive, less afraid and indecisive than he, is in love with his wife, and she with him. In close-up, a key turns to lock a door and is drawn out. We retreat across a room to a note left on a table: "Dear mother. Today there comes to an end . . . ." The husband sits. We see hammers playing a glockenspiel, champagne spilling over from one glass set within a lower one, and a hand lifting the upper glass and giving it to the wife seen beyond it. Her eyes widen. She drinks. She and the man she is with embrace and dance. Her lips sing. The husband in his room takes his glasses off, stands, and blows out the lamp. A fly on sticky paper struggles to free itself. The husband raises a revolver to his head. The fiddler stops playing as a shot is heard. The dancers stop. The eyes of each look upward. The hammers hang over the keys of the glockenspiel. The husband in up shot falls toward us. The fly still tugs its tangled feet. The husband's head falls back on the floor. Into an empty frame drops his hand, fingers holding his pince-nez. The fly no longer moves. The cellist lays his bow across the strings. The hammers of the glockenspiel sink slowly down to rest on their bars. Above the floor is the husband's misery, below in the ballroom, the lovers' happiness. As the shot is fired, all motion ceases, as if the stillness of death has filled the building (*Ecstasy*, Gustave Machaty).

13   By Sound

Norman McLaren's two *Neighbors* each covet the flower that grows on the line between their properties. As the savagery of their quarrel grows, we hear sounds like yelps and barks that say, "these men are animals."

A mixed company of refugees is waiting in an Alpine hut, during their escape from Italy to Switzerland. An American, one of three soldiers who have helped them, starts singing "Frère Jacques," using words beginning, "You are crazy." Little by little all in the room join in the round, each singing the words he knows in his own tongue. They are singing in different languages, but they are all singing the same song together: a common culture or a common humanity beyond the mask of speech (*The Last Chance*, Leopold Lindtberg).

A mother is cutting vegetables into a steaming bowl, and looks up. The cuckoo clock shows 12:20. A boy and girl are walking up the stairs, and the mother looks over the bannister to ask them, "Is Elsie with you?" We now see Elsie and a man buying her a balloon from a street vendor. The door bell rings—it is a man delivering a magazine: "Did you see Elsie?" We look down the empty stair well, and hear the mother's voice call "Elsie!" The cuckoo clock is 1:15. Hearing voices, the mother goes to the window and calls again. After this, we hear the name but never see the speaker: in the empty stairwell again the voice echoes; in a basement, with nothing to be seen apart from two bits of clothing hung on a line, we hear the voice. We see a dish, napkin, and glass waiting on a table. A ball rolls out of a bush and comes to a stop on grass: "Elsie."—very faintly. The balloon, rising in the wind, catches briefly on telegraph wires, and just barely heard is the last "Elsie!" The name, echoing in

empty space, a disbodied voice growing fainter, is like the memory of Elsie coming
back to her mother again and again for years to come, dimming with time, or, like
Elsie, slipping away (*M.*, Fritz Lang).

14 By Manipulation

What characters do with objects may be a metaphor.

Count Sparre has deserted the army, and Elvira has left her work as a tightrope
walker. They are spending the summer together. He will ultimately be caught and
punished, and they have a limited amount of money. They sit under a tree for a
picnic. He pours the wine and they drink. The bottle sits on the cloth and as he turns
he knocks it over. The red wine spurts out of the opening. We see each of them
somberly watching the bleeding bottle, but neither moving to right it. For the
moment they see their lives, like the wine, coming to an end, and watch as if there
was nothing they could do to stop it. Is spilling the wine that was bought with the
last of their money of a piece with the fecklessness with which they managed their
affair? Is it because they know that soon food and wine will not concern them (*Elvira
Madigan*, Bo Widerberg)?

Hynkel and Napaloni, as they talk in the barbershop, each jacks his chair higher
than the other's several times, in a casual way, so as to be looking down on the other.
One-up-manship in high places (*The Great Dictator*, Charles Chaplin). The effec-
tiveness of the Italian armistice in 1943 in the face of the German invasion is shown
by a paper crumpled up on the road with the word "Armistiso" showing (*The Last
Chance*, Leopold Lindtberg).

15 By the Dream

What would otherwise be non-diegetic may enter a narrative as someone's dream.
Joan Webster, from childhood on has gone after many things, and has always had
her way. At lunch with her father, she tells him she is going to be married. "To
whom?" She hands him a folding card. "But this is your work pass. The only name
on it is yours. You can't marry Consolidated Chemical Industries."

"Can't I?" she says.

"Have you got your ticket?" (She is traveling to Scotland for the ceremony).

"It's all arranged," she says. "Everything's arranged."

At the train, she says good-bye to her father, and Hunter (who is acting for her
future husband, Sir Robert Bellenger, chairman of the board). Her last words to her
father were "Don't worry. I know where I'm going," and as she takes out her
cellophane-covered wedding dress and hangs it up, we hear the Irish folk song, "I
Know Where I'm Going," which continues throughout the dream. Outside, the
train sweeps past. We see her head as she sleeps, and we hear her father's question
again, "You can't marry . . .," and we see her lips in sleep frame the words, "Can't
I?" We pan up from her to the cellophane bag, now empty. Dissolve to her in the
wedding dress, with glints to hint that both she and the wedding dress are wrapped in
cellophane.

A clergyman, right frame, backed by turning wheels and other industrial devices
sketched on white, looks up from his prayer book to ask, "Do you, Joan Webster,
take Consolidated Chemical Industries to be your lawful husband?"

She replies decisively, "I do."

The clergyman (also behind the cellophane that covers the frame) raises his voice, as if to reach the distant ears of a vast colossus, says, "And do you, Consolidated Chemical Industries, take Joan Webster to be your lawful wedded wife?"

A factory whistle answers. We see the fleeting train, the driving wheels and draw bar, and voices repeat in the beat of the wheels, "Everything's arranged. Everything's arranged . . ." We see her face, and we hear the words "Lady Bellenger" several times. Then there is a landscape of two tartan-covered hills, vaguely resembling deerstalker hats, and a tiny train with lighted windows winding across into a tunnel, and the whole dream faced with shiny cellophane. Here is a girl bent on wealth and position and who has taken all the necessary steps to come within a day of getting it. The wedding dress and she in it, the clergyman, and the highland wedding are all packaged as ordered, shiny, and expensive (*I Know Where I'm Going*, Michael Powell and Emeric Pressburger).

16   Used for Conveying Character

Looking now from the means to the purpose, a metaphor can give a visible shape to a character.

Henriette has just been reviled by a woman for being mean and spiteful, and trying to make others unhappy because she is ugly and nobody loves her. She goes to a mirror, looks at herself, and bangs her hand on the glass, and shatters it. Then we see her partial distorted image as the camera lingers on the mirror. It is she who has made herself ugly, outside and in. Later, she is told she can also make herself beautiful (*Flesh and Fantasy*, Julien Duvivier).

Pusya, the mistress of a German officer, is laying beauty clay on her face, and sharp words grow between her and a Russian peasant girl, Feodosia. "Get out," Pusya cries, rising to her feet. In the same frame we see the plain sunburned face of the peasant girl, and the gray finger-pocked expressionless clay from which Pusya's eyes look out, like something unnatural and loathsome (*The Rainbow*, Mark Donskoi).

A boy with a bloody knee, held by two others, is hit by a snowball and falls, blood running out of his mouth. As a grown man, he sits at a table, himself as a boy lying under his chair, bleeding. He reaches down and from inside the boy's jacket picks out a playing card with which he wins his game. In the adult world he is using wisdom gained from his boyhood sufferings (*The Blood of a Poet*, Jean Cocteau).

The photographer stands in a dancehall. The guitarist in the band, unable to make his playing loud enough, throws his guitar down, jumps on it, and after it is broken up, hurls the fingerboard out into the mass of faces around the platform. The photographer successfully wrests the fingerboard from competing hands, fights his way out of the mob into the street, outdistances his halfhearted pursuers, and finding himself alone in the street, flings the fingerboard on to the pavement. His life is one of short-term objectives, taken up one after another, not for the satisfaction they give but to avoid nonmovement. He takes picture after picture, drives around in his car, buys useless things like airplane propellers, and when he finds the clue to a murder by enlarging a chance picture, does nothing about it (*Blow-Up*, Michelangelo Antonioni).

17   Used for Conveying Situation

The meaning of a situation may be shown by metaphor with clarity, brevity, and power, and with great variety of means (pls. 13, 14, 15).

The itinerary of Joan Webster's journey to marry a millionaire, handed to her on starting her journey, has been followed punctiliously, until she stands on the wharf and meets the Laird of Kiloran. He is also waiting to go to the island, rented from him by the millionaire. They are standing in the wind, watching a raging sea, and are told that they cannot cross till the storm has passed. The itinerary is blown out of her hand, and floats away on the sea. The storm has wrecked her careful plans: after its eight days, she has fallen in love with the Laird (*I Know Where I'm Going*, Michael Powell and Emeric Pressburger).

Four Egyptians have tried to track down swindlers of the government—they have found out that gray trucks crossed with yellow and red lines have removed material from a factory the government is building. The investigators have been hindered by indifference and hostile high officials. After the Ten Day War, one of them, a singer, is leading a crowd of people over the bridge, singing as they go, "Let us die that our country may live." Going the opposite way, in the other lane of traffic, is a long train of the gray trucks, crossed by red and yellow. Corruption opposing patriotism (*The Sparrow*, Youssef Chahine).

Hester, a poor pupil in a private school, is befriended by a fellow-pupil, Clarissa. Hester later becomes the mistress of Clarissa's husband, and intends to become his wife. She gives Clarissa, when sick, an overdose of sleeping pills. We pan from Clarissa's face to her hand clasping Hester's, and beyond them both to the clock at five past twelve. Dissolve to the face of the clock now showing 3:00 and back to Hester. She breaks their clasped hands, opens the window, pulls the covers off Clarissa's bed, wraps them around herself as she crouches by the fire, and fiercely pokes the burning embers out. We hear her remembering Clarissa's kindnesses: "Now that Hester is staying with me, I am happier than I have been for years. . . ." Breaking their hands, wrapping Clarissa's bedclothes around herself and poking the fire out, are figures for Hester's intentions (*The Man in Grey*, Leslie Arliss).

The old hall porter collapses after lifting a trunk, and a page with some effort undoes his gold-braided greatcoat, and one of the buttons from it falls to the floor. The old man, like a plucked fowl in his thin shabby suit, looks down at the severed button. The overcoat, now hung in a cupboard, comes into focus, and we move toward it. The man's hands are taking it back again, when he sees the housekeeper coming across the hall, and he furtively takes the key of the cupboard instead. He has lost the source of confidence and self-esteem. The button has no use apart from the coat, nor the old man apart from his work. The key is his hope of getting the coat again, as if merely putting it on would give him back his occupation, and with it, respect (*The Last Laugh*, F. W. Murnau).

Stepa is unable to have children because of her husband's syphilis. She is traveling home from the mental hospital where she has been to visit him. Through the glass partition, she sees in the next compartment a little girl of seven or so and a large nun who is dozing. She smiles at the girl, who comes to the glass and places her palm on it. Stepa goes to the glass and places her palm on the girl's dirty one. She places her lips where the girl's lips are, and strokes with tenderness the place of her cheek. They touch fingers through the glass, and the girl strokes Stepa's face gently and kisses it, always with the glass between (*Oil Lamps*, Juraj Herz).

18 Used for Conveying Abstractions

Film is pictures; pictures are particular and concrete. Metaphor is therefore of value to express the general and abstract (pl. 29).

After a haze of steam has cleared away, a huge machine with men working on three levels appears to Freder, as he watches, to become a temple with mouthlike portal in the center, teeth at the top, and above it, eyes and nose. Nearly naked slaves plod up the last steps of an enormous staircase into the furnace glow of the entrance. They are followed by factory workers in caps and overalls trudging in step. The machine demands worship and sacrifice, like the Canaanite Moloch (*Metropolis*, Fritz Lang).

The most cited example is from *October* (S. M. Eisenstein). During the 1917 Revolution, we see men climbing a statue. It is a kingly figure, the czar, short sword in one hand, orb in the other. By ropes to the neck and other parts, head, hands, and other pieces of the statue are broken off. Then, in long shot, the whole chair and figure topple off the plinth. Later, after Kerensky comes to power, the parts come together, the figure sits again in its chair, orb and scepter rise from the ground and land in its hands. Kerensky is the new autocrat.

Death has been rendered in many various ways. Here are a few. It can be shown, the death of a queen, by a servant snuffing out the lights in a candelabrum (*Catherine the Great*, Paul Czinner).

Mumtaz speaks for the last time and dies, and the light on her side of the bed goes out and leaves her a black silhouette, while *Shah Jehan* sits fully lit still (A. Kardar). Gaffney is bowling. The camera follows the ball. The pins are scattered. Abruptly a shot sounds, and the last pin totters and falls. We know that Gaffney has been killed. In the same film, as Tony enters a door, he turns to the name on the glass and drives his fist through it. The name is Johnny Lovo. In a moment a shot is heard offscreen. Johnny is dead (*Scarface*, Howard Hawks).

There is imagination, a poetry, to these expressions of death, lacking in the recent literalities of gore and mutilation, which may gain in shock effect the first few times they are used, but for viewers of sensibility no more emotionally affecting, and perhaps in time rather blunting our feelings.

This is more complex. Frankie loses sixpence and steals Ronnie's balloon. Ronnie chases Frankie up in a ruined building and along a girder. Frankie suddenly turns; Ronnie falls back and off the girder, and is killed. Most shots in the sequence were up, to emphasize height. Now in the first shot pointing down, we see Ronnie on the ground. Frankie has let the balloon go and it floats down, landing beside Ronnie, its movement, like its owner's life, stopped. The object of the chase is now abandoned by both of them. It was not worth a life, and the thief no longer wants it: the owner no longer can use it (*The Yellow Balloon*, J. Lee-Thompson).

Von Aschenbach, a composer, has come to Italy to rest after a heart attack. In flashback, we are shown his earlier flight from an elegant brothel at the mere sight of the woman. Now he is drawn by the beautiful face of a slender boy in Venice with his family. Von Aschenbach feels this to be wrong and tries to leave Venice, but is frustrated by misdirected luggage. Learning of a cholera epidemic, which is being hushed up, he nerves himself to warn the boy's mother. Sensitive of his age, the composer goes to a barber, who suggests dying his graying hair and lightening his sallowness. He learns in the lobby that the boy's family is about to leave in any case, and abandons his purpose. He collapses on the way to his bathing box and is helped by an attendant to a deck chair. He weakly answers a wave of the distant boy that he wrongly thinks is to him, and dies. Down the cheeks of his canted head, a black trickle, as if from the dye on his hair, has nearly run to his chin. Death is suggested by several things: the color black and the trickle that looks like a crack in the solid structure of the head, like juice down the outside of a rotting melon, for death by disease. The dye too is not part of him, but something added on, like the inhibitions that hedged his life. But above all, it is an image that speaks directly to our feelings and no analysis can exhaust it (*Death in Venice*, Luchino Visconti).

19 Used for Conveying Inner States

Like an abstraction, an inner state is a nonmaterial, nonvisible event, which may, in a metaphor, shine through a material visible thing.

Seriochka is sick. His mother says that until he is well, he cannot come to Kholmogori, where his stepfather has a new position. Furniture and luggage are all in the van. The boy stands in the emptiness, as we move away from him to see how small he is in a large room. He looks, and we look, at a close-up of a jar that lies on the floor. It is upset, and a trickle of what was in it lies on the floor, and the empty jar is all that is left in the empty room besides the boy. He feels a void that grandma cannot fill (*Seriochka*, Georgi Danela).

Norma is on probation and has been forbidden to dance. She has fallen out with her boyfriend, and in a reckless mood has gone to a discotheque. As the sounds of the jukebox permeate the room with languid sweetness, our glance falls from her head and shoulders down to end on one of her crossed legs, where the foot, moving to the music, seems as if it were caged by the crisscrossing ties (*I Believe in You*, Michael Relph and Basil Dearden).

We see a man floating out of his car in a traffic jam, and ending in the clouds: this represents his inner state—he tends to be out of touch with everyday things. A man on the ground in a white uniform is pulling on a rope that runs up toward us as we look down to earth. The upper end of the rope is tied on to an ankle, just within the frame—it might be ours. A man in white, half length, is looking at a file, presumably the history of a patient and his treatment. He says, "Down, definitely down." In a long down shot of the ocean far below, we see a man falling and falling, finally plunging into the water. This is followed by a doctor examining a patient (*8½*, Federico Fellini).

The reflective power of the mirror fascinates the maker of metaphors. In *Dead of Night* (Robert Hamer), a mirror came to reflect, more and more often, not the room in which the looker stands but a room in which it had stood in the past, with other furniture, four-poster bed, candles, paneled walls, and blazing fireplace, reflecting, not reality but an obsession of the looking man. The jealous, crippled, occupant of the room seen in the mirror had strangled his wife and cut his own wrists in front of it. The hold the mirror has on the looker is thrown off only when his wife, who now sees the room too and herself in it, and is on the point of being strangled, smashes the mirror with a candlestick. The mirror had stored and reflected evil, and something sleeping within him had answered and absorbed it. There is often a hint of contagious magic in metaphor, and more in metonymy.

Professor Willingdon, a brilliant scientist, is convinced that his life's work, which he hoped would serve God and his fellowmen, is being used for evil purposes. He has served an ultimatum on the prime minister that if an undertaking is not given to cease making atomic weapons, he will detonate an atomic bomb in London at noon on Sunday. We first see Willingdon praying at the distant altar of a church, war-shattered and roofless. From him the camera pans to close-up of a pew in the nave, beside which is the bag that houses the bomb. Is the ruin to signify London after Sunday, his destroyed hopes, or the morally corrupted world he sees around him (*Seven Days to Noon*, John and Roy Boulting)?

20 The Part That Stands for the Whole

Here the meaning of the whole film is condensed into a single event or image (pl. 15). This adds force and clarity to the film's message. In Simile, under the same heading, three examples were given, the first of which was clearly a simile, the last of which could easily be a metaphor. Here the earlier cases are clearly metaphors, and the latter are long enough to be taken for allegories.

An innocent but solitary man, who keeps to himself, Desiré Heer, is wrongly suspected of murder, and later in *Panic* (Julien Duvivier), is pursued by a mob that is bent on killing him. He enters a trolley-driven electric car at a fair, and drives around a large circular enclosure. Alfred, the real murderer, and a girl with him, enter another car, and keep going after and bumping Desiré. Others, complete strangers, take up the bumping. Cars aim straight at us; cars, one after another, jolt Heer; in lower and lower angles bumpers of the cars rise toward us higher and faster, till at last Heer is packed in a hostile crowd and cannot move his car. The detective, watching, says to an assistant, "Did you ever see a hunt like that?" It is a figure for Heer's fate from then on.

To build a road to his house, a large property owner has had the land of a number of peasants confiscated. Among those whose land is taken is Mohammed Abu Swellem, an older well-respected man. The peasants try to harvest the cotton before their plants are all grubbed out. Cavalry come to drive them off. All flee but Abu Swellem who stands dazed and bewildered. A rifle strikes him and he falls bleeding. A rope from an officer's saddle is tied to his legs. At the first whip to the horse, Swellem's face on the ground, and his hands clutching the cotton plants do not budge. The straining horse and the unmoving man form a strong image. On another stroke of the whip, the stretched arms trail the ground, plants dragging from the fingers. After a little the fingers release the plants, but scratch the soil as if they were harrows. Then once again the fingers clutch plants, and the clutching hands are frozen as the film ends. "What is a man without land?" Abu Swellem had said (*The Land*, Youssef Chahine).

The Fellowes Feeding Machine avoids wasting time on lunch hours. It is a figure for the inefficient way that the capitalist system supplies people's needs, and this is the whole theme of *Modern Times* (Charles Chaplin). Tilting the bowl too quickly the gadget spills the soup on Charlie's clothes. Refilled, it throws the soup in his face. Each time the wiper comes politely to wipe his mouth, despite that not a mouthful of soup has reached his lips, and all the other mess is left untouched. The entrée is rammed into the mouth, one piece after another, together with two metal nuts, left on the plate by mistake during adjustments. The corncob moves across and back, turning to expose a new row on each run, like a typewriter carriage, but at such a rate that the eater's teeth resemble rapidly striking type, and a hail of single kernels hurtles over the table. The dessert feeder throws the pie in his face and holds it there, after which the wiper resumes its strictly limited attentions. At the end, the wiper, formerly so polite, delivers a series of rapid slaps on his mouth.

21 Repetition

Once a thing is charged with a gloss, a director may, with great economy of means, recall the gloss by showing the image. When Rainer in *Random Harvest* (Mervyn Leroy), recovers his memory, he finds in his pocket a key. It disturbs him. He wonders what it opens, for of all that had taken place in the time between he knows nothing. When we see the key in his hand, as he talks to his butler, sits in a theater box, or works in his office, we know he is troubled—about the door the key unlocks, and what else is locked in those hidden years.

A director, on the other hand, may give us an image, and hold back the gloss. As Isadora's car enters a tunnel, to a high shrill sound, she puts her hands to her face, and a pale frame appears in the darkness containing two faces, a girl's and a boy's, pale in color, going away from us. She emerges distraught from the tunnel. She (and we) see the image several times. The film alternates between the present when she is writing her life, and flashbacks of what she is describing. Later we see, as she tells us about it, horses dragging a vehicle out of a river and a nanny taking her two children away. She kisses them through the glass of the rear window before they are driven away. As she looks, the car goes—this is the frame she saw in the tunnel—and turns a corner. As she writes this, she sobs. On a dark and gloomy day we see a long bridge and a car crossing. The car swerves against, and breaks through, the guardrail. In up shot, it falls down toward us. Then we draw back from what can be seen of the car to a long shot of the whole river. The receding window was a figure not only for separation from the children as arranged with her husband but for their death almost immediately afterwards, and the paleness of color not only a figure for dimness of memory but for the sadness matched by the elegaic music heard with it (*Isadora*, Karel Reisz).

22 Intention

All the cases above presume intention. The viewer may speculate on the subconscious: I merely assume that as the director has deliberately assembled what we see in the frame, and the order in which the frames come before us, if I find what appears to be a figure, I am justified in giving to what I see whatever meaning an average viewer would.

There are two qualifications to this. First, it must be clear from the context that there was no reason for shooting or editing the image the way it was done, other than metaphorical. Second, if the style of the film, or the director's work as a whole, does not run to metaphor, it would be rash to find a metaphorical intent in a single case.

The Hindenburg begins with newsreel quotations in black and white, and it ends the same way, with other material added in black and white. The body of the film is photographed in color, with an elegant blueish cast. The effortless beauty of the vessel, the vast interior, and the fine decor create a romantic and sumptuous atmosphere. The pink of the explosion is followed by the final ten minutes of burning in black and white. I felt strongly the Damoclean luxury of the blue, dependent on controls designed to minimize the explosion of hydrogen, when seen beside the probabilities of combustion suggested by the harsh black and white.

Late in the film, too, the ship sails from the right, heading toward a sunset of yellow mists just above the horizon. Knowing the ship's fate, and that the film is nearing its end, it is tempting to read this as a figure for the end of *The Hindenburg* and perhaps of lighter-than-airships in general.

In both cases, however, the director, Robert Wise, assured me that no metaphor was intended. The newsreel quotations had been shot in black and white, and any added material had to match it; the second was "just a good shot."[17]

Anadiplosis or the Carry-Over

1 The Anadiplosis in Rhetoric

Anadiplosis is starting a sentence or clause with the same word or phrase that ends the previous one:

> O happy men that finde no lacke in *Loue;*
> I *Loue,* and lacke what most I do desire;
> My deepe desire no reason can remoue;
> All reason shunnes my brest, that's set on fire;
>   And so the fire mainetaines both force and flame,
>   That force auayleth not against the same;[1]

But the word, when repeated, may have changed its meaning: "The battle was won not by engines but men, men who had vowed to die rather than yield." The first *men* is "men as against machines," the second is "men of courage and resolution as compared with others."

Two words, the same in form and sound, may shift as their context alters, not merely in meaning or connotation but in the object they include, their denotation. A friend of mine brought home a collection of seashells. It was wartime. On being asked what was in his box, he said, "Shells." The customs officer, startled, said "Shells!" and called over two other inspectors. They removed the parcel very gingerly to the farthest counter, quickly cut the cords, and opened it carefully. The one was talking of mussels, the other was thinking of missiles.

Shakespeare wrote in Sonnet 93:

> But heaven in thy creation did decree
> That in thy face sweet love should ever dwell,
> Whate'er thy thoughts or thy heart's workings be,
> Thy looks should nothing thence, but sweetness tell.

Empson points out that line three, although clear in itself, can be read with either line two or line four, in each case with a slightly different meaning.[2] The line between, however, is written only once, not repeated, and our attention can sway forward or back in giving it meaning. In form it is not a strict anadiplosis: in function it is.

2 Strict Form: The Same Image Repeated[3]

In the strict filmic anadiplosis, the same image ends one scene as begins the next. A pen, for example, points on a plan of staterooms to B46, and this dissolves to the door of the room with B46 on it (*Champagne*, Alfred Hitchcock).

Boss Geddes threatens to publish the fact that Kane has a mistress, unless he withdraws as candidate for governor. Kane refuses. Geddes and Kane's wife have just emerged from the house where the mistress lives. The wife goes off right and Geddes left, leaving the lighted double doors and the number above them—185. The tone changes from dark gray to light, and we pull back to see the doors now on the front page of a newspaper, exposing Kane's "lovenest." The repeated image is stronger, from a cause-and-effect relation: the scandal as a consequence of Kane's refusal (*Citizen Kane*, Orson Welles).

In *The Mystery of Edwin Drood* (Stuart Walker) a scene ends on Jasper's legs walking down the steps of an opium den, from which we dissolve to his legs moving at the same pace, and retreat to show him as one of a church choir singing in procession.

The strict form can also be found in sound, especially in speech. Young Harris, questioned by his mother the second time, says roughly to her, "I told you never ask me what happened on Saturday night." "Saturday night, Johnny?" are Superintendent Hasard's first curt words, as he interrogates Johnny Fiddle in the following scene (*Sapphire*, Basil Dearden).

"You need me," says Frank Machin, a professional football player, to Margaret Hammond. "You're just a great big ape on the football field. We don't need you," she answers. Machin, head and shoulders, with a little square of window behind him, says quietly, "What do you want of me? . . . A great ape in a football field," as if he were answering her. Then in a longer shot, we see listening, not her but Machin's married friend, Maurice, seated beside him in a pub. "She makes me feel clumsy, awkward, big, stupid," he adds (*This Sporting Life*, Lindsay Anderson).

We feel in *Sapphire* that the scenes are going on at the same time. In *This Sporting Life*, the latter scene was clearly occurring later, and the carry-over bridged a gap in time. This is a double carry-over—in sound the phrase recurs in the same form, and the image of Machin could belong to either scene: a carry-over for both the eye and ear.

3 Variation I: The Same Pattern Repeated

What is often carried over is not the identical object, but the same pattern embodied in different objects.

In a beam of light from a circular window, Harriet Green sings in the witness box of a courtroom. The window in close-up dissolves to the lens of a spotlight, the song changes, an orchestra supports the singer, and the camera pans down the beam of light to show her on a stage (*Evergreen*, Victor Saville).

There are degrees of likeness between the two patterns. While his wife was in Venice, Warlock, in company with a friend, has met a girl who fell in love with him. As he and his friend ride home in a taxi, he tears up the paper on which the girl has written her address. "I'm only interested in one woman in the world," he says, "and her name's not Doris." The bits of paper, as he throws them out of the window, flutter against a black sky. The bits dissolve to black pigeons fluttering on a ground of white, and this dissolves to his wife and her sister lunching beside a canal in Venice

(*Cynara*, King Vidor).⁴ The skipper of a trawler is shown at his radio transmitter. The time by his wall clock is 8:07, and across the clock the shadow of a dangling rope sways to the ship's movement. We cut to a clock on the wall of the skipper's home, showing the same time, a pendulum swinging to and fro below it. We pan to follow the skipper's wife as she too goes to her radio set (*North Sea*, Harry Watt). Scrooge, lying on the ground, embraces the black-robed legs of the Ghost of Christmas Yet to Come, crying out, "I am not the man I was," from which we dissolve to him lying in his room, his arms around the feet of the figure carved on one of his bedposts, in size and posture closely matched, one imperceptibly becoming the other (*A Christmas Carol*, Brian Desmond Hurst).

The likeness may make us more aware of a contrast between situations. Johnny, collapsed in a bomb shelter, feels for his wound, sinks down, and the camera pans to his hand, lying limply on the floor. Cut to a policeman's hand rising quickly into an empty frame to stop someone, and in longer shot requesting an identity card. The exhausted fugitive: the brisk pursuit (*Odd Man Out*, Sir Carol Reed).

In *Abdul the Damned* (Karl Grune) the chief eunuch fastens a bracelet on the wrist of Thérèse. This is cut to a jailor locking manacles on the wrists of Talak Bey, the man she loves.

The art then is to find in a scene a shape or pattern resembling one to be found in the following scene; to make sure that the final shot of the one and the opening shot of the other contain this shape at the same spot on the screen; and not merely contain it, but to have them both shot from the distance and angle that will bring out the resemblance. It is better still if the shape or pattern used is of some significance in each of the scenes. We thus bridge an ellipsis in time or space with no loss of clarity, little effort, and the pleasure that comes from a deft piece of craftsmanship. It is using a simile to bind a narrative: an elegant figure.

But there may be no likeness at all in sound or image, and still some sense of carry-over. The carry-over may be merely of color. Levin's brother dies of consumption. On the white pillow by his head is a red splash of bright blood. The next shot begins with Betsy seen by a window, half-length, turning to speak to Anna, and on her white hat, cuffs, and bodice, the same bright red as on the pillow (*Anna Karenina*, part 8, television, Basil Coleman).

From the timetable where it reads "10–11 Music," a pyramid-shaped wipe up the center discloses a pyramidal metronome ticking during the following day's lesson (*Little Friend*, Berthold Viertel). In *Abdul the Damned* (Karl Grune), a circular wipe from the center blends into a ringlike pattern in the following ballet. This is a pseudo-carry-over: the wipe does not belong to either scene: it is no more than the shape of the opening between them.

This may also be done with sound. First with sound and image both. In *Cynara* (King Vidor) Jim Warlock hears of a suicide for which he feels guilt. He keeps bringing down his fist on his desk in an agony of self-blame. This cuts to a coroner pounding his fist on his desk to silence talk—it is the inquest. Then with sound alone. A pianist strikes the same note on a piano four times. This is cut to a door, on which someone is knocking in the same rhythm (*Seven Days Ashore*, John H. Auer).

There may be no likeness at all in the quality of the sound itself, but merely in a pattern of words. The Count hands Jeannie out of the carriage, and as the revolving door sweeps her in, it sweeps out a drunk from the other side, who staggers, raises his hat, and says, "Good Night." Cut to the following day, as Jeannie passes a page on the staircase and says, "Good Morning" (*Jeannie*, Harold French).

A solicitor bearing a boxful of money knocks twice on a door. A tap from the hammer of Morris Finsbury, as he opens a crate in the next shot, completes an even-spaced set of three beats. The knocks belong to the former, the tap to the latter shot, but the set of three belongs to neither; it is common to both, and that brings the next variation (*The Wrong Box*, Bryan Forbes).

4 Variation II: A Single Common Image

If the space is erased between the first and second showings of the image, it becomes a continuous one, which may be thought of as belonging, half and half, to each of the two scenes it brings together, a single image held, like a legal tenancy, in common or jointly.

Even when weak from the sweatbox or oven, Colonel Nicholson tells Dr. Clipton that he will not agree to have his officers work. Speaking of the two colonels, Japanese and English, the doctor says as he stands in the square just after this, "Are they both mad, or am I mad, or is it the sun?" He looks up. For three or so seconds a hazy sky with a yellow spot is held on the screen. Then Shears's head, red and unshaven, rises into the frame. In a longer shot, we see Shears by a sandy shore with driftwood, his water bottle dragging along by a strap. The sun, which is torturing Nicholson and is wondered at by Clipton, is also scorching the escaping Shears (*The Bridge on the River Kwai*, David Lean).

Kadar Pasha lifts up the paper signed by Thérèse, which fills the frame. The paper moves off the frame to reveal Abdul's face, as he finishes reading it. He hands it back, and says, "I knew she couldn't resist me." The paper belongs at the same time to the scene in which it is signed, and the one in which it is read (*Abdul the Damned*, Karl Grune).

It is a step from this to bridging the gap with an abstract shape common to an object found in each scene. "The fate of an entire province is in your hands." O'Hara goes out, carrying money to buy arms with, and closes the door. The man who spoke looks at the door, and we approach it thoughtfully, till the knob is all that is seen of it, white on a light ground. Suddenly the shape on the screen is a billiard ball, as another ball strikes it, and a longer shot shows the enemy, making plans as they play (*The General Died at Dawn*, Lewis Milestone).

Here the background was neutral and featureless. In other cases, a person or thing may remain on the screen, and the setting may change to a new one. In *The New Land* (Jan Troell), a sequence ends with five twigs of a tree bough groping down into the current of a river. This dissolves to the same twig frozen into the winter ice.

Tom's son, both legs painted black, afraid to come home, was found by his mother in a school lavatory. At home his father tries to explain that he would not join the strike on principle. His son says, "You're a dirty scab." Tom puts his hand up to his head and looks down. We pan from him in this posture to show the other men in the factory lunchroom. By making the setting nondescript and ambiguous, we could not tell where Tom was when he put his head on his hand, which made this part both of the scene at home and that in the lunchroom (*The Angry Silence*, Guy Green).

A person or object may move from one scene to another. This was done on the medieval English stage, where different *loca* or *mansions* stood for different places, and as the actor went from one to another, the audience understood a change of place.[5] This is sometimes done in the Noh plays.[6] In film, the camera pans with the actor or thing, giving an impression that the setting is changing, instead of the actor moving. In the Kabuki theater, as Eisenstein pointed out, changing a painted screen behind an actor signifies a change of place.[7] In present stage practice, revolving sets behind an actor may translate him from place to place, or action may freeze on one part of a stage and start up in another.

A magic chest, a reward for Bahir's courage, is stolen by Balchen a miser. By the use of certain magic words, Balchen, his wife, and the corrupt judge, an accessory to the theft, are drawn into the chest, willynilly, and it closes on them. The chest rises into the air, and remains there as the scene outside Balchen's tent changes into that of the rugged cliffs from whence the chest came. The cliffs now collapse and bury the chest (*Magic Treasure*, Dimitri Pavilichenko).

5 Variation III: A Single Ambiguous Image

In this variation there is a continuous flow of action or dialogue through a change of place or time or even of persons, as if two lines of narrative crossed and we switched from one to the other. A single image forms a pivot between the two, in which there is nothing that might place it firmly in either scene. It is unlike the previous variation, where half the common shot could be given to either scene. Here the pivoting shot is felt first to belong to the former scene, and then just as clearly to belong to the latter, between the two of which it floats ambiguously. It cannot belong to both; only to one or the other.

Take, for example, the scene from *Voice in the Wind* (Arthur Ripley) where Volny is practicing on a grand piano. All the furniture we see is covered with sheets. Maria comes to ask if his injured left hand is better; he asks her if she has his dress tie. The scene ends with Volny's left hand on the keyboard in close-up. The right hand enters to take up its part, and we retreat to discover him now in tie and tails, performing to an audience. Bridging this leap in time, playing continuously through both scenes, are Volny's hands. It is Variation II—we could allot half the close-up to each scene.

Now compare a scene from *Sapphire* (Basil Dearden). A detective opens a drain where he has seen a suspect drop something. In close-up we see a stick in his hand. But is it his hand? As the camera retreats, we see it is the hand of Detective Inspector Learoyd, from which Superintendent Hasard (we are now in his office) takes the stick. (pls. 18, 19, 20)

An airplane enters a cloud. We pan past the cloud to see smoke and flames on a mountainside. There is a close-up of the burning plane—but no: a retreat shot shows that the flames are in a hearth, past which a man crosses to a radio, where he hears of the plane's crashing (*School for Secrets,* Peter Ustinov).

Anthony leaves for Germany. We see his train. We approach the oval black entrance to a tunnel, which spreads to a black frame, during which the train sounds alter to German voices. The black shrinks from the frame edge to become again a black oval now drawing away from us. The other end of the tunnel, of course. Not so. It appears to be the mouth of a loudspeaker, tended by khaki-shirted young men. It is Nazi Germany (*England Made Me,* Peter Duffell).

Marianne, who is Dr. Borg's daughter-in-law, is sitting beside him, as he drives to Lund, and she tells him of something that passed between her and her husband. "Ewald was sitting where you are," she says, looking toward us where Borg sits; but in a longer shot, we see that it is not Borg but Ewald at whom she is looking. Her husband is against their having a child. "Your need," he says, "is to live and create, mine to be dead." As she listens, she looks toward where he sits beside her, but as the camera draws back, we see it is Dr. Borg who is sitting there, and we are back in the present (*Wild Strawberries,* Ingmar Bergman).

These are clear, straightforward examples. The variation lends itself, however, to trickery. Colonel Hyde has projected on a screen the parade ground of a military camp from which he proposes that he and his league of seven should steal arms for use in a bank robbery. We move closer to the picture, its frame edges off the screen, people enter and move, and we are actually there on the day of the theft (*The League of Gentlemen*, Basil Dearden). Now strictly speaking, it is quite clear that the still picture belongs to the former scene, and the moving picture to the latter, yet so imperceptibly does movement start that there is, at first view, an ambiguity much the same as in other examples of this variation.

Private Potter is charged in that he cried out during a night attack. He said he had seen God. During his interrogation, we see him and only the back of the questioning officer. Potter is noncommittal. "You are not trying to help me," the officer says. Now we first see the officer's face, looking down. "Why did you run away?" he asks. From him we pan to a wounded Cypriot, sitting in bed, being questioned at the same time. We never saw the face of the officer questioning Potter, and both questioning voices sounded much the same. We did not know beforehand of the second interrogation, and forgot for the moment that Potter had not run away. At the time we see the officer's asking, "Why did you run away?" we take it as part of Potter's interrogation, but later, by retrospection, it unobtrusively slips into place as part of the wounded Cypriot's (*Private Potter*, Casper Wrede).

The distinction between the second and third varieties can be shown by a case that belongs to neither one. Kiichi, the eldest boy of a family, feels that he is standing still and must leave home to go to school. He has worked since he was eight, and is now twenty-one. His mother is against his going, and his father upset at the loss of his son's wages. Kiichi has taken to staying out until late, missing his dinner, and going straight to bed—to avoid discussion. One night, at a street stall, he is eating noodles. He sets down his dish and looks at his watch. At this point, we expect a shot of his watchface. Instead of this, we see an old wall clock with enclosed pendulum below, showing the time as 10:50. Then we see his father looking at it. Both, for different reasons, are concerned about when Kiichi is coming home (*The Whole Family Works*, Mikio Naruse).

Now if this were Variation I, we should see Kiichi looking at his wrist, then a shot of his watchface, then the home clock showing the same time, and then his father looking at it. If it were Variation III, after Kiichi looks at his wrist, we should see a face showing the time, which could be either the watch or the clock, but is not clearly either, and then the father looking down from the clock. As it was done, it would have to be seen as Variation I, with one of the two similar images elided. This removes the repetition from a figure of repetition, and it becomes at most the ghost of a carry-over, for there was neither a repeated pattern nor a common or ambiguous image. And it fails to establish that both looked at the time simultaneously. If the clock were left out, and the son and father, both curious about the time, came in succession with nothing between, it would improve the carry-over. It is, in fact, a sloppy piece of editing.

At one time, bands often played *musical switches*.[8] In these a number of airs were arranged, each of which flowed into the next by means of a musical phrase found in exactly the same form in both tunes, the listener's anticipation being thus unexpectedly jolted into a new pattern. Looking back from the phrase, it belongs to one tune; to another, when looking forward. In film, we should see it as Variation III, but since the flow of sound is unbroken, it forms an easy transition to Variation IV.

6   Variation IV: Unbroken Sound or Horse-Swapping

In this variation there are neither two similar patterns, nor a single common image, nor a single ambiguous image. The images may, in fact, be visually unrelated, but a single continuous sound rides across the break between the scenes. It is something we experience in dreaming. I have dreamed of a boy playing a mouth organ and woken up to the horn of a railway engine holding the same note. It is like swapping horses when crossing a stream, not as imprudent in film as the proverb suggests.

In *The Thirty-Nine Steps* (Alfred Hitchcock), Hannay is on the train for Scotland. Cut to a woman's head and shoulders, turning toward us, mouth open, screaming, followed quickly by a railway engine bursting out of a tunnel opening, whistle screaming in the same pitch as the woman. We learn thus that the corpse was discovered when Hannay was on the train, and the common pattern of sound and image speeds us back there, hardly aware we have left it (pls. 16, 17).

But in most cases, the sound alone sustains the carry-over. When the source is unseen, sounds are more ambiguous than images. We have all heard the dripping tap that sounds like a ticking clock: it is easy for fancy to shift, on the least cue, between tap and clock.[9]

Anna Petrovich, a Yugoslav, is in Italy without papers. She sits on her couch, and a clock is ticking. A stout old man comforts her and leaves. We see the clock, we see him leave, we see her fall off the couch as the clock ticking loudens and its vehemence becomes a vehement knocking at the door. The street door opens and American military police and Italian soldiers enter, asking "Documents please" (*Women Without Names*, Geza Radvanyi).

The most frequent kind of unbroken sound is the human voice. A person may speak the letter he is writing, and his voice may continue after a cut to the person reading it (*The Magnificent Ambersons*, Orson Welles).

Something like a dissolve in sound is found in *I, Claudius* (part 3, television, Herbert Wise). The aged Emperor Claudius reads an old letter he has found. The image slowly dissolves to that of Tiberius, to whom the letter was written, also reading the same letter aloud years before. During the dissolve both voices are heard reading the same letter, and when it is complete only the voice of Tiberius.

Speeches by the same person on different occasions may be pieced into a single continuous whole. The district attorney points his finger at the governor's political adviser. "I'm not prosecuting John Doe," he says, "I'm prosecuting twenty-two citizens of Strand . . ." (we cut here to him in the courtroom, his finger still pointing) "which I can prove guilty of first-degree murder," and we pan from him to the accused (*Fury*, Fritz Lang).

A sentence may be split between two people, with continuity no longer of timbre and pitch, but only of grammar and meaning. To Robert Dudley, seated under a river boat's curtained canopy, a messenger announces, "Lady Dudley was found dead. . . ." "Of a broken neck," Lord Burleigh adds, informing the queen at business in her palace (*Mary Queen of Scots*, television, Charles Jarrott). When Citizen Kane runs for governor, Leland is telling an audience, "Kane, who entered on this campaign" (and Kane, speaking from another platform, continues the sentence) "with one purpose only: to point out the corruptioin of Boss Geddes's political machine. . . ." The two fragments form, and are spoken as, a grammatical whole, through the change of place, time, and person (*Citizen Kane*, Orson Welles).

A song may be split in the same way. We retreat past rows of sailors' backs on board ship, singing "Good King Wenceslas," and as they finish the line "Deep and crisp and even," the scene cuts to five boys who continue without break, "Brightly shone the moon that night," in high treble voices: Christmas on sea and land at the same moment (*In Which We Serve*, Noël Coward and David Lean).

An unbroken series of numbers may have the same effect. Hooper has written a telegram to the Association of British Ornithologists, and begins counting the words "One, two, three, four. . . ." "Five, six, seven, eight, nine," continues the school-mistress, her finger choosing from her class nine runners to call the village together (*The Tawny Pipit*, Charles Saunders and Bernard Miles).

7 Variation V: Substitution

In the fifth variation, an expectation is raised in the first scene and satisfied in the second, but not in the expected way.

A medium is describing the deeds of a dead man. We cut from her to him, as he raises his dagger and thrusts it into his chest, her voice continuing. Now falls, not the stabbed man but the swooning medium, her story finished (*The Rashomon Gate*, Akira Kurosawa). Fanny's hand rises to knock on a door. Just before it strikes, we cut to inside the door, and hear the knock from there (*Fanny by Gaslight*, Anthony Asquith).

In *Storm over Asia* (V. I. Pudovkin), the Mongol youth, whom invading armies were hoping to use for a puppet ruler, escapes by leaping down from a window, but his landing is replaced by a huge black explosion on a wide plain. This is cut to galloping horsemen, with him in the lead. Lord Rohan disparages his mother's choices for a wife, and throws dice on a table. Cut to a rolling ball, continuing the motion of the dice. A dog chases the ball and Clarissa throws herself on the floor to catch the dog. Her godmother then enters to present Lord Rohan. The dice have chosen Clarissa (*The Man in Grey*, Leslie Arliss).

This variation too runs to many forms. Here is a more elaborate form of the *Rashomon* example, where one person kills himself and another person falls. Fé, the daughter of one thief and lover of Henry, another one, arrives at a villa just as Henry is ready to drop from a balcony. We have seen him before drop from a third floor and catch the rail of the second floor on reaching it. She enters the grounds, an alarm rings, precipitated perhaps by her entrance, lights flood the garden and house, and we hear a watchman running. Now, in his own house, her father, seated with back to us, raises a revolver to his head. We hear the shot and expect the father to fall. Instead we see Henry, just letting go of the highest balcony. He misses the next one and falls to die on the ground. In one moment she has lost her father and lover. If the watchmen also fired a shot, and the one report we heard served as the sound for both his and her father's, then this is variation II as well (*Deadfall*, Bryan Forbes).

A glance creates an expectation, but here it is cut, not to what she sees, but what she will see the following day. Lermontov has discharged Craster as musical director for the company, and Serge comes to tell him and Vicky that the impresario is leaving for Paris tomorrow at 8:15. Vicky, sitting to the right, casts her gaze up to the top left frame, thus creating an expectation of seeing something there. The next shot is the railway platform, with a clock at top left at 8:03, and we pan down to where Lermontov is ascending the stairs to be met by his secretary (*The Red Shoes*, Michael Powell and Emeric Pressburger).

A tune approaching a tonic note creates an expectation. In *The Waverley Steps* (John Eldridge), a symphony orchestra reaches the leading note, but the tonic is played in the next scene by a dance orchestra. The Salvation Army lasses in *The*

Wrong Box (Bryan Forbes) have reached the line of "Onward Christian Soldiers" in which they were "Marching as to . . .," and instead of reaching *war* on the tonic, the inspector is cut in, seated on a piano stool, and he strikes the single final note, as he says to himself, "I think I'd better be paying a call on. . . ."

Here is a double substitution. The workers will not allow Walters, a time- and motion-study man, to enter the factory. He observes them through binoculars from the roof of another building. A large worker sees him, and jogs the arm of the worker beside him. Two windows are slammed closed one after another. The second closing we do not hear, because just as the window would have reached the sill, we cut to the observer's binoculars reaching his lap, and any sound they might have made on touching his leg was replaced by a vigorous final chord of music (*I'm All Right, Jack,* John Boulting).

The substitution may form an antithesis. A man, pleased with himself at having, he thinks, made a good impression on a certain girl, opens up a bottle of champagne. The cork flies up. We know it has to come down, but what comes down—in the next scene—is a shoe dropping into a suitcase, as the girl quickly packs to give him the slip (*Sunshine Susie,* Victor Saville).

In the last example, the carry-over is based on an abstract movement, semielliptical in shape, and embodied half in a cork and half in a shoe. Take another shape: a semicircle, whose radius, hinged on the bottom frame line at the center, moves through an arc of a hundred and eighty degrees, clockwise. Embody the first ninety degrees in the flap of a pocketbook, opening for police inspection, and the other ninety degrees in the closing of a trapdoor, so shot and edited that the opening flap and the closing door are the same size on the screen, and the movement continuous. This may be found in *Candlelight in Algeria* (George King).

8   Variation VI: Paronomasia, or Pun

If the pun is a play on words, and arises in English from its wealth of homonyms and the range of meanings its words possess, we should not look in film perhaps to find this figure, but since a carry-over may hinge on a single ambiguous image, as a pun on a single ambiguous word, there may be carry-overs that are also puns.

Some carry-overs are purely verbal. In *Quiet Weekend* (Harold French), one of the vulgar city girls asks another, "Have you heard about Paul Perry's new game? We are going to have a midnight bathing party with all the girls in . . ." "absolutely nothing," says Adrian Beresford, as we see him, the justice of the peace and a poacher sitting disgusted, after a barren evening's fishing, "we've wasted a whole evening." "Absolutely nothing," like the line in Shakespeare's "Sonnet Ninety-Three," refers back to a lack of clothes and on to an empty creel, and is amusing because, for a sudden incongruous moment, both notions are present at the same time.[10]

Where the figurative meaning of a word is confronted by its literal image, the pun is rather more filmic. A schoolmistress, driving in the rain, complains of how she is hindered in trying to help a pupil of hers, "You can't get anywhere in this world. People are always getting in your way." We catch a glimpse of the watery windshield with a cyclist close in front of her. Her companion grabs her shoulder to prevent a collision (*South Riding,* Victor Saville). As we see the police raising a car from the Thames, the voice of a radio commentator expresses the confident opinion that the thieves who stole the gold bricks "would find their loot too hot to handle." Two of them are now seen with tongs, lifting a glowing retort out of a furnace and pouring gold into molds of the Eiffel Tower. There are several such puns in *The Lavender Hill Mob* (Charles Crichton).

Even though the word is not used, the substitution below is clearly a play on two kinds of *bell*. Algernon is hungry, so Cicely tugs the bellpull to summon the butler, but what we hear is a church bell, and we cut to John stepping down from a cab at the front door. He is wearing full mourning, a tag of black crepe hung from the back of his top hat, for which the tolling bell seems like incidental music. We expected the sound of a bell; we heard a bell, but not the kind we expected (*The Importance of Being Earnest*, Anthony Asquith).

When an anadiplosis is also a pun, it is rarely quite free from the spoken word.

9 Variation VII: Forward Reference

A common means of bridging two scenes is for the end of one to refer forward, mostly in words, to the next, which

   i. may show the person or thing referred to;
   ii. may mislead us as to the person or thing referred to;
   iii. may answer a question put in the former scene;
   iv. may show the effect of something done;
   v. may contradict what is shown in the former scene; or
   vi. may make a comment on it, jocular, ironic, or otherwise.

   i. In talking of building a go-kart, a boy says, "I know what my mother will say." The next shot is a woman saying "No" to us (*Go Kart Go,* Jan Hedley-Smith).

Jaggers announces Pip's *Great Expectations* (David Lean), and leaves twenty sovereigns. Joe exclaims, "A gentlemen, Pip, a gentleman." Cut to a pair of polished shoes, from which we tilt up to show the whole of Pip's finery, to his wide-cravatted neck, as he stands by the front gate of Satis House.

A Wren from the Operations Room tells a man to look after himself. "I always do," he says. "But I know where you're going," she answers. Cut to ships on the horizon, guns booming, the sky filled with smoke and explosions, with planes and rockets (*The Cruel Sea,* Charles Frend).

Julie, frightened by the unexpected arrival of her brother, says that he might have been the Bournmouth Strangler. He might have had to go to the mortuary to identify her "poor crushed body." He pauses halfway up the stairs to say, "You mustn't use that word. It's not becoming."—"I meant a dead body, Morris . . . Body, did I say, body?" Cut to two porters rolling a huge keg along a railway platform, followed by Morris's brother. We know he is shipping a corpse to London, and this must be it (*The Wrong Box,* Bryan Forbes).

"How large is a UR bomb?" the superintendent asks in *Seven Days to Noon* (John and Roy Boulting). "About the size of a small typewriter," says Lane. "It could go inside a small suitcase," says the superintendent. Lane nods. Cut to a Gladstone bag sliding across a luggage counter to its owner (our first glimpse of him). This is cut to the prime minister asking a cabinet meeting, "Is he bluffing?" The first scene refers forward, and the third one back, to the second.

In all these examples, an object, place, or person referred to at the end of the first scene is shown at the start of the next.

   ii. This implies a certain trust in the director; he can just as easily show us someone who is not the person referred to. We incline to connect in meaning any two successive shots. Add to this that viewers have seen many truthful carry-overs, and it is easy for a director to hoodwink us and yet be able to claim, "I never said so."

Mrs. Stokes we know to be a spy. She meets a man in a shop, and tells him to go to Thrayle, for her brother will need him. She will write to her brother at once and the letter should reach him tomorrow afternoon. We cut to the postman, meeting Dimble who takes to the house his own and everyone else's letters. "Save you a journey," he tells the postman genially. We assume Dimble to be the brother: we find he is not (*Cottage to Let*, Anthony Asquith).

James Brewster has murdered Charlie Prince for three thousand pounds, and undermined his rival for Ann Horton's affections. He is taking her out on Thursday evening. In a half-length shot, he congratulates himself on all going so well "unless there is some snag—and what snag could there possibly be?" We cut to two police-men half length, giving the usual warning that "anything you say may be written down, and used as evidence against you." As we slowly move back, we discover that the person addressed is a bespectacled young man clearly not Brewster, and then a red curtain falls between us and them. It is the play that Brewster has taken Ann to. Not only does it mislead us for a moment into thinking there was a snag, and that Brewster is discovered, but it hints at Brewster's thoughts as he watched the play (*Nothing But the Best*, Clive Donner).

iii. The reference forward may be in the form of a question asked by one of the characters (Where? What? or Who?) and answered in the scene that follows the carry-over.

The colonel of a cavalry regiment notices an officer's absence, and asks, "Where is Lieutenant Sparre?" We pan the parade, and then cut to Sparre, half-length, sitting and cutting buttons off his uniform. He has deserted his wife and regiment and run off with a tightrope walker. As horses are led past on their way to the ring, the ringmaster asks, "Where is Elvira?", and then we see her, sitting and holding a mirror for Sparre as he sits on the grass and shaves (*Elvira Madigan*, Bo Widerberg).

Malnate says to Giorgio, "What do you want tonight, a woman or a movie?" In the next shot we are inside a cinema, watching Hitler saluting a march past of high-stepping soldiers (*The Garden of the Finzi Continis*, Vittoria de Sica). Bader sent a signal directly to the commander-in-chief that his squadron would not be operational until he received supplies. He was called before the commander-in-chief, repri-manded for not using the proper channels, and asked, "What exactly do you want?" Cut to a long convoy of trucks moving slowly toward us (*Reach for the Sky*, Lewis Gilbert).

Helen tells her daughter Jo that she is getting ready for Peter. "Who is Peter?" says Jo. Cut to a car salesman rising from his desk. He is wearing a bold checkered suit, smoking a cigar, and as he goes out, he pinches the middle-aged woman clerk on the buttocks (*A Taste of Honey*, Tony Richardson).

Prince Albert asks, "What time is it?" Cut to Lord Palmerston, sitting with his feet up. A servant enters and says, "It's three o'clock, sir" (*Victoria the Great*, Herbert Wilcox).

Asking and answering a question is the figure *hypophora*, common in oratory. "But why not a Catholic king, as well as a Catholic member of Parliament or of the Cabinet?" asks Sydney Smith, and answers, "Because it is probable that the one would be mischievous, and the other not."[11]

The question may be implied more than expressed, as when Robert Louis Steven-son ends a chapter thus: "up I jumped, and, rubbing my eyes, ran to a loophole in the wall." This implies the question "What did he see?" and the following chapter begins by giving the answer: "Sure enough, there were two men just outside the stockade, one of them waving a white cloth; the other, no less a person than Silver himself. . . ."[12]

In the same way, after his daughter Maggie had undertaken to look after him, Hobson opens the two doors of a creaking cupboard. It is quite empty. Clearly he is looking for something. It raises the question in our minds, what is it?; and in both his mind and ours, where is it now? In the next shot, a man is carrying out to the front of the shop a large basket. The basket is loaded to the brim with full bottles of liquor, under the eye of Maggie (*Hobson's Choice*, David Lean).

In *The Tawny Pipit* (Charles Saunders and Bernard Miles), Flying Officer Bancroft has asked his nurse to marry him, and as part of a group talking together, he says, "I have a question to ask Mr. Kingsley. . . ." We do not hear the question nor the answer, but the next shot is of Mr. Kingsley, the vicar, saying from his pulpit, "If any of you know just cause or impediment. . . ," from which we infer both question and answer.

iv. The reference may be forward from cause to effect, civil or criminal. Let us consider the civil causes first.

Barry Lyndon is drunk, slouched on a chair, his head sunk on his chest. Four men across the table are watching him. Lord Bullingdon raises his head with the tip of his cane: "I have come to demand satisfaction." Cut to a second, in close-up, tamping down the charge in the muzzle of a pistol (*Barry Lyndon*, Stanley Kubrick). Justin's wife Mary, not knowing that her husband is in the room, is waving good-bye to Stephen with whom she is in love. She comes in from the balcony just as her husband has left slamming the door behind him. Cut to a typewriter carriage slamming back to start a new line, and we read the document in it, "Petition for Divorce. *Justin* v. *Justin*" (*The Passionate Friends*, David Lean).

If the forward reference, which lies in meaning, is added on to one of the anadiploses based on sound or image, the effect is pleasing and the meaning strengthened. Because of good weather, a company of players at a seaside resort has been playing to nearly empty houses, and is near the end of its resources. We approach to a window streaming with water and hear the pelting of rain. Dissolve to a moving shot past rows of clapping people in the theater, every seat filled, the sounds of the rain and the clapping being continuous and indistinguishable (*The Good Companions*, Victor Saville).

And now the criminal cases.

A magistrate's gavel falls in close-up as he sentences James Allen to ten years on the chain gang. A hammer falls in close-up from the same direction coming down on a chain. It is the blacksmith forging on anklet an Allen's leg (*I Was a Fugitive from a Chain Gang*, Mervyn Leroy).Cause and effect are reinforced here by a repeated pattern. The boss of a gang is coaching a witness to perjure himself. The boss holds the picture of the man to be framed in front of his own face. Cut to the witness in court, pointing, as if to what we have just seen, "Dat's de man I saw," he says (*Criminal Court*, Robert Wise). In *Kamouraska* (Claude Jutra), Nelson draws a revolver and shoots Antoine in the head. This is cut to Elizabeth starting up in bed out of sleep, as if she knew. This is a "reaction shot" over a gap in space.

The chain of cause and effect may be greatly extended. In two films (*Dark Journey*, Victor Saville; *Confessions of a Nazi Spy*, Anatol Litvak) the first sending of a message is shown (in one film by semaphore; by telephone in the other). All the steps by telegraph and otherwise quickly follow, by which means the message comes to its destination (in one case, Berlin; in the other, a ship at sea).

v. The following scene may contradict the preceding, acting as a kind of antithesis.

It may be verbal. James Brewster says to Coates, "Oh yes, I know Adrian Slater very well." Adrian Slater says on the telephone: "James who?" (*Nothing But the Best*, Clive Donner). Mary, speaking in France: "I shall win her friendship. . . ." Elizabeth, slamming a book down in England: "Never!" (*Mary Queen of Scots*, television, Charles Jarrott).

The following sentence may not refer at all to the one preceding, but may in form sound like a contradiction and give this impression. From out of the coffin in which he lies Masterman Finsbury says to Michael (who is beside the hearse): "The tontine is ours." Cut to the solicitor inside the house of John and Morris Finsbury. As the solicitor rises to wrest the box of money back from them he says, "Well, it certainly isn't yours," not referring at all to Michael and Masterman, but still with a smatch of antithesis (*The Wrong Box*, Bryan Forbes).

A statement in words may be given the lie by an image. A general says to his advocate, "No French soldier would ever fire at me." Then, between the backs of two of the firing party, we see the general tied to a post. The officer commands: they fire (*The Day of the Jackal*, Fred Zinnemann).

A dramatic opposition can often only be effected by leaving out intervening action. When the two are wrecked on a desert island, the cook tells his supercilious former employer, who has criticized his every act during the voyage, that she must earn the fish she eats, that he catches. "Wash my pants," he says, throwing them at her. "Never," she says, but in the next shot is seen doing it. Some hungry hours must have preceded this capitulation (*Swept Away*, Lina Wertmüller). Mrs. Seymore's letter asks for Fanny as her maid. when Mrs. Heaviside has finished reading it, she says, "Not if I know it, she won't have you." After a brief shot of Mrs. Seymore's house, we see the back of someone lacing her, and the camera moves to show us Fanny tugging the laces. There is not a word of the argument that must have ensued before the matter was settled (*Fanny by Gaslight*, Anthony Asquith).

vi. The purpose, in a forward reference, may be ironic or humorous.

Trying to locate a former partner who had run off with their shares of loot, two thieves kidnap a boy. As they drive in the front seat, each boasts of what fantastic things he has. The nondriving thief says, "You see this scarf, it's from Japan; it's made of metal, but see how smooth it is." The boy will not believe it is made of metal. "I swear by my old mother," says the thief. "May she drop dead if I'm not telling the truth." Cut to a brief shot of an old woman falling over backward (*Shoot the Piano Player*, François Truffaut).

In many examples, all the elements of irony are present.[13] First, there are two levels, the situation as we, the observer, see it, and the situation as seen by the victim. In the second place, there is some opposition between the levels—between, for example, what the victim thinks and what the observer knows. There is, third, an element of innocence, as when the victim or alazon is confidently unaware of any upper level, or the ironist pretends there is none.

A little boy of six has discovered a car in the coach house below the loft where he and other children have a clubhouse. The car has been stolen, and a sergeant at the police station is telling two constables what one of the two thieves is said to look like, "A small dark black nasty-looking customer." Cut to the wheel of the car. Crouched behind the wheel, his gaze intent on the road, pretending to steer the car, is the six-year-old, looking as nearly as he can like the last tough gangster he saw on television (*Seventy Deadly Pills*, Pat Jackson).

The Emperor Napoleon declares to one of his generals that there is nothing to hinder agreement between him and Alexander. "When Russian meets Frenchman, there is a natural and immediate affinity." Then we see Pierre Bezoukov lying face up on the floor and, face down across his legs, Rampal, the French captain, both in a drunken stupor. Pierre has prevented a servant from shooting the captain, and the grateful Rampal has pressed the reluctant Pierre to dine with him (*War and Peace*, part 15, television, John Davies).

John Finsbury asks his brother in what kind of box they ought to ship the corpse. "Something," replies Morris, "of suitable size and robustness for a man in that condition." The next shot is of Masterman Finsbury's aged butler Peacock, reaching into a huge barrel on which he hangs limply, his arm down inside it packing dishes, head sagging, weary-voiced. What about a barrel like this, the director is thus suggesting? The bleary-eyed retainer, very nearly a man in that condition, seems to be trying it for size (*The Wrong Box*, Bryan Forbes).

10   Matters of Practice

Several matters call for thought and care. In a single ambiguous image, nothing must appear in the frame that is not common to the two things compared. In *Go Kart Go* (Jan Hedley-Smith), an engine is taken out of a lawn mower and placed in a go-kart. To show this, a girl takes a rag and begins to polish the lawn-mower's engine housing. In close-up, her hand continues polishing, and we pull back to show that the engine she is polishing is now installed on the kart—an economical way of showing it. In taking the earlier shot, however, part of the mower cover showed on the left, and in the later one, on the right, part of the go-kart: so the join shows between the two close-ups, and the ambiguity is gone.

Must there be a link in sense behind a likeness of image? Is it enough that the likeness glides us neatly, and often wittily, from one sequence to another? Or may a carry-over imply a connection where none exists and thus mislead us? Kaiser Wilhelm at a council of war complains testily about the blend of the tea, and helps himself in close-up to two cubes of sugar. The cubes, as they drop to the cup, are cut to Rasputin, falling into a river. No causal connection between the two events was hinted at (*The Secret War: The Fall of the Eagles* part 12, television, Michael Lindsay-Hogg).

It is doubtful if a single other shot should ever separate the two that form the carry-over, but it is certain that the more frames that come between the two the more a sense of carry-over is weakened.[14] Rath, just married, pleased with himself, smoking a cigar, is asked by Lola Lola for her bag. She is changing behind a curtain. As he lifts the bag, the catch opens and the contents are strewn on the floor, much of it picture postcards of her. "As long as I have a penny," he says, "these won't be sold." "You'd better hold on to them," she answers coolly. "They might be useful." Here the image fades to a black screen, to fade in on Rath in a shabby suit, seated in a cabaret. He presses out his stub of cigarette, hesitates, and then feels in his pocket for a black book. He takes from it a bundle of postcards, looks round to see if anyone is watching him, and shuffles round the tables, to hawk them with little heart (*The Blue Angel*, Joseph von Sternberg). Without presuming for a moment to suggest that the director should have made his picture any other way, consider the different effect of dissolving from a hand holding a picture picked up from the floor to the hand holding the picture out for sale.

Of what I term anadiplosis, or carry-over, Bela Balazs advised, "Use . . .
sparingly, otherwise it easily degenerates into an idle pointless formalism."[15] Is this
so? It may be, if a common image is irised in and irised out, as in his film *Narcosis*.
This is a busy obtrusive technical device, now almost entirely replaced by an approach to close-up, and is certainly no essential part of the carry-over. Can the figure
be used for all a film's transitions? At least for some styles and moods, the lyrical and
the witty, for example, it can with great advantage.

This can be demonstrated in *Moscow Nights*, directed by Anthony Asquith, in
which most sequences, if not all, are linked by carry-overs. It suits the romantic
mood of a story set in the last days of Czarist Russia. Here are a few of the
anadiploses used in this film, to show the dramatic effect as well as diversity with
which the director designed them. I use the term "design" advisedly, for, if the pieces
are to fit, the planning of a carry-over must be done before the camera turns on the
sequences linked. Otherwise it is a matter of chance whether an editor can manage it.

Captain Ignatov leaves the surgeon, closing the door behind him: Madame Sabline
opens a door and enters the room (variation II).

Madame Sabline rises and leaves Ignatov. He has lost all his money. We become
aware of string music as he tosses a coin. Cut to the orchestra that is playing the
music. It is now a restaurant, and we pan to a table at which Ignatov sits, as again he
tosses a coin. Madame Sabline enters to sit beside him (Strict form modified or IV).

One repeated pattern is more psychological than visual. Ignatov admits his debt of
eighty thousand rubles. General Kobline reminds him, "You know your duty as an
officer." As we move from head and shoulders to close-up, Ignatov's lip twitches; his
look is that of a person faced with distasteful necessity. In the next shot, Briokov
reaches with equal distaste for a piece of paper, and after some hesitation he writes a
receipt for eighty thousand rubles, as he has promised. The officer faced with
suicide, and his rival reprieving him from it, go about their tasks with equal reluctance (II).

Substitution is used in several places—including the following. Natacha, Ignatov's
nurse, with whom he has fallen in love, is promised in marriage to Briokov, a
wealthy peasant, a contemptible profiteer as the soldier sees him. Briokov calls to
take Natacha out for the afternoon. Ignatov makes a bitter comment on him.
Natacha points out how generous he is, reminding the captain that the table laden
with food beside his bed is a gift from Briokov. She turns with a smile to Briokov and
goes. Ignatov lies quiet, watching them go. He turns to look at the table, and in a
sudden fury sweeps the food off. The expected crash becomes an explosion as we cut
to a rising mass of black smoke, and we find ourselves at the war front. The explosion aptly tells his feelings. The moving shower of eatables on its way to the floor is
like the roll of drums before the beat in dance music arousing expectancy and giving a
bounce to the start of the next bar (V).

As we see Briokov at the telephone, we hear Natacha's voice say that she will come
to his party that night. He slams down the receiver onto its cradle, but before the
expected noise of impact, we cut to a tutti chord from a gypsy orchestra and we
continue to hear the music as we pan to a table, double doors beyond, and four
waiters running in to place the finishing touches before she comes. Substitution of
sound is combined here with a forward reference (V and VII iv.).

"Did you know our nurse is a general's daughter?" his neighbor says to Ignatov.
Cut to a portrait bust of a general, and the camera pulls back to show General
Kobline gesturing toward it, as he says to the girl's mother, "I don't know what her
father would say about it" (VII i.).

"You understand," says a general to a newly appointed intelligence officer, "You must suspect everybody—even me. These" (he points to his medals) "mean nothing. The spy may be your servant, your brother, a sweet young girl, or a kindly old lady." Cut to Madame Sabline, the very type of a kindly old lady, writing down a wounded soldier's letter to his dictation. Is it a hint or a red herring? (VII i. or ii.).

Here is a kind of double carry-over. An officer says, "There is only one man who knows the details of the position—Captain Petroski." Cut to Madame Sabline, speaking to someone whose presence is known only by the shadow he casts, "Captain Petroski—we must get to him before they do." Then to the captain himself, seated in a chair in his office. We pan to a clerk in close-up, who is bringing down files from a high shelf. He slowly turns with a couple of files in his hand, as if he heard a sound. He stands amazed. We pull back to see Petroski lying dead on the floor (VII i.).

One of the most interesting carry-overs occurs at Ignatov's trial. The prosecution produces a receipt, and alleges that what he received from Madame Sabline was not to pay his debt, because that had been paid, but for betraying military secrets. Madame Sabline is dead. Briokov is called by the defense. Will he honor his oath and tell the truth that he gave a receipt and got no money? Or will he damn his rival and say he was paid? The priest administers the oath. Briokov swears and kisses the cross. The president of the court asks the question "Did you receive any money from Captain Ignatov?" Briokov, head and shoulders right, a single candle left, and the wall behind him dark, is silent, impassive, withdrawn—in profile—in full face. The president, impatient, waves his hand, "Well, Mr. Briokov, you have heard the question." The camera approaches closer to Briokov, as he fingers the long chain he wears, and his lips move. His gaze fastens on someone and the camera moves away to show who it is—Ignatov, his eyes on Briokov, his face strained and waiting, and the camera comes to his face in close-up. Cut to Ignatov standing to attention, close to a wall. An officer ties a handkerchief over his eyes, rips off his shoulder straps and his decorations, and walks toward the firing squad as the camera moves back to long shot. A rank of soldiers, seen in up shot, rifles aimed. The officer lifts his sword above his head, and after a pause, cuts it sharply down. A volley is heard. Ignatov topples and falls. Dissolve to a plain wooden cross on a knoll. Cut then to Briokov, still standing beside the single candle. The president speaks brusquely, "Come, Mr. Briokov, what are you waiting for? Did you receive any money?" Briokov, full face, fingers the cross on his chain. He slowly speaks, "I have kissed the cross. I received no money" (VII iv.).

We assumed an ellipsis, a forward reference from testimony to execution, which implied the answer Briokov must have given. In what could ambiguously be either wish or event, we chose, as the director knew we should, the wrong one.

These few of the film's anadiploses are perhaps enough to show that far from being an "idle pointless formalism," the carry-over, used consistently throughout a film, can add flow and cohesion with great variety. On the other hand, the jump cut or asyndeton provides the raw material and lets the viewer make whatever connections he can. The two are thus limiting cases, the carry-over of coherence, the jump cut of incoherence; most films falling in the middle ground between.

The Figure in Film:
A Picture Summary

Alexander Nevski.
PLATE 1. SIGNIFICANT OBJECT. METONYMY.
The skull is a conventional symbol of death; the helmet, the armor and the embedded arrow speak of conflict, and all together mean death in battle. But if these things are taken as relics of one ancient encounter which happened at a particular place, as all that was left on the wind-swept steppe of one day's clash between the Asiatic hordes and Slavic Russia, the things are metonymic.

Hamlet. (By courtesy of the Rank Organization Ltd.)

PLATE 2. SIGNIFICANT OBJECT. INNER STATE.

A person, appearing large, placed in the foreground, expresses dominance. Here Ophelia, cast off by Hamlet, is distant, frail and small, a foil to the solid steps. Dwarfed by massy ashlar walls, lying prostrate and looking

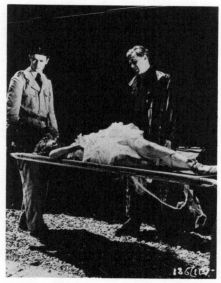

The Red Shoes. (By courtesy of the Rank Organization Ltd.)
PLATES 3 AND 4. REPETITION. ALLEGORY.
In *The Red Shoes* ballet (a story within a story), a girl is bewitched by shoes she cannot take off and is forced to dance until she dies of exhaustion. As she dies, she gestures to her lover to take off the shoes. Victoria Page, who dances the leading part in the ballet, is torn between her desire to dance and her devotion to her composer husband and, unable to choose between them, throws herself in front of a train. Like the girl she portrays in the ballet, her last words to her husband are, "Take off the Red Shoes." The two shots are composed alike, the man standing, and the woman lying supine in front of him. The allegorical ballet makes explicit the meaning that underlies the story of Vicky Page.

A Place to Stand. (Government of Ontario)
PLATE 5. SIMULTANEOUS REPETITION.

Two pictures of a ballet school occupy the screen, one in place of the two left frames, and one in place of the three right ones. These two are changed by installments to five different frames picturing the same woods and lake. This plate shows the moment before the last frame changes from ballet to woods. The change in colour is from brown to green and the lyrical ballet music runs on over the change.

A Place to Stand. (Government of Ontario)
PLATE 6. SIMULTANEOUS REPETITION WITH VARIATION.

These three pictures of two different shapes are projected at once on a sixty-six foot screen. The plane spraying water on the forest fire, the falling spray and the rising steam are three different views of the same event seen at the same time in a simultaneous repetition.

Music Academy. (Halas and Batchelor Cartoon Films Ltd.)
PLATE 7. SIMILE BY MANIPULATION. HYPERBOLE.
The way the pennyfarthing is used likens it to a harp. The posture and costume of the Welsh harpist, the music stand, the delicate plucking of the spoke establish the simile. Both machines are much the same in height. Both spokes and harp strings are thin wires, which, being plucked, give off musical notes. The incongruity is one of shape. The leap of reasoning is, that if you can play a tune on strings, why not on spokes? This is hyperbole, not quite fantasy.

King Size. (National Film Board of Canada)
PLATE 8. SIMILE BY MANIPULATION. FANTASY.
Here the "if" of fantasy is clearly seen. If we hugely increase the size, and alter the substance of a pack of cigarettes, cant it at the right angle, and add soldiers and wheels, we can see the likeness in shape to a rocket launcher. Both cigarettes and rockets, it is hinted, are destructive of life.

Nebule. (National Film Board of Canada)
PLATES 9 AND 10. SIMILE BY MANIPULATION. FANTASY.
The simpler the shape of a thing, the greater the number of other things the fancy can liken it to. A rope, a mere line, can coil to take the shape of a spring or can wriggle itself into the noses of a stair. If we add the rigidity it does not otherwise have, it can be so used.

Fantasia: Nutcracker Suite. (© MCMXL Walt Disney Productions)
PLATE 11. SIMILE BY EMPHASIS.
A motion picture artist may by adding and emphasizing draw a thistle to look like a Cossack, and says in so doing, "to me a thistle is like a Cossack." He also says here that a flower can look like a woman in crinoline.

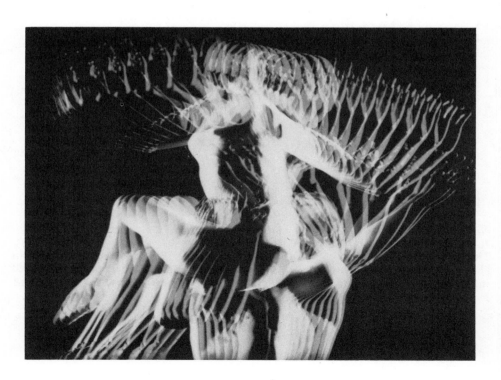

October.

PLATE 13. METAPHOR
Followed by two aides-de-camp at a respectful distance, Kerensky walks up a wide stair-
case, then a second and a third flight. Intercut in the course of his climb are titles:
"Minister of the Army," "Minister of the Navy," "Prime Minister," and then "Etc., etc."
The climbing of the stairs is a metaphor for Kerensky's rise in political position, or for his
rise in his own esteem.

e Deux. (National Film Board of Canada)
. 12. ACCUMULATION. SIMULTANEOUS REPETITION. SIMILE: INTENTION
lancer's image leaps to a new place, but not all at the same time. The laggard part
es up in a procession of like selves, which enter and vanish into the dancer standing in
·w place. The image has an elastic feeling, as if a moment in time were stretched and
·ed. When the movement pivots on one end, as when a leg moves, it seems like a fan
ng and closing. It is unlikely that Norman McLaren intended either simile. Can a
 not consciously intended by an artist, but found by the viewer, be said to be part of
essage? Or should we credit an artist with whatever any viewer finds in the film?
· figure accumulation is repetition considered as adding force or clarity. The proces-
·f identical images pursuing the same path enables us to observe the shape of the
·ment more clearly in another kind of simultaneous repetition.

The Red Shoes. (By courtesy of the Rank Organization Ltd.)
PLATE 14. METAPHOR.
Victoria Page has just alighted at the seaside villa of Lermontov, the impresario. He
about to tell her that she is to dance the leading role in a ballet to be specially composed
her. She has risen to the culmination of her career, for which the ascent of these steps
metaphor.

Part IV

Figures of Contrast

8
Antithesis

1 Theatrical Uses

At its simplest and least significant, *antithesis* may be nothing more than a technical deftness. An actor knows that to hold an audience, or merely to keep it awake, he must not stay too long on any one rung of the ladder of pace, pitch, volume, or intensity, and that a sudden change in any of these is highly, as we say, *dramatic*. A playwright knows that the greater the pride of Oedipus, the more overwhelming the catastrophe. Shakespeare puts his whimsical unruffled porter just before the discovery of Duncan's death, with its bells and outbursts.

Since, then, the quality of a scene or image is more vividly shown when set beside its opposite, it is not surprising to find antithesis in film, serving the same purpose here as it does on the stage. There is a cut in *Barry Lyndon* (Stanley Kubrick) from the yellow flickers of a flaming house to a still gray courtyard, lined with soldiers, and another from the yellow candles and warm browns of a gambling room to the cool grays of a terrace by moonlight and the Countess of Lyndon in white.

Fifty years before this, Abel Gance through most of *Napoleon* tinted inside scenes in orange or yellow; outside ones he left a normal gray or tinted blue or lilac. This was merely to point a change in place; but when Napoleon is sent outside by the teaching brothers after his eagle had been let out of its cage and he had undertaken to fight a dormitory full of his fellow-cadets, Gance's leaving the inside orange for the outside blue of the night, where he lay on the trail of a field gun with tears on his face, carried a further sense of defeat and frustration.

The same can be done within a single shot (pl. 22). Tommy Swann appears to be running away from us much faster than he is, for the director has a train on either side of him pulling toward us (*It Always Rains On Sunday*, Robert Hamer).

During the siege of their quarters, the chief spy, short, round-faced, and full-bodied stands beside Agnes, tall and angular. He is grinning sardonically at Ramon, the crack shot, whom Agnes has just threatened back to the window. At that moment a shot is heard and the face of Agnes twists with agony, while the chief, not knowing she is hurt, continues to smile at the Spaniard's discomfiture (*The Man Who Knew Too Much*, Alfred Hitchcock). A pan shot holds a European hunt, correctly attired, seen trotting after the hounds in Kenya, beyond a cluster of rondavels, and the backs of the watching blacks (*Africa Addio*, Jacopetti and Prosperi).

An antithesis may not go beyond the mere surface of words or images.[1] In *The Struggle* (D. W. Griffith), for example, a short man dances with a tall girl, his eyes

121

rolled up as he speaks to her. The next couple to enter the screen is made up of a tall man dancing with a short girl, her eyes rolled up to look at him. It is a mere passing joke, with no tie whatever to story or characters. It hardly needs to be said that in the most effective antithesis, a contrast in form is matched by a contrast in meaning that has some significance in the narrative.

The antithesis may use sound in various ways.

A father is speaking soothingly to a brainless nobleman whom his daughter detests, assuring him that she is most willing to marry him. At the same time, from beyond the door where they are standing, the daughter's voice is shouting, "Jamais! Jamais!" Something heavy strikes a wall, and a series of blows are followed by tinkles of glass (*Passionnelle*, Edmond T. Greville).

Mr. Memory, fatally wounded, has been carried off the stage of a music hall and laid in the wings. He sits up, is asked what he had memorized for a ring of spies, answers for a minute or so, and breaks off with his usual stage ending, "Am I right, sir?" Hannay tells him yes. Between the leg curtains, we see the girls of a chorus dancing, and we hear the orchestra. "It's the biggest job I ever tackled. I'm glad to get it off my mind." Mr. Memory's head sags in death, to gay music (*The Thirty-Nine Steps*, Alfred Hitchcock).

A pan shot past a house shows a dormer window hanging open. A pan shot through its deserted rooms, with little furniture left, passes a table with heavy carved legs, canted over on one that was broken. We hear the prosecuting counsel's voice throughout the pan, "he heard a shot outside . . . went out, was shot, dragged himself inside to protect his wife and children. . . ." We see from near ground level the broken table and a wine bottle on its side, empty, and hear water dripping. We rise to pass another empty bottle on the mantel, and stop on the wall beyond at a portrait, head and shoulders. It is a young naval officer, pleasant-faced, in white uniform. The prosecutor concludes, "killed his wife and children, and on his body were seventy-two panga blows. . . ." The violent past and the silent present (*Africa Addio*, Jacopetti and Prosperi).

There is an interesting ambiguity in a scene from *Sabotage* (Alfred Hitchcock). In a narrow alley, little more than five feet in width, we see on the right the rear of a cinema screen on which some highly emotional incident is being enacted. To the left, Detective Sergeant Spencer has shinned up a brick wall and is sitting on a window ledge, listening to four men inside, who are planning to set a bomb in Piccadilly Circus. On one side is the fabricated world of the film, on the other, a real situation, both equally melodramatic. At one remove further, we know that for us in the audience, the second one too is fabricated.

2 Oxymoron

From the clash of opposites, *oxymoron* draws a new meaning (pl. 21). Antithesis opposes two contrary things to one another; oxymoron joins them.[2] "If they are silent, they say enough."[3] Ben Jonson speaks of "the liquid marble of poetry." Coleridge, asked if he believed in ghosts, replied, "No, madam, I have seen too many to believe in them," combining an oxymoron with a play on words, and expressing a complicated answer very briefly.[4]

Here, as in the metaphor, the two extremes of the antithesis are not to be taken separately, but combined. On the screen, a gesture may do it neatly. An impassive butler brings down a respectful blackjack on Barry's head (*Saboteur*, Alfred Hitchcock).

An oxymoron is a form of lateral thinking, of bringing together things not commonly joined in thought, things whose joining, indeed, might be considered absurd.

A robust man in working clothes enters to a refuse can, carries it away down steps, around a wall, over the water's edge, and dumps its contents, yes, into a gondola. He enters the vessel, and punts away, singing "O Sole Mio" in a rich tenor voice and with an operatic flourish (*Trouble in Paradise*, Ernst Lubitsch).

In *The Wrong Box* (Bryan Forbes), two hearses gallop across a park where a military band is playing. Now a galloping hearse is in itself an oxymoron, but we know in addition that 111,000 pounds in notes are in one hearse, and that the second one is after it. Besides this, each time a hearse tears past, the bandmaster breaks off the chirpy tune he is playing, stands the band up, and has them play a few lugubrious bars, while he salutes. It is not the aptest match for a hearse at full stretch.

Jean Cocteau distinguishes the quick and the dead by oxymoron. In "The Zone," the country of the dead, along a narrow street between high, partly shattered buildings, Orphée, full length, walks toward us as we retreat, pushing, as if against a high wind, but with no ruffling of hair or clothing. In the foreground left, the guide Cegeste, head and shoulders only, glides with us through changing lights and shadows, as if impelled by an outer force, without movement of legs, without effort, hair and clothing fluttering as if in a strong wind. "You move but you are motionless," exclaims Orphée (*Orphée*).

3 Syncrisis

When the extremes of an antithesis come, not at the same time, but one after the other, it is the figure *syncrisis*, which has been defined as "comparing contrary elements in contrasting clauses."[5]

> But yesterday the word of Caesar might
> Have stood against the world; now lies he there,
> And none so poor to do him reverence.[6]

Hannay and a girl have escaped from spies, but with wrists joined by handcuffs. Concealing the handcuffs, Hannay rents a room at an inn. The landlady has said goodnight, closed the door of their room, and gone downstairs. Her husband asks her, "Do you think he's married to her?" "Ah dinna ken and ah dinna care," she says to him, "they're that terribly in love with one another." Cut to the girl struggling to open the door and Hannay preventing her (*The Thirty-Nine Steps*, Alfred Hitchcock).

On their marriage night, Paul leaves his wife Stepa. As she sits alone drinking in the kitchen, she hears a sound and goes to the window. She sees Paul chasing the servant girl across the yard, she trying to fight him off and he wrestling her to the ground. The next shot, as sedate as the other was vigorous, is of Paul and his wife at the breakfast table, she smiling a little, he with a ghost of a smile, as we hear the music of the waltz to which they danced when first they met on New Year's Eve (*Oil Lamps*, Juraj Herz).

Colonel Nicholson is released from the sweat box, to which he has been confined by Colonel Saito to compel his assent to his officers' doing common labor. Saito tells him that, as part of an amnesty to celebrate the anniversary of Japan's victory over Russia in 1905, "it will not be necessary for officers to do manual labor." As Colonel Nicholson returns to the parade ground, he shakes the hands of his officers as they are released from the punishment hut, and is carried across the parade ground on the shoulders of his men. Through a narrow door in dark walls, seated in a small room, is Colonel Saito. His hands are over his face, he shakes with sobs, and at last he collapses over on his bed (*The Bridge on the River Kwai*, David Lean).

The syncrisis may be one of darkness and light. Graham searches Joseph Banat's cabin by the light of a match. In its shadows anything might lurk. As Graham returns along the dark passage, the captain looms noiselessly up in the dark, points his finger, says "boom," and roars with laughter (he is amused at Graham's fear of being shot). Glad to be out of the gloom, Graham opens the door of his cabin, and in the bright glare of the light, Mueller is sitting and pointing a revolver at him, and then his eye is caught by his friend Kovetli, lying dead on the floor. Here, after expecting danger in the harmless dark, Graham suddenly meets it, bright lit, in his own cabin (*Journey into Fear*, Orson Welles and Norman Foster).

The syncrisis may be in sound. The wild boys from the slums of Moscow have set up a working community in the country, and Mustapha, one of their leaders, is to drive the first train along the branch railway line they have built themselves. Two former exploiters of the children have torn up a part of the track. Mustapha is singing as he pumps a hand-car on his way to the junction, and his voice, as we see him in long shot riding along the bottom frame line, seems to soar into the early dawn. A sudden stop, and he is flung into the air. In several short shots, he soars and falls. Then we see him lie, unmoving. The joyful song, and the dead silence (*The Road to Life*, Nicolai Ekk).

In a film that lends itself to antithetical treatment, rioters fight police, a man is shot, and an announcer expects that the present situation "might be the flashpoint that would set off a war. . . ." This is cut to a man interviewed in the street, who says, "I think there's nothing to worry about" (*The War Game*, Peter Watkins).

4 Montage

If the two extremes are shown more than once, the figure becomes a montage of antitheses. When Smith's opponents, controlling the press, prevented his home state from hearing of his filibuster, boy rangers ran the story off on a handpress. Handsetting is contrasted with linotype, handpresses, with automatic, and so on to wrapping and final delivery—each stage of production is a separate antithesis (*Mr. Smith Goes to Washington*, Frank Capra).

Stoker Thompson, threatened by gangsters, dresses quickly. His wife is seen as she buys beer, soup, and a hamburger. He leaves by a fire door into a blind alley, and walks along smiling. The light is now on in his room across the street: his wife is back. Four men turn the corner and fight him down. "You'll never fight with that hand again." Through the hotel window, we see Julie coming to stir the soup. She looks out, and we see a down shot of the empty street. Thompson rises, battered and spent, and stumbles over some pails. Through the curtains of the window, we see Julie taste the soup and come to look out. In a down shot, Stoker staggers out of the alley and falls. His wife, the waiting meal, and the peaceful room are a foil to set off the brutal beating (*The Set-Up*, Robert Wise).

5 Irony

Another form of antithesis is irony, and especially the form known as dramatic or Sophoclean irony.[7] In this form, a contradiction is present that is not apparent to some, or even to any, of the characters, but is to the audience. A simple case is a fellow player saying to the winning Huller, "He's lucky in cards and in love too"; and we cut to another man kissing his wife (*Variety*, E. A. Dupont).

Filmic ironies run from the purely verbal to the fully visual.

In the southern United States, white convicts, chained, trudge under guard to see a film after the evening service in a black chapel. The preacher tells his congregation beforehand, "I hope you will not by any word or action make them feel at all unwelcome. For we are all equal in the sight of God." He leads them in "Let my people go" as from floor level the chained ankles move right and left into the pews: free blacks, chained whites, and the preacher's charitable innocence (*Sullivan's Travels*, Preston Sturges).

A pianist practices, a girl (outside) listens. The *garagiste,* her father, is fixing the horn on a motorcycle, trying it now and then. As we approach the pianist through his window, there is a blast of the horn and he stops playing. He sets his hands again on the keyboard, snatching them back again on another blast. Down below, the father says to the cyclist, "How that piano gets on my nerves!" (*Les Belles de Nuit,* René Clair).

The irony, though not verbal at all, may lie in the situation and thus may be theatrical more than filmic. To identify the man whom he alleges held him up, Holland (the actual thief) walks along a lineup of suspects. We know, but the policeman with him does not, that the man he is looking for is not in the lineup, but walking beside him (*The Lavender Hill Mob*, Charles Crichton).

Trina refuses to give a penniless McTeague, her husband, anything out of the five thousand dollars she won in a lottery. She slams the window down with a mocking smile and goes back to her work, scrubbing the floor. Suddenly he is there beside her, demanding the money. On the street outside the school, two policemen meet, and, as they chat in a leisurely way, in the building behind them Trina dies trying to defend her treasure. The policemen exchange cheerful waves, and go on their way. McTeague leaves the school with the bags of money (*Greed*, Erich von Stroheim).

After reading some horrific story, a man cannot sleep. He tries to count sheep leaping a stile in the clouds that form his ceiling. All goes well, and he is almost asleep when a brown ram (all the rest were white) refuses to leap and settles down on the near side of the stile. Suddenly the brown ram is gone. The counter settles down to sleep, but becomes aware that the brown ram is now in the room. It climbs into the bed with him, and it too settles down to sleep. Our gaze rises up to the cloudy ceiling, where the sheep counter in blue pajamas is just about to leap the stile, and a number of others wearing the same face, but in white pajamas, wait their turn in line. He little knew that as he was counting sheep, the sheep might very well be counting men (*The Thirteenth Sheep*, Zofia Oraczewska).

6 Structure

The most extended form of antithesis is when two extremes of one make up the whole film story.

Night Mail (Basil Wright and Harry Watt) is the run of the mail train between London and Glasgow. All the way it drops mailbags and picks them up, in a continuous interplay between the train and the country it passes through. Visually, the film gives us in turn the passing town- and landscape as it looks from the train, and what the fleeting train looks like to those it passes.

Silent Dust (Lance Comfort) builds an antithesis by having the visual image oppose the spoken word. Stephen—the idolized son of a blind, newly rich industrialist—comes home, a deserter and a coward, and seeks to win sympathy by an account of his noble endurance under incredible trials. We hear his story as he tells it: we see it as it was:

What we hear	What we see
"You mustn't show fear . . . you must be inhuman . ."	Stephen, hat and all other carried equipment abandoned, runs toward us, leaving two other officers, who look around in surprise. An explosion kills them.
"I was left shell-shocked and wounded . . . it must have been a while before I regained my senses, more dead than alive . . ."	Stephen reaches down below the frame line for the papers of a dead soldier, puts his in their place, and looks around alertly.
"anything I made, I came by honestly . . . I kept my hands clean . . ."	Stephen thrusts back the tarpaulin of a military truck, hits the driver over the head with a wrench, throws him off, steadies the wheel, drives away.

And so, till the end of the story.

The first sequence of O Lucky Man (Lindsay Anderson) forms an antithesis to the rest of the film. This is a flickery, mock-silent, black-and-white passage, centered on the wide screen, of a native picker who dropped a few beans of coffee into his bosom, and had his hands chopped off as a punishment. The remainder of the film elaborates in color the enormities carried on today without the risk of any punishment. The leading character, Travis, is an innocent and harmless young man, imposed on by everyone he meets. In the course of the film, he is (among other things) tied and given electric shocks by two military intelligence officers; he is nearly operated on by a doctor trying to turn human beings into animals (to increase their chances of survival); he is nearly killed by down-and-outs to whom he is taking soup; and falsely accused by an employer he has trusted. At least, in bygone days, if the punishment was often too severe, there was a definition of right and wrong, and an unpleasant consequence for choosing wrong. Now, the film implies, no one sees the difference, and anyone can get away with anything.

The second half of the film Shame (Ingmar Bergman) consists of a series of situations, each of which contrasts with one in the first half, to show how quickly sensitive civilized people can sink into primitive savagery under the lawless anarchy of guerrilla war. In the first half Jon could not bring himself to cut a hen's throat in seeking food for a journey. He tries to shoot it, misses it and refuses to try again. Later he takes a young deserting soldier's rifle, while he is asleep, and after finding out from the soldier where a boat can be found, Jon shoots the boy and pilfers his boots. And so throughout.[8]

Six boys and two girls go for a swim one summer morning. One is a medical student, the rest are just out of high school. In great good spirits, they head a soccer ball, dive in the river for mud, and engage in other like frivolities. The climax is a kind of primitive corroboree. Two of them daub themselves with mud and hold biting bags in their mouths, and all dance around the fire they have built. We give no thought to it, when six only run up from the beach. One we know had not been swimming. Only when they stop for a picture does someone say, "Where is Gabi?" The drum, the tapping sticks, the stamping feet, and the waving arms, all the beat of the dance is now still. In the second half, we see the boys running and searching, and pan from one to another. We see six in long shot, looking small from across the river, giving a lonely feeling. They all dive. We plunge into the dark water. As they stand again in silhouette near the stump where they changed, the sky is dark, and we lose them in the shadowy poplars. The police boat purrs away from us, leaving a long tail of tremulous light on the dark surface, and as the motor dies away in the distance, the lapping of waves on the shore is all we hear. The following day, a car taking three away to study at Budapest, passes the church tower and the pump that four of them had passed the day before on their way to the river. The car crosses a bridge, and beyond the parapet we see the wide slip-off slope of the great meander where Gabi was drowned (*Current*, Istvan Gaal).

In many of Ozu's films, we feel a recurring antithesis between the transient—people, who come and go—and the moveless things around them, that outlive both them and their sufferings. We feel it in the empty rooms that come on the screen before his people enter, and stay after they leave. We feel it between scenes, when action is suspended, and he has us contemplate the stillness of a building, a treed slope, a stone lantern, a tower of steel, the sky or the sea, no man to be seen—things that abide without heed the passing of many people. In *Late Spring*, Noriko and her father's assistant cycle up a road and off right, past a diamond-shaped advertisement in the foreground, and the camera stays on the road and the sign for several seconds after they have left. The sign will outlast the passing of hundreds more. The poignant is the passing, and Ozu stresses this by contrast with the lasting and passionless. In the same film, her father has persuaded Noriko to leave him and marry, for although she was happy living with him and caring for him, he felt that he had to provide for her future. After Noriko has left, her father walks back to the house, where they had lived so long together, up the familiar lane we have seen walked by one or other of them five or six times in the course of the film. He hangs up his hat, sits, takes an apple from the table, and starts to peel it. We see his hands using the knife. We see his face and hear the peeling. We see the knife stop, the peel fall, and his hands hang. In a longer shot, his head sags. Then we see the breakers rolling toward the shore; not only the poignant and passing against the everlastingness of the seas, but a sense that over and over again the grief of parting must be suffered by daughter and father.[9]

5 Antithesis Combined with Other Figures

Other figures too may be antithetical. Even though its headline is "NO WAR THIS YEAR—10 OF OUR 12 CORRESPONDENTS SAY," the slow drift our way of a *Daily Express* in the littered water of a dock still tells us "War is coming." This too is the message of a steadily loudening roar of airplanes. The words in close-up explode from the center to reveal the title "Crete, May 23, 1941," and the gunfire of a naval engagement. It is an antithetical metaphor (*In Which We Serve*, Noël Coward and David Lean).

In order to go back for the girl he loved, a guide left twelve escaping Norwegians to find their own way, telling them how to reach the boat. On going back, he found that those committed to his charge had fallen over a cliff and perished. He returns to the place, unable to shake his guilt, and he dies with his arms reached out to the twelve he constantly sees on a never-ending journey over the snow. When first we see him and them asleep in a hut, it was weatherproof, the stove casting a cozy gleam over the sleepers. Twelve years later, it is ramshackle, only a rail or two of the door still on the hinges, the stove cold under a drift of snow. The two states of the hut reflect the change from the confident guide that was and his tortured irresolute present (*Cold Tracks*, Arne Skouen).

The heart of a repetition may be contrast. At Lola Lola's wedding, the stage magician materializes an egg and then another from the nose of her husband, Immanuel Rath. She leans her head under his and clucks cajolingly, and after some thought about how to respond, he crows. Delighted at the effect, he does it several times, and Lola Lola kisses him. Years later, the company returns to his hometown where against his will he appears on stage before his former colleagues and their students. He is now an encumbrance to Lola Lola, and acts as a butt for the magician. He, once again, draws eggs from Dr. Rath's nose, as Rath stands in a clown suit with painted leering face and shoulder-wide collar. He breaks both eggs on Dr. Rath's head, on which they stand like little horns. Rath's eyes keep straying to the wings, where Lola Lola's one visible eye looks doubtfully up from the embrace of her latest lover. The magician says "Crow" without response. Again and again the magician seizes the reluctant clown roughly and commands him, "Crow." At last Rath forces out a harsh agonized shriek, and the magician turns with a smile to the audience. The tormented Rath wanders offstage, and over and over again we hear his distant crowing (*The Blue Angel*, Joseph von Sternberg).

Anadiploses in Variation VII v are also antitheses.

When William Friese-Greene finishes making his first motion picture, he goes home and wakes up his wife. He opens a bottle of wine with a pop. "It works," he cries out. "In a couple of years we'll be millionaires." Quick dissolve to a brass plate in front of a building, *Official Receiver in Bankruptcy* (*The Magic Box*, John Boulting).

Where a part is put for a whole, the figure is synecdoche. Where two contrasted parts stand for two contrasted wholes, the image is at the same time antithesis. A glassblower rolls his pipe with one hand, with two hands, along a table, in the air, with palm and fingers, fingers only, with longer and shorter turns, but all with extraordinary grace, rhythm, flexibility, and care. They were thinking hands. Now we go to a bottle factory: coarse and clumsy fingers roll a cigarette, and light it on a just-blown bottle. The owner of the fingers leans languidly back (*Glass*, Bert Haanstra).

Julien has disposed of the body of a man killed by the girl he loves, but, hurt by what he learns about her, gives himself up to the police. She is being married to someone else as he leaves the church. He meets the gendarmes and holds out his clenched fists decisively. Her hands under her veil are seen coming together in a comfortably hypocritical gesture of prayer. We cut back to his hands as other hands snap the handcuffs home (*Passionnelle*, Edmond Greville).

An anamnesis (flashback) may also be antithetical. Pierre Bezoukhov, a prisoner, leaves the French baggage train to relieve himself. As he stands, he sees, jutting out of the snow, a drum, its head broken; partly covered by the snow, a sword and other gear; and looking up from a socket in the snowy counterpane, a skull. He kneels by the drum. As he looks up remembering, there is a cut to soldiers, full-length, fighting with zest in summer dust and bright sunshine, brilliant in red, gold, and blue, stabbing their bayonets down in great sweeps of movement. Pierre himself, an elegant bespectacled civilian with welltrimmed whiskers, looks around pained and bewildered. Again cut back to the mummified head peering out of its hollow, quiet in the snowy dusk, and Pierre now, in warm peasant coat and hat, his whiskers long and unkempt, without glasses, calm and resigned (*War and Peace* 18, television, John Davies).

To belittle the importance of something is the figure meiosis. It is also an antithesis between the belittling image and what it belittles. In *Dr. Strangelove*, (Stanley Kubrick), the director has shown an event of literally earthshaking significance—a series of atomic detonations that completely wipe out all life on earth. As we see the familiar images of rising and expanding clouds, a woman's voice is singing a wistful wartime ballad in leisurely tempo. We'll meet again, she says, some sunny day, and advises us to keep smiling through. Beside the size of the disaster, the song is an understatement so great, it is almost inept or irrelevant: it is the director's commentary on our incredibly casual attitude in the face of annihilation. It is both meiosis and antithesis.

9
Hyperbole

1 Disproportion

Hyperbole or exaggeration is a disproportionate alteration in one component of a set. The disproportion may be great or little, but, as a rule, unless it is great enough to be obvious and improbable, while it may be emphatic, it will not be amusing.

It will be clear that if all the members of a set are magnified in the same degree, the proportion between them remains the same, and we notice nothing untoward. This happens in all approach shots, and we do not normally speak of close-ups as hyperboles. It is the oddness of the one magnified member contrasted with all the others left unchanged that makes the hyperbole. The barbershop where Hynkel and Napaloni sat side by side and each raised his chair twice to look down on the other, was normal in all respects except that the barber chairs, instead of rising the usual inch or two on thrusting the lever, rose by the foot, ending near the ceiling (*The Great Dictator*, Charles Chaplin).

It will be equally clear that if one member is magnified or even left unchanged, and the rest of the set so reduced in value or visibility as to disappear, this is no longer hyperbole but abstraction. In Wheaton Galentine's *Night Lights*, we see a pair of bright glowing disks, but now and then passing glints in other parts of the frame suggest the hood of a motorcar. The motorcar,—apart from the headlights—has nearly disappeared. Since, however, a trace is left, enough to establish its presence, this may be considered hyperbole. As the film goes on, the glints on the hood vanish, the yellow disks are multiplied and move in a bright parade from corner to corner, with nothing at all to tell us what they are part of. They are as abstract as the dots of Norman McLaren.

2 Reductio ad Absurdum

Logic is the life of hyperbole (pls. 23, 24, 30). The merely irrational belongs to a world we do not recognize, but the reasonably absurd is the world we know, freed from its customary limits.

Charlie, the fireman, alone uncoils the hose, couples up, turns the hydrant on, and waters the fire, the other seven firemen waving him heartily on (*The Fireman*, Charles Chaplin). In *Modern Times*, (Charles Chaplin), his work is tightening two nuts with a wrench in either hand. These are on a large metal plate, carried past his place on a moving belt. The line ends where the plates and conveyor belt vanish into a curved metal cover. The speed of the belt was so increased that no time was allowed for simple emergencies, like rolling a sleeve up or flicking off a bee. When these occur, and plates go by undone, he has to leave his place, crowding with others near the cover, each trying frantically to finish his operation.

In all these, a familiar human trait is carried up to the limit, where, like much untempered logic, it becomes absurd. If a crew manages to finish a job with one of its members not pulling his weight, why shouldn't everyone "soldier," not merely doing less but absolutely nothing, all but one man—even Parkinson couldn't cut the number lower than one. If the dividend is increased by cutting the time between operations, the limit, of course, is no time at all: the absurdity of logic in human affairs.

The most enjoyable hyperboles are the most persuasive. If we treasure a lock of hair cut from a loved one's head, why not a severed hand? Why should it not be locked in a box, and pressed to a bosom? (*Le Chien Andalou*, Luis Buñuel and Salvador Dali).

In *Rhapsody Rabbit* (Isadore Freleng), Bugs Bunny seats himself at the piano, closes his eyes, and is about to start when we hear a cough. He turns and glares at us the audience. He concentrates again, and once more before he can start, the cough. He turns, draws a revolver, shoots, and the coughing stops. He watches long enough to make sure he has quite ended the cough, and then starts playing. Artists, awaiting a quiet audience, have been known to help the matter on by a thoughtful glance. Summary execution serves the same purpose, and is the next logical step—a look that can kill.

3 The Threshold of Hyperbole

Hyperbole begins at the last outpost of credibility (pl. 7).

Many scenes in *Wee Geordie* (Frank Launder) are just within the threshold of belief. We reflect a moment before we say, "Well, it is just possible." When Geordie is faithfully exercizing as Henry Samson, the body builder, tells him to, his mother staggers into the living room in the morning with a great black iron pot full of porridge and ladles it into a twice-normal size of porridge bowl. A kitchen could hold, but only a very very large one, the dishes we hear shattering on and on in *Helpmates* (James Parrott).

We draw close to a half-length shot of Queen Victoria, as she takes a sword from off a red cushion, saying, "In recognition of many and varied services to the Crown . . ." She seizes the sword in both hands, and brings it down out of the frame. "we dub thee . . ." She stops and we hear a thud. Her gaze falls. "Oh," she says, and pauses, "we are frightfully sorry, Sir Robert" (*The Wrong Box*, Bryan Forbes).

The Big Fellow, wearing roller skates, follows Charlie and Edna, waving angrily. Charlie blows hard, and the Big Fellow topples backwards; just beyond the normal instability of roller skates (*The Rink*, Charles Chaplin).

By degrees we move from the just possible to the barely likely. The twenty-eight boys, for example, who tumble out of a single taxi to catch a gang of criminals (*Hue and Cry*, Charles Crichton).[1] Or the running shower that fills a bathroom up with water in *Brats* (James Parrott): when Laurel and Hardy open the door, they are swept away in the flood. This is a door more tightly fitting than most of the doors we know, and a floor less penetrable. Or the comment made on a girl's cooking when her doughnut falls on a man's toe and he lifts his foot in agony (*The Pawnshop*, Charles Chaplin).

At the steps of a reputedly haunted house, Dizzy says, "Listen—it sounds like drums," and we certainly hear a hollow throb. Henry listens, and then points to a strong pulsing on Dizzy's left side, matching the sound. A heartbeat that bulges the jacket and is heard by the person beside you is doubtful biology but certainly only a modest hyperbole (*Henry Aldrich Haunts a House*, Hugh Bennett).

Breaches of the laws of physics can clearly be seen as hyperboles. We know that even a small dwarf could not hurl himself away with a sack by holding on too long; and that a dwarf, however large, could not open and close the door of his room, however small, by breathing out and in during sleep (*Snow White and the Seven Dwarfs*, Walt Disney and David Hand). Nor do we consider it at all likely that a man sliding into a swimming pool could glide all the way across and out on to dry land at the other side; or that two men, falling from one of the gondolas on the Big Wheel, could parachute to earth by opening umbrellas. There is a physical principle involved in each of these, but the cause adduced for each event has either no effect at all—like breathing on a room's air pressure—or it could not have had an effect of the size proposed—friction would slow the man in the pool, but would not make the umbrellas buoyant enough. Momentum in one case and friction in the other are vastly overstated (*Surf Girl*, Mack Sennett).

4 Fantasy: The Upper Limit of the Logical

As we rise up the scale of improbability, it is still the false analogy that intrigues us, however farfetched it may be.

If sprinkling dandruff gives us concern, it is perhaps a neurotic possibility to picture a man up to his neck in a pyramid of it (*Dandruff*, Jim Duffy). If a tuning fork can be seen to quiver when struck, and another in sympathy with it, is it very farfetched, when a clock is large and its chime deep, to show things in the room visibly quivering every time it strikes (*The Fall of the House of Usher*, Jean Epstein)?

Pluto escapes Butch by hanging on a dangling red thread, which he chews up as fast as he pulls it down. When the end of the thread pulls through the ceiling, Pluto falls, with some show of logic. So long as the slack is taken up as it comes, we fail to realize that a thread not fast at the other end will hold no one at all for any time at all, and the image generates a kind of specious physics—as if the friction encountered by the thread moving through the air equaled the pull of gravity on Pluto plus thread. Any tiny amount of friction is prodigiously exaggerated (*The Purloined Pup*, Charles Nichols).

Pablo the Penguin is making an ocean trip in a plugless bathtub. When he has bailed the tub out, he quickly affixes a shower hose to the hole, and by pointing the hose back at the water surface, the force of the water jet impels him forwards. There is a cavalier disregard of what we all know but forget for the moment, that water will not rise in the hose beyond the surface of the sea. The upward pressure in the hose is magnified beyond what is physically possible (*The Three Caballeros*, Normal Ferguson).

At its most extreme, the plausible becomes the clearly impossible. Pluto hides behind a door. Butch opens the door and leans his great bulk against it to make scratching easier. When the door is closed, Pluto is flush with the plaster, and when he wriggles free, he leaves his intaglio behind (*The Purloined Pup*, Charles Nichols).

Crow and fox each want the last grape on a plate, and their quarrel ends by each tearing down the other's house. The crow telephones the fox, turns the hose into the mouthpiece, and water sprays from the receiver, drenching the fox. Here is a metaphor: the wire is a pipe. The fox in return thrusts his hand through the mouth-piece, and it comes out the other end and grips the crow by the neck (*Grape Nutty*, Al Lovy). A mad inventor's rejuvenation fluid had shrunk a goose to a gosling. Laurel and Hardy make of the gosling, an egg. Hardy then falls into a vat of the fluid. After he climbs out, he sits on the edge, with his usual mock-patience but now as a chimpanzee (*Dirty Work*, Lloyd French).

The imagination seen at work here is the same as in mathematical notions like negative numbers, which are the extension of subtraction beyond the logical possibility of its application.[2]

5 Technical Means

The film as an art has a wealth of technical means for making hyperboles.

There is the frozen scene. An assassin drives up to a hotel to find out from his employers if any unfavorable happening might have led them to cancel his mission. It was a moment of pause in the movement of events. The Jackal stops his car. Not only his car but all the traffic on the street stops for a few seconds (*The Day of the Jackal*, Fred Zinnemann).

There is the moving camera. As Pip tugs the cloth to one end of a long table, the camera moves toward the other, hastening the movement (*Great Expectations*, David Lean).

There are different uses of editing. In *The Valley of the Giants* (William Keighley), for example, the fall of a redwood tree was taken from four angles, and the shots were not cut in true succession but overlapped in time. A part of the downward path of the tree, that is to say, was seen twice from different angles, so that the time of fall on the screen was greater than actual. In the same way the falling of coins from a bowl can be lengthened out. Two bowls of coins were poured over the czar at his coronation, no doubt to signify, or by some vestigial magic secure, prosperity. We saw shots of his feet with coins falling, shots from each side of an usher pouring them, and one from the front of the czar's face seen through a golden veil of them. The two bowls we saw could not have held enough coins at the rate of fall to fill the time the pouring took on the screen (*Ivan the Terrible*, S. M. Eisenstein). We saw the same event more than once from different angles. Buster Keaton, in his last film, traveled across Canada on a motorized maintenance vehicle. In the course of his journey, out of the two or three square feet of the storage box, he took dishes and cutlery, a large bearskin coat, a variety of food, including eggs, tablecloth, washing utensils, and sundry other items, the sum of which could not have gone in this puny chest. Because the film can edit out the putting in, and leave in only the taking out, it can give any container a nearly infinite capacity (*The Railrodder*, Gerald Potterton).

It is thickening a stroke beyond nature, by way of emphasis.

To this has to be added the nearly limitless possibilities of animation, which can, for example, so distort perspective that a fence may seem to rise hundreds of feet (*Chicken Little*, Walt Disney).

6 Parody

There is exaggeration in many parodies, which must catch exactly the victim's manner, yet mark unerringly the point of weakness, and by enlarging it, make it seem ridiculous (pl. 23). Two weak points in *The Old Man's Comforts and How He Gained Them* are the facile moral precepts, so general as to have no practical value, and the curious choice of a rollicking anapaestic meter in which to express them. Lewis Carroll made the advice more useless still:

> "You are old, father William," the young man cried;
> "The few locks which are left you are gray;
> You are hale, father William—a hearty old man:
> Now tell me the reason, I pray."
>
> —Southey

> "You are old, father William," the young man said,
> "And your hair has become very white;
> And yet you incessantly stand on your head—
> Do you think, at your age, it is right?"
>
> —Carroll

> "In the days of my youth," father William replied,
> "I remembered that youth would fly fast,
> And abused not my health and my vigour at first,
> That I never might need them at last."
>
> —Southey

> "In my youth," father William replied to his son,
> "I feared it might injure the brain;
> But, now that I'm perfectly sure I have none,
> Why, I do it again and again."[3]
>
> —Carroll

The lurking absurdity of the original appears in the intended nonsense of the parody, which keeps the form intact, and alters only the advice asked and given.

Chaplin treats the Western epic in much the same way. Extreme right, into a wide-screen saloon, a stranger enters. Extreme left, from behind the end of a counter that curves away nearly out of sight, a kneeling man fires at the stranger. In a leisurely way, the stranger fires at each of eight cowhands leaning against the bar, equally spaced around the curve. Each in turn, hesitates and collapses. Then the stranger by the door and the villain behind the bar fire at one another, turn about. The king, his ambassador, and all the audience we see behind them, swing their heads from side to side with each shot heard. The king and his friend go out, and as we follow them up the aisle to the door, the dreary procession of pistol shots goes on and on. Here is the conventional situation, the lone stranger surrounded by armed enemies. The eight he kills, as if they knew their preordained fate, did not attempt the futiity of defense, and meekly awaited their turn to bite the dust. The duel never finishes: if the marksmanship were not incredibly bad, there would be no suspense, so at twenty feet neither can hit the other (A King in New York).

In The Dance of the Hours, agility, music, and movement are as in ballet: what is exaggerated is the size and shape of the performers. We must all have seen a ballerina who seems a trifle bulky and whose legs are on the leaden side. But here we see a hippopotamus who wears ballet shoes, who rises and stretches elegantly and eats grapes with grace. She yawns, and we look down a monstrous throat to a huge uvula before she closes. She lies on a sagging couch, turns over, and modestly pulls the infinitesimal tutu over tremendous buttocks. As we near the climax of this glorious romp, the leading crocodile manhandles the première hipporina with more and more violent, not to say sadistic, recklessness (*Dance of the Hours: Fantasia,* T. Hu and Norman Ferguson; pl. 24).

Pleasant as it is, few take Ponchielli's piece very seriously—it has a touch of triteness to our ears—and the directors have matched this in their lighthearted treatment of ballet itself. It is movement that counts, not who makes it: women or elephants is no matter as long as they move to the beat all at once.

In both cases, there is present beyond the imitation that which, in Gilbert Highet's word,[4] "wounds" or belittles the original, if only slightly. They are caricatures not portraits.[5]

Part V

Figures of Omission

10
Ellipsis

1 Ellipsis Defined

Aristotle, writes Dr. Whately, gives us a choice of words from two classes, Kuria or Xena.[1] Whately translates the former as "proper, appropriate or ordinary;" the latter as "strange or uncommon," and these are the figures or tropes. Now one way of conferring strangeness on a thing or person is to leave part of them out.

I propose to use for this the term *ellipsis*. This is strictly a figure of syntax, where a word normally used is left out, thus,

Steal forth [from] thy father's house tomorrow night.[2]

Shall us [go] to the Capitol?[3]

The word in brackets readers must add from their knowledge of grammar. So long as we remember its first limited meaning, there is perhaps no harm, when dealing with a means of expression other than words, in extending its use.

2 Frame and Proscenium

What the director is leaving something out from is first, of course, the frame. This is a window on what is going on, which includes and leaves out, just as the proscenium arch of the theater is a window in the fourth wall of the room we see on the stage.[4] Frame and arch both include what the director wishes us to see, and keep out of sight what, for reasons of his own, he does not wish to disclose. The theater window, however, shows us the same square of space throughout a scene, and the director, from time to time, uses various devices to fix our eye on some one part. A moving or speaking actor, for example, will take our eye from a still or silent one. The resolute theatregoer may even so defy the intended focus, and look where he or she is not supposed to. But the filmic window gives a director a dictatorial control over attention. Throughout a sequence he constantly narrows or widens our view, brings in and leaves out, and points us where he chooses, with no rebellion possible.

In *Arsenic and Old Lace* (Frank Capra), Mortimer makes fun to Dr. Einstein of a play in which the hero sits while the villain creeps up to bind him with a curtain. As Mortimer describes it, Jonathan behind is fitting the action to the word. Now on the stage we may look to see if Einstein is going to warn, or Mortimer take alarm, or

Jonathan leap. The director likely intends this, but even if he did try to lock our eye to any one, we could still defeat him. On the screen, the director places us facing Mortimer, with Jonathan stalking behind, and only a rare glance at Einstein. We have no choice. Einstein is not there and the other two are, Mortimer talking and Jonathan moving.

3 Other Ways of Using the Frame Lines

Apart from controlling our attention, the frame line has been used as part of the setting. As a large band of wild children come in sight, we are shown a police call-box. A militiaman throws himself into the frame and makes an urgent call, like an actor making a sudden entrance "on stage" (*The Road to Life*, N. Ekk).

We feel this proscenium effect whenever the frame is used as a point of reference. To show Washizu and Miki lost in fog on a flat plain and circling round again and again to the same place, the frame is used as a landmark for them and us. Ten times they gallop toward us out of the mist, recognize where they are, and gallop away, or off to the right or left, twice remaining in sight and coming back. The tenth time, they walk their horses towards us, and the mist is clearing (*Throne of Blood*, Akira Kurosawa).

In *Fanny by Gaslight* (Anthony Asquith), the frame, by metaphor, is a mind reaching decision. A cabinet minister's wife has just given him two choices: to allow himself to be divorced, with a dearly loved illegitimate daughter named as corespondent, or to have his daughter's parentage made public. Victoria being queen, either choice would require Seymore's resignation and could result in the defeat of the government. He stands at right frame, with his back to us, by the dressing table at which his wife had been sitting. He picks up the letter that his daughter Fanny has left him. We see him in each of three mirrors, half-length, a profile in each of the side mirrors, full face in the center. Slowly we move closer. Seymore's back passes out of the frame, then each of the side mirrors. An eddy of music bubbles into the flow and continues. His voice, though not his lips, repeats a fragment from the letter, "better for both of us. . . ." There is a low rumble of drums. All things are leaving the frame except for the full-face reflection, large, tensed, and sweating. We hear the distant pulse of a train. His eyes are fixed on something far off, his lips are parted, and his face is glistening. The sound of the train is louder. The camera no longer moves: there is one Seymore only left in the frame, head and shoulders. Suddenly the reflected face turns from us, and from off frame right the man himself swings back before us. Mirrors, table, all that stood behind him has vanished into a flat black, and on the black, taken from below, is his face, looking upwards at something that stares with a hard white light and stamps on the face a mold of rigid fear. The rush and clatter of the train obliterates the music in an overwhelming crescendo. There is a last stabbing shriek from a train whistle, and an abrupt cut to a newsboy, oblique on the screen, skirted by a poster, and yelling, "Death of a Cabinet Minister!"

It was not part of the absorbing event, whose full force nonetheless I felt, it was not until I was outside walking the gleaming streets, that I said, "The three mirrors, of course, are three choices, and the floating of all but one off the screen is his weighing of them, ending in sudden decision with his quick swing round. Each image is a different self that might have chosen a different outcome: to be divorced, to acknowledge Fanny (either one of which would end his public life and perhaps bring down the government), or suicide. After his decision was made, all that befell signified little, could be passed over—all but the fearful moment before the steel struck.

4   Excluding the Irrelevant

The choice to exclude is a decision on the relevant.

Natacha is taking a kettle of water to Korozov. She has come to half-length, and both her hand and kettle have passed out of the frame, when she hears someone say that Sergei Korovin is dead. We hear a metal vessel striking the floor; we know she has dropped the kettle, but no irrelevant movement has drawn our eye from her face and the sound is metaphoric for the shock she has received (*The Girl from Leningrad*, Victor Eisimont). In *Monsieur Vincent* (Maurice Cloche), whoever threw the stones or poured the water is left unseen; what was important was that Vincent rescued the child from such human malignity.

When social workers interview the leader of the "wild children," what is important is whether he will fall in with their proposals, so most of the time we see his face, its glance and expression, and only hear the social workers (*The Road to Life*, N. Ekk). Much the same is seen at the start of *Butch Cassidy and the Sundance Kid* (George Roy Hill). The Kid is seen seated at a table, slowly handling cards. As we watch the unresponsive mask of The Kid's face, we hear the voice of someone, offscreen, "You haven't lost since you got the deal. . . . What's the secret of your success? . . . You're a hell of a good card player. I'm a hell of a good card player myself . . . and I can't even spot how you cheat. . . ." The purpose of the scene is to introduce The Kid: to show the speaker would bring in the irrelevant.

It is the same with even a great number of persons. Only now and then do we see the whole courtroom between the backs of the judges (*The Divided Heart*, Charles Crichton). We see the Slovene mother, her interpreter, and her counsel, taken between the backs of the German foster parents, and the German foster parents between the backs of the natural mother and her counsel. In a trial to decide who is to get the boy, separated from his natural parents during the war, we are interested in how each of the claimants feels as he or she listens to the other, and for most of the trial, this is what we see.

5   Ellipsis as Emphasis: The Mask

One way of omitting part of a scene is to black it over or mask it.

D. W. Griffith introduces the Girl at left frame, and masks the other two thirds of it. He then wipes the mask off to the right to show the rest of the room in which she is standing. Nothing distracts us from looking well at the Girl before the director allows us to see her surroundings. One part of the scene is emphasized by being shown first, shown longer, and seen in isolation from the setting. A round frame in a black mask bottom right shows us the priest of Imgur-Bel half-length. The mask wipes outwards to show us the walls of Babylon reaching across the screen into the distance, not merely to have us note the priest but to move our eye by degrees into the vista. Griffith sometimes matched the shape of the screen to the line of movement. When chariots raced across the screen, he blacked out the bottom two-fifths, making a horizontal frame for horizontal movement. When a soldier fell from the top of a city wall, he masked out all but the center third, leaving a vertical slot for the downward motion (*Intolerance*).

In a small square to the left of a wide black screen, Julie goes out by a side door. She looks to right frame, and the mask flings back off the screen to show a black servant leaving by the front and walking toward her. Julie returns quickly into the house till the servant is gone. This not only held our attention on Julie, but the quick drawing back of the mask as she turned her head suggested her sudden awareness of the servant—a trivial occasion perhaps for an impressive device (*Mississippi Mermaid*, François Truffaut).

Harold leaves the general manager's office, shaken by a reprimand. He stands left of the door, and leans to recover himself. His letters home have made him out as rising rapidly in rank and earning a large salary. His girl has come to town to surprise him, and as he is leaning, she sees him and smiles with pride. The full frame of Harold and the door shrinks to a small circle around the words "General Manager: Private," and then blacks out (*Safety Last*, Fred Newmayer and Sam Taylor).

In a less obtrusive way, the same thing is often done by using things in the scene instead of the mask. In *The Whisperers* (Bryan Forbes), for example, near the end of a sequence, Margaret Ross is shown entering a white vertical frame on the right half of the screen. A shadowed wall blacked out the left half, and the sky beyond her provided whiteness on the right.

6 Ellipsis and Emphasis: The Close-Up as Exclusion

The close-up has largely taken the place of the mask and the iris-in. Compare with the following the irised-in shot of the priest from *Intolerance*. The silken draperies in front of their couch rise and Anthony and Cleopatra lie before us, and only them. The camera draws back to take in more and more of the ship they are sailing on: dancers upon dancers, censers, the chased silver heads of oars, and at last the drum-beating stroke, timing the thrust of the blades with a ponderous double beat. In each case, the part emphasized at first has blended into the long final shot (*Cleopatra*, Cecil B. de Mille).

All of a scene may be left out but a mere part of one person's body. Superior Private Kaji, after a day's work in prison camp, wolfs his little meal: all we see is his chewing, bearded lips; a man is become a mouth (*The Human Condition*, part 3: *A Soldier's Prayer*, Masaki Kobayashi). Or when little Miles, possessed by the lustful Peter Quant, kisses his governess, she starts back, and a close-up of her face, of the mouth but not the eyes, betrays her shock (*The Innocents*, Jack Clayton).

Not only may a sequence be introduced by isolating a detail in close-up but this may be done for several details. We see the snowy steppe and then the following, all shot close: a leafless bush in the snow, part of a black-and-white striped post, the whole post, the head and shoulders of a man lying on the snow, his right hand holding a revolver, and then his left thigh with hand holding a note. A long shot now shows the snow-covered steppes, the post at the crest of a knoll, and below it the supine body. An insistent high note blends into jingling bells, as a sleigh enters. A policeman alights to examine the body, rises and says to a companion, "The Italian is dead" (*Petersburg Nights*, Grigori Roshal and V. Stroev).

7 Ellipsis as Synecdoche

If we think less of what is left out and more of what stays in, many ellipses are also synecdoches, where a part of something stands for the whole.

Simon Rawley, a deserter, has leaped through a window to escape arrest. We see only his shins and feet. His toes point to us, to right, to left, and then to us again; then they turn and run away from us over the cobbles (*Silent Dust*, Lance Comfort).

In showing a journey by night, Friedrich Ermler blacked out the sky, the trees, the road, and the carriage itself: all we see is a flickering white horse galloping larger toward us. Presumably a traveling light kept pace with the horse, and the flicker was caused by trees in between *(Peasants)*.

A visitor to a hotel who asks for Constantin Golas is told that no one of that name had registered within the month. The visitor buys a newspaper, and in profile sits and opens it. The next frame contains only the paper, the headline reading "DIMITRIOS MAKKROPOULOS FOUND DEAD." Hands come in from either side of the frame, crumple the paper, and remain tense (*The Mask of Dimitrios*, Jean Negulesco).

In *The Magnificent Ambersons* (Orson Welles), George Minifer's life from boy to man is given in four episodes to show us that he was always the singularly unlovable person we find him to be when he first meets Lucy. To present him as he was for so long a time in four brief episodes is clearly ellipsis, and just as clearly, synecdoche.

8 Composition

The composition of the frame is not within the scope of this book. This is merely to remark in passing that what is left in the frame must be so arranged as to send the eye quickly to where the meaning lies. We may spend an hour exploring the niceties of a painting, when we have but seconds to take in a shot. The director must give as much care to composing for immediate effect, as the painter gives to multiplying subtleties.

Jacqueline has revealed what was forbidden, and, surrounded by members of the witch cult she belongs to, poison is placed in front of her. Close to us is a black table, and all that is on it is the glass goblet of poison, so lit that it glows against the black. Beyond it she sits, face toward us, in black dress and black fur coat, and the white V-neck below her pale face is an arrow pointing down to the soft sinister glow of the goblet on the table below. The emphasis comes from leaving out of the frame all other white objects (*The Seventh Victim*, Mark Robson).

It will be understood that such pictorial emphasis will make any figure more effective.

9 The Use of Ellipsis: Mood

Ellipsis is often used in evoking a mood.

It might almost be said that a good director can be told as much by his shadows as by his lighting. Jessica comes slowly through a secret door to Tony, who had killed the man she loved. The doorway was dark, her face in shadow, darker perhaps because of a small semicircle of light beside her head. We are only aware of her two eyes, and the eye of a revolver muzzle embedded in the threatening darkness (*Scarface*, Howard Hawks).

The same suggestion of the sinister is found in *The Lady Killers* (Alexander Mackendrick). "Is there any reply to my advertisement?" says Mrs. Wilberforce, and we pan to a board with cards on it, and a light shadow of someone wearing a felt hat is printed there. On his first appearance at her door, he is a shadow on the frosted glass, and when the door opens, his lower left jaw is dark. As Marcus looks out at the railway cutting, a hanging curtain cuts off the right side of his face, hinting at someone unbalanced.

In a flashback of Czechs living under German occupation, there is a mood as of doomed people, whom no action could save. They listen, for example, to a playback of a concert in which Jan Volny played the forbidden *Moldau*. There is no movement on the screen. A man is wearing a coat. When next we see him, the coat is off. Someone turns around, but we see the man before and after the turn. By keeping all movement off the screen, the mood of resignation, of waiting for the end, is conveyed (*Voice in the Wind*, Arthur Ripley).

10   The Use of Ellipsis: Suggesting Not Showing

As Greek playwrights knew, an event may gain in power by happening offstage (or offscreen) and being conveyed by means of a thing or person.

A girl is being lavishly decked for a wedding. The man she is to marry has an evil name for cruelty. She does not love him; she is marrying to save her lover's life. She sits in a glittering dark dress. As the camera slowly approaches her and her maids from ground level, the oval hand mirror she is holding exactly blanks her face, and is framed by her hair. The concealment of the face by the featureless oval has an effect of horror hard to explain. An actress might achieve a set face of outrage, fear, despair, or listlessness, but the expressionless metal somehow adds a feeling of being wholly lost, withdrawn, of one who has lost her humanity (*Abdul the Damned*, Karl Grune). Few faces can match the infinite significance of the unseen.

In *Unpublished Story* (Harold French), Trapes, the dupe of a fifth-column enterprise, is being tortured. The Nazis wish him to telephone for the return of a letter he has written. Trapes is sitting facing us in center frame; standing behind him are two men, one of them Stannard, a Nazi. The left third of the frame is black—someone's back, standing close to the camera. Trapes refuses. Stannard says, "All right, Hayter." The black back at the left slowly spreads over to Trapes with a sense of approaching menace. Trapes's face, white-lit, glistening with sweat, looks in terror down as at Hayter's hands, hidden by his back from the camera. That is all we see of the torture.

In *Jane Eyre* (Robert Stevenson), the mad wife is never seen: her door, her shrieks, her sobs, a silhouette on a distant window, hands clawing her husband's throat from out of the frame, but never a face—that is left for the misty horror the human fancy shapes from such hints.

11   The Use of Ellipsis: Face or No Face

Leaving out a character's face from the frame is a special case of ellipsis with many applications.

When the real Hitler arrives for a gala theater night in Warsaw, Ernst Lubitsch never shows his face. We see only his back from his arrival outside to his walking into his theater box, his arm raised in salute, and the standing audience below, or now and then a very long shot. This prevents a minor character from gaining undue weight, as such an historical personage would (*To Be or Not to Be*).

In some cases who the persons are is no matter. Hoffman looks down through a fretted screen at a sexual orgy. Couches point in to the center of a ring. The heads of all are cut off, and all we see is pairs of twisting legs. In a later long shot all are wearing colored masks, which makes them less than men, and emphasizes more their animality (*Tales of Hoffman*, Michael Powell and Emeric Pressburger).

In a down shot of an alley, we pan with five English spearmen—each is only the crest of a helmet, a swinging arm, a shouldered spear—they are not seen as persons but the tools of an occupying power (*The Passion of Joan of Arc*, Carl Theodor Dreyer).

Tatsuhei carries his mother up the mountain, where old people who eat but cannot work are left to die. She will not speak. To each poignant word of his, she stretches out her arm and points him on. Her face we never see, bent as it is over his shoulder. Near the top of the mountain black vultures hover, and the camera's eye sweeps across a vast company of skeletons. We see the final embrace from far off. When it starts to snow, he runs back. He collapses left frame. "Mother, you must be cold," he cries. She bows and beckons him away. By not seeing her face or hearing her voice, we feel she has left the world of men already: she is a presence preparing to vanish (*The Ballad of Narayama*, Keisuke Kinoshita). The ellipsis has distanced us.

In the figure hyrmos, the face may be the fact withheld and needed for understanding. When Marie-Louise, an evacuee, is brought home by Hedi, she must gain her father's approval. The handle turns, but all we see of the man who enters the door is his middle part. His hand puts his cane in the stand, and his hat on a peg; legs and body cross the room with briefcase and paper; hand pats dog. But what sort of man is he? Will he likely approve? His face might give a clue, but this the director keeps out of our view (*Marie Louise*, Leopold Lindtberg).

12 The Use of Ellipsis: No Face in Satire

Ellipsis of the face is used in political satire. Like its literary counterpart, filmic satire attacks human vice, folly, or stupidity, and its form is fantasy.[5]

In *The End of St Petersburg* (V. I. Pudovkin), we see a row of chairs. One after another, eight men in court dress enter and are seated. The frame includes them all except their heads. One of a smaller group of five headless men rises to speak: "The czar and your country call." In a profile shot of the five, all are dressed the same, all their legs are crossed, and none have heads. Their dress and posture are uniform, they are people conditioned by class and education; they think and they say the same. By showing the garb and not the face, conformity is emphasized. This is an ingenious means of generalizing in a medium that finds the individual case easier to handle.

A long procession of men in bowler hats comes toward us, chanting "Dirty foreigners," and on their banners, La France Aux Français and À Bas La Republique. We see the proprietor of a bar leaning on his door jamb watching the procession pass with some amusement. At one point in close shot, he suddenly chants loudly "Vive Chiappe," and keeps it going with great vigor. In a shot from across the street, the procession marching by in the foreground, without even looking round at the source of the cry, switches over to his "Vive Chiappe." At a later place, they come from the left, and move away from us round a corner. With backs toward us, they seem but a faceless mass of round bowler hats, all in step marching into the distance, chanting they know not what, and the backs of their banners are now blank white. In three leaps, the end of the column jumps into the distance, and then is gone. A stormy sky, a flash of lightning, and the end. The Deluge (*The Diary of a Chamber Maid*, Luis Buñuel)?

13   The Use of Ellipsis: Surprise

It is hard for the film to avoid a kind of structural ellipsis, for it leaves out all that happens behind the camera. Besides providing a handy working place for the crew, it is, so far as we who view are concerned, a place behind our backs, where unexpected things are going on, and from which unexpected people come.

Tokiko and her husband Ida quarrel. He has pushed her away. There is a sound and they look toward us. We cut to their little son, sitting up in his bed, looking with what seems a stern glance (*A Hen in the Wind*, Yasujiro Ozu).

In *To Be or Not to Be* (Ernst Lubitsch), the Führer enters an office and answers a chorus of "Heil Hitler's" by raising his arm and saying "Heil myself." This is cut to a row of footlights, and beyond them in front of the stalls a man sits, who bangs his hand on a table and says sharply, "That's not in the script, Mr. Bronski." Up until this there was no sign of a theater. Hooker, out on probation, hears that his hated stepfather is home, and runs out of the hostel at which he stays. The warden says, "Phone his probation officer." We see Hooker hustled out of his mother's home by Tom, the stepfather, and thrown in the gutter. Hooker picks himself up, sobbing, humiliated. He seizes a big stone, pulls his hand back to throw—and a hand comes into the frame from the right, grasps his hand, and prevents him. A man follows the hand into the frame: it is his probation officer, Phipps (*I Believe in You*, Michael Ralph and Basil Dearden).

The camera thus has a great capacity for leaving things just out of the frame: it may also place them the other side of some person or thing. Annabella bursts into Hannay's room at night and runs toward us. We see her over the top of his bed, a map clutched in her hand. Not until she falls forward on to the bed can we see the knife in her back (*The Thirty-Nine Steps*, Alfred Hitchcock).

By choice of shot, part of a situation may be edited out. The crofter's young wife has aroused her husband's suspicions by her evident interest in the stranger. They sit at table, the crofter facing us, the others facing one another at either side. "Ye havna told me yer name?" "Hammond," says Hannay. "Well, if ye'll quit readin' the paper, I'll be for askin' the blessin'." He closes his eyes. Hannay's anxiety forces his gaze down to where he set the paper. Margie's eyes rest on the stranger, with calm interest and then follow his to the paper. We see the headline, "PORTLAND MANSIONS MURDER." Her eyes are again on Hannay, startled, questioning. He looks at her. We are again aware of the blessing, the words coming slower, like the last drippings of a tap, and as the crofter says, "and keep our minds from worldly things," they stop. Only then is the crofter seen again; the whites of his open eyes are clearly seen in his dark whiskered face, and his gaze is fixed on Margie. With no turn of his head, it flickers across to Hannay and back to Margie. A pause. "Amen," he adds (*The Thirty-Nine Steps*, Alfred Hitchcock).

The moving camera may disclose what is left out. We pan with a nurse as she leaves a girl seemingly asleep. Then we pan back to the bed and the patient is gone (*Vampyr* Carl Theodor Dreyer). Don Quixote has rescued a shepherd boy about to be beaten by his master. The camera sinks from nearly treetop level, first showing the departing Don and the squire, then the back of the grateful boy to the right, looking after them, and bringing in, left frame, at last, the boy's master, swinging an ominous rope in his right hand (*Don Quixote*, Grigori Kozintsev).

The unanticipated may also be hid under a tarpaulin of darkness. Presuming that the wakeful Abdul, who had commanded their performance, was asleep, the soldiers, dancers, and musicians quietly withdraw. Ali turns the lights out, and Abdul is lost in the black square of his throne, which stands out against a tall window. Noise is followed by stillness, and, of all the doings, only the searchlight steals across the dark room at intervals. We approach the throne, and as the beam crosses the room, Abdul's eyes, wide open, staring, gleam for a passing moment at us out of the darkness, deep in the black mood that consumes him (*Abdul the Damned*, Karl Grune).

14   The Use of Ellipsis: False Impression

In our daily lives we live in the context of what we see. We can turn our heads to follow its continuum. Peripheral vision spreads a lesser awareness around the more distinct foveal vision: the boundary between the two is uncertain. But what we see on the screen is cut sharply off by the sides of a rectangle, and this, without its context, may be quite misleading. If a camera pans up a building at gravitational speed, and nothing beside can be seen, it appears to collapse (*The End of St Petersburg*, V. I. Pudovkin). We can, on the other hand, run our eye up or down the moving steps of an escalator, even trying to hood out its sides, without our sensing any change of speed. Perception makes correction for our moving heads.

By ellipsis of all that would lead us to read the situation correctly, with misreading often actively encouraged, the director is able to surprise us.

In *Nothing But the Best* (Clive Donner), Brewster is bent on being accepted in high society. Charlie Prince, lying in bed, says, "Sorry about the ball." He had misdirected Brewster to the wrong country house for a hunt ball. Now we see another imposing mansion. Where is Brewster off now in pursuit of the upper classes? But the picture lifts up to disclose biscuits—it is on a lid. Brewster is still at home with his parents, and the biscuits are passed.

We may be misled by a title. Harold has implied in a letter that he is moving up in the business world and is growing wealthy. The Girl's mother is concerned at his carrying large sums of money on his person. "She Thinks He's in Danger." "Her Mother Instinct Was Right." Cut to Harold, his back to a wall, tie loose and crooked, hair tousled, shrinking in fear. A slow retreat reveals a counter in front of him, and on the near side, hordes of women fighting to reach the bolts and remnants of cloth displayed there (*Safety Last*, Fred Newmayer and Sam Taylor).

Sound out of context is useful. Alice in a pale coat is walking slowly, Irene, in a black fur coat, is walking fast. Both are walking along the same wall, but both are never seen in the same frame. We assume from the concrete wall behind them both that they are fairly close, and because Alice stops and listens for the fast steps. At last she hears nothing; she looks back and sees nothing. The shrubs above the concrete wall are jostling one another. Is it the Cat Woman gliding through them? As Alice stands wondering against the wall, there is a sudden soft but startling whoosh. A bus comes in abruptly from the right, and we see her through its open door. She looks up and then quickly turns and enters the bus. Whatever we thought before, it seems now like the sound of compressed air (*The Cat People*, Jacques Tourneur).

15   The Use of Ellipsis: Hyrmos—Meaning Suspended

Surprise comes when we think we know all there is to know about a situation, and find we are wrong (pls. 18, 19, 20, 25). When we are well aware that a piece of information is being withheld from us, and are waiting to find out what it is, this may be called the *hyrmos,* a word used of the periodic sentence. The word or detail indispensable to understanding the whole, and which we know must come sooner or later, is held back until the end.[6] Here is the literary form:

> "But I defy him!—Let him come." Down rang the massy cup,
> While from its sheath the ready blade came flashing half-way up,
> And with the black and heavy plumes scarce trembling on his head,
> There in his dark carved oaken chair, old Rudiger sat—dead.[7]

As with the term "ellipsis," it is convenient to extend what strictly applies to a sentence to longer forms. Many of the best short stories are based on this figure. Take, at random, one by Sir Arthur Quiller-Couch, *The Two Householders,* a story told in twenty-five pages.[8] A highwayman, benighted in the rain and wind, sees his first light for miles. The door of the house is open, and a yellow mastiff is sleeping under a table. The intruder cautiously takes off his shoes, and upstairs finds a man in the one lighted room. As the highwayman, pistol in hand, faces the man, armed with a poker, he learns that the man has that day discharged his butler for some wrong-doing. The man warms to his visitor, on finding him educated and having a nice discrimination in wine. He offers to take the highwayman on in place of the departed butler, shows him the butler's quarters, and gives him a nightshirt. The highwayman is still uneasy, and at dawn hears footsteps outside the house. Now here we are at page twenty-three, and neither he nor we know the truth, nor do we find it out until fifteen lines from the end of the story.

The frame is an obvious filmic means to keep us in suspense. A man is seated, reading, first in close-up of his head, and then in longer shots, in a small place, with various outside sounds, none of which are precisely identifiable. We are not clear where he is until he reaches out of the frame to tear off some paper (*Krasner, Norman: Beloved Husband of Irma,* Steven Goldstein).

The mask is a temporary frame. After Napoleon's two hours with Josephine, we see him in a circular mask, down on one knee, facing left and looking up. He must be proposing to Josephine, we think; but the mask widens out and off the screen to reveal the actor Talma, to whom we find Napoleon is paying his addresses, the actor giving instructions in how to do it (*Napoleon,* Abel Gance).

The unannounced photograph is a not uncommon variant. In *Peasants* (Friedrich Ermler) a dramatic scene has just ended with a vigorous declamation, followed by many voices in lively discussion. Then there is a sudden silence, and we slowly draw back from a woman standing, staring, stock still. Two by two persons enter on either side of a table, their faces toward us, intently still, one even gripping a tankard. They are clearly overwhelmed by some catastrophe. What can it be? When all the stern-faced company are in the frame, a sudden puff of smoke enters from the side, and a man carries a camera into the frame.

The final fact may be held back by editing. In *The End of St Petersburg* (V. I. Pudovkin), a battalion of soldiers stands on parade. Kerensky speaks; an agitator speaks; a peasant speaks. Officers command a squad of soldiers forward. On command they level their rifles. "Fire!" The volley is fired. But those at whom they fired are out of the frame—who are they? The revolutionaries? The next shot shows us: they have killed their officers.

What is withheld may be where someone is in relation to someone else, which is simply done by never showing both in the same shot. Here is a sequence from *We from Kronstadt* (E. Dzigan):

   i. The sole surviving Red sailor is shown on the shore of the sea, looking back, and pushing out a boat.
   ii. Two White guards leap down a bank to the beach.
   iii. The single sailor and boat are still struggling through the breakers.
   iv. Three guards, and then a fourth, run along the beach looking out to sea.
   v. The sailor is beyond the breakers, but close to shore.
   vi. Seen from the sea, the four guards kneel and fire at us (the camera position may be that of the boat, but may not).
   vii. Seen from the beach, the boat is well out beyond rifle range, the sailor rowing vigorously.

Not until shot 7 do we know how far from the guards, and how safe, the escaping sailor is.

The clue we need may be kept from us till the end of the film. Holland and a companion are chatting in a fashionable restaurant. A passing lady thanks Holland for a charitable gift. He calls over a jockey, praises his riding, and gives him a roll of banknotes. He does the like to a girl who greets him, for her birthday. She kisses him. His left hand stays on his knee. "You seem to have accomplished a good deal in a year," his friend remarks. "Unlike most men who long to be rich and have little hope of being so," says Holland, "I was in the enviable position of having a fortune literally within my grasp. . . ." Dissolve to his supervising the pouring of gold bricks, followed by how he stole them. It ends with his entering the underground after eluding the police. As we cut back to the luncheon, we are still unaware where he is or how he came to be there, and he has an air of impregnable confidence. What happened after that? A last passer-by praises the fine party he had given, and his friend asks, "Are you ready?" They rise, and now for a moment we see the handcuffs. By common accord, they hide the tie that binds them, and walk away from us at a leisurely pace (*The Lavender Hill Mob*, Charles Crichton).

Ana, a girl of seven or so, who cannot sleep, comes down to the front hall in time to hear a woman's voice in her father's room and see the woman run out of the door. She goes in, finds her father dead without surprise, and takes a partly emptied glass of milk to the kitchen. She washes it and carefully mixes it in with other glasses. During the film we learn that instead of throwing out a metal box as her mother had told her, she had kept it. When she pressed her mother as to whether the white powder in it was a poison, her mother said with a smile that a teaspoonful would kill an elephant. Ana later drops the powder into a glass of milk she takes to her aunt, who after her mother's death, becomes her guardian. During the night, as her aunt sleeps, she takes the glass from beside the bed, washes it in the kitchen, and puts it in among the other glasses. We now know that she must have placed the powder in her father's glass (he had been callous and unfeeling to her mother). And when, the next morning, as the servant is rousing the children for school, her aunt bustles in as usual, we and Ana learn that the powder, whatever it was, was not poison and she had not been the cause of her father's death (*Cria*, Carlos Saura).

16 The Use of Ellipsis: The Sphere of Awareness

We may include in the frame only what some character sees or could see, and thus show a subjective view of a situation.

In *The Passion of Joan of Arc* (Carl Theodor Dreyer), a priest's head may enter the frame from side or bottom to throw a question at Joan, as if he suddenly obtruded himself on her attention.

All the way to Waterloo Bridge, Nancy (and we) keep looking back, but the Artful Dodger is not to be seen. He was, however, following somewhere, for, as she talks to Mr. Brownlow, we pan past one of the piers of the bridge to see him listening (*Oliver Twist,* David Lean).

Nell, sleeping beside another woman guest in a haunted house, hears voices during the night, and reaches toward the other woman (who is out of the frame) for reassurance. When all is over, we see her fingers bent as if they had let go someone's hand. She turns toward the other woman; she is asleep and her hands are under the covers. "Whose hand was I holding?" (*The Haunting,* Robert Wise).

Len has been blackmailing a boy, Frankie. The two have gone to a station on the underground, no longer used. Becoming aware that Len intends to kill him, Frankie has run off and Len is looking for him. In a long shot, Frankie backs into an alcove between the mouths of two passages. We see the empty black mouth of a passage and hear Len's voice talking to Frankie. In several shots of each, we come from full-length shots to closer ones, at last only of Frankie's listening eyes and Len's head as he follows the beam of his flashlight, as it searches the walls. Len looks down, and the disk of light falls from ceiling and walls to the toes of a pair of shoes poking out from around the end of a wall. With stealthy feet Len approaches the edge. We face the alcove, as his arm flings around the corner across its emptiness, and the camera pans down to a pair of shoes, their owner gone (*The Yellow Ballon,* J. Lee-Thompson).

A frame too may leave out the unattended things that surround a person in thought, as when Dr. Borg, sitting in his car in the last stage of his journey to Lund, reflects on the events of the day. All we saw of the car around his head has given place to a featureless blackness (*Wild Strawberries,* Ingmar Bergman).

In these examples the camera never moves: it shows what a person sees from where he stands. The approaching and retreating camera can, as well, show a person's awareness shrinking or growing by discarding or bringing in parts of his surroundings; and the panning camera can glide into a scene and out of another both at the same time.

In close-up, Julian's hand slides idly off the telegraph key as he works in the post office, and he hears in imagination the laugh of the baron's daughter whom he loves, and her "bon soir." Her voice is now gradually overlain by other voices, those of people waiting at his window. We retreat from his hand and bring into the frame the window and the waiting people just as their angry voices enter his awareness (*Passionnelle,* Edmond T. Greville).

Where the river tumbles down over an outcrop, all but one of the party, (which was on its way to blow up the bridge) are bathing and laughing. The camera pans along the rock into unknown space offscreen with one of the Burmese bearers. The swiftly sweeping frame line lets in a Japanese soldier. The Burmese suddenly stops, and they face. We share the frightening moment, the unexpected antithesis of mood (*The Bridge on the River Kwai,* David Lean).

17   Ellipsis in Montage: Leaving Out Time

Only when we conceive a complete whole can we sense an ellipsis from it; only then can a director count on the viewer supplying what is missing; and the gap a viewer is most able to fill is one of time.

Showing only beginnings and endings of such events as journeys, meals, and rides on elevators is a common way of ridding a film of the trivial. Seven children and their teacher are seated at a dining table. During grace we pan from the left along the serving plates, with salad, potatoes, and sausages on them. Then we pan back from the right over several dinner plates with only the leavings on them (*The Lone Climber*, William C. Hammond). We see a bell ring. Firemen rush in from all sides, in various kinds of undress, they listen and rush off. Almost at once they are back in uniform, sliding down the pole (*The Fireman*, Charles Chaplin).

Noriko and her father, Professor Somiya, are standing in long shot on a station platform, and we see their train coming. In the next shot it enters a tunnel. (The stopping and boarding are left out.) Both are seen, half-length, strap-hanging. "You brought my manuscript?" he asks. She smiles, "Yes." From outside we see the traveling train. Now we see her still holding the strap and him sitting. He looks up, "Like to change places?" She shakes her head, smiling. From the rear of the train, we look along the side as it speeds to Tokyo. Now we see both of them seated and reading. This both condenses the journey, and suggests a side of the daily life they have happily shared for the years during which she has lived at home and cared for her father (*Late Spring*, Yasujiro Ozu).

This lends itself to the jocular unexpected. A girl in school uniform is demurely singing "Sioux City Sue." Articles of her clothing fly out of the frame, to reveal a dark, smart, close-fitting evening dress, slit up the thigh, and the style of singing changes to match it (*Seven Days Ashore*, John H. Auer). As Achille prepares to go in a hurry, the camera pans to a bed and a picture above it vanishes. It pans to a table and cigarettes are suddenly gone and over to a cupboard where a tie disappears from off a rack. Then we see Achille in long shot racing across the floor, tie in hand, as if he had now slowed his pace enough that the camera could catch him (*L'Eternel Retour*, Jean Delannoy). An eccentric detective steps behind a tree from one side, and reappears on the other side as a Cossack. He does it again to become a Turk, again to become an artist, and at last comes out as himself again. Not only was the camera stopped while he changed but while he went somewhere else to do it, for he could not have changed behind a tree barely a foot across (*Hellzapoppin*, Harold C. Potter).

It is a matter of indifference whether part of a shot is cut out, or whether it is never shot in the first place.

18   Ellipsis in Montage: Leaving Out Space

A gap in time is also a gap in space; but matters like meals or journeys are thought of more as occupying time. Now and then the notion of space is stronger, and we think more of a leap from place to place.

We see Buster Keaton, for example, leap off the parapet of London Bridge, after reading an advertisement for travel in Canada. Then he is shown wading out of the sea at Nova Scotia (*The Railrodder*, Gerald Potterton).

19   Ellipsis in Montage: Parenthesis or Bridge

Where there is a marked alteration of situation, as in the weather, or where the length of a time lapse, either felt or in fact, is a necessary part of the story, the director may stuff the gap where the ellipsis occurs, to make the lapse or change more plausible, or make us ready for it. Daniel Arijon uses the term pause;[9] it is also the figure *parenthesis*, described thus by Puttenham, "where ye will seeme for larger information or some other purpose, to peece or graffe in the middest of your tale an unnecessary parcel of speech, which neuer the lesse may be thence without any detriment to the rest."[10]

In logic, there must be a case where the space between is too small to be seen. Acknowledging applause, a dancer wearing a long white dress bows, quite out of the white patch printed on the fluted wall by a spotlight. Rising into the circle of light again, her dress is a black one. The time it took to change the dress is left out by merely stopping the camera while she is away. The place and the situation stay the same, and the director wishes to stress, not a lapse of time but a lapse of no time. There is thus no gap to fill (*The Common Touch*, John Baxter).

Ellipsis by compression may tell the lapse of time, if there is little change in the character of what is happening. As the doors open, students clatter into the gallery of a theater. They talk, they eat. Some are there to see the ballet and some to hear the music, which one of their professors has composed. As this goes on, a white line of capitals moves across the foot of the frame, "FORTY-FIVE MINUTES LATER," and as the words cross, we hear the orchestra tuning up. Since what went on during this time changed little in character, the director merely tells us that this went on twenty times as long as we see it on the screen (*The Red Shoes*, Michael Powell and Emeric Pressburger).

The most suitable filling between scenes may be nothing. In *Desert Victory* (Roy Boulting), we see men making ready, the tanks moving up at sunset, waiting troops. Narration continues to a black screen, and then a wrist with a watch rises into it, giving the time, a minute or two before zero hour. The blank screen catches the emptiness of waiting.

If what fills the gap is something more than mere space between, if it informs us, prepares us, moves the story along, it is less open to Puttenham's word, unnecessary.

Take two cases of bridging a journey. In *Candlelight in Algeria* (George King), Dr. Muller and Susan enter his car. Dissolve to a motor car wheel, seen from the side, full size on the frame. Dissolve to their alighting from the car. This scene is like a bump on the path of the narrative. As Peter Henderson rides in a car with two others, he asks them to deliver a letter for him the next day. "I'll tell you the story briefly," he says. Here follow three shots of the car traveling the streets. Then we are again inside the car as he is saying, "That's a rough outline" (*The Common Touch*, John Baxter). The beginning and end of a story or journey need something between them to signify a break in time, and in the second case the something had to do with the flow of the story.

In *The Third Man* (Sir Carol Reed), the caretaker of the building where Lime had lived says to Martins down in the street, "Come back at night, when my wife is out; she doesn't like me to talk." Inside, he closes the casement, turns toward us, and stands still, his eye held by some thing or person. Martins goes to Anna's flat, where she leads him on to talk about Harry Lime, until they leave. On reaching the building, they learn from the crowd outside that the caretaker has been killed. The talk between Martins and Anna does not forward the action or add much to what we know of Lime: it is to keep apart in time their calls on the caretaker.

Maryutka, a sharpshooter, with two other soldiers, is escorting a White Army officer across the Aral Sea, so that he can be questioned at the earliest moment. The rest of the company are marching around the sea. We see the boat in several shots of clear bright weather and brisk breeze. The officer, who likes to sail, enjoys the experience of "sailing himself into prison." Then we see the rest of the party, marching along the shore, the sky black, a gale blowing, and a hat blown away. "They'll have to sit the storm out at Maritzka," one of them says. Then we see the boat again in long shot, its hull small in a high sea, the sail collapsed, against a dark sky, in a high wind. The parenthesis here, bridging a change from fair weather to storm, prepares us by showing the storm's force ashore (*The Forty-First*, G. Chukhrai).

20   Ellipsis in Montage: Anadiplosis as Bridge

The neatest way of bridging a leap in time is the anadiplosis.

We approach a girl as she blows out her birthday candles, ending on the cake in close-up. This dissolves to the figures *1880*, which, as the camera retreats, we see to be on another birthday cake, ten years later. The leap is from birthday to birthday, through a pattern common to both, which gives a flow to the story despite the long break in time (*Fanny by Gaslight*, Anthony Asquith).

The commander of U-boat 37 has instructed a landing party to go ashore for provisions. Before the party leaves the deck he raises his hand saying, "Heil Hitler!" We expect the landing party to reply with the same salute. They do, but now they are lined up ashore. There is a substitution of the second salute for the first: left out are their journey from ship to shore, and the salute of the landing party commander, the one we see them returning (*The Forty-Ninth Parallel*, Michael Powell).

In *Knight without Armour* (Jacques Feyder) Fothergill is briefed as a British agent. He is in Moscow under the name of Peter Uranoff, to penetrate the revolutionary movement; "There is an Axelstein who keeps a bookshop . . ." This is cut to Axelstein speaking to Fothergill about one of the revolutionists, "I hope nothing has happened. He is such a hothead . . ." It is clear from the conversation that enough time has elapsed for the now-bearded Fothergill to have become a trusted member. The forward reference to Axelstein is the link. What is left out here as having no bearing—all the early stages of meeting and establishing confidence—could well be the heart of a different story.

The forward reference can be antithetical. Calvin B. Marshall is angry. Through a mistake of his secretary, the bath for a new house of his in the highlands of Scotland is being carried very slowly by a tiny vessel, the "puffer" *Maggie*. He manages to find and board the boat with every intention of taking the cargo off at the next landing. The skipper talks of a possible fog, which might make landing difficult. "How do you know?" Marshall asks. "Well," says the skipper, "by the way the wind is blowing, the time of the year. What you might call sailor's instinct." Marshall looks up at the clear sky. "Fog!" he says contemptuously. This dissolves to his face at the same angle peering through a dense veil of it (*The Maggie*, Alexander Mackendrick).

21   Ellipsis in Montage: Asyndeton or Jump Cut

The jump cut is an ellipsis which, in Louis D. Giannetti's words, "is confusing or disorienting in terms of time or place."[11] This arises from an absence of bridges, in story, in logic, in figure, or otherwise between shots or sequences. It is like *asynde-*

ton in literature—a lack of connection between a series of words, phrases, or clauses, normally provided by conjunctions:[12]

> The enemy said, "I will pursue, I will overtake,
> I will divide the spoil; my lust shall be satisfied upon them;
> I will draw my sword, my hand shall destroy them."[13]

> Caesar upon the victorie he obtained against Pharnax King of Bithinie . . . wrote to the Senate: Veni, vidi, vici . . . I came; I saw; I conquered.[14]

"It wants," writes Puttenham, "good band or coupling."[15]

In a series of shots, the surf is breaking on a shore. Abruptly a woman is lying in the surf; just as abruptly she is stranded above the surf; then on the sand, looking up, no sign of the sea is seen at all. She is then beside a huge root of a tree, reaching up and climbing it. If we disregard the small amount of movement, this is like a series of stills in a comic strip, between each of whose frames a clear leap is implied in time and often in place. As with a missing word in the literary form, the missing movement here is added by the viewer (*At Land*, Maya Deren).

Scarlet Street (Fritz Lang) provides a good example of the cumulation of elliptical snippets into a single event. A detective is seated in the foreground, with Johnny beyond his desk, seated in front of three plainclothesmen and a uniformed officer. The detective lifts exhibits from a drawer, saying as he does, "found in the murdered girl's car. . . . This is your handkerchief, her blood. . . . her diamond ring worth $300 . . . this ice pick is yours too—your fingerprints are on it. . . ." Then, one after another, people speak as if they were giving evidence, although nothing in the blank wall behind the chair that each sits in suggests a court:

JOHNNY:	She didn't paint the pictures.
STREET PAINTER:	He (Johnny) brought me two of them to sell.
DELLAROWE:	In my opinion she was a very great artist.
BARTENDER:	He was mean when he was drunk.
MARCHETTI:	He killed her with my ice pick.
MILLY:	She said, "Here comes Johnny." (Over the telephone)
JANEWAY:	She never let anyone see her paint—that was one of her peculiar characteristics.
ADELE, CROSS'S WIFE:	What Mr. Cross painted he just stole from someone.
CHRIS CROSS	(who actually killed Kitty, the girl who stole his paintings and gave the money to Johnny): What my wife, my former wife, says, is correct—I really can't paint. My copies were so bad I had to destroy them.
JOHNNY:	For God's sake, he's lying.

This is a masterly distillation from hours of testimony of the points that convinced a jury of Johnny's guilt.

Most western viewers today would hardly find these disorienting, but whether they are or not is related to what Bela Balazs calls the visual culture of the moment.[16] Cuts that in his time would quite bewilder an audience appear to be clear today.

In *Alice in the Cities* (Wim Wenders) Philip, a German reporter, finds himself in Amsterdam with a nine-year-old girl, whose mother did not, as she promised, come on the next plane. Here is one succession of shots:

Phillip at the hotel, dozing in bed.

Phillip and Alice at the roadside; there is a sound of traffic; she takes his picture with his Polaroid camera.

We see the picture with her face reflected on it.
The two of them walking in a city square. "I'm hungry. You walk too fast."
The two sitting in a restaurant. "Why do we have to eat in such a cheap place?"
Such asyndetons are not uncommon today.

The jump cut has long been accepted where several threads of a story keep return-ing. The Boy is with his confessor before leaving for the gallows. The governor's train speeds on its tracks. The Detective and the Dear Little One hurtle by car to intercept the train and prove the Boy innocent. In France, troops bent on killing the Huguenots enter the streets, and a man in a long cloak hides a child beneath it. In Babylon, Belshazzar and his Beloved speak of the city he will build her. Cyrus watches his passing troops from his chariot. To warn Belshazzar of the coming attack, the Mountain Girl on her chariot gallops like the wind. Prosper hears of the threat to the Huguenots, and sets out for the house of Brown Eyes. She wakes up. The Mercenary Soldier who lusts for her stops at her door. . . . The Rocking Cradle (theme) is followed here by Christ on his way to the Cross. The Bacchanale is being danced on the great steps of Babylon. . . . The Mountain Girl is still on the road. . . . The steaming pistons, the racing car, the priest, and the Boy talking . . .Brown Eyes cowers from the soldier . . . a foot pressing a pedal, train and car now in the same frame. . . . There is not merely a break of continuity at every switch from one story to another but the switches cover jumps in each separate story (*Intolerance*, D. W. Griffith).

The Day of the Jackal (Fred Zinnemann) is built entirely on showing, turn about, an assassin's preparations, and on the other hand, progress made by Inspector Lebel in finding out who the Jackal is and where he is. The Jackal nearly collides with another car. Both cars are off the road, and the other driver is dead. The Jackal examines the other car faced from inside by a fiercely barking dog. Then we see him busy painting it blue, having driven it somewhere else. We are not shown how he disposed of the dog nor his driving the car away, and between the two shots is a scene from the other thread of the story.

22   Inclusion: Simultaneous Montage

It has been pointed out by Jean Mitry that when two events are brought together, whether by editing one after the other, by panning from one to the other, or by showing both at once in the same frame, they combine in the viewer's mind with equal effect (pl. 26).[17] To leave some things out of the frame implies an intention to include what stays in. Ellipsis implies what may be called a simultaneous montage or intentional bringing together of all the events present upon the screen at one time.[18] In an effective ellipsis, as much rigor must go to choosing and arranging what is left in, as to choosing what should not be there at all.[19]

23   Inclusion: Creating a Relation

When Joris Ivens shows the counterweight in the foreground passing down and obscuring for a moment the bridge beyond, which is rising, he is showing the two as related parts of an operation (*The Bridge*). And the angle that shows clearly what an umbrella is for is down from above showing it pelted by *Rain* (Joris Ivens).

We see in a down shot the summit of the nearest building and all the storys down to the street. Large, in the foreground, a window cleaner emerges from a window and hooks on a safety belt. The man in relation to the place conveys the danger of the work (*Window Cleaner*, Jules Bucher).

Ivan, sad after the drowning of Miarichka, bends to drink from the river and is seen through the water. It was, from the shape of the lips breaking the surface, as if they kissed it, as if it were she, as if it were a way to follow and find her (*Shadows of Our Forgotten Ancestors*, Sergei Parazhdanov).

When a sculptured group is unveiled, Charlie is discovered reposing comfortably in the middle. He is shooed down and abused by speaker, police and public. As Charlie stands, he looks at the huge admonishing hand of one of the stone figures, and from where we see them, it looks as if the thumb of the hand and Charlie's nose touch, as if he were cocking a snook at all present (*City Lights*, Charles Chaplin).

Howard Justin went to the theater to discover that Stephen Stratton and Howard's wife had not used their theater tickets. He throws on the table the program of the play they would have seen. When the two arrive home, there is a close-up of her hand, pausing over the program on its way to a cigarette (*The Passionate Friends*, David Lean).

Carol has persuaded Stefan, partly against his will, that he can serve Poland best by composing music and raising money by concerts. They are riding in a taxi, seen from the side. His head and body partly obscure hers: they seem close. The voice of a newsboy shouts, "Germans in Paris: read all about it." Now we see them full face, a clear space between them as he reads the paper and she talks quickly to him. He is resolved now to join the air force, and the space we see between them reflects a divergence of purpose (*Dangerous Moonlight*, Brian Desmond Hurst).

24   Inclusion: Suggesting Separation

The arrangement of what is included can thus convey separation or no-relation. Frankie feels he has brought about the death of another boy. He is being black-mailed, but feels that he cannot speak to his parents about it. In one shot his parents are large in the foreground, either side of a table, and Frankie, much smaller, comes in through a door in the background. There is the same sense of distance in another shot where Frankie's face is in close-up as he lies on the floor, and his father, above, beyond and far off enters a door, tying his dressing gown (*The Yellow Balloon*, J. Lee-Thompson).

Smith enters the concert hall during rehearsal, and his cellist friend is to introduce him to the conductor. As he tries in vain to catch the cellist's eye from the edge of the stage, Smith, from where we see him, is barred from the great world of music by a fence of closely set wooden columns through which he reaches out as from a jail (*Tales of Manhattan*, Julien Duvivier).

After a mental illness, Lady Franklin regains her confidence by talking to a chauffeur, whose car she hires by the day. In time, he comes to contemplate proposing marriage. One evening, as he calls and waits by the car, we and he see Lady Franklin through the window, walking along the upper hall, in blue dress and fur coat, slowly, without a sound. She walks down the stairs, and at the foot speaks to the housekeeper. Seen through the diamond leaded panes, distant, small, unhurried, she moved at her own pace in another different not-fully-understood world (*The Hireling*, Alan Bridges).

25   Inclusion: Comparative Size

The poles of insignificance and dominance, whether felt or actual, are frequently shown by size.

Oliver Twist, coming toward us bowl in hand asking for more food, is tiny beside the beadle's right leg and the beadle's right hand holding a stick that fill the left of the frame (*Oliver Twist*, David Lean). The composer Smith, timid at meeting a famous conductor, enters the concert hall by the stage door. The camera looks distantly down from the roof, and in the broad converging planes of walls and floor, a tiny door opens, and in its little white patch is the speck Smith (*Tales of Manhattan*, Julien Duvivier). A peasant and his mother have come to St. Petersburg. Left, in the foreground, are the two great forelegs of an equestrian statue. To the right the peasant and his mother, very tiny, cross the square below. Beneath the feet of power, the powerless peasants (*The End of St. Petersburg*, V. I. Pudovkin).

A change in relative size can reflect a change in situation. Martin Schulz, who has come under the sway of the Baron von Freischer, a supporter of Hitler, enters by a door left, quite small. Elsa, his wife, to right frame, near us, is lighting candles at the table. He says they are invited by the Baron for the evening. Elsa says it is a great honor but this was the night her grandmother was coming. In close-up Martin curtly says, "We are going to Baron von Freischer's." Half-length, Martin's back is now large on the screen and Elsa small in the distance (*Address unknown*, William Cameron Menzies). Workers in *The Crab Canning Ship* (So Yamamura) burst into Asakawa's cabin. The superintendent's torso fills the left frame, his revolver covering the crowd that huddles at the right top corner. As the confrontation continues, the workers little by little come closer and seem larger. Then we see one the same height as Asakawa, face to face with him. Suddenly the worker strikes down the revolver, and the crowd seizes the superintendent. The growing size of the workers on the screen signifies their growing sense of power.

It should be noted that where, as in *Alice in Wonderland* (Dallas Bower and Leo Hurwitz), the actual, not the figurative, size, changes, distance from the camera (for which the eye corrects) is not enough. Objects that show the true scale must be kept out, and only those left in that show the supposed one consistently. We never see Alice growing smaller, but in two successive shots, the fan she is holding doubles in size. A glass-topped table, which comes to her waist, is eight times as high as she in the next shot. The phial she drinks from and puts down on the floor has a broad flange for a base, and later swimming out of the sea of tears, it is up on this flange that she and the rest climb ashore.

26 Inclusion: As Commentary

Assuming (as we must) that the edge of the frame and what it reveals is (like the hem of a skirt) a deliberate boundary, we can often infer from what it includes a director's comment.

Bader is a reckless airman and a natural leader. He has just been married. As he and his wife come out of the Register Office, he says in answer to something she says, "Me for the quiet life," and as they pass off right frame they uncover a news poster that reads "HITLER SUCCEEDS HINDENBURG." History will contradict his resolve, the director suggests (*Reach for the Sky*, Lewis Gilbert). Masterful Maggie has taken on the task of building the confidence of Willie, the shoemaker who works for her father, and is making clear to the daughter of the house where he lodges, that from then on he is walking out with her, Maggie. At one point, she has sent the intimidated-looking Willie outside. As he leans his ear toward the window to make out something of what is happening, a Salvation Army procession is coming down the street, whose large dark banner bears the words, Beware the Wrath to Come (*Hobson's Choice*, David Lean).

John L. Sullivan, a film director bent on gaining personal experience of privation, dresses up as a tramp, and on his first night out, sleeps in a hostel. In the morning when awakened for breakfast, he raises his head, and stares with disbelief toward us—where his feet would be. We move back, and in the outraged face between the big bare feet, we sense a director's comment—Sullivan had thought that all the poor were honest but exploited (*Sullivan's Travels*, Preston Sturges).

In such a figure, that would have been called *significatio*, it is for the viewer to piece together the meaning implied by the director, just as in law a plaintiff may prove an innuendo or secondary meaning in what may seem a perfectly innocent statement.

27 Inclusion: Inner State

A director may project, by what he includes, a character's inner state.

Defiance rages in the great fires that burn behind the burghers of Pskov, their gray heads bare, bound and on their knees (*Alexander Nevsky*, S. M. Eisenstein). Anger explodes in the steam that thrusts, puffs, and throbs from the factory behind the angry peasant Peter (*The Golden Mountains*, S. Yutkevich).

Chris Cross is smiling as he reads of an exhibition of his paintings. A messenger comes to say that a man outside, calling himself a detective, wishes to see him. We leap back from Chris to see him in profile, and the frame now includes the word "Cashier," large on the glass wall of his cage. We share his fear that his theft of money for Kitty has been discovered (*Scarlet Street*, Fritz Lang).

Two probation officers are talking about a client, sentenced for pilfering and drunkenness. "She was engaged to a pilot and he was killed . . . There must have been thousands of others who had the same thing happen to them . . . . There were so many ways she could have worked it off, and she had to take to drink." Miss Matheson added that she could not agree with Phipps that the girl should be sent back to jail to keep her from drinking. As she turns to right frame, we see beyond her, standing on her filing cabinet, the picture of a naval officer in white uniform. Phipps frowns, looking as if at the picture, and puts his cigarette out. We see the picture in close-up. Taken with what she has said, we guess, and think that Phipps does too, that she has suffered the same loss as her client (*I Believe in You*, Michael Relph and Basil Dearden).

There is an interesting variant in *The Passionate Friends* (David Lean). Howard Justin knows that his wife and Stephen did not see the play they had tickets for, but presses her politely for details. "Have a good evening? Where did you dine? How was the show? Good seats?" Her answers are short. Being uncomfortable, she moves out of the frame entirely, as if it stood for Justin's gaze, and she sought to escape it.

28 Inclusion: Background

Bela Balazs points out that however a setting may match the dominant mood of a scene on stage, it cannot vary from one moment to another as in the film, to strengthen every passing change in feeling.[20] Background and player together are the filmic picture, and the director may change the composition as he wills at any moment.

Luis Buñuel with down-pointed camera shows us Saint Simeon on his column, his arms uplifted, eyes raised, in the left foreground, and a crowd, evenly spaced out, moving down the frame like a texture beyond him, suggesting his immovable resolve as against the crowd below, constantly changing. Foreground and background are antithetical (*San Simeon del Desierto*, Luis Buñuel).

In early shots of the Tuckers' farm, two thirds of the frame was sky. After the rainstorm, all shots are taken down, with water always in the background, as when Sam and Tim wade and then swim to find their cow. The sky was never more than a narrow line at the top, and below it flowing water, or rainsodden, pool-patterned ground (*The Southerner*, Jean Renoir).

29 Inclusion: Offscreen Space—Synecdoche

Offscreen space is part of the background, and is implied from what we see on the screen or from sounds heard.

In *Forbidden Games* (René Clement), the heads of two feuding families are down in a grave fighting, as the rest on the ground above shout abuse. Now and then a fist pokes up into the frame to remind us of the doings going on below the frame line. The same applies if something leaves the frame for outside. In *Western Union* (Fritz Lang), after a duel of shots with his brother, Vance Shaw is mortally wounded. We see him lying on the steps of a barbershop. There is a close-up of his hand, the fingers clinging still to the ledge of the window. The grip slackens, and his arm and hand fall out of the frame to join the body that must lie there. Besides being a synecdoche, the hand's dropping from out the frame is the metaphorical departure from life of him whose hand it is.

If we are shown a part, by way of synecdoche, of a thing that continues off the screen, we project the space required by the rest. We follow Macheath as he gallops in silhouette across a dusky landscape to a gallows. When he pulls up his horse, only the corpse's boots are within the frame, and Macheath's head is below in close-up, reading a notice hung from the boots. Having seen the corpse from far off, the boots project an indeterminate space above the frame (*The Beggar's Opera*, Peter Brook).

If we see the effect of an offscreen event, we tend to fancy space where we place the cause. Dumbo falls with Timothy Q. Mouse down out of the frame. The three crows left in the frame, and the tree they are perched on tremble again and again, as the falling two (we assume) strike one limb after another (*Dumbo*, Walt Disney).

Patrolman Bandy was killed in Wanda Siscovitch's speakeasy. McNeil is trying to persuade her to change her identification of the murderer. She shouts back at him. The roar of a passing train drowns their speech, during which time they both turn to stare in our direction. By doing this they create an expectation of something behind us, and thus of space there. As the sound of the train dies down, we cut to a man in black leather jacket, pointing a revolver from the doorway (*Call Northside 777*, Henry Hathaway).

If we hear a sound from off the frame, the frame seems to expand in that direction. The chief of staff alone in the frame speaks toward the right, asking questions. An answer comes from off the screen, and the speaker walks into the frame from the right (*The Defense of Siberia*, The Brothers Vassiliev).

In the court sequence shown in *Phantom Lady* (Robert Siodmak), neither judge, jury, nor counsel is seen—they are only heard. We see the tall doors of the courtroom, the reporter's notebook, with the name of the case at the top and his hand beginning to write, Inspector Burgess mopping his forehead, observing someone, speaking to a constable, the public benches, Carol asking what the verdict was (for someone coughed), and her neighbor saying, "What did you expect—guilty of course." Here half the room was offscreen, projected by sound and glance.

The offscreen space may lie behind something seen on the screen, perhaps a wall. Dr. Riordan has kidnapped a man and is planning his undetectable murder. Hearing a knock, he carefully locks his laboratory, and standing in his anteroom, he sees a trail of white smoke drifting across the bright blank of a doorway. After a pause, during which we share the doctor's misgivings, a slight amiable man comes around the jamb, smoking a pipe, and introduces himself as Superintendent Finsbury (*The Hidden Room*, Edward Dmytryk).

Noël Burch rightly remarks that our sense of offscreen space is a fleeting one, lasting little longer than the stimulus arousing it, so strong a fence is the four-sided frame cut in the blackness.[21]

30 Inclusion: Superimposition

Superimposing an image upon another, both of which are seen at one time, is a way of including on one frame things that because of separation in space or time or other technical obstacle, cannot be brought together in one shot, or which it is more effective to show in two layers.

There is a superimposition we see every day. Davy is leaving home. His mother has made him sandwiches for the journey, and, with his father, he leaves. We pan from them as they walk away, to her as she stands looking through the window, and the two she is looking at are reflected in the glass, superimposed on her. After they have walked off the glass, only the shafthouse is left reflected. Suddenly she bows her head. The departing men in the glass were the source of the distress we see, and the shafthouse was the mine no longer part of Davy's life but still of hers (*The Stars Look Down*, Sir Carol Reed).

Most superimpositions are, of course, composed in the printing. Function may be conveyed by an eye imposed on a camera lens, or engine pistons imposed on a moving ship or on men stoking its furnaces. (*The Man With a Movie Camera*, Dziga Vertov; *Drifters*, John Grierson). Zahrat's face watching a carrier pigeon flying out of sight is superimposed on the pigeon (*Chu Chin Chow*, Walter Forde).

In *Reach for the Sky* (Lewis Gilbert), three parts of a situation are emphasized by superimposition. As Bader tries to walk for the first time on his artificial legs, we must, of course, come close to the legs. We must also be reminded of the tremendous effort and pain involved, expressed in the superimposed face. We should see too how the situation is judged from the outside, and for this his instructor's face is added. It would have been easy to show all three in one shot, but from further off. By superimposition, we see them all more vividly in close-up, and the implication of each with both of the others is much more strongly felt.

A like relation can be brought about, not by overlaying a transparent image but insetting an opaque one. In *Run Wild, Run Free* (Richard C. Sarafian), on a close-up of the eye of a pony, the pupil is replaced by a shot of the little boy, Philip, who is watching him.

31 Repetition

If we leave out from each of a series of events all that makes them differ, and leave in the ways in which they are alike, we are in effect drawing a likeness between them.

If these likenesses are shown one after the other, they may convey sameness, speed, or frequency.

A line of men is carrying bags from a sinking barge. When they work faster, all we see of each trip is a bag on its way from shoulder to pile. By cutting out the rest of each bag's journey, we see more bags fall in a given time, and presume a faster pace of work (*My Universities*, Mark Donskoi). Sergeant Troy throws up a sword three times as he stands nearly silhouetted on the top of a slope, and only the last time do we see him catch it, enhancing thus an impression of speed and agility (*Far from the Madding Crowd*, John Schlesinger).

When Itsuki returns to his office after a trip to Europe, we see him looking out of his office window. Then, in half-length shot, a clerk enters his door with papers, a second with a roll of blue prints, and a third announcing a meeting. All we see of each is his entrance. The ellipsis of the rest brings out the recurrent pattern of Itsuki's day, one person after another making demands on his time (*Kaseki*, Masaki Kobayashi).

Ellipsis—pruning a whole down to a part—and synecdoche—given a part, to build it into a whole—are two ways of speaking and of living. By ellipsis, the world becomes the small part we know; from this part, we try, by synecdoche, to reach the remainder. Memory works by ellipsis, leaping from time to time, salvaging synecdochical fragments from years of living, some from the joy or pain they brought us, some from a curious rhythm or pattern, and some—the merest trivia—for no reason at all.

11
Metonymy

1 Forms and Distinctions

It may be more dramatic to replace an image of a person by an image of what an audience knows belongs to the person, a voice, a shadow, a cap, a ring, or a footstep. A mere part may thus bring to mind a whole web of connected ideas and happenings, briefly but in a vague imaginative richness. If I say, "The Cross comforted me," it means that reflection on the sayings, sufferings, and death of Christ, and all the additions of two thousand years have made my life more bearable. Thirty-two modes of *metonymy* are in Macbeth, one of the fuller treatments.[1] Of these, the following may be found in film:

   i. Giving a tool instead of its user.
      Louis Kossuth said, "Even bayonets think" (those who wield bayonets).
  ii. Putting the effect for the cause or the product for the producer.
      She sowed the ground with larkspurs (with seeds that would grow into larkspurs).
 iii. Putting the cause for the effect, the source for the product.
      He was a slave of the grape (of the wine made from it).
  iv. Substituting the badge or attire for the person wearing it.
      The Crown approved the bill (the person wearing the crown).
   v. Using the container for what is contained.
      That is too dear for my purse (it would cost more than the money my purse contains).
  vi. Substituting a place for an event that happened there.
      He had fought at Dunkirk (in the battle fought there in 1940).
 vii. Using the abstract instead of the concrete.
      He heard more profanity that day than he had in all his life up till then (swear words).
viii. Using the concrete instead of the abstract.
      The old Adam was strong in him (a tendency toward the sin committed by Adam).
  ix. Putting the voice for the speaker, the sound for the object making it.
      The buzzer called him downstairs (the person pressing the button of the buzzer).

A few distinctions are important, remembering always that figures overlap and that the same image may be seen in more than one way. Aristotle indeed put together metaphor, metonymy, and synecdoche.[2]

Three floating hats, of sailors drowned by White guards, are carried further in to shore by every shallow wave. It may be the dead seeking to come back to mend their defeat, or the inevitable return of the Reds to rout their enemies, and thus the hats become a metaphor. Or the hats may remind us only of the sailors who wore them and are thus metonymies—not nouns but pronouns, that stand in place of their owners (*We from Kronstadt*, E. Dzigan).

A bowler hat is prima facie evidence that its owner has been in the room where it lies—like a pronoun it stands in place of its owner and thus is metonymy. If he were a policeman smothered by members of the Resistance, and his bowler hat falls under the table he lies on, its rocking on its crown with quicker and shorter oscillations until it stops may give by metaphor the noun Death (*Hangmen Also Die*, Fritz Lang).

Besides this, the pronoun is distinct from the adjective. If a person is stabbed with a hypodermic syringe, and instead of her cry, there is an offscreen wail from a departing train (*Judex*, Georges Franju); or if, instead of a moving acrobat riding his trapeze, we see a moving audience as he sees it (*Variety*, E. A. Dupont), we are switching a descriptive adjective to a noun it does not belong to. We are saying "The wailing woman" when the train did the wailing, and "The acrobat watched the moving audience" when the acrobat himself was doing the moving. This is hypallage or transferred epithet.

While substitution underlies all three figures, in metaphor the substitution is double. When Pericles said that the loss of the city's youth was as if spring had been taken out of the year, spring replaces the young men, and the year, the city; thus,

> Spring is to the year
> As young men are to the city.[3]

2 Metonymy and History

It may be remarked that many works of art start as metonymies. Saints' remains like those displayed by the "dexterous Capuchins" of Macaulay; statues like that of Shelley's Ozymandias; mementos like letters, pressed leaves, and remembered music; ruins restored and repeopled in fancy; scars that speak of battles; the shaman's and the sexual deviant's fetish, these are a few of the ways in which, by metonymy, imagination ekes a present fragment into a rich revival of lives long dead. Eisenstein has described the start of *Alexander Nevski*: "a few broken broadswords, a helmet, and a couple of suits of chain mail preserved in museums are all the relics of those far-off times."[4] He read what the chronicles said of Alexander, "He is taller than any man on earth, his voice is like a clarion call." He read the lives of the saints and trod the walls of Alexander's towns. In what still stood of Great Novgorod, Eisenstein looked at the land from the battlements and strove to imagine what might have been there in Alexander's day. He touched a pair of mildewed boots with pointed toes, long in the mud of the marshy Volkhov, a drinking vessel, an ornament worn on the breast. Within and around these fragments Eisenstein built his twelfth-century Russia (pl. 1).

3 The Modes: A Thing Instead of Its Owner or User

The most common mode in film is the thing that stands for its owner or user. It is hard to avoid a feeling that this is a vestige of the law of contact, by which principle of sympathetic magic things once in touch continue to act on one another even when separated (pl. 15).

i. The clue is this mode at its most familiar. As he passes Detective Sergeant Spencer, Stevie is carrying a couple of film canisters. The sergeant shows an interest, reads the labels and exclaims, "Bartholomew the Strangler!" Later, inspecting the site where a bomb blew up a bus, the sergeant lifts a battered metal lid, and we read on the label the title, *Bartholomew the Strangler* (*Sabotage*, Alfred Hitchcock). Another sergeant stops and warns a driver who has been traveling well over the speed limit. A devil with trident lunges ahead from his radiator. The sergeant is later called by radio to inspect a collision. He examines the wreckage. He stoops to pick up a cap thrown from the flattened car: a devil and fork now darting nowhere in particular. He throws it down (*Traffic with the Devil*, Gunther von Frisch).

Bridie Quilty, an Irish girl who has had a change of heart about helping the German Intelligence Service, German and British agents, and Lieutenant Baynes, who is in love with her, have all been seen among the crowd in a seaside ballroom. Several times her number is called after the raffle is drawn. Twice more we hear her number called, after the image has changed proleptically to gleaming cobblestones, lying on which is the ticket for 211. We follow the fingers that pick it up to the face of Baynes looking at it. This anadiplosis answers, not "Who has number 211?" (this we know) but "Where is the holder of number 211?" She must have passed along this street (*I See a Dark Stranger*, Frank Launder).

ii. These are clues found by a person in the story. Other signs are left by the director for us.

A homicidal psychotic had given sweets to a little girl and gone for a walk with her. Her ball bounces out from a clump of bushes and comes to rest (*M*, Fritz Lang).

Anthony Farrant is about to leave Germany with information prejudicial to Krogh and Heller, who have unsuccessfully tried to prevent him by winning his money. He puts down his bag and lights a cigarette. He always smokes Gold Flake. Heller's face enters the frame in close-up. A sideling camera keeps in the frame the stride of polished shoes. We approach Farrant who looks up and says to someone offscreen, "Hello." Later in a misty lake, we see in close-up a package of Gold Flake cigarettes, and we tilt up to see the hands and legs of a floating body (*England Made Me*, Peter Duffell).

Norman Maine, a former film star, is an alcoholic dependent on his wife. He has overheard her say that she intends giving up her highly successful career to care for him. He goes to the beach. In a shot of his legs, his dressing gown falls to the sand and he drops his slippers off. In long shot, we see him entering the water and swimming against the breakers. In close-up, the water laps up to the dressing gown, wets it, and then engulfs it (*A Star Is Born*, William A. Wellman).

In all these, in one way or another, the owner or user must be clearly established before the metonymy.

iii. Another use of the mode is to signify what cannot be seen, or what a director chooses not to show. The condition of a patient on the operating table, for example, is told by a bladder that shrinks and swells, slow and even for normal respiration, rapidly for agitated breathing, and when the patient is dead is still (*Green for Danger*, Sidney Gilliatt). Butch Cassidy and the Sundance Kid see their pursuers at night a long distance back as a cluster of torches. They have both ridden one horse, and set the other free to divide their pursuers. In a long down shot, we see the cluster divide into two and the two come together again as the ruse fails. By this the director holds our attention to the fugitives and away from those who pursue them (*Butch Cassidy and the Sundance Kid*, George Roy Hill). Early in *The Man Who Knew Too Much* (1935, Alfred Hitchcock), we learn that Abbott has a chiming watch. Later, the chime identifies him before he is seen, and at the end, in a seemingly empty room, it is heard from behind the door.

iv. It is of great use to convey inner states, also invisible.

Tommy Swann is an escaped convict, and his trousers are drying in front of the fire. Hearing her stepdaughter Doris enter the kitchen, Rose Sandigate covers the trousers with towels and picks up both together on leaving. Concealing his trousers means concealing Tommy. By a kind of negative metonymy, when Doris cannot find one of the dinner plates, and sets a pudding plate instead, the camera emphasizes the odd plate by moving toward it. The pudding plate is certainly not Tommy's, but it takes the place of one he is using (*It Always Rains on Sunday*, Robert Hamer).

In *City for Conquest* (Anatol Litvak), Burns and Peggy sign their first variety contract. She sinks into a chair and with a joyous kick flings her shoe off into a corner of the room. When the agent leaves, Burns approaches her caressingly. "Let me go . . . . my shoe, Murray, get me my shoe," she says. As she speaks, the camera slowly leaves them, pans over to the corner, and rests on the shoe. Her voice stops; the shoe stays; so does she.

Anna is given a British passport and is put on a train by the sergeant. Looking out, she sees Holly Martins at a counter in the station restaurant, leaves her compartment, and makes him confirm her suspicions that he has agreed to lure Harry Lime into the hands of the police, to get her a passport. Holly has placed his coat around her for the night is cold. In a shot of the two, she tears up the passport. Cut to the double doors of the restaurant, each swinging a different way, and pan down to Holly's coat lying on the floor and bits of torn passport beside it (*The Third Man*, Sir Carol Reed).

Hitchcock has used a bangle eight times in *The Ring* to express a variety of emotions. It was given to the Girl by Corby, when One-Round Sanders believed her to be engaged to him. When she and Corby next see Sanders, she keeps her right hand over the bangle. Just after Sanders has placed the wedding ring on her finger, the bangle slips down her arm to the wrist of the same hand. When Sanders waits at home for her after an important bout and finds her coming home with Corby, he rips the left arm from her dress, and seeing the bangle, tugs it off her arm. After Sanders knocks out Corby, she is standing in the ring by Sanders. Corby nods toward her and gives a slight smile. With her eye on his, she takes the bangle off deliberately. The bangle is given by Corby; it stands for him; snakelike, it has an insidious undertone; it circles the arm like a manacle. Its putting on is Corby's fascination; its taking off is Corby's dismissal.

v. Things often express an owner's personality. Mr. Hulot's car certainly does. It is a small car, with tires little more than bicycle size, and looking rather naked under the tiniest mudguards. The canvas top crouches over the seats at an angle we later see in the owner himself. A large car passes in a cloud of dust, and when we next see the little car, its right wheel is on the grassy shoulder, and it gropes its way back to the road blindly and uncertainly. A bus rounds a corner, and a dog lying on the road leaps up out of the way with alacrity and comes back after the bus has passed. The little car comes to a stop and hoots, but the dog only looks around and rests its head again (*Mr. Hulot's Holiday*, Jacques Tati).

The film with equal ease can keep all personality out. In a down shot, we pan with an umbrella moving toward us. We stop as it meets another umbrella. We see projecting toes and eloquent hands. Then the umbrellas go their ways. It could be anyone (*Sous les Toits de Paris*, René Clair). The soldiers on the famous Odessa steps are always seen in part—if from the side or front, only booted feet and rifles, only full length when facing from us. Thus far, a part for the whole; this is synecdoche. But the soldiers are seen as the tool of an oppressive government, for which they are taken to stand, not as people with personalities. In this sense, there is a metonymy (*The Battleship Potemkin*, S. M. Eisenstein).

vi. Another use of this mode is conveying number. An official explains in *The War Game* (Peter Watkins) that they take the rings from corpses for survivors to identify, and the camera pans down to a bucketful of the dead, represented by proxy. Horses are led off one by one. We hear a shot each time, and a man comes in to throw another collar on to the snow (*Scott of the Antarctic*, Charles Frend).

vii. A thing, of course, can also recall the person who used it. One of the most haunting of such metonymies is in *The Red Shoes* (Michael Powell and Emeric Pressburger). Torn between her husband, who wishes her home, and her impresario, who feels her talent must be used, Victoria Page throws herself in front of a train. That night, after the last chord of the overture, the curtain lights on and the baton poised, Lermontov appears between the curtains. "Miss Page is unable to dance tonight," he says and hesitates, "nor indeed any other night . . . ." The curtains open, and Lyubov holds up the red shoes, which in the story brought the wearer death. He dances as always, but where Victoria Page would have been, there is only the spotlight that would have been following her. The spotlight and the shoes both stood in place of her and her driving passion to dance that led to her death.

4 The Modes: Putting Cause for Effect or Effect for Cause

i. Putting cause for effect is fairly rare.

A soldier keeps repeating into a field telephone, "Kronstadt, Kronstadt . . . ." Smoke drifts over the frame, and as it clears, we see a single wire straggling up to a pole. We glide along the wire, hearing still the urgent call of "Kronstadt," but stop after passing a second post, for the wire trails discontinuously earthwards, and the voice stops. Receiving a message is easily shown; nonreceipt—the effect here—is harder. Showing the cause—the broken line—is also more dramatic (*We from Kronstadt*, E. Dzigan). Charlie in *City Lights* (Charles Chaplin) is a street sweeper. We are not shown what it is he is sweeping up. We guess what it is when he looks with some concern at a long procession of horses crossing the street, and turns suspiciously to watch an elephant pass him. In *Iphigenia* (Michael Cacoyannis), the slaughter of a whole herd of cattle is shown in many shots of a bowman winging an arrow, none of an arrow striking its mark, and only one brief shot, of a prostrate ox.

ii. The reaction shot is a commonplace, which hardly needs examples. Instead of showing the speaker, we see the effect of what he says on the listener, often of greater consequence to the flow of the story. A deaf mute provides a variant, for he cannot listen. He sits in a restaurant beside a friend. In a shot showing the back of a waitress, he smiles at her, but we see from the way the smile droops and vanishes, that he has been discouraged (*Together*, Lorenza Mazzetti).

Seven prisoners escape from a concentration camp. The commandant has seven crosses made on which to hang them when captured. The first man is soon brought back. We see a line of men pollarding a row of six trees to make them crosses. The men are looking toward us where the first cross must be, and so is the guard. On the guard's face is a smile of satisfaction. The workers looking up are still and somber; one of them faints (*The Seventh Cross*, Fred Zinnemann).

A halfwitted seller of newspapers is being chased for showing interest in a girl who sells drinks in the train. He has leaped into a railway carriage and is running toward us between the seats, when suddenly his head is jerked, and the papers under his arm spray out on the floor. There is no sight or sound of the stone that hit him (*Cairo Station*, Youssef Chahine).

iii. The shadow too is one of the commoner filmic metonymies (pl. 26).

On the cracked mud of a desert, an English officer lies prostrated by heat, and the shadow of a large bird glides across his body (*The Four Feathers*, Zoltan Korda). From inside a church, we hear shots. The hands of the priest startle apart, but come together again in prayer. The priest leaves the altar bearing the sacrament. Outside on the church wall, the shadows of helmeted soldiers march in and halt, and the only person we see on the frame is the informer knocking on the door (*The Last Chance*, Leopold Lindtberg).

Some shadows are more abstract. Three paintings of Chris Cross are hung on the wall of a gallery, and the viewing public are vague passing shadows cast upon them (*Scarlet Street*, Fritz Lang). Two pursuers leap from a cab and run. Hannay draws his head back into the window. His train starts moving along the platform. On a white ground, two pairs of running legs remain in the frame right, and an angular shadow moves left off the frame—the owners of the legs had missed the train (*The Thirty-Nine Steps*, Alfred Hitchcock). Johnny Belinda, a deaf girl, is learning to use signs and to read lips. At a dance, her teacher has had her touch a violin and feel the vibration. The dancers cast their shadows on the ceiling—age, color, style of dress all are gone: little remains of them but rhythmic movement, rhythm seen but not heard, as Johnny Belinda sees it (*Johnny Belinda*, Jean Negulesco).

iv. Things may cast lights as well as shadows. As Natasha looks out of a window, burning Moscow flickers on her face and neck (*War and Peace*, Sergei Bondarchuk). As the crofter and his wife wrangle over what he will ask from Hannay, to save him from the police, a light starts to waver slowly across them. It is the headlights of a car coming toward the house on a rough road, and shining through the window. Is it the police (*The Thirty-Nine Steps*, Alfred Hitchcock)?

v. An event may leave a sign or trace that lasts a little while after it is over.

A headwaiter ruffles among the coats behind which Hulot had hid himself. He then goes to the other side and looks down, and we see the prints of wet feet from there up the stairs. Hulot's canoe had sunk (*Mr. Hulot's Holiday*, Jacques Tati). In an air shot, the evasive action taken by an oceangoing tug under attack, is shown by the twisting white band of wake left behind her (*The Key*, Sir Carol Reed). As five people he had no wish to see waited for Ivo Kerns, Suzanne observed on the snowy street the circling tracks of a bicycle. She said with a smile, "He's not coming." A boy on a bicycle, who is much attached to Kerns, often scouted places out before he came (*The Man Between*, Sir Carol Reed).

After a slender dwarf has emerged, the corpulent Hardy thrusts himself into a crowded elevator. The gates close, and the hand of the position indicator flings itself across its half circle, bounces on reaching the basement, and the whole assembly falls from off the wall. The door of the lift opens, and there are the passengers, piled up on the floor (*Blockheads*, John G. Blystone). A soldier, one of six going through a South American forest, is suddenly tipped over and hoisted quickly up out of the frame by one of his legs. The soldier in front of him turns and goes back to find him. He is puzzled, and coming up to half-length, he stops. Just below his head on a leaf, drips of red fall down. He looks up, cries "Indians," and runs (*Aguirre, the Wrath of God*, Werner Herzog).

The most enigmatic sign is that of radar. *School for Secrets* is about how it developed. McVitie, a man of science, takes the first equipment up in a plane. The control room, using the screen, from time to time corrects the plane's direction, till finally the pilot is told that what he is flying toward is "straight ahead." The pilot, flying through an impenetrable mist, with sweat on his brow, replies, "I can't see it." All the time on the dial, the luminous patch comes closer to the center, the fixed end of the sweeping arm, and we know it stands for some object coming closer to the plane. The planes could collide; the other plane, if plane it were, might fire first. But the pilot helped by radar knew more than the other—he knew at least that something was there, and coming closer. It was a Junkers 88, and the English pilot was able to fire first (Peter Ustinov).

5 The Modes: The Badge for the Person

The badge here includes uniforms and insignia, official or occupational dress, and that characteristic of any class.

To start with the everyday, a line of cyclists enters a street and stops. Into an empty frame, with a piece of helmet seen bottom left, a white-gloved palm enters, facing us. It was not the man but the power conferred by his uniform that the cyclists obeyed, to show that is enough (*Rhythm of a City*, Arne Sucksdorf).

A boy is proud of becoming assistant stationmaster. When first he gets his official cap, his mother puts it on him. When he goes to bed, his cap comes off last. When he goes to bed with a girl, she has to take it off, and at the end she lifts it from the platform after he bombs a German train and is killed (*Closely Watched Trains*, Jiri Menzel).

When Her Royal Highness visits the school, there is a down shot of a great round picture hat entering the frame at the bottom, each girl in the line at either side bowing as the hat reaches her (*Mädchen in Uniform*, Leontine Sagan).

Twice at least in *The Battleship Potemkin*, Eisenstein keeps us in mind of the established order, by the priest's cross tapping against his hand and the eagle on the bow of the cruiser.

6 The Modes: The Container for the Contained

The container for the contained is hard to identify in film.

What of the seven crosses prepared for the seven men who escaped from concentration camp? They are not personal possessions that stand in place of their owners, but they are places prepared to receive their bodies, and bring them to mind whenever the crosses are shown to us (*The Seventh Cross*, Fred Zinneman). What of the huge keg that holds the corpse in *The Wrong Box* (Bryan Forbes)? Do we not think of the corpse when we see the keg? What of the shining white dots that shift around in the black rear window as Susan Ann and Dr. Muller drive away? He looks back and remarks that we like to have our friends near when we find ourselves in trouble. The white dots were a car, and the car was a container for the friends (*Candlelight in Algeria*, George King). What of Mr. Hulot's car, which looked and acted like him? Is it a container for him, or a thing used by him? (*Mr. Hulot's Holiday*, Jacques Tati). In fact, in literature, the container is rarely put for the people contained, as when we say, a castle repelled an attack, meaning those contained within who defended it, for in most cases, this is another mode, a thing put in place of the owner or user.

It is not possible to say in film, "He drank the bottle," for what we *see* is his drinking the wine that was in it.

Where we are most likely to find the mode is in such things as the glass of milk in *Suspicion* (Alfred Hitchcock). The glowing white glass stands for the poison we are sure it holds. The black bag of Dr. Willingdon stands for the atomic bomb we are told it contains (*Seven Days to Noon*, John and Roy Boulting). It is not the package carried by Stevie through the streets of London that gives us cause for anxiety: it is the bomb that we know is inside it (*Sabotage*, Alfred Hitchcock).

7   The Modes: A Place for an Event That Happened There

As in literature, this mode is allusive and relies on information possessed by the viewer. A honeymooning couple chat as they lean on the rail of a transatlantic liner. After they leave, we see the life belt that had been behind them, written on it, *S. S. Titanic* (*Cavalcade*, Frank Lloyd). This is taken directly from the play, and is verbal; but in such films as *The Immigrant* (Charles Chaplin), the Statue of Liberty stands for Ellis Island, and the legendary agonies of immigrants passing through it. Here the site we see is not that of a single event but a vaguely imagined class of happenings.

8   The Modes: The Abstract Instead of the Concrete

The chief abstractions used in place of the concrete are pictures for persons pictured and maps for their territories.

A map is greatly smaller in size than the territory it stands for; conventional signs represent real things, but the arrangement of things on the map corresponds to where they are on the ground. In making a map, too, for clarity, we abstract from all the things that are on the ground, certain ones only, perhaps roads, towns, height of land and annual rainfall, but leave out bus stops, schools, and fire stations. This choosing certain things to leave in, and leaving all the rest out, is what abstraction is: a skeletonizing of actuality. If movement through, and occupation of, territory is most of the story, it may be told almost entirely in maps. The English Civil War is such a story. Armies are places in motion, and Newcastle's force becomes a slowly moving black arrow. Fairfax, who harries him, is a white arrow darting out against the black and back again, over and over, quickly. Parliament besieges Oxford: the white arrow divides, going each way around the square that is Oxford and forming a circle, whose inside edge aims arrows at the town. The trained bands from London are a white arrow four times as wide as Prince Rupert's: his black arrow turns back (*The Unquiet Land*, Felicity Kinross).

A photograph may abstract from an actual person half his height, none of his color, and only the one expression he wore when the photograph was taken, and this may be used in place of the person. The Girl in *The Ring* (Alfred Hitchcock) turns the key in the lock to keep her husband out and hugs Corby's picture. Her husband later hurls it across the room (pl. 27). A corrupt police chief takes something from out a coat on a chair, saying that while he is alive his family is in danger. The voice of Driscoll, the investigator, is heard; "For God's sake, Bill!" Cut to Driscoll trying to restrain the chief, then to a half-length picture, surrounded by others of uniformed heads. We hear a shot and a shatter of glass. The face in the center picture is now a hole (*Underworld USA*, Samuel Fuller).

A shot may be part picture, part map. A sailor enters a ship's hatchway. Six decks rise into the frame, one after another, and vanish off the top. We hear the clatter of many feet, but see no men climbing down. Then we see a cabin, as the sailor we saw, and others, enter to meet. What we moved past could just as easily have been a cross-section plan. The scene was partly in this mode, and partly in the next (*We from Kronstadt*, E. Dzigan).

9 The Modes: The Voice for the Speaker, The Sound for the Object Making It—Offscreen Sound

Kathy, trying to shake off a detective, goes through a dance hall. She hurries out through a door, lets it bang, and runs. As we watch her running down the street, we and she hear the door again bang shut. She slows down. The detective catches up and speaks to her (*Odd Man Out*, Sir Carol Reed). Lines of light and black from window shutters are printed on the face of mademoiselle. A clatter of hoofs is heard, loudens, and fades, and at its loudest, a black shadow passes across the bars of light on her face. This happens three times. What is important is not the riders who pass but her listening (*We From Kronstadt*, E. Dzigan).

Whether the hideous crudity of killing or maiming is fit meat for an evolving human race, it certainly does not suit a light romantic mood and it may frighten the viewer more if never shown. *Chu Chin Chow* is thrust back to fall into an open grave. A spear is thrust into the grave, and all we know of his fate is the groan we hear (*Chu Chin Chow*, Walter Forde). One of a murderer's victims leaves to fetch her coat. The guests left in the drawing room are silent. Her steps are heard on the stairs. Our gaze rises to the chandelier as her steps continue along the upper hall. We hear an opening door; and a final scream (*And Then There Were None*, René Clair).

The voice for the speaker, the sound for the object making it—this mode lends itself to suggesting the invisible, though what we see on the screen at the same time may steal our attention.

The roofless church in the desert is peopled by voices as Malcolm the black man stands in the middle of it. We see the lectern and hear the voice of Father Vogelsang. We pan along pews made from tree limbs and hear the congregation answer out of a distant past. After the final "Amen," through the church's cross of tree boughs, we see Malcolm walk out, his mind on Father Vogelsang, "who taught me in the long ago" (*The Back of Beyond*, John Heyer).

As he reads in his room, Suvorin hears a cane tapping. He throws open the casement but sees no one. He looks along the hall, sees no one, and closes the door and curtain, but the door flies open and the curtain flings to the ceiling in a fierce wind, which swings the hanging lamp, upsets a table, and scatters papers. The tapping cane and a double scuffle of skirts and feet grow in loudness (three times we had heard the Countess walk like this when alive). We approach to a close-up of the shrinking Suvorin. The wind, the taps, and the scuffling all stop and we hear her voice echoing softly in space, "I am commanded to grant your request. The cards are three, seven, ace" (*The Queen of Spades*, Thorold Dickinson).

10 Undisclosed Principal

In some cases we are given the sign but not what it signifies.

This is the case with supernatural presences, for what they are is seldom disclosed or explained. In *The Haunting* (Robert Wise), the presences manifest themselves by a drumming or pulsing sound, loud banging, creaking, thundering, and rushing winds, to say nothing of the turning of knobs and the bulging of old and solid-looking doors, when all the known company is in the room.

A former-lawyer-now-bum decides to attend his class dinner. We see in the lobby a table top laden with silk hats. Over the top of these we see him enter the door in a borrowed suit. An opulent stratum of society is established by the line of hats, without their owners being identified. It is indeed a generalization about them (*Tales of Manhattan*, Julien Duvivier).

In the animated film *Jealousy* (Todor Dinov), two swords rise in a blue void and act as if hands thrust and parried with them. Two revolvers point at one another, are flipped into the air, twirl, and are obviously caught and aimed by invisible hands.

11 Hyrmos

Peters has received a bundle. He assumes it is money, and from Dimitrios, an elusive swindler. He enters his flat, opens the bundle of money, and embraces it with triumph. His eyes look down then with astonishment. A scarf and a hat are lying there on a hassock. Someone was there before him. Whose hat it is is later disclosed, so here are both metonymy and hyrmos (*The Mask of Dimitrios*, Jean Negulesco).

12 Structure

Metonymy may be employed in shaping the story.

Throne of Blood (Akira Kurosawa) starts with mountains and haze and the gusting of a strong, insistent wind. As we pass a clearing in the mist, a few courses of stone are seen, a few empty post holes, and then we reach a twelve-foot stela, telling of the great castle that once had stood there. This dissolves to the castle as it was, at the moment when a horseman rides up and knocks on the gates. At the story's end, after Washizo dies, a long shot of the fortress as it was dissolves back to the stela, set in its waste of legendary mists. We pass from the monuments to the happenings in their past, and back again.

The Dark Mirror (Robert Siodmak) starts with a pan from a clock showing the time as 10:50. It approaches through a doorway to show a floor lamp, toppled over but lit, and up to show a circular shatter where something had struck the mirror over the mantel. It then retreats over a couch to expose a man prone on the floor with a knife in his back. Effects of which the rest of the film traces the cause.

In the first shot of *Went the Day Well* (Alberto Cavalcanti), the sexton crosses the churchyard and speaks to us, "So you've come to have a look at Bramley End . . . nice old thirteenth-century church. But it won't be that you'll have come to see. It'll be the names on this gravestone. Queer, isn't it? German names in an English churchyard . . . Battle of Bramley End, that's what the papers called it. They wanted England, those Germans did, and this is the only piece they got. . . . It happened on Whitsun Weekend, 1942. . . ." And from there we cut back to the events that put the German names on the tombstone.

The director has begun by brandishing, so to speak, something used by a person or persons who are at the moment unknown to us, or the effect of something done by them, or a place where some event has happened, usually in a way that arouses our curiosity. Of what were these courses of stone a part, who killed the man, who were the six Germans whose names were on the stone, and how did they come to die there during a war with Germany? It is a very old way of telling a story, romantic and metonymic.

13 Silent Film Acting

Metonymy was a necessary part of silent film acting, where mime had to supply much that is now spoken. As the Dear Little One sweeps the room and nears the table, she stops, and her hand goes to the absent Boy's hat lying there (*Intolerance*, D. W. Griffith). Cutie kisses her sweetheart's picture, kisses the telephone when he hangs up, and throws on the floor the necklace given to her by another suitor, as she remembers her sweetheart away at the war in France (shown in flashback) and the ring that he had given her before he left (*The Girl Who Stayed at Home*, D. W. Griffith).

12
Synecdoche

1 A Special Case of Metonymy[1]

Synecdoche is a form of metonymy in which the part stands in place of the whole or (less commonly) the whole in place of the part. We speak of buying a hundred head of cattle, quite sure of receiving too the whole hide and all that is inside it. The figure likely has a name of its own, and it certainly has its own chapter here, as being the most widely used of all the modes. Whereas the other modes are rather pronominal, merely standing in place of a person or object, synecdoche is more adjectival, adding a quality, showing a person resolute or cruel, weak or watchful. The close-up (without which a film today can hardly be imagined) functions most of the time as a synecdoche.

I find it therefore quite remarkable that up till quite recently, I read only a single writer on film who used the word *synecdoche* in a passage that must be quoted for its uniqueness:

> . . . the dangling eye-glasses were made to symbolize their owner, helplessly struggling among the seaweeds after the sailors had thrown him overboard.
> In one of my articles I compared this method of treating close-ups with a figure of speech known as synecdoche. I think both depend on the ability of our consciousness to reconstruct (mentally and emotionally) the whole from a part.[2]

It is not surprising that this was written by the most scholarly and the most perceptive of all film theorists. What is surprising is that only a book or two written since this was printed have elaborated at all on this hint. Forty years later, the filmic simile and filmic metaphor are briefly glanced at in some books, declared impossible in others, and any figures beyond these are not considered at all. Arnheim, one of the more original and better written books, does consider cases where a part is used for the whole (it should be impossible to write on film without doing so), but without pointing out that this is synecdoche.[3]

In the broadest sense, any story-telling or character-drawing must be synecdochical. Certain parts—events or traits—are picked out that form a connected thread, or show the sides of a person that shape the story. It must be the salient part of the whole for the purpose in hand. Charlie reduces a dancer to a head and two feet in *The Gold Rush*, (Charles Chaplin) when he stuck a fork in each of two rolls and moved them to music, turning his head, just above, to match the feet.

173

In this wide sense, a story abstracts from a man's life only those events or parts that form a connected narrative. In the narrower sense, synecdoche abstracts at a later stage, parts of these events to emphasize. From the fraction of *Gatsby*'s years that make up an hour-and-a-half's film, synecdoche picks from one event the finger wearing the ring that Daisy gave him (*The Great Gatsby,* Jack Clayton).

2 Uses: Identification

When establishing who a person is depends on one of his physical features, a close-up of this feature stands for the person thus identified.

Annabella said before her murder that the chief spy whom Hannay must unearth lacks the last joint of his little finger. Hannay was asked by a smiling host, who saved him from the police close behind him, which finger it was that lacked the joint. Hanny thought the fourth finger. In a shot of the host's back, he raised into center frame in close-up, his right hand with fifth finger missing its last joint, "It wouldn't be this one, Mr. Hannay?" and Hannay realized that now he lay in the power of the man he had been warned against (*The Thirty-Nine Steps,* Alfred Hitchcock).

A film like *This Happy Breed* (David Lean), which covers twenty years, evokes the changing times through things in the public eye: Tickle's *Tours of the Battlefields* (1919), a minaret at the British Empire Exhibition (1924), the marching banners and barbed-wired buses of the General Strike (1926), the straight-sided silhouette of a 1928 pattern book, and on the day of the King's death, antennas against a twilight sky.

3 Uses: Characteristics

The actor's task on stage is to find the gesture, the director's on the screen to find the close-up, which in the part betrays the whole person.

What adjectives apply to these men? One sits in a restuarant, reading, his eyes ignoring his wife who is sitting beside him. She is smiling slightly at two performers with trumpets and a young couple dancing. With his newspaper the man swipes at a bee, and if falls on its back. There is a close-up of a metal chair's tubular leg being guided slowly and carefully down on the wriggling bee and killing it. Later we see her sit with another man, an engineer, who stopped her horse when it ran away, and who bound her sprained ankle. A bee alights on his hand, and in close-up he tilts it into the cup of a daisy he has plucked. As she beyond him watches what he is doing, there are superimposed shots of her husband, slapping down the bee, and a close shot of the chair foot that crushed it. She shudders. The engineer gives her the flower. She blows and the bee flies away (*Ecstasy,* Gustave Machaty).

A tall man stands in the office door of *Raymond Ney Detective.* A client opens his pocketbook. In close-up, slow reluctant fingers pull off one bill at a time. Another set of fingers are seen, smartly slapping the bills together and briskly rolling them into a bundle, later thrown onto a typist's desk (*The Love of Jeanne Ney,* G. W. Pabst).

Two pairs of legs, walking slowly in perfect unison, trousers well creased, shoes well polished, and with each pair of legs a matching umbrella, convey an air of self-assurance, a position of some importance, and identity of purpose or interest (*The Ipcress File,* Sidney J. Furie).

Harry Lime is elusive. Long before Holly Martins, his friend, persuaded Lime to a meeting, Martins finds but hints and glimpses of him. One night Harry's kitten lies on polished shoes, all that is seen of a man in a dark doorway. Martins, drunk, shouts at the man, and the light goes on in a second-floor window as a woman opens it up and abuses Martins for his noise. For the moment the light is on, we see a sardonic face in the blackness of the doorway. Before Martins can reach it, there is a clack clack of running feet, and, as he pursues, he sees a great shadow running along a lighted wall. Martins comes out in a silent, empty square. Parts to signify a presence: never the whole man (*The Third Man*, Sir Carol Reed).

On an otherwise dark map of the United States, the area of the Great Plains is shown in white. Keeping the same outline, the featureless white dissolves to show windblown grass, as if we saw it through a window. This tells us that all the Great Plains is covered by the same tall grass we see in the opening (*The Plough That Broke the Plains*, Pare Lorentz).

4 Uses: Physical or Mental State

Hands may show vitality or its loss. The Jackal and a woman are in bed. She tells him that the police were inquiring for him, that she knows now he has done something serious. She asks him to tell her about it. He leans forward as if to caress her. Her hand goes over his shoulder, and then slides down and falls on the bed. We cut to the commissioner. "This is a straight murder case," he says. "We can do away with the secrecy" (*The Day of the Jackal*, Fred Zinnemann). Harry Lime, wounded, slowly climbs a set of rungs to a manhole. This alone, of all the ways out, is unguarded. He looks up and thrusts weakly through the small square holes in the cover, as if through coarse bars that contain him. In the wide square above, looking from ground level, we see his fingers reaching straight up through the holes. Below again, light through the grid patterns his face. Above, his fingers fall back through. He cannot lift the cover: he is trapped (*The Third Man*, Sir Carol Reed).

Feet are also indexes to body and mind.

Before giving Alfie his treatment, Nurse Kerr draws the screen around his bed. Harry Clammercraft in the next bed and his visiting wife try to look away, but watch fascinated, for under the bottom of the screen one of the nurse's feet curls around the other ankle, and then both feet leave the ground. Alfie, it seemed, was giving the treatment (*Alfie*, Lewis Gilbert).

Captain Thorndyke walks out of a room with three Gestapo officers. On his return, we see coming toward us the trousers and boots of two men in uniform, and between them a pair of trailing legs, the toes of whose boots are scraping across the floor (*Man Hunt*, Fritz Lang).

In *A Soldier's Prayer* feet are used in various ways. There are furtive steps over sleeping people before a woman's hands enter to rifle Kaji's rice bag. There is a foot withdrawn in haste as Kaji fires a shot down in front of it: he is disobeying the command of an officer to join a last resistance against the Russians. There are the booted feet of ten Russian soldiers, followed by Chinese peasant militia—bare legs and loose trousers—advancing on a village. There are the feet of prisoners, running out of line and back again as they march, suffering from diarrhea. Near the end there are Kaji's own feet, walking in water ankle-keep; and as at last he dies, the camera panning his body stops on his feet, the space between the sole and upper showing his toes. The end of the war (*The Human Condition*, part 3: *A Soldier's Prayer*, Masaki Kobayashi).

Whatever the part may do to enrich the whole, there may be a reciprocal enrichment of the part by its context. It is because we know that she killed the artist who would have seduced her that the feet of the woman walking through the streets all night can suggest her feelings (*Blackmail*, Alfred Hitchcock). The feet running various ways, and scattering baskets of vegetables, clay pots and other wares express haste, but only for certain haste that springs from fear, because we have seen German soldiers enter the marketplace leading dogs (*The Taras Family*, Mark Donskoi).

5 Uses: Situation

One significant thing may summarize a situation (pl. 28).

A common synecdoche is a hand holding a revolver: intimidation—a threatening hand standing for a threatening person. The captain of a fishing factory ship has just received a distress call and is altering course to answer it. To avoid losing fishing time, the superintendent instructs the captain to ignore the call. The captain refuses. Then follows a close-up of a revolver being drawn from a trouser pocket, and the captain, silent, stepping back (*The Crab Canning Ship*, So Yamamura).

In a close-up of two full rolls of admission tickets, one on top of the other, the loose end of the top roll moves off the frame in a series of jerks—each jerk being a ticket sold. Then the tickets move off in a quick, smooth, continuous flow. This dissolves to the roll now still, but half the size of the whole roll beneath it: a full house (*The Ring*, Alfred Hitchcock).

A husband has surprised an actor with his wife. The husband is drunk and he talks as he shows them round his gunroom. He takes down a gun called "Colonel Young," promoted from "captain" because "it never misses." He fondles and oils it as he talks. He loads the gun and points it in the actor's direction. The wife cannot settle which man she wishes most. We see three sets of hands. The husband's first pat the rifle barrel; later his fingers are straying near the trigger. The wife's fingers first are twisting and wringing; later are taut and still. The actor's fingers move slightly up and down his lapel (*Tales of Manhattan*, Julien Duvivier).

What is meant by two pairs of yellow eyes racing across a black screen, as Butch chases Pluto through a sewer pipe? Does the black mean that neither can see the other? Do the eyes mean that they can, or are straining to, see (*The Purloined Pup*, Charles Nichols)?

6 Uses: Reminiscence

Events of a story can be recalled by showing things or places linked to them.

Three men search for gold and find it. One of them, Dobbs, makes off with the gold of the other two. He is robbed by bandits who have no use for the gold, but who steal his shoes and his horses. Howard, one of the two men robbed, goes with Indians, of whom he has made friends, to the ruins where Dobbs met the bandits. All that Howard finds is an empty bag that once had held gold. As the two robbed men part, we pan down to a cactus on which is impaled another empty bag—the only return for ten months' hardship (*The Treasure of Sierra Madre*, John Huston).

As they wait their turn to go to a fascist prison camp, Micole Finzi-Contini is comforted by the father of the man who loved her. The camera pans to a window, and we go out into Ferrara, into the streets, up to the house of the Finzi-Continis. We see the grove around it, the locked gates of wrought iron, the coach house where Giorgio and Micole had sat in a carriage together and through whose window he saw her with another man. We retreat from the empty tennis court, where Giorgio,

Malnate the communist, Micole, and her brother Alberto had all played and sat and talked. An intelligent, elegant, leisurely, circle of people, all scattered—only their things remain (*The Garden of the Finzi-Continis,* Vittorio de Sica).

If these could be taken as things that stand for their users, they might be seen as metonymies; but here they are fragments of incidents, mementoes, bringing back in a final reminder the whole tale and its theme.

7 Uses: Mystification—Amphibology, Hyrmos, Undisclosed Principal

Synecdoche is used for mystification, of which we may distinguish three kinds. First is pure amphibology, the subtlest use, which leaves equally open two or more meanings, any one of which would fit the images given. Second is hyrmos, the concealment of the meaning, followed by later disclosure. Third is the undisclosed principal, in which the meaning of the part is never told us—the least forgivable. (Did the director know?)

Amphibology, first. The police drag a pond and find only a dead dog, which frees Mathieu from suspicion of murder. Mathieu now wonders if the girl (who was to shoot the man she seems to live with) has made off with money given to her, all Mathieu had in the bank, and if the wrapped mass they threw into the pond was not a body at all. Mathieu goes back to the pond, and in a brown open patch in the frozen surface, he sees a white hand and runs back in glee, "She did it for me. She hasn't fooled me." For him the hand is the hand of her dead lover, and a sign of her devotion to him. But it could have been someone else's hand, and his logic false (*Belle,* André Delvaux).

If we find out later particulars we need to know to understand the part, such as who the person was whose hands we have seen, this may be seen as hyrmos as well as synecdoche.

At the sound of a door buzzer, a knife slicing through a roast chicken stops in its forward thrust. The housekeeper opens the door, listens, shakes her head. Martins insists, "I'm a friend of Harry Lime." In another close-up, the fork is withdrawn from the bird, and it and the knife are laid on the plate beside it. "Let him come," says a voice. Alertness and then decision, but whose (*The Third Man,* Sir Carol Reed)?

In hyrmos it is we who are kept in suspense by the nondisclosure. David Lean in *Dr. Zhivago* lets the audience know, but keeps important knowledge from those who are most concerned. As the band that heads the procession of workers turns the corner, we see the end of the street as it looks to them. It is black, with only little bright needles where light from the side has caught the edges of what we, but not they, know to be sabers, for we have seen the cavalry making ready.

The door must not be left out, as a source of concealment, especially the door at the end of the hall, slowly approached. In *The Seventh Victim* (Mark Robson), Irving August, a private investigator, is told by Mary that he must find out what the room holds. Now this particular door is not merely right at the end of the hall, facing us fully seen. It is on the side wall, a thin darker line in the night's gloom that mantles at the end of the hall. The reluctant August slowly merges in the shadows. We are behind him again as he walks back toward Mary, away from us, walking stiffly. He drops dead. He should have known. We have seen enough of them to know that doors at the ends of halls are fatal places. Here in addition the door lurked in darkness. Now the darker and more ill-defined a part is, the greater is the range of wholes our fancies may invent for it. The limit is, of course, a black screen, the range of whose possibilities is infinite: it may be a part of anything, at which point it becomes a synecdoche for nothing.

The undisclosed principal is not to be utterly damned in all cases; though the same could be said of most of them as Stevenson did of *The Pit and the Pendulum:* "He knows no more about the pit than you or I do. It is pure imposture, a piece of audacious impudent thimble-rigging."[4]

In *Vampyr* (Carl Theodor Dreyer), purely for mystification, we are shown a hand sliding along a bannister and stopping on the newel post. We never find out whose it is. This is a commonplace in mystery and horror films.

Then there are supernatural presences, of which the only visible part is the scurrying leaves along a curtained hallway or trailing muslin that looks like formless ectoplasm. The director, it seems, never felt obliged to tell us what wholes these were parts of (*The Fall of the House of Usher*, Jean Epstein). Bergman uses mystification in *Cries and Whispers*. Agnes is taken for dead, after a long illness. Thinking she hears Agnes calling, a surviving sister, Maria, goes to the bed and sits. From out of the frame, two arms reach up and the hands caress Maria's face. Maria flees in terror. All we are given are the yearning arms, and Agnes's voice begging Maria to talk and not be afraid. Agnes's face would have told us more but is out of the frame. Had Agnes only appeared to die, or had the affection she bore her sisters brought her back from the dead? This is an effective suggestion of a ghostly presence.

8   Uses: Generalization

To generalize is hard in an art like film, which, in its nature, deals in particular cases. What must be done is to show the special case as synecdochical for a whole class.

In *The Last Chance* (Leopold Lindtberg), two soldiers climbing through the Alps halt and look back. In a long shot, we see the little group of refugees whose escape from Italy the soldiers brought about, black on the white snow, moving slowly along the distant valley. The shot dissolves into another one, the same valley: a long line of tiny specks crawling endlessly across the entire frame. "Millions of them," one of the soldiers says.

A well-dressed man, with his wife and his two children, leave their flat and load their bags on a two-wheeled barrow. We have never seen them before. The children speak of "a vacation." "Will it be a long train?" "When are we coming back?" The answer to the last is, "Don't ask questions". In what they say and think and do, and how they look, this family is much the same as any of a thousand picked at random. The camera changes viewpoint and now shows us clearly, on the left breast of the husband's black coat, the Star of David. He now stands for the class, Jews, different and persecuted (*Romeo and Juliet and Darkness*, Jiri Weiss).

In Russian films especially, characters are often conceived less as persons than as types representing whole classes, and individual traits are suppressed in favor of assumed class characteristics. An English soldier executes a Mongolian boy in *Storm Over Asia* (V. I. Pudovkin). The English soldier's reasons, attitudes, or doubts are not explored at all; we see only the act. Our sympathies are thus forestalled and held for the victim, and the soldier, lacking any personal traits, is a general image of every foreign invader, a dehumanized killing machine (V. I. Pudovkin).

In generalizing like this, only the traits assumed in the class are displayed and individual features are almost entirely suppressed. In the following case, on the other hand, four contrasting individuals exemplify various forms of the same public indifference. Charleston has just completed a poorly attended lecture tour to warn England of Hitler. He is passing a cinema as "All the latest news and Pop-Eye" is announced. He goes in, and we hear the commentator describing Hitler's entering Sudetenland. Charleston looks left, and we pan to what he sees: a man and woman kissing and embracing, a man sleeping, another man patiently enduring boredom. Charleston looks right and sees a huge woman feeding herself peanuts and pushing away a child who is pawing for some. The camera retreats as the newsreel ends and we hear the start of Pop-Eye. The bored man comes to life, the sleeper awakes, the lovers are interrupted, and the peanut-eater pauses as Charleston edges past on his way out (*Thunder Rock*, Roy Boulting).

To take one of many fungible things, one of an anonymous crowd, suggests a random sampling, and that any other one would have done. After the letters "MUSIC HALL" have lit one by one, a hand pays at the box office and gets its ticket, feet walk to the ticket collector, and a hand rips the ticket in half and hands back the stub. Feet walk up the carpet, and our gaze rises to the back above the feet as they sidle to an empty seat. It might have been you or I or anyone who sat that night in the empty seat, found himself beside Annabella, and lived through all that followed (*The Thirty-Nine Steps*, Alfred Hitchcock).

The moving camera may reveal the whole, after we have seen the part. A girl and a soldier kiss in a close shot. The camera then rises quickly to show them as part of a whole long railway platform flooded with soldiers, all in various ways preparing to leave (*The Girl from Leningrad*, Victor Eisimont).

In the same way, Chaplin compresses the ghetto into a single street. When the storm troopers turn the corner, or a radio in one of its houses blares forth a speech, what is disturbing the nation reaches the ghetto (*The Great Dictator*).

As a later chapter will show, as a means of generalization, montage may be seen as a form of synecdoche. A series of synecdoches, with only a single feature in common, can build a stronger generalization than one. A filmic synecdoche cannot fully avoid the individual. However strictly we limit a person's acts and words to manifesting one ruling passion, we still must see and hear the person move, look, and speak in some one way as against all others. In a series of synecdoches, the individual traits cancel out, and the one class feature they have in common is given emphasis. *Lost Boundaries* (Alfred L. Werker) deals with middle-class blacks in the United States, in the story of one man who can pass for white. This, in itself, leads us to assess him independent of color. The total effect of each successive incident is to show that the one before is not exceptional but part of a course of conduct, the outer expression of a philosophy. We see the doctor at work at a forest fire, doing emergency medical work, performing artificial respiration on a boy who had fallen through the ice of a river, attending a patient late at night, and so on. He applied, as a black, for a post in various hospitals. Of four successive letters entering the frame, we hear part spoken, all to the same effect, "very sorry," "We regret to inform you," thus conveying through different forms of words a single attitude. The four letters stand for a larger number, and their tenor as found in four is clearer than it would be in one.

9 Synecdoche and Metaphor

Synecdoche can come close to metaphor (pl. 29), as the reader will have noticed, let us say, in *The Treasure of the Sierra Madre*. The casting off of a vessel's hawser and hauling it aboard is only part of what goes on when a ship leaves, but a most significant one. In *North Sea* (Harry Watt) we are shown the crew closing hatches, covering them over with canvas, tightening the clamps, and ringing the engine room. We see the prow edging away from the dock, the whole ship moving away from where we stand. But none of these reverberates into other images as much as casting off the hawser—into cutting the umbilical cord, untying a dog, letting go a balloon, and so on—which enrich the image of casting off and give it a metaphorical color besides what it does to carry forward the narrative.

Duddy's grandfather is on his knees, planting tomatoes and watering them in. "A man without land is nothing," he says. "If I got some land, would I be somebody then," Duddy asks him. His grandfather smiles, and pinches Duddy's cheek with his right hand. He has just firmed the damp soil, and some of it leaves a smear on Duddy's face. Duddy touches the soil on his face, and his fingers go to his tongue thoughtfully. His grandfather's belief has "rubbed off" on him (*The Apprenticeship of Duddy Kravitz*, Ted Kotcheff).

10 Synecdochical Structure

Synecdoche may be used in the build of the story.

As she sits in an open air café, we become aware of The Lady with the Little Dog in details, perhaps as Gurov notes them. We see her back, her skirt, her hand, her skirt and the dog, her back and her hand, and in the way she moves her hand we know that she knows that someone is watching her. Gurov holds a bone out, and the dog leaves her. She half turns: "He doesn't bite," she says (*The Lady with the Little Dog*, Joseph Heifetz).

In the *Romeo and Juliet* (Lev Arnstam) ballet, the frame is filled with a platter of grapes and apples, which moves away from us in a servant's hand, and shrinks in size to show a large hall being readied for a banquet. The principle is here the same as in early silent films, where a mask blacked out the whole of a scene except for a small circle that picked out a detail. The circle widened into the whole frame. What is better in the present case is that the part singled out is seen clear and large in close-up, and itself acts to mask out all of the scene but itself. As it moves away, it carries us into the scene with it. And being part of the story, it is not as if something outside like the mask were obtruding itself. The same can be done with a panning shot. In the same film, a frame is filled with lilies. We pan to find it part of a procession of welcome for the County Paris.

Perhaps the most thoroughgoing synecdochical story-telling is *Jeu de Mains* (Alain Pol). We may see the faces of minor persons, but never more than the hands of the man whose life is told.[5]

> We see a child in a christening dress;
> A hand pulls a bell rope;
> A hand passes a collection plate;
> A dish of jordan almonds vanishes under the attack of half a dozen hands;
> A hand opens a wine bottle;
> Hands pour and drink champagne;
> Hands with a rolling pin sprinkle and roll pastry;
> Hands sprinkle powder on a baby that lies on its back. . . .
>
> A hand in white gloves presses a button;
> Nervous hands turn the brim of a black felt hat;

A man's hand raises another hand to lips just inside the frame;
Hands are playing runs on a piano;
A woman's hand caresses a shoulder;
The piano player's hands end on a chord; .
Hands tie up a bundle of letters;
Hands in a mirror are tying a tie;
A hand places a ring on another's finger;
A hand passes a collection plate;
Another hand pulls a bell rope;
Glasses are clinked;
Flowers are placed in a vase in front of a mirror. . . .

Hands pin the Legion of Honor on a soldier's breast, and we pan down to show a
    steel hook where his hand ought to be;
The hook tries to open and hold down the pages of a book, with clumsy lack of
    success;
The hook tries to turn the knob of a door;
A wine glass slips from the hook and shatters. . . .

A hand lights a candle;
A body lies on a bed, its head not seen;
A hand stamps an identity book and closes it;
A hand throws a bundle of letters on the fire;
A hand puts the candle out.

11   Matters of Practice—Visual Culture

Bela Balazs used the term *visual culture,* in discussing how far a director can count
on the viewer's rounding out the whole, when shown the part.[6] He takes as an
example a scene like that in *Brief Encounter,* where a woman stands on a railway
platform, and the passing train is only seen in the flicker of light on her face from the
train's windows. Balazs wrote that at first sight he did not know what the flickering
stood for. He pointed out that much simpler film conventions were quite beyond the
grasp of African villagers, and that the subtle use of any mode of metonymy depends
on the growth of a visual culture in the viewer, and speaks only to persons possessing
this.
    An air attack on a ship is told in the upward looks of sailors, in a train of bullet
holes across a ship's hatch, a rattling gun, and the loudening roar of an engine (*The
Long Voyage Home,* John Ford). Regretfully, death by bullet and plane is part of the
European culture spread throughout the world. Even so, could every Inuit and Ibo
fill the meaning out from these four signs?
    At the swearing-in of Tennessee Johnson, we pan across the seated crowd to stop
on merely a stovepipe hat and the tip of a beard. How many, beyond the coasts of
America, would add to these parts the rest of Lincoln (*Tennessee Johnson,* William
Dieterle)? Consider then what the director of *An American Time Capsule* (Charles
Braverman) assumes in his viewers, where the whole history of the United States is
encompassed in under four minutes, through a series of paintings, prints, and photographs of people and incidents, each of which is shown on the screen something over
a second, some indeed as short as one frame in length.
    This applies especially to words, which are rich in allusiveness but restricted in

range to those who can understand them. Would everyone today, in even the English-speaking world, complete the story of Edward and Edith after they leave behind them in the frame the life belt on which is printed *S.S. Titanic* (*Cavalcade*, Frank Lloyd)? Or know at the end of *This Happy Breed* (David Lean) what Queenie was going to in 1939, by seeing her baggage labeled "Singapore"?

The director's task is complicated further by variations in personal visual cultures. Some creature bulges up the desert sands behind a guard who sits on a rock, exhausted (*The Adventurer*, Charles Chaplin). When I watched this I had recently seen *The Sands of Central Asia*, (F. F. Brusilovsky), where such a bulge hatched into a snake which ambushed some hapless victim, and this was what I expected; but no, it was Charlie—it was Charlie who broke through in a striped convict uniform. It was purely chance that the movement in the sand brought a snake to my mind, and there must have been few besides myself who gave it this meaning. Nonetheless, there is little doubt that individual differences in visual culture must now and then modify the message taken by the viewer.

Part VI

Figures of Sequence

13
Motion

1 Can Motion Be a Trope?[1]

Can mere motion confer a meaning that things or persons would not possess without it? If it can within the length of a single piece of film, we then may speak of a figure or trope of *motion*.

I MOVEMENT OF PERSONS AND THINGS

2 Moving Objects

It will have been observed that in a head-and-shoulder shot of a person walking, we have no means of knowing if the movement is that of the person or the camera—it could be either. Taken against a blank wall or sky, it is nearly impossible to say whether someone is rising into the frame or the camera sinking. Both kinds of movement must thus be considered, of the subject recorded and the instrument used in recording.

Users of screens that are large enough to engage our entire peripheral vision have certainly realized the strong effect, something of threat or danger, of masses, especially large ones, that seem to move toward us. We cross a bluish rippling lake at increasing speed and head for a tree-topped cliff, and in the nick of time we tilt up and over it, or follow a stream toward a waterfall, hesitate above the plunge-basin facing the flounced curtains of shattered water, approach the cracked yellow rock that splinters the stream, and rise to the smooth translucent blue above (*North of Superior*, Graham Ferguson).

On the conventional screen, a galley of Cecil B. de Mille, smooth, dark, and somehow menacing, approaches us at water level, swelling out all ways to fill the frame *(Cleopatra)*. The approaching train taken from ground level between the tracks is a commonplace. The motion here certainly adds a sense of being endangered.

A safecracker, being pursued, is on a flat roof. In a down shot from there, as he would see it, the tip of a fire ladder swings around, unmanned, until it aims toward us. The slow mechanical swing and exact stop of the ladder suggest his inevitable capture. Later a police inspector, giving instructions, is at the top, a black figure, looming closer and larger against a white haze (*Turn the Key Softly*, Jack Lee).

Margaret's mother is not well and her young sister has a date, so Margaret, as usual, does the ironing. The iron moves to and fro; her head moves to and fro as she irons; then the head, a white bulb, and a hanging cable all move to and fro to throbbing music. She stops; she has a terrible headache, she says, and cannot finish the ironing. She feels tethered and cannot go past a given point. It is almost a visible throb; and the cable that falls to the iron whose handle she holds is almost the tether itself (*Feeling of Rejection*, Robert Anderson).

In all these examples, motion tells us more than change of place: it conveys also states or feelings. It is a figure.

3   Moving People

People who move in an uncut scene are like enough to actors moving on stage, that within certain limits of space a scene can be transferred entirely from stage to screen. The life belt scene in *Cavalcade* appeared the same both in the play and the film (Frank Lloyd).

In *Tom Jones* (Tony Richardson), Thwackum first, Square, and then Mr. Blifil are seen coming down a narrow stair, Thwackum denouncing Tom as a "monster of depravity." As they are all coming down exactly in step, the movement implies three bodies all of one mind on the subject of Tom, and perhaps more—a hint of premeditation.

During a drought, a line of some fifty men dig an emergency irrigation trench, the head of the line with picks, the tail with shovels. They step and close on each of four beats, bringing their picks down on every other beat, digging and then throwing to the same rhythm. The concert in sound and motion expressed their common purpose (*Our Daily Bread*, King Vidor).

When the Beauty first enters the Beast's palace, we do not see her legs and are not aware of any effort of movement on her part. She is swept the length of a great hall toward us, tall curtains billowing out at the left, her head leaning, glance rapt, as if without will of her own, enchanted (*La Belle et la Bête*, Jean Cocteau).

4   Distortion of Movement—Speeded[2]

On the stage an actor may choose to make a gesture slow or fast. What the film director can do, however, is to take the actor's picture at normal speed, and project him faster or slower—and this is not the same. If I take four minutes to make my bed, I can do more and move more than if I take two. But if I am shot as I make the bed in four minutes and this is projected in half the time twice as fast, everything I did will still be there, at a pace that would not be possible in real life. Used with discretion speeded movement can add to a scene a meaning otherwise absent.

When Charlie climbs a burning building at breakneck speed and comes down as fast, it is giving form to a wish—the best way to enter and leave a fire is as quickly as possible (*The Fireman*, Charles Chaplin).

When the host and guests at an inn—ten or so—are discovering, chasing, and mistaking one another with little rhyme or reason, a pleasant satirical shot shows them tearing around a rectangle, up and down the stairs at either end, crossing between them, down below on the ground or up above along a gallery, at a frantic pace, each a machine powered by his "ruling passion" (*Tom Jones*, Tony Richardson).

Allegro (Paul Roubaix) is the rush and repetition of life in cities. Traffic stops for a second or two at lights, bursts away into the distance, and another batch of traffic accumulates. A train on the Metro stops, ejects and absorbs flitting forms of regular flow patterns, closes up its momentary mouth, and flashes off, and another takes its place. We see the gyrating pattern of strike-and-break in the boxing ring, and the quick repeated movements of human eating machines that sit in restaurants, without pause or enjoyment. At our normal pace, we are not so much aware of the robot in us.

Speeded movement adds excitement in *Seven Days Ashore* (John H. Auer). Danny and Annabella agree to marry, and in speeded movement they flit across the room, out of the door to a taxi, into the house of the Justice of the Peace, whose words are mere gabble, slowing down only to say clearly, "I now pronounce you man and wife." After a slow kiss, they speed again out of the house, into the taxi, out and up to the door, slowing to normal as Danny carries his wife over the threshold.

If, as in time-lapse photography, the camera stops and starts at regular intervals, movement, instead of being unbroken, would leap from posture to posture, in segments of interrupted movement. The time gap that separates exposures or groups of exposures has thus been lengthened. The phantom coach that comes for Jonathan Harker, and the man seen from Harker's window, who loads the wagon and enters the coffin, and the team that drives off on its own, are all jerky in movement, as if lifeless automata, nonnatural, therefore, supernatural (*Nosferatu*, F. W. Murnau).

5 Distortion of Movement—Slowed

V. I. Pudovkin calls the stretching out of a happening to fill more than its actual time, and the consequent slowing of its movement a "close-up in time."[3] It allows us to scrutinize the characteristics of motion as the common close-up does those of a surface. It is a means of emphasis, and may convey the subjective lengthening of a moment brought about by strong emotional states and heightened awareness.

Julia looks down into the cellar, and through a cobweb sees Michael looking up from the crate he has taken down. She moves out of the door in slowed motion, along the hall and into the drawing room with a gliding step, and pivots around with raised forearms. Michael follows up the stairs and into the drawing room, also in slowed motion, and there they slowly kiss to three quarter time. We sense a release, a lightness of heart, a floating up from the gravitational pull of a solid world (*The Wrong Box*, Bryan Forbes).

A boy of about ten who has not spoken from the age of five is sitting on an outcrop of rock on Dartmoor. His parents are impatient rather than encouraging, and his silence is a sad one. On this day, a white pony with blue eyes, which he has seen before, comes slowly toward him and nuzzles him. Its timid approach and the boy's gentle and happy caressing of it are slightly slowed, which gives a grace and a dreamlike feeling to their gentle meeting (*Run Wild, Run Free*, Richard C. Sarafian).

Within a hut, a bandit holds a child whose life he has threatened. A samurai enters at a run. The bandit glides out on slowed legs and falls dead, as one who would escape, but being in fact slain by the quick sword of the samurai, his body cannot second his wish (*The Seven Samurai*, Akira Kurosawa).

Four bandits make to draw their guns and Butch Cassidy and the Sundance Kid kill them all. In slowed movement the bandits roll over and down a slight slope. The dust slowly clears, and the drawn-out cries die away. Then we see Butch and the Kid perfectly still. The rapping of revolver shots, rapid arms, and quickly swirling dust is followed by slowed bodies, dying cries, a still haze, and then silence: a stretching out for emphasis of the slackening after tension, and perhaps reflecting Butch's feeling of first killing someone (*Butch Cassidy and the Sundance Kid*, George Roy Hill).

6 Distortion of Movement—The Still—Epizeuxis

If we slow motion as far as possible, we reach the motionless, the still—the limiting case. This comes from repeating a single frame, which thus freezes the movement in it, and lengthens out a single moment for emphasis. Likewise, in the figure *epizeuxis*, a word is repeated with no other words coming between, thus prolonging in the reader's or listener's mind the notion it stands for:

> Stay, stay
> Until the hasting day
> Has run
> But to the evensong.[4]

> O dark, dark, dark, amid the blaze of noon.[5]

> Many as fair as thou might be,
> But oh! not one—not one like thee![6]

The figure can suggest, with each repetition, a gain or growth in some characteristic:

> And I heard the bells, grown fainter, far behind me peal and play,
> Fainter, fainter, fainter, fainter, till they seemed to die away;[7]

The fabricated stillness of the same frame repeated is not the same as an actor standing still. Sanjuro and another samurai have allied themselves with opposite interests. At the end of the film they meet at a crossroads. Sanjuro does not wish to fight, for only one will leave the place alive; the other insists. They slowly draw their hands from behind their backs, and let them hang out of wide sleeves. For thirteen seconds they stand without a move, seconds in which we should have expected close-ups. Then, with a whirl of weapons, a spout of blood gushes out of the other, Sanjuro draws back, and the other falls (*Sanjuro*, Akira Kurosawa).

This is a live stillness, that of the actor. An actor may stand for some time without moving, but still with subtle signs of life, tiny changes in chest or eye that an actor cannot fully control and we may not be conscious of. On the other hand, when an editor takes a single frame, a fleeting slice of movement, and keeps repeating it, chest and eye are paralyzed, and the moment—it is the best word—is frozen, with all the absence of life that this implies. At the same time, it gives to the moment a length and emphasis beyond what it had in actuality.[8]

In *Tom Jones* (Tony Richardson) Tom visits Molly, finds her in bed, says he is sorry, and is upbraided by her as the only man she has loved. He is trying to answer, when the pillow she is whacking him with dislodges a sheet hanging beside the bed. It falls, to reveal Square, one of Tom's tutors, naked and embarrassed, holding an clout over his loins. Tom laughs and Molly laughs, but Square has not the heart to, and a shot of all three is frozen. The laughter seems to continue longer than a shot with normal movement, and we feel the indelibility of humiliation remembered.

The frozen frame is an effective ending. It is almost always of a leading character, as if the director were saying, this is how I wish you to remember him. The boy in

The Four Hundred Blows (François Truffaut), after an unhappy boyhood, is frozen in the act of running away along a seashore, in a final, perhaps forever futile, effort of escape. It might also be, as Murray Macquarrie suggests, like an old photograph, discovered by chance, which brings back what once we were, remembered now with lessened agony, even with detachment.[9]

The final frame of *Butch Cassidy and the Sundance Kid* (George Roy Hill), who were actual persons, is indeed yellowed so as to look like a faded photograph, but the stillness here is not that of a memory, dried and pressed, but of motion cut short by death. They are sought as bank robbers, and are wounded by the police before they can gain cover within a building. In a full-length shot the two emerge running and firing. As they reach half length, we hear a command and a volley, and the image freezes. Two more commands are followed by volleys. Their last moment of life is held in the still, and as we move back from it, as if in time, it fades to an ancient sepia.

The end of *Elvira Madigan* (Bo Widerberg) was equally in character. Count Sparre and Elvira have left their work, their friends, and their families; detection is imminent and their money gone. They eat their last meal under an autumn tree. Death, she says, is all that is open to them, but he cannot bring himself to shoot her as he holds her to him. "No! No! No!" he says over and over. She rises, catches sight of a late butterfly, and follows after it. She turns toward us. Sparre is kneeling under a tree, straight arm aiming a pistol. She raises two curved arms, and as they rise the height of her chin, there is a shot and the image freezes. And then another shot. Chasing butterflies.

There is in all these a hint of time having a stop, either when motion cut short is a figure for death, or when a moment is so charged with feeling that its image is beyond possibility of weathering.

There is another kind of stop in time in *A Matter of Life and Death* (Michael Powell and Emeric Pressburger). Peter Carter, his brain injured, has vivid hallucinations. He believes that a person, Conductor 71, was sent to earth to shepherd him hence at the moment of death. The conductor missed him when his plane crashed, because of a dense fog, and Carter argues with him that having in the meantime taken on responsibilities by falling in love, his term of life should be extended. Whenever the conductor appears, all life in the real world freezes. Two table tennis players may freeze poised in a rally, and stay so until the conductor vanishes, for as he says, "We are talking in space, not in time." However long the conversations may seem, none is more than a transient flash of thought, brought about by some cerebral impulse, shorter than the time between two film frames.

More normal states of mind are also well caught by the frozen image. In *Z* (Costa-Gavras), the assassination is described by counsel for the peace movement, and we see again Lambrakis being clubbed from a passing truck. The incident flows in one- or two-second bursts, at the end of each of which the last frame is repeated, freezing the movement, blurred from the speed of the truck, as if the speaker and the juge d'instruction were scrutinizing carefully what had happened.

In *Les Deux Timides* (René Clair), counsel for a man accused of wife-beating described the couple's idyllic life together. The court is disrupted by a scampering mouse and the counsel's notes are jumbled. When his address resumes, he comes to a missing sheet. He is describing the husband about to play the violin for his wife. The husband's image freezes, one foot off the ground, and his bow poised. The counsel starts again, speaking faster, like one taking a run to clear a fence. The scene is repeated, stopping dead again at the same place, in the same frozen posture.[10]

7 Distortion of Movement—The Still Sequence—Ellipsis

It is possible to tell a part or sequence of a story entirely in still pictures.[11] For what purpose? With what effect?

At the end of *Les Deux Timides* (René Clair), a timid young counsel and his future father-in-law spend some time drinking together. Full of Dutch courage, the counsel ("delivers a statement . . .") argues his client's case in court with unexpected vehemence. So much so that the defendant, a rival suitor, attacks him. After a long shot showing the start of the scuffle, we see a succession of still shots, each tableau catching and holding a moment. First the counsel down and now his rival, showing the ebb and flow of battle with sudden violent thrusts of movement, with greater force than if all the movement between were filled in. It carries further the jerky movement seen in *Nosferatu*. It is, in fact, an ellipsis of all but the salient moments.

Andrzej Munk in *The Messenger* accompanies a spoken narrative of past events, as if by snapshots of them, separating in this way past events from present. A former Schutzstaffel (SS) officer has gone to the United States and has married. She saw at Southampton a woman she thought was one she sent to her death at Auschwitz. Here are some of the stills: the SS officer at the rail of a ship, her eye apparently caught by something; a girl on the gangway, half turned, looking up; the SS officer, head forward, mouth open, appalled. It will be clear first, that if each of these shots had been, not a repeated single frame but a normal shot in motion, the movement would have been little more than what we saw; and second, that the length of time each frame is repeated is determined, as in any editing, by the pace desired.

Butch Cassidy and the Sundance Kid and The Kid's girl friend enjoy themselves on the way to Bolivia. This is a transition of little importance, and is condensed into its characteristic incidents, and these are depicted in sepia-tinted stills, as if they were faded photographs taken at the time. We see them seated in a railway carriage, posing outside the station, rowing on a river, shooting for prizes at a fair, looking over the rail of a steamer, dressed in tails, dancing. A railway carriage with *Nacionales de Bolivia* painted on the side passes left, and reveals their backs as they stand at a country station, and the sepia tint slowly dissolves into natural color (*Butch Cassidy and the Sundance Kid*, George Roy Hill).

La Jetée (Chris Marker) is told entirely in still pictures. It is a very moving story of a man after World War III, who is forced by technical means to travel into the past and into the future for knowledge that would help man survive. Before the war, when a boy, he had caught a glimpse of a girl at Orly airport and had fallen in love with her. He also knew that at that moment a man had died. In a number of journeys back, he meets her "ghost." He is sent to the future, and learns there that those who sent him will liquidate him when his purpose is served. Those in the future offer to keep him there, but he chooses to return to his boyhood when he saw the girl. At the airport he rushes toward her, sees in the crowd the director of the institution that sent him back, and is thus kept in mind that he cannot escape his destiny. At the moment in which he glimpses her, he falls dead—he was the man who died. Narration is well done, with a past reference, and the stills, being like pictured records of events past, succeed in overcoming the illusion that *moving* pictures give, of seeing events now happening, and this despite that all is set in the future.

8 Distortion of Movement—Reversed

To show an event reversed in time, an arrow, say, returning back to the bow, the film is shot, running normally forward, and then printed and projected end first, reversing what is by nature irreversible.

Inversion of normal or natural order is the figure *hysteron proteron*. It is always hard to resist quoting Puttenham:[12]

> Ye haue another manner of disordered speach, when ye misplace your words or clauses and set that before which should be behind, and *é conuerso*, we call it in English prouerbe, the cart before the horse, the Greeks call it Histeron proteron, we name it the Preposterous. . . . One describing his landing vpon a strange coast, sayd thus preposterously.
> When we had climbde the clifs, and were a shore
> Whereas he should haue said by good order
> When we were come ashore and clymed had the cliffs
> For one must be on land ere he can clime. And as another said
> My dame that bred me vp and bare me in her wombe.
> Where as the bearing is before the bringing vp.

It is emphasizing an event by putting it first and adding as an afterthought, almost in parenthesis, a prior condition that made it possible. Or it may be a turning round of the usual way of seeing a situation, done with satiric intent. Cicero is said to have had an undersized son-in-law, given to strutting around with a long trailing sword, and is said to have asked someone, "Who tied my son to that sword?"[13]

In literary use, we are always aware of the inversion. Not the event but the mode of expression is altered, and this we correct in reading as Puttenham does. In film it is hard to reverse the form without working a change in the event itself. Charlie is driving a horse-drawn fire engine. He looks back, and in longer shot we see there is no crew. At a furious pace, the engine gallops backward into the station to take them on. This is very literally, "the cart before the horse;" but it is not saying, "He picked up the crew and galloped back to the station," where the order of events is reversed. What the image actually tells us is "He galloped backward to the station." (*The Fireman*, Charles Chaplin).

Reversing a person falling does not equal the same person rising, for a person giving way to gravity, his muscles relaxed, has not the same look as one with muscles thrusting against a downward pull. When the lid is lifted off Dracula's coffin, he rises up rigid and planklike, as if he were hinged at his feet. This is more expressive of death and the supernatural than the bending of joints that such an act calls for. The actor likely fell back into a padded coffin and the shot was projected reversed (*Nosferatu*, F. W. Murnau). Approaching ocean breakers, projected backwards, have a different, stiff, and formal appearance as compared with ebbing water (*At Land*, Maya Deren).

Inversion, in fact, brings about in film a new event, not a new way of describing the same one. In *Barn Dance* (Ernest Reid) a single petal appears on a daisy's yellow disk, then three more appear to form a cross, and then all the rays to fill the circle. The incident must have taken place of course in the opposite order and been reversed in projection, but it is not a different way of taking petals off, for what we see is putting petals on.

A poet comes back from the land of the dead, out of a mirror. The camera here was mounted over a pool, and the poet fell backwards into the water, through a frame made to resemble the mirror's. But since the latter part of a fall is faster than the start of it, when the action is reversed for his coming out of the mirror, the poet seems to rise swiftly at first and then slower, as if he were hurled out (*The Blood of a Poet*, Jean Cocteau).

The hysteron proteron may be found in film perhaps only in stories that start by showing how they end. Kitty Foyle is to meet Mark at St. Stephen's Hospital. They are going to be married. On the same day, Wynn, a former husband of Kitty's, comes to her lodgings and her love for him seems to be rekindled. She had been his secretary, and his wealthy upper-class family had caused the marriage to be set aside. He had remarried a woman of his own class. He now asks Kitty to go with him to South America, unmarried, and tells her to meet him at Pier 49. As Kitty packs in haste, the events of their meeting, marrying, and parting are remembered in flash-back. She dictates a message through the taxi window for a young man who will call later, looking rather upset. The hall porter slowly spells out, "I will always love you in a special way . . . I am going to be married." She tells the driver, "St. Stephen's Hospital," up to which moment, we are uncertain which of the two she has chosen. This hysteron proteron is at the same time an example of anamnesis and hyrmos (*Kitty Foyle*, Sam Wood).

II   MOVEMENT OF THE CAMERA

9   The Moving Camera—Terminology

I propose to refer to camera movement in simple spectator's terms, not a camera-man's. A viewer may not be able to tell a dolly shot from a tracking shot or a crane shot and still be fully sensitive to a film's message. All he needs to communicate his impressions is a term for shots where the camera brings him closer or pulls him back. Here are the terms I shall use:

i. Subject Stationary Camera Moving	—Approaching Shot —Retreating Shot —Rising Shot —Sinking Shot
ii. Subject Moving Camera Moving at the Same Pace	—Following Shot —Leading Shot —Sid(l)ing Shot
iii. Subject Moving Camera Stationary but swivelling	—Pan(oramic) Shot

While some write "pan shot" when the path described by the lens is horizontal, and "tilting shot" when the path is vertical, I have found it convenient most of the time (for some paths are neither the one nor the other) to use "pan" for all such move-ment, adding the angle, if it is needed, by adverb.

10   Approaching Shot—Rapid

A rapid approach to an object may signal a sudden surge of emotion aroused by it, or the sudden awareness of a situation the object signifies.

Ali Baba and Kasim's widow are looking out of a window. Below in disguise are Abu Hassan and the cobbler. In a lightning approach, the camera pounces to a close-up of the rubies at the widow's neck. Then we see Hassan staring up with greed in his eyes (*Chu Chin Chow*, Walter Forde).

A girl who is introduced as the owner's daughter, and who makes her way around in a wheelchair, arrives at a house. During the night she wakes, and is aware of a flickering light. On looking out, she sees that it comes from the summer house. She wheels herself toward the summer house and finds the door unlocked. She pushes it open, rolls her chair in and stares. Facing us in long shot, propped up in a chair, dead, is her father. Again, we are shown her, staring. Now the camera starts where it was and darts to a close-up of her father's head and shoulders. We see her stare again, and once more spring to a close-up of his mouth and eyes only. The darting shots are brief, and each adds to the shock. Then we see her mouth as it opens to scream (*Scream of Fear*, Seth Holt).

As it is the quick leap of the camera that brings the shock of surprise, the effect is the same whether the approach is toward the person shocked or the thing that shocks.

A sea captain takes off his shirt, and a cuttlefish, a skull, and other wonders are seen tattooed on his chest. As the heads of two watching little boys poke together forward, mouths open, we leap down to catch them close-up, staring transfixed (*Seriochka*, Georgi Danela).

We are looking down at Napoleon from three or four times his height. A voice says, "The Old Guard has broken." Suddenly, in the second he takes to turn and look up, we plunge to a close-up of his face, like a dagger driven home. A sudden sense of peril swung him round, a leap of thought mimicked by the camera's motion (*Waterloo*, Sergei Bondarchuk).

To escape the jealousy of a devoted wife, who has learned that her husband has seen the "love of his life," who years before had turned him down, a man goes to drink with his friends. His wife enters to plead with him to come home to dinner. The camera flashes across the room to his angry face in close-up. "I'll come home when I like," he shouts, picks up a chair, and throws it at her (*The Merchant of the Four Seasons*, R. W. Fassbinder).

Two approaching shots are used in *Swept Away* (Lina Wertmüller), for each of two people is instantly aware that what they have seen will bring to an end their way of life together. Gennarino, a deckhand, has tamed an abusive, wealthy woman with whom he has been cast away on a desert island. He has forced her to work for her food, to stop insulting him, and at last he has brought her to love him. He is in a tree overhanging the sea, reaching to a nest for eggs, when his eye is caught by something at sea: a motor launch is heading for the island. The woman has dropped a bundle of wood on the beach beneath. He looks down at her. There is a quick approach to him in the tree from below, and a quick approach down to her as she looks up. It was like a question mark: the quick thought that the bond between them was threatened.

11 Approaching Shot—Slow

Disregarding where slow retreats or approaches fill time during, say, the reading of a document (*Monsieur Vincent*, Maurice Cloche), where the motion has no tropical value whatever, the most obvious use of the slow approach is emphasis. It is the gradual dispersal from the frame of the inessential, making large, clear, and few the things remaining, as if the director kept saying, "Not this, not this, or not this." The final object of interest is commonly centered, while all the others float away from it. Several means are thus used at once to fix our attention on it.

"What business is it of yours," says Dr. Riordan to Superintendent Finsbury, "if I happen to let off a revolver in my own house?" The superintendent brings out a pocket knife, pries a bullet out of the door jamb, and goes. In half length, the doctor, looking intently, comes a little toward us. We slowly approach the door jamb, centering on the empty hole. The doctor steps backward. We pull slowly back from the door jamb. The movement suggests reflection—on the bullet hole and the superintendent's interest in it (*The Hidden Room*, Edward Dmytryk).

The slow approach can arouse expectation. We approach the stone corner of a building and wait. Lieutenant Slobinski rounds the corner, and as quickly retreats when a peering electric beam finds his face and a voice calls "halt." To emphasis, the approach here has added expectation, for what point would there be in emphasizing a place, of no prior significance in the story, if nothing were going to happen there (*To Be or Not to Be*, Ernst Lubitsch)?

In *Young and Innocent* (Alfred Hitchcock), an approach begins as a pan, and only slowly discloses its destination. Barry is wrongly accused of a murder done with the belt of his stolen raincoat, given by the murderer, a man with a twitch in his eyes, to Wilf, a tramp. A Grand Hotel matchbox is found on the coat, when recovered, so Wilf goes there to find the murderer. From looking down on shifting heads in the lobby, we pass columns and over the wall into the ballroom. Still peering down, we pan across the crowd that sits or dances. The pan, we observe, has stopped and we are tilting up to the stage and the orchestra, whose leader is facing us, beating time as he sings "Drummer Man." He, on his feet, and the drummer high at the back stand out. We are coming closer, the leader slips off left, and we make for the drummer, to full length, to a close-up of his face, to his eyes. After a pause, they twitch.

A variation occurs in *Random Harvest* (Mervyn Leroy), in which we approach, not the place where something will happen but someone who will see it happen. A newsboy has pointed out the Mercury office, and Smithy goes off right across the street. The newsboy turns away to sell a paper. We slowly approach the boy and the spectacled buyer of the paper, who looks up in a casual way, and then with alarm, as he shouts, "Look out!" The slow approach, deliberately leaving Smithy out, warned us of something impending and ominous.

In a second variation, we move ahead of two little girls, reach their door before they do, and wait for them to catch up and reenter. Not merely is there a sense of prescience or perhaps omniscience but this takes the emphasis off the girls and throws it on to the place (*Fanny By Gaslight*, Anthony Asquith).

Another approach in the same film is slow nearly to imperceptibility. If less purposeful than a faster one, this approach is more reflective, as if the director were to say, "I am fascinated by all these people, but of those abroad on this fine April morning, I think I shall let the hawker go his way, and the one leaving the pub and the one that enters, and the two fine ladies with escorts, and see where the two little girls will take me, the one in the black dress and the one in the white, as they talk and throw their ball." All this time the girls are gradually growing larger, and the rest of the street is edging off the frame.

The approach may place a detail in its context. Take a long down shot of a large hall, and a wide staircase, the hall thronged with guests. As we slowly approach, among the figures drifting away to the sides we recognize, after a while, the constant center, Alicia. As we come closer still, the center is now her hand, and the final close-up is the key it holds (*Notorious*, Alfred Hitchcock).

12 Retreating Shots

The retreat is chiefly used in two ways. First and most obvious, it adds a sense of disclosure. As we move back from the close view with which we start, other things, one after another, float in from the sides and the composition grows from simple to multiple. The retreat can be, in the second place, used for surprise, revealing relations not known before between things or people. In René Clair's *And Then There Were None*, Lombard says to someone beyond the door that he has no revolver, at the very moment of placing one in his pocket. We retreat through a keyhole mask, to see Blore looking through it at Lombard. We retreat through another keyhole to see Dr. Armstrong watching Blore, and we pan through a right angle to observe the judge at the end of the hall, speculating on what the doctor is doing.

This means of drawing attention to two related things can be used equally well with still paintings: a retreat from a dead man's face to show the dissecting surgeon and those who are watching; or showing each of two men by himself, and then retreating to show the commerce between them (*Rembrandt*, Starcky Sayer).

In *Carnet de Bal* (Julien Duvivier), the slow reflective retreat is from the past back to the present through an ambiguity of sound and image. A pianist plays a waltz, which takes a woman back to the ball when last she had heard it. As we see the remembered scene, the tune flows without break from piano to orchestra. We are still in the past as the orchestra leaves the tune again to the pianist. We see his hands in close-up, and, retreating slowly from them, we find we are back in the present, the music having never stopped.

The retreat may convey a subjective state.

Two small boys are looking in at the window of Vassya's house. A family council is going on. The boy's uncle (a sea captain, here on a visit) asks how Vassya gets the money for cigarettes and points out his low marks at school. The uncle rises to his feet. "The boy needs a rod of iron," he says, and bangs his hand on the table. "Get out. He's going to thrash him," one little boy says to the other. There is a crash and a quick retreat both at once, which cuts the window down in size to a tiny square in the center. Two startled heads poke out of a sea of foliage. They had fallen from the window. The retreat conveys their wish to flee and their sudden lack of support, as they lose their balance and tumble into the shrubs (*Seriochka*, Georgi Danela).

The slow approach, which at the same time sets a scene and picks out a detail, as in *Fanny by Gaslight,* and the slow retreat from a starting detail to disclose or explain its context, are both common alternative means of starting a film or sequence. The retreat, however, may not merely reveal a setting to the viewers, but the setting as one of the characters takes it in, piece by piece.

Sergeyev brought from the sewers and slums of Moscow a number of "wild boys," to start them on a new life in the country. Coming back after a day or so away to their new home, an abandoned monastery, he stops at the refectory door, facing us, and looks about him somberly. The moment he stops, the camera starts pulling back in a continuation of his movement, exposing a jumble of broken chairs and tables overturned, as his eye moves from close to far in several fixations. The boys he trusted had gone wild again (*The Road to Life*, Nicolai Ekk).

It remains to notice the emphatic use of retreating shots.

Two mimes raise an imaginary balloon from waist level to above their heads, each using one hand. As they do this, the camera sinks from a close-up of their heads and arms, down their bodies nearly to their feet as if the balloon were drawing them up to the ceiling. The plain background and the nonappearance of either floor or feet helps the illusion (*Down the Ancient Stairs*, Mauro Bolognini).

13 Traveling Shots

Little time needs to be spent on traveling shots: they rarely add much figurative meaning. They merely keep a moving person the same size on the screen so as to be clearly seen.

It may be a following shot, chasing a cluster of leaves that blow along a floor and out a doorway (*The Fall of the House of Usher*, Jean Epstein). Motorcars are often followed, and a common leading shot is one that looks back on the driver and passenger (*Face to Face*, Ingmar Bergman).

The sidling shot has been used as a means of shifting an attribute from one thing or person to another one, the figure hypallage. A notable sidling shot is the long traverse even-pace with the charging French knights at Agincourt (*Henry the Fifth*, Laurence Olivier), by which the speed of the fleeting countryside beyond shifts to the knights, the camera moving sideways at the same speed, and keeping them at the same place in center screen.

Motion can be quickened by shifting a sidling camera closer to things passing between the camera and the person centered, or by changing from a leading shot, where the background alters little, to an air shot, where the ground a horseman is galloping over flows constantly past him (*Tom Jones*, Tony Richardson).

14 Panoramic Shots I—Relations

A pan shot is not the same as turning the head. When we do this, we switch our gaze from the thing seen before we turn to the thing we turn to see. We do not attend to, or even see, the things passed on the way.[14] In film it is otherwise: we are watching the screen, and all that passes across it claims our attention equally. A common use of the pan shot is thus to relate things in space, making one part of another's context. Sidling shots past stationary subjects are included here with pan shots, as both are used for the same purpose.

We pan the countryside, keeping centered a distant stagecoach traveling along the road. Quite close, a rock intrudes into the frame from the right; then a revolver lying on it, and last, Captain Starlight, whose hand is holding the weapon (*Robbery under Arms*, Jack Lee).

"Where are you, Robin?" says one of the escaping outlaws. We pan obliquely upwards, pass the portcullis, and reach the figure of Robin on top of the wall, about to climb over. "Here I am," he answers (*Robin Hood*, Michael Curtiz and William Keighley).

We stand at a corner. Marshal Kane is coming toward us along the main street. To right frame are the five or six steps that rise up to verandas in front of stores. We pan a quarter circle past a corner: four men, sworn to kill the marshal, are coming toward us here. We, but not they, can see that their paths, if nothing intervenes, will cross close to the corner (*High Noon*, Fred Zinnemann).

Space, as always, brings time with it. A slower pan hints at a longer distance and pans may be from one time to another.[15] We pan from Morgenhall interviewing his client in prison, to a prior incident at Fowle's home or on to his trial, passing a neutral gray wall to reach the other time, like panning past successive incidents on a Grecian crater (*The Dock Brief*, James Hill). Since we cannot at the moment move in time, we cannot say what a pan across the days would look like, so a flat neutrality is sensibly substituted.

Where it can be done, it may be clearer to relate things by showing them both at once. Prince Andrei opens a book while waiting for Suvorin. We first imitate his glance by panning from a sheet of notepaper he finds as he opens the book to the facing page. Then we see side by side a letter printed in the book, "I revere you. I esteem and admire you . . ." and the same letter, copied word for word on the sheet of paper and addressed to Lisaveta Ivanovna. Relation in the same frame enables the viewer to go to and fro between the things compared, so as to confirm a first impression, desirable in such a case as this (*The Queen of Spades*, Thorold Dickinson).

15 Panoramic Shots II—Anticipation

The panning camera imports purpose—we are on our way somewhere and this arouses anticipation.

This is obviously so where a character looks off the frame, and the camera pans to satisfy the curiosity aroused. In *The Man in Grey* (Leslie Arliss), Hester enters left into the entrance hall of a school and stands in profile, a porter bringing her trunk behind her. She looks offscreen right. We pan right slowly, to stop halfway up an impressive staircase on the figure of Mrs. Patchett, headmistress.

Even without the added strength of a glance, any such traverse makes us curious. A shell-shocked soldier, his memory gone, escapes from hospital and is found and befriended by an actress. She fears to leave him alone in her dressing room, so, when she is called, she puts a chair on an iron balcony in front of her door from where he can see the stage, and sets him down. "I'm all right really," he says. It is armistice night, and the audience rowdy, and they clamber on the stage after the curtain. As we look down on the lighthearted commotion, we are aware that our gaze is moving into the wings, past the flats, past the balcony rail, and we suddenly say to ourselves, "Oh yes, how has Smithy been doing all this time?" We reach the chair; it is empty, and on the balcony floor beyond it Smithy lies unconscious. A straight cut from stage to Smith would have been a sudden shock, which would have been out of place in this romantic tale and would not have aroused the question before showing the answer (*Random Harvest*, Mervyn Leroy).

Its mood of curiosity makes a pan shot a good beginning. From a tower clock at midnight, we pass disturbed birds and a prowling cat, and hear a loud knocking. We travel along a row of houses, with windows lighting up, two remaining dark (heavy sleepers), and some with heads poking through. To a growing murmur of talk, we sink down close to a front door as a constable knocks again. Inside, we pan down the same policeman, across to Diana Baring, who sits and stares, across the carpet, past a poker and come to stop on a body (*Murder*, Alfred Hitchcock).

Rising and sinking shots that stay on the same place and people do not arouse this anticipation and thus can surprise us. Seen from tree height, twenty or so Norwegian soldiers run out of a wide gate. We slowly sink with camera still on them, as if to show them closer. A hoarse voice warns "Here they come!" and into the frame rise the backs of German machine gunners, just in front of us (*The Moon Is Down*, Irving Pichel).

16 Panoramic Shots III—Description

There are two alternatives to this opening of *Murder*. Each particular, cut in a separate shot, would have been as clear, but this would not have shown the relation of each to the other. Two long shots, one outside and one in, would have shown the relation, but at such a distance that no particular came to the eye clearly. A pan or sidling shot can do both.

When Philip first enters Mildred's room, there is a close-up of his hand as it hangs up his hat, from which our eye traces a tortuous course past every squalid article till it reaches Mildred. So might his eyes have moved as he and we learn something of her from what she lives with (*Of Human Bondage*, John Cromwell).

At the end of *Robin Hood* (Michael Curtiz and William Keighley), King John's men are surrendering their weapons. That their number is large is shown by a sidling shot along a row of shields, as swords and spears are thrown down on them, the angle slowly rising to bring in the file of men walking alongside and ending at last on

Robin Hood and the king. The varying angle allows a lengthier shot without monotony, and the longer the movement lasts the greater the conquest appears to be.

Each of these moving shots depicts a whole and its parts at the same time. The parts are near enough to yield their full meaning, but are shown to belong to a larger continuum where their meaning lies.

In *The General Died at Dawn* (Lewis Milestone), the director stressed the size of an advancing army by fusing two motions. The troops approach toward us. We neither move toward nor away from them, but we sidle along a line parallel to theirs. As we move, the smooth calm gray of a grassy knoll is broken by an unquiet bobbing up and down of a few black dots above its horizon. As we keep moving right, along the knoll, the dots acquire shoulders, and then bodies. They become bobbing men and then rise up on legs, walking. The first jerky bobbing of things unknown, almost abstract, unidentifiable, arouses disquiet in us. A camera standing still would show only a small squad advancing. The squad, as we move, becomes an endless horde, dominant and irresistible as the soldiers grow higher and larger. This is an excellent figure.

17 Panoramic Shots IV—Adding Speed

The speed of a thing may be added to by camera movement.

In the second episode of *Dusty Bates* (Darrell Catling), as police and criminals engage, the camera in up shot, hand-held, sways with different pairs, as they struggle to and fro. When a body falls, the camera sinks with it. The instability of those engaged, and of the situation itself, is strongly felt.

Less easily noticed is a camera panning left as it photographs a thing moving right, thereby enhancing speed. In *We From Kronstadt* (E. Dzigan), the speed of warships was quickened by this means, for the sea between the ship and us also moved right. And so in *The Defense of Siberia* (the Brothers Vassiliev), as men slide down an iced hill, we pan slightly up to increase their apparent speed.

18 Panoramic Shots V—Adding Animation

A camera travels past and quite close to yellow leaves, and through gaps between them, we see people in various colored costumes. The yellow speeding past gives a sense of pace and gaiety, and yet we find in later, longer shots that everyone we saw was merely standing (*Shadows of Our Forgotten Ancestors*, Sergei Parazhdanov).

This is useful in films composed of stills. Moving slowly down the backs of prospectors, we almost feel their line trudging away from us through the snow. In the same film, *City of Gold* (Roman Kroitor), a band is performing, and as we pan from it through the listening crowd, we hear a hymn tune played by a band. We pause several times on a man's face, looking down reflectively or soberly, his thoughts perhaps on other happier times when he had heard the tune before. In another place, the camera takes us from a man's intent face to the pan of gravel below it, in close-up.

19 Panoramic Shots VI—Pause

A pan can strengthen a pause. In a prisoner-of-war camp, Pasqualino has gained the woman commandant's favor, and is put in charge of Stalag 23. She tells him to pick six for execution—if not, she will execute them all. He reads the names. Two prisoners run out of line, saying they cannot stand the strain. One plunges into a tank; the other is brought to his knees. Pasqualino is marched along the line to him, and is handed a cocked revolver. "I'd rather die," he says, "I won't do it." The kneeling man looks up, "They'll do it anyway. I'd rather you did it." Pasqualino points the revolver down, shoots at the head, and the body falls. There is a sudden furious brief barking of dogs. We see the leashed Alsatians between booted legs; we retreat from them to the corpse and a few drops of blood beside it; from there to show Pasqualino's face in close-up, from which we pan up to a long shot of the large hall, dull green like a limbo of lost souls, filled with kneeling men in prison dress, their heads looking down, their prisoner supervisors standing in line beside them. We circle back once more to Pasqualino, and approach to close-up of the revolver barrel pointing down from his hanging hand. From there we rise past his head, past the roomful of moveless men, and into a green mist. And all in silence, barely broken by sparse notes of music (*Seven Beauties*, Lina Wertmüller). We feel the enormity of what he has done sinking slowly and inerasably into his depths.

20 Panoramic Shots VII—The Streaking Pan[16]

A slow and a quick pan in contrast, may signal a change in events. Miss Richmond is beautiful, well-connected, and respectfully treated. She is on her knees when the headmistress, followed by a servant, enters the dormitory. Mrs. Patchett tells the servant to put the candle out in ten minutes, when Miss Richmond has finished her devotions. As the two leave, we pan slowly with them. The moment the door is closed, we pan quickly back to show Clarissa dropping her sanctity with unseemly alacrity and a gleeful smile, and the whole dormitory awakes to life. The quick pan launched us into the lively scene that followed. It was the movement more than what it showed that affected us, since both pans passed the same things (*The Man in Grey*, Leslie Arliss).

This is especially true of what I call the streaking pan, for its speed dismembers all shape or identity in the things traversed, and any effect must come from the rapid sweep of mere streaks of light. It is common experience that when a train is going the other way past our own, vertical bars or lines, like the mullions dividing windows, grow narrow in width and at higher speeds, vanish. Gaps between cars are merely flickers in the horizontal band of gray that the whole course of windows now has become. On passing walls, the lines that remain are those that parallel the line of movement, those between courses of tile or brick. The mortared space between the bricks in a course is wiped out. All shapes are now dissolved into fleeting rods and blobs of broken light, flowing the opposite way to our own movement. Their narrow, linear horizontal shape, combined with speed, makes the word *streak* an irresistible description.

The first meaning conveyed by the fleeting streaks is obviously speed.

Several such pans may cumulate their effect. We hear a bell ringing below decks. There is a streaking pan to a dark room, which ends with men rolling off their bunks. From the head of a man waking, the camera streaks to a hat; a hand enters and grabs it off the hook. Pan to a coat from another waking head, and a snatching hand whips it off the frame. From a third head, we streak down to sea boots; hands grab and pull them on feet. The effect in part is the contrast between the rush of light and the object suddenly still when the motion stops (*In Which We Serve*, Noël Coward and David Lean).

To this first meaning of pace, it is easy to add a sense of sudden awareness or sudden action.

Hannay shows the bullet hole in the Bible, in telling how he was nearly killed by Jordan. The sheriff is reassuring and friendly, just waiting for some official to come. Hannay, as he talks, rises and walks to the window, casting a casual glance through the panes. We cut to the sheriff sitting near the door. A police sergeant and two constables enter. "I arrest you, Hannay, on the charge of murder," the sheriff says. There is a quick streaking pan from them to Hannay staring at them, stunned by the sudden change in front, stone-still. A pause; and with a sudden leap he breaks through the window (*The Thirty-Nine Steps*, Alfred Hitchcock).

Marshall Tyler presented a titled lady with a silver dish, in which he had placed a poisoned chocolate. She did not eat it, but nonetheless died of natural causes. At the reading of the will, Tyler catches sight of his fiancée discovering the silver dish, and about to put the chocolate into her mouth. Held in center frame, he races across the room, which streaks by behind him, seizes the chocolate, and hurls it into the fireplace. "Well," Rowena says, "You'd think it was poisoned" (*Flesh and Fantasy*, Julien Duvivier).

From speed it is a short step to distance, for how fast the streaks are moving past we cannot tell—we could be covering any distance. A streaking pan is used in *North Sea* (Harry Watt) to suggest the speed of radio waves, and thus the tremendous distance covered by them. Her antenna damaged in a storm, the trawler *John Gilman* cannot reach Wick Radio. We have seen men climbing the vessel's mast, repairing the wires. The skipper sits in front of his radio, and says, "We'll try now." From a close-up of the *John Gilman's* microphone, as the skipper starts to speak, there is a streaking pan left, ending up on an operator listening to the voice that continues through the pan. It is Wick Radio receiving. The pan, of course, is impossible, if seen as one from place to place in space. The camera would have to be high enough to overcome the effect of the earth's curvature and equipped with a telephoto lens of great power, leaving out of account some means of seeing through walls. The imaginary camera position, however, does remind us that what is simulated is a normal use of the pan, raised greatly in dimensions.

As with place to place, so from time to time. In *The Mystery of Edwin Drood* (Stuart Walker), the streaking pans between conversations is the gossip "spreading like wildfire"—"in no time at all".

III   OTHER FIGURATIVE USES

21   Abstraction—Movement as Meaning

It is clear then that as camera movement alters the shapes of things and persons to passing patterns of light, the concrete becomes the abstract, the outer form is of no consequence, and the motion is everything. The meaning lies in the motion.

There are many examples of this in *Night Mail* (Basil Wright and Harry Watt). In an air shot, the roof of the train is a narrow vertical band, held in the center, and the countryside is merely a vibrant surface pouring down the screen at either side in vertical streaks.

To suggest the speed of a stooping falcon, we are shown a mere speck of black, swelling toward us at a tremendous rate, but on the screen we see it so briefly, that whether or not what we saw was a bird, we really cannot say (*The Falcons*, Istvan Gaal).

Veronica has married Mark, a home-staying musician, believing that his brother Boris was killed in the war. In her hearing, her Uncle Fedor has spoken bitterly of women who marry rats who will not fight for their country. Veronica runs and we travel with her, centering now her feet, now her head and her shoulders. Between her and us are the pales of an iron fence. So quickly do we pass them by that they narrow into a mere quivering of the running girl's image, vividly suggesting her inner turmoil. She mounts the steps of a bridge, seeming in telephoto lens less to climb than to pulse upward. Slow and afraid, she approaches the rail of the bridge and covers her face with her hands. Down the screen the train pounces, fearful in black smoke, her scream embedded in its roar (*The Cranes Are Flying*, Mikhail Kalatozov).

Even with no distortion, the mere quality of motion can often by itself command our feelings.

Unusual happenings in the village of Piedmont have led the authorities to call a "Wildfire Alert." The excitement aroused by this action is conveyed by the teletype machine, typing out the top secret clearance of the men involved. Besides its noisy chattering, the irregular popping up and down of the type carriers, the steady flow of the carriage sideways despite the rapid staccato with which it pours letters out into words and sentences—this is itself exhilarating (*The Andromeda Strain*, Robert Wise).

A wide screen used throughout a film has little figurative meaning; but when Napoleon has reached the plain of Lombardy and made himself master of the army there and those who lead it, the single center frame leaps out to three times its size, and this is electrifying. We feel that Napoleon's world has enlarged and he is no longer merely a notable Frenchman, but one that all Europe must take account of (*Napoleon*, Abel Gance).

Griffith in *The Birth of a Nation* uses white smoke in battle scenes, in single spurts, in drifting sheets blotting or exposing patches of struggling men, and in unexpected swirls from which someone may emerge. The slow diffusion of smoke, so different from the sudden violence of battle, resembles clouds that float without haste across continents, undisturbed by doings far below them, and makes the fighting glimpsed in its windows part of a slow sweep of historical change.

22 Metaphorical Uses

Wartime shots of troops rising out of trenches and running, and six horses galloping with limber and gun are followed by the phrase, "the Canadians threw themselves at Vimy Ridge. . . ." To the sounds of battle, we move through the air in a slow and steady approach over a coppice, and down a path cut across it pointing us to the twin pylons of the Vimy Ridge Memorial (*Graves of Sacrifice*, Donald Brittain).

Jack Sanders wins a bout that qualifies him to challenge the champion. In great good spirits, he invites five circus friends home to drink to "My wife and happiness." He comes out unhappily to say that his wife is not home, but invites them in. He hears the elevator stopping and eagerly pours the wine, which bubbles vigorously. It is not his wife. They wait. In a down shot of the six glasses, the now halfhearted bubbling soon stops. Four of the guests are crowded on a couch, one sleeping, the others glumly silent. Jack is standing at the window (*The Ring*, Alfred Hitchcock).

23 Montage

Montage may suggest movement.

Strauss's wife, nearly full length, stands in a dark opening, dressed in white. Her husband is rehearsing a new work in the opera house. For six bars of a waltz, we leap back on the first beat to a farther-off shot. In the last bar we see her as if from the stage, a tiny white figure surrounded by darkness. It is like a visual pulse. The shrinking image is perhaps the draining away of a resolution to challenge her rival, who was singing Strauss's music with such verve (*The Great Waltz*, Julien Duvivier).

Norma, searching in the mountains for her brother Elie, slips and tumbles down a snowy slope. Rising to her feet, she sees Elie hanging from a tree root on the side of a precipice. Surrounded by a circular black mask, one quick face follows another, but even after seeing them three times, I cannot say whose faces they are, so brief is their passing. It is nothing to the point that looking at each frame by itself could identify them.[17] What the images are is in fact of little consequence: it is the quick twinkling of contrasting masses that works the impression—of an agonized whirl of thought, of searing consternation (*La Roue*, Abel Gance).

Norman McLaren has devised various distortions, by abstracting and repeating the same phase of a movement. In an early film, quoted by Gavin Millar, a man crosses a yard, his heels together all the time. Another man glides as if skating on one leg, a third comes down a fire escape, sitting all the way, and yet another keeps removing innumerable pairs of glasses. The heels-together position was presumably a recurring phase in making a series of side steps. By leaving all else out and editing together only the frames containing this phase, by montage, that is to say, the director has abstracted from reality an unnatural, automatic, or puppetlike motion. It is at the same time a figure of ellipsis, motion, and montage (*The Eye Hears and the Ear Sees*).

The same director showed us two neighbours floating above the ground as if on their knees. His actors must have found this more strenuous, each making some three hundred leaps, with his lower legs bent up, each one a little away from the last. By editing together the highest points of the leaps, the two appear to be sledging around on their shins, in thin air (*Neighbours*, Norman McLaren).

A change in the direction of movement may signify a change in situation. The gray Russian citizen-soldiers are swept down the frame to the bottom by a surge of white-cloaked Teuton knights, and later, by movement the opposite way, the frame changes to gray again from white (*Alexander Nevski*, S. M. Eisenstein).

24 Inner State

It was noted above that when we turn our head, we are aware of what we see before we turn, and of what we turn to look at, but not of what is between them. When a pan, then, is to simulate a person's glance, the emphasis must lie on the start and the finish. Charlie looks at Chris's daisy, a magnificent pattern of gold painted on black. "Do you mean to say?" he asks Chris, "that you see this when you look at that?" and we pan from the canvas to a glass of water holding a wilted flower, with nothing to catch our attention seen between (*Scarlet Street*, Fritz Lang).

Having read the advice, "When you want to get control of the masses, begin with the stupidest," Foxey-Loxey strolls along observing various fowls, reciting their names in the voice of one weighing their qualifications. The camera pauses on each as he says its name, and the last is Chicken Little. We pan beyond him to an empty frame, and then back to look him over again, as Foxey-Loxey's voice says with conviction, "Yeah, he looks nice and stupid" (*Chicken Little*, Walt Disney).

The viewer thus may personate one of the characters and see with his eye through the camera, whose movement is that of the character. The squire and his sister are thrown from their chaise when it loses a wheel. The camera swings from the road up to the sky and the trees, as if they were tipped over to land on their backs (*Tom Jones*, Tony Richardson).

The first-person camera, however, is not the only way to express inner states by means of motion. Norma, out of jail, falls out with her boyfriend, goes to a discotheque, a place forbidden to her during probation, and dances with another boy, Geordie. As they dance, in half-length shot, Geordie murmurs, "Good-bye, Charlie Hooker." She draws quickly back against the vaguely dark discotheque and sparks of light from a circling glass ball move slowly across her face and the darkness, reflecting a mood of uncertainty, even fear (*I Believe in You*, Michael Ralph and Basil Dearden).

A like uncertainty is felt by Anne in *Day of Wrath* (Carl Theodor Dreyer). She is Pastor Absalom's wife, but she is in love with her stepson. She cannot forget that her mother was a suspected witch, and asks herself if she is one. The camera swings from profile to full face, and the background whirls dizzily behind her.

As Carol speaks to Stephen on their first meeting, and later when she feels that the war may take him from her, the camera several times pulses toward her slowly, as if to match an upsurge of feeling (*Dangerous Moonlight*, Brian Desmond Hurst).

25 Coupling Motions Together

Two converging movements increase the weight of emphasis. In a high down shot, a tractor-trailer enters a square, moving to down left on a shallow diagonal. The truck stops and the driver alights and continues to walk in the same direction. During this we approach a refuse bin on the ground bottom left, reaching a close-up in the same frame of both the bin and the driver. We see a pair of women's legs sticking out of the bin. The convergence of the approaching camera and the path pursued by the truck and the driver give a sense of inevitability (*Panic*, Julien Duvivier).

While Strauss and Carla waltz to *Tales from the Vienna Woods*, the camera at first circles as they are doing, clockwise, and then slowly starts to circle back the other way. The couple now seems to turn at a faster, giddier pace, and everything beyond them, dark and indeterminate in shape, seems to swirl with them. All we see in the frame is now in motion, faster and faster (*The Great Waltz*, Julien Duvivier).

26 The Range of Motion

When using still pictures, on which, by a kind of hypallage, the camera confers its movement, the motion must be varied in order to avoid monotony. In a film composed entirely of prints by Daumier, we retreat from a single visitor to a long shot of the Paris Botanical Gardens; we tilt from a windlass down a mine cable, to show two children hanging on to the end; we retreat from a hand holding a glass of wine, and pan to show a long table running from us, with a man at the far end on a rostrum speaking to an excited audience; we approach to the head of a dead boy, and pan along a wagonful of the dead (*1848*, Victoria Spiri Mercantor, Marguerite de la Mure, and Albert Sadoul).

The same treatment has been given to things in the round, which may appear to be moving sideways, falling over, turning round, or moving closer, all by grace of the moving camera. Driftwood and carved figures are treated in this way in *The Banshees* (John Straiton).

In a film such as *Night Mail* (Basil Wright and Harry Watt), one of whose themes is the speed of the train taking the mail to Scotland, the skill lies in how many different ways this can be shown:

By *antithesis:* Section men standing still by the track and the train speeding past;
    As the wheels and lower carriage are sweeping by on the tracks above, a newspaper, dropped from the train, lies on the gravel, still;
By *metonymy:* The shadow of smoke pouring from the engine's funnel is gray on the passing grass;
    A mail bag hangs from an arm. From the right the train tears out from behind an embankment. After the sixth car has passed, the bag is gone. With just as little to show how it is done, another bag is suddenly in the catching net;
    In an air shot, the train is only seen as a long streak of steam on a dark landscape;
    Lines of light race past us, almost entirely abstract—they might be a passing train or a station, a light in a tunnel, or lights of a passing village, all identity streaked out;
By *montage:* The wheels of the engine streaming with exhaust steam are cut in with a black dog and then with rabbits running from us, with birds rising from cover;
By *hypallage:* (movement transferred from the train to something else):
    In down shots of the tracks from the front of the train, the rails writhe off into sidings and back into the main line again;
    In sidling shots from the train, telegraph wires swoop down and up between poles;
    Shot from an airplane at the same speed, the countryside streaks by the still train;
    In shots from the top of the train, bridges and gantries rise over above us;
    The engineer and the fireman of a train waiting on a siding are looking out of the cab towards the left—their heads turn quickly to look right;
By *using the frame:* The train suddenly bolts into the frame from bottom right, and rapidly recedes in size into the distance;
By *coupling movements together:* The train approaches us from right frame, and as it passes, the camera swivels with it in a quick pan, to show it vanishing into the distance on the left.

14
Montage

1   The Nature of Montage

More has been written on *montage* than on any other aspect of film; "avant-garde" magazines like *Film Art*[1] pondered on it in almost every issue; so all that is needed here is to deal with its use as a figure.[2]

Eisenstein speaks of "the montage trope," to which he adds a literary definition, "a figure of speech which consists in the use of a word or phrase in a sense other than that which is proper to it," and he gives as an example the word *sharp*, properly used of a *sword*, but figuratively said of *wit*.[3] When two pieces of film are put together, their meanings, according to Eisenstein, collide, and the consequence of the collision is a meaning not present in either piece by itself.[4] In an often-cited passage, he draws a parallel to ideographs. The signs in Chinese for *water* and *eye*, if written together, give the meaning *weep*. The signs for *dog* and *mouth* collide in the meaning *bark*. The Haiku too is the agglutination of several observations:

> Veiling me from sun
> A cedar lapped me in scent
> As I sawed its trunk.[5]

Not only do three distinct images—the sun through the leaf sprays, the pungent scent, and the destroying saw fuse in a single experience, but only together do they yield some such sense as ingratitude. It is in the reader's mind, says Eisenstein, that this whole forms and arouses his emotions.[6]

As Arnheim writes, a film is a sequence of many single frames projected one after another, so it cannot escape a figurative character, since every frame and every piece must in some degree be colored in meaning by all the frames or pieces projected before it.[7] He points out, for example, that a head, seen in profile and then full-face, gives the impression of having turned.

Roman Jakobson writes that "Combination and contexture are two faces of the same operation."[8] Any piece of film or succession of single frames embeds in a context the frames or other smaller units that make it up. This piece, in turn, will find a context when it is spliced with other pieces in a longer whole. This is a quality found both in film and in human experience, for "the present like a note in music, is nothing but as it appertains to what is past and what is to come."[9]

Kuleshov wrote that each art is built on a raw material, the arrangement of which was its means of expression.[10] It could be words, pigments, or strips of film. This, of course, implies that photographing people and places is not art, any more than compiling a dictionary or placing an order for paints is. Each art, in the second place, assembles its material in its own way. Words are ordered in sentences, pigments are mixed and brushed on a surface, and pieces of film are spliced in sequence with others. Thus we are into syntax, which, by controlling the order in which words or impressions are received, imputes a relation between them.[11]

Christian Metz points out that milk is broken up into cream, butter, skim milk, and so on, and these are put together with other substances to form new wholes, glue, or a cup of coffee.[12] Likewise, says Eisenstein, a director starts with an impression he wishes to convey, and picks the situations or visual images whose blending in the viewer's mind will arouse this impression.[13] It is like picking one rising agent (baking soda, baking powder, yeast), one fat (oil, butter, lard), one flavoring, one flour, and the rest, which, when all combined, will make the bread intended. The impression the images leave in the viewer's mind will not be quite the one the director started with, for each viewer's temperament and experience will combine with and color the images, which find in each viewer a new context. The film is a joint creation of director and viewer.

The situations and images used in giving visual form to an idea are its denotation or extensional meaning, which Hayakawa describes as putting one's hand over one's mouth and pointing rather than speaking. Two of the rules that Hayakawa gives for extensional meanings are: (a) Meaning is determined by context and (b) The meanings of words are *not* in the words (and the same is true of the images we see on the screen); they are in *us*.[14]

2 Fractional Synecdoches

To exhibit a person's character by showing how he behaves in a situation is to use a synecdoche, since the minutes we see are but a part of a life. If several situations are shown, to reinforce or enlarge our concept, each is no less a synecdoche because it supports the others.

The director of *Ecstasy*, Gustave Machaty, shows us the behavior of a husband on his marriage night. We pan from his feet in patent leather shoes to a hand with a key, which is trying to open a door. With a choice of two locks and three keys, the hand, with much deliberation, opens the door by the last possible option. Still holding his bride, whom he has carried over the threshold, the bridegroom pushes off each shoe with the opposite foot, and we see on his face the only contented smile he gives. He removes his jacket, and stiff in white waistcoat he bends over to the fringe of a rug and brushes with his fingers something too minute to be seen in close-up. When both have donned pajamas, the bride enters the bathroom and playfully and gently takes the toothbrush out of his hand, and puts it in the glass on the shelf. He takes it out and places it back again, its bristles up. She sits on his knee and invites him to undo the catch on her necklace. In doing this, he pricks his finger. He fondles the finger with concern, and hardly seems to notice her leaving him. He lets her go to bed unattended, while he sits and dozes in the bathroom. These events combine to convey a man who is unpractical, passionless, easily deflected by trivia, and unresponsive to the feelings of others.

Directors and physicians are both seekers of symptoms, the outer signs of inner events. Robert Anderson shows us a man who has slept in, and is going to be late for the office. He looks at his tongue, picks up and lays down both orange juice and bread, does an exercize, and pants heavily. He telephones his wife to say he is sick; he asks her to make a doctor's appointment for after lunch, and then to telephone his office for him. He is not dressed when she comes to drive him to the doctor. He asks her what tie to wear, wonders where he left his pocket-book, and then finds it after some search in his jacket pocket. The director brings in a physician to discuss the symptoms we have seen, and we see that they both share a common procedure, the search for visible signs, which, whether observed or invented, either by doctor or director, would lead the viewer in this case to a diagnosis of *Over-Dependency.*

In the same way, a director may choose from the details in a scene those that carry the same abstract notion, such as danger. An up shot from down in a valley brings out the flimsy make of a planked scaffold that hyphens parts of a mountain road around a hairpin bend. A close-up shows a truck's rear wheel skidding on the scaffolding's wet planks, and we hear the creak of timbers. A hand thrusts a bunch of twigs in front of the wheels, which grip and slowly move away from the edge. But the scaffolding hangs from cables, and a lug on the side of the truck hooks one of these and, unknown to the driver, tugs it into a deepening V as the truck advances. We see the hook that links the upper and lower parts of the cable straightening under the tremendous pull till at last the two pieces fling apart. In a long shot, the scaffolding breaks into its component logs, and careers down the slope into the valley, the truck's rearmost wheels just barely resting on the rocky edge (*The Wages of Fear,* Henri-Georges Clouzot and others). Each of these particular shots could yield the meaning "danger." Piling one on top of another stretches out the time the message is on the screen, and gives it, with each additional image, greater power.[15]

3 Congeries or Accumulation

A succession of things, persons, or situations, all with a similar drift, is called *congeries* or *accumulatio,* a piling or heaping up.[16] The *City Night Piece* is almost a filmic treatment:

> The clock just struck two; the expiring taper rises and sinks in the socket, the watchman forgets the hour in slumber, the laborious and the happy are at rest, and nothing wakes but meditation, guilt, revelry, and despair. The drunkard once more fills the destroying bowl, the robber walks his midnight round, and the suicide lifts his guilty arm against his own sacred person.[17]

How easy to find a parallel to this in Jules Dassin's *Naked City* or *The Man with a Movie Camera!*

In congeries, as distinguished from repetition, items may not be the same in shape: they shape the same theme; they fuse, like the sounds of a city, in a single meaning.

Visual patterns may be accumulated, all with a single common characteristic. The best example of this, even though it is fifty years old, is found in *The Battleship Potemkin* (S. M. Eisenstein). Nearly every shot of what the director has called act 1, "Morning of June 14, 1905," has a similar visual pattern, small movements that vacillate or circle within the frame, never challenging the limit set by the frame lines. There are sailors forming and breaking groups; the heads of other sailors peering at sides of meat; maggots aswarm on hanging carcasses; two officers who enter, stop, and look back to scrutinize; sailors on deck walking to and fro as they talk; a cleaning rod running in and out of a gun's muzzle; hands rubbing to and fro to polish a bollard or trunnion; a spoon stirring a cauldron; mess tables hung from the ceiling swaying to and fro to the ship's roll. Not every shot conforms to this pattern, but most of them do, enough to set a mood of indecision, instability, discontent. With great skill, the director has found in the setting itself, not merely the incidents that led to the mutiny but visual patterns that through their mere form, conveyed the covert resentment that went before it.[18]

In *The Angry Silence* (Guy Green) thirteen men decide not to comply when a strike is called. "I know what I'd do," says one picket. Cut to

a hurled brick shattering a window;
a refuse pail being dumped out on a front step;
greenhouse panes being struck through one after another;
a clothes line being cut down and the washing trampled;
a bicycle being thrown on the ground and hammered;
a car burning.

All these were done by night, the movement quick with a sudden breaking of silence and the faces unseen.

In most cases however, the director is content with a series of situations that are unlinked by likeness in the visual images. In *Happy Anniversary* (Pierre Etaix) a line of cars is held up at a city intersection. A driver reading a book, puts it down, pulls his goggles down over his eyes, starts the car, drives six inches forward, pushes up his goggles, and opens his book again. We pan down to the stub of a cigarette he has thrown on the road, pan back to a cluster of a dozen stubs, up to a man sitting in another car dictating a letter and then to the back seat, where a secretary sits at a portable typewriter. We pan on to a man, equiped with cloth and pail, who with much care and no trace of haste, is washing down a white car. It is, of course, hyperbole, but we gain the impression of long delays in city travel being so normal that people plan their days to make provision for it.

Congeries can place before us a time: the depression—queues of people seeking relief, soup kitchens, walking feet, men leaping on freight cars or rummaging for food in refuse cans, factory gates closing, signs like "no men wanted" (*The Drylanders*, Donald Haldane). It may suggest a place: the Australian desert—blowing sand, a camel wagon, dry bones by a roadside, steaming water bubbling out of a bore-hole, skeletons of cattle hung on a tree by floods, a crawling snake, crumbling walls of an abandoned house, "the only shade the shadow of a truck," a tiny tuft of cloud and the rainmaker's chant, by night the clear moon, and the howling of dingoes. One of the strengths of this film (*The Back of Beyond*, John Heyer) is that every shot in the film adds another face of the desert or of man as he lives with it.

A congeries may be intermittent. In between shots of the various tasks that fill a farm day, we see the stages of baking bread: taking flour to the doughtray, the setting of the yeast, mixing the dough, kneading the dough, placing it in pans, covering the pans with a quilt, firing the oven with bundles of wood, thrusting the pans into the oven, drawing the peel out with baked bread. The impression is that all the farmer does in a day is but a means of gaining his daily bread (*Farrebique*, Georges Rouquier).

The message conveyed by an accumulation may arise from the pace of cutting, not from what is contained in the shots that make it up. Felicity, on a scooter, disturbed by quarrels between her parents, races rebelliously ahead of her governess, down a slope from a park. Miss Drew, in anxious close-up, calls out, "Stop at the gates." Felicity is seen in long shot careering down the slope at a speed that must carry her out into the street, which seems to be empty. This is followed by six quick flashes, which, even when seen twice, are hard to remember and order, and no doubt equally hard for anyone concerned in such an occurrence: a motorcar approaching fast, a man applying brakes, and an arm sweeping Felicity out of the way are some of the shots, in none of which did we see the girl in front of the car. But content is of less importance here, for the message is quick sudden action, and this is expressed in the cutting (*Little Friend*, Berthold Viertel).

Three applications of this figure, which are masterly both in their pace and variety, are the search in *M* (Fritz Lang) by police and underworld for the murderer, the search for the atomic scientist in *Seven Days to Noon* (John and Roy Boulting), and the evacuation of London in the latter film. They cannot be dealt with here because of their length and intricacy. Consider, though, as an interesting exercize, some of the images that might be found, let us say, in the third. An operations room, of course, where all is plotted. Who are some of the people to be evacuated?—elderly pensioners, cripples, hospital patients. What kinds of transport could be pressed into service?—buses, bicycles, horse carts, police vans, private cars. What about pets? Works of art? Looting? Reaching everyone? What are the complicating factors?— profiteers, religious fanatics, children, "My little girl was on that bus—I went back to get her doll." A little boy whispers in an elder's ear, who says, "You little devil. I told you to go before we started." Both films maintain suspense from the pressure of time and multiplication of instances.

There are five films, each an impression of a day in a great city. Dziga Vertov moves through the day from dawn to night, compiling an exhaustive congeries for each stage. In dawn he shows a poster of a man with finger to his lips, a woman asleep in bed, and babies in cots, empty tables in open-air restaurants, a man asleep on a park bench, a drinking fountain unfrequented, rows of deserted houses, drivers lying asleep on their carriages, a shop window with wax dummy using a sewing machine, another one with three hairdresser's blocks, tools of daily use lying still— elevator, car engine, telephone cradle, bobbins above a loom, keys of a typewriter—a smokeless chimney and breezeless poplars (*The Man with a Movie Camera*). And so for the rest of the day. Alberto Cavalcanti in *Rien Que les Heures*, Walther Ruttmann in *Berlin*, Arne Sucksdorf in *Rhythm of a City*, and Gordon Sparling in *Rhapsody in Two Languages* have each done the same in his own way for the city of his affection.

An unusual congeries is found in *Rembrandt* (Starcky Sayer). Portraits made by Rembrandt of himself in the order in which they were painted are shown in fairly quick succession, perfectly matched in size and placing on the screen so that we see the artist's face changing with age.

4   Montage as Commentary: Abstraction, Slanting

In many of the above passages, it is easy to find a single word or phrase for the impression made by the course of images: indecision, the stillness of dawn. Congeries is a filmic way of expressing the abstract. The placing of shots in sequence is an act of will, and what we find of irony, of ridicule or condemnation, is thus deliberate comment. A different set of images can almost always be found, to make a different comment, to slant the opposite way.

Through her lorgnettes a woman admires the chief justice's handsome face, and a second woman remarks that the sentence is sure to be stiff. The defense counsel is drunk and hiccuping, and the chief justice tells him, "Save your eloquence: there isn't any jury." A second judge appears to be making notes, but from another angle is seen to be drawing a horse. A third has trouble keeping awake, and is seen several times looking at something under a sheet on his desk, that we later discover is a watch. The impression to be left on the viewer is, quite unmistakably, *justice mocked* (*Mother* V. I. Pudovkin).

In the Burmese jungle, Joyce, with knife in hand, looks for a Japanese soldier known to be there. Joyce is suddenly confronted by the soldier, who rises grasping a rifle. The young men face, neither willing to kill the other. Major Warden quickly steps between them, and kills the Japanese with his knife. This is what happened; what follows is commentary. Warden turns away with remorse in his face. We see the dead soldier's arm lying on the ground, his pocket book open beside him at a girl's picture. And the sky fills with a thousand black silhouetted birds that screech as if in outrage (*The Bridge on the River Kwai*, David Lean).

Avec Tamboures et Trompettes (Marcel Carrière) professes to do no more than record the Régiment de Zouaves de Québec during its official occasions. They are camped on a school playground. A soldier in resplendent uniform is clumsily trying to tie a flag to its lanyard. His mouth works as he fights his fingers, and he looks behind him to see if it is time to hoist. When the guard comes to attention, exaggerated precision almost topples it, and in changing the guard, the corporal pushes the drummer out of the way to allow the old guard room to march. Two of the fingers holding a sounding trumpet are also holding a cigar. A soldier crossing the parade ground is holding up an umbrella. The slope-shouldered colonel goes to shave, towel over his arm; he is wearing his undervest, civilian trousers, and military gaiters. He later congratulates the wrong soldier for something somebody else did well, and occupies an interminable time trying to fasten the clasp of a medal. And a soldier pops a fire cracker out of the muzzle of his rifle. Do these soldiers really exist? They strike the satirist-commentator dumb. There is nothing he could say that they have not said of themselves with greater pungency.

Slanting is little more than a subtle form of repetition. Although an image may not be exactly repeated, each different image carries a similar message. In *Traffic with the Devil* (Gunther von Frisch) we see crowded streets: motorcars at a stand, a woman driver beaten to a parking space three times over, pedestrians climbing over bumpers, men squeezing out of partly open car doors. Then we see a series of traffic signs, No Parking, No Right Turn, No Left Turn, No Stopping at Any Time, followed by a faster series of signs, showing in each only the word *No*. The final staccato pounding of noes drives home the reductio ad absurdum of private cars. There is a like sequence in *The City* (Ralph Steiner and Willard Van Dyke).

A comment may be wrapped up in a likeness.

In *The Plough That Broke the Plains* (Pare Lorentz) the men at the front and the men on the farm are seen as being equally parts of a war. The spout of a combine enters bottom left into the upper frame and pours grain into an unseen wagon. From the same angle bottom left the barrel of a large field gun thrusts at the moment of firing, black smoke pouring out of its mouth. A row of tractors rolls from right to left across a field of grain, followed by tanks rolling from left to right across a field of battle, a cloud of dust in one case, a cloud of dust in the other. A likeness of image purports a likeness of purpose.

Some directors assume an air of merely showing the situation to the viewer and letting the viewer form his own opinion. Even so, a strong point of view tends to filter out conflicting images, and leads to a sharper impression; and it may be, as Chesterton wrote, that "when we want any art tolerably brisk and bold we have to go to the doctrinaires."[19]

A comment may come from the clash of contrasting images.

Viridiana spends her share of her uncle's estate in supporting beggars, her cousin Jorge uses his share to improve the property. Viridiana standing among her kneeling beggars during the Angelus is intercut with Jorge and his laborers, tipping gravel, mixing mortar, piling fenceposts, sawing logs, demolishing walls. Meditation and action contrasted. But the beggars become drunk, smash dishes, break furniture, and rape Viridiana. It is hard to avoid concluding that the director speaks in the words of Jorge who says that what Viridiana did "only helps a few, and solves nothing" (*Viridiana*, Luis Buñuel).

The images that close *The Legend of Lylah Clare* (Robert Aldrich) join in the viewer's mind to form what would at one time have been called a moral. Zarkan has seen the première of his masterpiece on the life of a dead protégée, a worthless woman he has idealized, in the course of which his present protégée falls to her death. He photographs her dying moments before he allows anyone to help her. On the screen, as she dies, she says, and really to him, "I love you, Lewis," followed by *The End*, printed on the swing of an empty trapeze. The clapping audience leaves, and Zarkan sits by himself in a desolation of empty red seats. Rosetta, a friend of both girls is seen in two shots loading a revolver. An usher comes to take Zarkan out for an interview. We see Rosetta watching the television screen, where an announcer burbles the expected banalities, "terrible tragedy . . . unqualified triumph . . . say a few words . . . how much due to her actual tragic death? . . . How much is fact? . . ." Zarkan slowly answers, not now on the television screen but to us, "You thought you had at last learned something . . . When you gathered up your courage to try again, you find that all you've learned is how to make the same mistake again. In this cast, Miss Campbell . . ." But the announcer cuts him short for "an important message from our sponsor, Barkwell . . . all the minerals too . . . good friend to you . . . zesty food for dog lovers . . ." Here on a television screen and then on the full screen, one after another, dogs of different breeds and colors leap in toward, and overturn, a bowl of dog food. The final frozen shot is a close-up of the open jaws of a dog. A predatory culture, a confusion of corrupted values.

II METHODS

5 Montage Reinforced by Visual Image

If the fractional synecdoches in a sequence all in some way look alike, they are more easily taken in as a whole. Of two trains of events intercut, Napoleon tossed on the sea is tinted blue and the tumult at the Convention orange-brown (*Napoleon*, Abel Gance). Other examples have been given in discussing congeries.

A variant of this is to use the common visual image to bridge the shots in a sequence by anadiplosis. Tom Curtis's children suffer at school from his not having walked out on strike with his fellow workers (*The Angry Silence*, Guy Green). A picture of the two children moves off the frame in the hand of a reporter holding it, to show Anna, their mother, being interviewed. Bundles of papers are pushed round a corner, boys pulling them off and cutting the ties. The union organizer, Phil, lifts up a copy to read, and disappears behind it. The paper is put down, but by Joe, a neighbor, who rolls it up and walks to the left, up to a close-up of hand and paper. Our gaze rises to show that the hand is now that of a maid, who is taking the paper to the managing director at breakfast. As the paper lies on the table, he glances at it, frowns, and looks closer. We see the front page and the picture of the children. The page moves away as the paper is laid on the table, but now by Anna, the children having rushed in in high spirits. They are full of having their picture in the paper, which once more is lifted up to fill the frame. A finger enters to push a pin through the boy's eye, and we move back to see Connolly and other union men around the notice board on which the picture is pinned.

A highly coherent set of images in every sequence of a film makes for a strong, clear statement in the film as a whole.

The careful control found in *The Battleship Potemkin* of the visual character of the shots throughout a sequence, and the sharply contrasted character of neighbouring sequences, cannot be looked for in every film, but every director can bear it in mind with profit. *The City* (Ralph Steiner and Willard Van Dyke) contrasts a New England village of the last century, a modern city, and a possible city of the future. Much of the film's point was made in the leisurely pace of cutting in the first and third parts, the frantic pace of the second, and a matching contrast in the visual images. In the middle part, we see people standing or sitting, speaking to no one, and eating, then rows and rows of people doing the same. Intercut with close-ups of a man sipping coffee, a knife cutting a sandwich, and a mouth biting one, are shots of bread slicers, pop-up toasters, meat slicers, hands spreading butter, slices of ham falling, a sandwich topped and sliced, and pancake batter falling from a spout on a round, rotating pan. A hand wipes a table, a woman wipes her mouth with a paper napkin, and the silent lunchers leave. The people are hardly less predictable than the tools that feed them.

The compositions in *Barry Lyndon* (Stanley Kubrick) are clearly modeled on eighteenth-century painting, in poses, facial expressions, groupings, furniture, costumes, and coloring. Few period pictures have been steeped so completely in the way the period saw itself as this one.

6 The Montage Sequence

Karel Reisz has pointed out the variety of meanings to be found for the word *montage*.[20] In France, it is merely a synonym for editing; in Russia, it is the creative use of editing, which Eisenstein had in mind when he spoke of the "montage trope"; in English and American studios, it is used in the phrase "montage sequence," a series of glimpses that condense a long stretch of time or many changes of place. Especially in musical films, montage often does little more than sketch an itinerary and signify a lapse of considerable time.

In *One Night of Love*, (Victor Schertzinger) score after score of operas march and countermarch across the screen. Trains, fleeting tracks, passing landscapes, orchestra pits, harps, flowers, and applauding audiences roll above the horizon as Mary Barrett sings the round of Italian provincial opera houses. These might well be her own confused impressions of crowded months.

The elaborate montage sequence in *Thunder Rock* (Roy Boulting) does more—it forwards the story by summarizing the events that led Charleston, a foreign correspondent, to give up his work, to become the keeper of an isolated lighthouse and cut himself off from the world's doings. He had done what he could to make the English aware of their impending peril from fascism. We see a heading, "VII SPAIN", followed by such shots as men in trenches, or lying in and firing from shallow redoubts, and superimposed on it a news poster, "CHARLESTON WRITES FROM SPAIN"; a street with shattered buildings, with superimposed a typewriter and hands; another poster "GUERNICA BOMBED;" a lorry unloading refugees. And so with "FASCIST ITALY MOVES" and "GERMANY'S STRENGTH." Charleston accuses the editor of toning down his dispatches, and saying, "Thank

God there are other ways," he walks out of an editorial meeting. We see hands typing; we see a hand pulling a book from a shelf, *Report from Outside* by R. H. D. Charleston. This dissolves to him speaking from a platform, which in turn dissolves to a map, on which we move north on the western counties, as posters are superimposed announcing his meetings. A poster "BRITAIN AWAKE" floats across at Birmingham, and back again at Manchester. From different setups we see Charleston speaking as we move south on the map on the eastern counties. A hand gives a pamphlet, a gavel falls. We see Charleston's face as he speaks, a fist pounds a hand. The map dissolves out, leaving a poster "GRAND FINAL RALLY," and a hand enters to paste on "To-Night." We retreat from Charleston speaking to show two less-than-interested reporters and pan to show entire empty rows, not one with more than four listeners. The comments heard from those going out are critical of Charleston and as he leaves the woman holding out his book at the door gives him a faint grin.

No doubt Charleston gave the same speech each place, but this is not suggested as it is in *All the King's Men* (Robert Rossen). We hear Willie Stark as he gives a single continuous speech, as the screen shows us the words spoken from a dozen different platforms, at night by torchlight, by day in the sun, coping with various interruptions. It is a just impression, for during a campaign, a candidate may often repeat a speech with local modifications, or put another way, all that is said in the course of a campaign is one speech, consistent in tenor, uttered through a montage of only-half-remembered halls and audiences.

7 Montage Reinforced by Sound

Another common means of giving unity to a sequence is to underlay the changes of shot by continuous music. Such a montage too may be merely transitional, but may also convey not merely the kind of event that filled a period of time but its emotional character, and may form thus an essential part of the story.

Mary Justin has dined with Stephen Stratton, with whom she had been in love before her marriage. In a mood of reminiscence they kiss on a balcony. Then we dissolve to one brief glimpse after another of the week her husband is away—she receiving a box of flowers that Stephen had sent her, the two of them seated at lunch, in a riverboat, walking arm in arm on the street, in evening dress dancing, and then by a fire, she lying left on the floor and he sitting right foreground. This is all backed by continuous romantic music (*The Passionate Friends*, David Lean).

Work has stopped for the day in a monastery, and we see monks walking, singly and in procession. We see a steady drip from a gargoyle, and hear its beat as it strikes a surface of water. Then follows a recapitulation of all the work we have seen the monks doing, the blacksmith, baker, gardener, planer, illuminator, and all the others, every shot cut on a beat of the drips. Then the shots lengthen, giving a visual rhythm that lags behind the sound. This falling behind of the rhythm established by the drips suggests a slowing down of work at the end of the day. And the monks quietly depart from the frame, and leave it empty (*Life in a Benedictine Monastery*, Harold B. Stone).

8 Montage Reinforced by Speech

A single unbroken speech may straddle a series of glimpses. Epiphania in *The Millionairess*, (Anthony Asquith) starts talking to her physician. We then see the two of them again, she lying on his couch, then in a change of dress she is sitting up, then sitting in another place in still another dress, and then the two of them outside sitting in a park. Through all the changes of place and costume, her voice continues unbroken, suggesting a stream of self-revelation continuing over a long stretch of time.

The spoken underlay to the sequence of shots may be a single passage but spoken by a succession of different people, as in *Martin Luther* (Irving Pichel). The secretary to the Pope starts to read a papal bull demanding the retraction within sixty days of Luther's opposition to the sale of indulgences. The reading of the bull continues unbroken, but through successive speakers, as monks, students, courtiers, and burghers read it aloud—in a largely illiterate society,—and ends in the mouth of Spalatin. Melancthon and Luther approach him to ask, "When does it expire?" and he says, "Today." We hear the contents of the bull, which bear on the story, and equally important, we see its wide circulation at all levels of society. At the same time, the beginning and ending of the bull subtly suggest the beginning and ending of the term of sixty days.

9   Simultaneous Happenings—Alternation[21]

Of the means open to film for showing separate happenings going on at once, the one most commonly used is montage.

What other means are there? The screen may be split into two parts in various ways to show in each part one of two simultaneous happenings. In *War and Peace* (S. Bondarchuk), there is a long shot of Russian armies marching under a sky of lightning. Inset in a circle center, smiling confidently, French soldiers cry "Vive Napoleon!"

The two actions may be superimposed. In *Under the Frozen Falls* (Darrell Catling), as he rides his horse a boy carries a lead cylinder, intending to melt it into toy soldiers. Two boys and a professor, knowing that the cylinder holds a secret formula, are crossing a lake by boat on purpose to intercept him. There is the usual alternation between rider and boat, and then a shot of the front half of the boat superimposed on the front half of the horse and rider.

Showing scenes turn about is much more lively than showing them side by side in the same frame, it shows each scene in larger size, and with greater clarity, it is free from the strain of attending to two flows of events at the same time, and it lends itself, through shortening or lengthening the strips of each scene, to variety and climax.

The pattern lends itself to many changes. There is the figure *collection*, a universal statement is broken into its parts.[22] Instead of saying, for example, "The soldiers have no share in this honor," Cicero says, "The centurion has no share in this honor, the lieutenant none, the cohort none, the troop none." Likewise in *Elizabeth R.* (Claude Whatham, television), a hand shoots a bolt on the door of a cell, and we pan up to a small window to see who the prisoner is—Archbishop Cranmer. In a second and third repetition of the shot bolt and a window, we see Northumberland and Lady Jane Grey also in cells. We are shown, that is to say, the particulars making up the statement, "The principals in the revolt were all arrested and imprisoned at the same time." In the nature of film, and apart from the use of words, it is easier to use the figure and give the particulars, than make the collective statement.

Any treatment of alternate editing must start with an obeisance to Griffith. In *Death's Marathon*, a man at a telephone is bent on shooting himself. As his wife tries to keep him from hanging up, a friend rushes out to a motorcar. From here on, three simultaneous actions are intercut, now and then the friend on his way in the motorcar, but mostly an alternation of the husband and wife on the telephone. The woman pleads, coaxes, scolds, has their child brought in to speak. The would-be suicide brings out the revolver, talks, smiles sadly, puts the telephone receiver on the desk, writes his will, but at last fires the revolver into his mouth. His friend arrives, leaps out of the car, and breaks into the room; but coming too late, all he can do is report the death to the wife.

The alternating events may show antithesis. On the day the girl he loves is to marry someone else, Harold is told that the groom-to-be is a bigamist. As he tears through the streets to stop the marriage, some of the means of travel used by the hero are a hi-jacked street-car, a commandeered policeman's motor-cycle, and last a dump wagon. When one of the wagon's wheels rolls off, he leaps to one of the horses, on which he gallops up the long garden to smash down the French window just as the minister is about to say "I now pronounce you . . ." The sedateness of the marriage proceedings is cut between shots of Harold's continually checked but undeterrable dash across the city, not only for suspense but contrast (*Girl Shy*, Fred Newmayer and Sam Taylor).

To edit together two continuing and intersecting events sets going within us a kind of meter, which ticks off the distance to be traveled (never quite clear) or the time available (often precisely stated) before they meet. Inge stands in a food queue with twelve million marks in her hand. The butcher comes out from time to time to chalk up the price (in millions of marks): "8–9," "9–10," "11–12," and then, with only two people between her and the door, "15–17" (*Isn't Life Wonderful?*, D. W. Griffith).

The effect may also be felt even without a scale of size or number. In *Way Down East* (D. W. Griffith) halfway through the sequence where David steps from one ice floe to another to rescue the girl floating down the river, as we wonder if the ice floes are stable, if even so he can reach the one she is on, and if he does, can he carry her back to the bank, the suspense is heightened further by bringing in a waterfall. We assume that the fall is downstream, from its mere presence, that it must be close, and that every time we see it again it must be closer, though at no time did any shot inform us whether the fall was even on the same river.

Alternating two threads can imply an allusion from one to the other.

Into a convent that starts a chain by which Jewish children escape from a German prison camp, a rabbi secretly comes to conduct a Yom Kippur service. The Rabbi with candles and altar is intercut with the Kyrie Eleison sung at the nuns' mass, suggesting a common culture or purpose (*Conspiracy of Hearts*, Ralph Thomas).

Poison pen letters, that have brought strife to a small village, are revealed as the work of the vicar's sister. We cut from him in church saying evensong, to her, packing to flee as she has a vision of Connie, who hanged herself on the belfry rope, and of Len Griffin, who was murdered in consequence of her letters. As she hears the detective outside, she escapes through the window. As she opens the church door and looks in with tears in her eyes, her brother, in surplice and cassock, is distant in the chancel. At last, she climbs the moor and leaps over an edge. This is followed by the vicar giving the benediction, "Unto God's gracious mercy we commit you . . . and give you peace, now and for evermore." Her dead body is seen small from the top of the escarpment, and we end outside the church to the sound of the sevenfold amen (*Poison Pen*, Paul L. Stein).

"Don't forget Nina," says Modeste, as he and his brother Peter dine sumptuously in a private room. Peter's wife, Nina, her hair cropped, ignoring her overdressed mother and clearly withdrawn from the world around her, goes to sit on a basement grille, up through which men's hands come to fondle her. "I have many lovers," she says. "Your Sixth Symphony needs a name," Modeste says. Peter goes to the piano, plays a few notes, and says, "The Tragic." At the asylum Nina snatches the food of a neighbor while she is gone. "Her mother says she is well cared for," says Peter, and asks for water, brushing off the waiter's warning about cholera, while Modeste, still eating with gusto, says, "Call it the Pathetic." "My requiem," replies Peter, as his hand, which has been hovering between wine and water, settles on the water. Nina says, "He hates me," runs violently against a wall, and is placed in a straitjacket. Modeste and a doctor agree that neither will speak of Peter's drinking contaminated water as suicide. We see Peter's scabbed face as he says, "I tried to love her." Cut from Peter in a bath of scalding water (a form of treatment then) to the chain on -Madame Von Meck's door (also a source of agony), and then to Peter's mother also in a bath of scalding water (for she too had died of cholera). There is a lambent play of allusion from the words "tragic" and "pathetic" to Nina's destitution and madness and her husband's prosperous melancholy, to the self-destruction sought by both of them, to his rejection by Madame von Meck and Nina's rejection by him, and his and his mother's death both from cholera, if not from its harrowing treatment (*The Music Lovers*, Ken Russell).

Proximity may cause a simile: on the same train, on the footplate the fireman feeds coal into the furnace, and in the dining car, a passenger shovels food into his mouth (*Rome Express*, Walter Forde).

Things may briefly give us the course of simultaneous events. In a montage sequence of incidents in the lives of traveling performers—reviews, trains, marquees—billboards announcing *Burns and Company* show their names in ever larger letters. In the same sequence, on other billboards, the name of Young Sampson, a boxer in love with Peggy (the company), is moving further down the bills from preliminary to main event (*City for Conquest*, Anatol Litvak).

Alternate editing is usually confined only to part of a film. *The Day of the Jackal* (Fred Zinnemann), however, is a whole film based on alternation. Inspector Lebel is trying to intercept a professional assassin who he has reason to believe is on his way to murder Charles de Gaulle. We switch throughout the film from the present state of the assassin's preparations, to the inspector's developing awareness of the assassin's identifying marks and whereabouts. Here are two examples:

> Madame La Baronne is flirting with Duggan (the Jackal) in the lounge of a provincial hotel. "I am fascinated by combine harvesters. I should like one as a pet." It is 9:55 in the evening. Cut to Inspector Lebel, listening on the telephone, "Duggan entered France at Ventimiglia five hours ago."
> Lebel arrives at the hotel to find that the Jackal left at eleven. He examines the staff. Cut to the Jackal spraying his white car with blue paint. There is the sound of a plane, and we see a helicopter passing over. Cut to the plane landing on grass, and Lebel disembarks to question Madame la Baronne.

And so, turn about, we see them coming closer, until on the day planned for the fatal shot, Lebel and the Jackal come face to face.

10 The Montage of the Nonexistent

A director starts with a notion he wishes to convey. He puts together images, which, he believes, will recreate in someone else's mind the notion he started with. He can take the facade of one house and the inside of another, and make them one by editing, as Jack Cardiff did in *John Cassidy*.[23]

There is a simple case of this in *The Four Feathers* (Zoltan Korda). Troops are embarking for Egypt. Two officers say good-bye to a general and walk up the first feet of a gangway. Women behind a wooden paling, singing "Auld Lang Syne," and the general in front of the fence look up as if at the deck of a ship, and we hear the siren. All are facing toward us. We never see the ship which is placed (in the audience) by movement, glance, and sound. It is a part of the whole that we supply ourselves; it never existed.

It is possible to make one composite person out of two. In *Reach for the Sky* (Lewis Gilbert), we see Bader's back as he walks away on crutches, his right leg very clearly missing, its trouser pinned up. We know that the other leg is artificial. Whenever Bader faces us, however, we see him, say, with legs under a table or half-length. It is tolerably certain that the actor whose back we saw is not the one whose face we now see, and yet in the context we lump the two into one person.

Francis Bacon Paintings 1944–1962 (David Thompson) is wholly made up of this artist's work. There is a brief passage of three pictures of what seems to be the same person in the same red jacket, each with a different posture and facial expression. Shown one picture after another, we had an impression of a person restlessly fidgeting, despite our knowing that what we were looking at were still paintings. The director imposed on them, and on us, a nonexistent movement.

A keeper in *Catch of the Season* (Mary Field) is seen cutting grass at a river bank. Then we see him in up shot through rippling water—a fish's viewpoint. This is followed by a trout looking at us through the water, its mouth open and moving as if it were speaking. The trout suddenly turns and makes off as fast as it can. It is highly unlikely that man and fish were present at the same time, or perhaps at the same river. We have no means of knowing why the trout bolted when it did but as the film is edited, it looked as if it bolted from fear of the keeper or what he was doing.

The film can then compose places, persons, movements, and situations that never were.

11   Nonexistent Space-Time

The Japanese sentry leans over the rail of the bridge, makes a joking remark to his fellow sentry, and spits. We see the spittle splash an inch or two from the dark-stained face of Major Shears. In the nature of filmmaking, it is almost certain that the spittle that struck the water was not the one we saw launched from the bridge, but place the two together, and both cohere into one event (*The Bridge on the River Kwai*, David Lean).

The nameless woman in *At Land* (Maya Deren), cast up on the seashore, gains consciousness, crawls up to the huge roots of a fallen tree, and climbs them with effort. We see her hand clutch the topmost root, and in the next shot of a dining table, her hand reaches over the edge, clutching the white cloth just as it had the root in the last shot. Her head and then her eyes rise over the edge. She looks up: from a glass chandelier, bathed in smoke, we pan down to the table lined with guests. We are never shown where table and root meet, and yet, as edited, the sandy shore, the root, and the dining table are one unbroken space.

12   Nonexistent Happenings

An event that never took place can be seen apparently to happen from viewing a succession of shots in the right order. When Lermontov in *The Red Shoes* hears that

Victoria Page has married Craster, we see him in a red smoking jacket, facing us above a mantel shelf in the foreground, as if reflected in a mirror above it. He suddenly and vehemently punches toward where the mirror would be. To the sound of a crunch this is cut to a shot of part of his back and his fist pressing now against an actual mirror, and spreading out from his fist, a web of cracks. But although we are sure we do, we never see the fist strike the glass. In the ballet itself, the demonic shopkeeper, a shoe in either hand, stabs them down to the floor where they stand erect on their toes, large in the foreground, and the girl who covets them is seen beyond. She runs toward us and leaps, and her feet appear to land into the shoes. What we actually see is a cut from the untenanted shoes to the shoes with her standing in them, the same place on the screen but closer and larger (*The Red Shoes*, Michael Powell and Emeric Pressburger).

In *The Cheat* (Sacha Guitry), the speaker says that he has always thought that the "toy army" of Monte Carlo would look rather quaint if they did a quadrille, at which point, by using reversed film, the soldiers are made to march forward and back, as if they were dancing.

The decisive importance of order is quite clear in a passage from *The Overcoat* (Aleksandr Batalov). We see a full-length shot of a baby. A man looking into a book is saying, "What shall we call him? Mokkiah?" We see the baby again, with a look as of one considering. The man with the book tries another name: "Sossiah?" The baby seems to be giving it serious thought. "Khuzdozod?" The baby is doubtful. A group of three women is sitting in front of the man reading the book. One of them says, "Name him after his father—Akady Akadyevich." The baby bursts into a loud howling.

Her German captor hands Mrs. Collins a clogged pepper shaker. She unscrews the top, and impulsively hurls the contents offscreen. In a down shot, the soldier reels back in his chair by the table. In a short shot, a hand seizes a long wooden shaft leaning in a corner. In a steep up shot of Mrs. Collins only, she brandishes an axe above her head, and with a wild look in her eye, swings it down out of the frame. Now we see at greater length a supine hand up left, at bottom a revolver, both in shadow, and the rest of the frame is a bright litter of shattered white crockery, doubly still from having followed quick sudden gestures. No axe is seen cleaving a skull, but it is hard to see how simulating bodily harm in full bloody color, however vivid, could convey the shock of the deed with greater power (*Went the Day Well*, Alberto Cavalcanti).

It is only a short step from what is not to what is impossible. The Princess, one of the forms of Death, materializes walking across a street. She enters an arch, but never comes out the other side (*Orphée*, Jean Cocteau). The three retainers of Shibiky Heinai vanish the moment the samurai thrusts his blade through them, but suddenly as he laughs and leans on the sword, he is aware that they are standing somewhere else in the courtyard (*Kwaidan*, Masaki Kobayashi). In each case the set showing the people and the set without the people are placed in succession, and according to the order of editing, they appear or disappear.

13 False Impression—Surprise and Ambiguity

Putting off until later a disclosure of all the surrounding circumstances makes for surprise; neglecting to disclose it all can keep afloat an ambiguity.

In *Hue and Cry* (Charles Crichton), we look down on two boys climbing a tall spiral staircase to the flat of an author, whose serial story seems to describe crimes before they happen. The boys' tall shadows climb the wall with those of a fleeing cat and the curling bannisters. Another time they are tiny specks in a down shot of the stairwell, as words echo loudly in it, and they stop dead, "Your fate is in my hands. . . . You are alone with me. . . . I have a silencer on this gun. . . . You have only five minutes to live." Then through a partly-open door, a man with loose tie and an open waistcoat closes off his dictating machine and comes toward us. It is the author.

Mere succession may mislead us. A double-barreled gun is to be shot at an actor, Julian Gordon. Mae Feather, his wife, has changed one of the two blanks for a live round. Two scenes are being shot at the same time. She is tied to a post and gagged in one scene, while her husband plays on another set in the same studio. The director says to the villain, "Shoot as soon as Julian breaks the door down." The panels are smashed through, Julian is seen, the villain shoots, and the frame goes black. A close-up of the live bullet Mae had put in the gun is superimposed on slowly circling lights, and through this we approach to Mae, lying unconscious and slowly coming to. Julian at the broken door says, "Wouldn't it have been more exciting to let off both barrels?" The black screen suggested a loss of consciousness. We assumed it was Julian's, and later find it is Mae's (*Shooting Stars*, A. V. Bramble and Anthony Asquith).

Michael and Julia Finsbury are absorbed in a very long kiss in close-up. Cut to Joseph Finsbury half-length, running across the park outside, crying "Stop!" Not until we have gone with him all the way to his door do we find that he was shouting to men delivering a box, not cutting short the long kiss (*The Wrong Box*, Bryan Forbes).

We change focus in life between the outer world and the inner one of imagination and memory, but most of us can tell one from the other. Some directors give us no signs by which to distinguish them, and the viewer, like those afflicted with some forms of mental illness, cannot tell the two worlds apart.

Mathieu Gregoire in *Belle* (André Delvaux) is infatuated with a girl who lives in a ruined farmhouse, and whose dog was injured by his car. We may have an order of shots rather like this. Belle distant in a field. The dead dog, creamy-brown, blood on the ground, in close-up. Mathieu, his wife, and Victor, a colleague, at Mathieu's home; Mathieu, during the conversation, asking his wife to bring some brandy. Now we see Belle in a hazy brown autumnal field. Hemlock leaves in close-up are dripping with rain. Mathieu, at home, quotes a poem, "I am soaked . . .," and his wife completes it, "in love." Mathieu closes the door on Victor, who leaves rather drunk. The moon is seen under branches. Mathieu alights from his motorcar saying, "She no longer has her dog." He stands on a railway platform with a woman (their backs are to us). She is partly naked, and later wholly so. She looks around. We see his wife in bed asleep, and Mathieu beside her awake and breathing heavily. He is driving his car, and we see his face in close-up. He parks his car on a country road, and emerges in the upper floor of the ruined farmhouse to see Belle lying in bed. "Why do you stay here?" he asks, and as always is unanswered. He walks over dead grass. He enters a grocery shop, a chemist's, and a bank. Now he is giving a drink to Belle. She spits it out. He then makes her a stew that she eats.

The theme of the film is Mathieu's infatuation with Belle. We see its injurious effect on one of his lectures, and on his wife. It is reasonable that shots of Belle are constantly cropping up obsessively. We are likely right in assuming that being on a railway platform with a naked woman is imagined. If that woman is Belle, he may be thinking of going away with her, for which he goes to the bank to withdraw all his money. We may take it that Victor's visit really happened; but what of Mathieu's drive immediately afterwards—to nowhere? After we see him lying awake in bed, does he rise in the night and drive off in his car, or merely imagine it? Or does he imagine it first, and then do it, one image serving to tell us both? And so throughout the film we hover, as Mathieu may also do, not sure which thing is done and which is imagined.

14 Movement in Time

Movement in time should have a brief word. The least movement in time is perhaps to be found in *The Blood of a Poet* (Jean Cocteau), which starts with a tall chimney collapsing. Halfway to the ground, the falling chimney is cut, the body of the film is inserted, and the last shot is the rest of the fall from where it was interrupted. The action of the film took place in an instant of thought, in "no time at all."

It has been observed that there is no past tense in film—what we see is always happening now. As between two adjacent passages, the director should, therefore, tell us unequivocally, unless for good reason, if they are simultaneous or successive, or if one is in the historic present relative to the other (anamnesis or flashback).

The Jackal inspects his new rifle in Switzerland. The hands of a clock stand at 7:00. The minister in Paris, presiding over a long table of officials, tells them of a possible threat to de Gaulle's life. It is not clear in which place the clock hangs, but because it stands between the two events, we take it as the time for both (*The Day of the Jackal*, Fred Zinnemann).

It is usually clear that certain events must follow others. For example, in *Sapphire* (Basil Dearden), Sergeant Cooke is talking to a shop assistant who had sold a red petticoat to Sapphire. "I was very surprised," says the clerk, "because the man with her was a big colored fellow." We cut to a close-up of Sergeant Cooke, as she repeats to the clerk, to avoid any mistake, "Colored?" We cut to Superintendent Hasard walking toward us in his office, as we hear Sergeant Cooke reporting, "A big colored fellow." These events must happen one after the other, not at the same time. Most film events do, and the action here makes this clear.

Hill 24 Doesn't Answer (Thorold Dickinson) starts with three men and a woman lying dead. As the name of each is called, the person rises into the frame alive. Since life and then death is the normal order, and here we see death before life, this warns us that what we are about to see has occurred in the past.

The director may rely on dialogue to separate the tenses. In *Z* (Costa-Gavras) a fig seller is sitting in a car beside the juge d'instruction. "The boxer brought me to see him. . . ." he says. Over the top of another car, we see the fig seller standing with, we assume, the boxer. The camera sinks down to the window of the car to show us the back of someone inside, who says, "The meeting is tonight. You must be there." The fig seller answers, "That is impossible." We cut back here to the juge d'instruction, as the fig seller explains, "I had a shipment of figs coming." We return to the other car, as the man with his back to us hints that if the fig seller is not at the meeting, his license might not be renewed. This combines a telling now of what has happened, and our seeing the event itself, both in the present tense; which event is the historic present is clear from the dialogue. Seen with no subtitles by someone with no French, it would have been anything but clear, because nothing visual clearly asserts an order.

How far we have leaped in time is harder to show in images. The director must often assume that the viewer knows how people dressed, worked, or traveled in other times; how fast plants and people grow and how they show age; how long it takes to recover from an illness; and other signs like these. Thérèse is said to suffer from a psychosomatic lameness. Calvero persuades her to leave her bed and holds her hand as she tries to walk again. We then cut to her in street clothes, still touching his hand, but walking with greater sureness. Weeks or months must have passed (*Limelight*, Charles Chaplin). Distance into the future can be less precisely shown, lacking some of these aids, and is often dated, as in *Things to Come* (William Cameron Menzies).

A director, however, cannot be faulted for not making his time sequence clear, if time is not material. For example, in *Kaseki* (Masaki Kobayashi), four people are seen dining. The narrator tells us, "The topic of conversation is a place for sale. Madame Marcelin came to see it. . . . It is supposed to be haunted. . . ." In two gray-green compositions, we see the four going to and entering a gate in the wall of a manor house. After this, we return to the warm reds and browns of the restaurant, the narrative going on unbroken. They are either by anamnesis talking about a visit they have just made, or else by the figure vision discussing one they are going to make. It is of no consequence to the story which it is.

15 The Limits of Ellipsis

Not only can moments of time be swollen or shrunk in length as compared with clock time, but by way of ellipsis bits of any event may be snipped out. The goal of editing, as it must be of style in all arts, is the constant cutting away of what can be cut away without loss of meaning, the continual choosing and rechoosing of what exact words or images will most concisely, and yet most fully, pass to the viewer the story, mood, and character as conceived.

Bela Balazs warns us that an elliptical cut may leave a viewer wondering where a character is and how he got there, and any technique that baffles the viewer raises doubts if the director is reaching his audience.[24] At the same time, Balazs points out that what he calls visual culture has altered over the years. The following might have given pause to a filmgoer of Bela Balazs's time, but would not today, at least in the Western world or in Japan:

Squire Allworthy is just barely holding in the horse as he drives himself and Mistress Blifil along a country road.
A close-up of a wheel parting from the axle.
Our view suddenly soars to the sky and the trees.
Allworthy and Mistress Blifil lie sprawled on the ground.
The canted-over one-wheeled chaise is still dragged by the horse.
Tom is riding cheerfully. A pan shot from him as he stops shows us Blifil, beside a hearse, weeping.
Tom comforts Blifil and runs off to Allworthy on learning that he is not expected to live.
A metal plate with "Bridget Blifil, 12 December 1698" sinks away on a coffin into a grave.

Despite the ellipsis of many events between Mistress Blifil traveling and Mistress Blifil buried, a strict order of time helps us fill the gaps, and a minor event has been held in length to no more time than its weight warrants (*Tom Jones*, Tony Richardson).

In other films, the bond is loose, connection is obscure, the gaps between shots are more obtrusive, and the narrative ambles, often jerkily. Consider this from *Strawfire* (Volker Schlondorff):

> Elizabeth, who is newly divorced, is driven part way to her destination in the motorcar of a young man she meets. "I must prove I lead a moral life to keep my son."
> A train arrives, and she alights.
> She enters the door of her house, speaks briefly to a friend.
> She takes her bicycle out of the hall into the street.
> She alights and parks her bicycle.
> She enters a house, greets her son, kneels, and says she has no present for him this time.
> She and a friend and the son are talking.
> Close-ups of the son's drawings.
> Before she goes out to get some green beans, her husband's mother asks her to "patch it somehow."
> She talks to her husband over coffee, without warmth.
> In an employment agency, she declines all that the interviewer offers. "You don't really want a job," he says, "You just want to satisfy your ego."
> She is guiding Japanese visitors around a trade fair and is photographed with them.
> Her singing teacher tells her that her voice is immature. "Try Mahler." "I'd like to sing in musicals."

Now the director may have intended an impression of living in disconnected pieces, without purpose or direction—it is certainly the effect of the editing. We feel that he lacks a firm principle of judgment, by which to cut a shot or leave it in. We see her mount her bicycle; then she alights and parks it—what do these add to our portrait of her? He could have dissolved from one to the other of two visits to friends or shown her briefly riding between the visits. On the other hand, she turns down all jobs, and with no reason given is seen working.

Dziga Vertov considered that everything happening in a city at the same time of day converged in a single theme. Peter Baylis carried the matter a step further. He believed that he could take any six random shots different in subject matter, and with the right twist of commentary make all express a single theme.[25] Can one then say that everything happening in the world at a given moment, or during a given century, expresses a single theme? Or anything happening at any time or place on the same planet? I felt some such approach in *21-87* (Arthur Lipsett). The choice in so vast a field must be almost a matter of chance. There were some interesting sounds, but neither sounds nor images conveyed a theme or mood. Each canceled the last without adding to it. The mind seeks gestalts or wholes, and when it fails to find one, feels frustrated. In *21-87*, spread over many items, dimly if at all related, whatever conception had brought them together was diluted past possibility of discovery, lacking the twist of commentary, which Peter Baylis felt would give them a common voice.

> an acrobat performing;
> a chicken being sawed;
> mechanical fingers pouring some radioactive substance;
> an old man walking;
> pigeons flying;
> a boy chewing;
> a monkey;
> a puff of steam. And so on.

Each item, we assume, is considered as adding as much to the meaning as any other, but the director who chose the items chooses to conceal his principle of choice and lets his assembled shots fuse into what they will in the viewer's mind—if anything.

In the film from which the following comes, the directors expressly rejected any approach to rational narrative:

A man, half-length, sharpens a razor.
He goes through a door to a balcony.
There is a full moon in a black sky.
A woman's face.
A full moon with a cloud horizontal across the center.
The woman's eye in close-up as a razor slices across it, and
   the aqueous humor oozes out.
A man who wears a kind of pinafore rides a bicycle.
The cyclist superimposed on a road.
The keyhole of a striped bag.
A girl holding the bag,
The cyclist wearing the pinafore.
The woman looks down from a window (her eyes unharmed).
The cyclist falls, and the bicycle wheel continues turning.
The girl turns to a man in the room and kisses him.

This goes on for some length in much the same way (*Le Chien Andalou*, Luis Buñuel and Salvador Dali). As Max Ernst wrote, "No conscious intellectual direction (either of reason, taste, or will) being permissible in an absolutely surrealist work of art, the active part for the person till now described as the author of the work is greatly reduced. It is as a spectator, either passionate or indifferent, that the author assists at the creation of the work.[26]

This is the limit of ellipsis, in which the viewer supplies the intended but unexpressed. This the viewer cannot do here, for the director neither intends or knows of any bond, for his purpose is, on purpose, no purpose.[27]

I have no advice for the viewer. To try to supply a connection that the director strove to avoid is to behave just as irrationally as he. Ellipsis has now become the figure *Enigma*, "which for the darkenesse, the sense may be hardly to be gathered . . . being a figure of deepe obscuritie. For indeede this figure is like a deepe mine, the obtaining of whose mettal requireth deepe digging, or to a darke night, whose stars be hid with thicke clouds."[28]

16 Pace

In *Scott Joplin* (Jeremy Paul Kagan), stills of Joplin's childhood and his youth dissolve quickly one into another: Joplin having a piano lesson, his mother smiling, the family around her coffin, his father looking with disapproval, Joplin leaving home, all tinted in sepia monochrome, as if from a family album. At the end, as Joplin plays for an impresario, we see the main events of the story in brief reminders. Quickly touching on many incidents is the figure *epitrochasmus*.

Pace or tempo rests in great measure on two matters: the speed and amount of movement within the shots and, second, the length of shot—the number of changes of shot in a given time.[29]

A slow tempo—twenty- and thirty-second shots—matches the pace of Peter's thinking. This is varied now and then by shots of rapid content: Cossacks galloping diagonally or tearing away from us; tracks in sinuous motion, seen from a train at full speed; the whirling by of an iron fence as Peter flits past it (*The Golden Mountains*, Sergei Yutkevich).

When one shot follows another, there is often a change of tone, texture, or color between any part of the screen and that same part in the next shot, from dark to light, vertical lines to horizontal, red to blue, and this change affects the eye as movement. If this happens once a second, we feel a faster pace than if it happened every five seconds. There is a passage in *Desert Victory* (Roy Boulting) of quite short shots of guns at the moment of firing, each, turn about, pointing in to the screen from the opposite side to the one before and after, giving a staccato pace from short cuts and contrasting lines.

The struggle between Kolka's mother and one of the wild children in *The Road to Life* (Nicolai Ekk) takes up a dozen shots or so. These shots are very short in length and greatly contrasted in composition, with, say, their legs in one shot, their heads and shoulders in the next, from greatly contrasted angles, and, from being in close-up, with greatly exaggerated movement.

On the other hand, the slow passing of time for men standing to attention under the tropical sun is emphasized by greater length of shot, as is also, in another place, the stunned incredulity of the English soldiers, when Colonal Saito slapped their commanding officer (*The Bridge on the River Kwai*, David Lean).

17 Chapter, Act, and Sequence

Most narratives are felt, as well by the audience as by the storyteller, to fall into smaller wholes of time, place, or action, and a pause between these refreshes our interest. So in the novel, play, and film, we have the chapter, the act or scene, and the sequence. The same need leads to a like solution.

The close of a film sequence is like a stage curtain, and should be as carefully calculated. It is high praise for a playwright to say that every scene has a good curtain. Young Harris, in *Sapphire*, (Basil Dearden) is appealed to by his mother to say where he was on Saturday night, for he is under suspicion of murder. "Never ask me what happened on Saturday night," he says, and turns away. His mother is silent, disturbed, and then the scene is cut. An effective curtain.

Some film sequences end with what even look like curtains. Tony Richardson in *Tom Jones* draws a blank panel from either side, like sliding doors, before Tom and Molly Seagram embrace in the woods. He reopens this door from center to sides, to start the next sequence, thus confirming the impression. In *Hello Moscow* (Sergei Yutkevich) a similar panel enters from only the right. It is light gray, hazy, and wrinkled, and is drawn back to the right again to show the next shot. Voltaire himself is brought into *Candide* (James MacTaggart, television) as a means of keeping ironic remarks on the action, most of which would otherwise have been lost in filming the story. After Candide has eagerly joined a lady of Paris in bed, Voltaire enters to say that he is drawing (which he does) a tactful curtain. He then pulls the curtain open again, to show Candide afloat bound for Venice. To the like effect in *Our Town* (Sam Wood), the stage manager places his hand over the camera aperture, taking it away again as he introduces the scene that follows.

Where the sliding door is not blank, but shows the next setting, it is like turning the actor into a stagehand setting a drop scene. In *Thicker Than Water* (James W. Horne) Hardy crosses his living room to right frame and pulls across the room what seems like a sliding door, on which we see the front of a bank. He and Laurel walk out of the door with all of Hardy's money. Later, when Hardy's wife has knocked him unconscious, Laurel feels his pulse, and after yelping frantically for his hat, he comes back to draw across the screen another sliding door, this one showing the front of a hospital. Halfway across, the door slips from his grasp and springs back and off the screen.

A variant of this is found in *Seven Days Ashore* (John H. Auer), as two sailors court Lucy and Carol. We see the four in a car, under a beach umbrella, on a roller coaster, dancing, and each scene, as if it were hinged on one side of the frame, lifts, like a page being turned, to show the next scene underneath.

A wipe is a line crossing the screen with the going scene on one side of the line and the coming scene on the other. It does as Voltaire did in *Candide*—draws the curtain on one scene and opens it on another—but with twentieth-century abruptness, it compresses the curtain into a mere line.

To show a lapse of time on the stage, the light may dim to a blackout, and then go on again. And so in film a scene fades, the screen is briefly blank, and then the next scene fades in. This again has much the same effect as Voltaire's curtain. The blank screen, which is usually black, may also be red, as it is in *Cries and Whispers* (Ingmar Bergman), or any other color.

A variant of this is to iris out the frame to a small circle, and pause on the circled image before blacking it out. The next image is seen in part in a small circle, which then expands to show the whole scene. This is as if a stage were blacked out, all but a spotlight on one player. It is useful to stress a detail in each scene. In *Nosferatu* (F. W. Murnau) the iris at the end of a sequence isolates the host of an inn, who slowly shakes his head as he comes toward us. The circle that starts the next sequence shows us a wolf leaving cover, and, as it expands to show the whole scene, we see horses galloping wildly away.

If the black frame is left out, and the fades in and out overlap, we have the dissolve. The modern stage provides the analogy of a going scene revolving little by little out of sight, and the coming scene spreading in from the other side, some bits rising up to the flies, and others flying down to the new set.

As there is in film no actual curtain or sliding door, no stage to revolve or page to turn, each of these ways of changing a scene is a visual simile, likening the frame to a stage, a room, or a book.

If the fade or iris, out and in, is left out, we have the shots leaded out by nothing more than blank black space. *Days and Nights* (Alexander Stolper) tells of the love affair, during the Battle of Stalingrad, of a nurse and a captain. It is made up of episodes too short for chapters. The events are briefly spaced by a black screen, which emphasizes recurrence, the relentless hammering of incidents, one after another. In *Attention, the Children Are Watching* (Serge Leroy), changes of place and leaps in time are so conveyed. Dimitri, one of four children, devotees of television violence, fires at a strange man who has settled in their house. The man falls on the television set; it flashes and the lights go out. This is cut to a black screen, and then to the next scene in which the children explore the dark room with a flashlight. This is cut again to a black screen, from which another cut brings us outside the house the next morning. *O Lucky Man* (Lindsay Anderson) uses a rather longer black screen between longer installments, after one of which the sound of the General Confession (for Travis collapses in church during a service) dwindles out in the blackness after the cut.

Another way of spacing sequences is to hold the final shot on the screen after all the characters have left, as Joseph Losey did in *Accident*. On the stage, this would be a slow curtain. Stephen and Francesca leave her flat. She turns out the light, and for some seconds we see the darkened flat before the cut. In another place the tree, the cricket stumps, and the sky remain after Charlie is bowled out and has left the screen. This gives a reflective brooding quality, as if the storyteller were thinking of what has happened before going on. Because the eye has something to focus on, it perhaps enables a longer suspension of action than would a black screen. It fitted the general slow pace of the film, and is a means of emphasis, of letting a mood settle and clarify.

Yasujiro Ozu is perhaps the most frequent user of the slow curtain. He often shows a setting before a character enters, and holds it after everyone has left. In *A Hen in the Wind*, Ozu shows us for some seconds Tokiko's kitchen and living room, with no one to be seen, before she and her little boy enter. This has the incidental, but likely unintended, effect that we take in the room's character and furnishings more fully than we should if their users too insisted on being looked at.

To slow the transition further, and shed a more leisurely, contemplative tone, Ozu uses what Edward Branigan calls a *modulation*, a series of shots of places, usually unpeopled, between the last action of a former sequence and the start of the next.[30] If the musical analogy is just, it implies a sufficient difference in mood or tone or otherwise between the shots that are linked, and a careful choice of scenes that will divest our minds of the former and make them ready for the latter. But such a difference is very often absent. It is more a lifting of the mind out of the action, and setting it down again much as we do the tone arm of a phonograph. It is more a meditative hiatus to still the mind, a moment of rest or calm.

A modulation may be a single shot, which in its neutrality from the action lifts us out of it quite as much as a black screen. Professor Somiya and his daughter, whom he is trying to persuade into marriage, are watching a Noh play, at which she is disturbed at seeing the woman whom, it is hinted, her father will marry after she has left him.

A wide-branching tree, gently moving in the wind, fills the frame, as the Noh chanting continues.

After this, we see their backs as they walk along a road (*Late Spring*, Yasujiro Ozu).

A modulation may be shots clearly within the house where the character is. Taeko Satake, a supercilious wife, scorns her husband's table manners, the cigarettes he smokes, and other habits that he was brought up to and she was not. She has deliberately turned up too late to see him off to Uruguay, and been scolded for it by a friend and her niece. She goes to his room, sits at his desk, and picks up an empty cigarette package. Now we see

the hall outside his room, as the lights go out there;
a short slow retreat from a cabinet in the living room, as we hear a chime;
a dark hall with a lighted room at the end;
a lighted table lamp in the left foreground of a room.

Then we see the head and shoulders of Taeko, lying awake in bed. The transition could be taken as showing the route from her husband's room to her bedroom, but it has a slow reflective pace that fits both of the scenes it separates (*The Flavor of Green Tea Over Rice*, Yasujiro Ozu).

In *Tokyo Story* (Yasujiro Ozu), when his doctor son-in-law tells an old man that his wife will not live until dawn, the old man says, "Not live—so—not live . . . So

this is the end." He remarks that his son Keizo will not be in time, and goes out.
Now we see

the dock, harbor, and hill beyond;

a large stone lantern in the foreground, a boat crossing the harbor, and hills
beyond it;

three sailing boats tied up side-by-side;

a wet quay with a building beyond; and

a train in the foreground below, and a ferry crossing the harbor beyond it.

We then see the four children kneeling around their dead mother. The old man may
have been watching the harbor, for he is fetched from where he is standing on the
terrace when Keizo arrives. He says it will be another beautiful day, and likely hot.
The function of the *suspending passage* (a closer description perhaps than modulation) is twofold. It signifies a lapse in time, for the son-in-law spoke at night, and
when the old man was called in, it was day and his wife dead. And it stops, rests or
suspends the flow of the story, the unhurried scenes with no or little movement
filling the space between with quietness, as no black screen could have done and at
greater length.

18 Lengthening the Gap

There is thus a scale of pauses to choose from, either to fit the pace of the story, or
the separation required at any point. These are the means discussed, from short to
long:

Cut

Wipe

Other variants of the curtain

Dissolve

Black screen

Fade or iris out and in, to and from a black screen

Suspending passage

Any one of these but the cut may be longer or shorter, slower or faster. Two of them
need a little further comment.

19 The Wipe

It is likely fanciful, as has been tried, to find a figurative intention for each of the
many possible ways of wiping.[31] It may be said that a wipe that prepares the eye for
the coming composition is close to an anadiplosis or carry-over. In *Tom Jones* (Tony
Richardson) there is a spiral wipe starting center frame to a bronze knocker center
frame in the next shot. An up shot of a tall building is wiped down to a shot of a
window cleaner scraping down the water off a window (*The Window Cleaner*, Jules
Bucher).

It is pleasing too when the wipe is diegetic. In *The Christmas Carol* (Brian Desmond Hurst), the Ghost of Christmas Yet to Come is black cloaked and hooded.
When he fills half the frame and lowers his arm on the other half, his black drapes are
a curtain that, as they fall, wipe out the scene and rise on the next.

Another device, equally rare, is to show the characters half length, kill the lighting on them to make them silhouettes, keeping the setting behind them brightly lit, then by wipe to replace the setting with another, after which the figures in front are once again lit. The characters are now in a new time and place without ever having left the screen. This is an adaptation to film of a way of using sets in Kabuki theater (*The Ballad of Narayama*, Keisuke Kinoshita).[32]

The wipe is used in *Tom Jones* to suggest that the two events thus joined are happening both at once. It is, when seen as a surface, a pair of wipes, one starting at each side of the frame. They meet in the center and wipe back to the sides. But it is as if the frame revolved on a center axis through half a circle, one side of it showing the going scene, the other the coming one, as if we were turning a wall to see what was going on at the other side at the same time.

Squire Western is lying beside a woman on a pile of hay. His sister comes along and they trade sharp words. At something she says, he leaps up waving a hayfork, trips and falls. The scene revolves to Allworthy resting on a couch listening to the two tutors who stand behind him, talking, "Tom was whistling drunk the day of your great danger." We then revolve to Miss Western outside, speaking to Sophie, "Many couples dislike one another." She is pressing Sophie to marry Blifil. Sophie answers, "I have a very solid objection to him—I hate him" (*Tom Jones*, Tony Richardson).

20 The Dissolve

The orator links his units of discourse by the figure *metabasis*. It brings together in one sentence what you have done and what you propose to do:

> I have hitherto made mention of his noble enterprises in France, and now I will rehearse his worthy acts done near to Rome.[33]

The film dissolve does the same. There are two images on the screen at once, the older growing fainter and the new one stronger, and the new image seems to arise from the old. "This," it says, "is what I am finishing, and this is what I am starting," but in its filmic form, in its blend of images it is more. There is a point at which neither image is clear. It shows, in Leonard Hacker's words, "forms and events in growth and transition," a sense conferred on the figure by picture and motion.[34]

The most common use of the dissolve—common enough to be called an idiom—is dissolving a clock face to itself at a different reading, to show a lapse of time. In *Les Deux Timides* (René Clair) a shy young man has called on a father to ask for his daughter's hand. The young man sits on the wrong chair, and is pointed over to another. He temporizes by blowing his nose, drawing on his gloves, and other irrelevant activities. The clock face dissolves from 3:30 to 4:25. The father offers the young man half the paper. The clock now dissolves from 4:25 to 5:20. The father is asleep, and the young man is addressing him with bold and assured, but voiceless, gestures of insistence. The clock dissolves from 5:20 to 7:05. They are both asleep.

In *Seven Days to Noon* (John and Roy Boulting) the landlady is sitting, looking up, listening to the lodger walking to and fro in the room above. Approach to the clock on the mantel: 11:15. Dissolve to the clock at 3:35 and still we hear the sound of walking feet above. Pan to the landlady, seated, smoking. She stubs out the cigarette and leaves the room. This does not state, but suggests, that the feet have never stopped for over four hours.

Many other things than clocks have served as measures of time, the most common of which is the cigarette. We have a rough idea how long it takes to smoke one, so if an ashtray with one stub dissolves into the same tray with four stubs, the passage of time is shown by metonymy (*Blackmail*, Alfred Hitchcock). The same applies to a cup of coffee. In *Les Deux Timides* (René Clair), Frémissant is waiting to appear in court, charged with assaulting a rival suitor. He and his future father-in-law each order a cup of coffee, drink it unhappily, and sigh in unison without looking at the other. Dissolve to the table with four saucers in front of them. Both are talking volubly and waving their hands. Dissolve to eight saucers. Now their gestures are larger, even belligerent. Each leans toward the other. They swing their arms. On their way out, the suitor slaps the face of another customer, and the usually meek father sweeps the man's hands off the table.

Dissolves may vary in length. After Oliver, who was sent out with books and money, fails to return, Mr. Brownlow waits, disappointed but hopeful. A man merely waiting cannot be kept on the screen for very long. The next shot is of the steps where Fagin is expected, but he does not come at once, and the image of the waiting Mr. Brownlow perseveres in a long dissolve well into the shot of the empty steps, which also suggest absence. We are held by the change, but still kept in mind of the waiting benefactor (*Oliver Twist*, David Lean).

The longer the dissolve, the more it is like a superimposition. It may not merely work as a bridge, but while the two shots are on the screen, their presence together may convey a message as in *The Inheritance* (Maseki Kobayashi). Yasuko feels obliged to drink tea with a young man she knew in her humbler days. She thinks, "My day is messed up. . . . How can I stay with this disgusting creature!" Superimposed on the hand that stirs her cup is a white figure 4, and then a 5 and a 6. We feel she is counting the seconds until she could have her tea drunk and be gone. But it is the slow dissolving in of an elevator's position indicator, and the bright white figures are all we can see until the fade out is nearly finished.

Metabasis is close to metamorphosis, which Norman McLaren makes of it in *La Poulette Grise*. This is a folk song accompanied by drawings, parts of which—and usually not the ones you are looking at—are all the time dissolving slowly into something else. The things we see are not moving, and yet are constantly changing, giving a sense of mystery or magic. Almost imperceptibly the hen becomes the egg inside her, or changes to a cloud. It is most apt for a quiet lullaby, telling of different colored hens who laid their eggs away in odd places, a church, a tree, a cupboard, and the moon.[35]

The question occurs, can there be metabasis in sound? Apart from where people are seen listening, as to a radio, sound and image would normally dissolve together. And the ambiguity of much sound (are we hearing rain, peas rolling over a drum, or an audience clapping?) often requires words or images to make its message clear. Some separation was tried in *Candlelight in Algeria* (George King). Thurston, a secret agent, says, "I'm going to stage a car smash." Susan Ann jumps out of the car into the brush. The car moves off the screen, leaving our gaze on her, and we hear a vibrant screech and crash. The beat of the screech merges into the rhythm of bubbles, and then the image of Susan Ann dissolves to that of the conning tower of a submarine submerging. As there is no break between the screech and bubbles, we tie the bubbles to the car, sent over a cliff into the sea. After the dissolve is complete, we may think the bubbles are caused by the submarine. Perhaps both are intended, in an anadiplosis or carry-over. All that is certain is that neither meaning would have reached us without the words or images that kept them company.

21 Transitions as Figures

What these devices add to the straight cut, and gives them a figurative quality is to signal a break in the continuity of place, of action, and most of all, of time. They are like the three points in print that signal an ellipsis of words that are lost or left out. A boy is sitting on his bed, putting on a second sock. We wipe to him putting a second boot on, and again to a shot of him pulling on a jersey. We can be made aware of the time he takes to dress, and still leave some part of it out (*The Lone Climber*, William C. Hammond).

These devices also have a subjective color. Each time Leydon finds an informant who can add a piece to the story of Dimitrios, we shift from now to the flashback's historic present, by way of a slow wipe, which takes the shape of a rolling distortion of the two blending images it separates. It is as if it were mirrored in a flowing band of water, as if a barrier in time were melting, or the person remembering were bringing his past into focus (*The Mask of Dimitrios*, Jean Negulesco).

III MONTAGE AND OTHER FIGURES

22 Several Figures

Other figures may blend with montage to give a rich texture.

Mary Justin has just renounced the man with whom she has fallen in love, but her husband, in a sudden passion, has told her to leave his house. We see her going down steps, passing ticket vending machines, and floating down an escalator as if with no will of her own, past the postered wall. She reaches the railway platform. We see her and four shining curved steel rails in the same frame, and then a close-up of the gleaming rails by themselves. In an up shot the destination sign changes to "Acton." The signal lights change from red to green. In close-up her face is dark, but a strip of light stresses her eyes. The gleaming rails quiver in center frame. We watch her shadowed face as the roar of the train loudens, then her head and shoulders, in brightening light, her hair blowing, the roar of the train rising to its loudest. In close-up she leans forward, but suddenly turns her head. In a longer shot, her husband holds her in his arms (*The Passionate Friends*, David Lean). The train's presence is told in synecdoche (its roar) or metonymies (the signal lights, the change of sign, her moving hair); there are ellipses (of the train itself, of her husband's arrival) and emphases (of the tracks, of her eyes).

23 Anadiplosis—Variation IV

To lap a conversation over a change of place, time, or person may be seen as a form of anadiplosis: the same conversation seems to open the second scene as closed the former.

In the simplest form the same persons are in both scenes. Inspector Callahan is lying on a couch, having an injury dressed, and answers the telephone. We cut to the doctor at the other end of the line: "A hundred and fifty pounds. Pale complexion." We cut now to Callahan, fully dressed, facing the doctor in person, and putting the obvious next question, "He didn't give his name?" (*Dirty Harry*, Don Siegel).

Mr. Stringer is reporting to Miss Marple on a will. "First," he says, "he only gets the income and not the fortune." "Secondly" (but it is now the sergeant who has been inquiring into the same will speaking to Inspector Craddock) "the fortune goes to the children on his death. . . ." The description of the will is unbroken, but the person speaking, spoken to, place, and visual pattern are all different (*Murder She Said*, George Pollock).

This is continued over a longer time in *Citizen Kane* (Orson Welles).[36] Jedediah Leyland is talking of Kane and Emily, Kane's first wife. Dissolve to the first of a series of breakfast table conversations, speech and image alternating between the two. The last speaker in each scene is always Kane, and there is a streaking pan to Emily, who starts the next scene. The conversation sounds continuous, both because of their manner of speaking and because throughout, he is to the left of the table and she to the right.

They are both in evening dress, having been to six parties in one night. He says he adores her, and agrees to put his morning appointments off to the afternoon. On another morning we see them in dressing gowns. She complains of his keeping her waiting while he went in to his office "for a few minutes." On a third morning, wearing a dark dress with a wide cravat, she chides him for attacking her uncle in his newspapers: "He *is* the President." She asks on a fourth morning (Kane, dressed this time in a black suit), "Does that monstrosity of Bernstein's have to stay in the nursery?" "Yes, it does." "What will people think?" she says on the fifth morning. "People think what I tell them to think" is the answer. On the last morning, both are silent. The music alters from sweetness to dissonance, and the mood shifts from the warmth of love to cold hostility.

Four members of a family are each interrogated by a different person, the questioner always on the right and the arrested person somewhat lower to the left. Question and answer come alternately, but the question put by the first interrogator is answered in the next shot by the second accused. The second interrogator puts the second question, which is answered in the next shot by the third accused, and so on. That someone other than the person questioned gives the answer tells us that all four are being asked the same questions, and perhaps that all are giving the same answers (*Hangmen Also Die*, Fritz Lang).

24 Repetition

Repetition can lend conciseness.

Children seeking a treasure left by evicted monks in Tudor times find a shard of pottery that, fitted with one they have, completes the incised outline of a bell. Grouped around a fallen statue where the shard was found, they exclaim, "A bell!" Two listening bumpkins, who had knocked the statue over without finding the shard, say to one another softly, "A bell?" Inside the abbey, the man who has paid the bumpkins repeats, as if he had just heard them reporting, "A bell!" (*Five Clues to Fortune* part 3, Joe Mendoza).

Williams, an elderly ex-convict, returning from a public toilet, cannot find her wiry-haired terrier. She hesitates, but asks a policeman, who tells her politely that he has not indeed seen such a dog. She looks around, and there is Johnny, standing where an arcade opens to the street. She cries "Johnny!" and turns from the constable. She runs toward us and ends in a close-up of her face. The constable turns, looks alarmed, runs toward us, and ends in close-up. A fast-moving car comes toward us, and with a screech of its brakes, comes to a close-up of its right headlight, which fades to a black screen. The viewer supplies the accident himself, prompted by the quick repetition of three round bodies making swiftly toward us, growing rapidly to fill the frame, one after another (*Turn the Key Softly*, Jack Lee).

Repetition may show direction. In *Thunder Rock* (Roy Boulting), Miss Kirby defies her father and releases her fiancé, in order to continue the writing they disapprove of. We see her before a judge in each of four different courts, her clothing becoming plainer and poorer and her sentence increasing from twenty-eight days to three years penal servitude.

Repetition may bring out a likeness or abstraction. As Colonel Geddes walks in the park, he sees three old men on a bench. Shortly after this, we see his face, thoughtful. There is a close-up of each of the old men he saw, followed in each case by a close-up of himself, taken from the same angle. Only in this way could the shots of either the men he saw or himself give us his thought, "I too am old" (*Clubman*, L F. Lauk).[37]

A whole film has been built on repetition, to show a likeness between two lives. A young man and a young woman live in adjoining rooms, but have never met. Not only are they both lonely but their working days follow a like pattern. Her clock: 7:15: she rises, yawns, and dresses leisurely. His clock: 7:35: he wakes, yawns, sees the alarm at *silent*, leaps out of bed, and dresses in haste, with repeated glances at the clock. She walks, he runs, down the steps. Both are seen in the subway, he munching the last of a doughnut. At her locker, she powders her face; he pulls his overalls up and furtively edges his way to the machine where he works. We see several shots of each as they work, and around the edge of the frame are the figures of a clock, the hour hand slipping slowly from IX to XII, when a factory whistle is superimposed. One life repeating what the other does goes on for much of the film. Each, with a face of cheerfulness, declines, when invited by a couple to join them in an outing. Each goes home, and finds no joy in cards, records, magazines, or the radio. Each hears a band advertising an amusement park, dresses up and goes there. They meet, are together through a series of entertainments, and an accident parts them. Each seeks the other, each is soaked by a rainstorm and returns home disconsolate (*Lonesome*, Paul Fejos).

25 Antithesis

Antithesis is another effect of context, for its nature is to set side by side extremes or opposites of color, image, verbal statements, or movement.

A tall slim aristocratic black man who wears a goatee (the son of a bishop) sits beside a black girl waiting in an elegant car for him. He has been questioned on what he knows of Sapphire Robbins. "He'll never find out I was ever at the Tulip," he tells the girl, expressing contempt for dim police wits. "If my father did, he would disinherit me." Cut to Superintendent Hasard saying to the inspector, "That fellow was hiding something" (*Sapphire*, Basil Dearden).

In a device of classical Greek drama, stichomythia, two persons in turn speak single lines:

MESSENGER:	I am not your father, neither is Polybus.
OEDIPUS:	How comes it then that I was called their son?
MESSENGER:	I will tell you. You were given to him—by me.
OEDIPUS:	Given? And yet he loved me as his son?
MESSENGER:	He had no other.
OEDIPUS:	Was I . . . found? Or bought?
MESSENGER:	Found in a wooded hollow of Cithaeron.[38]

This lends itself to antithesis:

K. RICHARD: Say I, her sovereign, am her subject low.
Q. ELIZABETH: But she, your subject, loathes such sovereignty.
K. RICHARD: Be eloquent in my behalf to her.
Q. ELIZABETH: An honest tale speeds best being plainly told.
K. RICHARD: Then plainly to her tell my loving tale.
Q. ELIZABETH: Plain and not honest is too harsh a style.
K. RICHARD: Your reasons are too shallow and too quick.
Q. ELIZABETH: O, no, my reasons are too deep and dead.[39]

The film can switch persons too, as well as places and occasions. We hear a speaker for McGinty, "These are the things he has done for you and you and you . . ."; and a supporter of Honeywell says, "the worst crook since last year's big wind." We cut between the two:

HONEYWELL: On the one hand virtue, and on the other . . .
McGINTY: Forty thousand men working . . .
HONEYWELL: He gutted the treasury . . .
McGINTY: Forty thousand full lunch pails . . .
HONEYWELL: He raided the taxes . . .
McGINTY: Forty thousand happy families . . .
HONEYWELL: He built useless buildings and bridges, each a monument and testimonial to graft . . .
McGINTY: and has given you the most beautiful city in the world (*The Great McGinty*, Preston Sturges).

Contrast of image may take various forms. Butch Cassidy and the Sundance Kid, during their escape, are often shown half-length and close-up, rarely smaller than half the height of the frame. Their pursuers are mere specks or tiny torches at night—never really people, only a presence, pursuing without haste or deviation, later with barely heard hoofbeats (*Butch Cassidy and the Sundance Kid*, George Roy Hill).

In color, an actor, still in a Nazi uniform, chatting after a performance, remarks, "I am the only Nazi left in the country—I am the only one who admits that he wore a brown shirt." Cut to a black-and-white shot panning over a huge square with acres of arms raised in the Nazi salute, as thousands of voices shout "Heil Hitler." We return to the actor in color, as he says, "That's me" (*The Memory of Justice*, Marcel Ophuls).

Pieces of contrasting action may rub elbows: the quiet of a church during a baptism, in which Michael Corleone vows to renounce the devil and all his works, is intercut with assassinations carried out on his orders, all to the sound of the priest's voice and religious organ heard throughout both sets of events (*The Godfather part I*, Francis Ford Coppola).[40]

A whole film can be based on antithesis. A poorly disciplined and gaudily but sloppily dressed company of would-be soldiers go clumsily through the routine of camp life on a school playground. Intercut with scenes of their military ineptness are those of Zouaves in action, as pictured in romantic fiction—sentries—deserter under arrest—bishop in white canonicals coming to counsel him—an attack and the prisoner is given back his rifle—a few survivors return, the deserter mortally wounded—he dies, is draped with a flag—the bishop in up shot prays—an officer bows his head.

What they are, and what they would like to think they are, are shown side by side throughout the film (*Avec Tambours et Trompettes*, Marcel Carrière).

Stillness and great speed are a strong antithesis, motion and no-motion.

As Kaji and his men approach a hut in a forest, a Russian soldier rises from the undergrowth. Two half-length shots of both Kaji and the Russian are followed by the eyes of each in close-up—all quite still: we share the surprise and the tension. The Russian's head and shoulders move quickly, then Kaji's. A shot, and the Russian falls (*The Human Condition*, part 3: *A Soldier's Prayer*, Masaki Kobayashi).

In *The Road to Life* (N. Ekk), a farm for the rehabilitation of "wild" orphan children brought from Moscow is being undermined by two of their former exploiters. They have set up a brothel, which Kolka, Mustapha, and some few more have taken upon themselves to close down. In long and close shots, the owner, on this their first visit, makes them, the leaders, most welcome. Wine pours into a glass and overflows, in close-up. Mustapha winks at Kolka and empties his wine on the floor. A woman plays an accordion, Zhigan his balalaika. Mustapha, with hands above his head, dances away from his table. Kolka follows. During the dance, their heads come close and Mustapha whispers, "Get ready." The floor fills with dancers, and the whisper passes around them. Three heads of Mustapha circle slowly clockwise. A woman in white is seen standing, watching. In another prism shot, the roomful of dancers begins to eddy the opposite way. The camera starts panning slowly past the dancers around it, who pass from right to left at ever-increasing speed. Suddenly when they are hardly more than streaks fleeting across the frame, there is a cut to a hand pointing a revolver, quite still, held for several seconds.

26 Apophasis

In *apophasis*, a number of possible answers are given, and all are rejected but one. JR constructs airplanes and has become a legend in the industry. Tony and his bride, who is JR's daughter, alight from an airplane at the factory. A small car comes to a stop under the wing—presumably JR, to welcome his daughter. But no, it is Will, the designer. A Rolls-Royce pulls up, surely it brings JR now; but it is merely a car to take them to him. Tony carries her over the threshold and into a room, where an arm and a newspaper poke out beyond the back of a wing chair. Tony sets his bride on a couch and he turns the flank of the chair to find her younger brother. A hand half opens a door, and its owner says firmly to someone outside, "Well, cancel the order then." He enters toward us. This is JR (*Breaking the Sound Barrier*, David Lean).

27 Climax, or, the Ladder

In the pieces making up a congeries, *Dawn in the City*, say, every piece must contain the theme, adding its own difference to the fullness and clarity with which the theme is presented.[41] Something found in many or most pieces may change from less to more or more to less, or in any other way give a sense of movement or change in some direction. *Climax, or, the Ladder* implies a consistent order.

First, then consider more and less. It may be merely coming closer and growing larger. When Abel Magwich comes back to London, and Pip slowly grasps the trend of his questions, in each succeeding shot we are closer to him—at first we can see the third button of his jacket, at the end we see the top one only (*Great Expectations*, David Lean).

There is an amusing parody of this in *The Wrong Box* (Bryan Forbes). Julia floats in slowed motion into the drawing room and Michael follows. Julia sinks into a chair full-length. We approach Michael to half-length, as he stands looking down. We approach the white shoes and stockings that show below her dress. We approach Michael again to head and shoulders, looking down still. We see her bosom as it palpitates, white lace over pink silk. She, half-length, looks up. We pan up his bare arm with rolled-up sleeves. We see her face, his face, her eyes, his eyes, one of her eyes, one of his, her lips, his lips, these both again. We approach to each head in turn. They kiss.

The parcel given to Stevie to check in a baggage room contains a time bomb. We know this but he does not. He is held up by his curiosity, by his tendency to dawdle, by acts of other people. The director makes us aware of the great variety of clocks to be seen on the streets of London, but what we look for in each clock is how far the minute hand has moved from where it was. In the final clock, the minute hand is at 1:45, and the second hand is reaching for the final moment (*Sabotage*, Alfred Hitchcock).

In *Romeo and Juliet and Darkness* (Jiri Weiss), Pavel has hidden Hana, a Jewish girl. When she is discovered, she runs away and is shot. The element of change is a lessening number of shots including Hana, and a growing number of Pavel:

Hana	Pavel		
1		1	Pavel's mother opens the door, and an actress, a friend of the soldiers, sees Hana.
2		2	Hana slips out,
	3	3	Pavel's mother prevents his following Hana.
4		4	Hana coming down stairs, in up shot, pauses.
		5	Grandfather on stairs, says, "Come with us, lassie."
		6	Actress on stairs shouts at grandfather.
7		7	Grandfather holding Hana by the arm, defies the actress.
	8	8	Pavel on the stairs, his mother still holding him.
		9	Actress shouting.
10		10	Hana and grandfather.
	11	11	Pavel breaks from his mother, seizes actress by the throat.
12		12	Hana runs down the stairs from grandfather.
	13	13	Pavel turns to run after Hana.
14		14	Hana in courtyard running toward us.
	15	15	Pavel throwing off his mother who has again taken hold of him, "I hate you."
		16	Mother on the balcony shouts to the caretaker, "Lock the gates."
	17	17	Pavel runs across the court to the gate, tries to open it.
	18	18	Pavel shouts to the caretaker to open the gate.
	19	19	Pavel's head slowly turns toward us, as we hear shots.
	20	20	Pavel turns to face the gate again, bangs on it with his hands, crying out, "I won't allow it."

Another, and common, way is to change the length of the shot. The viewer (but only on second or later showings) may school himself to measure the shots in seconds, if only roughly. My count, for example, of the length of shots in *Things to Come* (William Cameron Menzies) just after we see the sign "Stand to Arms" was (in seconds) as follows:

62525 4221 111111 321232 1111

This shows a shortening in length toward the climax.

In the third place, the speed or quality of movement in the shots themselves may change by degrees. The actors themselves may move slower or faster, or the camera may come closer to them, so that their movements cross more of the screen and seem faster. Motion may be conferred or increased by technical means like panning. In *Sons and Lovers* (Jack Cardiff) as Miriam and Paul walk in the woods and sit by a stream, we hear a sound as of thunder. "It's the mine," says Paul, as he rises and runs. We pan with him, passing a flitting landscape as he tears downhill, Miriam running behind him. We see a street with others running more slowly. As the street becomes more and more crowded, the pace is slower still. A large sheave-wheel, its hub at bottom left, gradually stops turning, a distant line of people slowly crossing its barely rotating rim. We are now in front of a standing crowd, in half-length shot, with Arthur's mother thrusting through them toward us. Then the mother standing still, Paul to the right, and Miriam just reaching them. A sequence that starts with running downhill ends in stillness.

A fourth way is to tell us what is going to happen, but not the circumstances, not the outcome. In *Death of a President* (Jerzy Kawalerowicz) the mere title tells us, apart from hearing from the start the assassin's confession, intertwined with all the events that went before, that Gabriel Narutowicz is going to be killed. We feel the flow toward the expected event. The Albert Hall sequence of *The Man Who Knew Too Much* (Alfred Hitchcock) is built the same way in both versions, but with rather fuller detail in the second. We hear the record played and know at what point in the music the shot will be fired. Mrs. Lawrence does not know. The questions raised are, What will she do? and Will she do it in time? She cannot tell the police, for the assassins are holding her daughter. Our sense of direction is kept on the move by six threads intertwining, each with its own lesser climax, all blending to make a strong impression.

The first is the diplomat. He is greeted in the lobby, sits in his box, and, near the end, he leans forward listening with interest, making a better target.

The second is the gunman. As he crosses the lobby, he presses Betty's brooch into Mrs. Lawrence's hand by way of reminder. He looks right out of his box, measuring his mark, the box on which the flag hangs, and sinks back into the black of his own, the only one whose lights are not lit. The girl with him follows the score, until the time when she closes the score and is also lost in the shadows. A muzzle slowly pokes out from the curtain, and turns to point its ringed black threat at us in close-up.

The third is the performers. The seated women singers are still, and the players are idle with soundless instruments; two large cymbals rest on a chair. Soloist and conductor enter to clapping. The choir stands. The orchestra starts with an ominous seven-note theme in a minor key. As we near the forte passage, we see the percussion scores—twenty-four and thirty-six bars rest. One percussion player after another rises to his feet—the kettle drummer, his eye on the score, sticks poised; a second ready to strike a gong; a third brandishing two huge cymbals above the score his eye is fixed on. The conductor's whole body is caught up in the beat. The men singers in full voice quickly turn a page. The camera pans along a double staff, passing the words *poco a poco crescendo*. The camera pans along a single staff, the notes closer, bigger, and blacker. The music is faster and louder. The conductor's beat is stronger and bigger. Drums, cymbals, gong—their players all stand with muscles tensed.

The fourth is Mrs. Lawrence. From the time she is seated in the stalls, she is glancing around the hall and the camera gives us what she sees—the draped box, a run along the row of boxes, passing and then coming back to the one with no lights, its curtain sometimes shaking, an inspector coming in and speaking to the policeman on duty, her hand as it opens to show us Betty's brooch. At last the orchestra goes out of focus.

The fifth is Abbott, his gunmen, and Mr. Lawrence, their captive listening to a broadcast of the concert. A microphone at Albert Hall comes into focus, we pan to a radio, and in longer shot we see them listening. Abbott has threatened Lawrence and Betty with death if the assassination is thwarted. We are here listening with them when the music reaches its climax.

The music—thread six—reaches a fortissimo chord, Mrs. Lawrence screams, the diplomat collapses forward. He has however not been killed but wounded.

Climax is found in abstract film, using similar elements. A tiny square may grow or multiply or split into many smaller ones. Coils may wind into larger ones. Lines may grow from fine to bold. A single shape may enter, and then groups and larger groups of the same shape. A dot of yellow may swell till it nearly fills the screen (*Motion Painting No. 1*, Oscar Fischinger).

28   Hyperbole

Some hyperboles may be seen as elliptical montage. In *Magic Treasure* (Dimitri Pavilichenko) the miser Balchen riding away on his camel shrinks in size more quickly than even a rocket in flight. This may be seen as a series of cuts. Projected at a speed of twenty-four frames per second, two hundred and forty frames would show the distance covered in ten seconds at actual speed. We could increase the rate of travel twenty-four times by cutting twenty-three frames from each second, and leaving in every twenty-fourth, projecting thus one frame per second of movement instead of twenty-four. This exaggerated speed of movement is thus an effect of montage, even if done in shooting.

This can be seen in such a film as *The Magician* (Ivan Renc and Pavel Hobl). The magician on his way to an island castle riding a dolphin travels in four stages. We dissolve from the dolphin, quite near, to a place further distant. In two more stages each further off, the magician is at the castle. If straight cuts had replaced the much more leisurely dissolves, the dolphin would have sped as fast as the camel.

Montage can change actual speed from what is barely perceptible to supersonic, from smooth to jerky, from which range a director may choose the most appropriate. The hubbub caused by Cat Ballou when she and her helpers hold up a train is shown when it reaches the station. The crew and passengers leap from the coaches, run to the station, collide with people meeting the train, and leap on horses, all in ludicrous haste (*Cat Ballou*, Elliott Silverstein).

It is also hyperbole to make things fall more slowly than gravitation does. This is done by increasing the number of exposures per second above twenty-four. This may be done to have us ponder longer on, to observe more closely, an event that is normally fast: throwing a bag of books on a fire (*Fahrenheit 451*, François Truffaut); the elegant movements of athletes jumping, throwing the discus, and hurdling (*The Man with a Movie Camera*, Dziga Vertov). It can also suggest decay, ruin, collapse, neglect, or slowly wasting, as in *The Fall of the House of Usher* (Jean Epstein). Books, for example, topple slowly from their shelves behind curtains. This magnification of a moment, this "close-up in time" can also be looked upon as an effect of montage, the adding in of a number of frames, much above the normal.

29 Hypophora

Hypophora raises a question, either express or implied, and then provides an answer.[42]

In *The Testament of Dr. Mabuse* (Fritz Lang), four of the men resisting arrest have dropped their revolvers through a slit in the door. They then emerge, their hands above their heads. "Where's number five?" asks Inspector Lohmann. Cut to a shaggy rug, on it a revolver, and, hanging down into the frame, we see the hand that had held it.

A scene that is cut before its outcome is clear may raise a question. Shunsaku's mistress agrees with his daughter Kimiko that he ought to return to his wife in Tokyo, and gives him the money he needs to pay his expenses. Still he sits on the floor, unpersuaded. The next scene starts with moving landscape, the moving engine, and seated inside the train, Shunsaku and Kimiko (*Kimiko*, Mikio Naruse).

But a director, perhaps, like a cross-examining counsel, should ask only questions to which he knows the answer. In *Vampyr* (Carl Theodor Dreyer) a vampire-bitten woman sits in a tall oaken chair, her eyes fixed offscreen on the ceiling. They move slowly right to left and back, as if they followed something—something never shown or explained.

30 Hyrmos

Like hypophora, the hyrmos arouses curiosity, because a clue we know we need for the understanding of a situation is held back and sprung upon us at the end.

Roberta's father has been imprisoned for a crime he did not commit. She, her brother, and her sister wave to an elderly gentleman who passes every day on the train and who waves back. He proves to be kindly, and helps them when their mother is sick. They tell him about their father. One day Roberta, out walking, meets the porter, Mr. Pearkes, on the station platform. He has only time to tap his newspaper, to say he is pleased, and kiss her on each cheek, before hastening away to his duties. Someone had alighted from the train, lost in the cloud of steam that hazed out the platform as the train left. What was Mr. Pearkes so happy about, she wonders. We cut between her as she looks at the departing train and the clouded platform, each time the steam less dense. A faint shadow of someone standing there becomes clearly a man. At the moment of recognition, we are standing beside her father, seen full-length. She runs toward us, slightly slowed, as if unable to go as fast as she wishes. As a person of some importance (he owns the railway) the elderly gentleman had an inquiry made which cleared her father of the crime (*The Railway Children*, Lionel Jeffries).

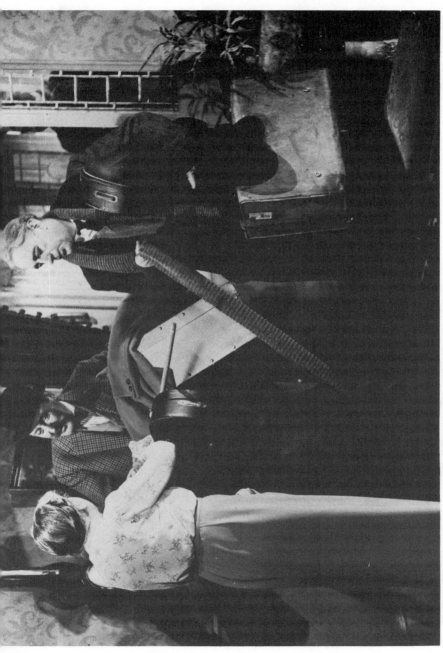

The Lady Killers. (EMI Film Distributors Overseas Ltd.)

PLATE 15. METAPHOR. METONYMY. SIGNIFICANT OBJECT.

The five bank robbers who take lodgings at Mrs. Wilberforce's do not seem able to disentangle their fates from the disastrous doom she seems to bring upon them. Several metaphorical incidents hint at this. Twice, for example, Professor Marcus finds himself tethered to her by his muffler on which she is standing. This might also be seen as a metonymic use of his scarf and her shoe.

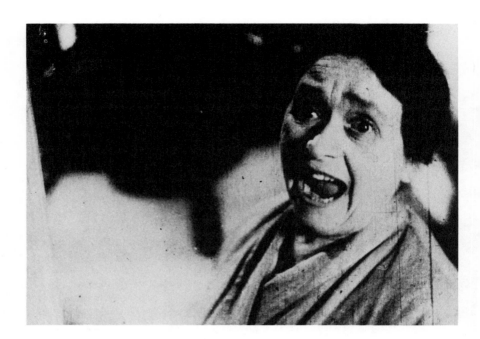

The Thirty-Nine Steps. (By courtesy of the Rank Organization Ltd.)
PLATES 16 AND 17. ANADIPLOSIS, VARIATIONS IV AND I. ZEUGMA.
Hannay is on the train for Scotland, suspected of murder. Cut from him to the head and
shoulders of a woman, who screams and turns toward us. Cut to a railway engine bursting
out of a tunnel opening, the continued scream now becoming that of the engine whistle.
The circle formed by the woman's chin and the labio-nasal shadows occupies the same
space on the screen as the circle of the engine's boiler, and the scream tends to draw our
attention to the mouth in the same circle. There is thus a hint of a like pattern carrying
over the cut (anadiplosis, variations IV and I). A common sound given off by two contrasting images may also be seen as a zeugma, where a verb applies to two contrasted
subjects in different senses.

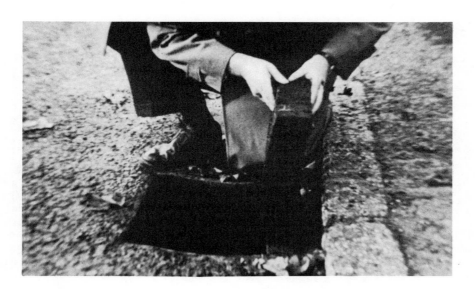

Sapphire. (By courtesy of The Rank Organization Ltd.)
PLATES 18, 19, AND 20. ANADIPLOSIS, VARIATIONS VII AND III. SYNECDOCHE. ELLIPSIS.
A detective opens a drain into which he has seen a suspect drop something. We expect him to pick it out. In the next shot, a hand, presumably his, holds a short wooden stick. But as the camera retreats we see that the hand is Inspector Learoyd's, from which, in the third still, Superintendent Hasard has picked the stick. This is anadiplosis, variation VII, a carryover from action to consequence. There is also a single ambiguous image. There is not enough background in the shot of the hand for us to be able to determine whose hand it is or where it is. Knowing only what has gone before, we assume that it is the detective's hand, and later find it is someone else's (variation III). The hand for the person is synecdoche. The ellipsis of the rest of the body and the finding of the stick we supply, as in all ellipses.

Things to Come. (London Films)

The Bridge on the River Kwai. (Columbia Pictures International Corporation)
PLATE 22. ANTITHESIS. DEAD METAPHOR. INNER STATE: VIEWPOINT.
The Japanese commandant is large and close in contrast to the tiny distant prisoners of war below him. This conveys a position or posture of power. We grasp the meaning usually without observing that it comes from a dead metaphor, the commandant being "above" the prisoners of war, and by being larger, therefore stronger than they are.

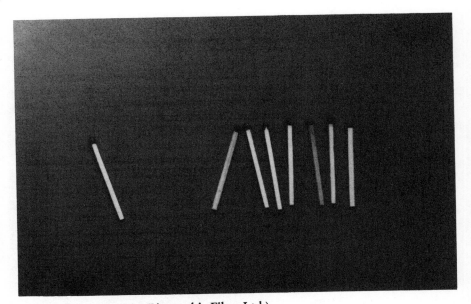

Do It Yourself Cartoon Kit. (Biographic Films Ltd.)
PLATE 23. HYPERBOLE: REDUCTIO AD ABSURDUM. PARODY. ABSTRACTION.
Figures pursuing each other around a Greek vase, bits of paper in full flight from others,
or as here, a gang of matches after one which is trying to escape them, have nothing in
common but flight and pursuit. From this the director has evoked the generalization
"chase". He has kept the form of the chase but altered the participants, to demonstrate the
reductio ad absurdum that the filmgoer is not concerned with who is chasing or who is
being chased; it is flight and pursuit that holds him. This is a parody of Hitchcock's work,
who never identified in more than the vaguest way the "McGuffin" his chases were about,
but concentrated his attention on the chase itself.

Fantasia: Dance of the Hours. (© MCMXL Walt Disney Productions)
PLATE 24. HYPERBOLE: REDUCTIO AD ABSURDUM. PARODY.
Here music, agility and movement are as in ballet: what is not the same is those who
perform it. It is all in the movement: as long as they make the movements required, all at
once on the beat, those who perform can be men or women, elephants, ostriches,
crocodiles, or a hippopotamus. As in caricature, there is in parody that which wounds or
belittles.

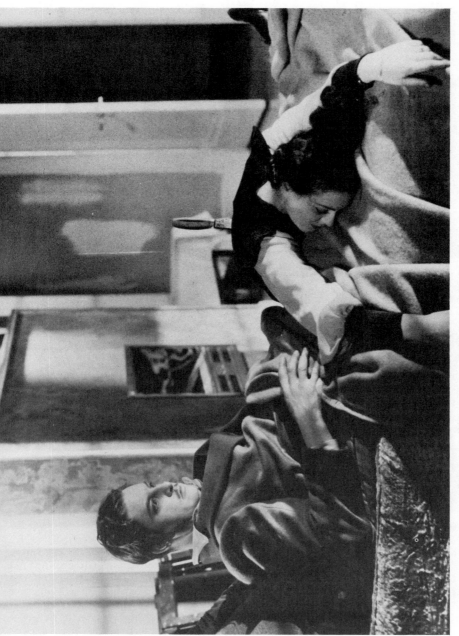

The Thirty-Nine Steps. (By courtesy of the Rank Organization Ltd.)
PLATE 25. ELLIPSIS. HYRMOS.

After Hannay and the unknown woman have gone to sleep in different rooms, we see an open window with curtains flying in the wind. Hannay's bedroom door opens, and the woman rushes in with a map grasped in her hand. What has happened? We do not know until she collapses on Hannay's bed and we see the knife in her back. Keeping back till the end a detail needed for understanding is hyrmos.

M. (Atlantic Film AG)

PLATE **26.** ELLIPSIS AND INCLUSION. METONYMY.

The shadow is one of the commoner filmic metonymies, an effect placed for the cause. Here too as well as leaving out the person who is casting the shadow, three things are deliberately included in the frame: the shadow, the advertisement it falls on, which offers a large reward for the killer of a child, and a child with a ball. The three things together irresistibly suggest that the shadow is the murderer's and the child in peril.

The Ring. (EMI Film Distributors Overseas Ltd.)
PLATE 27. METONYMY.
In silent films inner states were often conveyed by metonymy, by the heroine kissing the telephone after calling a lover, caressing a necklace he had given her, or (as here) clutching a picture of the man she was in love with, an abstract image put in place of the person it stands for.

Chicken Little. (© MCMXLIII Walt Disney Productions)

PLATE 28. SYNECDOCHE. SIGNIFICANT THING. APOSTROPHE.

Foxy Loxy has panicked a flock of hens into the Cave. The commentator says (to us), "Don't worry, folks, everything's going to be all right." Then we cut to the above shot, where Foxy Loxy is picking his teeth with a wishbone. In the foreground are the wishbones, like gravestones, each standing for the hen of which it had once been a part, now eaten. The commentator protests. "That isn't the way it ends in my book," to which

Part VII

Specific Areas of Use

15
Sound

1   Sound and Image

In the film today, there is a flow of sound as well as a flow of images. These flows may be seen in metaphor as horizontal and parallel, and what eye and ear take in at the same instant, as simultaneous and vertical. If a figure can arise from the putting together of two successive images, surely it can from two successive sounds; nor is there any reason why a sound and an image perceived at the same time cannot also work on one another, transmuting, as figures do, their meanings.

This is a simple notion, but one often clouded by an unfortunate use of terms.

2   The Term "Contrapuntal"

The term "contrapuntal" comes from the theories on sound of Eisenstein, Pudovkin, and Aleksandroff.[1] Pudovkin has written that film sound must not be circumscribed by the sound a thing makes in the actual world, the throbbing we hear from a motor or the words of a speaker, and that any sound from any place or time could be put in its place, to add to the image, emphasis or comment.[2]

Eisenstein had already conceived montage as the cutting together of several different events or different lines, one line perhaps the shots of crowds, another of individuals coming nearer, and a third of a railway train slowing down.[3] These three simultaneous events were parallel only in his mind, for, on the screen, only one line could be seen at a time, its place taken in turn by a shot from one of the others. Sound then appeared to Eisenstein as just another line to add to these. So taken was he by this analogy that he made little of one critical distinction, which is that sound and image are presented and are perceived at the same time, while the lines in the images are seen turn about, and, as in any montage, the meaning of a single piece of any line takes its meaning, not so much as part of its line but from what we see before and after it.

In the early days of sound, when wonder it was merely to hear an actor speak from the screen, this was a needed statement, but the tagging to sound of the label "contrapuntal" did more to darken than clarify. Unless to those who are well versed in music, counterpoint suggests a round or canon, and as anyone knows who has sung

"Sumer is acumen in" or "Frère Jacques," each voice in a canon sings the same notes, but each in turn starts a bar or two after the one before it. The austerity of unison is, so to say, sloped in time into the richer texture of counterpoint. By merely having all the singers start at the same time, unison returns.

The first notion then that comes from the word "contrapuntal" is likeness of the lines of sound and image. But we cannot speak of a sound as "like" an image: a white horse is not the same as its neigh, nor is a pianist, like the chord he plays. The point made by Eisenstein and Pudovkin is that each of the two voices of sound and image must be free to be "unlike" the other. They were thinking surely of the simultaneous differences, in interval, in assonance and dissonance, between the notes of the several voices heard at the same moment. When they spoke of counterpoint, they were thinking harmonically, and though it is true that in counterpoint, one must compose up across the staff and along the staff as well, if we draw on music at all for an analogue, we had much better speak, not of contrapuntal sound but harmonic. If sound and image are in unison, or perfect in interval, the sound will say what the image also says, each in its own way—a form of emphasis. If the two clash strongly, a message may emerge that is not expected from either, often ironical.[4] The coupling of sound and image suits the "two-story" nature of irony, with its dissonance between the two levels. And the element of "innocence"—the victim's unawareness of any other level—is ensured by the freedom to add whatever sound we like to the victim's image.[5]

In *The Lady Killers* (Alexander Mackendrick) Major Courtenay pursued by Harvey has fallen off the roof with a chimney pot. The major was making off with more than his share. His fellow thieves have to dispose of his body. "One-Round" Lawson lays him out on a wheelbarrow, feet toward us, and wheels him down the garden path to the parapet of a railway tunnel. Professor Marcus follows the cortege, to the sound of a solemn, organ-hymn-like music. A train engine hurls a spreading drape of steam above the parapet as it enters the tunnel. Against it for a moment we see Marcus and Lawson each holding one of Courtenay's legs, the rest of the body cut off by the parapet. The steam whites them out, and when it clears, the legs are gone. The music was an ironic reminder of other more dignified exits.

Each thief is killed by another till Marcus, the sole survivor, having dropped Louis down to an empty wagon, is himself struck by a signal arm dropping down to danger, and also falls below into the wagon. Now we hear a coy "peep peep" from the engine, about to steam away with the two final installments. It takes the edge from a rather macabre episode, and invites us to treat the whole story as a fantasy. It may also signal the irony of the briefly victorious Marcus being shipped off on the same train as his victim.

In both cases—religious solemnity at the callous dumping of a corpse, and after two dark deaths, a lighthearted good-bye—we feel a harmonic dissonance. Unknown to the persons in the story, the director is adding a tone of color to it, for us in the audience, as if clothing a melody in unexpected harmonies.[6]

3 The Term "Synchronous"

It is common to class sound as synchronous or not. It is synchronous when it comes from a source to be seen on the screen (moving lips, fingers pressing piano keys, a glass crashing to the floor). In this case, as it starts, grows louder, and stops, the sound must fit what is seen to be taking place. All other sound is asynchronous.

Is this distinction important for the viewer, any more than the kind of rig that carries a moving camera? Is it indispensable to his understanding, is it even peripheral, to know that when a person turns his back, what he says is no longer synchronous? Must the viewer, in short, add this to the words he needs to talk of the films he sees? In my view, the answer is no.

In *A Cup of Tea*, an episode from *Kwaidan* (Masaki Kobayashi), one of the characters, whenever he drinks, sees a face looking back from inside his cup, however much he tries to be rid of it, however often he pours out his cup and fills it again. We hear at the same time the buzzing of a fly, an apt metaphor in sound for the face that will not cease. Presumably, if the fly can be seen, the buzzing is synchronous, and when the fly alights, the sound must be stopped. If the fly is there but cannot be seen (my eyes could not see it), or when it soars out of the frame, the sound is asynchronous. The viewer's response is still the same, whatever difference it makes to the sound recordist.

But there is an adjective the viewer needs: it is "diegetic."

4 The Term "Diegetic"

We do need to distinguish sounds that are part of the flow of the story from those that are not. I have, therefore, borrowed from Jean Mitry and Christian Metz, reluctantly but gratefully, the term "diegetic." I say reluctantly, for it seems to me that unless we add a new term reluctantly, and only after a thorough search fails to unearth an existing one, that is equally specific in meaning and convenient in use, we erode the language more than enrich it by bringing in a new word, whose meaning can be clearly expressed by an older one. I have found no term as concise and unambiguous as "diegetic."[7]

The narrative or discourse is the diegesis. As I shall use the term diegetic, it comprises all sound that a person could hear if he stood at the place and the time shown on the screen. It will apply not only to words said, instruments played, or tools used by those we see, whether or not their backs are to us, but also to sound entering by a window we see but do not look through, music played by a band that is in the room but out of sight, or sounds whose origin the eye cannot reach because of intervening things or distance.

Of nondiegetic sound, some is the words of a commentator, some is music added after shooting to support a mood, some is a means of irony or satire, some belongs to a later shot, begun before a prior one has left the screen (it is diegetic for the later, but not the prior, shot).

And what of apostrophes delivered off the screen to us the audience? What of soliloquies heard when the speaker's mouth is closed? The speaker is part of the narrative, the words a reaction to it, but they cannot be heard by the other characters, and may be a means for ironic or satirical comment.

II DIEGETIC SOUND

5 Diegetic Sound—Peristasis I—Realism

The figure *peristasis* is described in Lanham as "Amplifying by describing attendant circumstances";[8] and this is certainly something done by sound. In *The Seventh Victim* (Mark Robson) as Mary goes down steps to a basement restaurant, we hear the tinkling of a hurdy-gurdy mingling faintly with an unaccompanied voice in an Italian aria. She opens the door, and the aria loudens. As she slowly shuts the door behind her, the tinkling stops, and we hear only the singing. We see the source of neither sound, for neither is important in the story; the shot without the sound, in fact, would give us all we need; yet the sound evokes the atmosphere of the place, and strengthens the change from street to restaurant.

The realistic use of sound must, of course, differ from reality. A director will not burden our ears with every clattering dish, closing door, or passing motorcar. From all the plausible sounds a place may supply, he will choose only those that serve the story, that establish a place or situation, a time of day, an atmosphere, the mood of a character, who, as we all do, will hear only those sounds that suit his feelings. He will hold a sound only so long as it serves his purpose. He knows too, that we soon cease to notice any unvarying long-continued sound, like that of machinery. So, until he intends us to hear it, he will delete a sound that in life would not be noticed and in film might lessen emphasis on a sound of greater weight in the story.

Tokiko lives in an industrial district, and the pumping sound we sometimes hear likely keeps going all the time, day or night. But the director lets us hear the sound only at certain times. When Tokiko is in the kitchen and finds her little son, Hiro, unconscious on the floor, and carries him to the doctor's office, we hear it. When she is looking at herself in the mirror, trying to make her mind up to earn money in a brothel (she cannot pay the child's medical bills), and suddenly covers her face, again we hear the throbbing pump. As she sits by Hiro at night placing a bag of ice to cool his forehead, she begs him to get better, wondering what she would do if he died, and the silence is broken by a distant engine whistle. There must have been many trains pass during the action, but this alone the director lets us hear (*A Hen in the Wind*, Yasujiro Ozu).

Sound can place us vividly in someone else's shoes—the figure *ethopoeia*. A warder opens the door to three prisoners, whose terms are up. Through the door they see the open streets, and the silence is invaded by the roar of traffic, the sounds of horns, the throbbing of engines, and the whole distant undertone of a great city (*Turn the Key Softly*, Jack Lee).

As the Japanese soldier he is seeking rises up from the undergrowth in front of Joyce, a bird screeches. The screech startles us more than the silent soldier does. It strikes like a blow, as it must have done to Joyce (*The Bridge on the River Kwai*, David Lean).

6 Diegetic Sound—Peristasis II—Situations and Places

Reality, especially when charged with emotion, is hard to convey without sound, whose impression on us is more thalamic than cortical, whose message comes less to the mind than the feelings.

A flock of sheep has blocked the road and allowed Hannay, handcuffed to Pamela, to escape from the spies who had kidnapped them. We see the houseless hills of Scotland, the road lost in dust, a confusion of sheep, the spies vainly searching, Pamela wondering if the man she is hiding under a bridge with is a murderer—the whole turmoil admirably captured by the senseless agitation of bleating sheep (*The Thirty-Nine Steps*, Alfred Hitchcock).

Who that saw *The Wages of Fear* (Henri-Georges Clouzot) will forget the moment when the starting trucks filled with nitroglycerin crept slowly and nervously towards us. From a low angle, the massive engine, the fringe of tiny lights, and the huge word *Explosives* were intimidating, but it was the ominous racing of the motors that struck the fear to our hearts.

The first train is seen coming along the branch line, which the boys of the training school had built themselves. Mustapha was to drive the train. Their band begins to play with enthusiasm, but as the train comes closer, we can see on the cowcatcher a body—a dead body—the body of Mustapha. The music dies out, and we hear the train gliding quietly to a stop, and then the only sound is the last sighs of steam escaping from the valves (*The Road to Life*, Nicolai Ekk).

Ashenden and the Hairless Mexican enter a Swiss church, whose organist, a former German agent, has information for them. They kneel in a pew and light three candles, the sign agreed upon. From the moment they enter, we have a sense of unease, at odds with a quiet country church. Around a pillar, we see the back of the organist. He is bent over his instrument, but gives no sign of knowing they have come. After waiting a few fretful minutes, the Mexican draws a knife, and the two approach the organ. We now discover the cause of our unease, for it grows louder as we and they approach the instrument: from the time we entered the church, the organ has been sounding the same unchanging discord. On either side of the player they stand. At the Mexican's touch, the player falls back dead and the discord stops. A hyrmos (*The Secret Agent*, Alfred Hitchcock).

The situation in *The Lavender Hill Mob* (Charles Crichton) is less dramatic. Two fleeing thieves in a stolen police car misdirect the police to a corner where the visibility is poor, where one police car after another piles into those already there, one of which is a civilian car with a radio playing. We see two long antennas tangling and hear a rollicking rendering of "Old Macdonald Has a Farm," genially unconcerned at the stunned paralysis of police activity.

7 Diegetic Sound—Peristasis III—Reminiscence and Commentary

The sounds of a place may not merely change the mood of those who are there: the mood may arouse memories. When Tokiko's husband Ida returns from the war and hears of her having gone to a brothel, he scolds her. He goes to the brothel himself, and carefully verifies that his wife had gone there once only. He asks for a girl to be sent to him. There is a school beside the building, and we hear children singing to the organ, their voices filling the calm of a sunny summer day. He finds out from the girl that she is twenty-one, the eldest of several children, and is supporting the family, for her father cannot work and her mother is dead. She stands at the window and looks out. She had gone to that school, she says, and played in the yard below. For both of them, the sound returns them in thought back to their younger days, whose problems, looking back, seem to have been simpler and much more manageable. He gives her something and leaves (*A Hen in the Wind*, Yasujiro Ozu).

Where the face of the outer world seems to match an act, good or bad, it may carry a director's comment or suggest a character's feelings. Lacombe Lucien, having gone to a Jewish tailor for a suit, covets the tailor's daughter, and having joined the Gestapo, Lacombe feels that there is no limit on what he may claim. The night he comes in a dark suit, knocks on the tailor's door, and first makes his purpose plain it is raining outside, and there is a roll of thunder (*Lacombe Lucien*, Louis Malle).

8 Diegetic Sound—Offscreen Space—Metonymy

"Noises off," "Alarums," "A cry of women within" are directions quite familiar to readers of plays. The knock on the door is found from *Macbeth* to *The Monkey's Paw*. The offstage scream is found in David Campton's *Frankenstein* and Alexander

Mackendrick's *The Lady Killers*. It is a device then shared by stage and screen, a convenient and effective metonymy.

We look in one direction, we hear from all directions, so the "attendant circumstances" added by sound may be outside what we see on the screen, in what has been called "offscreen space." We extend the space on the screen by adding to it the place from which the sounds we hear come, and they may come from things or people we have just seen.

The camera leaves Vincent walking along a narrow cobbled street, to scrutinize the houses across the road, but the sound of him and his footsteps keep him and the cobbles as part of the scene (*Monsieur Vincent*, Maurice Cloche).

Thorold Dickinson has made a theater from four listening people seated in a box, brightly lit from the right, by adding the sound of the opera (*The Queen of Spades*).

We may place the action offscreen, to let our imagination work upon it. Joel starts downstairs in pajamas and blanket. Our gaze remains on the head of the stairs as Joel falls out of the frame, and we follow his downward progress by the sound of his bumps. We feel that the director is washing his hands of him; it is certainly easier on Joel (*The Palm Beach Story*, Preston Sturges).

We may keep the action onscreen and place it in context by sound only. As Major Shears and Joyce work in silence to mine the bridge, we are at water level with them. The bridge and the sentries on it are brought to us by the sound of marching boots, the camp full of prisoners of war by cheers from a faroff concert they are putting on, and the waterfall upstream by its distant sibilance (*The Bridge on the River Kwai*, David Lean).

Harry Lime, in flight from the police in Vienna, finds himself in a large square brick chamber, part of the sewers. He stands irresolute and looks in turn at the many ways out. The chamber swirls with reverberations, he knows not where from, that make the ambiguous black of each hole an endless corridor peopled with pursuers (*The Third Man*, Sir Carol Reed).

Perhaps the most thoroughgoing use of sound in this way is in *Un Condamné à Mort s'est Échappé* (Robert Bresson). The German prison guards are rarely seen, and are distanced from us, as from the prisoner, by sound. We come to identify the musical passing of the one who runs his keys along the metal bannisters, and the squeak of the one who uses a bicycle to make his rounds of the "moat." We hear German phrases passing by. We are alert for the cough of the neighbor across the hall, warning us of someone coming. We hear the train roaring by and a piece of glass breaking—somewhere. The camera never leaves the cell, which adds its own sounds, tapping a neighbor's wall, grinding a spoon to a chisel on the stone floor, or the slushing of water (together with broken glass) out of a ventilating duct. These, and the absence of human talk, make up the solitude and the silence.

The incident may happen behind a door. One of Dr. Mabuse's men, who is firing through a slot in a door, stops to reload. A detective lying on the stairs aims his revolver carefully. We see the letter slot again; we hear a shot, followed by a cry of pain (*The Testament of Dr. Mabuse*, Fritz Lang).

A common practice is to bring in the next shot by installments, first as offscreen space by sound, and then on screen. As Colonel Nicholson is taken out of the corrugated iron hutch they call the oven, which lies alongside the parade ground, we hear the voices of his men singing "For he's a Jolly Good Fellow." Then we are shown a long shot of the parade ground and the men we heard singing (*The Bridge on the River Kwai*, David Lean).

Offscreen space, disclosed in a sudden sound, can surprise us with an unexpected circumstance. Twice in *Moscow Nights* (Anthony Asquith), when Captain Ignatov and Natacha are together, we hear her name uttered offscreen by Briokov, whom then the camera pulls back to show us. On the first occasion, she goes with Briokov; on the second, he leaves alone.

9 Diegetic Sound—Sound without Image—Amphibology

We can only imagine offscreen space, if what we do see (and hear) provides a sufficient clue to what we cannot see. This is true of the examples above; but a sound whose source we cannot fix may suggest many different ones. Thus we have the figure amphibology.

In *The Innocents* (Jack Clayton), the invisible world, the world of revenants, comes to us mostly in sound, in screeches, rattles, thumps, and creaks; in the sudden whoosh of a window blown open; in a high-pitched whine as of distant insects; in whispering, weeping, and echoing laughter; and in a silence oppressed by hollow footsteps and the hum of bees.

When the image is dark or the frame black, we have to assume that what is heard is the sound of something on the screen that cannot be seen in the dark, for there would be little sense in showing a dark screen unless its diegetic night were the source of the sound. A man who resembles a suspected murderer has gone down a dark alley. Inspector Callahan follows him. We lose sight of the inspector in the dense blackness, and while the frame is black, we hear the clang of a resonant, metallic object and a squeak (which might have been given out by any one of a score of objects). Then a window comes into view from the top of the screen, as the inspector's head rises into it silhouetted. We are free to imagine the unimportant objects he had to assemble to let him climb up to window level (*Dirty Harry*, Don Siegel).

A form of this is to show a loudspeaker, through which an event is heard but not seen. We listen at headquarters to the two men who landed at the village of Piedmont. They speak of finding bodies lying dead throughout the village. We hear the sound of a car, they speak of something coming toward them; we hear a scream, and there is silence (*The Andromeda Strain*, Robert Wise).

III NONDIEGETIC SOUND

10 Nondiegetic Sound—Confirming the Image

Nondiegetic sound comes from somewhere other than the space, on or off screen, in which the events of the story are taking place. It is, in the nature of the matter, a director's gloss or commentary, in musical or nonmusical sound, or in words that convey a viewpoint or further details we need to know. An anonymous voice, or a character not present, may speak the words, or a character seen on screen may turn to speak to us the audience—in the figure apostrophe. The sound may, by peristasis, amplify or confirm the message of the images, or, by some other figure, change the meaning of the image by what it adds.

There is, as there must be with all distinctions, the sound that may be diegetic or not. As Tom, sought by the police, says good-bye and kisses his father, we hear a train whistle. There might well have been tracks within earshot, though none were shown, but it certainly is a metonymy, that for most of us will stand for long journeys, often final ones (*The Grapes of Wrath*, John Ford).

We see Stephen on his way to meet Francesca, ringing at her door, entering, sitting and talking, and helping her on with her wrap, and through a restaurant window, we see the two of them drinking and eating. We see little or no movement of lips, and we hear, well spaced out, free from any other sound, of traffic, dishes, or telephone, as if in a vacuum, the usual words one says to avoid saying nothing or to show pleasure in the other person's company. "I was in my bath when you phoned . . . Ten years? It can't be . . . It must be . . . You don't look a day older . . . That is a beautiful dress . . . and a beautiful coat . . . I'm in consumer research, did you know? . . . It's quite fascinating . . ." These are their words and these the situations in which they said them, but the conversation is taken apart and reset and given a leisurely pace, which fits the unhurried mood of the images, better than the continuous talk from which it was abridged. Not exactly diegetic, not fully nondiegetic (*Accident*, Joseph Losey).

In *Farrebique* (Georges Rouquier) his fingers tell the grandfather's death. In close-up, we see them lying supine, slightly bent. We hear a chopping sound, which might be coming from outside or not, for we are never shown who is doing the felling. In a close-up of a vein, the old man's blood throbs to the beat of the chopping axe. The chopping stops, and we hear a tree sliding and crashing, and as we listen, the pulse too that we see on the screen weakens and stops and the camera pans down to rest on the supine fingers. The sound is almost certainly nondiegetic; it is, in fact, a simile in sound.

A thing may seem then to give off a sound like something else. A troop train pulls out of a station, its engine almost lost in steam. The rattle of the drawbar, the puffing of the steam, sound like the beat of a drum; a metaphor (*Baltic Deputy*, A. Zarkhi and Joseph Heifetz). A submerged submarine is sending a message. The music suggests the tapping key of the telegraph sender and throbbing engines; the figure onomatopoeia (*Escape to Danger*, Victor Hanbury, Lance Comfort, Mutz Greenbaum). In *The Black Panther* (Ian Merrick) what starts as diegetic sound becomes nondiegetic, with a hint of cause and effect. As Donald Neilson, intent on stealing a motorcar, tries the handle of one, a dog leaps at the window and barks fiercely. Neilson runs, and the beat of the barks dissolves into a throb on a kettle drum, suggesting the beating heart of startled flight.

The most common of nondiegetic sound is music. Anthony Asquith wrote that, in moments of intense feeling, music may be used as a substitute, a metaphor, for speech, and quotes Mendelssohn that the emotions music arouses cannot be rendered in language, for music is an exact expression of feeling, and words are ambiguous.[9] It is a metaphor for speech and inner states.

Three of those conspiring to inherit Yawahara's millions are named in his will: his widow, a child alleged by the widow to be his illegitimate daughter, and his secretary. Yasuko, the secretary, proves that the child was not Yawahara's. She thus disqualifies the child and, at the same time, disqualifies the widow, because of the fraudulent representation. With no change in her customary self-possession, the widow turns toward us as if to look at Yasuko. Only a guttural growl of brass reveals her fury (*The Inheritance*, Masaki Kobayashi).

After some talk of Lime's death, Anna says to Martins, "If it really was an accident." Martins, at the window, turns abruptly around, as the zither music rises in sudden loudness, accenting the leap of his thought (*The Third Man*, Sir Carol Reed).

Hamlet enters behind the praying king, and in half-length he raises his dagger above the king's head to rising music whose pitch reaches its height as the dagger does. We hear his unlipped words, "Now might I do it pat . . ." The upsweep of the dagger is as one screwing his courage to the sticking point, but before the dagger's point can plunge down, reflection countermands it. The music is linked both to the raising of the dagger and the mounting resolution (*Hamlet*, Laurence Olivier).

In longer passages, the mood evoked by the music is often more important than the trivial or broken conversation it likely replaces. A young woman, depressed at being unable to find work, meets a young man in a park. Through a window, we see them trying to eat with chopsticks and laughing; between their backs we see a distant ballet; we see her gasping at a daring circus act; we read the printed program of a concert; and we hear her say, as they stop walking in front of her house, "Oh Philip, I've had such a nice time since we met." Under all this montage, these were the only words, the rest was happy and romantic music (*The Suspect*, Robert Siodmak).

Non-diegetic sound is often used by peristasis to fill out the image, where sound, for example, is added on to historic stills. In *1848, the Year of Revolution* (Victoria Spiri Mercantor and others) the events of the revolution are shown in photographs of the time. We see firing guns, and cut to shotholes in the walls of buildings, but the guns we hear are not those that broke the holes in the walls.

11 Nondiegetic Images

Now and then with some success, the reverse is tried. The director starts with music and invents images to match its character. *Fantasia* (Walt Disney) has not been excelled in this: volcanic eruptions to match the violent brassy beats of Stravinsky, the early crust of the earth to match the early rites of man, facetious elephants conferred on Ponchielli, and abstract shapes on Bach.

Several times in *The Music Lovers*, Ken Russell takes Tchaikovsky's music and adds a montage from Tchaikovsky's thoughts and experience, in Russell's conception of them. The *1812 Festival Overture* accompanies moments of triumph and eminence; the Sixth Symphony is matched with Tchaikovsky's own death from cholera and Nina's madness. We see him at the notorious private concert for Rubenstein, seated at the piano, starting to play the andantino movement of his first piano concerto. He looks toward the audience. His sister gives him an answering smile, and, as he plays, we leave the concert hall. We see her crossing a field of daisies; the two of them running through a birch grove in slowed motion; he, she, and a little girl in one of two rowboats gliding side by side, with languid spray and oars, low sun, and calm water. Tchaikovsky in up shot is scything wheat, and his sister runs through waist-high grain with water for him, which he drinks as he leans on the scythe. He carries the little girl piggyback, and as the andantino becomes a duo for cello and piano, we see him and his sister playing it. The director has found in the music the composer's joy in their summer days together.

Although it was not so, I have sometimes felt, in seeing *Brief Encounter* (David Lean), that the film was composed as incidental images to Rachmaninoff's second piano concerto, which is heard between and behind the film's poignant incidents—the story of a happily married woman who finds herself in love with a man she meets only eight times and never sees again, and who could not confide what she felt to anyone.

12 Nondiegetic Sound—Transforming the Image

Nondiegetic sound may not only strengthen the intention of the images but give quite another color to the impression left by the images taken alone, for a director can add any conceivable sound to any piece of film.

We *see* the country folk of Ceylon, the men climbing for coconuts; the women picking, packing, and baling tea. We *hear* the distant voices of brokers and buyers, whose doings bring the tea to the drinker and pay to the picker: "August prices firm . . . contract to rise . . . one and a quarter to one shilling a pound. . . ." The soil, the plants, and the people that grow the tea are pictured clear in detail, the destinations and the distances of ocean-spanning commerce are lightly sketched in sound (*Song of Ceylon*, Basil Wright).

We are shown but a tiny part of the still northern snows and one day of a prison camp set in the midst of them. But a sustained chord with a vibrant high note, suggesting the sound of high-tension lines on frosty winter nights, heard at the start and at other times in the story, carried a quality of endless continuance, both of the snow-laden Siberian desert, and the uncountable days, every one the same, of those immured there for tens of years (*One Day in the Life of Ivan Denisovitch*, Casper Wrede).

Perhaps the most effective use of nondiegetic sound is imposing the past on the present, like the cries of schoolboys and the sharp voice of a master on the somber, empty courtyard where the poet Rimbaud had gone to school (*Le Bateau Ivre*, Alfred Chauvel).

This was done with ingenious variety throughout a whole film on war graves by Donald Brittain (*Graves of Sacrifice*). We are shown a sightseer, head and shoulders out of a bus, photographing a wall in Italy. We then see, as if we were he, one wall after another, each with festoons of bullet holes in it, quick pans like sudden alert glances, pans with short rests on doorways and windows, a house with one wall gone and no roof, and a final pan up a wall that seems to lean as if it were about to collapse. Through these we hear single shots, ricochets, submachine guns, and all the other sounds of street warfare. In another place we see a tarmac landing strip, grass luxurious in its cracks and foundered hollows, tossing in a whining wind under a gray sky. We see the officers' mess, partly unroofed, with dead voices chatting; a building with dark, doorless entry and glassless windows, and singing heard. We see a low ditch between two buildings, sheep charging down one side and up the other to urgent voices, bustling sounds, a signal, and the shouted word "scram". The camera pans along the tarmac past the control tower, slowly but gaining in speed, and then rising to stop with its gaze on the sky, as the sound of an airplane fades to nothing.

When Pip returns to Satis House, now deserted and for sale, he opens a creaking gate, and as he steps through the door, slowly and reminiscently and up the stairs to the room where he first met Estella, we hear in each successive place the words he heard when he first entered the house. He looks up and we hear a window opening: "What name?"—"Pip."—"Quite right." He walks along the hall: "Don't loiter, boy." He walks with a candle up the side stairs: "Whom have we here?" The words are as much sounds from the past as the submachine guns of *Graves of Sacrifice*, but more—they bring the past back to us, who have seen it, as well as to Pip, as if we were he, remembering (*Great Expectations*, David Lean).

In *I Know Where I'm Going* (Michael Powell and Emeric Pressburger), a woman's voice tells the legend of Moy Castle as Kiloran defies the curse by going inside it. As he looks at each place, the voice tells what happened there—the dungeon with nine feet of water, the stone in the center that only one could stand on, the curse carved on the parapet. There are two pasts here, that of the legend and that of the time when Joan and Kiloran (and we) first heard the legend.

A place or time of day may revive our personal past. A rising stage curtain dissolves to a cell door as a warder raises the shutter. We see Diana Baring seated inside, convicted of murder, and we hear the calls, "Third Act beginners," and "Your call, Miss Baring," as she used to hear them at this time of night in her dressing room. Here the recall is strengthened by anadiplosis (*Murder*, Alfred Hitchcock).

13 Nondiegetic Sound—Humor, Satire, Allusion

Sound may add a touch of humor or whimsicality of which the image is innocent. Louis has been most successful in making money from other people's labor. A large disk with an "L" on it is followed on the screen by the disk of the time clock, from which we retreat as men punch in, each time to the sound of a cuckoo. It is not clear if this alludes to Louis's exploitation of them, or mocks the clock's plainness, compared with a more elegant relative, or jeers at the rituals of industry and those who conform to them—it might be all three (*A Nous La Liberté*, René Clair). It is amusing too when a glassmaker blows his pipe, and we hear the sound of a trumpet (*Glass*, Bert Haanstra), or when a man in red huntsman's tunic and black cap grins to expose long upper teeth (distorted surely) and we hear a horse's whinny (*Africa Addio*, Gualtiero Jacopetti and Franco Prosperi). A boy who has sprained his ankle and fainted is brought to the home of The Railway Children. As the camera pans the bed on which he lies, a whimsical hint of the drama with which their imaginations have invested the incident is given by hearing a few bars of the Dead March (*The Railway Children*, Lionel Jeffries).

Sound has been used for satire. Two men and a woman unveiled a statue. Their voices had a kazoolike timbre, broken up into phrases with normal inflections, but with no articulation into words, as if this conveyed as much of a message as what is normally said on such occasions (*City Lights*, Charles Chaplin). Someone trying to persuade a dog to fetch sounded like a trumpet, with groups and inflections but no words, no sense, perhaps the way it sounds to a dog's ear (*Let's Keep a Dog*, Ternovsky Bela).

Allusions must be rare in a mass medium that crosses cultural borders. It is certain that many who see the film will not know the source and fail to catch them. The situation is usually clear without them, and they are there to enrich the film for those who recognize them.

Mrs. Wilberforce is troubled. Professor Marcus has warned her that as the innocent carrier of stolen money, and thus (he says) an accessory, she must not inform the police. If she does, she will be imprisoned. As she sits in thought, she catches sight of her "dear late husband," a sea captain whose portrait hangs on the wall, and this hastens her decision: it is no good, she tells Professor Marcus; she will go to jail if she must. As her husband's picture comes on the screen, some stirring bars of "Rule Britannia" ring out in the score. But if this is not enough, there follows a long down view of the house in greenish light, with trains pouring white steam behind it, two flashes of lightning, and a loud peal of thunder (*The Lady Killers*, Alexander Mackendrick).

A captured American general insists on his food being served on tin plates according to the Geneva Convention. The queen (whose government engineered the invasion, to gain postwar aid) wonders if they have tin plates. The other soldiers captured at the same time are shown eating in luxurious surroundings, talking to handsome women and eating off china. As the general eats from his tin plate, alone down in a greenish dungeon, he prides himself on "not budging an inch." "I showed them," he says in triumph. "No tin plates, eh?", and as he speaks we hear Colonel Bogey whistled by a choir. To hear the tune is mock-heroic enough; to recognize the allusion to *The Bridge on the River Quai* is doubly so (*The Mouse That Roared*, Jack Arnold).

We hear "Blue Skies" as Doris and Warlock float on the river, happy. Later in London, we see her taking a taxi, and an altered situation is told by "Blue Skies" heard again, but now with discordant harmonies and ending with a sudden braying sound (*Cynara*, King Vidor). This is both an allusive use of a tune the listener is taken to know, and a repetition with variation.

14 Nondiegetic Sound—The Narrator

Narration or commentary is a separated flow that does not impede, as diegetic speech may do, the pace of editing that fits the action. It may range from eking the image out with further facts, as in documentary film, to adding a meaning not found at all in the images, both by what is said and how it is said.

In the course of *The Dandelion* (Mary Field), every violence of biological, mechanical, and chemical warfare is inflicted on this unfortunate plant. At the end, a tiny shoot thrusts up, undaunted, out of the ground, and E. V. H. Emmett winds up his comments, laced, as was his way, with humor and irony, by announcing in the tones of the boxing ring, "Ladies and gentlemen, the winner."

In story films, an omniscient narrator may sometimes mediate between us and the action, placing its persons at a distance, as historical events we can view with calmness and reflection, rather than feeling that we ourselves are undergoing their turmoils.

Itsuki opens the panels of his house, we see his daughters and granddaughter sleeping, and a voice informs us, "This is the story of Tajihei Itsuki, a self-made man. Two thousand employees work for him. He is just about to make a trip to Europe . . ." (Facts.) In the airplane, we see his face in close-up, as he lies back on the seat, and the voice resumes "Itsuki thinks about Kiyoko, and is overwhelmed by a surge of emotion. . . . He feels alone, never so alone . . ." (An inner state not otherwise known to us.) We see him raising a glass to his lips at a dinner given in Paris by some compatriots. The camera circles his fellow guests and returns to him as he rises, "Itsuki . . . carries his drinks well. But he felt a nausea on smelling the liquor. . . . He wanted to go to the washroom but couldn't get up . . . He felt that he could if he made a great effort." (Here he rises slowly, and he and his secretary walk slowly out through a doorway.) "He feels pain . . . he feels like crouching . . ." Subjective sensations.) In a quiet Romanesque church, he leans his head on one of the columns. "He would like to stay here in this place . . . He doesn't know why . . ." Narration is interspersed with normal diegetic dialogue. Despite a seeming detachment, the narrator brings to the film a tone of compassion (*Kaseki*, Masaki Kobayashi).

The onlooker's voice in *Tom Jones* (Tony Richardson) is a fount of irony. Lady Bellaston sits on her bed. "In town, it is not considered polite," she says, "to keep a lady waiting." As Tom quickly joins her, the narrator declares, with equal amounts of innuendo and elegance, that, "with our usual good breeding, we shall not pursue this conversation further."

The story may be told in the first person, one of the characters giving us his own feelings and reflections on what is happening to him. Isak Borg starts the film by describing a strange dream. He stops on his way to Lund at the house where he spent his childhood, and remembers some hours of his life there. During this and other events by the way, he reflects on his youth, his parents, the girl he loved, his failures and his wish to make them good, his sense of being a spectator, and, flowing out of this, a sense of peace. As we see him in the academic procession at the university, which is conferring on him a doctorate, *honoris causa,* we hear his musing voice, "During the ceremony, I kept thinking of the events of the day, and there seemed an extraordinary logic to them all . . ." The mood of the film owes as much to his spoken thoughts as to the images (*Wild Strawberries,* Ingmar Bergman).

Such first-person accounts are, in fact, soliloquies that run (with many breaks) the length of the film, for the voice is heard but no lips are seen to shape the words. They become more abundant from Olivier's *Henry V* to his *Hamlet,* and in such films as *Wild Strawberries,* they form the very frame on which the film is built.

15   Nondiegetic Silence—Image without Sound

Silence being the absence of sound, if there is nondiegetic sound, there should be nondiegetic silence, silence, that is to say, where in the place and at the time seen, we know there is sound; silence that works the way sound can, to confirm or transform the image.

In *The Story of Mandy* (Alexander Mackendrick) Mandy runs into the street to fetch her dog. She sees a truck coming toward her, quickly, but walks across the street without haste and bends over to pick the animal up. The truck looms up and comes to a sudden stop. Tall, in an up shot, the driver scolds her loudly and crossly. In a close down shot, she looks up wondering. We see the lips articulating under the angry eyes, but all in a void of silence: Mandy is deaf, and we have entered the world she lives in.

Michael Mallet, deep in thought, passes a children's playground. Beyond the wire-mesh fence, the children are swinging, sliding, and running without a sound. Then the camera reverses; we are with the children, looking through the fence at him, and their shouts are loud around us. As the time and place are the same, the nonhearing must be in Michael (*The Reckoning,* Jack Gold).

Two White Russian cruisers are nearing Kronstadt and about to bombard it. In the casemates gunners are laying sights on their targets. Some noise is unpreventable despite the strictest instructions—of metal on metal, of engines, orders, hoists,—however carefully subdued. But in this surprise attack, by night, noise is cut to the limit—zero, dead silence, a form of hyperbole (*We from Kronstadt,* E. Dzigan).

IV   SOUND AND OTHER FIGURES

16   Simile

The two things compared in a simile are neatly kept apart by having one seen and the other heard. We see a kangaroo, swaying back and forth with its young in its pouch, we hear the rocking chair to which it is likened. We see a stream of peanuts fired from Dumbo's trunk; we hear a machine gun (*Dumbo,* Walt Disney).

Suvorin begs the Countess Ranevskaya to give him the secret of the cards. She looks at him in silence and shrinks from him. His voice becomes threatening. She turns her head from him. He draws a pistol. "Are you going to tell me the secret of the cards, or are you—" As he breaks off, we are aware that a clock has stopped ticking. She is dead (*The Queen of Spades,* Thorold Dickinson).

Both parts of the simile may be heard. Philip, traveling on the *Train of Events,* tells the girl he is with that she plays a B flat where it should be a natural. They look at the score. She gesticulates and he points, "B natural."—"That's what I play."—"You don't." There is a cut from her screaming at him to two trains passing on parallel tracks, each whistle keeping on her note as it screams at the other train (*Train of Events*, Sidney Cole, Charles Crichton, Basil Dearden). The simile is partly situational, a person and then a train, both screaming, but we find it amusing because of the unexpected likeness in voice between the train and the woman.

Where one of two sounds compared is not heard, is it still a simile? Is it not now rather a metaphor, or even hypallage, the transfer of a pattern, from a sound we cannot hear to one we can? Tony returns to his house, believing that Vera and his servant Barrett were visiting their sick mother. He turns from the sink in the kitchen to see Vera, barefooted, standing in the doorway. During her explanation—she had felt sick at the station, had come back, had heard someone entering, had been glad she was not alone in the house and so on,—we hear the dripping. Could he get her a drink of water, he asks, and now the drip falls twice as fast, suggesting a faster heartbeat, and thus that she had gained her end of arousing his desire. The quickening tap we hear is like the quickening heartbeat we cannot hear (*The Servant*, Joseph Losey).

17 Metaphor

Thérèse kills the son of the butler, who said he was going to expose his affair with her, and persuades a postal clerk in love with her to dispose of the body. We see her left frame playing a harp. The camera changes focus, and through the strings of the harp, we see her mother. She is standing at the head of a few steps to say that the dressmaker has just come. She turns and goes. Still watching through the harp strings, we see Thérèse mount the same stairs, when a string suddenly snaps with a taut reverberating ping: an inner tension revealed (*Passionnelle*, Edmond T. Greville).

18 Antithesis

Loudness and silence form the most obvious antithesis. Throughout much of *Zulu* (Cy Endfield), sound and silence, activity and stillness are contrasted. As a column of mounted volunteers nears camp, the men stop their busy piling up of breastworks. Lieutenant Chard seizes the reins of the commander's restless horse and shouts above the scuffle of hoofs, "We need you. Don't go." He is refused, and in long down shot the horsemen leave the screen and their hoofbeats die. The camera pans along the wall of grain bags and the men behind them, and back the other way past others, all standing still and silent, looking toward us, their last hope of help riding away.

Two contrasting diegetic sounds may be heard at once. Kaji, as a new recruit, had suffered beatings and other cruelties. When he becomes a superior private, in charge of a hutful of men, we see him passing among his new recruits, some of them older men, in an easy friendly way, advising one to keep a nude picture concealed in his loin cloth, inquiring of another about his home. As he does, we hear shouts and cries of pain from the other huts (*The Human Condition*, part 2: *The Road to Eternity*, Masaki Kobayashi).

Two girls in a schoolroom write as their master dictates, "The Fuehrer is our best friend." They look up for a moment as we hear a shouted command outside followed by rifle fire. We know it is their father being shot (*The Divided Heart*, Charles Crichton).

It may be sound and image that clash. Don Jaime, who is fond of religious music, plays the "Hallelujah Chorus" on the phonograph, as he embraces the drugged unconscious body of Viridiana. It is played also by the beggars during their banquet, while the leper dances in Don Jaime's wife's corset and veil, and the blind man, unable to find the man who lay with his woman, smashes food and plates, and two women tear each other's hair over their children (*Viridiana*, Luis Buñuel).

So linked is feeling to sound that a change in sound is nearly always also one of mood. In *Moscow Nights* (Anthony Asquith) Natacha asks Briokov how he will speak at Ignatov's (his rival's) trial. He rushes across the room, raises an imaginary rifle, and cries "fire". He turns, blows a candle out with a vehement breath, and in a mounting frenzy cries, "He is finished—finished—finished." We see his head bottom left of the frame. There is a short pause, and one soft word from Natacha, "Please," softer and lower from following after his fury.

There may be a change of weight between alternating pairs of sounds, as these are repeated. Christmas in London shows us a boy looking into a shop window at warlike toys, a woman buying a turkey, a holly seller, a pavement artist finishing up a design of "Merry Christmas," cheerful crowds leaving a hotel, a cinema, a theater. In the same scenes, perhaps on a newsboy coming at us out of the crowd, on a wall above or a stall beside, on the front page of a newspaper, are ominous headlines, "WAR SCARE," "WAR STORM BREWING," "WARNING TO EUROPE," growing in frequency, and at last displacing all else on the screen. Through this, on voices or instruments, we hear "The First Nowell," "While Shepherds Watch Their Flocks by Night," and "God Rest You Merry Gentlemen," the verses of which are spaced out by chill martial fanfares of trumpets, that seem to intrude more and more as the sequence continues (*Things to Come*, William Cameron Menzies).

19 Tautology

Tautology is a form of repetition: it is saying what has already been said, in a different way—usually, adds the *Oxford English Dictionary*, as a fault in style. In film, it arises chiefly when sound and image express the same event.

Tautology, clearly, can be a serious fault. In a film on motor racing, best left nameless, we see through a yellow-lit factory window three men talking around a table. We know that they are designing a car. Then in tones weighty with sinister meaning, a narrator tells us, "Three men stayed up late," at which the audience, very properly, burst out laughing. The image told us it was night; we could see the men were three; and there was nothing before, during, or after the scene, to justify the portentous tone of delivery.[10]

It is not, as such, tautology to present an event both in sight and in sound, for this is normal experience. In filming a performance, runs on the piano may be shot in close-ups of rapidly twinkling fingers, or a harpist's glissando in a sweep of the player's arm to match the image as close as may be to the mood and pace of the music (*Adventure in Music*, Ernest Matray and others). As it is two signals from a single event, the likeness between what is seen and what is heard cannot be damned as tautologous, nor are they sufficiently different for a proper simile. Can you liken a thing to itself?

It is otherwise with fantasy, which is much less confined in choice of angle. When Liszt's Hungarian Rhapsody No. 2 courses across the keyboard from bass to treble, *Rhapsody Rabbit* shows the fingers in exaggerated perspective at keyboard level, remotely small and hugely near. The rabbit virtuoso tramps with heavy feet up to the treble and flits back on tiptoe to the bass. Image and sound are not coming here from the same event: the piano we see is not the one we hear. Its enormous length is hyperbole; tramping feet for a loud phrase, an acceptable simile (Isadore Freleng).

When then is tautology a fault? When Elektra lies on her father's grave and wails, and the camera sweeps the cloudy sky, matching its pace to the pitch of the wail, faster as the wail rises and slower as it sinks, what does the matching image add (*Elektra*, Michael Cacoyannis)?

An owl perches on the limb of a tree. It oscillates into several images as a deer below rubs its antlers up and down the trunk, and the musical accompaniment imitates the motion, its tremulous triplets merging in a single note as the owl's multiple images lessen to a single bird. What is added by this doubling in sound (*Bambi*, David D. Hand)?

Music reinforcing a mood might be seen as tautologous. Four thieves in a car follow Mrs. Wilberforce's innocent and long-drawn-out progress home with the stolen money. She goes back for a forgotten umbrella, she stops to berate a hawker for hitting a horse that was eating his grapes. The car and the four exasperated passengers crawl along the streets to the sound of a dreary oboe. The mood we see in the men is doubled in the music. It could be wariness; it could be anxiety or exhaustion; whatever it is in words, the oboe states it with clarity. This is less tautology than emphasis (*The Lady Killers*, Alexander Mackendrick).

Explaining a point at length, and then providing an "abridged repetition," is recommended by Archbishop Whately. "They will *understand* the longer expression and *remember* the shorter."[11] A restatement serving a new end is justified: it is a test that should be made of each tautology both by director and viewer.

Whately's dictum applies to the popularizing of music. The story of *The Sorcerer's Apprentice* can be read in Goethe's ballad, in Lucian, or the program notes, but the film tags on a particular image to every passage and makes the course of the musical story clear to the tyro listener. The sorcerer, giving over his evening pastime of making bats and butterflies from vapors, goes yawning to bed in the languorous opening. A clash of sound fits the desperate apprentice wielding his axe on the fast-breeding broomsticks, with equally violent color changes on the screen, to red, to yellow, to blue. The brigade of innumerable brooms marches with disciplined pace to a strong beat, gaining in vigor as it crosses the floor of an ocean it poured itself, and it seems as if no one could stop it. But stopped it is: gone with a few sweeps of the magician's wand. The music has said it all, and what we see is mere tautology, justified perhaps by rephrasing Whately: the listener may *remember* the image, and *understand* the music (*Fantasia*, James Algar).

It is hardly possible to render what we see into words or sound, so much more precise is the image than the word. "She kissed him" compasses every kind of kiss; the visual image can show us only one. To give in words then what we see on the screen would seem to be an unprofitable waste of time, and unimaginative. And yet Noël Burch describes a film I have not seen and one not likely to be widely shown, where effective use is made of what would seem to be tautology.[12] As described by Burch, *Un Simple Histoire* (Marcel Hanoun) tells of a woman who, having come to Paris with her child, can find neither work nor housing and is taken in by a kind woman after spending the night on a piece of wasteland. At first face, the woman seems merely to be telling the events that are shown on the screen; yet an attentive listener comes to notice discrepancies, interpretations, omissions, reflections, and feelings of complaint and resentment in what the woman believes to be a plain account of what happened. It shows us abstraction in the making: none can hear or see all that is going on around us, of what we can see and hear we notice only a part and remember but part of that, quite likely in some distorted form.[13]

20 Metonymy and Repetition

One of the modes of metonymy is *The voice for the speaker, the sound for the object making it.* To represent a man by the sound of his voice is an act of abstraction. It may also slant for or against him, depending on whether his voice is the most or least impressive of all his traits. As Kaji, a prisoner of war, eats his meal, he hears the Russian guard singing a folk song in several parts, and thinks, "When they sing, I feel they must be good" (*The Human Condition*, part 2: *The Road to Eternity*, Masaki Kobayashi).

A common form of repetition is planting a sound as part of a happening, and when it recurs, repeating only the sound. Men are carrying furniture out of the house of Sir Thomas Seymour, a prisoner in the Tower. Lady Jane Grey and her tirewoman are trying to dissuade them. A gun sounds, and Ellen tells her mistress that one is fired whenever a prisoner is executed. This one, they realize, had sounded for Thomas. King Edward VI is addressing a banquet, when again a gun is heard and the young king at once taxes Warwick with breaking a promise to spare Thomas's brother. At the end the headsman raises his axe above Lord Guildford Dudley. Before it falls, we cut to the parapets of the Tower, a gun resounds, and the birds rise from the walls (*Tudor Rose*, Robert Stevenson).

We hear a whistling sound as General Fitzjohn pursues a maid behind a pillar. Then we see the source, a U of rubber hose hung on the wall. The housekeeper puts the nozzle to her ear, and answers the question, "Is he there?" Four or five times in the film, we hear the whistle, and we know it is the general's wife asking where he is or demanding his presence. Is the director, in a sonic pun, suggesting that she is whistling for him (*The Waltz of the Toreadors*, John Guillermin)?

We see a vessel sinking at sea, torpedoed; we hear the words, "I'm not kidding, I tell ya, I'm sailing for Hawaii at 10:30 by the Navajo." We had heard the words before. We had then seen a soldier speaking them over a telephone, to explain to his girl why he could not take her to the beach the following day. Someone had heard him (*Safeguarding Military Information*, U.S. Army Signal Corps).

Where the sound repeated is music, it is usual to speak of a leitmotiv. We hear the beginnings of the Warsaw Concerto, when Carol and Stefan Radetsky first meet in a bombed building in Warsaw. It is her encouragement that leads to its completion. The concerto comes to stand for the bond that holds them together. We first hear the Military Polonaise of Chopin, chimed on Radio Free Warsaw, when Stefan is flying a fighter plane in Poland. It expresses the pull Stefan feels to return to the air force. Mike often hummed The Rose of Tralee, and when Stefan plays this in the officers' mess, smiling as he does, we know he is thinking of his dead companion-at-arms. These are symbols in sound, standing, as symbols often do, not merely for people they call to mind but for abstract notions like love, loyalty, and comradeship (*Dangerous Moonlight*, Brian Desmond Hurst).

If the sound, when first introduced, is described, but not heard, the sound itself may take us by surprise for a moment, for we have to recognize the new sound as the one the words described. In *Right, Left and Center* (Sidney Gilliatt), a Conservative candidate meets on the train a young woman economist. She quotes with scorn from a woman's magazine that someone gave her, where a girl in love is described as hearing "the tintinabulation of glass bells." He joins in ridiculing the phrase. He later discovers that she is his Labour opponent, and more than that, he falls in love with her. When the two speak in the same factory yard, he listens admiringly and hears, not her words, but a sound of glass bells tintinabulating. His inattention leads to his being mobbed, but he recovers his wits, and speaking to the few remaining listeners, he attacks her arguments with vigor. Her fear that the crowd might harm him turns to respect for his undismayed recovery, and, as she stands and listens, the clamor of the hostile crowd is lost in the same tintinabulation.

21 Sound as Sound—Onomatopoeia

Onomatopoeia is the use or formation of words that sound like the events for which they stand, where

> The *Sound* must seem an *Eccho* to the *Sense*.[14]

Stephen Spender describes *The Express* as it starts:

> After the first powerful plain manifesto
> The black statement of pistons, without more fuss
> But gliding like a queen, she leaves the station.[15]

We are quite clear that we are not listening to the shafts of steam spewed from the cylinders, but a simulation in words of what they sound like and we enjoy the skill with which the sound is suggested.

In film, however, if the simulation is well done, we are not aware that we are not listening to the sound of the event itself. If we are not completely deceived, we think that the imitation is poorly done, and certainly do not enjoy it. If a sound we know is intended for an engine whistle does not seem to our ears like those we have heard, we are critical; if it does, it becomes the whistle itself, and there is no imitation felt at all.[16]

Onomatopoeia, strictly so called, can only apply to the use in film of music or verse. In *Night Mail* (Basil Wright and Harry Watt), as the engine climbs a steep slope in Scotland, we see coal, shoveled into the firebox, a steaming piston, moving wheels, passing trees, village chimneys, dawn hills, a bridge sweeping overhead, and a stream deep in a glen, but the natural sound is replaced by words and music, with a strong regular beat like that of the pistons. W. H. Auden's verse, as Karel Reisz tells us, was spoken to a visual metronome, with the pictures cut to fit the recorded words, and as Benjamin Britten recorded the music, he was at the same time hearing the recorded words.[17] This is genuine onomatopoeia, and more evocative than natural sound.

At one remove from the strict meaning, we may use sound, not so much as linked with a diegetic event but, so to say, as imitative of some character's feelings, by finding a sound that would evoke in us a similar tension. It is the use of sound for the immediate thalamic response it brings, untempered by thought. In *Romeo and Juliet and Darkness* (Jiri Weiss), the shrill yelp of the dog is like the chalk that shrieks on slate. We hear it when the actress and her German officer are mounting the spiral staircase, and Pavel hastens Hana to her hiding place in the attic. The actress is suspicious. She and another girl, as they leave her flat, corner Pavel to talk to him, and the dog yelps again. On a third occasion, someone tries the door of the attic, the dog is loose on the stairs and we hear him once more. Each time our nerves are on edge, in part from the fear of discovery, but quite as much from the kind of the sound itself.

22   Emphasis—The Close-up in Sound

A microphone mixes into a composite signal all that is within its range at the point where it is placed. A human being, on the other hand, can, within limits, through effort of attention or an eager interest, keep out of his awareness all but part of the signal, and listen to Bach on the radio instead of the silly remarks of the person beside him. Film has the means for doing this too, in what may be called a close-up in sound.[18]

A close-up in sound may come about by raising the volume of one sound above all the others, or by lowering the level of all sounds but one.

There is a long down shot of a lane in a crowded market, with stands on both sides. From this we approach close to Inspector Fothergill, who is slowly picking his way through the crowd. All we can hear is the noise of traffic, the puffs of Cheap Jacks, and the conversations of sellers and buyers. As we reach the inspector, a reporter is asking for a story on Swann, who has recently escaped from prison. During the conversation, the market's clamor fades to a quiet background, and when the conversation is over, it rises to its former level (*It Always Rains on Sunday*, Robert Hamer).

A close-up in sound may also come through making one of many sounds distinct and the rest a fuzzy confusion.

Alice White is coaxed by an artist she has just met into going with him to see his studio. He makes sexual advances, and in a panic she kills him with a knife. She spends a distraught night walking the streets, but manages to get to bed just before her mother comes to waken her. Her parents' living room adjoins their shop, and as Alice sits at breakfast, a customer is leaning on the doorjamb talking of the murder, of which he has just read in the morning paper. We see her face, her attention indrawn from what is happening around her. All the talk in the room is a blur of sound, except when someone speaks the word "knife," which cuts clearly through the murmur. At last her father catches her attention, and asks her (in clear sound) for the bread. Her hand goes to the breadboard slowly, and her fingers grasp it, her eyes fixed and absorbed. The word "knife" comes now for the ninth time, suddenly louder than the others, and the knife flies from the board into the air. Her father picks it up from the floor, "You want to be careful, girl, you might have cut somebody with that." The word is an arrow that pierces her stupor (*Blackmail*, Alfred Hitchcock).

Keeping off the sound track all sounds but one is a kind of emphasis: it is part of the drive the artist feels to discard the inessential. As in all forms of emphasis, stress is laid by loudness or clarity, on one sound out of a mix of sound, just as a close-up in space imports a larger space out of which the detail is chosen, of which larger space, we are, in some measure, always aware. This said, even a single sound heard by itself, may be larger than life, like the match struck in *Fahrenheit 451* (François Truffaut), near the end, by which its threat is enhanced.

23   Prolepsis

We often speak of two events together, one of which could only happen after, or in consequence of, the other; we say it happens before it happens. If I say "I am wiping the bowl clean," so long as I am wiping the bowl, it is not clean. If I speak of the "fatal carelessness" of a man poisoned from failing to read a label, it was not clear at the time of the careless act that it was also fatal; I have linked in a single statement an act and its later outcome—the present and the future. Hamlet, living, says "Horatio, I am dead."[19] Because he can say it, what he says has not yet happened. This is *prolepsis*.

Normally an image and its diegetic sound begin at the same time. The easiest form of prolepsis in film is to start either one ahead of the other. The later event may result from the former. His sword is handed back, as the court-martial acquits Captain Ignatov. During this, a march played by a military band wells up in volume. We cut then to the band, as it marches along a street, *its music having anticipated its appearance*. The band is followed by troops on their way to the front line, one of whose officers is Captain Ignatov. He is marching with them because he was acquitted. This is close in form and use to Anadiplosis VII iv from cause to effect (*Moscow Nights*, Anthony Asquith).[20]

Margaret Hammond is dead. From inside, we hear the front door handle rattled, and then the door is broken in by her footballer-lodger who had loved her, Frank Machin. He goes through the house, and utters her name softly. At last he grips the lintel of a door frame, cries "Margaret" loudly, hangs by one hand, and then sinks down, his head on his knees, lost in a black shadow. The roar of a watching crowd breaks in softly and grows in loudness before we cut to him on a football field, as he is knocked down by another player, and without zest rises to his feet. *This Sporting Life* (Lindsay Anderson) intrudes on private grief.

In *Far from the Madding Crowd* (John Schlesinger), Bathsheba runs away from Sergeant Troy, as he juggles his glittering sword in the setting sun. As she runs, we hear women's voices talking in eager gossip. They continue until and after her arrival at the kitchen window, where she hears them. She enters angrily. Sergeant Troy is nothing to her, she says. She may have been thinking of possible talk as she ran, or else the proleptic talk suggests by exaggeration the speed at which word of her doings had passed.

This can be done the other way: the image can change, and the sound that belongs to the image displaced may continue. In a warm yellow light, we see Jennie, then Professor Jacobi, and then the roomful of people, all shadowed but the two of them, as they listen to the Fantasia in C minor of Mozart. Through a narrow doorway to a second room we see the distant performer, a woman distinct in yellow, and we move, one by one to some of the other listeners. Then we see Jennie through a windshield, scenery flashing dull-green up the surface, we cut to Jacobi, the driver, and back to her again. The car stops in long shot and they alight. Now comes the final chord of the music, and in the next scene they enter his door. The continuing music, as they ride away from the concert without speaking, tells us that the music's mood continues through their silence (*Face to Face*, Ingmar Bergman).

The unspecific nature of many sounds can add surprise to prolepsis. The general has gone upstairs to tell his fiercely jealous wife that he is going to divorce her and marry Ghislaine. As we see Ghislaine waiting in the drawing room, we hear a thundering rattle. We share her fear that his wife had heaved Fitzjohn down the stairs, but the noise continues into the next shot: it comes from the doctor's car, whose repertoire of sounds is nearly inexhaustible (*The Waltz of the Toreadors*, John Guillermin). It is not indeed a great hyperbole to say with Keith Learner (*The Do It Yourself Cartoon Kit*), "The crash is good for nearly anything," which he demonstrates by tacking it onto a woman striking a man on the head, a butterfly landing on a flower, and a kiss.

24 Apostrophe

In *apostrophe*, a speaker or writer breaks off what he is doing, the thread of his discourse or his interplay with other actors, to speak directly to some person, present or imagined.

At the end of each verse of *Prothalamion*, for example, Spenser turns aside from his description to address the river:

> Sweet Thames! run softly, til I end my song.

Soliloquies in melodrama were often given as if in confidence to the audience, as when Lady Audley moves downstage and says:

> It must be my aim to stand well with this young man; he is my husband's favourite, I know
> . . . he may prove a dangerous rival in my path. . . .[21]

More recently, there are those on stage who talk without subterfuge to us who watch, as Peter Pan does, most memorably, in Act Four. In Thornton Wilder's *Our Town* (Sam Wood), and in the film version, the stage manager drops a word in our ear from time to time. At the start:

> Well, I'd better show you how our town lies. Up here is Main Street. Way back there is the railway station . . .

and at the end,

> Most everybody's asleep. . . . There are the stars. . . . Eleven o'clock in Grover's Corners.—You get a good rest, too. Good Night.[22]

There are films too in which someone now and then takes us into his confidence, asks us to back him up, tips us off to something we did not know, or stops us from looking at something he had rather we did not see. Alfie often speaks his reflections, not as a lips-closed soliloquy but looking at and addressing us, because he is the chatty kind, who likes to think himself a philosopher, especially on women, and likes to feel that we are seeing things his way. He starts off by scrambling out of a car, after which a girl does the same, and he walks across to us, "I suppose you think you're going to see the bleeding titles. Well, you're not. . . . They never make cars big enough. My name is Alfie. . . . I always find that if you can make a married woman laugh, anything can happen after that . . ." The film establishes the convention that when he is talking to us, no one else present on the screen can hear him. During a physical examination in the hospital, he throws a word or two to the doctor, and then turns to us with his next sentence, the doctor behaving as if she were unaware. (To the doctor:) "ninety-nine . . ."; (to us:) "you can always replace a bird, but a son, now he's something different . . ." (*Alfie*, Lewis Gilbert).

This occurs here and there in *Tom Jones* (Tony Richardson), and makes us feel part of the spirited goings-on we are seeing on the screen. Tom is routed out of bed by the landlady. He says he will pay her handsomely for the entertainment provided, but he cannot find his five hundred pounds. They argue. "Did you take it?" He taxes her; she denies it. He turns to us, "Did you see her take that note?"; and then back to her again. Near the end, as Allworthy and Western talk at the left, Mrs. Waters, at right screen, turns to us and says, "No, he is not my son . . . and that is what it says in the letter."

A director has even gone to the length of apparently planting someone among us to talk to. Jeff (the hero) and a Miss Wren are singing a love duet, he up a stepladder and she at the bottom, when a white-lettered sign, which partly covers them, asks, "IS STINKY MILLER IN THE AUDIENCE?" After a short interval, another sign covers them over to say, "STINKY MILLER—YOUR MOTHER WANTS YOU." We naturally expect a third message. Knowing this, the director keeps us waiting, but it comes, "STINKY MILLER—GO HOME." The singers have had enough of this: they look out at us, annoyed and impatient. An eccentric detective, who keeps cropping up, opens a door toward us and says firmly, "Go on home, Stinky." We return to the disgruntled singers. A silhouette moves onto the screen from the right, turns, grows smaller, and vanishes off the bottom. It is fantasy, of course—a metonymy for a nonexistent person. Of a film within the film, one of the screen viewers remarks, "That guy doesn't look like a Russian prince; he's only a cheap four-flusher." The person spoken about, in the film within a film, turns, as if he had heard the remark, and (now filling the whole screen) looks with menace toward us (*Hellzapoppin*, Harold C. Potter).

Between us and the actor is a one-way glass of lenses and emulsions. We can see him, but he cannot see us. He appears to speak to us; in fact, he speaks to the camera, which thus he treats as a person. In practice, then, apostrophe in film must seem to imply personification or prosopopoeia too.

Where apostrophe is used only once in the course of a film, its usual purpose is persuasion. "You," it says to us, "are responsible"; or "This", it may say, "could happen to you"; or it may merely say, "What do you think?"

In *The Road to Life* (Nicolai Ekk), as Kolka, his mother murdered and he beaten, wanders the streets of Moscow during a storm, a voice says to us, "Suppose it were your son?"

In *The War Game* (Peter Watkins), we travel past head after head of those who have suffered burns of more than 50 percent, their arms congealed with bloody tissue. No one in this row will receive medical treatment. One of the orderlies turns to us and remarks, "Call this defense?"

An editor is facing a deputation of citizens who protest his giving front page space to news about gangsters. He retorts that he is going to keep on doing it until those who read it will do something about it. He leaves his chair and coming toward us points to members of the deputation. It is, he says, for you and you and you to see that the violence is stopped. He is now, however, nearly alone on the screen, full face to the audience, and as he points to the deputation, it looks too as if he pointed at us (*Scarface*, Howard Hawks).

Chicken Little (Walt Disney) has two apostrophizers, one that we only hear and one that we see and hear. When Foxy Loxy has panicked all the hens into the cave, he follows them in and closes the entrance with a stone. Its legend reads "Lunch is served." The commentator says (to us), "Don't worry, folks, everything's going to be all right." We cut to Foxy Loxy, who leans on his Red Book, and picks his teeth contentedly with a wishbone. The commentator says, "That isn't the way it ends in my book." Foxy Loxy looks at us and says, "Don't believe everything you read in books, brother" (pl. 28).

In a documentary film, whose purpose is to present or press a viewpoint, a director may use apostrophe to place his persons directly in touch with us. We are moved more strongly by those who can say to us with feeling, "This happened to me" than by a mere fact passed on by a commentator. It is not an accident that commercial television is constantly apostrophizing us.

One recent example will show this, *Les Ordres* by Michel Brault. It reconstructs what was undergone by five persons (out of four hundred and fifty) who were arrested under The War Measures Act in 1970 in Canada, and released, no charges having been laid, within three weeks. We see, for example, a family at breakfast in their kitchen. During this, we hear a voice, "My name is Jean Lapointe. I play the part of Clermont Boudreau. . .," and then some personal details. Then we see him facing us, and answering someone who is neither heard nor seen: "Do I go to church? Yes. Politics? No, I've never taken much interest in politics. My union work keeps me pretty busy. . . ." The reconstructed scenes are in color, and are intercut with others of the people we have seen in prison interviewed in black and white some months later over a glass of beer or a cigarette. Boudreau says to us, "I'll never forgive them for putting my wife in jail . . ." We see Richard Lavoie, in color, taken from his cell during the night in his underwear, told to walk the length of a long cellar, and fired at by a guard. His otherwise tautologous narrative of what was done, heard as we see it happen, adds his inner anxieties to his outer plight. This continues into an apostrophe in black and white, as he says directly to us, "The bastards were trying to scare me. They only used blanks. But it was such a shock that I fainted. When I woke, I was in my cell . . ."

Apostrophes, which one would assume must always be said and heard, can also be silent. When Anthony Asquith, director of *Cottage to Let*, has thoroughly confused us as to which of his characters are spies and which detectives, in a silent apostrophe two people helping to set booths up at a garden fete challenge us on his behalf by carrying across the lawn a sign reading "Can You Guess?" The Devil, going by the name of Mr. Scratch, has some success with Jabez Stone till thwarted by Daniel Webster. In the last shot of the film, the Devil fingers through his book for another promising subject. He glances up thoughtfully, slowly smiles as he thinks of a likely name, and looks and points—at us (*All That Money Can Buy*, William Dieterle).

25 Zeugma

In *Zeugma* (pls. 16, 17), a single word, commonly a verb and used once only, goes with two or more other words, in different senses. Useful tools in framing couplets, zeugmas abound in Alexander Pope:

> Here thou, great Anna! whom three realms obey,
> Dost sometimes counsel take—and sometimes tea.[23]

> Learn each small People's genius, policies,
> The Ant's republic, and the realm of Bees.[24]

In the second couplet, *learn* does not agree grammatically (in the absence of the preposition *about*) with *the Ant's republic*, and, where this is so, the figure is not zeugma but syllepsis.[25]

The pleasure given by zeugma is in the leap from one sense to another, whereas in the pun or paronomasia both meanings are held in mind at the same time. If we say, "She painted with oils and abandon," the grammar is correct, but from "placing oil paint on a canvas" we leap in meaning to "composing a design with more dash than subtlety," with no change in verb, which is used first of material things and then of an abstract notion, less expected.

In film, what is described above as the fourth variation of anadiplosis, "Unbroken sound or horse-swapping," is also a zeugma.[26]

A similar use is found in *The Maggie* (Alexander Mackendrick). "The harbormaster has got your message to *The Maggie*," the lady at the telephone is telling Marshall. "Good, then tell him . . ." "But, Mr. Marshall, the boat has turned round and sailed out again." As Marshall turns round, the doorway frames his head and shoulders. His mouth is open and we hear a roar. Then we cut to a shot of his plane taking off. Hearing its roar before we see the plane is prolepsis, using the same voice for engine and man is the figure zeugma. In one sense the natural sound of an engine, in another, an apt venting of Marshall's fury at being again outwitted.

In *We From Kronstadt* (E. Dzigan), Mademoiselle, beside a cot in the children's home, softly sings a lullaby. Then we see a great hall, its floor covered with sleeping soldiers and sailors, their rifles piled here and there and the lullaby, still continuing, seems to be sung to the sleeping men too.

16
Inner States

1 The Unseen and the Unheard

To reveal what is not seen or heard—thoughts, dreams, fancies, memories—is clearly to use figures, because something seen must be pressed into service to show what is unseen, and something heard must speak what is unspoken.

We are concerned here with outer behavior, with sounds, montages, comparisons, distortions of image only as the signs of motives and feelings. We are concerned less with events that persons move through than with what goes on in the person who moves through them. Nearly all the novelist's viewpoints are used for this purpose, the perspicacious observer, the omniscient reader of minds and motives, and the eye of the participant.[1] As film rarely leaves the present tense, we catch the flights of thought as they happen.

Documentaries and pseudo-documentaries mostly confine themselves to the outside, and few will be found here. In *State of Siege* (Costa-Gavras), for example, whether or not people wear masks, like the Tupamaros, all we see of anyone is his body's mask, often only his label. We are told that a man we see is a cabinet minister, director of seven companies, three of them American-controlled, and that is all we see of him. We see merely the roles that people play—they are president, policeman, Tupamaro, American agent, liberal, capitalist tool. The action is smooth as clockwork, each dealing with others according to his specified role in the social machine. Kidnappings and arrests are done each with equal precision, and at the end, all is much as it was before it all began. A dead body is found and the question is asked, "Who is Mr. Santore?" The rest of the film purports to answer the question, but at the end, after his long interrogation by the Tupamaros, all we have really learned is that he is in the pay of the United States and hates change. We never see their opponents as close or as often as we do the Tupamaros, and our sympathies are by this preempted for them. Even so, by the end of the film, we still do not know who they are, who Mr. Santore is, or anyone else.

I OBJECTS

2 Speech, Light, Gesture, and Costume

Words may convey day dreams or feelings as in the theater.
Catherine Howard's words to Lady Rochford not only picture for us Henry

265

VIII's old body but lay open the loathing she feels for it (*The Wives of Henry VIII,* part 5: *Catherine Howard:* television, Naomi Capon).

On the wall of a house captured from the Germans, Ivan has read, "We were eight, all under nineteen, the Germans will kill us in an hour. Avenge us." His imaginary vengeance is partly seen in his crawling across the floor of the empty room and hurling a bottle to douse the light, but more as his flashlight searches the walls and we hear his voice, "Don't let them leave the building . . . Come out, you won't get away . . . We haven't forgotten . . ." and as his disk of light stays on a hanging coat, "You are trembling . . ." (*Ivan's Childhood,* Andrei Tarkovsky).

Light is a means to be used both in film and in theatre. Napoleon sits in his room, writing and listening to the crowd on the street below his window, where some unfortunate man is being hung from a lamppost. Though Napoleon's features change little, bright light and shadow flitter across the heights and hollows of his face, with now and then darkness blotting it all: the quick-winking light speaking of racing thoughts, and the black of sombre ones. His fingers dart across the table to the handle of his pistol, stop short, and snap closed with decision. Following this is the document headed "A Declaration of the Rights of Man" (*Napoleon,* Abel Gance).

From theater comes the gesture.

Professor Rath has lost his respected post as teacher, because of his affair with a cabaret singer, whom he later marries. He lives by selling pornographic pictures of her, and is humiliated on returning to his own town by appearing on the stage as a clown, and seeing the strong man making love to Lola Lola. His stiff jerky shuffle and furtive glances back as he walks from the cabaret to his old school reminds us of when we first saw him, jaunty and upright. He hastens up to the classroom where he had taught. The caretaker later finds him dead, seated at his desk, his arms across it, his head sunk, and his taut fingers, clutching the corners, cannot be loosened (*The Blue Angel,* Joseph von Sternberg).

We never see the streetcar, with which the boy is obsessed, in *Dodeska-Den* (Akira Kurosawa). In dirty white gloves, a white belt with a pouch behind, and a peaked cap, he edges sideways along a concrete strip, and wipes imaginary dust off with his index finger, disapprovingly. At the far end, he faces us, unsteps, and with upturned gaze and alternate hands he lets something up, wth a click and the starting sound of a compressor. He walks to the other end of the concrete strip, looks up, grasps with his hands, and takes three steps in place. He faces us again, and looking ahead, he twists each wrist as if turning brake and controller, and shuffles toward us, saying over and over again, "Dodeska-Den, Dodeska-Den," the sound of the tracks.

Theater also uses costume. Before Martin, the pastor's son, arrives home, Anne, the pastor's wife, wears a plain linen collar and a close-fitting cap with two points. When she reads *The Song of Songs* at breakfast, she wears a lacey collar and white lace cap. When she enters to Martin alone, she wears no cap, and her curls are loose (*Day of Wrath,* Carl Theodor Dreyer). Two twins are dressed the same at first. As it becomes apparent that Terry is unpredictable and malevolent, we see her in darker costume, and Ruth in lighter. In the final scenes, Ruth is dressed in white and Terry in black. It is specially useful here as the same actress plays both twins (*The Dark Mirror,* Robert Siodmak) (pl. 30).

3 Manipulated Objects

A whole chapter could be filled by examples of Chaplin's telling us what he is thinking by how he handles things. As he lies at the top of a slope, looking down and laughing at the two warders he has toppled over to the bottom, a foot steps on his hand. He quickly pulls his hand out and heaps earth on the foot—pretending it is not there (*The Adventurer*). Fearful before a boxing bout, Charlie sees a black boxer circle his face with a rabbit's foot. He does the same, adding a dab or two of his own. When the black man is carried in unconscious, he snatches a towel and hurriedly wipes wherever he dabbed the rabbit's foot, as if wiping off an ointment (*City Lights*). He catches flies one by one, carefully slips them into his trousers pocket, and then with a single big slap he kills them. He could not bear to pinch a fly to death in his fingers, but his conscience is easy when a slap on his pants pocket happens to kill them. A paradigm of much we do: we would eat the meat, but would not kill the ox (*The Vagabond*).

Professor Rath lays out on his desk three pictures of Lola Lola, on to which feathery skirts have been pasted. He has confiscated them from his pupils. Although alone, he looks round, gently blows up the skirts, looks round again, and repeats the blow. It is our first hint that the professor could be seduced (*The Blue Angel*, Joseph von Sternberg).

The despised servant girl, who has wished for the rape and death of her master's daughter, picks up a stone to throw as she watches the rape. Her two hands hold the stone tight for she cannot bring herself to throw it, and when the deed is done, it is dropped, and rolls down a slope into a stream, her hatred spent (*Virgin Spring*, Ingmar Bergman).

As Ackland was taking a child home, their bus hurtled into the wall of an underpass. A train was passing overhead at the time, and his hand was holding a bunny, shaped from a handkerchief to amuse the child. He had kept her late and a sense of guilt for her death is revived by the sound of a train whistle, at which times he is often found obsessively clutching a handkerchief shaped like a rabbit. When he finally lays to rest an impulse to throw himself in front of a train, the steam from the train clears from the bridge he is standing on, and we approach to close-up of the handkerchief bunny, lying mangled on the track where it had fallen from his hands—his obsession is destroyed (*The October Man*, Roy Baker).

A scarf slips through a man's hands, as a woman slowly draws it from them in reluctant parting (*The Defense of Siberia*, The Brothers Vassiliev).

4 Unmanipulated Objects

Things may express inner states without being touched, and this is less theatrical. It is the director who brings person and thing together, mostly by angle and editing.

Angle. James Brewster says on the telephone, "Yes, I think I could work it in on Friday." In the same frame we see his appointment book, with not a single entry (*Nothing But the Best*, Clive Donner).

A boy of the bayous, raised far from technological marvels, sees a drilling rig for the first time. The barge and how it is towed cannot be seen for the canes and grasses, beyond which the tall white steel tower floats past slowly and silently like a cloud, embodying the sense of wonder with which the boy sees it (*Louisiana Story*, Robert J. Flaherty).

In *Waterloo Bridge* (Mervyn Leroy), Myra Lester steps down to the pavement as a rumbling, thundering sound grows louder. She walks away, and we see beyond her a train of trucks approaching across the bridge. Then as she walks toward us, half length, we notice the lights of the trucks flashing in a steady beat on her near cheek.

One after another, evenly spaced, they rise bolder out of the fog and pass, their lights blacklidded, slanting down, bodies high, no drivers visible. The camera seems to sink lower and lower, giving the wheels increasing emphasis, and as each truck passes, it rises till its wheels nearly fill the frame. Turn about, we see the flashing face and looming trucks, and feel the same hypnotic rhythm in both. Myra's gaze turns to the source of light, and she walks more quickly. The suicide is told in a few flashes: her eyes in close-up; a truck's radiator with a painted cross rises above us; locked wheels skid; the radiator comes to a stop; men scramble out of the cab. A long slow approach from high up ends on a stretcher.

Editing. As Peter runs across the rotunda, his madness is hinted at by cutting in flashes of a gilded heraldic eagle mounted on a newel, one distant, one close, as if it leapt at us, and three later ones from sharply contrasted angles, sudden wild whirls in the flow of thought (*Catherine the Great*, Paul Czinner).

To evoke the mood of a schizophrenic, the things that Polanski shows are not out-of-the-way in themselves but all the things that catch her attention in a given environment, seen one after another, show an abnormal bias. Distorted reflections on a tea kettle, the glare of a light shade hung from the ceiling, her brother-in-law's razor, a skinned rabbit, wizened potatoes with hairy roots writhing out of them, a woman seen upside down talking with eccentric lips, her boyfriend seen through the lens on the door, his chin and forehead grotesquely narrowed: these picked from all the things around, and the rest ignored, create a sense in us of a distorted consciousness (*Repulsion*, Roman Polanski).

Motion. Katie Brady kisses Eugene Gaillard, a married man with whom she is infatuated. This is followed by the road, the countryside, slopes with fields and hedges, swooping toward us with elation (*The Girl with the Green Eyes*, Desmond Davis).

5 Verbal Objects

To know what someone is reading is to see into his mind.

Professor Willingdon walks to and fro during the night. He surprises the landlady listening at his door, and remarks politely, "I find that my mind is clearer in the early morning, Mrs. Pickett." She watches him leave through the window curtains, looks at the heading of the newspaper she is holding, "Landlord killer at large," and telephones the police (*Seven Days to Noon*, John and Roy Boulting). A woman writes, concerned about her sister, who had gone to Reunion to marry Mahe. We see the letter as he reads it, we hear her voice speaking the words, and, superimposed on the letter, we see her face as she speaks them. He is thinking both of what the letter says and of her who wrote it (*Mississippi Mermaid*, François Truffaut). In *The Man in Grey* (Leslie Arliss), we never see the text of the letter at all: we hear Rokeby's voice speak it and see Clarissa's face, responding to what he writes as she is reading.

What applies to words applies also to other printed matter. Mahe and his wife, in flight from the police, have reached a chalet in Switzerland. He knows that she was privy to a murder. He has had ample evidence of her avarice and lack of scruples. He has been spreading rat poison that she had brought from the village. He begins to vomit and feels weak. While she is away in the village buying medicine, he leans out of bed in order to pull a sweater toward him. As he tugs it off a newspaper, a comic strip catches his eye. We pan along the story of Snow White, to where the witch gives Snow White the poisoned apple, and the pictures go out of focus. He pauses, gathers his strength, rises from bed, and goes out to flag down a car (*Mississippi Mermaid*, François Truffaut).

6   Nondiegetic Objects

Something may be brought in to symbolize an experience, entirely from outside the story's ambience.

Scotty is a union president, one of the older leaders, who gave up much in the early days and saw little of his son as he grew up to the stranger he now is, because of the time and concern he brought to the cause. He is now being ousted from his post by younger men. Now and then his bewilderment is given form by a very short shot of a rapidly rotating wheel (*Do Not Fold, Staple, Spindle or Mutilate*, John Howe).

The thing may be an abstract pattern. The White officer's face is up left, and that of Maryutka, the Red Army sharpshooter, down right. They have been shipwrecked on an island, their roles have changed, and the officer, his mind enriched by much reading and schooling, has become the guide of her with little of either. The only words we hear are, "In Liverpool there lived . . ." To romantic music, we approach them and then her face to close-up. Superimposed, as we see them in turn, are the fire blazing in the room and a sparkle as of light on choppy water, a hint of her eager listening, of the prickle of adventure. He with dramatic gestures narrating, she concerned or smiling, and the excitement of tiny lights (*The Forty-First*, Grigor Chukhrai).

The accident in *The October Man* (Roy Baker) shows the rod as it comes loose from the wheel, the brake pedal thrust full down, the driver trying vainly to control the direction of the bus, the bus in long shot heading for the wall of the underpass, the wall through the windshield rapidly coming closer and brighter, Jim Ackland's arm around the little girl, his face fearful, the wall about to strike, and in a dark frame, a white star bursts from the center.

The abstraction may be a color. Payton, a game warden, is wounded in his thigh. Warned by a chatter of birds, he takes up his rifle. He sees a leopard and keeps his muzzle on it. He fires to no effect. The leopard runs. Payton in close shot shouts, and across the shots of both him and the leopard, there flash pulses of red, suggesting the quickened activity of the body in time of danger (*Ivory Hunter*, Harry Watt).

II   COMPARISONS

7   Simile

Windrush is about to start work for a confectionery firm. They are showing him round the factory. He has eaten two chocolate bars and two ladles full of some liquid. He leans on a gadget, which goes up and down, putting cherries on confections with a rising whushing sound of bilious persuasion. Then he sees a machine, whose barrel-shaped side bulges out, and every four minutes, it spews from a mouth-like aperture a flow of white liquid. It is then that Windrush, with staring eye and bulging cheek, bolts from his guide, and the camera pans to the swollen barrel, which at that moment vomits its white contents (*I'm All Right, Jack*, John Boulting).

The simile may be the character's, not the director's. In *Morgan: A Suitable Case for Treatment* (Karel Reisz), Morgan feels that human relations are too much for him, and that, if born a higher ape, he would have been happier. Not only does he sometimes don a gorilla costume, but in people he meets he finds the marks of other animals. A short, large-headed, fleshy ticket collector yawns, followed by a hippopotamus yawning. Morgan then bends forward, arms dangling apelike and ambles toward a fellow-subhuman. There are three elements: a close-up of Morgan's face with a happy smile, telling us he has found another jungle mate; a sensory cue, like the workman looking down from a metal scaffolding, holding onto one of the braces; and then the likeness he finds, in this case, a gorilla swinging from limb to limb on a tree.

8 Metaphor

He is embarrassed, his neck and shoulders are tense. We know this, for he takes an oil can and oils his neck (*The Fireman*, Charles Chaplin). In the bottom half of the frame the glutton is in bed. In the top half is a casserole, backed by black, from which three imps leap and belabor his head with hammers, at which, still asleep, he winces and fidgets (*The Dream of a Rarebit Fiend*, Edwin S. Porter).

Artinelli stands ready to launch his dive, but Huller, on his trapeze, crossing toward him and away again, waves him back. Huller is wrung by jealousy of Artinelli, whom he suspects of having an affair with his wife. He has just imagined Artinelli dead on the ground, as if he, Huller, had let him fall, and he cannot let Artinelli start with his mind as it is. The swaying of Huller, the rising and falling of Artinelli and Bertha-Marie on the platform, as he sees them, of the stars on the ceiling as he looks up, the sway to and fro of the audience, whose eyes and heads are following his trapeze, these are an image of Huller's indecision (*Variety*, E. A. Dupont).

The tenant of a flat, from whose window a woman had thrown herself, comes to feel that the place is imposing the same role on him. At the end, when he has bought a wig, made his face up, and put on the woman's dress, he faces the window. We come from behind his back, through the two white net curtains waving in the wind, and look down into the court. As we pan past the windows they open, lights go on, people look out and start applauding. They come in groups, the windows now are alcoves like theater boxes, girandoles of tiny electric lamps are on the walls; some of the men are in evening dress. For a moment the music is an orchestra tuning up, and this is followed by a roll of drums, as before a circus act. We approach up to the window, where the tenant stands on the ledge. There is a shot of a box with five in evening dress looking eagerly up. Then he falls (*The Tenant*, Roman Polanski).

A man plunges into a mirror, which absorbs him like a surface of water. It is an entering into himself, a self-scrutiny. Through one of the keyholes in a long hall of doors, he sees a man in Mexican garb standing by a wall. A firing squad shoots him. He slowly falls to the ground, and rises quickly again to stand where he was. The firing squad returns to shoot him again. Do we suffer in fancy first and then in reality (*The Blood of a Poet*, Jean Cocteau)?

Convalescing after abdominal surgery, Aleksandrov sits in pajamas and dressing gown, depressed. Suddenly in down shot, he finds himself standing in the street, still in hospital clothing. He looks round, and in longer shot, he sees all the passers-by dressed the same. Can it be that they are as sick as he (*The White Room*, Metod Andonov)?

III   THE UNUSUAL

9   Anastrophe—The Unusual in Film—Angle

Anastrophe is an unusual arrangement, an inversion of what is logical or normal, in literature of the words in a sentence, in film of the image, in angle, in focus, and in lighting. It comprises all forms of technical distortion. It is clearly a figure to be used rarely, and it is not always certain if it has the effect intended.

What could be more unusual or inverted than showing someone upside down? After learning of his incurable cancer, Itsuki locks his door, and we see him lying spread-eagled on the bed, upside down. No expression can be read on such a face, so it may as well be a blank oval, but its upside downness is clear, and, though the image appeals more to the mind than to the feelings, it may be taken as "a turning upside down of his life or its values" (*Kaseki*, Masaki Kobayashi).

And yet the image may speak directly to us. As Orphée leaves the Zone of Death followed by Eurydice, the Princess (who is his Death) and he spend a brief moment with one another, and their heads are seen as they kiss upside down. We cannot make out the lines on their faces; they are less people than bodies. But more than this, a reversal of the normal is implied: it is life and death embracing, Orphée more in love with death than with life, Orphée returning from the Zone of Death to life. We need not read their faces; they are more symbols than persons (*Orphée*, Jean Cocteau).

Again, in the *Ballad of a Soldier* (Grigor Chukhrai), one of two signalmen is killed, and the other runs, pursued by a German tank. In a down air shot, the camera pans with tank and man, and at one point the scene turns, placing the ground up, the sky bottom right, the chase continuing. Is it the disoriented panic of the man fleeing wildly without plan, or the manic mind of the tank driver, pursuing one man, when he should be addressing himself to the destruction of companies, when, in fact, he could shoot. A bizarre act seems to call for an anastrophic treatment.

After walking for days with little or no food, Kaji leaves the forest for the open plain. He is weak and lightheaded. The horizon sways to an angle of forty-five degrees. He passes corpses, birds of prey circle overhead, flies are swarming around him. He raises his hand up to his mouth and nose, and the horizon sways up further, recovering only slowly. He seems to be tottering downhill, giddily (*The Human Condition*, part 3: *A Soldier's Prayer*, Masaki Kobayashi).

In *Brief Encounter* (David Lean), the tilting is an upsetting of normal values, a woman's briefly thinking of suicide. As an approaching train whistles, the camera slowly tilts her head left. On the same diagonal, she runs from us to the door and onto the platform. The train rushes from top to bottom frame in a flash of steel and vapor. Her face is still tilted as her hair is blown and the pulse of the passing train flickers on it. As the sound of the train dies, we are aware that the tilt has left her.

Things that come between a face and the camera may stamp a mood on the face. In *Dodeska-Den* (Akira Kurosawa) a woman tells of going to seduce a middle-aged man, whose feelings were "dead," she said. She opens the door, hears a groan, sees him sit up in bed and say "Ocho" in a low tone, like a ghost, and she runs away. As she describes it, her long hair hangs in strands over her cheeks and mouth, thus laying stress on her staring eyes and how the experience had frightened her.

Davy's wife talks of Joe Garland, whom he had seen leaving his house as he came home, "You've always liked Joe, haven't you . . . He's going to get you a job . . ." Davy's back says nothing, and at last she sinks back into silence and the pillows, where black shadow lines from a window stamp her face. It is hard to find a word for what we strongly sense, shame, guilt, perhaps hate (*The Stars Look Down*, Sir Carol Reed).

Agamemnon has said that before he will sacrifice his daughter, as Calchas demands, he will send the soldiers home. The army, having heard that the priest has been told by the gods a way to bring the wind that will take them to Troy, is jubilant with torches as Agamemnon leaves his lodging to face them. In the hot air from the torch just within the frame, the image of Agamemnon's face begins to waver; we sense a melting resolution (*Iphigenia*, Michael Cacoyannis).

10 Anastrophe—Lens and Lighting

Anastrophe by the use of lens and lighting is used for conveying unusual states of consciousness.

Indistinct image—general awareness. To avoid writing a letter in his own hand, Mitchell in *The Captive Heart* (Basil Dearden) contrives to injure his right hand. As he steadies a post being hammered into the ground, he slips his hand on top of the post. He turns his head away. In up shot, a soldier standing by shouts "Look out!" Waves throb across the image of his averted head and it melts into that of the woman he is writing to—the vibration of pain and the loss of consciousness.

One-Round Jack in *The Ring* (Alfred Hitchcock) is knocked out and saved by the bell. Five round blurs of white on a darker ground slowly come into focus as ceiling lights.

The old hall porter creeps unsteadily to work along a wall the morning after his daughter's wedding party. Whenever the camera looks with his eyes, people and streets are blurry. But when at last he sails around a corner and sees the *Atlantic* hotel across the street, the new hall porter standing in front of the door is painfully sharp and clear. His glory is gone; he had forgotten (*The Last Laugh*, F. W. Murnau).

Indistinct image—sight only. Harry Palmer, sitting in a lecture hall, takes his glasses off to wipe them, and all is blurred. Something catches his attention, he puts the glasses on, and quite clearly, halfway down a row, we see the American agent, smoking (*The Ipcress File*, Sidney J. Furie). Isadora's last glimpse of her children, walking away on either side of their nanny, hand in hand, is blurred by tears (*Isadora*, Karel Reisz).

Indistinct image—romantic convention. McTeague in *Greed* (Erich von Stroheim) is in love with Trina. As a dentist, he has given her gas. He looks at her, as she lies in the chair unconscious, every feature softened and hazy. He clenches his fists as he checks his feelings. She comes into sharp focus again, and he pulls her tooth.

Distorted image. When a deaf girl is in church, the lips of the choristers make enormous gestures. As she reads what they say, her eyes are less aware of other features (*Johnny Belinda*, Jean Negulesco). As Harry Palmer is "programmed," we see him half-length, tied in a wheelchair, and as his face winces with pain, his chin and skull seem to stretch apart, as if on a rack, and his face changes color (*The Ipcress File*, Sidney J. Furie).

Negative image. In *Silent Dust* (Lance Comfort), a wealthy blind man, Robert

Rawley, who had set great hopes on his only son, presumed dead in the war, has caught from what he hears those around him do and say, that something has happened that they are keeping from him. He enters the drawing room alone, to piece it together. As the camera enters in his place, the room is a drab gray, heavily lined, thickly tangible, suggesting, by the use of negative film, a world of touch. "Something has turned up . . . *someone* has turned up. . . ," he says. We hear words as he remembers them, "Who's there?" (Simon, the son, a deserter, had come home and was then in the room, but never answered.) The camera pans past the table of decanters. (Robert had felt from the weight that someone had drunk most of the whiskey.) "I dropped my compact." (Angela's excuse for running and closing the door to keep Simon out). The camera goes on searching the tangible room, and we hear all the incidents as Robert brings them to mind. When only one conclusion is possible, the clear positive image of Simon glows in on the negative ground, standing by the piano, and then vanishes.

Light and shadow. Anne withdraws to where shadows mask her face, as her pastor husband speaks of sin, and she comes listening eagerly into the light as he speaks of his own death (*Day of Wrath*, Carl Theodor Dreyer). When Laura refuses to go with Dr. Harvey to his friend's flat, she leaves him silhouetted against the bright wall of an underpass, his face black, nearly featureless (*Brief Encounter*, David Lean). Mario confesses to Natalia that he has not taken her letter to the lodger, for he himself loves her. Her face is a sequence of dark and light reflected from water, as if opposing feelings were swaying her between the two (*Le Notti Bianche*, Luchino Visconti).

11 Anastrophe—Superimposition

Showing a man's thoughts is a common use of superimposition. Joe Wilson is listening on the radio to the trial of the men accused of killing him. He had escaped unseen from the jail they had set on fire. He finds himself being softened from his vengeful purpose by listening to what his fiancée says as a witness. He snaps the radio off and stands, and there is superimposed a panning shot of the twenty-two accused (*Fury*, Fritz Lang).

Dr. Baum is reading notes made by Dr. Mabuse, a former patient, now dead. "Domination by terror . . . man does not exist as an individual. . . ." We see rows of masks, helmets, and skulls. Seated across the desk from Dr. Baum is the superimposed and wraithlike figure of Dr. Mabuse, as if, in Dr. Baum's imagination, the dead man's words had brought him to life. The phantom rises, moves round behind Dr. Baum, sits in the same chair and vanishes, as if in to the doctor. The ideas of Dr. Mabuse, if not his revenant soul, have entered into Dr. Baum and rule his life (*The Testament of Dr. Mabuse*, Fritz Lang).

Two lonely people meet at an amusement park and fall in love. They are separated by accident. Back in his room, the young man, disconsolate, plays his record of "Always." The girl (who, unknown to him, lives in the next room) has also returned. She unpins her hair but cannot rest. She walks around the room and cries. She cannot put out of her mind that at last she has met someone to love and has lost him. Where her head is centered in the frame, there is also, superimposed, the circling record. It likely told the viewer of silent films, that she could hear the music, but it also gives an impression, perhaps more strongly now, of an agonized thought, going round and round her mind obsessively, driving all other thoughts out (*Lonesome*, Paul Fejos).

12 Anastrophe—Speeded Movement

Mike is coming toward us, trying the handle of every parked car. Finding one unlocked with key in the ignition, Mike opens the door and bows Colin in. In speeded movement they both duck into the car and off they drive. They drop over a brick wall after a theft, and in speeded movement run to the end of the street (*The Loneliness of the Long Distance Runner,* Tony Richardson).

IV THE CAMERA AS A PERSON—PROSOPOPOEIA

13 Up and Down

Prosopopoeia is "making into a person," treating inanimate things as if they can hear or feel or exercise other human attributes. The thing chiefly personified in film is the camera (pl. 2, 22). One way—and perhaps the most common—of showing that one person dominates, or feels that he dominates, another, is to photograph the dominating person with camera pointing up, and the person dominated with it pointing down. What it really signifies is that a person looking up from the same angle as the camera, would feel he was dominated by the person above him, so in fact we are attributing to the camera a human reaction. It may also be the feeling of a person in the story who sees the dominating person from that angle. In this case the camera sees, and makes us feel, as this person does.

It would be possible to illustrate this from several hundred films.

In all the visits, for example, of Jaggers the lawyer to the Gargerys, respecting the *Great Expectations* (David Lean) Pip might hope for, all shots of him are up shots, with less wall than ceiling behind his figure. When Jaggers straightened up, not only was he huge in bulk but Olympian in the glance cast down upon us (and Pip), and when he bent down toward us, he was large and emphatic.

14 Distancing—Viewpoint

Almost as common is to engage our sympathy for certain characters by showing them full-length and in close-up, and giving enough detail of them and their surroundings to make them interesting and attractive. Those on the other side, on the contrary, are shown either briefly or too far off to be clearly seen, and little is told about them. They are strangers to us, but often with a touch of menace or absurdity. Christ's trial, by both courts, and the release of Barabbas, are seen from far off from behind the heads of the crowd. We are the common people, watching remote and incomprehensible decisions being made (*The Gospel According to Saint Matthew,* Pier Paolo Pasolini).

Whenever we see the Teuton knights in *Alexander Nevski* (S. M. Eisenstein), visor and helmet hide their faces; they seem less than human—anonymous automatons of destruction (pl. 31).

In *The Four Feathers* (Zoltan Korda) the English soldiers are often shown in close-up, full face; we hear them speak; we come to know them as persons. The other side, the Fuzzy-Wuzzies, Arabs, Dervishes, are seen mostly in long shot, and even when a charge brings one or two of them closer, we meet them as strangers. The camera is behind the backs of the British and the others are charging *us.*

This is not the same as the first-person camera, which shows us a scene as one character sees it; it shows it rather as the director sees it. One set of people is larger and closer; we see more of their faces, their clothes, and their things; we hear their voices. We live with one side; the other side are not our kind.

15 Ethopoeia—Leaving Out—Ellipsis

By leaving out of the frame what a person cannot or does not see, and including only what he can or does, we are putting ourselves in his place—the figure *ethopoeia*. It is, when seen in another way, an ellipsis, the one that always lurks behind our backs.

Bridie Quilty, an Irish girl working for a German agent, is sitting in the visitors' gallery of the Manx Parliament. She is groping for, and finds, a notebook hidden in the stuffing of the seat. At that moment, she (and we) hear a voice, "Don't move. Stay where you are." She freezes. After a flash of light, a voice says, "Thank you," and in the next shot a photographer emerges from behind his camera. We had seen him taking pictures for a guidebook (*I See a Dark Stranger*, Frank Launder). Philip Marlowe is sitting in his office, looking out of the window. The camera retreats from his back to bring in a shoulder, head, and hat of Moose Molloy, and as it does, something prompts Marlowe to turn his head. He and we become aware of Moose at the same time (*Murder My Sweet*, Edward Dmytryk).

Our attention selects and may leave out part of what is right in front of our eyes. Jones is attending a luncheon to see more of a young woman he has recently met. The chairman rises to introduce the speaker, his daughter. The screen shows only him and a girl to his left, prim, plain, and with glasses, who is smiling up at the chairman. Jones listens glumly. The chairman sits, and the girl on his other side, the one Jones knows, rises and speaks. Our eye had been on the wrong girl: it had clearly not entered the mind of Jones that a good-looking girl could give a talk (*Foreign Correspondent*, Alfred Hitchcock). "It is our noticing things that puts them in a room," Marcel Proust remarked, "our growing used to them takes them away again"; and it is often because we need things that we notice them.[2] When *The Juggler of Our Lady* makes his call on the musician or the other brothers, the outline of an arch appears on the bare brownish background, and after he has paid his visit, it vanishes (Al Kodzel).

One of the most written-about shots is that in which the boy Pip first meets Magwich. The day is dull, bleak, and windy as Pip climbs over a stone wall to place flowers on his parents' grave. As the wind mourns, its wail is flecked by an occasional bird call. He looks round uneasily. The black limbs of a tree lash wildly; a pollarded, warted stump of willow fills most of the frame with its black mace. The boy leaves his flowers, and hastens left in half-length shot. The frame line races ahead of his nose by only an inch or two, till the two hands of a burly, grim-faced man enter like a pair of buffers to seize him and stop him dead, and our gaze rises to the head and shoulders that follow and the eye that glowers. Closeness to the camera made movement quick, there was a sense of bodily collision between the hands and the boy, and even though, since Pip was in the frame, we did not see with his eyes, we felt the shock of the unexpected encounter the moment he did (*Great Expectations*, David Lean).

16 Ethopoeia—The Expected Missing

The leaving out of the frame of something expected in the normal course of events, or conversely, including the unusual, is a sign that what we are seeing may only exist in the awareness of one of the characters, projected into the world outside.

In a photograph of grandmother, father, and mother, the father's head is out of the frame—rejected or unremembered (*The Quiet One*, Sidney Myers).

A person who finds the pantry hard to resist looks at himself in the mirror, and firmly decides that he has had enough to eat. We see him in the mirror going to bed and pulling up the covers. Now the man himself tips on stealthy toes toward the kitchen, and, passing a mirror on the way, there is no reflection; the man he had seen in the mirror, the man he would like to be, is in bed asleep (*Tomorrow We Diet*, Jack Kinney).

Persons or things whose comings or goings are unaccountable we commonly consider imaginary. Lori sees a boy swinging in a playground. She looks away, and almost at once looks back. The swing, the whole wide playground, is empty, with not a sign of any departing boy. In an instant, he had vanished (*Necromancy*, Bert I. Gordon).

When two persons view the same scene, and one sees what the other does not, we assume again that the difference lies in the mind of one observer, perhaps of both.[3]

In *Blithe Spirit* (David Lean), three people are seated in one room. In the two other chairs, as seen by the husband, Ruth and Elvira are both seen and heard, for although Elvira is dead, her husband can see her ghost. As seen by Ruth, one of the two other chairs is empty.

Dr. Macfarlane and the student Fettes have dug up a coffin. They are in a gig, driving back to the hospital, the coffin standing upright between them. The doctor hears Gray's voice (the resurrectionist he has murdered) calling his familiar name, "Toddy, Toddy, Toddy" in a rhythm the same as the gig's, and then the words "Never get rid of me" over and over again. He stops, tells Fettes to bring him a lamp from off the gig, undoes the cerecloth, and finds the body, not of the buried woman but the murdered Gray. Macfarlane drives off in a frenzy, leaving Fettes behind, the naked white body of Gray nudging against him. His gig topples off the road onto a slope and he is killed. When Fettes catches up, and lifts the cerecloth, we see by the light of the lamp, the upper half of a dead woman's body, on which Macfarlane had projected the image of the man he had murdered (*The Body-Snatcher*, Robert Wise).

17 Ethopoeia—The First-Person Passive

The person whose eyes the camera sees with may be the target of other people's actions. This may be called the first-person passive.

It may be the fist that punches right into the lens at *Oliver Twist* (David Lean); or the hands that slap at each side of the camera, as on a woman's cheeks (*Voice in the Wind*, Arthur Ripley); or the inspector's palm that bars our way to the two condemned men about to be shot—"That's far enough" (*The War Game*, Peter Watkins).

It may take the form of a millstone rolling down toward us—enemy agents (*Cottage to Let*, Anthony Asquith); or the hangman's hood coming down over our head and eyes, blotting out the cart and crowds that we and Macheath can see through the noose that awaits our neck (*The Beggar's Opera*, Peter Brook).

Since scenes are most frequently shot from head or shoulder height, when a surface of water rises to just below the camera lens, we take it that hardly more than our head is still above it (*The Stars Look Down*, Sir Carol Reed).

Even when an injury is self-inflicted, it still may be first person passive.

Dr. Peterson walks away to the door, having satisfied herself that Dr. Murchison, whose desk we occupy, has committed a murder. The top of a huge revolver held in a hand points toward her, and follows her to the door, where she turns and says, "I'm going to fetch the police." She closes the door slowly, the revolver turns sideways, hesitates, and then, big on the screen, the barrel swings to point its black hole at us. A shot is heard, a puff of smoke is seen, and the image fades (*Spellbound*, Alfred Hitchcock).

Matters of practice. Three films present interesting questions. The pointed red-hot pole to blind Polyphemus with is aimed at us by the men who bear it, all of whose eyes are looking at us. The shot is vivid—but Polyphemus is sleeping. His eye is closed; he cannot see the pole. It is not the situation as he sees it, for he is unaware of the situation. It is not ethopoeia. If the back of Polyphemus's head were also shown, this would abandon the first person, but also avoid the subjunctive (hard for film to manage), "This is what you would have seen, had you been Polyphemus, awake instead of asleep." As it is, we are told that he is both awake and asleep; this is contradictory, not conditional (*Ulysses*, Mario Camerini).

The sole of a shoe comes down toward us, as Stephen helps Anne out of a wrecked car but stops her from tramping on the face of a dead man. Is this an ethopoeia? If we were in the dead man's place, would we be aware of a foot about to step on us? Has the first-person camera any value here? It cannot, as it is edited, be Stephen imagining a foot approaching his face (*Accident*, Joseph Losey).

Using the camera to show what a person can see should surely be avoided, when the person concerned is either dead or asleep, unless in a dream or other fantasy.

Handful by handful, a tramp is grabbing up the banknotes he has dropped while crossing railway tracks. A train approaches. He delays, mistakes which of many tracks it is on, and is run over. To us, who see the train approach with his eye, there is no doubt which set of tracks the train is on; we do not share his confusion. This is again a flaw, of which Preston Sturges himself was not unaware. He had intended, he told me in a letter, that the train should come on one of many tracks curving toward us, and this would have made the confusion plausible, but he could not find a curve with a sufficient number of lines (*Sullivan's Travels*).[4]

18 Ethopoeia—The First-Person Active

When the person through whose eyes the camera sees is not the mere butt of other people's movements, but moves himself, we then have the first-person active.[5]

Bartolomeo, squire to the king, victim of a jealous husband, is dragged behind a galloping horse. We see blurred banks of brown leaves, of stony roads, branches, leafless trees, and outcrops of rock, either flashing across the screen from near the ground or else rushing toward us at ground level under the beating hoofs and swaying traces. The image is oscillating to and fro as if the squire were constantly flung from side to side, or shaking as if he continually bounced from a rough surface (*Blanche*, Walerian Borowczyk). Passive too in a sense.

In *The Great Adventure* (Arne Sucksdorff), a fox is seen making off with a hen in its mouth. A laborer levels at us a double-barreled shotgun. The camera travels fast, its eye down on a gravel road, and then enters past the trees of a wood. Abruptly, movement stops, all is silent, the scene slowly hazes over and goes out of focus. The laborer weaves through the woods, stoops for the stolen hen, and sees the dead fox.

Movement may be implied by editing. Four people are coming down stairs. A triangle of three men in dinner jackets waits at the foot of the stairs. We cut to each group in turn, but the angle from which we see the three men is lower each time, placing us with the four descending the stairs (*Notorious*, Alfred Hitchcock).

The searching eye is the most common use of the first-person active. An invisible commentator tells us that Grand Fenwick is the smallest country in the world. As he speaks, the camera roves to and fro on the map of Europe. After a slight pause, the voice says (to us) "Excuse me." For a little longer the camera silently seeks, and at last finds, a puny red point (*The Mouse That Roared*, Jack Arnold).

19 Ethopoeia—The Hand-held Camera

The jolting uneven motion that a handheld camera gives the image is often used as a signal that the camera's eye is to be taken as that of a person. In *The Drylanders* (Donald Haldane), for example, as Daniel, a sack of flour on his back, approaches his own window, glowing with a single candle, its image yaws from side to side as the handheld camera trudges in slow unsteady steps toward it.

As has, however, been pointed out, in life we make a continuous correction for the effect of bodily movement on how we see, and we do not, when we are walking, see a fidgeting world, unless we take pains to see it so.[6] An agitated image, then, from whatever source, cannot be justified on the ground of realism, but only as adding some figurative meaning.

One meaning that can be thus conveyed is physical weakness. Terry has stood up to a union boss and been beaten. His fellow stevedores respect his courage, and say, "If Terry doesn't work, we don't." He is bloody and dazed, but his friends persuade him to try. He is helped up and walks unsteadily along a line of watching longshoremen. The camera is now and then out of focus, it rocks a little, sways up to the roof in a sudden lurch or turns unsteadily to take in the watching line of men (*On the Waterfront*, Elia Kazan).

Mental unbalance may be suggested, as if our habit of correction had been disturbed, and the outer world appears to move instead of us and lack stability. After Abel Magwich dies, Pip, beside himself with grief, leaves for home. Quick iterations of interrupted streaks of light flit across the screen, to a buzzing and a rumbling and a shrieking rush of music. Wavering unsteadily, we approach the names of *Pip* and *Pocket* printed on the wall beside a door. Slowly and with a slight sway we cross a room to a corner cabinet, where the image trembles and pauses; we swing to the right, a door opens, and we plunge down quickly toward a bed (*Great Expectations*, David Lean).

20 Ethopoeia—Matters of Practice

As with anadiplosis, doubts have been expressed about the use of ethopoeia throughout a film. It is to be used, says Jean Mitry, in small doses, and cut in with outside, third-person shots of the character portrayed.[7] And yet in the novel and the tale, such a precept is disregarded. Unless the technical means are missing, or unless it runs against the grain of the medium, why deny this use to film? A warped sensibility has shaped most of the images in *Caligari*, and large parts of *Repulsion*, but neither has kept its protagonist off the screen and used the first-person camera consistently.

Let us look for a moment at *Lady in the Lake* (Robert Montgomery). After Philip Marlowe's opening words, the rest of the story is told by ethopoeia. Someone holds a cigarette case out to the audience. A hand comes in from bottom right, takes a cigarette, and smoke rises later from the bottom of the frame. "What is the time, Mr. Marlowe?" we are asked, and our glance turns to where a clock stands on a mantelpiece, and quickly back to catch a blow from the speaker's large fist. The image blurs and sways and the light fails to featureless black. Another time, we see our shadow on a door, hat in hand, and our jaw moving in talk. Throughout the film, the frame lines enclose the field of our awareness: the number on a door, the hand that opens it, the slow scan of a new room in wary examination, the quick dart back in sudden suspicion or guess, the finger which dials a telephone number or presses a bell button, the two hands that steer the car below the windshield.

That there are problems cannot be denied. The objectivity the screen seems to imply is quick to reassert itself, and the viewer must be constantly reinstalled behind the eyes of the character telling the story by some reminding sign. Where Marlowe, for example, is convalescing and sits for a while watching Fromsett, smoke rises from bottom frame, so as to keep us sitting where he sits.

Showing two speakers in turn, which gives animation to conversation, the first-person director must deny himself. He must make up for this by such means as moving the camera to show a change of place or turn of thought.

A third problem is perhaps more serious. Without intending to disparage a bold and intriguing experiment, it must be said that now and then a succession of metonymies, meant to suggest the person behind the eyes, do not pull together into a person. In the last sequence, Marlowe is knocked down in an accident. Our gaze rises to a telephone booth and falls to the wet gravel. Hands enter to claw our way across the gravel, and then in turn to seize the jamb of the doorway. A shadow falls on the telephone, a hand enters to take off the receiver and insert the coin. We hear gasps, the rattle of gravel, the shuffle of shoes, the voice, "Come and get me." But the whole, the suffering person, is hardly more than a ghost haunting the screen. It is almost a set of signposts pointing behind the eyes—to nothing.

I still cannot agree with Jean Mitry that this film was a failure, and that such a treatment should not be tried again.[8] It is just as likely to become another convention, with viewers accustomed to it and the means refined, and every new convention must make head against inertia. Whoever makes the next film all in the first person will certainly have to study *Lady in the Lake*.

It is useful to examine *Murder My Sweet* (Edward Dmytryk) for comparison. The story is threaded on a first-person narrative, a statement made to the police; it begins as the film begins and ends as the film ends. We hear the narration recurring often, but its continuity is broken by the sounds and voices of the flashbacks that form the body of the film. The scenes with diegetic speech all have Marlowe in them, and his voice narrates during all the others, which gives a persistent sense of the first person, despite that the film we *saw* was almost entirely shown in the third person.

Besides this, in three places, Marlowe gives us impressions received while semiconscious, heard in his words and shown on the screen. He leans on a car, we hear a thud, and he collapses (we do not see, and he was not aware of what struck him). We hear his narrating voice, "I felt a black pool closing in at my feet . . ." The solid image is now traversed by waves, with black edges rippling in from the sides to cover the frame. The literary metaphor of light for consciousness and black for its loss is even more telling perhaps when seen on the screen.

The most elaborate montage occurs when Amthor knocks Marlowe down. A shadow again closes in from the sides. He is dragged along the floor by the legs in a wavering image. He circles toward us in a black void. He climbs upstairs toward us in slowed motion. Molloy and Amthor look down from the top of the stairs with large glaring faces, "Where's the necklace?" Marlowe falls back down the steps and his image rotates. On a dim ground, a line of four door frames flips upright, growing smaller into the distance. Marlowe is able to open and go through two of the doors, but only with effort, as the watching faces of Molloy and Dr. Soderberg are superimposed. As Marlowe fumbles at another door, Soderberg appears left, as if waiting for him, syringe in hand. A thumb presses home the barrel of a syringe. The scene floats away like a lighted box. As it shrinks to a mere spot on the black screen, it is drowned in a white whirling, which slows down to become the white frosted bowl of a ceiling light, from which we pan down to show Marlowe lying in bed, as if seen through a dirt-streaked glass, or, as his words describe it, "like a web woven by a thousand spiders . . . wondered how they had got them all to work together. . . ." He reasons himself into action, "you have been zapped twice . . . you have been pumped full of dope to keep you quiet or make you talk . . . Now let's see you do something really tough, like pulling your pants on. . . . That's a beautiful bed. . . . *Stay off it* . . . *Walk*. I walked I don't know how long. . . ."

The way the narrator speaks tells us much of the sort of person he is, and this is borne out by the third-person images, as if we felt the events from within and saw them outside at the same time. It satisfies one of Mitry's criteria and avoids the spectral emptiness felt in some parts of *Lady in the Lake*.

V SOUND

21 Diegetic Sound

If a person's feelings are expressed by something heard in the place where he happens to be, not by a sound felt to be added on, this economy of means is itself a source of pleasure.

Durga and Apu have quarreled and made up. Dreamily each leans on one of a set of four poles holding up the wires of a power line, and we hear the even hum of the current. It captures the boundless, clockless universe of childhood (*Pather Panchali*, Satyajit Ray). The strain felt by those robbing a factory comes to us inside, as the money is handed over, in the beat of machinery, outside, as the nervous driver waits, in the throb of the car engine, and as they run for the car, in the continual dinning of a bell (*Odd Man Out*, Sir Carol Reed). The sounds may be made by the persons whose minds we are penetrating.

Tchaikovsky is standing, speaking, "I have composed nothing since I was married. There is nothing left in me." Nina, his wife, is crouched on the floor, distraught, her clawing fingers rasping the carpet (*The Music Lovers*, Ken Russell). Stoker Thompson, seeking escape from gangsters waiting at the front, scatters away through the clattering chairs of the arena, clangs noisily on two crash doors without effect, and breaks through a third into an alley, whose emptiness is soothed by music from a distant dance hall (*The Set-Up*, Robert Wise). Joe on his motorcycle goes to find the two men who had beaten and blinded Curtis, for not walking out on strike. The men run. Joe catches up and runs over the ankle of one of them. He turns back down the slope to deal with the other. All the time the snarling insistence of the motorcycle speaks of his fury (*The Angry Silence*, Guy Green).

Just as the screen is sometimes used only to show what one character sees, the sounds we hear may be only those that penetrate the awareness of one character. Sleet is beating silently on a window as we approach it. The sound of the sleet is gradually added, and then we see Emily just awakening and looking up at the window. She looks right, and the sound of flames is brought up. Then we are shown the fireplace (*This Is Tomorrow,* Irving Pichel).

The form in which a sound is perceived may suggest the state of mind of the person perceiving. In *Blackmail,* discussed above, only a single searing word strikes out of a meaningless blur. Thorndyke is not seen after he is beaten by the Gestapo. The officer in charge, who stands by the sitting doctor, demands an admission of intent to assassinate Hitler. The officer's browbeating voice, Thorndyke's brief answers, and the nondiegetic music all have a distant quality, and they suddenly rise and fall in loudness, as in the hearing of one who makes a great effort of concentration and then lapses from exhaustion (*Man Hunt,* Fritz Lang).

Inattention may be suggested by keeping the speaker off the screen entirely, and showing only the listener. Mrs. Ashton returns to a house where her parents were killed in an air raid. Her brother's solicitor sees her there, and comes to talk to her, but she answers nothing. In such a conversation, the camera commonly shows each in turn. Here it stays only on Mrs. Ashton, largely on her eyes. There was no sinking in the sound level, but because of the dominance of eye over ear (as a stage director knows), we find that we listen to what is said as little as she does (*A Family at War: A Separate Peace,* television, Gerry Mill).

Diegetic music may strengthen the mood. Laura, in *Brief Encounter* (David Lean), is sitting at home, mending. She goes to the radio, and tunes in a concert: she hears the Second Piano Concerto by Rachmaninoff. She sits, an engine whistle is heard, and she breaks into tears. Only a few weeks ago she had met Alec Harvey with whom she has fallen in love. She has seen him in town every Thursday. He has now gone to Johannesburg, and they have agreed not to write. The train whistle brings back the sounds of the station at which they used to meet, and where they parted. The music matches her mood. Between the details of their Thursday meetings, as these come to her mind in flashbacks, we return to Laura mending and listening to the music. Strictly, the music should only be heard when we are with her in the room, but it leaks over into the flashbacks, as if the present (in the music) and the past (which we see on the screen) were both present at once.

Offscreen sound reflecting the feelings of one of the characters has a modern name, the pathetic fallacy, dealt with more at length below. Diegetic sounds are heard, not as events in themselves but as if the outer world were in sympathy with a character's mood, thus giving the sound a figurative meaning. Robert, his possessive wife, and the young orphan they have taken into their house, of whom he has come to be fond, are sitting watching fireworks. He is trying to decide whether or not to leave both his wife and the girl. Not only the flickering light but the constant rattle and frequent explosions reflect his inner turbulence, as he looks first at one and then at the other (*The Wolf Trap,* Jiri Weiss).

Both noise and music are blended in *The Cranes Are Flying* (Mikhail Kalatozov). Veronica's father and mother have been killed in an air raid, and the man she loves has left for the front without her having said she will marry him. In self-punishment, she refuses to take refuge during an air raid, and Mark, who also loves her, stays in the room with her, playing the piano. "If it were not for the war, I should be playing this for you in the Tchaikovsky Hall," he says. As explosions mount around them, he plays tempestuously, and bombs and music blend in a passionate vehemence. A hit close to the building strews the floor with glass, the lights go out, and the curtains are blown to the ceiling. She runs to Mark in fear; he tries to kiss her, saying he loves her; she cries "Niet, niet, niet."

22 Silence—Ethopoeia

The example from *Man Hunt* given above is strictly a form of Ethopoeia, for as the sound of the outside world loudens or dies away, we are hearing it with Captain Thorndyke's ears. Where the blockage between the source and the mind is complete, there is silence.

The sound may be blocked out by the person's own act. After her parents are killed in a bombing, Veronica rushes into their room, now open to the sky, and on a still-standing strip of wall, a clock is ticking. As she faces us with flames and smoke flickering on her face, the ticking loudens. She claps her hands to her ears, and it stops (*The Cranes Are Flying*, Mikhail Kalatozov).

A physical wall may come between the person and the source of the sound. A suspected criminal is being questioned. Then behind a glass partition, we join two journalists, who are standing, watching, both pairs of watched lips now mute (*Call Northside 777*, Henry Hathaway). James Allen, who escaped from a jail farm and is being pursued by dogs, blows out a reed, and, breathing through it, hides under the surface of running water. Looking with him from underneath, we see the legs of the guards walking the bank, water-hazy and soundless (*I Was a Fugitive from a Chain Gang*, Mervyn Leroy).

The barrier may be a bodily one, like deafness. When Beethoven enters a smithy, the hammer is mute, regaining its voice when he leaves. He runs his fingers over silent strings, and a boy writes on a board with chalk that he can hear them (*The Life and Loves of Beethoven*, Abel Gance). A rich range of sound, of children's talk, sirens, noon whistles, traffic, and much more begins the tale of two deaf mutes. As the two friends walk slowly over a rubbled waste, music takes the place of actual sound, and their speaking hands are emphasized by angle (*Together*, Lorenza Mazzetti).

The barrier to sound may itself be an inner event. The dishes of a schizophrenic girl crash to the floor without sound, for the world outside is distorted or lost (*Repulsion*, Roman Polanski). Colin Smith has run well ahead of his public school competitors, to the satisfaction of the governor. He begins to think of his past revolts against authority. To be loyal to his fellow prisoners, he feels he cannot do what the governor expects him to, "Whose side are you on, anyway?" He stops within sight of the tape, is passed and loses the race. The lips of the shouting waving crowd are devoid of sound, as if he had switched off everything outside and was quite alone. His past had paralyzed his present; he had withdrawn from a world where movement forward was impossible (*The Loneliness of the Long Distance Runner*, Tony Richardson).

What affects us as silence need not be a total absence of sound. The words that pass between two people may be spaced, and the syrup of silence in which they float may outweigh the particles of sound (*Accident*, Joseph Losey). The solitude of an old woman living alone is filled with drops of water, slow soft tinkles on a harpsichord, a faint quarrel from upstairs, a distantly crying child, and a tap on the wall or ceiling. The remoteness of the sounds, and the long spans between, compose the silence (*The Whisperers*, Bryan Forbes).

23 Nondiegetic Sound—Projection and Reverie

Projecting into the world our inner fancies is a step further from walling part of it out. In the theater this presents a dilemma: which sound should the audience hear—

what one character hears, or what all the others hear? Take the well-known case of *The Bells*. Fifteen years from the stormy night on which Mathias killed the Polish Jew, just such a blizzard came again. Conversation turns to the Jew and the blizzard, and as he sits to eat his supper, Mathias hears once more the sleigh bells he heard as he followed the Jew to murder him:

MATHIAS. Do you not hear the sound of bells upon the road?
WALTER
HANS. *(Listening).* Bells? No!
CATHERINE. What is the matter, Mathias? You appear ill.[9]

The audience hear the bells too; the other players on the stage affect not to hear them.

Film here has the advantage of showing only the person who hears the sound. Craster hears from Lermontov that he is to write the music for *The Red Shoes* (Michael Powell and Emeric Pressburger). We see Craster's face in close-up. His gaze falls. Lermontov's voice is wiped clear by a sudden confused chord of music. Craster's eyes focus again on the impresario, and the music stops. Lermontov, a puzzled eye on Craster, slowly stops on the word "shoes."

There may not be an outer cue to start the fancied images. The streetcar of the backward boy in *Dodeska-Den* (Akira Kurosawa) is wholly prompted from within. The click as he mimes hanging up his watch, the hiss of the brake as he turns his wrist sideways, and the siren when he presses down his toe; these are real sounds but without visible source. When he bears down on the artist, and we see them both, the siren sound is one made by his mouth, which both hear. The artist hastily shifts his easel and is told he must not sit on the tracks.

In *Passionnelle* (Edmond T. Greville) Julien has dumped the corpse of a man murdered by the woman he loves. We see his feet in a flowing gutter, and hear the hiss of a whispering voice, "Police, police, assassin."

Many of the inner voices are soliloquies, nothing more abnormal than talking to oneself. It is an accepted convention that if a character is seen alone, his voice heard but his lips closed, that we are hearing unspoken thoughts, and the change from spoken to unspoken is quite clear.

Hamlet speaks the soliloquy, "O that this too too solid flesh would melt," with his lips closed, but for the lines, "Nay, not so much, not two," he uses lip movements. Once more he continues, lips closed, till he stands between the two chairs on the dais, a hand on each, when again he bursts out aloud,

and yet within a month—
Let me not think on't—Frailty, thy name is woman![10]

We thus are able to follow the train of unspoken thought that leads to the spoken lines (*Hamlet*, Laurence Olivier).[11]

Radev is speaking up to Aleksandrov's hospital window. His lips closed, we hear Aleksandrov's thoughts, "He is looking worn out . . . pretends to be gay. . . . I have doubts about being old . . ." During this, his face is replaced by that of Radev, mouthing words, but we are quite clear that we are still hearing Aleksandrov's voiced thoughts (*The White Room*, Metodi Andonov).

The inner words may be recollected, an anamnesis in sound.

Mahe comes home, finds his wife gone, pries open her trunk, and finds that it belongs to someone she has impersonated and possibly killed. As he drives back to town in his car, we hear his own voice, in unspoken thought, "I want my wife to use my account. . . . I have to see M. Hoardeau. . . . I know you are closed but I must see my account. . . . How much have I?" Another voice answers, "This morning you had twenty-eight million. . . ."—"How much have I left?"—"A hundred and fifty thousand francs. . . ." These events led up to what he is now doing (*Mississippi Mermaid*, François Truffaut).

A woman whose school has had to be closed because of the war walks into an empty dormitory. She stops at the end of a bed, we hear a coy child's voice, and she turns to left frame with a smile. Other voices come from the right. She turns, and with a smile, puts her finger to her lips. We hear running water. She quickly enters the bathroom, and runs along the handbasins, turning all the taps, none of which is running. No water runs indeed, even when she turns a tap on. It is reverie, projection, or something of both (*Portrait of a Woman*, Jacques Feyder).

If the remembered voices are sinister or obsessive, they may be distorted. When Chris Cross enters his room at the end of *Scarlet Street* (Fritz Lang), Kitty's voice echoes out of a great space. She had sold Cross's pictures to give money to Johnny. "Johnny, Johnny, I love you, Johnny . . . You killed me, Chris. . . ."

When dead people speak, we are using the figure *eidolopoeia*. After an air raid in Rouen, we pan along a row of coffins, each with a name and date, as rain is falling. As we pass each coffin and read the name, we hear the dead person's voice. *Elise Masson*, "I wish I could have lived to see peace. . . ." *Henri Laine*, "I left a wife and three children" (whom we are shown). *Jeanne*, "I was a couturier . . . next month I was to have been married." Then we see the mourners, two men and a woman, weeping (*Marie-Louise*, Leopold Lindtberg).

A common means of reinforcing, often the sole means of expressing, an inner state, is nondiegetic music. A man is on his way to meet the boat that brings his bride from France. He drives out of a tunnel, and as the white circle of day explodes to the edge of the screen, a joyous exuberant crash of music is heard (*Mississippi Mermaid*, François Truffaut).

The music may be so contrived that we are not sure whether or not it is diegetic. Finding he has only a year to live changes a clergyman's attitude toward advancement. He has entered a cathedral where he is to give a sermon on which (unknown to him) his fitness to be chaplain to a famous school is going to be judged. His eye rests on the stained glass window. The music (heard throughout the scene) is now exalted, his face content. He sees the pulpit and a frown of trepidation appears to evil omens in the music. The music thus responds to his mood, as nondiegetic music is able to, and yet it is played on the organ; he might well have been hearing it (*Nearer to Heaven*, Charles Frend).

VI   VISION—IN SLEEP—THE FILM AND THE DREAM

24   The Figure Vision

A vision is something that is seen otherwise than by ordinary sight, an obtrusion into conscious life, either from sleep or during an abnormal state.[12] It is also a figure, in which a past or future event is described, as if it were actually passing before the describer's eyes.[13] Owing to the film's natural present tense, any departure from the diegesis also gives the impression of happening now "before the describer's eyes."

Vision is considered under the headings of *Dreams*—Vision in the unconscious state, *Vision while awake,* and the *Recall of the past.*

25   Some Characteristics of the Dream

The film is, or certainly can be, dreamlike. I have for some time examined my dreams from this viewpoint. I hesitate to bare to the reader the secrets of my psyche, but I must support the statement. I observed these traits, mostly in a single dream:

i. *I see as through a first-person camera, with a strong sense of angle, and limited view.*
To the left, potting plants . . . was my mother. She asked me to help her . . . On my way down to the cellar through a trapdoor, my waist at floor level, I look up at her.

ii. *I know certain facts, not visually apparent. They might come in film from titles or commentary.*
A woman I felt was my mother, although she seemed taller and her face different . . . Ten packets arrived of what I knew were Petri dishes.

iii. *Scenes are enlarged in detail, as if in close-up.*
Out of a package no more than six inches long, I took a small gadget. It unfolded in my hand, and I knew it to be a respirator.

iv. *Simile by manipulation. The gadget becomes whatever I use it as.*
I set the respirator down on the lawn—it was a sunny summer day—and found a cord by which to start the motor. Despite pulling the cord and adjusting the only lever I could see, it would not start. . . . (The cord and the lever were not there when the gadget was first seen.) A passing postman sat beside the machine, now about a foot-and-a-half square. He adjusted the levers (now two) and it started. I backed the machine up. It now had four wheels and I was sitting on it.

v. *Ellipsis in time. I am in a different place, with no sign how I reached it, or any reason, in what went before, for being there.*
After opening the Petri dishes in the house, I then found myself outside, walking past University College, on the lawn outside which I found the package, one of a number . . .
It was now night. It stopped again, and the cord would not pull. I saw that, in backing, the exhaust had embedded itself in a pile of sand. Furious at this, I found a caretaker, and told him that the sand should not have been there. He brought a shovel, and as we walked, I became aware that, instead of one, there were now three walking in line beside me along a cloister. When we reached the place where the pile had been (I thought of it now as snow, for it was winter), it was gone.

vi. *A piling-up of situations may shadow forth an abstraction or the dreamer's feelings* (montage).
I am sitting for an examination . . . no subject is stated at the head of the question paper . . . I am writing on a spongy damp surface, on which neither pen nor pencil leave a mark . . . The lights go out, and I move my desk to the window . . . I try to write a description of the pineapples I see through the window, growing on trees, but the room is moving backwards, and they pass at such a speed that I cannot see them clearly. . . . The teacher in charge tells me that pineapples do not grow on trees . . . There is half an hour to go and I have written nothing . . . (The final message of all this together is the notion of difficulty, thwarting, and the inner state of the dreamer frustrated.)

vii. *My thoughts are projected in metaphors.*
I am speaking to Albert P. on the street. He is quiet, lean, and weathered. Now I am looking up to where he is standing, at the top of a slope fifty feet high. He rolls down to the bottom, and now, a wet, toadlike creature, gapes, picks himself up slowly, and

makes for a safe place, soft and vulnerable. (This is a metaphor for the kind of man I took him to be.)

I saw my father enter the door in uniform. I recognized a characteristic smell. He was robust and ungrayed, as he was when younger. He smiled in passing on, as if in approval of what I was doing. I was surprised, for I knew he was dead. Upstairs, I looked in the glass, and saw him reflected, instead of myself. As I realized the incongruity, my own image was superimposed on his, and kept going and coming. (The mirror is a common filmic metaphor.)

viii. *Superimposition.*

A military action is taking place in open country. A man's arm reaches across the screen from bottom left. It is transparent, and the battle is seen beyond it. Something like a lightning bolt flashes up across the forearm. A gap is seen just above the elbow and the forearm slowly disappears, leaving a stump at bottom left, which grows opaque. (A soldier, perhaps, remembering the battle in which he lost an arm.)

ix. *Various forms of the impossible (special effects).*

The two clusters of street lamps, which give out a pale eerie glow, glide from their places back into the court, and pass into a downstairs flat through wall or window.[14]

A red-headed man is floating in the air, and thrusts his head into a woman's snood, also floating there.

x. *A dream within a dream.*

I dreamed that I woke from a dream of my dead mother, with tears in my eyes, clear that I had seen a dream within a dream.

Readers will themselves have noticed other likenesses. We seldom sense the tension of muscles in dreams, and never in films. In one of my dreams, a boy of twelve began to tell a story, and when he spoke its last words, he was a young man in flight lieutenant's uniform, smoking a pipe, suggesting thus how long the telling took.

26 The Dream in Film[15]

Jean Mitry is reported as believing that film cannot convey a dream.[16] Some space must, therefore, be given to showing that in fact film has done so clearly and effectively.

There is a difference in quality between the life we lead in dreams and in actuality that a director tries to capture in various ways, in tone, color, movement, or editing.

In *The Shop on Main Street* (Janos Kadar), the young man who has been appointed custodian of an old Jewish widow's shop, drops off to sleep there. He fancies himself and her when she was younger going out of the shop and down the street, past where a band is playing. The images are in shades of white, and movement is slowed.

Moonbird (John Hubley) is a dream by two children of a bird escaped from its cage, which they try to recapture by leaving bait (sweets), digging a hole, and leaving open the door of its cage. The images are shadowy, transparent abstracts of the things they stand for, and are done in tones of blue. The bird when caught and led home in twice the size of the cage. The sound is the slow drowsy words of children to one another, that flows without stop or much change of pitch or pace, almost hypnotically.

Sindbad seems to be the broken dreams in his death moment (not his deathbed, for he dies in a cart) of a man given to loving and eating. This we take from the woman's remark, as she sends the cart back where it came from, "It looks like the end of him—Go back to your lover, Telka." There is no order of time in the scenes that follow—in some he is young, in some he is old. Some scenes are long enough to be lucid wholes: he eats a huge meal, as the waiter tells of his wife's leaving him;

Sindbad at the end informs the waiter that he was the man she went to. Other scenes are glimpses, like the flower girl who threw herself from a window. While Sindbad is with one woman, there is a quick flash of another, as perhaps he suddenly thinks of her. Most frustrating are the flashes, only a few frames long, barely long enough to take in the contents and never long enough to discern the meaning they may have had for Sindbad; a drop of red oil, a flower, a patch of lichen, a naked woman rolling toward us. They may be pieces of other episodes, brought back by what is happening now, a director's commentary, or things remembered merely for their beauty. [17]

A difficulty seems to be that it is only after we wake that we notice any lack of relevance and reason in a dream's happenings. While we are dreaming, we accept the course of events with as little surprise as we do what occurs in our waking life. The artistic problem seems to be to present a montage of incoherence, and yet give us a Godlike view, by which we see its logic. Merely editing in a flash of a flower during the flow of a scene does not in itself confer value or meaning on it. Baffled viewers find little pleasure in being told, as enigmatic editing does, how much more perceptive the director is than they are. The film, nonetheless, for all its enigmas, is one of great senuous beauty and creates a mood of nostalgic melancholy (*Sindbad*, Zoltan Huszarik).

A dream is a non-diagetic metaphor or chain of metaphors for a state of mind, often one of anxiety, whose roots in experience are sometimes easily traced. Anders has spent all his money in buying fish for an otter hidden in the barn. We see the boy's restless head on the pillow. We then see his pet's head, huge, guzzling endless fish in speeded movement, and hear the loud slosh of mastication. We approach the boy's head. We hear the ominous voice of his teacher, and he wakes with a cry. (Arithmetic was giving him trouble too.) (*The Great Adventure*, Arne Sucksdorff). A widower from a farm finds life with his son in the city aimless and oppressive. In long underwear, the widower lies in bed, tossing. Through the small pane on the door of an elevator, we see his face as he bangs on the door. From inside, one floor after another passes the window. Back in bed, the widower suddenly sits up, sweating. Confined in a small space, and unable to escape—this was how he felt his life to be (*Tree without Roots*, Hristo Hristov).

Metaphors are combined and worked out at greater length in *Wild Strawberries* (Ingmar Bergman). Professor Borg, a man advanced in years, tells us of a strange dream he had the night before he set out for Lund. As we hear his voice, we see the images: "During my morning walk, I lost my way, and found myself . . ." He stops in a street empty of people, and looks up at a clock above the walk. It is shaped like a pocket watch, but without hands. He pulls out his own watch, and it too has no hands. During this we hear the double thud of heartbeats. He looks up the street, and we see in an otherwise deserted square, a man dressed in black, who stands with his back toward us. Borg approaches and places a hand on the man's shoulder. The man turns to reveal a head, egglike in shape and smoothness, with fine lines for features, all crinkled up and eyes closed. Borg looks down, and there the man lies, his frail head cracked and bleeding dark liquid. We hear a knell tolling. A driverless hearse comes round a corner into sight. A rear wheel of the hearse catches a lamp post, the axle is tugged again and again against the post. At last the wheel is wrenched off, rolls toward the watching Borg and shatters. The coffin stirs and creaks on the sloped floor of the hearse. With a sudden start, the horses trot away, the coffin slides off on the road, the lid bumps loose and a hand is jolted out. Struck by the strangeness of this, Borg approaches the coffin and bends over it. The head moves, and the hand from the coffin grasps his. In a series of close-ups, we see in turn Borg's face and the one upside down within the coffin: they are the same. He wakes to the ticking of a clock. The meaning is clear: the stop of time, the fragility of the body, and the dreamer face to face with his own death.

A psychoanalyst may be put in the cast for our benefit. Liza Elliott floats in space, and the floor has dissolved into a wilderness of mist with two leafless trees. Her costume suggests a man's tail coat. She comes to a coffin-like box, labeled on top, "Editor-in-Chief. Private." (This was her work.) From a rope trailing behind her, she takes a key, at which the lid of the coffin slowly opens to let out a blue dress, which floats away. She runs after and catches the dress, clasps it, and circles round with it; suddenly she is wearing it. How does her analyst interpret this? When she was five, she heard a man say that she could not possibly be her mother's child, so plain was she, so beautiful her mother. Soon after that her mother died, and Liza sought to console her father, to whom she was devoted, by putting on her mother's blue dress, which her father, she knew, had liked. He was angry. "How dare you wear that dress. Don't ever do that again," he said. She felt that the man she had loved most had turned on her. At school, only once had a boy taken her out, and he had left her during the evening for another girl. From then on, she had "never been interested in men." She did well in her studies, found a man-size job as editor of a magazine, and wore mannish suits. She strove to escape hurt by not competing with women for men's affections. The analyst unlidded the coffin and gave her back the power to love that she had striven to bury (*Lady in the Dark*, Mitchell Leisen).

Dreams allow the escape which life does not. In *Les Belles de Nuit* (René Clair), a music teacher who can find no one to perform his compositions is beset by pneumatic drills and motorcycles outside his window, pursued by well-intentioned friends concerned for his sanity, and invaded by bailiffs repossessing his piano. He escapes into dreams. There he is a famous composer in prerevolutionary France about to elope with a beautiful heiress, a member of the Foreign Legion making perilous love in a harem, and so on. The dream stories are straightforward narratives in the present tense, more like waking imaginings, but, especially near the end, the switches from one dream to another, the attempts to return to an interrupted dream, and the insistent guillotine of reality capture the dream's abrupt shifting of time and place.

Dreams give us the power that life denies. A surly shopkeeper refuses to pay boys for bottles returned, or to let a little boy fetch his kitten from the cellar where it had strayed. In the boy's dream, he is standing beside a very important official, in front of a huge crowd. The official (in dumb show) makes the merchant bring out the kitten, take the bottles in, bring out the money, and even go in again for the empty bag. The merchant is given a scolding and is suitably humbled. Speech is replaced by music (*Porcupines Are Born without Quills*, Dimiter Petrov).

An old man has been taken off his post as a hall porter, where in gold braid he commanded some prestige, because he is no longer able to lift and carry trunks. After his daughter's wedding, he is sitting bemused by wine, when a smile comes over his face. He is in his uniform and the hotel's revolving doors, vertically stretched, are superimposed on his face. Six porters lift a trunk from the roof of a taxi. He approaches and waves them away. He seizes the trunk by the handle at one end, and hoists it without effort, and carries it toward us, balanced vertically. He floats through the revolving doors with trunk still poised, all vaguely out of focus. Superimposed are guests and members of the staff standing in the lobby, applauding. He throws the trunk into the air in slowed motion, and catches it as it falls. Then we dissolve back to him at home smiling (*The Last Laugh*, F. W. Murnau).

The change from dreamless to dreaming sleep is shown in *Little Friend* (Berthold Viertel), as well as the way in which, hearing sounds as we wake, we devise dream images to match them. The film begins with a flickering white flame pouring from the bottom of the screen, widening toward the top, against a dark ground, a metaphor for the sleeping dreamless mind. The flame grows and broadens, flowing smoothly. Momentary white spots now come and go in the field around it, each to the sound of a light metallic tick. The heart of the flame opens to show an oval glow like a candle wick. A number of brief shots follows, nearly all taken looking up. A man with a sweeping gesture of his hand says, "No children here." Three stern landladies all say the same, "No children here." A scholastic gentleman with beribboned glasses points to us and says, "No schoolchildren here." A policeman with a large hand says, "Go away." An inspector, flanked by a constable, both canted obliquely in the frame, points his finger and says in a loud voice, "For the last time I tell you . . ." A child suddenly wakes in a dark room, and hears faintly from beyond the door of her room, "For the last time I tell you I won't stand for it." The child cries "Mummy" and there is silence. There is a pause and the door opens. The child's mother comes in to soothe her, and a man in dinner jacket is seen in the open door.

An event that wakes the dreamer up is sometimes quickly changed into a lengthy happening. Bridie Quilty awakes from a dream in which she reenacts some of her doings of the day, ending with tipping a dead man down the face of a cliff toward us, out of a wheelchair. She starts up in bed, suddenly awake and frightened, and we cut to the fireplace, where the dead man's hat, which she had hidden in the chimney, is seen sliding down into the fireplace with a cloud of soot, the sound of which we assume has awakened her (*I See a Dark Stranger*, Frank Launder). It is a sound heard in waking (not an image) that alters into the tail sound of a dream: here a likeness in images is used by hypallage for a likeness in sound.

The capacity to move in time, during dreaming, in either direction, forwards or backwards, has, curiously enough, been seen in film less than would be expected.[18] *Dead of Night* has been discussed.[19] *Flesh and Fantasy* (Julien Duvivier) also touches on it. Just before a performance, the Great Gaspar dreams of walking his tightrope. He is seen from the ground, slightly out of focus. One stage dissolves to another, till he slips and falls to the ground in slow motion. A woman screams, and there is a long rapid approach to the audience, to the one woman in black where the rest are gray, to a close-up of her ear alone, from which hangs a lyre-shaped earring. Gaspar sits up on his couch, startled. As he enters the big top, and again as he walks the tightrope, we see him on the left half of the screen falling in slowed motion. Some time later, he sees the woman he dreamed of, wearing the lyres on her ears.

Neither stage nor literature has been able to capture as vividly as film the dream's obsessiveness; its minuteness of detail; its unpredictable shifts of place, person, and event; its transformations; the concreteness it gives the impossible; its inventions of metaphors in which to vent our anxieties, and at the same time to invest it all with the unsurprised logic, which a dream, for all its fantasy, holds for the dreamer while the dream lasts.

27 Dreamlike Films

Films that are not said to be dreams may wear the marks of a dream; for dreams are often extended metaphors that express feelings, and films, in a more conscious way, are often the same.

The Blood of a Poet (Jean Cocteau) does not profess to be a dream. No accepted convention is used that might suggest this. A chimney starts collapsing as the film starts, and reaches ground in the last shot of the film, so that what is between is an instant of thought, as a dream well may be. Irrational or impossible incidents happen—the lips of a drawing move, they are wiped off by a hand and stick to its palm, the eyes of a statue open, and a child steps off the top of a ladder to stay on the ceiling.

The mood of *The Red Shoes* (Michael Powell and Emeric Pressburger) ballet is one of evil wizardry. After the girl wearing the shoes leaves the bustling fair, a cluster of Arabs carry away her lover. A clawing shadow on the empty street draws her away from her blind mother. In open country with contorted clouds, night spreads. A newspaper swirls up from the ground and becomes a man, on whose mast-forehead is printed *Le Journal*. He dances with her and swirls back down again to flatness. Dancers in yellowish animal skins with hideous masks close in on her. The demon shoemaker who gave the shoes gives her a knife, but as she slashes at the shoes that force her to dance, it becomes a leafy twig (pl. 38).

In Buster Keaton's films, events that could never really happen, happen before our eyes, and, more than this, are taken for granted as normal, as in a dream. He leaps through a double hoop, on which a dress is spread, and lands on the other side in an old woman's weeds. He stops at a safe, turns the combination lock, opens up, and walks through the safe to the street. Riding on the handlebars of a policeman's motorcycle, he has not seen the policeman bounced off the saddle into a ditch. The machine with Keaton goes on ahead. Reaching the other side of a level crossing just before a train sweeps across it, he says to the driver that isn't, "I never thought you'd make it" (*Sherlock Junior*, Buster Keaton).

The frustration that often shapes the events of our dreams dogs the engineer of *The General* (Buster Keaton and Clyde Bruckman) as he chases a stolen train. Coupled behind is a flat car, on which there is a mortar. He loads the mortar, aims it to fire over the engine, and lights its fuse. He unwittingly uncouples the car, which nonetheless keeps following closely. The mortar, by little nods, drops its elevation to aim at him. Hastily climbing up to go back to the cab, his foot is caught in the loop of a chain, and he is hove to on the back wall of the tender, a target for the mortar.

VII   VISION—IN THE WAKING STATE—REVERIE

28   Dream and Reverie

In a work that may have come from the pen of Longinus, vision is said to be "When the imagination is so warmed and affected, that you seem to behold yourself the very things you are describing, and to display them to the life before the eyes of an audience."[20] The figure is still so described in the twentieth century.[21]

Pity thy offspring, mother, nor provoke
Those vengeful Furies to torment thy son.
What horrid sights! How glare their bloody eyes!
How twisting snakes curl round their venom'd heads![22]

I see before me the slaughtered heaps of citizens lying unburied in the ruined country. The furious countenance of Cethegus rises to my view, while with a savage joy he is triumphing in your miseries.[23]

Is this a dagger which I see before me,
The handle towards my hand? Come let me clutch thee.
I have thee not—and yet I see thee still.[24]

The vision may be something vividly imagined, projected on, or transforming the outer world, or drawn from memory. There is a relative disappearance of the outer world as what is imagined grows in vividness. A vision presupposes a person who sees it. Where what is seen is something remembered, the vision resembles the flashback or anamnesis, a nonpersonal narrative device of the director to be dealt with later.

It is rare to find the traits of the dream in the reverie, which is more under conscious control. Its events are closer to those of actual life. Any playing fast and loose with actuality we take for mental unbalance.

i. *Substitution.* It is a common experience that when we imagine a person or scene, our awareness of our immediate surroundings, even with eyes open, sinks to zero. There is a disappearance of the actual, and what we envision completely takes its place. In film it would be a cut from the outer scene to an inner.

Cleo, a singer, is walking down the street. The first-person camera records the passers-by who look toward us. We hear the click of our heels. Suddenly, from time to time, in place of the passing people, we see Cleo's lover, her maid, the two men who have written and composed a song for her, the wig she has taken off and left by her mirror. These are unmoving, seen in full face, and are clearly different from those who pass on the street (*Cleo from Five to Seven*, Agnes Varda).

In the same way, Gaber Zaidan, waking in the morning, sees, instead of the room around him, his brother in army uniform, striding briskly in the bright sun of a desert. Later, a street in Cairo, along which he is walking, is replaced by a flash of his brother's head, streaming with blood (*The Sparrow*, Youssef Chahine).

The visions here were clearly set off against reality by contrast—in movement, lighting, place, and what was happening.

Despite the switch from the world the person shares with others to one apparent only to himself, the same set of eyes is doing the seeing in either case, which links the otherwise unconnected shots. If the switch, however, is not from a shot of what a person is looking at but from a shot of the person who is looking, we are not seeing through the same eyes in both shots. We cannot assume that a person's face is always followed by a shot of what he is thinking: it may be what he is looking at, or it may be a mere cut to another scene. Even closing off the imagined images by showing again the face we saw at the start will not, without other hints, make the shots in between a reverie, for the screen image of all the shots is equally real.

Some means of distinction is needed for a lucid syntax, and one possible means is sound. Luis is lying back in a dentist's chair in *Blindfolded* (Carlos Saura). He is a stage director and a member of a commission which is bringing to light acts of terrorism. A strong light whitens his face, and the dentist begins drilling. The glare of the light fills the screen. This is cut to a woman, her hands tied, and strips of adhesive tape are across her eyes. The screen image cuts to and fro between the seated man being treated by the dentist and the seated woman under duress by inquisitors, and in the last we see of her she is fleeing across rough ground, pursued by three men, who catch her, and as they drive her away, tape her eyes. Then the passage ends with Luis in the dentist's chair. Without more, this could be two events occurring at the same time, but there is more: the sound of the dentist's drill has continued unbroken through all the shots of the woman, and now, on the last return to Luis, it stops. The sound belongs to only one of the two flows of action cut together, and keeps us in the dentist's chair with Luis. It maintains a continuity of place, person, and situation as we see in turn the outer man and what he is thinking.

In *No Reason to Stay* (Mort Ransen) the unbroken sound is not heard but suggested. A teacher speaks of the spread of Christianity. Christopher Wood, a pupil, does not seem to be listening. We cut to soldiers in battle, black men rioting, piles of burning books, a woman dying in Indochina, an airplane dropping incendiary bombs, and other such scenes. Here, instead of the classroom sound continuing over the imagined images, it occurs by prolepsis only at the end of the reverie, as the teacher, observing Christopher's inattention, imposes his voice clearly and loudly on the distant scenes, and then in person replaces the daydreams. "What was the third cause of the spread of Christianity?" the teacher asks. Becoming gradually aware of the voice before we see the speaker, whose role had been well established before the start of the reverie, our sense is that the voice had never stopped. We can hardly escape the sound and feel of a dentist's drill, but most of the time, as we daydream, fancy obliterates the sound as well as sight of what is around us.

ii. *Thinker and thought both seen at once.* Thinker and thought may be shown at the same time, instead of one after the other.

A copy of Charlie steps out from the one that stays in his chair. The copy kicks the tightrope walker who is making a more successful play for Merna, knocks him down as he turns, and kisses Merna before sinking back into the quietly dreaming Charlie, still in his chair (*The Circus*, Charles Chaplin).

During a game of anagrams, Beaky builds up the words *Mud, Mudder, Murder.* As Lina sees the last word completed, we see superimposed steep cliffs, the sea below, Johnny pushing Beaky over the edge, Beaky falling, his coattails swept up, sea and cliffs fleeting past him, and we hear choking and gasping. She stands and faints (*Suspicion*, Alfred Hitchcock).

A riveter working on the hull of a ship stops for a moment, and we see superimposed on him the passengers-to-be playing deck tennis, knitting, reclining in deck chairs, and dancing to a band. The riveter mutters, "dressed in natty clothes— wonder if they'll ever think of the men that made it" (*Shipyard*, Paul Rotha).

iii. *Inner and projected visions.* Some visions are wholly generated in the mind of the character; some are cued by, and projected on, something they see in their surroundings.

Having partly opened the general manager's door, Harold overhears him say he would pay a thousand dollars to anyone who could find a way of bringing more people into the store. There is a dissolve from Harold's head in the partly open door to his roommate climbing the face of a building, and back to Harold again (*Safety Last*, Fred Newmeyer and Sam Taylor).

A railway signal failing to work has caused a collision. The signal is a metal disk with a black dot at upper right. From the window of his cab, the signalman shakes his fist at the disk and cries, "Assassin." The disk now shows another dot at the left, which makes a pair of eyes, below it a faint crooked nose and a leering mouth. This personification gives us his mood, whether or not he believed he saw the face (*La Roue*, Abel Gance).

Stranded in the desert when their car stops, Laurel and Hardy see on the sand a pair of skeletons. These dissolve to Laurel and Hardy asleep in the same posture, and then back. We see the two looking glum—will this be their fate (*Jitterbugs*, Mal St. Clair)?

In *The Manxman* (Alfred Hitchcock), Peter's wife has left him for love of another man (the deemster). She is not in when he comes home. His eye is caught by the dinner table. One place is set, and a second setting dissolves in and out opposite the other chair, her chair. Why is only one place set?

Captain Ross, on a rescue tug bound for a damaged merchantman, is convinced that its breach of radio silence has doomed him. He sees his dead predecessor entering his bridge, when it is in fact, and later changes into, the radio operator (*The Key*, Sir Carol Reed).

Whether or not they are used so in reality, mirrors or blank spaces in film are used for screens that invite projected thoughts. In a close-up of the fire on which she is burning bits of a doll, Lori Brandon sees on the back wall her initiation as a witch. Later, when she is looking into a mirror, she sees, in place of the normal reflection, the continuation of the ceremony. There is more here, of course, than mere projection: the image may have been conjured by witchcraft (*Necromancy*, Bert I. Gordon).

iv. *Hallucinations* (pl. 32). Whether it is the director making visible for us the thoughts of his characters, or whether what we see is an image projected on the outer world by someone during an abnormal mental state, and which he believes is really there, the same quality of realism is usually given the image, and only the circumstances, including the character's behavior or state of mind, can tell us which is intended. This is laying out of consideration cases where ghosts or departed spirits are shown transparent by superimposition, and the character knows that what he sees is physically nonexistent, as when Ulysses talks to the shades of Teiresias, of Elpenor and his mother (*Ulysses*, television, Franco Rossi). The following visions are certainly hallucinations; one or two of the above may also be.

Mrs. Verloc has fainted. She opens her eyes and looks round at the circle of heads above her. Her dead brother's head and shoulders appear in the space between two of the heads. As she walks the street, he runs toward and past her, but when he turns, it is someone else (*Sabotage*, Alfred Hitchcock). Men materialize from nowhere and lie beside a paranoid schizophrenic woman, no sound heard but the quiet ticking of a clock. As she leans on a wall, hands thrust through the plaster and clasp her breasts (*Repulsion*, Roman Polanski).

Oddmund, the guide for twelve escaping men, leaves them in order to take the girl he loves back to safety. He comes back to find that all have fallen over a cliff and perished. Years later, his guilt brings him back to where it happened. The twelve pervade the place. He is always seeing the seemingly interminable procession of skiers darkening the snow of the present: crossing near us; as distant specks below in the valley; trudging away from us, heads down, to lose themselves in a snowy haze, or coming faceless toward us. They never become people, only an obsessive pattern, the symbol of Oddmund's remorse (*Cold Tracks*, Arne Skouen).

It is about the time when Itsuki, in Paris, learns that he has an incurable cancer, that he often sees a beautiful woman in a black kimono somewhere near him. She reminds him of things he has forgotten to do or see, of friends, and of the cherry blossoms. She says she is his alter ego. She is a memento mori, and, as Dr. Johnson has reminded us, there is nothing like the imminence of death to sharpen our thoughts (*Kaseki*, Masaki Kobayashi).

v. *Faces.* The distinction between the director's projection and that of a character is perhaps most interestingly studied in the use of faces.

Manuela's mother is dead, and her yearning for a mother has been transferred to Fraulein von Bernburg, who has treated her kindly. The headmistress disapproves, and has insisted that the mistress tell the girl never to speak to her again. "Good-bye, dear Fraulein von Bernburg," Manuela says, and with sagging head she slowly passes beyond the door jamb and out of sight. Groups of girls are seen talking, concerned about her. Von Bernburg offers her resignation to the headmistress: "I cannot bear to see these children frightened the way they are." While she is doing this, Manuela is climbing the stairs toward us, murmuring the Lord's Prayer. At the landing she looks around as if in a dream. In an up shot of the stairwell, whose height has been planted in three previous incidents, girls are heard shouting; in a down shot, Manuela is hanging over the rail, and girls are crowding the lower landings. In the head-mistress's study, von Bernburg's face in close-up slowly dissolves into that of Man-uela. The fraulein rushes out of the study. In a full-length shot, Manuela is outside the railing, in a posture of crucifixion, her eyes closed, her head askew. Girls are looking up, "Manuela is crazy." On the upper landing, the girls surge in to grasp her and pull her back. Throughout the dissolve, the outer line of the face remains the same: only the features inside it alter. From this persistence, we feel the closeness between the two persons, and something like a message passing between them. Simple but masterly (*Mädchen in Uniform*, Leontine Sagan).

"Yes, it is easy; just a plunge, and it is all over . . ." We hear an echoing voice, and then see a down shot of water, with Henrietta and a bearded face reflected upside down. Then in an actual shot of her and the old man, his voice no longer echoes. He takes her to a shop that sells masks. She picks out a "sweet appealing face" (which covers a sharp shrewish one). A friend has told her that she is mean, spiteful, and ugly, bent on making other people unhappy. This was a last chance, but the mask had to be back in the shop by midnight. She meets a discouraged law student about to go to sea, and persuades him to start again. When the hour comes to take the mask off, she is afraid to, but finds that her own face has changed. The owner chases them out of the shop, and in the window they see, and we approach it, the face mask of the old man who had counseled her (*Flesh and Fantasy*, Julien Duvivier).

Here it is the director who has used the face to tell us of inner imaginings—of the danger of someone not present and of a possible new personality. Now it is a person in the story who projects a fancied resemblance onto a real face and responds as if it were true.

Gippo betrays Frankie, to get money for Katie to go to America. As he sits in an Irish *shebeen*, opposite an English girl, her face dissolves into Katie's. He has drunk too much. He gives her five pounds to go home to England (*The Informer*, John Ford).

A similar confusion of two women is conveyed by Ingmar Bergman by having both parts played by the same actress. Professor Borg returns at the age of seventy to the house where he spent his youth, and sees in reverie, the girl Sara, whom he had loved but who later married his brother. As he resumes his drive to Lund, where he is to receive an honorary doctorate, he gives a ride to a young woman of the same name, Sara, and the two young men with whom she is traveling to Italy. He gains pleasure from finding that she likes him. She confides that she finds it hard to decide which of her two companions to marry. She enjoys his stories and is impressed by his coming doctorate. He in turn is taken by her simple, frank, tenderhearted youth-fulness and relish for life. She and her friends watch him receive his degree, and that night below his window, they sing to him. In dressing gown, he goes to the French window, opens it, and looks down. She calls up to him. The two men leave, and in the darkness of the garden she stands alone in white. We are not sure which of the two Saras he feels he is hearing, when she says, "Isak, it's you I really love, today, tomorrow, and always," for both Saras are played by the same person. Indeed, so much does the past suffuse the present, that the journey to Lund is almost a single reverie (*Wild Strawberries*).

vi. *Reverie in structure.* Some films are built on recurring patterns of reverie.

Walter Mitty escapes in daydreams from the fecklessness that blights his daily doings. In dramatic tones we hear a narrator: "Dr. Walter Mitty approaches the operating table . . ." A warm welcome, "So glad you've come, Mr. Mitty. Dr. Burlington, Dr. Remington. . . Mr. Walter Mitty." When the anaesthetic machine stops, Mitty asks a nurse for her fountain pen and uses it to replace a broken part. "That will hold for ten minutes," he says with calm assurance. A nurse murmurs worshipfully, "He is not only the greatest surgeon in the world, but a mechanical genius." One of the surgeons exclaims, "Correopsis has set in. Poor devil! Will you take over, Mr. Mitty?" "If you wish . . . There is only one chance in a million." "You mean the operation that Heintzleman performed on a rabbit?" And as Mitty operates, he asks the nurse for things his mother had asked him to buy on the way home, speaking with a surgeon's curt command, "Sock stretcher . . . sprinkling can . . . cheese grater . . . floor wax . . . number 2 thread . . . needles."

In a like manner, his fancy fired by a headline, a billboard, or a word heard, he dreams off into other heroic roles (*The Secret Life of Walter Mitty*, Norman Z. McLeod).

Morgan envies the simpler problems of the higher primates, and escapes from his own by donning a gorilla suit. At last he rides his motorcycle into the Thames, and clambers, dripping, up stacks of reinforcing rods. He wrestles his head mask off and lies exhausted. Now his fantasies turn bitter. His former wife's present husband, cigar in mouth, drives a locomotive crane up with aplomb, its arm trailing a strait-jacket. Morgan, inserted into the jacket by a policeman, is lowered into a barber's chair, which stands ringed by heaps of metal refuse. "Have you anything to say?" asks the policeman. "I just can't remember," says Morgan. Large poster pictures of Lenin, Trotsky, Stalin, and Marx, on which his parents brought him up, fill the screen as loudspeakers intone quotations liturgically. His parents expected him to lead the revolution, instead of which he became an artist, lost his wife, and aped the apes. What look like nineteenth-century workingmen rise from behind the refuse and level rifles at him to the sound of "Tannenbaum" and marching feet. His former wife rides in, brandishing a rifle. The reverie done, he scrambles up a pile of empty cans, his face in agony, perhaps from effort, perhaps from the bitterness of having failed in everything (pl. 33) (*Morgan*, Karel Reisz).

Some films are nearly all one continuous reverie.

The Cabinet of Dr. Caligari (Robert Wiene) is the tale of the doctor's criminal use of hypnosis. Only at the end of the film do we learn that the teller of the story is a mental patient, and we notice that the face of the doctor in charge of the hospital is the same as Caligari's. Seen briefly at the end, the medical director walks relaxed, erect, his toes out, his mien commanding. As a character in the patient's imaginings, his gait is jerky and pigeon-toed, his shoulders hunched, and his mien furtive. He moves through a town whose walls are warped, windows wedge-shaped, buildings askew and shadows artificially curved, and beyond them back-drops painted with stylized woods, roofs, or walls; furniture is vague or scanty; it is a world only dimly present. People in authority sit on high stools. The resemblance between the director and Caligari, and the reappearance in the dayroom of the hospital of those we were told had been killed, are further clues to the story's inner origin.

Zero de Conduite (Jean Vigo) is clearly a dreamlike film, though whose projection it is, is not expressly stated. But when we observe that the rituals are without significance, the deeds without reason, that other absurdities are found in the conduct of teachers and that a life without restaint is lived by the pupils, it can fairly certainly be taken as a schoolboy's reverie. The headmaster wears a beard nearly as long as he and a bowler hat carefully stored in a huge bell jar, to which he makes obeisance. His dwarflike stature and long-reaching steps make his attempts at majesty unimpressive. He is given to unpredictable manic phases, and he sits on a high stool behind his desk. A new teacher stands on his hands on his desk, and, balancing on one hand, he draws on the blackboard. The second row of chairs on prize day is filled with stuffed and painted effigies. These are all derisive images (pl. 34).

29   Collective or Mass Vision

The Wedding (Andrzej Wajda) is set in the Polish landscape, where armies and conquerors have marched for a thousand years. Wine and exhilaration, and later weariness, seem to evoke strange visions in the guests at a wedding party. Inside the crowded room, guests in half-length, vigorously dance the polka to the beat of an orchestra. Outside, the ground around the house is not long losing itself in a ruddy mist, in which all that stands out clearly is a line of sheaves, standing erect and alert like visored sentinels. All we hear of the music is a far-off bass beat, with a vague treble haze lurking obscurely behind it. Three riders in uniform, carrying carbines, ride silently up to us from out the mist, as if the softness of it had muffled their hoofs; they gallop into the mist again to vanish. The bridegroom is a poet who is marrying a peasant girl, and he, a playwright, and another poet sally outside into the intriguing mist. They and a stableman, a little girl, and an editor all suddenly see people wearing costumes two centuries old. The editor glimpses among the dancers a red-lit man, in the clothes of a jester. He talks to the man, pursues him through the crowd, and loses him through a trap in the roof. The bridegroom sees a man with bloody hands, a king with a scepter and a table covered with coins, who talks of the czarina's bastards. Another sees the severed heads of men being passed through a hatch, and being paid for with a couple of coins each by a languid soldier who puts the heads by the hair into a large basket. Through the window another sees the Hetman, "I have come with orders . . . I am the leader of your peasants' revolt . . ." He leaves a golden horn and a young man gallops into the mist with it, his mission being to arouse the peasants. Pikes are handed out from under the hay. The little girl sees the straw men right at the window ledge as the window swings. The young man is back by dawn, but the golden horn has vanished. The pikes have fallen from the hands of the drowsy revelers, and the magic, like the mist, has lifted in the light of morning.

VIII.   PAST AND FUTURE—ANAMNESIS AND PROMNESIS[25]

30   Anamnesis

Anamnesis is "a figure whereby the speaker calling to mind matters past, whether of sorrow, joy, &c, doth make recital of them."[26] It has also been used in medicine as a term for the past history of an illness, as told by the patient himself.

And on the tenth dark night the gods brought me nigh the isle Ogygia, where Calypso of the braided tresses dwells, an awful goddess . . . There I abode for seven years continually, and watered with my tears the imperishable raiment that Calypso gave me. But when the eighth year came round in his course . . . she sent me forth on a well-bound raft . . . For ten days and seven I sailed . . .[27]

> Once more I came to Sarum Close . . .
> 'Twas half my home, six years ago.
> The six years had not alter'd it. . . .
> And some one in the Study play'd
> The Wedding-March of Mendelssohn.
> And there it was I last took leave:
> 'Twas Christmas: I remember'd now
> The cruel girls, who feign'd to grieve,
> Took down the evergreens; and how
> The holly into blazes woke
> The fire, lighting the large, low room,
> A dim, rich lustre of old oak
> And crimson velvet's glowing gloom.[28]

31 Anamnesis I—Beginning at the End—Narrative

We may be shown the end of a story, and then by anamnesis told how it came about. This is also hysteron-proteron, the cart before the horse. It may be the end of a life, or one phase of a life, or the end of a thing like a ship, but in any case, a past requires a point of departure in a present, and, unless ambiguous time is part of the story, the relation between the two must, in some way, be made clear.

There are many ways of beginning at the end; death is an obvious one. A tank commander is blown up in pursuing retreating Germans over a bridge, and the rest of the film is his life up till then in chronological order (*The Rake's Progress*, Sidney Gilliatt). *Sunset Boulevard*, (Billy Wilder) starts misleadingly with police finding a corpse, which, as we learn at the end, is that of the person telling the story. As the story moves from diegetic speech to his narration, the action takes on a personal color. "He was a top producer and had a couple of ulcers to prove it . . . An old house has an unhappy look . . . She sat coiled up like a watch spring."

We see a destroyer built, and we see it sunk, and the rest of the film takes place in the time between. The survivors of the sunken vessel are seen holding on to a raft. For each of seven episodes, we dissolve from one of the survivors to a scene he remembers, whose image at the start is rippling as if seen through or on water. Each of the first three anamneses deals with one man (Captain Kinross, Chief Petty Officer Hardy, and Ordinary Seaman Blake). At the end of each episode, we come back to the raft by a rippled image (*In Which We Serve*, Noël Coward and David Lean).

The present, like a detective story, may pose a question, the answer to which is found, piece by piece, in flashbacks. Colonel Merton finds that the man who has broken into his rooms and then bolts, thinking the colonel has called the police, had served under him during the war. His curiosity aroused, he goes to see four ex-servicemen whom he thinks would have known the man, Ginger Edwards. What each man knows of Ginger is shown in flashback. At the fourth place, he finds Ginger himself, by which time we have come to understand why Ginger broke into the colonel's rooms (*Intruder in the Dust*, Guy Hamilton).

The subtleties and forms of anamnesis are explored in the work of Akira Kurosawa. The story in *The Rashomon Gate* is told on three levels. The pillars of the gate are fallen, its roof broken, the square littered with wreckage. It is pouring rain, and the two depressed men who have taken refuge there are joined by a third. Of these, the firewood gatherer, upset by what he has heard at the police station, starts telling of what happened in the forest, "There were three of them . . ." After the tale is told, the three men discuss it. The discussion is Level A. Level B in flashback is what the firewood gatherer found in the forest. In Level C, each of the witnesses describes the incident as he saw it, kneeling against a wall, speaking directly to us, as if to the police (whom we never see)—the priest, the bandit with hands tied behind his back, the wife of the traveler attacked by the bandit, and lastly a medium, who makes mystic manipulations and becomes the channel through which the husband— the traveler—tells us his story. The medium falls at the end, as the husband says he kills himself. As each speaks, we see on the screen his account of what happened. All three levels are intricately intercut—each of the five retellings adding to what we know, each putting its teller in the best light, and each inconsistent with the others. The group at the gate is morally perturbed both at the incident and the lies it engendered.

Kanji Watanabe never missed a working day for thirty years, and as a civil servant he avoided making decisions, passing anything contentious on to someone else. In a first set of flashbacks he finds out that, having cancer, he has at most six months to live. He learns too that his son's family is chiefly concerned with his money, generous though he has been to them. We see father and son at various times: when the boy is eight, and his mother dies, when the boy is playing baseball, during an operation, and when the boy leaves for the front in wartime. We see Watanabe's receiving a watch for twenty-five years' service. Disturbed at hearing of his illness, he misses work for the first time. The only kindness he meets is from a girl clerk in his office, who is soon bored with him. When they last have dinner together, something she says arouses in him a desire to push through, before he dies, a petition for a park, one of the matters he has been putting off deciding. The second set of flashbacks arises out of the wake or *tsuya*, after his death, and sketches the events of his last months. Each of these anamneses (twelve or so) follows a remark made by one of the guests:

> Wouldn't take no for an answer. My chief used to run when he saw him coming.
> Even more amazing . . . a section chief defying the mayor.
> I saw him one day on the park site.
> Must have known he had cancer. . . . I remember what he said one day.

Last was the constable who brought in his hat:

> I met him last night on the parksite, sitting on a swing in the snow. I thought him drunk.
> But he looked so happy, singing sadly in a voice that went to my heart (*Ikiru*).

The ways of quilting together past and present are limited only by the line at which they begin to bewilder the viewer. A more intricate example is *Seven Beauties* (Lina Wertmüller). A young, good-looking man, the pride of his family, but over-proud of himself:

> i. kills a pimp exploiting his sister;
> ii. is arrested, and expects death;

iii. pleads insanity, enters a mental hospital, and when war begins, receives a new test, and is released, as a sane convict, into the army;

iv. is captured, and avoids the flogging and other rigors of prison camp by pretending to be infatuated with a fat and hideous prison commandant, who even while she uses him, treats him with contempt;

v. escapes from the prison camp, and the commandant's clutches.

In each predicament he feels "Nothing could be worse than this. I want to live." At the end, in close-up scarred by a black shadow, he makes the equivocal remark, "Yes, I'm alive." The order in which the events are presented is 5142434. In a set of episodes whose essence is "from the frying pan into the fire," this disguises the sameness of the pattern. It keeps the prewar incidents in time order, and, by dividing it in three, it lays more stress on life in the prison camp.

32 Anamnesis II—Personal Remembrance

In many cases, the anamnesis is not the frame of the narrative. It is casual, incidental, brought to mind by something seen or heard, a trace in the present of the past, as when Eurycleia brought the water to wash the feet of the disguised Odysseus, and he turned away, fearing her recognition of the scar on his leg. The boar hunt, in which he suffered the wound that left the scar, passed through his mind in all its detail.[29]

To Catherine's agonized memory, the lighting of a match by Joe's brother sets the whole screen on fire, and in its midst is Joe, looking out of the burning jail (*Fury*, Fritz Lang). Garadoux, who has been to prison for wifebeating, is suing for the hand of a reluctant young lady. Through a window, he sees approaching the young man she is encouraging. As he looks, the man dissolves from street clothes into a barrister's tabs and gown, and back again—it was he who defended Garadoux in court (*Les Deux Timides*, René Clair). The round bathroom mirror reflects one eye of the deputy's widow, and looks like a speculum. It is followed by a glass screen, on which glow X-ray plates; the large ceiling light in an operating room flickers on and off, and a white-coated man covers a body. This last is seen twice more, as if it kept coming back despite herself (*Z*, Costa-Gavras).

The recall may be subconscious and show only in symptoms, as it is in *Audrey Rose* (Robert Wise). Ivy Templeton, who has bad dreams, and, especially on her birthday, runs blindly around the room, upsetting furniture, and beating her hands on the windows. In a hypnotic trance, she is taken back to her infancy, and is to wake on the count of five. First she smiles happily, then becomes troubled. We cut to a car crossing the median line of a road, seen through a windshield. It comes toward us, and soon in a glaring crash, the windshield is shattered. The child shrieks and collapses on the floor. The hypnotist counts from one to five without avail. "Can you hear me, Ivy?" he asks. "She isn't Ivy," murmurs the man who is sure she was his child in a former incarnation. She suddenly rises, and runs around the glass-walled room, banging on the glass. As we see her through the window, flames rise from the bottom of the screen, and, faded in above them, are shots of a child peering through the window of an overturned car that is starting to burn. Her anamnesis is back to a former life. She is indeed no longer Ivy: she is now Audrey Rose.

It may be something heard that is remembered. Hannay stands, a map in his hand, looking at "Alt-na-Shellach" circled in pencil by Annabella, her face superimposed on it, as we, and he, remember her words the night before her death, "only a matter of days, even hours, before the secret is out of the country . . ." (*The Thirty-Nine Steps*, Alfred Hitchcock).

33 Anamnesis III—The Interplay of Past and Present

A peasant woman's husband, weary from drinking or dancing, lays his head on his wife's lap. A closer shot of only her is briefly displaced by a flash of an artist, dressed in white, painting an orchard in spring. In a later shot she moves through the blossoms to see him again, her voice heard, "You did not come . . . Where are you now?" In the present again, the chin on her lap is pointing the other way—we see it is the artist's. Her husband is standing, "What was the matter? You were pale . . ." "Come to me," she says. "You are the one I want" (*The Wedding*, Andrzej Wajda).

A woman of about thirty-five leaves a car and enters the grounds of a school. It is summer, and the grounds are empty and silent, except for a single girl in school uniform, who sits on a bench sobbing. The woman watches a moment and goes on. Inside the deserted building, she opens a door. From inside the room, not she but the girl Thérèse enters and goes to the window. Seen from outside, the leads between the panes converge on her mouth, as if her face were tied and gagged. The headmistress enters and introduces herself. At the window the grown woman turns. The headmistress advances and meets, not the woman, but the girl. Places and remembered words recall happenings, and the visitor, turn about, is now the compassionate observer, now her suffering younger self (*Thérèse et Isabelle*, Radley Metzger).

Ana, a girl of nine or ten, has come downstairs at night and opened the refrigerator. We see a woman behind her who coughs and folds her arms, and asks her if she knows what time it is. After telling her solemnly and sternly that it is very late, she lifts Ana up, smiles, and kisses her. We see this woman, whom we suppose is Ana's mother, several times, and after the second occasion, as Ana tells her sister, the sister exclaims, "But mummy is dead," and thus we learn that this real-seeming person is real only for Ana. Since all the mother's doings are commonplaces of a child's life, they could as easily be remembered as projected by fancy, but in either case the past is vividly present (*Cria*, Carlos Saura).

A rehearsal is canceled. The première danseuse receives by mail an old diary. The pages turn, and a young man, superimposed, comes toward us. On going out, she meets David, a journalist, with whom she has been keeping company. Her coldness leads to a tiff, and on impulse, she takes the ferry and makes her way up a cliff to a one-roomed cottage built at the top. As she sits there, we see in flashback, the summer she spent with Henrik, whom she met at the spring dance of the ballet school. The flashback stops when she leaves the cottage to go to her uncle's house. The furniture in her study there is draped; there is no sound but the rustle of wind and the three notes she touches on the piano. Her uncle, who is fond of her, tells her that it was he who sent the diary. She returns on the ferry, and as she sits by night near a swaying lantern, the flashback resumes. She had said that her dancing must come before her marriage. It is two days before it is time for her to return to ballet school, and him to university. Henrik, swimming alone, dives from a cliff top, strikes a rock, and later dies. Back in the theater, David comes to see her, and she lends him the diary to read. The film captures the delight and the sadness of love, of what can be enjoyed once and never again. Of what is too brief to be fully savored. The past reverberates in the present, and we speculate how it will shape the future (*Illicit Interlude*, Ingmar Bergman).

It is in this interplay of past and present that sadness is found.

34 Anamnesis IV—Past and Pluperfect—A Flashback within a Flashback

The director of a school is trying to interest a scenarist into giving his students parts in the film the writer is working on. The two are in a box wat ~ Oleg

Bobrov, a small boy, on the stage. He is singing and playing a full-size accordion. The director tells how the instrument came to Oleg.

"I shall have to take you to another small industrial town, where there lived a retired factory foreman and his daughter Tania . . ." We see the foreman, Nikanor Ivanovitch, eating in bed. Suddenly he turns and asks about his accordion. Tania struggles to lift it. He calls her over to tell her the story of it. "It was forty years ago . . ." (Music starts.) "Konstantin Slatoganov told me that the only true friends he had were me and the accordion . . ." Now starts the inner flashback, set off from the flashback itself in three ways: (i) It starts with a wipe from left to right, which leaves a gray hazy curtain across the screen. This wipes back again to start the scene. (ii) There is a hazy edge to the frame, suggesting old, partly faded pictures. (iii) There is no natural sound, only Nikanor's narrating voice and music. "It was in 1906 . . . Death doesn't spare even the good-natured . . ." and he tells how his friend was shot by a soldier during a street riot, and he took the accordion to remember him by. The curtain wipes back again to return us to Nikanor in bed (*Hello Moscow*, Serge Yutkevitch).

After an operation, Aleksandrov turns back in dream and reverie to episodes in his life. The quality of the shot is the same in past and present, and there is nothing other than cuts between them, but seeing the unshaven Aleksandrov, in pajamas and dressing gown, in his hospital room, tells us that we are back in the present. From him, as he sits on a chair, a book in his hand, we cut to the day when one of his students was walking beside him across a park. As the student speaks, we cut from a close-up of his face with unlistening eyes, three separate times, to shots of Ryna, with whom he had once had an affair, long shot and a closer shot, both of them brief, and a third in which they are side by side. He finds that she is married. He declines to talk of their past or the shortcomings of her husband, and then she goes away. Back in the park, the student says to Aleksandrov, "I think you're the most wonderful person in the world," and quickly leaves him. All is quite clear: in the present he is wearing a dressing gown in his hospital room. In flashback, he wears a suit and it is summer; in the flashback within a flashback, he wears a winter coat, Ryna, furs and a muff, and the ground is covered with snow (*The White Room*, Metodi Andonov).

35 Anamnesis V—Spoken Reminiscence with Images

In the view of Jean Mitry, as the film is always perceived as happening in the present, a spectator entering during a flashback would not place it in the past. The question might be raised whether films are made for viewers entering in the middle, any more than a novel is written for those with only time to read the second half. For Mitry then only a commentary placing the action in the past, an anamnesis in words as well as images, can make a flashback of any scene.[30] Other means, however, of passing into this historic present are discussed below.

The link between what is said and what is seen may be looked at in two ways. The words may be quoted from some document, and the images going with them are the visual equivalent, in a sense a visual quotation. The words confer an autobiographical authority, even though the verbal quotations, used for bridging scenes, may break off, and the speech of those we see take their place.

In *Letter from an Unknown Woman* (Max Ophuls), a man on the eve of a duel receives a letter from a woman who has just died of typhus. In the letter she tells how, when she was eighteen, she had heard him play the piano and had turned down a suitor because of him. She had met him when watching for him outside his house, had spent an evening with him, had borne a child in consequence, and married another man because of the boy. Her voice, in the words of the letter returns as he reads between flashbacks. She had met him once again, "Suddenly in that moment everything was in danger." She had gone to his rooms, "I had come . . . to offer you my whole life; but you didn't even remember me." In *The Man in Grey* (Leslie Arliss), Clarissa's hand, writing her diary, dissolves to the events recorded, as she speaks the entry. Her voice adds emotional depth to the mere image.

In *Feeling of Rejection* (Robert Anderson), we hear the patient's voice throughout, giving what is in fact a medical history, accompanied, as we should say of a book, with an artist's illustrations, no doubt with a like amount of interpretation.

Spoken reminiscence can immerse a film in a mood or attitude, and this is its principal value.

A narrator's mere tone of voice can take us inside his mind and feelings. We hear spoken "A Brief History of the Events Leading Up to This Moment"—the moment when the tenth Duke of Chalfont is awaiting hanging. As we often hear the duke on the screen as a person in the action, his nondiegetic narration is said in a confidential voice, closer to us, an urbane and wholly heartless gloss on the incidents we see. One by one, he has killed off those who stood between him and the dukedom. Edith D'Ascoigne, over tea on the lawn asks him if she did right in persuading her husband to come to the country, where his enthusiasm for photography has driven out all other activities. Rising smoke from beyond a brick wall tells us that Henry has just been blown up according to plan. Louis confides in us, "I could hardly point out that Henry now had no time left for any kind of activity", so he went on talking of Henry's future. "Sometimes I had bad news, as when the duchess had twins. However, an epidemic of diphtheria evened things up again, and even brought me a bonus in the death of the Duchess . . ." And again, "I decided to write a carefully phrased letter of condolence to the father" (whose son he had drowned). The narration supplies what the images cannot fully convey, the plotter's calculating relentlessness, his contempt for his victims (*Kind Hearts and Coronets*, Robert Hamer).

When an autobiographical voice is heard only in a film's first and final minutes, it is almost impossible to sustain for an hour-and-a-half a sense of past events or the emotional cast given by the speaker's words. *The Hour of the Wolf* (Ingmar Bergman) starts with Alma sitting outside her cottage, to the sound of the sea and wind. She speaks to us thoughtfully, "I've no more to tell you . . . and you have the diary . . . We didn't want to meet people . . . We unloaded the boat into a barrow." We cut from her to a boat approaching the shore. In time her husband comes to see people who do not exist, and dies, he would have felt, at their hands. Alma speaks to us next at the end of the film, as she turns up an oil lamp, "When a woman lives with a man for a long time, doesn't she at last come to be like him, to see as he does . . . Was that why I began seeing the others . . . so many questions . . ." Her function perhaps is merely to raise these questions for us to ponder.

36 Anamnesis VI—Spoken Reminiscence without Images

Stefan Brand looks up from reading a letter from Lisa, and the nurse's note that a patient who had died at the hospital had left it to be delivered after her death. In brief shots without voice we are reminded, as he had been by the letter, of how he and Lisa had spent their one evening together, their meeting, dining, dancing, buying a toffee apple, and his playing the piano for her. He covers his face with his hands: he had entirely forgotten her, and her letter had ended, "If only you could have recognized what was always yours" (*Letter from an Unknown Woman*, Max Ophuls).

Showing again on the screen the incidents remembered seems to be so clearly what is needed that it is perhaps to be noted when a director chooses not to do it.

In *Tudor Rose* (Robert Stevenson), as Lady Jane Grey mounts the scaffold, her eyes looking up, her changes in fortune are recapitulated in sentences that she and we remember, her face responding to each. We hear her mother's voice, "Tut, girl, this is a great chance"; Ellen her maid's, "London is the Devil's playground"; Warwick's, "You will stay"; and Lord Guildford Dudley's, "He (meaning himself) won't marry you unless you want him to, I promise." We have already seen the occasions on which the words were spoken, and in her last minutes of life, the emphasis is better placed on Lady Jane.

37 Anamnesis VII—Distorted Memory

Critics are not alone in having memories that fade or ones that remember things they never saw. Isadora often remembers the last sight of her children before their death in an accident. In the flashback that shows us this, the colors are bleached nearly to a monochrome. Is it a memory softened and faded? Is it one she has striven to forget? Is it one she cannot bear to think of in stark reality (*Isadora*, Karel Reisz)?

Monika, during her summer with Harry, has been quarrelsome, demanding, has had relations with other men and has left him at last with a baby to care for. She is not handsome, she chews, she has vulgar habits, is sleasily dressed, and walks with a negligent gait. We have seen her tearing meat from a joint with her teeth. But the precredit shots of her, and the last shots of the film as he recollects their setting out to sea that summer, show her as she never was, quiet, thoughtful, elegantly dressed, and beautiful—it was what the summer meant to him; it was how he wished it to be remembered (*Monika*, Ingmar Bergman).

38 Promnesis (Diabole)—Vision

Projections into the future are felt by some to belong to the figure vision. In the film, movements backward or forward in time must both somehow neutralize the natural present tense of the screen, and it seems only logical that this likeness appear in the names of the figures, anamnesis and *promnesis*, keeping the figure vision only for those imagined events that, if placed in time at all, are placed in the present.[31]

Promnesis is not common. Carlos is in a telephone booth talking to Nadine. "Where shall we meet?"—"Maison Bullier." Here we see briefly an impressively wide building, and her seen from inside through double glass doors running toward them and coming in. We return to the telephone booth, and the conversation continues (*La Guerre Est Finie*, Alain Resnais).

Near the end of *A Man and a Woman* (Claude Lelouch), shots of Duroque and Anne in bed together alternate with shots of them elsewhere, lying in the snow, kissing, walking through a flock of sheep in the country, and strolling together in a park. He is about to ask her to marry him. The film offers no clues as to whether these doings had been done, or might be done after marriage. Since none of the scenes had been shown before in the film, the better presumption is the latter.

IX TRANSITIONS

39 The Separation of Inner and Outer

Films like *Sindbad* are like a collage in which past and present events are cut together regardless of time sequence, and with little help in sorting it out, perhaps with no intention that we should. Unless the viewer is ready to accept this (and in the present state of film culture, it cannot be said that we are quite comfortable with it), the director must find means to tell his viewers when he is leaving the present and outer world, and when he is returning.[32] Has the film its quotation marks, italics, or verb tenses, which separate the kinds of literary discourse?

40   Punctuation   I—The Cut

A director may merely cut into the past, relying on content or narration to mark the change.

A man sitting on his bunk, says, "I cast off wife and kids for her." We approach as a man leaves a woman's room. The woman sees in the hall the man we heard speak and invites him in. The scene ends with his hands around her throat. We are back on the ship at night, and the man is standing on the rail. He leaps into the dark and we hear the splash. The anamnesis fills the ellipsis in time between the man's ending his tale, leaving his bunk and climbing up to the deck for the suicide. The change of place is clear, if only because there are no women on the ship; the narration gives the tense; we start with and return to the narrator (*The Crab-Canning Ship*, So Yamamura).

In *Death in Venice* (Luchino Visconti) showing the composer with wife, child, or friend, whom we know are not with him in Venice, places all flashbacks but one clearly in the past.

The repetition of a death must also be recollection, as in *War and Peace* (Sergei Bondarchuk). A boy is tied to a stump and shot by the French. After a shot of Pierre lying thinking, the shot is repeated, as if it were something no detail of which he could ever forget.

41   Punctuation   II—The Return

To start and end a vision or anamnesis with a picture of the person whose imagination we are exploring is something very close to quotation marks, and is usually clear. The face may be approached and retreated from, it may be dissolved from and back to, or in other ways like change of focus, it may be given an emphasis lacking in the cut, suggesting too by its character the movement in time or in from the outer world.

A Czech is escaping from the Germans by posing as Mitchell, an English officer. As he stands in a train, we approach to his face. He is looking away from the camera as if remembering. His face dissolves to an up shot of the edge of a shellhole, into which he leaps. We hear machine guns. He touches a dead man, who rolls into a puddle, face down. He burns a number of pictures, and puts the rest of the man's papers into his pocket. This dissolves to Mitchell's face, from which we retreat to show again the crowded railway car (*The Captive Heart*, Basil Dearden).

In *Waterloo Bridge* (Mervyn Leroy), the anamnesis begins and ends with an anadiplosis. It is 1939, and Colonel Cronin leaves his car to walk across a bridge, having plenty of time to catch his train. He stands looking over the parapet, and as we approach in several stages, he takes off his right glove and brings out of his breast pocket a small, white fetuslike charm. The camera rises to a head-and-shoulders shot, as we hear his voice (without lip movement), "but I can't take your good-luck charm. . . That's wonderfully kind of you" and a woman's voice, "Think you'll remember me now?" There is a dissolve from him as he is wearing a greatcoat and a gray moustache, to him the same size on the screen, wearing a trench coat and a dark moustache. He is now a captain and younger. The girdered bridge in the background with no one passing becomes a stone bridge with passers-by. There is the sound of an air-raid siren. He turns, helps a party of ballerinas to find a shelter, and meets Myra Lester. After she has killed herself, there is a long slow approach down to a stretcher on the road and the legs of the crowd around it. This dissolves to a further approach to a close-up of the good-luck charm as it lies on the asphalt surface. Now we see the same charm in a hand, and the camera rises to show the head and shoulders of Colonel Cronin, who puts the charm away and continues across the bridge to his waiting car.

As Stefan Brand prepares to leave to avoid a duel, his valet brings him a letter. The first line catches his eye as he dries his hands. He lights a cigarette and leans over by a lamp to read it. We hear a woman's voice, "By the time you read this, I may be dead. . . ." As her voice goes on, we move closer to Brand and the image goes out of focus. This is cut to another blurred image, which comes into focus on a harp as men carry it into a house, "When I came back from school, I found a moving van in front of our building. . ." As her parents were leaving Vienna, she runs away and waits on the stairs for Brand, who comes home late with a woman. "And so there was nothing left for me. I left for Linz." The shot is blurred out, and Brand, reading the letter intently, comes into focus (*Letter from an Unknown Woman*, Max Ophuls).

Z (Costa-Gavras) uses the returning image, but with cutting only of quite brief shots. The deputy stops by a shop window. He sees an assistant lifting a wig from a block and smiling at him. We cut to another woman taking a wig from off her dark hair. He smiles at her. We return to the shot of him by the shop window.

Christopher Wood is quitting school. He runs down the school steps, and is frozen at the bottom. We see a girl and hear his voice, "I quit." We see his mother's head and shoulders, and hear his voice again. "I quit." In front of the city hall, the camera makes a long down approach to him, as he shouts, "I quit." A secretary enters a meeting and whispers in the prime minister's ear, who announces to his cabinet, "I have been officially informed that Christopher Wood has quit school. This is a bad thing for the country." Cut back to Wood frozen on the bottom step. He comes to life and continues running (*No Reason to Stay*, Mort Ransen).

The astrologers had agreed that sunset was the most propitious time, so Natu Godse, the assassin-to-be of Gandhi, waits in the room he has rented at the railway station. While his pillowed head remains on the screen at the right, the left two-thirds of the wide screen is blacked out, in which space his mother fades in, drawing water. His head now also dissolves in to the new scene. We see him last as he works for a newspaper. Coming back to the present, the right third of the screen dissolves to his head, lying as we left it. The remainder fades to black and then in to fill out the room at the railway station. By this means, the remembering person and what he remembers are briefly seen together, and the black mask on the partial screen, between past and present, is like the emptying out of present concerns that often preludes the spontaneous arising of memories (*Nine Hours to Rama*, Mark Robson).

42 Punctuation III—Camera Movement

Movement in space can be a metaphor for movement in time.

In *Les Belles de Nuit* (René Clair), Claude, an unhappy, poor, and laughed-at music teacher goes to bed. From a shot of the ceiling light, as it goes out, there is a pan down—not to his bed again—but to a girl singing and playing at a grand piano, and him standing beside her wearing tails, "the famous composer beloved of all."

When he—in his dreams—is in eighteenth-century France, a pan from the garden door from which he has emerged into a Paris street and along a wall, shows him on a cot in a prison cell (where he now is in the present). He wakes, turns over again, and a pan up the wall brings us to Algeria, where now he stands under the French flag in a nineteenth-century soldier's uniform.

Jean the coachman is saying, "We were seven children and a pig . . . across the river, the orchards . . . a kind of paradise guarded by fierce angels. . ." We approach between them, and thrusting them out of the screen at either side, we continue over the river beyond them to a cottage, where boys are being chased by dogs and a woman wielding a stick. But when we look across the river the other way, through the crotch of a tree, we see Miss Julie and Jean, talking still in the present. What does this mean? It cannot mean that the boy Jean foresees the conversation. Perhaps the director is stressing the gap in time and in situation between the boy and the man.

In a variant of this, as Miss Julie sits in the present, her mother and herself, aged eight or nine, come from behind her and go off right as she talks about them. As she speaks of her husband, he stands left, reflected in a mirror, and a pan takes us to the man himself, with her father and his friends, as Jean makes the comment, "So you were betrothed to the district prosecutor." We feel the past in and affecting the present (*Miss Julie*, Alf Sjöberg).

43 Punctuation   IV—Color and Tone

A director may change from color to black and white or monochrome, or use a contrast of tone or color to tell past from present, real from imagined, story from commentary, and the inner and outer worlds in which a character lives.

Dr. Borg is seated on the grass in sight of the house in which he spent his youth. His falling into a reverie is signaled by a shot of the house, as its wall changes from dull gray to glowing white. Inside the house too, so long as the reverie continues, the walls are a shining white, and the furniture, and the clothing, as if all that happened then had a vivid freshness (*Wild Strawberries*, Ingmar Bergman).

In *The Memory of Justice* (Marcel Ophuls), the narrator speaking now is in color, and the past events described are in black and white. A witness at the Nuremberg trials tells how, having run out of gas, the SS guards threw children into the fire alive. Then in color, speaking in the present, she says, "I felt responsible to those friends who had died to tell what happened and to tell it all . . ." Her narration continues as in black and white we see her leave the witness box and cross the courtroom. "This was the moment of my life. . ." She looks to the left and her image is frozen. Then we see the accused in the dock, also frozen. "I looked at them closely. They looked like ordinary people."

Before the days of color film, this was done by tinting. In Abel Gance's *Napoleon*, the scenes of the siege of Toulon are tinted red. As Napoleon is seen, head and shoulders, eyes intent, drenched by bloody rain, we cut back in untinted gray to the snow fight he won as a cadet at Brienne, cool then too in the heat of battle.

Through the darkening turbulent air Dorothy throws herself, in black and white, and enters her house, which is swept into the air by a cyclone. The house whirls around in the sky and falls toward us. We are inside when it falls with a bump. She rises from her bed and walks to the door leading outside, which now is yellow. She opens it on a garden of yellow sunflowers, a gray stone bridge over a blue stream, and walks into a colored fairyland. At the end, a whirling house again comes toward us, blacks out the screen, and is cut to her lying in bed, in black and white. Her eyes are closed, a compress is on her forehead, and she is murmuring the formula given by the Good Witch to take her back, "There's no place like home" (*The Wizard of Oz*, Victor Fleming).

A recreation of two beggars, a man and a boy who live in an old car, is describing "the house we're building." On one occasion they discuss the kind of gate, on another the style, changing it as we watch from European Rococo to Spanish Mission. Size, shape, and color change, as the old man describes it and the boy agrees. That the house is imaginary, its great plasticity is in itself a sign, and the intent glance of the speaker, the circling of his right palm as he conjures it up, the recurrence of romantic harp and wind music, the absence of people and plants, and the unnatural gaudy colors of sky and house. It is unearthly (*Dodeska-Den*, Akira Kurosawa).

Mahe is a man of average honesty. He has been drawn into the world of one Marion Vergano, has lost most of his money, and has just killed a private detective whom he himself had paid to find Marion. Twice, as we see Mahe sleeping, in a room where dark green predominates, there is a flash of the detective Comolli, wearing a sand-colored suit in bright sunlight, just at the moment when the bullet struck him. The short bright shot is a sudden shock, but long enough for us to recognize the man we had seen killed, which placed it in the past, and thus in Mahe's mind (*Mississippi Mermaid*, François Truffaut).

In full color, Squadron Leader Carter drops through an escape hatch of his bomber. He comes to, lapped by the sea on a sandy shore, meets and kisses the operator with whom he had last spoken by radio before his drop. Now we dissolve to lilac monochrome, and read on a paper, "Invoiced 91,716; Delivered 91,715." A supervisor is reprimanding Conductor 71 for failing to fetch Carter. Conductor 71 alleges a heavy fog by way of excuse. He is instructed to proceed to earth immediately. He sniffs at the rose in his lapel. Its monochrome becomes a glowing red, and he proceeds through flowering shrubs in color to find Carter. Carter has vivid visions of proceedings in heaven, relating to his misconducted survival. During his fall, his brain was damaged, and as his condition improves or worsens (in color), so does the course of the heavenly proceedings (in lilac monochrome). His doctor is killed in an accident, at a time when Carter and Conductor 71 were having trouble choosing a counsel for the trial. Carter lies on the operating table. There is a large shot of the overhead light, as what seem to be brown, veined eyelids close it slowly over from top and bottom. We pan down a wall, its yellow-brown growing fainter, and little by little becoming a lilac-tinted floor with crowds of people. Conductor 71 relieves another conductor (John Bunyan) of Dr. Reeves, and informs him that Carter has chosen him for his counsel (*A Matter of Life and Death*, Michael Powell and Emeric Pressburger).

In *Jonah Who Will Be 25 in the Year 2000* (Alain Tanner), any departure from the story is shown in sepia. Marco, a history teacher, has cut up a blood sausage, to show a class the arbitrary divisions of historic time. In sepia, Max, a journalist, rises from bed. He takes a revolver from a drawer, levels it first at his image in the mirror, and then fires at his clock. We then return in color to the history lesson. It is, we suppose, a footnote on man's handling of time. Max ends a talk on inflation by telling the young students, "I hope you are all here by the year 2000." The desks are instantly filled by middle-aged men and women, in sepia.

Voice, color, and split frame are all used at once in *The Legend of Lylah Clare* (Robert Aldrich). We hear Rosella's voice giving a version of Lylah's death by a fall from a staircase. This is shown on the screen in sepia, its detail scumbled. Along the top and bottom is a rough band of red, and at bottom left we see in full color the head of Elsa Campbell as she listens to the story of the woman whose life she is to reenact on the screen.

44 Punctuation V—Cartoon

Dreams may be shown in animated cartoons. A change from natural motion and appearance to geometrical lines, a different articulation of movement, and more abstract backgrounds, from shooting life to shooting drawings, clearly set off the dream from actuality (*Peasants*, Friedrich Ermler).

45 Punctuation VI—Superimposition, Mask, Wipe

In *Thunder Rock* (Roy Boulting), what Charleston, alone in his lighthouse, reads in the log of the wrecked vessel is superimposed on his image—the outside of the lighthouse, the bell buoy, the dark lake, the approaching vessel, waves foaming on the rocks below the lighthouse, and in a close-up of the logbook, the prow of the vessel thrusting out of the waves. He looks up intently, the leaves of the logbook blow back to the start. There is a high throbbing note, the sound of wind, and the slam of a door. The wind and the flittering pages come to rest. A shadow appears on the wall, and the camera pans to show, dimly seen, the captain of the wrecked vessel.

In a night of dark green, Adele tosses in bed, desperate from being rejected by Lieutenant Pinson. Superimposed in bright yellow is someone struggling to keep afloat in dark waters. It is either a recollection or a metaphorical dream; in either case it aptly expresses her state (*The Story of Adele H.*, François Truffaut).

Norma is poor, and a wealthy man has asked her to marry him. In the black border of the oval mask in which she stands, horizontal ovals open one after another, to show a case of jewels, a motorcar, a roast chicken, an array of dresses (*La Roue*, Abel Gance).

Catherine de Medici in *Intolerance* (D. W. Griffith) tells the king of the past acts of the Huguenots, and the flashbacks of these are inside a soft-edged mask. Unfortunately for consistency, the same device is used for events that are not in the past.

When the person remembering and what is remembered come in succession, instead of giving the vision or anamnesis a different look, the two may be linked by a metaphorical bridge. It may be one of the curtainlike devices discussed under montage, like the rippling muslin that blows across the screen and then off in *Passionnelle* (Edmond Greville), as if a secret were being unveiled. In *Thunder Rock* (Roy Boulting), Charleston is exploring the lives of six people, all of whom had been drowned on the rock ninety years before. He opens a door in the upper part of the lighthouse, as if into the past, and sees Briggs working at the kilns in the Potteries, the day his brother-in-law brings the steamer tickets, a step toward a new life in America. The opening of other doors reveals the earlier life of the other five.

46 Punctuation VII—Association, Anadiplosis.

A like pattern of image or sound, ending the present and starting the past sequence, may, by a kind of anadiplosis, bridge the two. Survivors of a sunken destroyer float in the sea around a life-raft. As one of them plays the tune on his mouth organ, the rest sing "The Beer Barrel Polka." During a dissolve from Chief Petty Officer Hardy's face, the surface of the coming image ripples as if it were seen through water. It shows, as it grows still, Hardy, his wife, Ordinary Seaman Blake and his fiancée (both men among those at the raft) sitting in a music hall. The same song is heard from the stage of the music hall, the audience joining in. The last image ripples like the first, and then dissolves to the raft again (*In Which We Serve*, Noël Coward and David Lean).

The doctor-deputy has been seriously injured. His wife sits in the hospital beside a screen that glows with X-rays of a skull. The doctor, after having briefed police officials, turns toward her and says, "Your husband has a wonderful heart." Cut to a half-length shot of her husband as he turns toward her with a smile to say, of one of his patients, "If his heart holds out, he'll survive." Then we return to her by the X-rays (*Z*, Costa-Gavras).

In another kind of anadiplosis to the past, the Birling family is assembled in the drawing-room, with Gerald Croft, the daughter's fiancé. "This time," says Inspector Poole, to Mrs. Birling, "you did not know her as Eva Smith or Daisy Renton, but as . . ." Cut to the head and shoulders of Eva saying, "Mrs. Birling." In a longer shot, we see her, the only person in a room of empty chairs, being questioned by a committee of nine women seated on a rostrum, one of whom is the Mrs. Birling to whom the inspector was talking (*An Inspector Calls*, Guy Hamilton).

47 Punctuation VIII—Sound

Speech is always available to bridge transitions in time and assert the tense.

Abigail, a singer, and a young lieutenant have been brought together by a storm, which forced his plane to land. She is telling him about her husband, now in prison. "I first met him," she said, "at a symphony concert." This is followed by a panning shot from an orchestra, across the audience, to a balcony in which the two are side by side. Her voice recurs at intervals during the flashback, which helps to keep us in the past. We retreat from her, as she sings to Robert's accompaniment, Irving Berlin's "Always," and we hear her speaking from the present, "Those six months were the happiest of my life" (*Christmas Holiday*, Robert Siodmak).

A change in the character of sound is also a means of separating inner and outer events. Jennie goes to bed in the room she occupied as a child. She tries to read a book, and puts it away. Her breathing and a ticking we hear louden as we approach her. She sits up in bed and the ticking and breathing stop. A severe-looking relative appears round a doorway, in a scene in which dark green predominates (its hue perhaps a metaphor for an obscure or somber memory). The relative comes toward us, her face in shadow. Jennie cowers on the bed against the corner of the wall, her color now also dulled. Her mouth opens in a scream but no sound is heard. In a half-length shot, the relative covers Jennie's mouth with a black-gloved hand. Then the light goes on. We hear Jennie collapsing on the bed, and again we hear her breathing (*Face to Face*, Ingmar Bergman).

48 Punctuation IX—The Limited Convention

A convention may be devised, valid only for the film in which it occurs. One is especially needed in *The Secret Life of Walter Mitty* (Norman Z. McLeod), since the incidents of his real life were as extraordinary as those of his dreams. Here the conventions included the following: we slowly approach, the lighting takes on a bluish hue, the shot of Mitty dissolves to the dream action, a voice narrates in the third person, Mitty is addressed as befits his dream role, and the onomatopoeic phrase, "tu-pocket, tu-pocket, tu-pocket" is used by the speaker, which might in a particular case be the engine of a ship or a Spitfire, or horses's hoofs, depending on whether Mitty is becoming a sea captain, Group Captain Mitty, or Mitty the Kid. "As the huge anaesthetic machine goes tu-pocket, tu-pocket, tu-pocket, Dr. Walter Mitty approaches the operating table . . . 'We're so glad you've come, Mr. Mitty.' . . ." The costume in the dreams was elaborately accurate, and the action hyperbolic, expressing power, with always an admiring audience. A blow of his fist was enough to shatter solid things, like chairs and wheels.

49 Punctuation X—The Misleading Transition[33]

The cut lends itself to ambiguity because of a natural bias to suppose that filmic events are continuous in time and happen in the outer world, and also because of our expectations formed by seeing hundreds of films before. The director can count on our making certain assumptions, and this allows him to surprise us, when in a particular case the assumption is wrong.

In *Moscow Nights* (Anthony Asquith), Ignatov sits up in his hospital bed, aligns his hands and eye as if to aim, and cries "Fire." This is cut to artillery firing and other scenes of military action. It looks like a new sequence, joined by anadiplosis. A nurse is cut in, standing by his bed. "There now," she says, "that's all over." Then we see him still sitting up, awareness of where he is returning to his eyes.

What we take for a flashback to Bernard's life as a conscript in Algeria, is disjointed, rather flickery, often underexposed in pale black and white. Not only, we feel, is the difference in quality a good separation of the anamnesis but the paler, colorless, disjointed image suggests the fallibility of memory. The flashback over, we see it was projected on a screen in Bernard's studio. In a sense it is a recall, though not an inner one, but perhaps inner as well (*Muriel*, Alain Resnais).

During the American Civil War, a man about to be hanged stands on the edge of a bridge. A pan along the projecting plank on which he stands shows his bound feet, then rises to his tied hands, the noose around his neck, and his sweating forehead. We see a woman in spreading white dress, with a girl on a swing. She rises and comes toward us, half-length. In the mist of dawn, we see the bridge from above and from below. A tear on his face, the bound man sobs and twists his wrists. In long shot he falls, rope and all, into the water, and frees himself. He comes to the surface, sees the leaves in the morning sun, dives to avoid the shots fired, comes to shore, runs down a glade, reaches a tree-lined road, runs along a water-bordered causeway and pushes open iron gates. In facing shots, we see his eyes closed. His feet move slowly, as if against resistance. The woman comes out on a terrace, looking eagerly. In full-length and half-length, he runs between trees, but gains no ground. They meet, he from the right, she from the left, both smiling. There is a crack, he straightens up, and his head jerks back. In a long shot of the bridge, he falls and hangs (*An Incident at Owl Creek Bridge*, Robert Enrico).

A director may sometimes leave undeclared which of two possible meanings he intends. He may, for example, present as equally real the outer world accessible to all his characters, and the projected world seen by one only of them. In *8½* (Federico Fellini), the almost unbelievable imitation of life lived every day by a film director, and the growing vividness of his inner fancies, hardly more strange, are matched by a lack of contrast in either quality or color of image between the way they are shown. Guido himself slips from one of his worlds into the other, as quickly as a cut between the shots of them. A girl in a smock holds out a glass of mineral water right beside him. He does not see her, for his attention is on a white-draped woman with bare feet, a glass in her hand, who does not appear again among the guests or in the film. A scriptwriter keeps on objecting during a screening. Guido points with a finger. Two men cover the writer's head with a black hood and hang him in the rear of the theater, but the body is not to be seen in a later longer shot—it is only imagined.

50 Punctuation XI—Matters of Practice

Should one means of punctuation be used throughout a film? In *The Secret Life of Walter Mitty* (Norman Z. McLeod), each time we see the established convention, it is more amusing. In *Juliet of the Spirits* (Federico Fellini), before the first of Juliet's daydreams, her eyes close, her head sinks on her chest, and a wide inverted-bowllike hat drops like a curtain entirely over her face, and the dream that follows is shown in muted colors. We expect a like punctuation for other reveries, but each is different. Did the director feel that, seen several times and even if all her hats were as well cast, the drooping prelude might become tiresome?

In *Ivan's Childhood* (Andrei Tarkovsky) also, each of the boy's dreams is set off in a different way. The film starts on a sunny summer's day in a glade, with a deer, a butterfly, a cuckoo's call, and the boy laughing with pleasure. We glide swiftly down a steep slope to a woman far below. The boy runs up, tells her of the cuckoo, and drinks from the pail she has set down. The image swirls to the sound of a cry, and the scene cuts to the boy waking at night in a barn. He dons a jacket and cap, runs across a field, wades through a flooded river bank, and reaches a military post, wet, cold, dirty, and hard-faced. This is a striking contrast. The second dream begins with water dripping into a bowl by his cot at the military post, and carries over to water dripping into a cribbed well, where his mother is filling a pail. Suddenly the bucket falls toward us, but before it strikes, it is cut to a bucket standing on the ground, splashing out as if something had fallen into it; on the ground beside it, his mother lies, dead. Ivan wakes in Lieutenant Galtsev's cot. The boy asleep at the start and waking at the end and the presence of his mother, set the dream off from the flow of the present. The third of his dreams is almost entirely of Ivan eating apples. As he rides on a truckful of them, he is in ordinary lighting, but the fleeting trees behind him are a fluffy spectral white against a black sky. The switch in tone to negative film to warn us of a change from outer life to inner life gives a sinister impression. The device is unpleasing, unjustified, and even upsetting to the story. While this may come from trying to suit the mood of each dream with a special punctuation, it may be smoother, clearer, less obtrusive to choose one means that suits the whole story and use it throughout the film.

The Little Island. (Richard Williams Animation Ltd.)
PLATE 29. SYNECDOCHE. METAPHOR. PROSOPOPOEIA. ALLEGORY.
Good shoots his hand into the sky, from whence it comes down like a hand of God, charged with supernatural authority. This hypostasis of part of himself into a power outside himself frees him to do whatever he wishes to do without feeling guilt. Here the hand of Good seizes Beauty, bent on squeezing out his life.

Morgan: A Suitable Case for Treatment. (EMI Film Distributors Overseas Ltd.)
PLATE 30. INNER STATE. HYPERBOLE: REDUCTIO AD ABSURDUM.
We use clothes to express our image of ourselves, what we would like to be or be taken for. Morgan envies the simpler problems of the higher primates, and endeavours by donning a gorilla suit to escape from his own world into theirs. It is a *reductio ad absurdum* of the language of clothes.

Alexander Nevski.

PLATE 31. INNER STATE: VIEWPOINT.

Our sympathy is engaged by those we see large and in close-up, and of whom we know enough to make them interesting and attractive. It follows that those we see at a distance, of whom we know little (and that little touched with menace or absurdity) invite hostility. In this film the Russians are rarely seen with covered faces, and we come to know them in everyday life. On the other hand, the only expressions of the two Teuton invaders whose faces we see are the Grand Master's set sardonic stare and the demented organist's toothy jowl, merely caricatures. The other Teutons are masked by visor and helmet; they are less than persons, hardly more than anonymous automatons of destruction.

The Great Dictator. (© MCMXL Charles Chaplin Film Corporation)

PLATE 32. INNER STATE: HALLUCINATION.

When Charlie goes to "check the fuse" of a dud shell, it swivels with a whizzing menace to point its nose at him wherever he runs: a hallucination arising from fright.

Morgan: A Suitable Case for Treatment. (EMI Film Distributors Overseas Ltd.)

PLATE 33. INNER STATE: REVERIE.

He rides his motorcycle into the Thames, climbs dripping up a tip of scrap metal, and wrenches off his gorilla's head. He lies exhausted, convinced that he is a complete failure. His parents had expected him to lead the revolution; instead, he has become an artist, lost his wife, and yearned for the life of the apes. As loudspeakers intone quotations from Marx and Lenin, he sees all these people he feels he has betrayed standing on what might be a figure for the wreckage of his life. They are all bent on destroying him.

Zero de Conduite.
PLATE 34. INNER STATE: REVERIE. FANTASY.
In a dreamlike film of a school as it appears to schoolboys, the headmaster is an insignificant dwarf, trying ineffectually to be dignified beside a tall impressive uniform, and the back row of Very Important Persons on Prize Day does as little to enliven the proceedings as a row of stuffed and leering dummies.

The Third Man.
PLATES 35 AND 36. PATHETIC FALLACY. SETTING AS SIGNIFICANT OBJECT.
Life in postwar Vienna is one of remembered loss, of disillusion, of men growing rich on
the sufferings of children, of suspicion, of life narrowed in comforts, food, and hope of
change. The story takes place in scenes of wet cloudy days, at night among ruined buildings, and in winter of leafless trees, surroundings that match the doings and feelings of
those who live there.

Dumbo. (© MCMXLI Walt Disney Productions)
PLATE 37. PROSOPOPOEIA. SIMILE BY DISTORTION.
An engine that leans back on its heels in a sudden stop is likened, by distortion from its usual iron rigidity, to a horse.

The Red Shoes. (By courtesy of the Rank Organization Ltd.)
PLATE 38. INNER STATE: DREAMLIKE FILMS. FANTASY.
Various traits found in fantasy—the absurd, the impossible, the supernatural and the allegorical—can be seen in *The Red Shoes* ballet, which is danced in the course of the film. A newspaper is swept up from the street by the wind of dawn, and as it swirls, takes little by little the shape of a man, clad in a newspaper. Here the paper is seen in transition from thing to man.

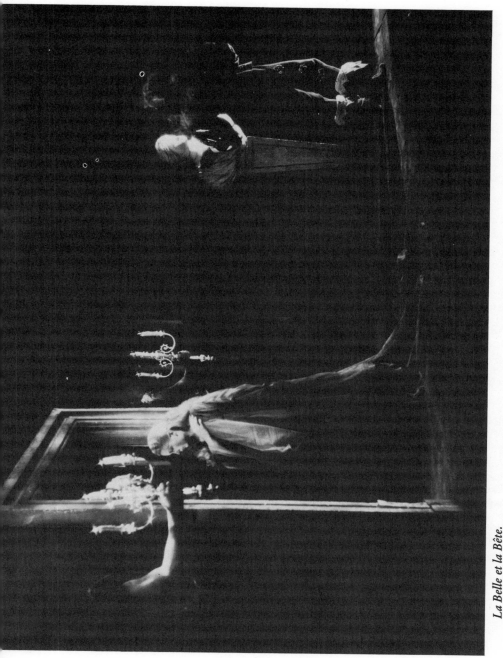

La Belle et la Bête.
PLATE 39. FANTASY: THE SUPERNATURAL.
The girandoles, here living human arms holding candlesticks, are a mark of the animistic or supernatural native to fantasy.

The Little Island. (Richard Williams Animation Ltd.)

PLATE 40. ABSTRACTION. SIMPLIFICATION. SIGNIFICANT OBJECT.

Cartoon at its most accomplished can express ideas with great exactitude. *The Little Island* exposes the enormities to which a narrow-minded and intolerant pursuit of truth, beauty or goodness can lead. The idea of sanctification by belonging to an institution is seen in the horizontal line of black or sinful figures, which become (by passing through the gate of goodness) a vertical line of white figures rising heavenwards.

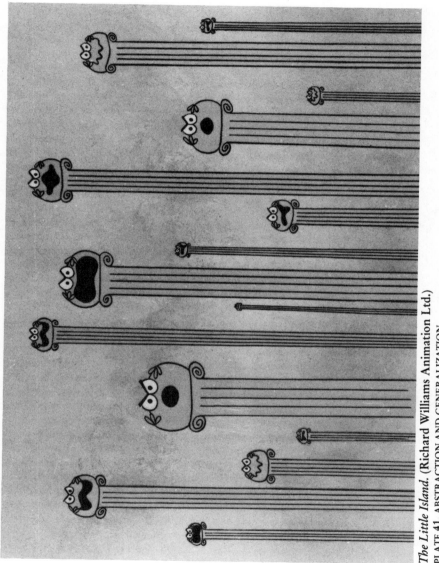

The Little Island. (Richard Williams Animation Ltd.)

PLATE 41. ABSTRACTION AND GENERALIZATION.

Ionic columns of various sizes, topped by unceasing mouths, rising in competition with one another and babbling in an unintelligible confusion, suggest the unprofitable theorizing of those who talk about art.

Anna Karenina. (London Films)

PLATE 42. THINGS WHOSE MEANING LIES BELOW THOUGHT.
Anna is a doomed woman: the choices she has made leave her only one choice, death. The locomotive, which glides, slow and unpausing, with never a wheel or driver seen—a tall, quiet, black shape with three white eyes, unswerving on its tracks like some irresistible, ineluctable force—can be seized by the mind as an image of destiny. But it is also a shape that speaks directly to our feelings, and as it comes closer to destroy Anna, we feel, without recourse to thought, that it also overwhelms us.

Part VIII

Less Common Uses

17
Minor Figures

1   Amphibology—Hyrmos—Irony

Then haue ye one other vicious speach with which we will finish this chapter, and is when we speake or write doubtfully and that the sence may be taken two wayes, such ambiguous terms they call Amphibologia . . . Thus said a gentleman in our vulgar, pretily notwithstanding because he did it not ignorantly, but for the nonce

> *I sat by my Lady soundly sleeping,*
> *My mistresse lay by me bitterly weeping.*

No man can tell by this, whether the mistresse or the man, slept or wept.[1]

Doing it "ignorantly" is clearly to be avoided; sloppiness is not a figure. Intentional ambiguity is perhaps harder to construct than the unequivocal message, for two or more possible meanings are placed before us at once. In literature they both may be expressed by a single word. This is William Empson's Type Three.[2] There seems to be something like this in those forms of anadiplosis that use a common shape—the doorhandle in close-up that ends a sequence is seen to be a billiard ball at the start of the next, as in a retreating shot we see it on the table. And yet, at midpoint, before it becomes a billiard ball, it is still a handle, and there is no other meaning present in our minds. It is not, therefore, a case of amphibology, and the proper term for it is anadiplosis.

If a director, by not disclosing all the context at one time, creates an impression found later to be false, this again is not an ambiguity. The weak and thirsty Shears looks up at the sky as he drags himself along the ground. We see what looks to us (and, we suppose, to him) like a black, red-headed, white-tailed bird of prey hovering and watching, a symbol of death, which must follow a loss of the will to go on. It alights by Shears's head. The Burmese villagers running to recover their kite find him and help him on his way (*The Bridge on the River Kwai*, David Lean).

From a shattered wall against a moonbright sky, we retreat past the crotch of a dead tree, and suddenly a hand enters to drive a knife hard into the trunk. As we glide further back, an unprepossessing figure in dingo skins comes on the screen. It is Jack the Dogger, who makes a living trapping dingoes for a bounty of a pound a head. In an audience of habitués, the director could count on the sudden plunge of the knife at such a place and hour to awaken sinister expectations, without a doubt

315

the overture to a murder: in the event, the overture to a pleasant meeting in mid-desert. The director let us deceive ourselves (*The Back of Beyond*, John Heyer).

At closing time, Chris Cross, the teller, takes from the safe an envelope of money he intends to steal. "I've caught you just in time" says a voice. Cross looks up, startled and wary. J. J. Hogarth, his employer, is looking down from an upper landing with what could be severity. Down at the wicket Hogarth says, "Cash this for me—personal" (*Scarlet Street*, Fritz Lang).

The two last are examples of the figure hyrmos, in which what we know we lack for the understanding of a scene is held back.

The director may help us deceive ourselves by using expectations arising from the nature of the story. We saw Otley open a suitcase, which later exploded and killed someone. Otley, lodged now in an expensive hotel, crosses the lobby past the reception clerk. He opens the front door, and out of the night a stranger comes with shadowed face, and hands him an attaché case. Back in his suite, Otley sits on the bed, opens the case cautiously, and unwraps the package it contains. The course of the story up till now has predisposed us to expect something more dramatic than fish and chips (*Otley*, Dick Clement).

The hyrmos lends itself to a dramatic opening. The plot is yet unknown, and the director can fob off on us almost any incident, as if it were the actual story. *Sullivan's Travels* (Preston Sturges) opens by night on a high railway embankment. Tearing around a curve toward us is a column of smoke from a train, with a long jet of steam issuing sideways from it. The noise of the train and galloping triplets of music build in a furious crescendo. Two men on top of a boxcar are fighting desperately, the wind of the hurtling train fluttering their clothes. One of the men falls between the cars but regains the top. The other draws a revolver and fires. The wounded man staggers, closes with the other, and both men topple over the edge. On a shot of them both plunging into a river, we see the words "THE END." The lights go on in a viewing room. John L. Sullivan rises, and points the moral, "You see the symbolism of it . . . capital and labor locked together in a death struggle." There is no ambiguity at all. For us, what we saw was the start of the film. The context, which placed it in the story was kept from us till "THE END."

We have all experienced the likeness of sounds from different sources. My cat growled at being dislodged from my chest. As the growl seemed long-drawn for the size of its lungs, I listened more carefully and found that a passing airplane had carried on the sound in the same pitch and quality. But here again there was no ambiguity, only material for a simile. The sound was first the cat's and then the plane's. Our gaze sweeps across the desert sands, and we hear clop-clop, clop-clop, which, being where we are, we take for a horse. As our gaze reaches a road, an ancient car with a trailer is traveling along it, its radiator bubbling plop-plop. Again, it is not a case of holding two different meanings in our minds: either we decide we are hearing a horse, or we keep an open mind until we find out where the sound is coming from (*Jitterbugs*, Mal St. Clair).

How many can tell the sound of a blank from that of a live round? Finding a middle-aged lawyer with his wife, Count Malcolm proposes Russian roulette. The count loads a single chamber, and he and the sweating lawyer place the revolver to their temples turn about and pull the trigger. The lawyer has aimed the revolver, and we cut to the countess and an actress outside as they turn toward us on the sound of a shot. Which one is dead? We are not holding two relevant meanings in our minds, both being true at once. It must be either the count or the lawyer, and the cutting suggests the last. The count is seen through the window: it cannot be he. He comes out and suddenly laughs. The women are concerned. "What!" he says, "Risk my life for a shyster. I loaded with a blank." Not an ambiguity, but hyrmos, the truth postponed. The sound in itself did not exclude the possibility that the round was blank, but in the situation it never occurred to us that it was other than live, and only when the context was fully disclosed was the presumption we had made rebutted. We deceived ourselves, with a little help from the director (*Smiles of a Summer Night*, Ingmar Bergman).

If all meanings to which an expression is open must be taken as intended, this is the door to both amphibology and irony.[3] The aging D'Ascoigne, rector of the parish, is entertaining Mazzini, who is posing as the bishop of Matabeleland. The rector insists on hearing the bishop speak Matabele. He stares astonished at the gibberish Mazzini improvises, and says, "If I may say so without disrespect to my superiors, my Lord, your visit has brought me something I could not expect from any churchman in this country." Mazzini has just finished poisoning the rector's port, to which the statement also certainly applies (*Kind Hearts and Coronets*, Robert Hamer).

In *King and Country* (Joseph Losey), after a level, plantless, wet, cloudy landscape has been established, we see a uniformed corpse, the skull to the left, lying on its back, a uniformed, handless left arm bent under the chin. This dissolves to a soldier lying in the same position, on a pile of hay, his left arm folded under his chin as he plays a mouth organ. A retreat shows us a door barred with an old bed end, and a guard beyond. The simile could mean that this—the corpse—is the man's destiny, or that this is what he is thinking of, or that the man in some spiritual sense is dead. If all three are true, it is Empson's Type Four, in which the possible alternative meanings are all alive at once, blending into a dense interplay.[4] If so, it is clearly *amphibology*.

With *Dead of Night* (Alberto Cavalcanti, Charles Crichton, Basil Dearden, Robert Hamer), we reach Type Seven, where the only two possible meanings are contradictory, the writer vacillating between them.[5] The film is described above under Repetition. The reader will remember the circular story, beginning and ending with the same sequence of shots. Up a road lined with trees a car approaches. It stops, and the driver, Walter Craig, looks, perplexed, at a half-timbered house away from the road; he then drives up to the front door. Inside, he tells his host he has met his fellow guests here before, every circumstance the same, in a dream. He even finds his way unerringly to a concealed cloakroom. He says at one point, "You're still there. . . . It isn't a dream this time." After strangling the skeptical psychiatrist, Craig flees through unexpected shifts of place, where he meets his fellow guests and people from the stories they told, ending at last locked in the same cell as Hugo Fitch, the ventriloquist's dummy, who crosses the cell to where Craig crouches on a bed, and strangles him. This recedes to a tiny square on a black screen, to the sound of a ringing bell. In the next shot, Craig wakes to the sound of a ringing bell. It is Elliot Foley, whom he had never met before, inviting him to come on the visit we have just seen. "Strange," he says, "wonder why the name seems familiar." Then we see the opening shots again. Did it, or will it, happen? The cyclical form, a *moto perpetuo*, makes a choice impossible.

Various writers have noted that what is seen on the screen seems to be happening in the present, and it is hard to sustain a sense of past or future.[6] *Last Year at Marienbad* (Alain Resnais) makes the most of this characteristic. It first establishes a timeless atmosphere. The stranger's voice is heard, "Once again I walk on . . . down these corridors . . . in this . . . enormous, luxurious, baroque, lugubrious, hotel— where corridors succeed endless corridors—silent deserted corridors overloaded with a dim cold ornamentation . . . from another century." The camera slowly searches the shapes of the pargeting. Speech and image combine hypnotically, "among which I was already waiting for you. . . . Are you coming?" The answer to this we hear in a woman's voice from offscreen, as we travel back across a large reception room, where men and women in evening dress are seated in rows: "We must still wait . . . a few minutes . . ." And now we are shown a stage, with an actor and an actress, and she continues the speech. It is not she to whom the stranger spoke; it is not he whom she was answering. So in the second place, our impressions are constantly shown in such ways to be unreliable. The stranger seems to be trying to seduce a woman away from the man who seems to be her husband by reminding her of previous meetings between the stranger and the woman last year, of which she professes no remembrance whatever. His quiet assured voice accumulates the irresistible detail, "One day, but it was most likely later on, you even broke one of your high heels. You had to take my arm for support." She says at last, "I don't know any more . . . It's all wrong . . . I don't know any more. . . ." She comes to be half persuaded that she had previously met and loved him. As we see the events he describes, the director never allows us to be sure as to whether what we see is happening now (it is as much in the present as any other incident), or did happen last year, if indeed they had met, or whether by constant suggestion he is making her believe that they did what he says they did, or is, in fact, persuading her to do it in the future, whether it is fact or fantasy. "You were not waiting for me, but you seemed to be everywhere . . . the same as you were in the gardens at Fredericksbad . . . You were alone, I remember." The buildings imbrued in the past, the statuesque stillness and unhurried pace of people rich in hours, make any happenings there seem to float unattached in time.

The stranger's insistent speaking of time past has cast adrift the present we seem to see, and since it is only in relation to the present that there is a future and a past, we (and she) are finding it hard to place ourselves in this uncertain tense. The woman says, "All I'm asking is that you wait a little. Next year, here, the same day, at the same hour . . . and I'll come with you." Does this speech point forward or backward? Did she say it a year ago, or is she saying it now? The husband comes to the meeting place only after she has gone in the stranger's company. Is it after the long siege of persuasion, or had she gone last year? We are never certain.[7]

2 Aposiopesis

Aposiopesis is stopping in midcourse, leaving a statement unfinished, as if unwilling or unable to proceed. It is a "falling silent," as when Macbeth says, "If we should fail. . . ."[8]

It is distinguished from ellipsis by intention. If the director's concern is merely to leave out the inessential, the figure is ellipsis; if it is unwillingness to show something he does not wish to contemplate, and assumes that neither would we (the Latin word for the figure is *reticence*), it is aposiopesis.

The following is almost certainly aposiopesis. Captain Thorndyke is going into hiding. He has given Jerry Stokes a slip telling her where his brother should write in three weeks. She is absorbed in thought as she enters her door, but once inside, stops fearfully. The Gestapo chief is seated at a table in the center, his dim face featureless in silhouette; a man is sitting either side of him. She runs out but is turned back by a policeman with a German accent. "Sit down," says the chief. "We must have a little chat." This is cut to a sign "LYME REGIS": Thorndyke is seen at the Post Office.

The means used for finding out from Jerry where Thorndyke was, and with what success, we do not find out, for the scene is not completed. To be an aposiopesis, we must recognize the statement as incomplete, from a purposed cutting off of part of the meaning, which we, if not in any precise way, can supply (*Man Hunt*, Fritz Lang).

The last shot of *Kind Hearts and Coronets* (Robert Hamer) also gives a strong sense of aposiopesis. Sibella has produced a suicide note signed by her husband and obtained a reprieve for Mazzini within a few minutes of his being hung for her husband's murder. Mazzini is standing outside the prison when a man comes up and makes him an offer for his memoirs. Now he suddenly remembers that on the table in the cell he has just left is a full account of the six undetected murders committed by him. He turns to the door. It is closed and impassive. The camera slowly approaches the title page of the memoirs that lie still on the table, "A Brief History of the Events . . . written on the eve of his execution." It is as if the camera were inviting us to think, "If anyone should read these before the Duke reclaims them. . . ." But here the film stops without letting us know if anyone does.

3 Emphasis

Ellipsis is leaving out or subduing what a director does not wish us to see, because it is unimportant or inexpedient for his purpose. *Emphasis* is thrusting upon us that which he does not wish us to miss. Leaving out is in itself a means of laying stress on what is left in.

Focus is used in the theater in the sense of emphasis. In film it is literally possible to place a part of a scene sharply in focus, leaving the rest blurred, and thus to emphasize it. In *Instruments of the Orchestra*, (Muir Matheson), the brass, for example, when spoken of by Sir Malcolm Sargent, is well lit and clear and the rest of the orchestra darker lit and out of focus.

When the washerwoman sees Elvira Madigan walking away with the clothesline, she follows. Elvira uses the clothesline as a tightrope, and between her legs (out of focus) we see the servant in the distance, at a gap in the fence, looking at us amazed. Then she blurs out of awareness, the legs are clear, and our mind is on Elvira (*Elvira Madigan*, Bo Widerberg).

Angle. Two children are sidling slowly along a ledge. It is shot from below, to stress the ledge's narrowness and, therefore, its danger. Shot from above, it would have seemed wider (*Dusty Bates*, Part 2, Darrell Catling). To bring out the length of lake boats, the cameraman shot one from above as it moves along the frame's diagonal, its longest line. Hatch follows hatch to an almost incredible number until at long last, the stern with mast and funnel brings the series to an end (*Great Lakes*, Uncredited).[9]

A director may start (or end) a scene with a *close-up* of some small part, that he wishes us to notice, to remember, or to understand. We see the upper half of a straw doll, the crinkled bark of a tree behind it. In a retreating pan, we see four dolls, one after the other, each with a spike through it. During this we hear a spike being hammered, and now we see a hand as it spikes another doll to the tree. In a longer shot, we see Madam, three flaming candles upon her head and a wand in her mouth burning at either end, walking around the tree, casting a spell (*The Conspirator*, Daisuke Ito). Four men on a raft divide up the last of the water, to do as they wish with. The man whose idea it was upsets his cup. He turns away. The cup on its side, in close-up, rolls to and fro as the raft rides the swell (*Forty-Nine Days*, G. Gaba).

The mask served Griffith like a close-up. Within a circular mask, Elsie and her brother sit in the stalls of a theater. The mask irises out exposing all the stalls, the galleries and Lincoln's box *(The Birth of a Nation)*. The captain of the Fire Department searches a dour-looking man with an open coat who looks to him to be suspicious. As the two stand on the right half of the screen, a mask moves in to cover the left half, and moves off again when the search is over *(Fahrenheit 451,* François Truffaut).

Part of the set may serve as a mask, as when Julia and Michael Finsbury look at one another through the mail-box. All we see is their eyes, first open and then drooping in rapture *(The Wrong Box,* Bryan Forbes). Part of another person may serve as a mask. Abigail's husband, escaped from the penitentiary, accuses her of being unfaithful and advances threateningly toward her. His dark body masks all of her face but a pale triangle, in which the white of her wildly peering eye catches the light and glitters—the only bright and moving part of the frame *(Christmas Holiday,* Robert Siodmak).

Size. A large foreground image can draw our attention even from background movement. In *Shadow of a Doubt* (Alfred Hitchcock), the two Charleys are seated close to us, talking. It was not until a second viewing that I noticed Louise, the waitress, sauntering away into the distance of a large room, placing the order and serving another customer, and a man rising to let a woman out of a cubicle. These other characters are tiny in size, and the space on the screen covered by their movement is small. In *A Tale of Two Cities* (Jack Conway) a sound is heard on the balcony, and the steward opens the door to look. In a long shot, our attention is caught first by a large carved head, larger than a man's, but where the head of a standing man would be. It is to the right of the French windows and brightly lit. Further right, beyond it, is the head of the intruder, smaller, half hid in the ivy, and with only a tiny gleam of light on it. This negative emphasis gives the impression of concealment, and makes plausible the steward's finding no one.

A moment or posture may be stressed by *freezing*—repeating a single frame a number of times. The commentator says, in *The War Game* (Peter Watkins), "This man is forced to take eight persons into his house, and if he refuses, he is liable to a heavy fine and imprisonment." During this, a shot of the man, in shirt and waistcoat, gesturing defiantly at a policeman, continues without movement.

Music may also emphasize, as italics do in printing. When Superintendent Hasard hears "Dr. Robbins" announced, he turns, but his smile freezes with astonishment, his whole body is still, and the length of the stillness is underlined by a single, sudden, sustained, brass chord. The murdered Sapphire Robbins to all appearance was white: her brother is black *(Sapphire,* Basil Dearden).

Converging movements draw the eye to the point of convergence. Tommy Swann, an escaped convict, is being pursued by the police. The rear end of a train is shunting toward us; we are moving toward it, from the side of the screen Swann is running toward the point of convergence, to throw himself in front of the train *(It Always Rains on Sunday,* Robert Hamer). This one example is merely to suggest that motion is a common means of emphasis. In parts of the chapter on motion, on approach and panoramic shots, for example, other ways may be found of using motion for emphasis

The still painter's means of guiding the eye are used of course by directors, but these have been fully dealt with in other books.

4 Epistrophe

Epistrophe is a figure in which the same word or phrase ends each of a series of clauses or sentences: "We are born in sorrow, pass our time in sorrow, end our days in sorrow."[10] In *The Thirty-Nine Steps* (Alfred Hitchcock), nearly every sequence ends with a still scene from which Hannay has just vanished, which is held long enough to establish the stillness. The bus with Hannay and Annabella pulls away left off the screen and leaves the facade of the Music Hall, with no one in sight. The journey to Scotland ends with a lengthy shot of the Forth bridge, looming dark against a clouded sky with nothing moving; Hannay had disappeared from the train. Hannay and Pamela, handcuffed, escape from two bogus detectives, and hide beneath a falls. The last shot is of the two pursuers in trench coats, standing on a knoll, bright gray on a dark frame, one higher than the other, looking out over the countryside, silent and unmoving.

5 Hendiadys

Montage is bringing together things, persons, or places that may never, in the real world, have been related. *Hendiadys* is taking apart things that belong together. As found in language, a noun and adjective for a single idea become two nouns joined by the conjunction "and." "He climbed the icy cliff" becomes "He climbed the cliff and ice." Instead of one danger, a slippery ascent, the climber has met with two, steepness and slipperiness. The added emphasis of the separation has made us more aware of the risk faced.

How can we separate the parts of an image? In *The Best Years of Our Lives* (William Wyler) three soldiers home from the war are passing down Main Street in a taxi, and through the side window we see the ballpark, fire station, shoe shine, Woolworth's, hot dog stand, and a boy driving a car with a naked engine. We see the three men in the back seat, pointing out the familiar sights. But the meaning of the scene is neither in the sights themselves nor in the animated men: it is places in these men's past, reseen after a long absence. The director therefore shows the passing street, several times, as seen from inside the car, and in the small frame of the rear-view mirror above the windshield we are looking through, he shows the three watching men as if reflected there. The director has separated out, but related in the same frame, the two parts of "Men remembering a town" into "The town, and those who remember it."

In *The Andromeda Strain* (Robert Wise), Dr. Leavitt remembering a conversation, a single event, is broken into two images: a black mask covers the screen, in a small square to the left of which is the thoughtful face of Dr. Leavitt, and in another larger square to the right, she is seen listening to another scientist say that intelligent life on other planets might be very small.

6 Hypallage or Transferred Epithet

Hypallage, or transferred epithet, is placing an adjective with a noun to which it does not logically belong. It is not the night which is restless; it is the person who could not sleep. It is a happy morning only to a happy person.

> On Thracia's hills the Lord of War
> Has curbed the fury of his car
> And dropped his thirsty lance at thy command.[11]

It is not the lance that is thirsty for blood, but the Lord of War who wields it.

It will be seen that hypallage sometimes trails a smatch of simile. In *Zulu* (Cy Endfield) a rifleman is shot and collapses against the bags of a breastwork. A slash in the bag above the soldier's head, caused perhaps by his bayonet as he fell, rains a trickle of grain. But what comes to our minds is not a bag bleeding grain, but a body trickling blood—his life seeping away. The leak is transferred from the soldier to the bag. In another sense there is a simile, in which the two flows are likened. The difference is that if the figure were a simile the trickling grain and the trickling blood would both be seen. In hypallage, there is but one image, dressed with a characteristic borrowed from the other. As Carter is given an anaesthetic on the operating table, it is not his eyes we see closing, but the round ceiling light, slowly overspread from top and bottom by two brown, veined, eye-lids (*A Matter of Life and Death*, Michael Powell and Emeric Pressburger).

Seriochka's pleasure in showing his birthday bicycle to other boys is spoiled when the bigger boys keep the machine to themselves and give him no chance to ride. Beside his hand in close-up is a large leaf carrying drops of water. One of the drops falls. The director respects the boy's feelings and does not show the tear he wishes to hide (*Seriochka*, Georgi Danela).

Hypallage can also be seen, not as displacing an adjective but as substituting the wrong noun for the right one. In *The Purloined Pup* (Charles Nichols, Walt Disney), a pipe rises up out of a moat, the top of it bent over toward us, to look like a periscope, and a pair of eyes peers from its dark opening. The eyes are those of the creature under the water holding the pipe. Instead of saying, "the watching animal," the director says, by substitution, "the watching pipe." In one of the *Pink Panther* films (Isadore Freleng), the Panther backs an insolent visitor off the edge of a cliff. He has ignored the signs reading "No cameras." The camera flies up as the man topples over, the Panther seizes it, takes a picture of the falling man, and pulls out the print. In a down shot we see the Panther's head, the edge of the cliff, and the print. After a second or two, the print shudders, as if it were jarred by striking the ground, like the man too far below to be seen—a reverse homeopathic magic, in which a man affects his image, instead of it affecting him.

In the same way, a sound can be distinguished from the thing that makes it, even in silent films. In *The Fall of the House of Usher* (Jean Epstein) on each stroke of a clock, Roderick's hands begin to quaver violently, lessening in amplitude until the next stroke, when again the quavering starts with new vigor. The bell is struck: the hands vibrate. It is easier still in sound film. Jacqueline Favreux is walking out of a railway station. Daisy, who seeks the Favreux fortune, dressed in a nun's or nurse's habit, steps behind Jacqueline, raises her arm, and brings down what seems to be a dagger into Jacqueline's shoulder. (It is, as we see in a later close-up, a hypodermic syringe.) As the victim's head falls back, her mouth opens to the sudden, loud offscreen shriek from a train leaving the station. By displacement of nouns, the shrieking or whistling *engine* is made into the shrieking or whistling *woman* (*Judex*, George Franju).

Stationary things between an object photographed and the camera sidling with it will take on the speed of the traveling camera; and the closer they are, the faster they seem to move. In another view, the apparent speed of the things between is taken by the viewer as the speed of the distant object, which, however it seems to stay in the same place, must, we know, be moving as fast as the camera. In *Peasants* (Friedrich Ermler), we and a single source of light are traveling even-pace with a white horse galloping along beyond a row of trees. We see the horse against the black night through gaps in the white leaves that streak swiftly by.

Hypallage may blend with metonymy. Colonel von Keller suggests to Lambert, the superintendent of a village and a collaborator, that he make up to the sister of an executed saboteur, to discover who else had been taking part. "You don't think I would do that," says Lambert. Von Keller comes over, touches and looks at the rose he has playfully put in Lambert's buttonhole a little before, and says, "I'm sure you will." After the colonel goes, Lambert throws the rose on the floor. We only hear it fall, for our eyes are on his hands, which take a revolver from the drawer. We look to the wastepaper basket, and, on the floor beside it, the rose. We hear a shot, and in a quick approach, we see the rose shudder (*This Land is Mine*, Jean Renoir).

Where a nondiegetic sound replaces an actual one, an event that would have affected the actual sound may have the same effect on the sound that replaces it. Mathieu Gregoire is driving to the country, ostensibly to arrange the settlement of an action for assault brought against him. He is being followed by a car with two men in it. He thinks they may suspect him of committing a murder. His state of mind is disturbed, and the steady throb of the car is replaced by more expressive music. He stops the car, and the moment he turns the key the music stops, as if it were the motor. An effect suggested perhaps by car radios (*Belle*, André Delvaux).

The characteristics of a person that might be marked in words by an adjective, like blushing, ascending, shaking, or approaching, may be displayed instead by the screen image. When Tom and Sophie first kiss, during his convalescence, before the scene dissolves out, the screen blushes, instead of Sophie (*Tom Jones*, Tony Richardson). *Graves of Sacrifice* (Donald Brittain) is a reconstruction of war, years later, often using still pictures. In one of these, on a sound of firing, the camera quickly and instantly pans from a cloud of white smoke to the muzzle of the gun it came from, recoiling in place of the gun.

The first-person camera, to which I have likened the figure ethopoeia—putting oneself in the place of another—can sometimes be looked upon as hypallage. In *The Clock* (Vincente Minnelli), Joe meets and marries a girl during a seventy-two-hour leave. As the hours pass, the tentative relations between them become warmer. In a series of shots of Joe in up shot and her in down shot (as if from one another's eyes), the camera continues to come nearer to them. We do not see them coming closer. It is we who come, in the person of each in turn, closer to the other.

If the transfer is concealed, can we say there is a figure? When astronauts are seen shaking during a blast-off (*Journey to the Far Side of the Sun*, Robert Parrish), or when parents and child under a table shudder to the shock wave of an atomic bomb (*The War Game*, Peter Watkins), it is hard to avoid reflecting that it is easier to shake the camera than to shake the set, and that the movement seen is likely that of the image, not the people. Perhaps all that can be said is that for the viewer who takes the movement as that of the camera, there is a figure; otherwise there is not.

What is happening to the visible image may be transferred from what is taking place in someone's consciousness. The dark figure at the door was Troy, returned, it seemed, from the dead. He interrupts Boldwood's toast. "Come, madam," he says to Bathsheba brusquely, and makes to pull her away with him down the staircase. As we slowly approach Boldwood, the voices echo distantly and indistinctly, and his image goes out of focus as if he had lost touch with what was going on. Logically, though, what should be going out of focus is not his image, but the image of the world outside with which he was losing touch. The adjectival distortion has been transferred from its proper subject, Troy and Bathsheba (*Far from the Madding Crowd*, John Schlesinger).

A tramp and a dog are fighting over the contents of a garbage bin. Desiré enters from the right, and kneels on one knee to take a picture of it. As he looks in the viewfinder, we approach him rapidly. Perfectly still, he snaps the picture, and then we retreat quickly again to the whole scene. Our sudden concentration on the single figure of the photographer transfers to us his concentration on the subject of his picture. His frozen pose also suggests in the placing of the figure and the lack of movement, that we, not he, were composing the photograph (*Panic*, Julien Duvivier). In *The Private Secretary* (Leonard Grover), there is a masked shot of a hand holding a key, and a door beyond it shifting erratically, as if evading the steady key, whose drunken wobbles have been given to the door instead.

One of the most striking transfers is in *Men of Two Worlds* (Thorold Dickinson). Kisenga, a composer and pianist of some reputation, returns as a teacher to his people in East Africa. The witch doctor opposes him, and makes it clear that Kisenga will die. Kisenga is shown under a mosquito net (in itself a symbol of capture). Hands enter to hold him down as he struggles in delirium. In an up shot of Mangole, the witch doctor, his hands, large in the foreground, come down upon us. Our gaze rises up the net to a death charm. Kisenga, in half-length shot, his arms raised before him, forearms and hands white like a European's, comes toward us, toward the death image, and, seen through the nets, many drummers are beating. We slowly approach Mangole. Kisenga turns to another part of the net, where a symphony orchestra is playing. He pulls the net aside and is going to the piano, pushing aside his father, who is trying to keep him back. Mangole rises up above him, raises a knife, and brings it down, and a gash of red rips the screen, obscuring the image.

And what of this? Charlie knocks out another waiter, and after getting a cordial for him, drinks it himself, at which the unconscious man at once revives as if he had drunk it. There is clearly a substitution of one drinker for another, and a transfer of both the drink, and its effect, if these can be considered adjectival in character. Is it hypallage, is it purely fantasy, or is it both (*The Rink*, Charles Chaplin)?

7 Meiosis

Hyperbole says much more than it means, *meiosis* much less. "If you diminish and abbase a thing, by way of spight or mallice . . . such speach is by the figure Meiosis," says Puttenham, who gives the example, said of a man with a load, "a heavy burthen, perdy, as a pound of feathers."[12] Falstaff says, "And this same half-faced fellow, Shadow; give me this man: he presents no mark to the enemy; the foeman may with as great aim level at the edge of a penknife."[13]

Richard Massingham in *Read Any Good Meters Lately?* (Richard Massingham) remarks, "I am a little absent-minded," and we then see him lying down in the bath fully clothed, wearing a bowler hat and smoking both cigar and pipe.

Hyperbole as well as meiosis is found in a scene from *The Great Dictator* (Charles Chaplin). So wild are Hynkel's face and arms, so savage the consonants of his mock-German, that the microphone shrinks back in fear. The commentator's translation is terse and matter-of-fact, "His Excellency has been referring to the Jewish people."

Meiosis in film thus appears to require a visual image, and a further description in words or other sound of the same subject, which "diminishes" or belittles the message conveyed by the image. It is possible to emphasize a river's perils by filling a frame in close-up with its foamy turbulence; it is equally possible to understate them by taking the river from far away, to show it barely flowing (*Morning on the Lièvre*, Grant Crabtree). In the absence of anything more, however, to compare it with, we take such an image as a plain statement of what the river is like, and are not aware of any hyperbole (where a like disproportion must also be present) or any meiosis.

8 Mimesis

Mimesis is "an imitation of word or gesture"[14] or a character's expressing himself "in his own words", or, we might say, in his own movements.[15] The camera thus might simulate the movement of a person or thing. Where the view through the camera is that of a person or animal, it is better to view it as the camera personating the character, ethopoeia or prosopopoeia. Where, however, the movement imitated is that of a thing, it must be seen as mimesis.

Mimesis may be done by movement of the camera. A composer plays a waltz, and the camera, as it pans to Cleo's maid, sways ever so slightly from side to side, in time to the music (*Cleo from Five to Seven*, Agnes Varda). A machine gun is heard outside, and the camera pans toward the window across the café in a long succession of tiny jerky steps that imitates the strepitant rattle of the gun (*Vivre Sa Vie*, Jean-Luc Godard).

Mimesis may also be done by editing. Eisenstein, in a much-cited passage, shows us two shots, turn about, each two frames long. In one shot a machine gun, shield, barrel, and muzzle, is seen against a light ground. In the other, on a darker ground, is the gunner, head, shoulder, and hand, as he sights and fires. Both shots are composed on the same diagonal, but one, for the most part, is light in a place where the other is dark. The quick change of image simulates the clattering rhythm of the firing (*October*).

8 Paronomasia or Pun—Simile

The play on words, *pun*, or *paronomasia* must not be confused with other tricks with words that are rather like it.

For the earlier writers, the play is between two words, nearly but not quite the same in sound, differing, as John Smith says, in one letter only. "He was bolder in a buttery than in a battery." "Friends turned fiends."[16]

It is not used either for the "mental juxtaposition of ideas, with the sensation, but without the reality, of connection,"—the Irish bull. An Irishman is alleged to have said, "This is a darling saucepan. Sure, I wouldn't be after partin' with it, if it wasn't to get some money to buy somethin' to put in it."[17]

A change of meaning during the flight of a word is a staple of comedians.

"Give me three fingers of rye," says Wayne.

"And you, sir?"

"I'll have three fingers," says Shuster.

"Three fingers of what, sir?"

"Just three fingers—I'm hungry."

The unexpected slip out of one meaning into another, from finger, as a unit of measurement, to finger, as meat for eating, is again not a pun.

These are all, in some sense, plays on words, but paronomasia, as used here, is none of these. It is Empson's Type Two, in which two apparently unconnected meanings, which the reader is prepared to hold in his mind at the same time, are given simultaneously, as where two ideas, both of which could apply in the situation, are given in one word in which they clash.[18]

If the pun is a verbal matter, dependent on the large number of homonyms that English provides, perhaps the pun does not exist on film, except verbally. Allen, escaped from a prison farm, is being shaved. Behind him, a policeman enters the barber shop, tells the barber the news of the escape, and gives a description of the escaped convict. We see Allen's head, as he eyes the barber intently and asks, "Could I have a hot towel, please?" When the towel is taken off, he pays the barber, keeping his back to the policeman. He sweeps his hat low over his eyes and rubs his face. "Close enough?" says the barber. "Plenty," says Allen and goes (*I Was a Fugitive from a Chain Gang*, Mervyn Leroy). "Close shave" and "Close escape from recapture," both relevant, both different, both intended meanings, are held in the mind at the same time, when Allen says "Plenty."

We never see the parade itself, but as each unit passes, the eyes in the reviewing stand scan from right to left. "Hynkel's heavy tanks" are announced, and heads turn to a loud clanking sound; "Hynkel's light tanks," and heads turn to dead silence. Thistledown is *light* and noiseless, but a *light tank*, so classed by weight of armor and bore of gun carried, will make some noise. This is meiosis in sound (*The Great Dictator*, Charles Chaplin).

The literary pun is a single word used in two meanings. The filmic pun must abandon the word. What, in film, matches the play on words is the play on shapes or sounds, and these are all to be found in the chapter on simile. The gestures of a traffic policeman and those of an orchestra leader are both "conducting" the movements of many people (*Capriccio*, Ole Askeman); the notion "religious war" is neatly implied in the likeness between the spire of a church and the spike on a soldier's helmet (*The Little Island*, Richard Williams); a cut between the like-sounding strepitation of a fighter plane's machine gun and a typewriter suggests the sword and the pen—two ways of fighting an enemy (*Things to Come*, William Cameron Menzies).

9   The Pathetic Fallacy

Since John Ruskin devised the term, *the pathetic fallacy* (pls. 35, 36), it would be presumptuous to present it in other than his words:

"I want to examine the nature of the . . . error . . . the mind admits, when affected strongly by emotion. Thus, for instance, in Alton Locke,—

They rowed her in across the rolling foam—
The cruel, crawling foam.

The foam is not cruel, neither does it crawl. The state of mind which attributes to it these characters of a living creature is one in which the reason is unhinged by grief. All violent feelings have the same effect. They produce in us a falseness in all our impressions of external things, which I would generally characterize as the "Pathetic fallacy."[19]

David Lean makes good use of this figure. It is no accident that the transient love that spans a few weeks, of two middle-aged married people, takes place mostly in autumn: when boats are put away for the winter, trees are leafless, breath is occasionally steamy, and the weather is dull and rainy (*Brief Encounter*). Despite her letter of good-bye, Stephen insists on seeing Mary Justin. As he waits, a stock exchange ticker chatters, the wind gusts curtains into the room, rain slaps the panes in sudden pulses, and papers flutter and rustle on the desk. It is an unquiet room, but cold and passionless. He turns as she enters, dressed in black, "I can't come with you" (The Passionate Friends). In Oliver Twist, a woman undergoing labor pains makes her solitary way up a hill to the workhouse during a thunderstorm, and leans for a moment against a tree with its branches toothed by thorns. The pains of her body are matched by the lash of the rain, the plunging jag of light, and the jabbing threat of the tree.

Having offended the rival bosses of a village, Sanjuro, a samurai, has been beaten. His innkeeper took him away from the village, fed and nursed him. Sanjuro learns that because of him the innkeeper has been tortured. He rises in anger, takes the sword that the coffinmaker brings him, and returns to the village. He stands on a raised terrace at one end of the village street, small in size but bold and still, the only figure in sight. Around and behind this avenging figure, a storm wind swirls banners of dust, and we hear the pulse of a cymbal (Yojimbo, Akira Kurosawa).

In all these third-person narratives, the surroundings express the character's feelings, as we take them to be, as the director intends us to take them. We are nowhere told that this was how the character felt the world around him to be, which is strictly what the pathetic fallacy is.

By a change of treatment, by suggesting that the images are those of the character's choosing, not the director's, and putting us thus in the shoes of a character, the true pathetic fallacy is regained. The pregnant woman could well have felt the storm as a sign, a metaphor, of the world's hostility.

It is a commonplace that our present mood chooses from the sights and sounds around us, those that run with it, and ignores the rest. Thus, in the same place, different moods can find their proper food. Dick, an American soldier, is shown into the anteroom of a church official. Dick is unsure of himself and what he is going to do. He looks around. There are quick shots of two statues, watching out of the corners of their eyes, and then of one staring at him in glowering disapproval. Other works of art must have been there, but the ones he noticed were those that enhanced his uneasiness (A Yank in Rome, Luigi Zampa).

There is in this a kind of animism, a sense that the world around is not indifferent, but responsive to, and active in, our affairs. In The Captive Heart (Basil Dearden), Captain Haček a Czechoslovakian, to escape detection by German police, took the papers of a dead English officer. In prison camp, he felt he had to answer letters from the Englishman's wife, as if he were her husband. When he is exchanged for a German prisoner, he calls to tell her of her husband's death, and why he had written as he did, but adds, "I want you to know that I meant everything I said." She comes to love him, and on Victory Day, when she is watching the fireworks, she is called to the telephone. In between voiceless shots of her as she runs to the house, and of both her and Captain Haček as they speak to one another, are shots of rockets exulting into the sky,—darkness filled with spreading ecstasies of light. And in Snow White and the Seven Dwarfs (Walt Disney), trees claw at Snow White in the forest, their trunks glower, their fallen logs gape with crocodile jaws.

10   Prosopopoeia or Personification

To give a human shape or human qualities to an animal, thing, or idea is the figure prosopopoeia.[20] It hides a metaphor,[20] as when John Donne compares the morning sun to a busybody shouting through the window to wake us up:

> Busie old foole, unruly Sunne,
> Why dost thou thus,
> Through windowes, and through curtaines call on us?[21]

Prosopopoeia in film has several forms. There is the first person camera, which may be seen either as ethopoeia—putting oneself in another's place—or prosopopoeia—making the camera into a person, through whose eyes we see. When the game warden in *Ivory Hunter* (Harry Watt) is charged by a wounded elephant, we approach him from the height of an elephant's eyes, a small figure hardly seen between the trees, his rifle raised and then shooting. The camera tilts, obliquely, slowly, and sideways, and sinks to the ground—for the moment, we are the elephant.

It is certainly prosopopoeia when a car, having bounced up and down on a bumpy road, goes on bouncing after it is back on a paved highway; like a person coming ashore, and finding his muscles behaving as if he were still at sea (*Girl Shy*, Fred Newmayer and Sam Taylor).

When a dead person speaks or moves, it is called eidolopoeia.

Sullivan is trapped by a widow, who commands the only door to his room and has made amorous advances. We have seen on the wall a picture of Joseph, the widow's late husband. As Sullivan ties the rope of sheets for his final successful attempt at escape by the window, we see Joseph's eyes widen. For a moment the painted canvas appears to live (*Sullivan's Travels*, Preston Sturges).

Epiphania talks to her dead father's portraits (*The Millionairess*, Anthony Asquith). As we hear his voice giving her advice, raising an objection, or giving an answer, we may be looking at her or at one of the many carved or painted figures of him that seem to inspect every room in the house. We may be looking at him as she replies. At last, he is pictured in sun helmet, seated amid a group of blacks, and in silence he holds out the handle of his revolver. The figure conveys the effect of the dead on the living (and the number of portraits proves his great wealth).

Seen from another direction, turning ideas into people, is like stripping a person of all but a single quality:

> In gallant trim the gilded vessel goes;
> Youth on the prow and Pleasure at the helm.[22]

This can also be seen as metonymy: abstract for concrete, Youth for young people. The process is clearer still in interludes like *Everyman*, whose characters have such names as Friendship, Good Deeds, Strength, Kin, and so on.

This is found in the animated cartoon, in which simplified features are matched by simple characterization. Bugs Bunny is *cunning;* the Seven Dwarfs even have names like *Happy, Bashful,* or *Dopey* (*Snow White and the Seven Dwarfs*, Walt Disney). They are paper-thin predictable people with only one response. It is found also in Oliver Hardy, who could fairly be described as *slow-witted and conceited,* and Stan Laurel, as *slow-witted and timid.* It is clearer still in a film like *Happiness* (Aleksandr Medvedev), where prosopopoeia treads the same ground as allegory. Khmyr, a peasant, finds a purse, by which means he buys tools and a horse, and raises a glorious crop. A title (the film is silent) reads, "One in the field, seven to feed." One after another a priest (the church), a soldier (the army), and a tax collector (the state) come in and drive off with bags of grain. The final wagon pulls down the fence. Two nuns (charity) and three beggars (sloth) apply to Khymr for food, and the latter, because Khymr has nothing left, beat him with his own stick. But this is not all. Two men (theft) come during the night, wrench the lock from off his little house, pull out a trunk and pry its hinges off, force the lock of the chest within that and find an empty purse, whereupon they abuse Khymr for going to such pains to hide nothing. None of these persons is long on the screen or developed in character beyond his function as a pillager of peasants, whenever, once in a long time, they prosper. Those who plundered Khmyr were merely ideas with legs.

Another form of the figure in literature is making parts of a man into persons, with wills of their own apart from the whole to which they belong.

> Send home my long strayed eyes to me
> Which (oh) too long have dwelt on thee;[23]

What a brave soul it is that is always prepared to leave the body.[24]

In the same way, in *The Little Island* (Richard Williams), Good sends his hand up out of the frame, which later comes down as if it were an independent blue hand, quite disowned by him, which forces him into actions he could not otherwise justify. He thus hypostatizes his own desires into a force outside himself to which he owns obedience (pl. 29).

Analogous to talk between soul and body is the dialogue in *Flesh and Fantasy* (Julien Duvivier) between a reflected image or a shadow and the man they belong to. They signify another self or new intruding motives. Marshall Tyler has been told by a palmist such minor things as where to find his lost pocketbook, and then, reluctantly, that he is going to murder someone. He stops at a shop window and looks at his image in it. "I don't want to murder anybody . . . but there is the pocketbook." "A shot in the dark," his reflection answers. After the colloquy is over, Tyler turns away. His reflection does too, but not with quite the same gesture; and it says, with its eye on the man it should be imitating, "Pull yourself together." As Tyler sits by the fire, his shadow leans on a piece of furniture, and says, as it points a thoughtful finger at him, "If you had the chance to kill someone a thousand miles from here, old and utterly worthless to anybody, would you do it?" "Of course, without hesitation." The shadow chuckles, "So it's only the distance that counts."

Tyler is going over the names on a list, and ends with Lady Pamela Hardwick. "Perfect," he concludes, "nobody'd ever miss her—absolutely useless." From the reading glasses that sit on the table, his twin reflections answer back in unison, "She is always sick." "How old is she?" "Seventy or seventy-five." Outside on the street he continues, "But she's good for a number of years yet."

From a mirror that hangs on a post, his other self replies with a question, "Weeks?" Tyler answers, "Well, months." To a shop window further on he puts the point, "But she's fond of me", and the window image answers, "Well, of course, if you're going to let sentiment stand in your way. . . ."

The easiest means to prosopopoeia in "moving pictures" is using animation to give human shape and motion to lifeless things.

A train at the top of a hill sniffs at a flower before swooping down the other slope. Holsters even spread themselves to receive Panchito's revolvers (*The Three Caballeros*, Norman Ferguson). A steam engine is given eyes, piston chambers that thrust like feet when it pulls, and a mouth and voice that cry "All aboard" (*Dumbo*, Walt Disney and Ben Sharpsteen; pl. 37). A building hoist falling at breakneck speed politely slides across to the next shaft on meeting someone, sliding back again after it has passed him (*Rhapsody in Rivets*, Leon Schlesinger and Isadore Freleng). A mere line, the soundtrack in *Fantasia* (Walt Disney), is gifted with human feelings, joy, and bashfulness. Even the little wandering black blob, which interlopes into several successive patterns like a questing fly, is a feckless halfwitted unit of design that will not stay in shape or keep its place—the comic relief (*Fiddle-De-Dee*, Norman McLaren).

It may also be considered prosopopoeia (though not within the usual definition) to make inanimate things into animals. In *Tales of Hoffnung: Music Academy* (John Halas and Tony Guy), as Liszt's *Hungarian Fantasia* breaks loose into its wilder passages, the piano becomes excited. It throws up its hind legs, and the pianist has to lash at the floor with a whip to hold back its bearlike charges. A spray of buckshot becomes a swarm of bees, tormenting the horse at which they were fired (*Jail Birds*, U. B. Iwerks). A cloud of smoke, when a door is slammed on it, sneaks round a corner, finds a knothole, draws back its head, and plunges through (*Smoked Hams*, Dick Lundy).

It is easier to make a person out of a dog, for dogs are very much persons themselves. *Let's Keep a Dog* (Ternovsky Bela) instructs us on real or fancied uses of dogs, one of which is the teaching of children. The dog who demonstrates this has a long, narrow nose, fitted with pince-nez, and a paw, which, when he raises it, has long, narrow, elegant fingers. The slight adjustment in the features and adding fingers was enough to make us sure that we had known someone just like him.

Groups like orchestras, who work together to create a single impression, can also assume a single personality. The *Light Cavalry Overture* slackens pace, and pauses lengthen beyond the authority of the score or any reasonable conception of rubato. At last the music stops entirely, and then as one man, players and conductor sneeze. If they play as one man, why should the habit not reach to their other doings too, perhaps to all.[25]

11 Tapinosis

Puttenham seems to consider that the figure *tapinosis* (bathos or anticlimax) is never carefully conceived but unwittingly committed: "If ye abase your thing or matter by ignorance or errour in the choice of your word."[26] He cites a certain "serjeant" who said to Queen Elizabeth's coachman during one of her magnificent progresses, "Stay thy cart, good fellow, that I may speake to the Queene." Treble and Vallins, on the other hand, quote from De Quincey's *Murder Considered as One of the Fine Arts*, a sentence undoubtedly deliberate, "If once a man indulges himself in murder, very soon he comes to think nothing of robbing; and from robbing he comes next to drinking and Sabbath-breaking, and from that to incivility and procrastination."[27] But whether from choice or neglect, we encounter the humdrum when expecting drama, the trite when expecting the tragic, disorder in place of dignity.

The best examples are from Chaplin, and are certainly not slips. Captain Schultz turns up as Charlie, the barber, is about to be hanged. At the captain's command, Charlie is let fall to the ground. At a further command, he is helped up to his feet by a yank of the halter. Charlie makes to lean on the gate post with defiant arrogance, but misses it and falls again. In the same film, Hynkel stands on the red carpet with all his dignitaries, awaiting Napaloni. Napaloni's carriage stops at another place. There is an unseemly scramble to where his carriage is. The train then backs up to the right place, and they scramble again.

On another solemn occasion, five dedicated men are eating pudding. It is agreed that the man whose helping holds a coin will bomb Hynkel's palace. Each man, as he probes his pudding with apparent indifference and feels his fork meet metal, furtively slips the bite containing the coin to his neighbor's plate (for, thinking the whole thing silly, Hannah placed a coin in each piece). Charlie in the center, richer by four coins, watched by four pairs of expectant eyes, swallows each coin, giving no sign that he knows it is there. He coughs. There is a rattle as of a jackpot in a pinball machine, and one by one he coughs the coins up. An enterprise of great pitch and moment ends in ignominy *(The Great Dictator)*.

18
Fantasy—Allegory—Abstraction

1 Four Forms of the Fantasy

Critics have spoken of the stubbornly realistic nature of the film.[1] Yet its images can falsify the world, can stand less for the things they show than for other meanings at one remove beyond them.

One approach to tampering with photographic fact is *fantasy*, the realistic depicting of what we know is imaginary, highly unlikely, or presently impossible. It is spoken of as a tone or mode of expression, a genre, not a figure; and yet, in fantasy's four kinds are happenings hinting at meanings beyond themselves, and that is what figures are: (i) absurdities; (ii) inner experiences; (iii) the supernatural; (iv) fantasy which is also allegory.

2 The Absurd

The farfetched is a first step to the absurd; it is the utmost reach of the (just barely) possible, a kind of hyperbole (pl. 34). The operative word here is "if" (pl. 8).

Donald Duck is on a suspension bridge. The last rope frays and snaps, and he is holding an end of the rope in either hand. He pulls the ends together and ties them into a knot. If the power of the human muscle were multiplied by the right figure, it could be done (*Saludos Amigos*, Walt Disney). If a hippopotamus could perform ballet and could spin sufficiently fast, no doubt its bulk would rise and bulge out by centrifugal force (*The Dance of the Hours: Fantasia*, T. Hu and Norman Ferguson). If objects moving at the speed of light become shorter, why should not a canoe too shrink in length when the stern paddler works harder than the one in front and the stern thus goes forward faster than the bow (*Jolly Fish*, John Foster and George Stallings)?

If the fabled botchery of builders goes a bit beyond what they are now accused of doing, some of the mishaps in *A Home of Your Own* (Jay Lewis) could conceivably happen. When the not-so-newlyweds (they have waited a long time for their house) take possession, three men try to open a door without success. The door is then pushed out and a man emerges: the hinge and the handle are on the same edge. The handbasin tap roars when turned. The elegant-looking rose for the shower asks, "Number please." The bathroom switch starts a stream of water through the socket.

In one hand a man holds the horn of a phonograph, and in the other hand he holds

332

its diaphragm the two joined by a wire. The record lies on top of a tree stump. The man races around the stump to the sound of music, appearing to keep the needle in the groove of the record (*The Running, Jumping, and Standing Still Film*, Dick Lester).

A second kind of absurdity passes beyond the barely possible into the unbelievable.

In *L'Homme de Têtes* (George Méliès), a conjurer takes off his head as if he were doffing a hat. He does it three times and lines up his discards on a table. To a guitar accompaniment, he and his three severed heads perform a quartet. The Diabolical Pickpocket baffles pursuing gendarmes by walking through a locked gate or becoming a rug, patterned like his jacket (*The Diabolical Pickpocket*, Georges Méliès).

The communication cord on a train is severed from its handle, but a downward pull on the handle still stops the train (*All a Bird*, Isadore Freleng). He fingers a nonexistent violin, but as he plies his bow, we hear the street-player's music (*Zazie dans le Metro*, Louis Malle). An elephant blows a soap bubble, and as it rolls, he leaps on it and balances (*The Dance of the Hours: Fantasia*, T. Hu and Norman Ferguson). Laurel sees on a white wall the shadowed lines cast by an open window, with flower pot and blind. He seizes the shadow blind and pulls it down (*Blockheads*, John G. Blystone).

In *Hellzapoppin* (Harold C. Potter), Olsen and Johnson face toward us, hail the projectionist, and tell him to keep them in the frame and not follow the girl in the bathing suit—something only the cameraman could do. The screen image then, by reason (it is implied) of a violent argument in the projection booth, starts to wobble and the actors on the screen reach to the top of the frame to hold it steady. The frame line falls down to near center screen. The top halves of two actors are seen below it, and a third is crouched in a narrow attic between the fallen line and the top of the screen. "How did you get up there?" they ask him.

A third kind of absurdity is making a mere concept, a palpable, visible thing. Pablo the Penguin's vessel made of ice butts against a yellow-tawny equator floating on the surface and bounces back from it. Neptune rises out of the water, lifts the equator up, and Pablo sails beneath it. Giving a physical form to what is imagined is not a great remove from prosopopoeia, by which we give eyes, voice, and a will to a steam engine (*The Three Caballeros*, Norman Ferguson).

3 Inner States

Children are most apt in shaping the seen into the wished-for, the everyday into the far-off, the real into the fancied.

There is no logic or plausibility to the way the boy's bed becomes *The Truck That Flew* (George Pal). Disney would have found an ingenious way that would satisfy the adult mind of discovering or making the wheels, engine, and cab from some oddments lying around the nursery. Here there is no fuss at all. The bed moves out from the wall, and the engine, cab, and wheels are suddenly there.

The same director has used color and monochrome to set the imagined off against the real. In monochrome, a boy's legs walk down steps and along the street, as his voice tells us that his father had told him always to observe carefully wherever he was and then to tell his father what he saw, and all he had seen was a horse and a wagon on Mulberry Street. This dissolves to the other side of the street, with horse and wagon and milk cans on the curb. How much more exciting, the voice continues, if the horse were a zebra (a yellow zebra takes the place of a monochrome horse), if the milkman were a charioteer (a full-color charioteer springs onto the screen). And so with all the oddments added on—a sleigh, a band, a snake charmer, and so on. But all he tells his father is that he saw a horse and a wagon (*And to Think That I Saw It on Mulberry Street*, George Pal).

A dozing projectionist in *Sherlock Junior* (Buster Keaton) adds an adult ingenuity to similar fancies. As he leans on the second projector, a second self rises out of his body, enters the auditorium, and climbs up into the frame of the screen. He is kicked out of the screen, off the stage, and over the piano by the villain. When he tries to reenter, the film cuts to a door being closed on his face. At another place, he picks himself up to sit thoughtfully down on a stone bench, and on the change of shot, he just avoids sitting down on the road in front of a car. He turns to walk off the road and pulls himself up on the edge of a cliff.

Her fantasy is kinder to *Ninotchka* (Ernst Lubitsch). She is a peasant delegate from revolutionary Russia, and sybaritic Paris has led her to abandon her spartan principles as far as to spend a night out with a count and his wine. When she wakes up the following morning, she looks with remorse at the picture of Lenin standing beside her bed. A smile appears to soften his resolute features.

Fantasy can deftly convey feelings.

When Charlie goes to "check the fuse" of the dud shell from the Big Bertha gun, the shell begins to swivel with a whizzing noise, like the hand on a gauge, to point its nose at him wherever he runs. It is more than a gag: it is fright giving rise to hallucination (*The Great Dictator*, Charles Chaplin; pl. 32).

When *The Juggler of Our Lady* (Al Kodzel), sees his fellow-brothers—the cook, the musician, the sculptor and others—working, he feels that what he can do is worth little, and he shrinks in size.

An animal-person is standing on a jut of rock, whose neck someone else cuts through. The unsupported rock does not fall till the person standing on it knows it is severed. Then it drops. This is a fantasy on what is common knowledge; that a blindfolded person may stand on a plank just off the ground, quite stably, but if he is told he is high above the ground, he loses his balance (*Scrambled Aches*, Chuck Jones).

Fantasies may be symptoms of morbid states of mind. The morning after a night of drinking, Hobson sees (and we see) a huge fly half the width of the screen coming at us and growing larger (*Hobson's Choice*, David Lean). A burly winter-coated policeman enters the door. A cocaine smoker snatches up a knife and the policeman vanishes—a sense of power (*Drug Addict*, Robert Anderson).

4 The Supernatural

It is natural for fantasy to be supernatural, even if it is not so declared (pl. 38). When it is, says E. M. Forster, it may bring into everyday life the strangeness of a god, a ghost, an angel, a monster, or a witch; or bring an everyday man into a strange world, in the past or future, the core of the earth, or the fourth dimension.[2] The film, which can show with ease the presumed impossible, lends itself to the legendary supernatural.

Dracula has lingered with Nina till after sunrise. He leaves her bed, and as he passes the bright window, he turns, raises his arm as if to ward off the sunlight, and vanishes. We see steam rising from the floor of the room. "The Master is dead," says Renfield (*Nosferatu*, F. W. Murnau).

Many of the events in *Vampyr* (Theodor Dreyer) have a tenuous connection with the action but bring about a supernatural atmosphere. A shadow glides away from a man with a peg leg who cast it. It glides back to its proper position, and man and shadow leave, tied as usual. Shadows of men slip along a river bank with no one to cast them. The sockets of a skull that sits on a table move like eyeballs to follow Marguerite as she crosses a room. It is as if an invisible world were dropping hints of its presence by synecdoche.

A woodman sees the Snow Maiden breathe into his companion's lips and kill him. The woodman promises not to tell what he saw. He meets a strange girl (who later proves to be the Snow Maiden), chases her over the withered grass, and marries her. We feel a spell cast over everything. We see an eye in the sky, and the sun is a pair of lips. The grass by the blue sea is red, and the sky is yellow and black or pink and yellow (*The Snow Maiden: Kwaidan*, Masaki Kobayashi).

This animism is also found in *La Belle et la Bête* (Jean Cocteau). As La Belle enters a hallway, the girandoles on either side are bare arms reaching out of the walls, which wave her along the hall, and the candles light up just as she reaches them. The arm holding the candlestick in the center of the table unclenches itself and pours the wine. The bed clothes creep off the bed in welcome to her (pl. 39).

Metaphors have been made by using film negative. As Jonathan Harker rides by coach to Dracula's castle, the image changes from positive to negative. The trees are a wraithly white instead of being in shadow, perhaps to suggest the reversal of good and evil, certainly to suggest that Harker has left the world of normal values. Coach, horses, and horse cloths with deep eye holes, remain black, suggesting that a different, white coach was used for the negative shots (*Nosferatu*, F. W. Murnau). And in *Orphée* (Jean Cocteau), when the motorcar crosses the railway, passing from the world of the living to that of the dead, the image again changes to negative, for the dark underworld of the dead, the world of the shades.

5 Allegory

Allegory should strictly be placed with metaphor, for it is a story whose whole is a single metaphor, but it is the longest and most elaborate of all figures; if it came anywhere else but at the end, it would seem anticlimactic. The use of the allegory has been traced from late Roman times to Orwell, Kafka, and Pinter,[3] but it is so much in the way we think and speak, to find in what we see something to stand for what we cannot see, that few descriptions escape a touch of symbolism.[4] If, as we follow the persons through the story, we find ourselves considering how widely its course is true in human affairs, the story is then a symbol, worked out in all of its particulars, for something beyond itself, and thus an allegory.[5] Not all allegories were intended as such when written. "We cannot speak, perhaps we can hardly think, of an 'inner conflict' without a metaphor," says C. S. Lewis, "and every metaphor is an allegory in little."[6]

There is a pleasure in balancing together at one time the image and the gloss, the story of particular people, and the shadows of thousands like them confirming the universal that lurks beyond them. Early in the story, we must be alert for the second or moral meaning, so as to enjoy its details with greater subtlety.[7]

Boccaccio found three classes of allegory: the Fable, the Myth, and the History, and these apply just as well to film.[8]

6 The Fable

To give speech, feelings and attitudes, as the fable does, to lifeless things and animals, is manifestly a use of prosopopoeia; as when a lock, tired of the key daily entering his bowels and churning up his stomach, stopped up the keyhole, by reason of which the owner tore off the lock and broke it; or when Silver charged Iron with making wars, and Iron retorted that centuries of wrongdoing, from adultery to treason, had come from love of Silver.[9]

In many animated cartoons, the allegory is not clearly conceived and these are of little interest here, but in other examples a gloss is readily found.

A broad red band along the top of the frame is the goal striven for by the characters, though what it stands for we are never told. One with a kind of jack nearly succeeded before he dropped back; another was lifted on the backs of a swaying pile of people, another was raised up on a woman's shoulders, and another still climbed on a pile of bricks. The one who at last attains the top hangs down by his feet and frightens or disturbs the others left on the ground (*The Top*, I. T. Murokami).

An angular figure, singing a cheerful but monotonous tune as he takes his ease on a beach, blows into a number of small triangles. One enlarges into a bed, another into a pillow, and another still into a barbecue. He deflates his car, inflates a rod, and then a fish, which he catches and eats. He inflates a milk bottle and then a girl. At first the girl will not grow big enough. When at last her size is right, she will not do as he wishes: he thereupon deflates her. He blows up the car, deflates everything else, and throws them in the car. He inflates the road, deflates the lake and puts it away, drives away, runs off the road, and collapses himself. Starting with normally inflatable things like a bed and pillow, this means of providing for our wants is step-by-step made more absurd in poking fun at the hollow substitutes for life, which seem to satisfy many city dwellers (*Substitute*, Dusan Vukotic).

In *The Island* (F. Khitrouk), a meek-looking common man on a small desert island, is exploited by various interests. First, he is ignored—by a barge of new cars moving left to right and a barge of scrapped cars moving right to left. A tug tows a huge statue to the left. Shortly afterwards, a launch labeled *Interpol* stops, questions him, takes him away, comes back with the statue in tow, and puts him back on the island. A man shakes his hand, and the launch leaves him. A boat comes from a steamer, cuts down the only tree on the island, and again goes off without him. A lofty structure of stained glass glides in from the left, from which a priest comes in a boat, raises a cross, blesses the castaway, and then departs, leaving him again alone and unprovided, except now for a Bible.

I prefer not to describe *The Little Island* by Richard Williams, a half-hour animated film in which we are shown, without a word spoken, the highly abstract thesis that those professing the pursuit of either Truth, Goodness, or Beauty may, by intolerance of the other two, be led to acts of hideous violence against them. To try in a paragraph to describe this richly figured fable would be to understate its many excellences (pls. 29, 40, 41).

These fables are also satires.

7 The Myth

In the myth we seem to see human beings, but they are as much universal types as individuals. In the medieval morality, *The Castle of Perseverance*, we see, as in any other drama, people in conflict, but their names are Backbiter, Folly, Sir Covetyse.

Glynne Wickham tells us that in medieval times the appeal of Troilus and Cressida was as symbols respectively of constancy and faithlessness, as having meaning outside their own time and experience.[10] At the same time, it is useful in rehearsing a play like *Everyman* to ask the actors in what relation they stand to Everyman. Beauty will likely think herself his mistress, Five Wits his mother, and so on, for this will keep alive in their imaginations the dualism of the myth, in which someone who lives in a certain time and place is just as clearly shaped in the mold of some recurring type of person or passion, a universal.

This double view of the characters lasted long past the Middle Ages. In Ben Jonson's *The Alchemist*, Sir Epicure Mammon is described as "a swaggering avaricious knight"; Lady Sneerwell and Snake live up to their names in Sheridan; in plays like Priestley's *They Came to a City* or *The Rose and Crown*, or Max Frisch's *The Fire-Raisers*, even if characters are not named as types, they are easily placed as such; and Death is to be found in *The Rose and Crown*, and Biedermann, "the common honest man" in *The Fire-Raisers*. As Louis MacNeice puts it, "Too Much Character Spoils the Theme."[11]

Satire is found here too. In *Mrofnoc* (J. J. Sedelmaier) a man ascends a stair into the street to find everyone walking backwards. Puzzled at first, confused, and jostled, he watches. Tentatively, and then with growing confidence, he himself starts to back up, and when last we see him, is able to thread the throng with ease, and thus to *conform*.

The Fat and the Lean (Roman Polanski) appears to portray the Cunning Employer and the Simple Exploited Worker. The Lean One dances to the beat of the Fat One's drum, shines his shoes, brings his dinner, holds his target for shooting, brings a cigar, plays the fiddle, and rocks him to sleep. Once, beguiled by the look of the distant city, the Lean One tiptoes away, but is brought back by the Fat One, who tethers a goat to his ankle. All his work is complicated now by the inseparable goat. Again the Lean One tries to flee, with the goat. Again he is brought back. This time, the Fat One unshackles the goat from his ankle. The Lean One is so overcome at the Fat One's making his work so easy now (forgetting that it was the Fat One's goat that had made it hard in the first place) that he plants artificial tulips around the sleeping figure of the Cunning Employer, and with his back to the city, leaps for joy.

Perhaps the most memorable scene in another myth of capitalism, *A Nous la Liberté* (René Clair), is near the end. A suitcase slides down the slope of a roof, and as it springs open, a gust strews the bank notes it contains over a large courtyard, where an array of directors in top hats and morning coats are declaring the new factory officially open. As they see the shower of bank notes, they swarm from the rostrum in hasty companies and appear to be blown across the large yard as if they were bank notes, grabbing for as many of these as their hands can hold. Their dignity of costume is contradicted by what seems to be a compulsive grabbing of the tokens of wealth, without enquiring where they came from or to whom they might belong.

Strictly speaking, the medieval allegory dealt with what is the nature of God and of Man.[12] It might, as a byway, satirize Man.

Adolescence and independence appear to be shown through the third keyhole in *The Blood of a Poet* (Jean Cocteau). A woman in nineteenth-century costume beckons a child up a ladder with gestures of a whip and off the top of the ladder on to the wall. At the end, the child floats in a corner of the ceiling, feet down, tongue out and cocking a snook at the woman who drove him up.

Birth and growth seem to be shown in *At Land* (Maya Deren). Laboriously she pulls herself up, one hand at a time, through the water-polished tentacles of a tree root that lies on the sandy shore where the sea had thrown her up. Then over the end of a dinner table, fingers appear, eyes, and then mouth. The eyes look up. From the glass chandelier they see, we pan down through rising smoke to the table from cloth level. Down the length of the table men and women are seated at either side in formal attire, chatting. Her foot thrusts down on the dead root and her knees mount over the edge of the table. She crawls on her hands and knees along the center of the table, in her tattered nondescript garment, ignored by the elegant guests. In all the passages of life depicted in the film, she is shown unchanged, with full adult stature, just as we feel ourselves to have always been the same, as far back as memory can go, through growth of body, duress of circumstance, and final fragility.

While allegories proper dealt with *what is*, those described as "moral allegories" took for their concern *how we should act*.[13]

Fritz Lang's *Destiny*, set in the Middle Ages, has most of the marks of medieval allegory. A tall, stern-looking man lives in a garden, whose high wall has no apparent gate. A young man who has recently been betrothed goes off in his company. When he fails to return, his betrothed seeks out the stern man, and finds him in a room with many burning candles. Her lover's time had come, the man told her, but, pointing to a bracket of three burning candles, if she could stop even one of those from going out, she could, he said, have her lover back. Here follow the stories of three women, in Baghdad, in Italy, and in China, each of whom strove to save her lover from death, and failed. Touched by her grief, Death gives her another hour of grace, in which to find a life to give him in place of her lover's. She rushes into a burning house, in which she hears there is a baby whom no one can rescue. Death is about to accept the baby from her, when she draws it back and lets it down in a curtain out of the window. Here is *the quest* of the young woman for a way to save her betrothed, the *psychomachia*, or battle of motives within her; *personification* of the abstraction Death, as a man weary of an unending task, and the magic or *supernatural events*. Among these last events are the wall through which departed spirits can pass, but only one way, and through which Death can pass either way; the burning candles that measure human lives, the Christian infidel left for the gardener to bury, who dissolves into the stern gardener Death.[14]

These traits will not all be found in every filmic allegory. Strangely, perhaps, the most persistent is magic, the impossible, the unexplained, which film is very good at.

The man with the black waistcoat, white sleeves, and eye shade, said before he left, "Don't touch anything. If you did, it would stop Niagara Falls." So Tommy and Penny Twidgett were alone with all the facelike dials, tiny lights blinking on and off, and levers poking out of black boxes. "I don't believe it," says Tommy. He grasps a handle and it comes away in his hand. We see the water backing up to a trickle and leaving the rocky escarpment bare. The dial faces pale; from a first sinister droop of the lids, the eyes close blackly. The hum of machinery whines down to nothing. "Now you've done it," says Penny. Men pour out of idle factories, a pen-printed issue of the Niagara Falls News, posted on a board, tells how the handle was stolen, and we pan down to the crowd reading it. Toasters don't heat, elevators are stuck, broadcasters face dead microphones, and so on, as Tommy and Penny walk around and see the consequences of Tommy's action. It is wise to do what those whose knowledge is greater than ours tell us to do (*The Boy Who Stopped Niagara*, Leslie MacFarlane).

Miracle in Milan (Vittorio De Sica) is the fight between generosity and greed. There is a touch of the supernatural sprinkled through it. The characters are simple in their motives, and the moral might be Carlyle's advice on how to change the world;

"Start with yourself, and then you'll be sure there's at least one honest man in the world." Toto the Good was not attempting to be that honest man: he took no thought for himself at all; he was born generous, cheerful, and helpful, never desiring for himself, but only for those he lived among. Starting from his enthusiasm, a large piece of wasteland at the edge of a city and all the destitutes who lived in hovels there were turned into a neat village of helpful people. This drew well-dressed (and greedy) newcomers. His dead foster mother brings him from heaven, illegally, a dove that will bring him whatever he asks for. He asks little for himself, but gives others all they ask: fur coats, chandeliers, goats, pianos, greater height, and steadily mounting sums of money. Oil is found and used and makes life in the village easier, till one of the villagers, for personal gain, informs a millionaire, who sends in truckloads of police to dispossess them, so he can set his oil derricks up. Before pursuing angels repossess the dove, Toto has foiled the police (when they turn their hoses on, every villager's hand is suddenly holding up an umbrella), freed the arrested vagrants, and sent them all to heaven on broomsticks.

Borderline cases are always instructive. Is *Metropolis* (Fritz Lang) an allegory? There is an allegorical gloss, however faint, in all creative writing; this is widely accepted. But there is a scale, at one and of which the gloss is barely discernible, at the other of which the gloss absorbs our interest.[15] Where does *Metropolis* lie? Most filmgoers have seen its regiments of workers, one entering, one leaving, marching with leaden feet, their eyes down, all wearing the same somber caps and overalls, doing the same simple task ten hours a day, open to death or hurt from exploding steam. Filmgoers will call to mind the capitalists, intriguing to keep the workers docile, substituting for an enlightened leader a robot who incites the workers to riot, and the capitalistic offspring luxuriating in sexual pastimes. A possible solution may come from the love of the master's son for Maria, the workers' leader. There are hints that, as allegories are sometimes said to do, the film is saying one thing (telling a story) and meaning another (propounding a universal moral).[16] There is a touch of magic (even if of a technological kind) in the robot made as a speaking image of Maria. The love of the master's son for the workers' leader brings about conflicting motives in both. The characters are simple to the point of merely embodying typical attitudes, and the quest of both lovers is a way to bridge the apparently conflicting interests of the different social classes to which they belong. There is perhaps on the whole more weight on the gloss than on the story.

8 The History

The writer of novels or plays, and the critic who reads a long succession of them, cannot but be aware that, shorn of the accidents of dress, houses, customs, climate, occupation, and forms of energy, there are patterns in the lives of people that happen again and again, which forms the matter for proverbs: "Do what you will, says God, but pay the price." It is only because of this that plays written as long ago as *Oedipus the King* can still command our feelings.

In this third kind of allegory, the characters are present in all their uniqueness of looks, costume, temperament, strengths, and failings—it is not here that the allegory lies. But we feel that the path of the characters' lives is one that we or those we have known have also traveled, or could easily do. The universal is found in the pattern of the story, not in the types of its people.

A Breton and a Cornish family come together in wartime. The families both have been fishing folk for generations, and they find that there is more in their like ways of using nets and navigating, of cooking and wrestling, of building houses and running households, to bring them together, than there is to keep them apart in such things as who rules them and how they speak. It is a horizontal bond that lies across the boundaries of states and languages, to offset the hates of national wars (*Johnny Frenchman*, Charles Frend).

In *The Falcons* (Istvan Gaal) a young man goes to the country to study the training of falcons. He sees the overfeeding of the birds to make them kill more than is their nature, and the demanding of implicit obedience (not only from the birds but from the trainer's four assistants). He sees the relentless hunt for a magpie hiding in a flock of sheep, letting a heron be half killed by the falcons by way of practice, and putting the wounded bird back in its cage to be used again. He sees the luring of wild falcons by pigeons and the killing of a hundred and twenty-six herons as practice for the falcons. Terez is the woman who prepares the meals, enjoys the furry softness of the mice and coypus for which she cares, and goes to bed with the men. The young man is at last revolted and runs away, but not before he says to Terez that pretending she has no guilt when what she does is part of a system based on cruelty is a lie made up to deceive herself.

An allegory often has a number of meanings from which a viewer may choose, not all perhaps intended by its maker.[17] *One Flew Over the Cuckoo's Nest* (Milos Forman) is an allegory of anarchism and order; it is also an allegory of conformity and nonconformity. It is the apotheosis and sacrifice of the social rebel, and its meaning may be taken in other ways. The routine of the mental hospital shown in the film is needed by the timid many, most of whom are voluntary patients, ones who could leave at any time but prefer to stay, for the choices required in the less-ordered world outside were beyond their powers. The head nurse, a firm but benevolent despot, administers the rules. McMurphy, sent by a court for observation, is a strong personality who frets at any rules at all and opposes the nurse whenever he has the chance. When he insists on the patients' voting on an issue, we wonder how much their votes are worth, since they do what the nearest strongest person tells them to do. The values in whose name McMurphy seeks to destroy the order of the ward seem to be lechery, drunkenness, gambling, and assault. He incited one of the patients to leave. The remainder took their medicine daily (they knew not what for), they played their cards and watched their television. Between times they stood or sat with no apparent purpose. McMurphy suffered for trying to destroy the order, without which the others could not live.

The Bridge on the River Kwai (David Lean) too provides a choice of meanings. In a Japanese prisoner-of-war camp, Colonel Nicholson, though undergoing torture, declines to allow his officers to work at common labor in building a bridge, for this would violate the Geneva Convention. When the Japanese commandant yields to Nicholson, the colonel's professional interest (he is an engineer) is engaged by the undertaking. The bridge, he points out, is being built on clay, and he starts building a new bridge on solid rock. To meet the time-limit imposed on the commandant, the colonel himself asks his officers to do common labor, and when the bridge is mined by a British demolition party, tries, but fails, to stop them. We may read in the film that war destroys men and their work and leaves all as it was; that those who endure suffering defeat those who inflict it; that those who insist may lose, but giving way, may gain more than ever they could have commanded; or that men must do what seems to them right, however tragic or even absurd the consequences, as did Antigone.

The story within a story, the one serving as gloss to the other's meaning, allows a director to specify the sense he wishes the viewer to take from the whole—that which both stories have in common. In the film *The Red Shoes* (Michael Powell and Emeric Pressburger), we see Victoria Page rise from pupil to première danseuse. She marries the company's musical director, who composed the music for a ballet entitled *The Red Shoes*, in which Victoria danced her first important role, that of a girl bewitched by a magical pair of shoes. While the shoes are on her feet, she cannot stop dancing, and, finding herself unable to take them off, she dies of exhaustion. Despite a happy marriage, Victoria's yearning to dance draws her back to the company. Between her desire for marriage and an equal desire to use her talent for dancing, personified by conflicting pleas from husband and impresario, she finds it impossible to choose, and throws herself in front of a train. Each of these women—Victoria and the girl in the ballet—had to dance, even though it killed her. By gesture in the dance, by words on the railway platform, her last request of the man she loves is "Take off the Red Shoes" (pls. 3, 4).

All films that are worth our time to see and worth remembering show a spine or kernel of allegory.[18] Those that are not worth seeing, which neither are fable, myth, nor history, are provided for in Boccaccio's fourth class—Old Wives' Tales, with no truth at all, hidden or visible.[19] Of these too we have our modern instances.

9 Alienation

Some writers have deliberately lifted the painted veil of the story and exposed themselves or their theme undisguised. Fielding, at the start of each book of *Tom Jones*, talks directly to the reader, keeping before us the storyteller as well as the story. Berthold Brecht rejects the illusion of reality. He places his lamps in full view of the audience, gives his players no sets or furniture, projects words or pictures above them on a screen, or has a player discuss his part with the audience. This is to prevent the literal story from arousing feelings that might make it opaque to the moral or intention, the sole justification for telling the story: "This is not a tale about real people. It is merely an anecdote, which illustrates a point I wish to make, for you to think about." So the playwright might say: now and then a film director seems to be saying the same.

At the end of *O Lucky Man* (Karel Reisz), Travis, during a screen test, is asked to smile. When he answers back, "What is there to smile about?", the director slaps him. He then slowly does begin to smile, and we cut to him as one of a dancing crowd. The tense, unsmiling director and those who in one way and another have exploited the anti-hero during the story are now smiling and enjoying themselves in the crowded ballroom. They were just playing parts in the director's anecdote—nice people really.

In *Marat-Sade* (Peter Brook), the director of the asylum (whose patients are performing the play) reproves the director, de Sade, for some of the dialogue, and then turns to speak directly to us. Properties are mimed instead of being made, some film is whited out by overexposure, and figures become indistinct while speaking, leading us to listen to what they say instead of watching. This keeps us reminded that we are seeing events at more than one remove away from reality: it is written and performed by mentally ill persons, whose perception of the outer world is distorted in the first place. They have trouble being persons other than themselves, little is done to establish place and time, and what is done may not be clearly photographed—only remotely real, nothing to seize our feelings, only a few scenes and words to think about.

Speaking with all the confidence of omniscience, a man tells us we are in Vienna, and continues, "It is the past—it is more restful than the present, more certain than the future." He speaks of "My puppets," and as he speaks, he passes across a stage lit by gas flares ("Is it a stage?" he says to tease us), and then past a spotlight and a microphone boom ("Is it a studio?"), to a merry-go-round. He calls over a woman, who approaches with very willing smiles. "No," he tells her, "I'm not in the game. Put yourself at that street corner. There will be some soldiers coming. Yours is the sixth." Then he gestures her away and announces the first scene as *The Soldier and the Girl.* At the end of the scene, he leads her into the future as one of two characters in *The Parlormaid and the Young Man.* After this is over, the master of ceremonies reenters, makes his usual ironic remarks, and lets the young man stay as one of the two for the episode of *The Young Man and the Lady.* In this way, one of the two players in each scene continues into the next with a new partner, until in the end, the soldier of the first scene and the Count from the last, pass each other in the street.

The manipulation of apparently casual meetings by the master of ceremonies, whether as God or the stage manager, leads to a sense of seeing a fanciful tale void of reality, or of a destiny that may not be defied, or of the transiency and ultimate insignificance of the people we see. With a passing pang, we feel their ecstasies and disappointments, but are always reminded after each scene that, as the master of ceremonies says to the husband who leaves, unsatisfied on the stroke of 12:00, "It is not important." There is only one embrace in a film whose theme is the many kinds of love: if Hollywood could only have left sex to Max Ophuls *(La Ronde)!*

10   Generalization

We glance, in allegory, first at a particular story and then through and beyond it at a pattern of life, considered apart from any single example of it, or as it might be found in a thousand examples, that is to say, at a generalization or abstraction made from the story. It is easy to write of such an abstraction as beauty; it is harder, in words, to describe things or people in such a way that the reader infallibly concludes, "This thing or person is beautiful." In film, the reverse is true: since a film always deals with particular things or people, it is less a problem to show them as beautiful than to state the notion beauty to which they all conform (pls. 23, 40, 41).

It is easy to show a cruel act, but how in film do we state the abstraction "cruelty"? Here are some of the incidents in *The Crab-Canning Ship* (So Yamamura):

   i. A seaman falls off the ship, when lashing down a boat during a storm. "What's a man or two: the boat is worth more to me," says the superintendent.
   ii. To avoid a loss of time, the superintendent forbids the captain to help a ship in distress.
   iii. A homesick boy is found hiding, is placed in a washroom, and nailed in with a plank across the door.
   iv. A storm warning is ignored, and men are forced out to fish: one small boat is lost and two men are drowned.
   v. The man in charge of the lost boat is slapped on the face, and is told that the cost of the boat would be taken off his pay.
   vi. The foremen in charge of those filleting fish carry clubs, hooked sticks, and whips, and those who collapse from working long hours are beaten.

If we sought a single word that would fit all of these, it would be such a word as callousness, brutality, or exploitation, and this is a generalization from the whole congeries. The director, who is to express an abstraction in film, must find or invent the first-order happenings, which, when seen by the viewer, one after another, will fuse to form in the viewer's mind the abstraction intended. This is considered better writing too. "By describing the blood on the victim's face and torn clothing, the torn ligaments hanging out of the remaining stump of his arm. . . . Instead of telling the reader, 'It was a ghastly accident!' *we can make the reader say it for himself.* The reader is . . . *made to participate . . . by being left to draw his own conclusions.*"[20]

The battle on the ice begins with fifteen shots or so, cut in more or less the same length, which move evenly forward like the steady tick of a grandfather's clock, and in each of which there are groups of persons, almost completely still and looking intently. It is perhaps a strength of film that this abstraction is felt, without our having to formulate it as stillness, waiting, power, concentration, or confidence, any one, or all of which, it could suggest (*Alexander Nevski*, S. M. Eisenstein).

Abstraction may determine angle. In *Berlin* (Walther Ruttmann), we see a man from the back, but only in part. The man later opens a book. He is, as a person, of no concern to the director, who is building up a highly abstract image of what goes on in a day of a great city. This explains the angle. If we had seen the man from the front, in light gray suit, small moustache, pince-nez, flower in his buttonhole, wing collar, and well-brushed hair, smiling at something remembered as he opened up the book, we should want to know more of who he was, and certainly why he smiled. We should barely notice the book and hardly at all its meaning: "The working day starts." If, on the other hand, we see the book in close-up, and a hand enters to open it, our attention is unduly directed to the kind of the book and its contents. As it was done, an anonymous man, seen from the back, opens a book of some kind, we know not what, and in context with other shots, it becomes "the start of a day."

The maker of *Tokyo Earthquake* (photographed by Shigeru Shirai) had the whole event spread before his eyes. He mostly had to decide what to leave out—the greater part of the event. What parts, when seen by the viewer together, would most completely define the abstraction, earthquake—that was the director's problem. All the kinds of human events that follow such a disaster should be included.[21] What we see are the effect on buildings, railway lines, and roads (fallen statues, cracks in roads, railway cars flattened, houses fallen all but their chimneys), fires, makeshift houses in open railway cars with washing hung and roofed with sheets of corrugated iron, mobile clinics, soldiers with fixed bayonets patroling against looting, and boy scouts removing rubble, to look for possible survivors.

The director of *The War Game* (Peter Watkins) has had to start at the other end. He is defining "atomic war." He has no blast and aftermath to photograph, so he has to invent what he cannot find, the first-order events that seem to him to be likely after a blast: the burning of thousands of dead; rings by the bucketful for identification; soldiers with pistols keeping relatives out; rows of people in category 3, with more than half their body burned, who will die in pain without drugs and are likely to be shot by the police; a woman, tired and dirty, saying, "We have one tubful of water for five days. We've had to drink and wash out of it"; a man saying he was offered a pound for a loaf he was bringing from his mother's, "but you can't eat a pound note"; and the mesh fence of Food Control Center No 3, from which we pan down to three dead policemen.

The gods "give power" to Donald Duck. What kind of "power" and how much? First we approach to a huge picture of his head, sharp dovetailing teeth seen in his open beak—immense physical growth. He lights up an electric bulb screwed into his beak, and lifts up a whole long fence, instead of opening the gate. He hurls a piano into a wall by a touch, makes it into a smoking mass of wire by a flip of his fingers, and saws off the edge of a cliff with the side of his hand (*Trombone Trouble*, Walt Disney).

Diffidence and fortitude are ideas—void of emotion. But it reaches our feelings to see a man whom war has deprived of hands, using his hooks to open the knobs of doors, drink from a glass, play "Chopsticks" on piano keys, and place the wedding ring on his bride's finger. Even his words are deeds: "Do you think I can't sign my name? . . . I've got a match, Captain, I can light it. . . . You ought to see me open a bottle. . . . I can even put nickels in a juke-box." His diffidence is not seen by everyone. When his fiancée embraces him at their first meeting, he is tense and straight, with his hooks held stiffly down beside him. She must see the worst, he feels; she must come to his room and put him to bed. "I can get out of this harness myself . . . but then I'm helpless. If that door is closed, I can't even get out of the room. . . . I guess you don't know what to say. I don't blame you. . . ." She says she loves him and will never leave him. Her hands move toward him as he shrugs into his pajama jacket, but she draws them back and offers no help until he says, " . . . but I can't button it." Then she helps him and smoothes his collar down affectionately (*The Best Years of Our Lives*, William Wyler).[22]

The feelings aroused, the notion formed in our minds, come not from the situation treated but from the incidents a director chooses from it. Mark Donskoi in *My Universities* and Charles Chaplin in *Modern Times* both deal with unemployment, managerial incompetence, poverty, speeding up of work, unhealthy and uncomfortable sleeping quarters, unfair distribution of wealth, agitation, and arrest. Gorky ponders, tries to preserve his self-respect, and tries to understand, but the film projects resentment and hopelessness. Chaplin, on the other hand, takes things as they are with no care for tomorrow. He finds what joy he can in the present, and when he finds he cannot win, he compromises. He leaves us hopeful that man can triumph over all things.

We choose from the facts of experience those that satisfy, those that confirm or express the view of life our temperament imposes.

11 Simplification

In a well-known story, an Eastern despot, on acceding to his throne, commanded his learned men to compile a history of men, to be his guide in becoming an enlightened ruler. After twenty years, they brought him a hundred great scrolls. "I shall not live," said the potentate, his time taken up with his duties as a ruler, "long enough to read a hundred scrolls. Condense them." After twenty more years, they brought their history back, now in forty scrolls. "I am older than I was," the Great One said, "with a smaller store of years in which to read and in which to use what I read. Abridge your history further." But when in five years the scholars had shrunk their history to five great scrolls, the king was aging, his body weak, and his mind weary. He sent the scholars back to their studies, from which the surviving few returned in two years and once more addressed the High Seat, "O King, live for ever. We have spent many days and nights in sifting out what might be briefly said of all the men that have lived and their mighty deeds. We find it is this: They were born, they suffered, and they died."

To generalize is to simplify, to pare away the particulars in which men, for example, differ and leave the one or two in which they agree. When Busby Berkeley's girls, dressed in white and holding white flags, are shot against a black glass floor from far off, they are nothing more than white spots on black, one with the moving dots of Norman McLaren (*Three Cheers for the Girls*, Jean Negulesco). The same can be said of athletic displays. Starting from the inmost of six concentric circles, joined arms rise and point out like opening petals. In a row stretching away from the camera, each man swings his head in turn from right to left, and a wave passes down the line. Man is a head-turning animal (*Russia on Parade*, W. Bielyev).

Cartoon is but a short step further. It is not clear if the Chinese Dance is done by large-hatted people; by mushrooms; or by darning eggs with scarlet heads, beige handles, and rudimentary feet; but people certainly cannot match their attack. Two of them are tall and lean, two are short and fat, and two are somewhere in between. The seventh, an infant mushroom, though more erratic, never misses a beat. In the Russian Dance, thistles dance like men with cossack hats. They have no fingers on their arm-leaves; no feet on their stems; and no eyes, nose, or mouth on their flower-faces. These features are barely perceptible in those who play or dance in large arenas: cartoons take it one stage further (*The Nutcracker Suite: Fantasia*, Samuel Armstrong).

Simplification, then, follows from distance, which often brings a surprising transformation. As an airplane lifts us above a city, what first shrinks to nothing is its maker, man. For a while longer we see his houses, part for the whole, as roofs, but increasingly see them as groups and rows, and less as single buildings. Later, all that survive are the roads between them, the houses altogether lost in dark lines, belts, or geometric patches. And, at last, before it is fully lost from sight, the city is only a cobweb of hairlines.

Composition too may be simplified by purging the frame of all but the images that build the intended effect.[23] We see Ivan's head, the orrery on the table beside him, and his great shadow faint on the wall behind, nothing more. Ivan dark in an arch against the snow below, where a long dark line of penitents is winding to beg his return: images of dominance (*Ivan the Terrible*, S. M. Eisenstein).

As *Rouli Roulant* (Claude Jutra) proceeds, the boys on their skating boards are caught against the haze and the sky, swaying and swerving, their context lost, their motion almost abstract, hesitating as each side swing slows and halts before the inevitable return, like a pendulum, like a flower lithe in a breeze, a swooping bird. This loss of place, of person, of all identity, of all but motion brings us close to their sense of rhythmic speed and bodily mastery.

The diagram is another means of simplification by abstraction. Dr. John Kay is traveling along the ground at eight hundred and fifty miles an hour. Intercut with him are two reference lines on a blue ground, vertical and horizontal, cutting at right angles. Above the horizontal line a jagged yellow tracing is being recorded. We are not told its purpose, but intercut with Dr. Kay who is strapped into the vehicle with cables coming from various devices on his body, the tracing conveys first, measurement, and secondly, from its angular path, stress, both messages being abstractions (*Journey to the Far Side of the Sun*, Robert Parrish).

Political cartoons perhaps are oversimple abstractions. In *The Charge of the Light Brigade* (Tony Richardson) contemporary cartoons were used as a source for animated ones, in which the Russian Bear pounces over the northern horizon of Europe to savage Turkey, and the Lion of England and the Eagle of France come from the west and wrestle the bear down.

12 Below Thought

In every art there is the stroke that stirs our feelings directly, without benefit of "thought," without our mind understanding how. It would seem that the primitive part of our mind, the thalamus, is not merely the seat of our feelings but is the vestibule through which sensations come on their way to the cortex (pl. 42). Feelings take shape there below the level of thought and words. This experience below thought is given many names, thalamic,[24] ineffable,[25] extraloquial,[26] unspeakable affective states,[27] and may be conveyed as well in film as in words.[28] It will not come from the same images to all viewers, nor can such an experience be fully conveyed in words, so it is not to be expected that each example given below will have the same value for all readers.

Annabella and Hannay say good-night. Then we see, right of center, a window, a frame for the black anonymous night in the warm, white walls at the end of a hall. To its left, a black figure nearly the height of the window stands on one leg and points toward it. The sash is up, the sill glinting, and above it, blown by a violent wind, warm white curtains reach for the ceiling wildly, their flutter just barely ruffling the silence. In the next shot, Annabella throws open the door of Hannay's room and falls with a knife in her back. The square of night, the black figure, the fluttering curtain, gave me a chill of apprehension past accounting for (*The Thirty-nine Steps*, Alfred Hitchcock).

It is night. A car enters a garage, its engine stops, a woman alights and walks away. A voice whispers, "Helen?" At the door of the garage, James Allen's head catches the light. He is an innocent man, who after escaping once from a southern jail farm, went back to the state to clear himself, and was sent back to the farm. He has escaped once again. He said he would have come sooner, but had been afraid. They embrace, and there is a clank of metal. He shrinks away, "I've got to go," he says. "Where can I find you? What are you going to do?" On a screen that is all black, his face and shoulders are less and less distinct as he backs away into the dark night: "I don't know. I don't know. I don't know" (*I Was a Fugitive from a Chain Gang*, Mervyn Leroy).

There is a long shot of a cliff in *We from Kronstadt* (E. Dzigan), as eleven sailors file to its edge to be executed for mutiny. Their hands are pinioned behind them, and rocks are tied around their necks to hang on their chests. The White commander points to the first sailor. He steps forward. "Good-bye comrades," he says. His balalaika, held by a White Russian soldier, catches his eye. With a sudden movement, he kicks, and the balalaika flies from the guard's hand, all the strings resounding in harmony. In a down shot the balalaika shrinks in size till it strikes the foaming sea. The twanging vibrance quickly softens, as if spreading to immensity. Now we are shown three sailors' caps, floating on a swelling sea. In a long up shot of the cliff and its one tree, a single distant White Russian soldier looks over the edge. He straightens up and walks away. The feeling is heroic, legendary, the dying resonance of the strings as if it were the tale itself resounding in time, as future tongues tell it again and again:

> . . . old, unhappy, far-off things,
> And battles long ago.

Things with meanings beyond themselves is where this inquiry started and where it ends. It is no accident that we speak in figures. We know only tiny parts of wholes, and live by synecdoche: of a city from knowing several buildings in it, of the universe from living on a single planet, of man from a few companions.

We are distorting mirrors, like waters of Dutch canals, where the tops of milk vessels pop up and down like Jack-in-the-boxes, houses wobble in slow round bulges, tall buildings are convulsed, and the trees vomit sprays of bouncing bubbles.[29] These broken bits we piece into working fictions, by which to find our way. Only metaphor can describe us.

For Jacob Boehme, the visible, tangible world was a figure for an inner one of greater significance;[30] to Sallustius the universe was a myth, beneath whose outer shell realities exist that we must seek for.[31] The quickening of things to express meaning much beyond their first and outer seeming is art—and life—at its most perceptive: "Raise the stone and there thou shalt find Me; cleave the wood and there am I."[32]

List of Books Cited

Books are referred to in the notes only by the word or word and letters that stand before their entries in the following list. The figures following each entry refer to chapter and note, e.g., 7/3 means chapter 7, note 3.

Short Form	Author and Title
Antoine	ANTOINE, SISTER M. SALOME. *The Rhetoric of Jeremy Taylor's Prose: Ornament of the Sunday Sermons.* Washington: Catholic University of America Press, 1946. 7/14, 8/2, 17/15
Arijon	ARIJON, DANIEL. *Grammar of the Film Language.* London: Focal Press, 1976. 7/3, 10/9, 14/21, 16/11
Arliss	ARLISS, GEORGE. *Up the Years from Bloomsbury.* New York: Blue Ribbon Books, 1927. 1/13
Arnheim	ARNHEIM, RUDOLF. *Film as Art.* Berkeley and Los Angeles: University of California Press, 1957. Good on angle, Chaplin, and simile by manipulation. Good scattered comments on similarity and contrast. A view from the 1930s, rewritten only to improve the expression. 7/3, 12/3, 13/18, 14/7
Arnot	ARNOT, PETER. *The Theatres of Japan.* London: Macmillan, 1969. 7/6
Aurelius	AURELIUS ANTONINUS, MARCUS. *Meditations.* Translated by Jeremy Collier, revised by Alice Zimmern. London: Walter Scott, n.d. 17/24
Balazs	BALAZS, BELA. *Theory of the Film.* Translated by Edith Bone. London: Dennis Dobson, 1952. First published in 1945. The author has grasped, perhaps better than any, the possibilities of the figure in film. 7/3, 7/15, 10/16, 10/20, 12/6, 13/15, 14/24, 14/37, 15/16, 15/18, 16/3
Barrie	BARRIE, SIR J. M. *The Plays.* London: Hodder and Stoughton, 1929. 4/3
Bell	BELL, DAVID CHARLES, AND BELL, ALEXANDER MELVILLE. *Bell's Standard Elocutionist.* New York: Funk and Wagnalls, 1916. 10/7

Bettetini   BETTETINI, GIANFRANCO. *Language and Technique of the Film*. The Hague: Mouton, 1973.
4/2

Boccaccio   BOCCACCIO, GIOVANNI. *Boccaccio on Poetry, Being the Preface and Fourteenth and Fifteenth Books of Boccaccio's Genealogia Deorum Gentilium*. Translated by Charles G. Osgood. Indianapolis: Bobbs-Merrill, 1956.
18/8, 18/19

Boehme   BOEHME, JACOB. *The Signature of All Things*. Translated by William Law. London: Dent, Everyman's Library n.d.
18/30

Brecht   BRECHT, BERTHOLD. *Brecht on Theatre: The Development of an Aesthetic*. Translated and notes by John Willett. London: Methuen, 1964.
1/21

Brownlow   BROWNLOW, KEVIN. *The Parade's Gone By*. London: Sphere Books, 1973.
12/5, 13/17

Buchanan FM   BUCHANAN, ANDREW. *Film Making from Script to Screen*. London: Faber, 1937.
14/21

Buchanan PW   BUCHANAN, ROBERT. *Complete Poetical Works*. London: Chatto and Windus, 1901.
13/7

Burch   BURCH, NOËL. *Theory of Film Practice*. Translated by Helen R. Lane. New York: Praeger, 1973.
Good on ellipsis and use of the frame.
1/9, 10/21, 15/12, 15/18, 17/6

Carroll   CARROLL, LEWIS. *Alice's Adventures in Wonderland and Through the Looking Glass*. London: Dent, Everyman's Library, 1965.
9/3

Chesterton   CHESTERTON, G. K. *Heretics*. London: Bodley Head, Weekend Library, 1928.
14/19

De Bono   DE BONO, EDWARD. *The Use of Lateral Thinking*. London: Cape, 1967.
5/7, 5/9

Detzer   DETZER, KARL. *Carl Sandburg*. New York: Harcourt, 1941.
7/4

Donne   DONNE, JOHN. *Poems*. Edited by J. J. C. Grierson. London: Oxford University Press, 1912.
17/21, 17/23

Dunne   DUNNE, J. W. *An Experiment with Time*. London: Faber, 1944.
16/18

Durgnat   DURGNAT, RAYMOND. *Films and Feelings*. London: Faber, 1967.
3/4

Eisenstein FF   EISENSTEIN, SERGEI MIKHAILOVICH. *Film Form*. Translated and edited by Jay Leyda. New York: Harcourt, 1949.
Includes his comments on montage and the ideogram, how the Japanese teach composition in drawing, and his use of the term "montage trope."
6/15, 7/7, 10/19, 12/2, 14/3, 14/4, 14/6, 14/15, 14/32, 17/19

Eisenstein FS   EISENSTEIN, SERGEI MIKHAILOVICH. *The Film Sense*. Translated and edited by Jay Leyda. New York: Harcourt, 1942.

Part I, *Word and Image,* appears in *Notes of a Film Director* in a different tr. as *Montage in 1938.*
14/2, 15/3

Eisenstein ND EISENSTEIN, SERGEI MIKHAILOVICH. *Notes of a Film Director.* Translated by X. Danko. London: Lawrence and Wishart, 1959.
Perhaps one of the first to do so, he writes here of the synecdoche in film.
5/8, 6/12, 11/4, 12/2, 14/13, 14/18, 14/40, 14/41

Eliot ELIOT, T. S. *Selected Essays.* 3d ed. London: Faber, 1951.
18/22

Empson EMPSON, WILLIAM. *Seven Types of Ambiguity.* 3d English ed. New York: New Directions, 1966.
1/10, 7/2, 7/10, 17/2, 17/4, 17/5, 17/18

Fletcher FLETCHER, ANGUS. *Allegory: The Theory of a Symbolic Mode.* Ithaca: Cornell U.P., 1964.
18/14

Forbes FORBES, BRYAN. *Notes for a Life.* London: Collins, 1974.
1/17

Forster FORSTER, E. M. *Aspects of the Novel.* London: Edward Arnold, 1927.
16/1, 18/2

Fowler KE FOWLER, H. W., and FOWLER, F. G. *The King's English.* 3d ed. London: Oxford University Press, 1931.
4/1

Fowler MEU FOWLER, H. W. *A Dictionary of Modern English Usage.* London: Oxford University Press, 1926. 2d ed., rev. by Sir Ernest Gowers, 1965.
6/10, 15/25

Frazer FRAZER, SIR J. G. *The Golden Bough.* Abridged edition. London: Macmillan, 1922.
11/5

Frye FRYE, NORTHROP. *Anatomy of Criticism.* Princeton: Princeton University Press, 1957.
1/11, 18/15, 18/17

Furness FURNESS, R. S. *Expressionism.* London: Methuen, 1973.
16/17

Giannetti GO GIANNETTI, LOUIS D. *Godard and Others: Essays in Film Form.* Madison, N. J.: Fairleigh Dickinson University Press, 1975.
5/4

Giannetti UM GIANNETTI, LOUIS D. *Understanding Movies.* Englewood Cliffs, N. J.: Prentice-Hall, 1972.
6/16, 10/11

Goldsmith GOLDSMITH, OLIVER. *The Citizen of the World and The Bee.* Edited by Austin Dobson. London: Dent, Everyman's Library, 1934.
14/17

Gray GRAY, THOMAS. *The Poems.* Edited by A. J. F. Collins. London: University Tutorial Press, 1924.
"The Progress of Poesy" (17/11) "The Bard" (17/22)

Grenfell GRENFELL, BERNARD P., and HUNT, ARTHUR S. eds. *New Sayings and Fragment of a Lost Gospel from Oxyrhynchus.* Edited with translation and commentary. New York: Oxford University Press, 1904.
18/32

Grierson GRIERSON, JOHN. *Grierson on Documentary*. Edited by Forsyth Hardy. London: Collins, 1946.
1/15

Grube GRUBE, G. M. A. *Aristotle on Poetry and Style*. Indianapolis: Bobbs-Merrill, 1958.
11/3

Hawkes HAWKES, TERENCE. *Metaphor*. London: Methuen, 1972.
6/1, 6/9, 6/11

Hayakawa HAYAKAWA, S. I. *Language in Thought and Action*. New York: Harcourt, 1949.
14/14, 18/20, 18/21

Herrick HERRICK, ROBERT. *Complete Poetry*. Edited with an Introduction and notes by J. Max Patrick. New York: Anchor Books, 1963
13/4

Highet HIGHET, GILBERT. *The Anatomy of Satire*. Princeton, Princeton University Press, 1962.
9/4

Hobbes HOBBES, THOMAS. *A Brief of the Art of Rhetorique* in *Aristotle's Treatise on Rhetoric*. London: Bohn, 1957.
11/3

Hodgart HODGART, MATHEW. *Satire*. New York: McGraw-Hill, 1969.
10/5

Holaday HOLADAY, PERRY W., and STODDARD, GEORGE D. *Getting Ideas from the Movies*. New York: Macmillan, 1933.
1/18

Homer HOMER. *The Odyssey*. Done into English prose by S. H. Butcher and A. Lang. School ed. London: Macmillan, 1921.
16/27, 16/29

Huss HUSS, ROY, and SILVERSTEIN, NORMAN. *The Film Experience*. New York: Harper, 1968.
5/4, 14/31, 16/6

Jackson JACKSON, HOLBROOK. *The Reading of Books*. London: Faber, 1946.
6/9, 16/2

Jacobs JACOBS, LEWIS. *The Emergence of Film Art*. New York: Hopkinson and Blake, 1969
13/10, 14/10, 16/20

Jakobson JAKOBSON, ROMAN. *Selected Writings*. vol. 2 *Word and Language*. The Hague: Mouton, 1971.
14/8, 14/27

Joseph JOSEPH, SISTER MIRIAM. *Shakespeare's Use of the Arts of Language*. New York: Hafner, 1949.
All the most-used figures as found in Shakespeare and contemporary treatises on rhetoric; clear, brisk, and richly provided with examples.
12/1, 17/16

Kawin KAWIN, BRUCE F. *Telling it Again and Again: Repetition in Literature and Film*. Ithaca: Cornell University Press, 1972.
4/1, 4/7

Kayser KAYSER, WOLFGANG. *The Grotesque in Art and Literature*. Translated by Ulrich Weisstein. Bloomington: Indiana University Press, 1963.
8/8

Kennedy   KENNEDY, GEORGE. *The Art of Persuasion in Ancient Greece.* Princeton: Princeton University Press, 1965.
8/1, 18/16

Koestler   KOESTLER, ARTHUR. *The Act of Creation.* New York: Macmillan, 1969.
5/11

Korzybski   KORZYBSKI, COUNT ALFRED. *Science and Sanity.* 2d ed. Lancaster, Penn.: Science Press, 1941.
18/24, 18/27

Kracauer CH   KRACAUER, SIEGFRIED. *From Caligari to Hitler: A Psychological History of the German Film.* Princeton: Princeton University Press, 1946.
18/18

Kracauer TF   KRACAUER, SIEGFRIED. *Theory of Film.* New York: Oxford University Press, 1960.
Useful on sound.
18/1

Kuleshov   KULESHOV, LEV. *Kuleshov on Film: Writings of Lev Kuleshov.* Selected, translated and edited with an introduction by Ronald Levaco. Berkeley and Los Angeles: University of California Press, 1974.
14/10, 14/23, 18/23

Landor   LANDOR, WALTER SAVAGE. *Imaginary Conversations.* A Selection by Ernest de Sélincourt. London: Oxford University Press, World's Classics, 1915.
Aesop and Rhodope (14/9)

Lanham   LANHAM, RICHARD A. *Handlist of Rhetorical Terms.* Berkeley and Los Angeles: University of California Press, 1969.
More accessible, but similar in treatment to Taylor, to which, despite some overlapping of examples, it usefully adds.
1/1, 1/2, 8/5, 13/1, 14/16, 14/22, 15/8, 15/25, 17/14

Lewis   LEWIS, C. S. *The Allegory of Love: a Study in Medieval Tradition.* London: Oxford University Press, 1958.
18/3, 18/4, 18/6, 18/18

Lindgren   LINDGREN, ERNEST. *The Art of the Film* 2d ed. London: Allen and Unwin, 1963.
6/16

Lodge   LODGE, DAVID. *The Modes of Modern Writing.* London: Edward Arnold, 1977.
14/17

Longinus   LONGINUS, DIONYSIUS (attrib.). *On the Sublime.* Translated from the Greek by William Smith. London: printed by F.C. and J Rivington and others, 1819.
9/5, 14/22, 16/20, 16/22, 16/24

Lubbock   LUBBOCK, PERCY. *The Craft of Fiction.* London: Cape, 1965.
6/9

Macbeth   MACBETH, J. W. V. *The Might and Mirth of Literature: A Treatise on Figurative Language.* London: Sampson, Low, Marston, and Searle, 1876.
Chatty, readable, and anecdotal; covers a wide range of figures with copious examples; some peculiarities, as in defining trope.
1/1, 1/2, 8/4, 11/1, 13/13, 17/17

MacCann   MACCANN, R. D. *Film: A Montage of Theories.* New York: Dutton, 1965.
1/15

MacNeice   MacNeice, Louis. *Varieties of Parable.* Cambridge: Cambridge University Press, 1965.
Good, brief, and readable discussion of allegory.
18/3, 18/4, 18/5, 18/11, 18/15, 18/18, 18/25, 18/28

MacQueen   MacQueen, John. *Allegory.* London: Methuen, 1970.
18/18

Manvell   Manvell, Roger and Fraenkel, Heinrich. *The German Cinema.* London: Dent, 1971.
18/18

Metz FL   Metz, Christian. *Film Language: a Semiotics of the Cinema.* New York: Oxford University Press, 1974.
14/12

Metz LC   Metz, Christian. *Language and Cinema.* The Hague: Mouton, 1974.
1/12

Milton EP   Milton, John. *English Poems.* Edited by R. C. Browne. London: Oxford University Press, 1870.
13/5

Milton MP   Milton, John. *Milton's Prose.* Edited by Malcolm Wallace. London: Oxford University Press, 1925.
5/12

Minto   Minto, William. *Logic, Inductive and Deductive.* London: Murray, 1893.
1/7

Mitry   Metz, Christian. "On Jean Mitry's L'Esthétique et Psychologie du Cinéma. Volume II." *Screen* 14, nos. 1-2 (Spring/Summer 1973).
5/3, 6/14, 10/17, 15/4, 15/7, 15/13, 16/7, 16/8, 16/16, 16/30, 17/6

Monaco   Monaco, James. *How to Read a Film.* N.Y.: Oxford University Press, 1977.
12/3

Montagu   Montagu, Ivor. *Film World.* Harmondsworth, England: Penguin, 1964.
Of the Eisenstein school. Very good on sound and montage.
1/23, 6/16, 13/14, 14/2, 14/21, 14/29

Montgomery   Montgomery, James. *Poetical Works.* London: Warne, "Chandos Classics", n.d.
13/6

Moody   Moody, Raymond A., Jr. *Life After Life.* Harrisburg, Pa.: Stackpole, 1976.
16/14

Muecke   Muecke, D. C. *The Compass of Irony.* London: Methuen, 1969.
7/13, 8/7, 15/5

Nesfield   Nesfield, J. C. *Senior Course in English Composition.* London: Macmillan, 1903.
16/13, 16/21, 16/23

Nock   Nock, Arthur Darby. *Sallvstivs: Concerning the Gods and the Universe* Edited with prolegomena and translated. Cambridge: Cambridge University Press, 1926.
18/31

Nowottny   Nowottny, Winifred. *The Language Poets Use.* London: The Athlone Press, 1962.
3/3, 6/5, 11/2, 14/11, 17/3, 18/26

Ontario   ONTARIO. THE ROYAL COMMISSION ON VIOLENCE IN THE COMMUNICA-
TIONS INDUSTRY. *Interim Report.* Toronto: Queen's Printer, 1976.
1/17, 1/19

Pargeter   PARGETER, EDITH. *The Soldier at the Door.* London: Heinemann, 1956.
16/33

Partridge   PARTRIDGE, BERNARD. *Usage and Abusage: A Guide to Good English.* 4th
ed. rev. London: Hamish Hamilton, 1948.
5/1

Patmore   PATMORE, COVENTRY. *Poems.* Edited with an introduction by Frederick
Page. London: Oxford University Press, 1949.
"The Angel in the House" (16/28)

Payne   THE PAYNE FUND STUDIES. *Motion Pictures and Youth:* 9 vols. New York:
Macmillan, 1933.
1/16

Peacham   PEACHAM, HENRY. *The Garden of Eloquence,* 1577, facsimile reprint, unpaged. London: The Scolar Press, 1971.
12/1, 14/28, 14/33

Plato   PLATO. *The Republic.* Translated by Benjamin Jowett. London: Oxford
University Press, 1908.
1/21

Pope   POPE, ALEXANDER. *Poetical Works.* London: Macmillan, 1869.
"Essay on Criticism" (15/14) "Rape of the Lock" (15/23)
"Essay on Man" (15/24)

Pratley   PRATLEY, GERALD. *The Cinema of David Lean.* London: Tantivy, 1974.
16/32

Price   PRICE, CECIL. *Theatre in the Age of Garrick.* Oxford: Basil Blackwell,
1973.
1/21

Priestley   PRIESTLEY, JOSEPH. *A Course of Lectures on Oratory and Criticism,* 1777.
London: The Scolar Press, 1968.
6/3

Pudovkin   PUDOVKIN, VSEVELOD ILLARIONOVICH. *Film Technique.* Translated and
annotated by Ivor Montagu. Enlarged ed. London: Newnes, 1933.
Excellent introduction to montage, with suggestive chapters on slowed
motion and sound.
6/15, 13/3, 14/2, 14/21, 14/42, 15/2

Puttenham   PUTTENHAM, GEORGE. *The Arte of English Poesie.* Edited by Gladys
Doidge Willcock and Alice Walker. Cambridge: Cambridge University
Press, 1936.
The third book of this pleasantly written Elizabethan treatise, *Of Ornament,*
contains definitions of many figures, with examples.
10/6, 10/10, 10/12, 10/14, 10/15, 13/12, 15/25, 17/1, 17/12, 17/26

Quiller-Couch   QUILLER-COUCH, SIR ARTHUR. *I Saw Three Ships and Other Winter's
Tales.* London: Cassell, 1892.
10/8

Reisz   REISZ, KAREL. *The Technique of Film Editing.* 2d ed. London: Focal Press,
1954.
Excellent treatment of montage. It examines a number of sequences, with
the script, piece by piece, often with a frame from each piece.
14/2, 14/20, 14/25, 14/36, 14/37, 15/7, 15/17

Richards   RICHARDS, I. A. *The Philosophy of Rhetoric.* London: Oxford University Press, 1936.
5/5, 5/6, 6/2, 6/6, 6/10

Robbe-Grillet   ROBBE-GRILLET, ALAIN. *Last Year at Marienbad,* Text for the film. Translated by Richard Hughes. New York: Grove, 1962.
17/7

Rowell   ROWELL, GEORGE, ed. *Nineteenth-Century Plays.* London: Oxford University Press, 1953.
Lady Audley's Secret (15/21), *The Bells* (16/9)

Ruskin   RUSKIN, JOHN. *Modern Painters,* vol. 3. Orpington: George Allen, 1888.
17/19

Scott   SCOTT, A. F. *Current Literary Terms.* New York: Macmillan, 1965.
17/20

Shakespeare   SHAKESPEARE, WILLIAM
Coriolanus 10/3 *Hamlet* 2/2 15/19 16/10 *Henry IV, Part II* 17/13 *Julius Caesar* 8/6 *King John* 12/1 *Macbeth* 2/3 16/24 17/8 *Midsummer Night's Dream* 10/2 *Much Ado About Nothing* 12/1 *Richard III* 14/39 *The Tempest* 12/1 *Twelfth Night* 12/1

Sheridan   SHERIDAN, RICHARD BRINSLEY. *Plays.* London: Dent, Everyman's Library, 1906.
4/4

Smith MR   SMITH, JOHN. *The Mysterie of Rhetorique Unveil'd.* London: printed by E. Cotes for George Everden, 1657.
8/3, 14/28, 16/26, 17/10, 17/15, 17/16

Smith PP   SMITH, SYDNEY. *The Letters of Peter Plymley to His Brother Abraham Who Lives in the Country.* London: Dent, 1929.
7/11

Sophocles   SOPHOCLES. *The Theban Plays.* Translated by E. F. Watling. Harmondsworth, England: Penguin, 1947.
14/38

Southern   SOUTHERN, RICHARD. *Stage Setting for Amateurs and Professionals.* London: Faber, 1937.
10/4

Southey   SOUTHEY, ROBERT. *Poetical Works.* London: Longman, 1847.
9/3

Spender   SPENDER, STEPHEN. *Poems.* London: Faber, 1933.
15/15

Spottiswoode   SPOTTISWOODE, RAYMOND. *A Grammar of the Film: An Analysis of Film Technique.* London: Faber, 1935.
1/15, 5/2, 10/18, 13/14, 14/21, 15/10

Stevenson ELC   STEVENSON, ROBERT LOUIS. *Essays Literary and Critical.* Tusitala ed. London: Heinemann, 1923.
12/4

Stevenson TI   STEVENSON, ROBERT LOUIS. *Treasure Island.* Tusitala ed. London: Heinemann, n.d.
7/12

Taylor   TAYLOR, WARREN. *Tudor Figures of Rhetoric.* Private ed. dist. by University of Chicago Libraries, 1937.
Concise comprehensive list of figures, with definitions and examples.
1/2

Treble   TREBLE, H. A., and VALLINS, G. H. *An A.B.C. of English Usage.* London: Oxford University Press, 1936.
17/27

Tudor   TUDOR, ANDREW. *Theories of Film.* London: Secker and Warburg, 1974.
1/15

Tuve   TUVE, ROSAMOND. *Allegorical Imagery.* Princeton: Princeton University Press, 1966.
18/7, 18/9, 18/12, 18/13

Vaihinger   VAIHINGER, HANS. *The Philosophy of 'As If'.* 2d ed. Translated by C. K. Ogden. London: Routledge, 1935.
5/7, 9/2

Vernon   VERNON, M. D. *The Psychology of Perception.* Harmondsworth, England: Penguin, 1962.
4/5

Vickers   VICKERS, BRIAN. *Classical Rhetoric in English Poetry.* London: Macmillan, 1970.
1/2, 1/3

Vidor   VIDOR, KING. *A Tree Is a Tree.* New York: Harcourt, 1953.
13/2

Watson   WATSON, THOMAS. *The Hekatompathia,* or *Passionate Centurie of Loue.* London: Imprinted by Iohn Wolfe for Gabriell Cawood, c1582.
7/1, 7/15

Wellek   WELLEK, RENÉ, and AUSTIN, WARREN. *Theory of Literature.* 3d ed. New York: Harcourt, 1956.
6/4, 6/7

Whately   WHATELY, RICHARD. *Elements of Rhetoric.* New York: Harper, 1854.
10/1, 15/11

Whitford   WHITFORD, FRANK. *Expressionism.* London: Hamlyn, 1970.
2/1

Wickham   WICKHAM, GLYNNE. *Early English Stages 1300 to 1660* vol. I. London: Routledge, 1959.
7/5, 18/10

Wilder   WILDER, THORNTON. *Our Town.* New York: Harper, 1938.
15/22

Wrottesley   WROTTESLEY, FREDERIC JOHN. *The Examination of Witnesses in Court.* 2d ed. London: Sweet and Maxwell, 1926.
1/6

Notes

Chapter 1—Introduction

1. Lanham, pp. 101–2; Macbeth, p. 157.
2. So used by Lanham, pp. 101–2; Macbeth, p. 157 and elsewhere; Taylor's book *Tudor Figures of Rhetoric* contains both *tropes* and *schemes*. Vickers points out, p. 85, that while up to that point he had been referring to all rhetorical devices as *figures*, yet, properly speaking, there were two classes of rhetorical device, the one called tropes or figures, and the other called schemes.
3. Vickers, pp. 93–114.
4. *ETC: A Review of General Semantics,* 3, no. 2 (Winter 1946): 91–105.
5. "If the critic becomes too far removed from the reader of literature . . . he will tend to develop a technical jargon of his own and to regard himself as a necessary mediator between the creative writer and the ordinary reader. Indeed, in so far as he will be intelligible only to fellow experts, he will not even be a mediator between writer and public, but a barrier indicating the impossibility of non-professional appreciation of good literature." Quoted from David Daiches, *Critical Approaches to Literature,* p. 287, by Andrew McTaggart, *Screen* 10, no. 6 (1969): 69.
6. Wrottesley, p. 87.
7. Minto, p. 286.
8. "Richie's Ozu," *Sight and Sound* 44, no. 3 (Summer 1973): 176.
9. Burch, p. 31, note 1. On the other hand, on seeing *The Cat People* for a third time, I was sure that the bus and its sound (in a passage I cite later) came at the same time, and only the assurance of a fellow viewer that he had heard the sound first persuaded me to leave this example in.
10. Empson, p. 205.
11. Frye, p. 87, has written that the exploration of a work of art can only be undertaken on the assumption that, as it stands, it sets forth its author's final intention.
12. Metz LC, pp. 225–32.
13. The same observation has been made on the theater. Arliss, p. 228, is quite firm that until the day comes when a member of the audience is free to stand and ask an actor to speak a passage again, it is the duty of the writer to make his meaning clear, at one sitting, to someone of average intelligence, for the audience will not pay to see it again, unless it has understood and enjoyed the play.

Claire Johnston, "Rethinking Political Cinema", *Jump Cut* nos. 12/13 (1977): 56, reports that in *The Nightcleaners,* the screen goes black at intervals, to give the audience time to reflect on what they have seen, the editor having inserted black leader.
14. Note, however, that the making of difficult and still more difficult films is growing in the Soviet Union, as a form of artistic expression appealing to those with brain power, an influential class in Soviet society. See Herbert Marshall, "Andrei Tarkovsky's *The Mirror,*" *Sight and Sound* 45, no. 2 (Spring 1976): 95. It is a matter of having a large enough filmgoing or poetry-reading intelligentsia, or low enough production budget, for the film or book to return the cost of making it.
15. Spottiswoode, pp. 263–68 (teleological theories: Plato, Tolstoy, and Marx); Tudor, p. 49 (Eisenstein on the moral aspect of film); Grierson, pp. 122–31 ("Films and the Community," but the same viewpoint pervades the book); Ingmar Bergman quoted in MacCann, p. 5.
16. Payne, passim. About the same time (January 1930), Dr. Fred Eastman wrote a series of articles to the same effect in *The Christian Century.*
17. Ontario. *Interim Report* (1976), Section 3, "Interim Report of the Director of Research", pp. 7–17. The commission cites Howard Muson, *Media Violence* (New York: Harper & Row, 1972), p. 21, to the effect that the average American child, by the age of fifteen, has witnessed more than thirteen thousand murders on television.

The press provides regular confirmation of this. Here are two instances. A father, aged twenty-seven, stabbed his three-year-old son, saying he was possessed of a devil. The father was influenced, according to his statements, by recent films about children possessed by the devil (*The Sunday Sun*, Toronto, 26 Sept. 1976). A boy of fourteen, reenacting the role of Clint Eastwood in *Dirty Harry*, shot and killed his eleven-year-old brother with a derringer (The *Globe and Mail*, Toronto, 12 Sept. 1977).

Professor Leonard Berkowitz of the University of Wisconsin found in experiments too complex to recount here, that they "cast considerable doubts on the possibility of a cathartic purge of anger," and "that, in fact, motion picture or television violence can stimulate aggressive actions by normal people as well as by those who are emotionally disturbed . . . under appropriate conditions." See "The Effects of Observing Violence," *Scientific American* 210, no. 2 (1964): 35–41.

Producers seem to turn a blind eye to this evidence of the effects of their actions on their fellow men. Brian Forbes has written:

> Every producer I came in contact with seemed determined to find instant success by outdoing his nearest rival in the violence stakes . . . the same old parrot cry of "give the public what it wants" totally ignored the fact that audiences were still declining . . . What was actually meant was "give a particular section of the public what *it* wants and ignore the rest."
>
> I cannot embrace the idea that the calculated exploitation of violence or degrading sexual acts has any place of honour in a civilized society.
>
> . . . I do not think it is difficult for men of reason and intelligence to define filth (*Forbes*, pp. 373, 343).

The occasional, more sensitive, producer may come to accept the fact and face the consequences of his influence. When the public relations officer for London Transport read the script for a film set in the London Underground, he begged the director, Ted Kotcheff, to cut the first scene, in which a man standing on the platform was thinking of killing himself by leaping in front of the train. The day after the broadcast, at least half a dozen people would actually do it, he said. Kotcheff was skeptical and made the film as it was written. The day after the play was aired, five people jumped in front of trains. Kotcheff said, "it was the first time I really began to concern myself with the relationship between myself and my audience. Does television offer models to translate appetites and impulses into action?" Canadian Radio-Television Commission, Symposium on Television Violence, 1975. Cited by Charles Oberdorf, "Censorship: Protection from What and For Whom?" *Homemaker's* magazine (October 1976):50.

In a film purporting to be made by a "Church of England Film Unit," a bishop is shown behaving like a gangland boss, striding along the street in miter and cope, elbowing passers-by. Two black-suited, dog-collared clergy slouch on either side of him, their hands in their pockets. The suggestion is that even religion, to gain access to an audience conditioned to violence, must conform to their violent expectations to gain a hearing (*Monty Python's Flying Circus*). Dr. Richard Palmer, president of the American Medical Association, has called television violence an environmental issue that is more threatening than pollution (*Eastern Province Herald*, Port Elizabeth, 8 Feb. 1977).

18. Edgar Dale, "Child Welfare and the Cinema," *The English Journal*, College ed., 26, no. 9 (November 1937): 699–701; Holaday found that false detail shown in films was usually taken as true. See Holaday, p. 66.

19. Ontario, pp. 11–14.

20. "4.5 Millions in 1970," *Screen Education* 9 (Sept.–Oct. 1968): 8.

21. Art, says Brecht, is never without consequences. Every performance in some way must shape the attitudes of those who watch it, p. 151. Two and a half centuries ago a reviewer asserted that Congreve's *Sharper* had made many pickpockets, and the example of Valentine many spendthrifts; and that when vice is made familiar to us in jest, our power of resisting it is lost, even in those who wish to oppose it. Price, pp. 134–5. Indeed Plato remarks in the *Republic* that everyone begins to excuse his own vices when he is convinced that similar wickednesses are always being perpetrated by the kindred of the gods, and would not allow such tales to be told either of gods or men. Plato, 391B, 392B.

22. Christian Metz, "Methodological Propositions for the Analysis of Film," *Screen* 14, nos. 1–2 (Spring–Summer 1973): 90.

23. Montagu, pp. 142–43.

24. Hitchcock in a television talk (WNED, Buffalo, 26 August 1976) said that he was indifferent to content in the same way that a painter does not care whether the apples he paints are sweet or sour, and that the way the story is told is the art of the film.

Chapter 2—The Trope and Its Translation

1. Stéphane Mallarmé quoted in Whitford, p. 27.

2. *Hamlet*, act 1, sc. 2, lines 129–30.

3. *Macbeth*, act 2, sc. 2, lines 62–63.

4. Station WNED, Buffalo, 15 November 1978.

Chapter 3—Symbol or Significant Object

1. Norman Swallow believes that this sequence of *October,* and other ones of "eccentricity" or fantasy, were Aleksandrov's. See "Alexandrov," *Sight and Sound* 48, no. 4 (Autumn 1979): 247.

2. In a broadcast on *Madame Bovary,* 5 November 1958.

3. When a motorcar and a train run side by side, with Jennifer in the train and her fiancé in the car, and the road swings sharply away from the railway line, what we know of the situation makes us feel that Jennifer's fiancé is leaving her, and we take the parting of the ways for a parting in their lives. Winifred Nowottny would say that this showing of one image as if it were another is metaphor. See chapter 6, section 10.

When Henri pushes a figure of the Laughing Buddha out of the window, he is not merely breaking a bit of philosophical pottery. In the film the Buddha was greatly prized by its owner, whose family was cold toward Henri's family: one of its members had said that Joel, Henri's retarded brother, when old, would look like the Buddha, and now at this point in the film Joel, of whom Henri was fond, is dead and will never live to be old. This is why Henri breaks the figure. The Buddha, as Nowottny would say, is a symbol or a significant object—a thing so presented that we see it not only as itself, but as standing for a situation or situations beyond itself. There are not two things, one taken as if it were the other, but one thing, glowing with reflected significance. See chapter 3, section 23. (Nowottny, p. 175.)

4. Durgnat, pp. 248–50, has an interesting summary of things used by Bergman in *The Seventh Seal,* in meanings attaching to them in Western culture.

5. In remarks after the showing, Ontario Film Theatre, 29 October 1975.

Chapter 4—Repetition

1. "Significant repetition" is preferred by Fowler KE, p. 218. Kawin, p. 4, makes a distinction between *Repetitious,* "repeated with less impact on each recurrence: repeated to no particular end, out of a failure of invention or sloppiness of thought," and *Repetitive,* "repeated with equal or greater force at each recurrence." He mentions too that the growth of a work makes exact repetition impossible, and that near repetition is the most that can be done (p. 7).

2. Discussed in Bettetini, p. 26.

3. Barrie, act 4, p. 131 ff.

4. Sheridan, act 4, scene 3, p. 285.

5. Vernon, p. 159.

6. In a conversation. Chapman's term for his practice is the "multiple dynamic image": multiple as using several subframes at once, dynamic because of the possibility of changing the size or shape of a subframe as the audience is viewing it. The width of the screen for which *A Place to Stand* was first made was sixty-six feet. His composition was based on his estimate that it took half a second, or a lapse of twelve frames, for a viewer's eye to cross the screen. Subsequent showings on smaller screens have modified the effect thus obtained.

7. Søren Kierkegaard. *Repetition: an Essay in Experimental Psychology.* New York: Harper, 1964, p. 33. Quoted in Kawin, pp. 176–77.

Chapter 5—Simile

1. Partridge, p. 284.

2. Spottiswoode, pp. 251–53.

3. Mitry, pp. 71–72.

4. See Huss, p. 93. Giannetti GO, Chapter 3, answers some of the reasons given why figures are said to be impossible in film.

5. Richards points out that a word, like an image, may support several different likenesses at the same time. See p. 118.

6. Richards, pp. 123–24, quotes André Breton to the effect that the highest task of poetry is to compare two objects as remote from one another in character as possible, and offsets it by Dr. Johnson's objections to "far-fetched" comparisons.

7. Adam Smith, writes Vaihinger, pp. 19–20, interpreted all human actions *as if* their only driving force was egoism, ignoring such causes as mutual aid and habit. This must be done, however, knowing that the assumption does not fit reality, a fraction of which is substituted for the whole range of cause and effect.

De Bono, p. 73, shows that a simple geometrical figure can be fully described in a variety of ways, the choice of one of which could be made from habit, simplicity, or convenience. The observer should be aware, when choosing one, that he could equally well have chosen one of the others.

8. Eisenstein ND, p. 181.

9. One way of escaping from rigid habitual classifications is to think, not, as we usually do, in words, but in images, which are fluid and plastic as words never are. Another way is to make the effort of turning things upside down; seeing walls, for example, as hanging from the roof, instead of holding it up. Humor comes from a sudden change in the way we view a situation—a view just as valid as the one we abandoned (De Bono, pp. 82, 83, 90, 91, 92).

10. "Man in an Apron," *Punch* 236, no. 6187 (11 March 1959): 353.

11. Whether what emerges is a humorous comparison, poetic image, or scientific discovery, the quest in each case is for some likeness hitherto unnoticed. See Koestler, frontispiece and p. 27.

12. *Areopagitica* in Milton, p. 280.

13. Other images evoked by this music may be found in *Hungarian Rhapsody* (William Cameron Menzies) and *Rhapsody Rabbit* (Isadore Freleng).

Chapter 6—Metaphor

1. Hawkes, pp. 71–72.

2. At its simplest, says Richards, p. 83, a metaphor is made up of two thoughts of different things held in the mind, bound by a single word or phrase, whose meaning flows from the play of one on the other.

3. Priestley, p. 170.

4. Samuel Taylor Coleridge quoted in Wellek, p. 188, speaks of the translucence of the special in the individual.

5. Nowottny, 52–54.

6. Richards, p. 100.

7. Wellek, p. 207, uses the term "gloss" once in this sense; "thus in Donne's 'Songs and Sonnets', his poems of profane love, the metaphoric gloss is constantly drawn from the Catholic world of sacred love."

8. A friendly critic points out that in Hardy's novel, the valentine is what kindles Boldwood's love (he would not have courted Bathsheba without encouragement), and his love is never quenched. I can only say that what the director placed on the screen evoked this response in me, and I must assume that, making allowance for any eccentricity of mine, this was intended.

9. Hawkes, p. 72. This is only a special case of the reader's, and viewer's, responsibility to the works he peruses. Lubbock, for example, p. 17, wrote that the reader must not suppose that creating the experience of a book is solely the author's affair—the reader is a joint author. Or, as Sir Hugh Walpole put it, the author merely collects and presents notes, from which the reader, each one in his own way, writes the book (quoted in Jackson, pp. 72–73).

10. Fowler MEU, s.v. *Metaphor;* Richards, p. 91, although he dislikes the term "dead metaphor," p. 102.

11. The term "background" is from Mukařovský, discussed in Hawkes, p. 73.

12. Eisenstein ND, p. 63.

13. Described by Charles Wolfe, "Resurrecting *Greed,*" *Sight and Sound* 44, no. 3 (Spring 1975): 172.

14. Mitry, p. 71.

15. The most famous is the three lions in *Potemkin,* sleeping, wakening, and rising, which, shown quickly in this order, suggest an outraged lion leaping up in protest. This is described in Pudovkin, pp. 88–89 and Eisenstein FF, p. 56 and figure 8.

16. Giannetti UM, pp. 90–91; Lindgren, pp. 93–96; Montagu, p. 164.

17. In conversation, after the showing at the Ontario Film Theatre, 12 December 1975.

Chapter 7—Anadiplosis or the Carry-Over

1. Watson, no. 41 (unpaged).

2. Empson, p. 50.

3. Arnheim and Balazs both give examples of anadiplosis. Balazs describes a scene from his film *Narcosis.* The hero's suitcase is seen in his room. The image is then "narrowed" by irising out, so that only the suitcase is left. Slowly the suitcase begins to shake, the diaphragm of the camera is opened up again, and now the viewer sees that the suitcase is no longer in the hero's room, but in the luggage net of a moving railway carriage. A pan from the suitcase to the hero seated below shows that he too is on his way. All of the unimportant events between were neatly bridged by the suitcase, which never left the screen between the room and the train. (Balazs, pp. 149–50.)

When two shots alike in form are joined by a dissolve, Arnheim speaks of a neutral zone between them, undefined in image, except for what is common to both shots, the mere abstract oscillation, say, of a pendulum and a child going to and fro on a swing (Arnheim, pp. 119–20).

Arijon, pp. 582–88, gives, but in no systematic arrangement, ten examples of this figure.

None of the three gives the figure a name, either its classical one, *anadiplosis,* or the English one that I propose, *carry-over.* None identify it or treat it as a figure.

4. It is clearly based on a simile. Carl Sandburg wrote, "Poetry is the establishment of a metaphorical link between white butterfly wings and the scraps of torn-up love letters" (Detzer, p. 146). Note here the ominous difference in comparing the torn-up letters, not to white butterflies but black pigeons.

5. Wickham, pp. 159, 175.

6. In some Noh plays, there are "simultaneous" settings, as, for example, where the Hasigakari or walkway from the dressing room may represent a boat, and the stage proper an island, or where the walkway may represent a village, and the stage the site of a hovel outside it. Walking from one of these to the other is to change one's place from boat to island, or village to hovel (Arnot, pp. 99–100, 269).

7. Eisenstein FF, p. 22.

8. *The Man from the Sea* by Eric Coates provides a good example of the musical switch. The last three notes of the sea shanty "Johnny Come Down to Hilo" are the same as the first and last three notes of "Three Blind Mice," and the composer uses these notes with great skill to move quickly between the two tunes with no sense of transition at all: now we find we are in the one, and now in the other.

9. Not knowing the source of a sound sharpens one's perception of its character and possibilities. A director then, by context, may exploit this, deliberately leading a viewer to take the sound for a like one from another source. Several times on waking I have caught the still reverberating sound of a clock's final chime, and taken it for a whistle, a voice, or an organ, before I had determined what it must have been.

10. Empson places sonnet 93 in Type Two, but the pun in Type Three, where the two unrelated meanings, both applicable, are given in one word. He quotes an example from Pope's Dunciad, book 4, lines 201–2:

> Where Bentley late tempestuous wont to sport
> In troubled waters, but now sleeps in Port.

Here we think of a ship sailing from stormy water into—and at this moment in a flash the image of a harbor becomes a bottle of wine. Yet the pun would not be amusing unless the harbor and wine were jointly present (Empson, chapter 3, especially p. 108).

11. Smith PP, p. 30.

12. Stevenson TI, pp. 121–22.

13. Muecke, pp. 19–20.

14. Sister M. Salome Antoine describes as imperfect anadiploses where other expressions come between the word and its repetition. (Antoine, p. 87.)

15. Balazs, pp. 149–50. All but one of the 18 lines of the poem by Thomas Watson, part of which starts this chapter, and which he called a "sonnet," is linked to the one before by anadiplosis. His deprecating note above the poem hints that he shares the doubts of Balazs, "This passion is framed vpon a somewhat tedious or too much affected continuation of that figure in Rhetorique, which of the Grekes is called . . . anadiplosis." But what a fascinating challenge the poem was, how neatly shaped!

Chapter 8—Antithesis

1. *Rhetorica ad Alexandrum,* quoted in Kennedy, p. 65.

2. Antoine, p. 149.

3. Smith MR, p. 99.

4. Macbeth, p. 133.

5. Lanham, p. 97.

6. *Julius Caesar,* act 3, sc. 2, lines 116–18.

7. This term goes back in English only to 1833, and was not fully accepted as late as 1907. See Muecke, p. 8.

8. According to Wolfgang Kayser, the grotesque is an experience of a strange, alien, and meaningless world of the monstrous, which contradicts the laws of the one we know, which is at once absurd and terrifying, whose deformations combine surprise and horror. See Kayser, pp. 31, 53, 184, 186. It is not a figure but a tone, and is of no direct concern here. It will be clear, however, that some antitheses and hyperboles have a grotesque tone, perhaps the following:

The humiliation of Dr. Rath in *The Blue Angel;*
The conclusion of *Dr. Strangelove;*
The blowing up of Henry D'Ascoigne in *Kind Hearts and Coronets;*
The various corruptions of *O Lucky Man;*
The transformation in the second half of *Shame.*

9. There is an interesting discussion of this antithesis in Don Willis, "Yasujiro: Emotion and Contemplation," *Sight and Sound* 48, no. 1 (Winter 1978–79): 44–49.

Chapter 9—Hyperbole

1. "We really did cram twenty-eight boys into one taxi." Charles Crichton, "Children and Fantasy," *Penguin Film Review* no. 7 (1948): 47.
2. Vaihinger, p. 57.
3. Southey, p. 124; Carroll, pp. 39, 42.
4. Highet, pp. 68–69.
5. In the view of Longinus, p. 200, hyperbole is stretching something beyond its natural size, either too large or too small. All the filmic examples I have found, however, are of enlarging. Belittling something by overstating its triviality or smallness would seem to be close to meiosis (chapter 17) as when someone bathed in blood says, "It's just a scratch."

Chapter 10—Ellipsis

1. Whately, p. 192.
2. *A Midsummer Night's Dream*, act 1, sc.1, line 164.
3. *Coriolanus,* act 4, sc. 6, line 150.
4. Richard Southern emphasizes this breach-in-the-wall aspect of the proscenium arch. See Southern, p. 81.
5. Hodgart, p. 31.
6. "Ye haue another maner of speach drawen out at length and going all after one tenure and with an imperfect sence till you come to the last word or verse, which concludes the whole premisses with a perfit sence and full periode" (Puttenham, p. 176).
7. Albert G. Greene, *The Baron's Last Banquet* in Bell, p. 336. Albert Greene never published a collection of his verse.
8. Quiller-Couch, pp. 243–67.
9. Arijon, pp. 590–601.
10. Puttenham, p. 169.
11. Giannetti UM, p. 84.
12. Where the unconnected parts are words, and not sentences, the figure is brachiologa: "Enuy, malice, flattery, disdain, / Auarice, deceit, falsed, filthy gaine" (Puttenham, p. 213). He adds, "If this loose language be used, not in single words, but in long clauses, it is called Asyndeton." Without implying any opinion in the argument as to what corresponds in film to the word or sentence, I include under the better-known term "asyndeton," all forms of jump cut.
13. Exod. 15:9.
14. Puttenham, p. 175.
15. Ibid.
16. Balazs, chap. 4 passim; and see pp. 273–74.
17. Mitry, pp. 43–44.
18. Spottiswoode, pp. 51, 229, 237, uses the term "simultaneous montage" for the joining of image and sound. Nonetheless, bearing in mind Eisenstein's use of the term "the montage trope" and the like effects that Jean Mitry finds evoked by adjacent images, whether seen at the same time or one after the other, it seems convenient to use a single term for the same effect on the viewer, distinguishing one from the other by adding to the word *montage, simultaneous* or *successive.* It follows from this that if a description is needed for the interplay at the same time of sound and image, a different word should be found—it might be *vertical.* See chapter 15, section 1.
19. S. M. Eisenstein observes that in teaching drawing in Japan, the student is given a number of frames of different shapes, rectangular, square, or circular, which held up to a scene, "hewed out" a piece of actuality, and feels that the lens ought to be applied in like manner (Eisenstein FF, p. 40). The use of such a frame, where what is left out and what is left in are visible both at once, makes the frame's two functions quite clear. The exclusion is ellipsis, the inclusion is simultaneous montage, two sides of one action.
20. Balazs, p. 96.
21. Burch, p. 21.

Chapter 11—Metonymy

1. Macbeth, pp. 202–18.
2. Nowottny, p. 49.

3. Hobbes, p. 336; Grube, p. 90.
4. Eisenstein ND, pp. 36–39.
5. Frazer, pp. 37–45.

Chapter 12—Synecdoche

1. The same image may be taken as a different figure by different people, according to how each one sees it: or (a quite different matter) depending on the definition.
Sister Miriam Joseph, justified by a passage in Puttenham, quotes the following as examples of the figure emphasis:

> Farewell, fair cruelty. (*Twelfth Night or What You Will*, act 1, sc. 5, line 307.
> Shrug'st thou, malice? (*The Tempest*, act 1, sc. 2, line 367.

To me this is abstract for concrete, and clearly a mode of metonymy. If it has an effect in emphasizing the trait, it is surely reason for using any figure that it gives at least a modicum of emphasis.
She also classes "Pour down thy weather" (*King John*, act 4, sc. 2, line 108), and "Put up thy weapon" as synecdoches, for her definition includes "genus for species." To me, weather is a higher level abstraction, whose particulars include rain, snow, fog, humidity, and temperature, not to be seen with any great exactitude as species. While dagger is readily differentiated as a species of weapon, the two may also be seen as different levels of abstraction (Joseph, pp. 112, 153, 315).
Peacham too includes as synecdoche the signifying "By the matter the thing made of it, as, they eate the fynest wheate, drincke the sweetest Grapes, and weare the fynest Wool, by Wheate we understand Bread, by Grapes Wine, by Wool Cloth." It is hard to view grapes as a part of wine; they are an antecedent stage in making wine, more easily seen as a cause, and therefore again a metonymy (Peacham, s.v. *synecdoche*).
That an image may be several figures at once, or different ones according to viewpoint, is an acceptable consequence of applying any set of categories to a work of art or literature. But that this should arise from floating definitions is, to me, unacceptable. Certainly for the present purpose, it is better to limit synecdoche to where a whole and part are clearly to be seen, beyond contention, as, for example, "Done to death by slanderous tongues" (*Much Ado About Nothing*, act 5, sc. 3, line 4). I treat as metonymies all cases where the whole alleged is better conceived as a higher step in abstraction.
2. S. M. Eisenstein "The Twelve Apostles" (1945), Eisenstein ND, p. 28. See also "Film Form: New Problems" (1933), Eisenstein FF, p. 133.
3. Arnheim, p. 80–81. Some recent writers are correcting this neglect. Monaco (1977), for example, includes a brief treatment of metonymy and synecdoche.
4. Stevenson ELC, "The Works of Edgar Allan Poe," pp. 180–81.
5. As far back as 1911, a Larry Trimble filmed a story with two characters, using simply shots of their hands and feet. The players were seen as wholes only at the end. Brownlow, p. 16.
6. Balazs, Chapter 4 passim, esp. pp. 35–36.

Chapter 13—Motion

1. That a trope works a change in meaning and a scheme a change in form seems to be a modern distinction. See Lanham, pp. 101–2.
2. I am concerned here only with speeded motion which is seen as such by the viewer. King Vidor tells how after increasing the metronome timing of the diggers in *Our Daily Bread* as much as he could, he gradually speeded their movement further by reducing the number of frames exposed per second, but not beyond the point where the viewers would credit the cameraman instead of the diggers (Vidor, p. 225).
3. Pudovkin, pp. 146–54.
4. Herrick, "To Daffodils," p. 171.
5. Milton EP, "Samson Agonistes," line 80, vol. 2, p. 209.
6. Montgomery, "Incognita," p. 374.
7. Buchanan PW, "The Green Gnome," p. 99.
8. Arnheim, pp. 117–18, adds that some of the postures caught by a single frame could not be held by an actor.
9. Murray Macquarrie, CBC Radio, 19 June 1966.
10. Seymour Stern describes a use in a film I have not seen. Speculators have caused the price of flour to keep rising. A baker comes to change the price of bread posted on his window. The queue of people waiting to buy freezes. Their money steadily buys less—would they have the price of a loaf when their turn comes (*A Corner in Wheat*, D. W. Griffith)? See Jacobs, p. 60. It is an expression of collective shock more than emphasis.

11. It is beyond the scope of this book to discuss composition. However pleasing a fine composition may be as an arrangement of elements, it rarely has the effect of a figure. It would not be proper, though, to pass without mentioning William Cameron Menzies. His compositions have a balance of tones, movement, and areas, of contrasting shapes, of the distant and the close, of blackness and light; triangular forms and converging lines varied with skill; and a precise use of emphasis, falling always where it should, at the right strength. Add to this a simple elegance and a sense of order, as of one who finds a shape and pattern everywhere, as of a detached Olympian looker-on, never so distracted by the sufferings or concerns of his characters that he is unable to find beauty and order in them. This is very close to a tropical addition of meaning, but it is rare in film and must be seen in the compositions themselves, especially in *Address Unknown*. It crops up now and then in films he designed, like the funeral ceremony in *Our Town* (Sam Wood), on a rainy day, composed only of umbrellas, taken from overhead.

12. Puttenham, p. 170.

13. Macbeth, p. 133.

14. This is noted by both Spottiswoode, p. 157, and Montagu, p. 101.

15. Balazs, pp. 141–42.

16. The term "swish pan" has come into use for this. *Swish*, however, is an imitative word for a hissing "sound." *Streak*, on the other hand, throughout its history, has stood for a "visible" stroke, scratch, or line, and seems more appropriate; and in such phrases as "a streak of lightning," has also been linked with swift movement.

17. The actual content of the sequence could only be ascertained, not by watching the screen, but by scrutinizing the film, frame by frame, as Kevin Brownlow must have done. He tells us (Brownlow, p. 628) that the faces of Elie and his sister Norma alternate, starting with three and six frames, then a series of three and two frames in length, leading to a climax of single frames of each and ending with three frames of him, before his hand slips and his body falls.

Chapter 14—Montage

1. Published in the years 1933–34.

2. I refer the reader to the following excellent treatments: Pudovkin; Eisenstein FS; Montagu; and Reisz.

3. Eisenstein FF, p. 240.

4. Ibid., p. 33.

5. By the author.

6. Eisenstein FF, pp. 29–30.

7. Arnheim, p. 100.

8. Jackobson, p. 243.

9. Landor, p. 13.

10. Kuleshov, pp. 48–50; and Dwight Macdonald, "Eisenstein, Pudovkin, and Others," in Jacobs, p. 127.

11. Nowottny, p. 9.

12. Metz FL, p. 35.

13. Eisenstein ND, pp. 68–69.

14. Hayakawa, p. 292.

15. Eisenstein FF, p. 133, goes as far as to tell us that film makes use of the figure synecdoche, but so far as I know, without consulting Russian sources, nowhere carries this further by pointing out that montage is only a piling up of synecdoches.

16. Lanham, p. 96.

17. Goldsmith, p. 311. Lodge, p. 79, following Jakobson, writes that montage is metaphoric and the close-up, synecdochic. However, although it may be possible to say of repetition, simile, and anadiplosis that all are the children of likeness, montage is not wholly of the family of any other figure. It may bring together bits of the same event (as here, a night in a city), each a synecdoche. On the other hand (as in *Potemkin*, below) it may make us aware that the bits have the same look, by way of simile. Which of these two it leans toward rests in the director's choice, and often in the viewer's awareness.

18. Eisenstein ND p. 55 divides *Potemkin* into five "acts." He speaks of like moving patterns as being *synonymous*. "The Fourth Dimension in Kino. Part II," *Close Up*: 6, no. 4 (April 1930): 264. See also chap. 4, Repetition, sections 3 and 4, *Accumulation* and *Leitmotiv*.

19. Chesterton, p. 294.

20. Reisz, p. 112.

21. The common terms are "simultaneity," "parallellism," or "cross-cutting," e.g., Buchanan FM, p. 69; Montagu, p. 122; Pudovkin, pp. 48–49; although Spottiswoode, pp. 227–30 uses "simultaneous

montage" for the combination of image and nondiegetic sound, and Arijon uses "parallel editing" for the alternate use of different set-ups as well as of different events, pp. 10–11.

The word "parallel" is especially inept, for we never see the two happenings together as the geometrical term suggests, nor are the two of necessity sufficiently like in character to make the word appropriate, and the two actions, rather than never meeting, nearly always converge. "Cross-cutting", suggesting a switch to and fro between two events, is better.

The term that describes what is actually being done is "alternation" or "alternate editing" and its use is certainly not confined to suggesting simultaneous action.

22. Longinus, p. 150. The quotation from Cicero's Oration for Marcellus is given in the note. *Collection* seem to differ from *Diaeresis*, at least as it appears in the example given in Lanham, p. 33.

23. Kuleshov, p. 52, did the same in the early 1920s.

24. Balazs, p. 148.

25. Reisz, p. 194. Quoted as epigraph to the chapter.

26. Quoted in Edward Ashcroft, "Surrealism: What Is It, Its Influence On Cinema," *Film Art* 1 (Summer 1933): 8.

27. Roman Jakobson notes that in aphasic patients, where combination and contexture are deficient, and selection and substitution are stable, this "gives rise to infantile one-sentence utterances, and one-word sentences . . . word order becomes chaotic, the ties of grammatical coordination are dissolved. . . . Conjunctions, prepositions, pronouns, and articles disappear first, giving rise to the so-called 'telegraphic style'" (Jakobson, p. 251).

28. Peacham, s.v. Aenigma. John Smith uses exactly the same words, but without crediting Peacham, p. 83.

29. Montagu, p. 133.

30. Edward Branigan "The Space of Equinox Flower," *Screen* 17, no. 2 (Summer 1976): 75. Other interpretations of Ozu's unpeopled screens will be found in Jonathan Rosenbaum, "Richie's Ozu: Our Prehistoric Present," *Sight and Sound* 44, no. 3 (1975): 179; and Kristin Thompson and Davis Bordwell, "Space and Narrative in the Films of Ozu," *Screen* 17, no. 2 (Summer 1976): 41–73. Some of the choruses that separate what could be called the "acts" in the plays of Euripides, in say, the *Heracles*, have just as tenuous a tie to the action they have halted, and seem to have a like function, of taking us out of the turmoil of a particular incident to the calm of a more reflective, secular viewpoint.

31. Huss, p. 60, shows in a chart more than a hundred modes of wipe. He suggests, for example, that a clock wipe (by an arm radiating from center screen, starting perhaps at 12:00) is a metaphor for the passage of time, p. 92.

32. Eisenstein FF, p. 22, discusses filmic analogies to the Kabuki theater.

33. Henry Peacham, quoted in Lanham, p. 65.

34. Leonard Hacker, "The 'Dissolve,'" *Film Art*, no. 3 (Spring 1934).

35. This is the "perpetual dissolve," whereby one image grows out of another. Leonard Hacker proposes this both as something uniquely possible in film, that matches the nature of thought, and as the best alternative to what he considers the perfect, but practically impossible, film, consisting of one continuous evolving scene with no joining of pieces whatever. See, besides the previous reference, Leonard Hacker, "Raymond Spottiswoode Criticised," *Film Art*, no. 10 (Spring 1937): 16–21.

36. An analysis of this passage, piece by piece, with running times and illustrative frames may be found in Reisz, pp. 116–20.

37. Reisz, p. 195, cites, from World War II, the use of the same shots in American and German propaganda films to arouse the opposite reactions in the viewers, for it does not follow, he reminds us, that the final impression left will be a truthful one, however authentic the shots from which it is gained. Balazs, pp. 120–21, has a striking example of how changes in order changes the meaning of a shot. In *The Battleship Potemkin*, the court-martial and the parading for execution of the sailors who protested against maggoty meat were transferred to a later part of the film. Without the provocation of a savage sentence for what was hardly an offense, the sailors appear unjustified in shooting their officers, and the court-martial, coming near the end, suggested, against the fact, that the mutiny had been quelled.

38. Sophocles, *Oedipus the King*, p. 57.

39. *Richard the Third*, act 4, sc. 4, lines 362–69.

40. Eisenstein ND, pp. 59–60, points out that in "Act IV" of *Potemkin*, not only is there a "leap in the opposite direction" from the carefree applause by the citizens of the revolting sailors to their panic-stricken flight before the fire of the Cossacks in the second half but also within the second half between, for example, the rhythmic marching feet of the soldiers and the helter-skelter of the crowd, the march of booted feet down the steps, and walking up, the woman whose arms carried her dead son.

41. Eisenstein ND, p. 65.

42. Pudovkin, p. 45.

Chapter 15—Sound

1. S. M. Eisenstein, W. I. Pudovkin, and G. V. Aleksandroff, "The Sound Film: A Statement from the U.S.S.R.," *Close Up* 3, no. 4 (October 1928): 10–13.
The statement declares that "The first experiment with sound must be directed towards its pronounced non-coincidence with the visual images," and goes on to speak of "a new orchestral counterpoint of sight-images and sound-images."
Robert Herring remarks a few issues later, "Sound Imagery," *Close Up* 4, no. 3 (March 1929): 39, "The new tag is obviously going to be 'contrapuntal.'"
2. Pudovkin, pp. 55–56.
3. Eisenstein FS, pp. 74–78.
4. Jean Mitry has reservations about the propriety of the term "counterpoint" in this context, and refers to it as a "rather muddled notion," which is generally intended to suggest some kind of *contrast*, which he considers a better word (Mitry, p. 55).
5. Muecke, pp. 19–20.
6. The late Michael Doran kindly drew my attention to Richard Wagner's practice, especially in the Ring Cycle of adding to a scene dramatically free of any premonition of evil, a chord or motif that warns the audience, but not the participants, of what is to come.
7. Such possible terms as "narrative" and "nonnarrative" sound could also suggest sound that might be diegetic, but is unrelated to the story. For a scene at a shop, for example, every passing bus, every boy that shouts, and every ambulance siren are plausible diegetic inclusions, but may be of no value in telling the story, may even detract from it. They may thus be diegetic, but nonnarrative. On the other hand, nondiegetic sound, like music, may help the story. Mitry, p. 72, wrote, for example, of diegetic metaphors. Reisz, p. 272, uses the word "actual" for "diegetic."
8. Lanham, p 76.
9. Anthony Asquith, "The Tenth Muse Climbs Parnassus," *Penguin Film Review*, no. 1 (1946): 25–26.
10. Spottiswoode, pp. 226–27, cites *Industrial Britain* (John Grierson and Robert J. Flaherty) as an example of this.
11. Whately, p. 220.
12. Burch, pp. 80–87.
13. Christian Metz discusses the question as pleonasm (redundancy, or lack of economy in expression), not as tautology (repetition, or stating a message more than once), and quotes Arnheim (Mitry, p. 51).
14. Pope, *Essay on Criticism*, p. 365.
15. Spender, p. 53.
16. Balazs, p. 216, makes the point that any exactly simulated sound has the same characteristics, as to wavelength and so on, as the sound imitiated—it is not really an imitation; it is the sound itself. What we see on the screen, on the other hand, is merely an image of the object photographed, lacking many characteristics of the object.
17. Reisz, p. 166.
18. Balazs, p. 210, writes of an "acoustic close-up." Burch, p. 91, writes of an "auditory close-up."
19. *Hamlet*, act 5, sc. 2, line 322.
20. See Chap. 7, sect. 9, Anadiplosis, Variation VII iv.
21. C. H. Hazelwood, *Lady Audley's Secret*, act 1, sc. 1, in Rowell, p. 245.
22. Wilder, pp. 3, 106.
23. Pope, *The Rape of the Lock*, Canto III, lines 7–8, p. 78.
24. Pope, *An Essay on Man*, Epistle III, 183–84, p. 212.
25. Opinion differs in the use of syllepsis and zeugma. The *Oxford English Dictionary* says of zeugma, "also sometimes applied to cases of irregular *construction* in which the single word agrees grammatically with only one of the other words to which it refers (more properly called Syllepsis)." Fowler MEU says, on the other hand, p. 622, "The difference is that syllepsis is grammatically correct, but requires the single word to be understood in a different sense with each of its pair . . . whereas in zeugma the single word actually fails to give sense with one of its pair." Sir Ernest Gowers in the second edition of Fowler (1965), s.v. Syllepsis, has made no substantial change in this passage.
Puttenham supports the *Dictionary*. For the Zeugma, or Single Supply, he gives the example, p. 164,

> Fellowes and friends and kinne forsooke me quite

where *forsooke* agrees grammatically with all three subjects. For the Syllepsis, or Double Supply, he gives, p. 165,

Here my sweet sonnes and daughter all my blisse
Yonder mine owne deare husband buried is,

where the *is*, essential to the rhyme, agrees with husband, but not with *sonnes and daughter*, which require *are*. Lanham, pp. 95, 104–5, supports this usage also.

Without abating my respect for Fowler, I follow Dr. Onions and the *Dictionary*.

26. See Chap. 7, sect. 6, above.

Chapter 16—Inner States

1. Forster, p. 75.

2. Quoted in Jackson, p 108.

3. Balazs, pp. 94–95, gives the examples, of which I have no note, from Dovzhenko's *Ivan*, of the Dnieprostroi Dam being shown four times, first as seen by Ivan, a peasant boy; then by him as a worker in industry; then by a mother whose son died in building it; and last by her later, when she came to be proud of her son's dying on a dangerous task he had volunteered for.

4. Dated 28 June 1942.

5. The first-person camera is sometimes spoken of as a "Point-of-View Shot," as in Edward Branigan's analysis of it in "Formal Permutations of the Point-of-View Shot," *Screen* 16, no. 3 (Autumn 1975): 54–64.

6. Huss, pp. 151–52.

7. Mitry, pp. 415 ff.

8. Ibid., p. 47.

9. Leopold Lewis, *The Bells*, in Rowell, p. 481.

10. *Hamlet*, act 1, sc. 2, lines 129, 138, 145–47.

11. Arijon, p. 48, uses the phrase "internal voice" for this, and "external voice," where lip movement is seen.

12. *Oxford English Dictionary*, s.v.

13. Nesfield, pp. 13–14.

14. Superimposition does not seem to be a normal state for the living, waking person, whose attention cannot well absorb two visual events at the same time. Film makes a single visual event of them. Something similar is described in Moody, pp. 55–56: A patient, suffering a postpartum hemorrhage, describes losing consciousness and feeling herself to be sailing across a large body of water. She could see on the far shore her dead loved ones, and yet at the same time could see from outside, like a spectator, the doctors and nurses trying to revive her body, as if one scene were superimposed on the other.

15. Luis Buñuel is said to draw on his dreams in planning his films. Axel Madsen, "Phantom of Liberty," *Sight and Sound* 43, no. 3 (Summer 1974): 171.

16. Mitry, p. 45.

17. These may be the absolute metaphors discussed by Furness, pp. 18–19, 105. These are metaphors in which image and gloss are no longer given together, but the gloss alone, as if the drop of red oil on a paler ground looked to Sindbad like the nipple of one of his many women, and we are shown the drop of oil but never told of the nipple. Furness says it is as though adjectives were cut free from their nouns, a "glowing" or "hissing" floating free from things that glow or hiss; glosses perhaps blending with other glosses to create a tissue of impressions, descriptive no longer, whose link to the real world is apparent only to the author, if he remembers it.

18. See, for example, Dunne, part II.

19. See above, chap. 4, sect. 14.

20. Longinus, p. 115 ff. It is well established that children and exceptional adults like William Blake project mental images into the outer world. Lewis Jacobs points out in *The Rise of the American Film* that perhaps the earliest example of vision in film is where a shot of Annie Lee is interrupted by a shot of her husband on the desert island where he is shipwrecked (*After Many Years*, D. W. Griffith). This is reprinted in Jacobs, pp. 43–44.

21. Nesfield, p. 13.

22. Euripides, *Orestes*, quoted by Longinus, pp. 116–18.

23. Cicero *Fourth Oration against Cataline*, quoted in Nesfield, pp. 13–14.

24. *Macbeth*, act 2, sc. 1, lines 33–35, quoted in Longinus, p. 117, footnote.

25. Looking into the future, or prediction, is the figure diabole: "For he shall be delivered unto the Gentiles, and shall be mocked, and spitefully entreated, and spitted on" (Luke 18:32). But, looking forward and looking back are often linked. See Chapter 4, Section 12. In such films as *Last Year at Marienbad*, it is not always possible to be sure when a flight from the present is forward or backward in time. It seems logical then that the terms for the two movements ought to suggest a likeness of movement but opposing directions. I, therefore, propose with diffidence that the word "promnesis" replace

"diabole," for looking forward, which makes a better pair together with *anamnesis,* looking backward. *Promnesia* has already been used for the experience of remembering what is happening or about to happen, "false memory" (*Oxford English Dictionary,* s.v.).

26. Smith MR, p. 249.
27. Homer, p. 111.
28. Patmore, p. 66.
29. Homer, pp. 322–25.
30. Mitry, pp. 45 ff.
31. See note 25.
32. "I've seen several films lately which have got some marvelous things in them, but personally I don't quite know what was going on on the screen at various key moments. I don't know if, for instance, a woman was supposed to be thinking about what I was seeing on the screen, dreaming it, or whether it was in fact actually happening to her. Now, in my book, that's not good film-making. I may be terribly wrong, but I like to tell a story, plainly and as simply as possible." David Lean, quoted in Pratley, p. 198.
33. The ambiguous cut is also found in the novel. As the rector enters his pulpit at a memorial service, his eyes looking around the congregation meet those of a young man he had seen before, attentive, troubled, angellike. "You will know," he felt the boy said, "what you have to say." It was the twentieth chapter of Exodus, the thirteenth verse, "Thou shalt not kill." We hear the sermon based on this text, "all killings are fratricide, all wars are civil war. . . . Be not deceived! God is not mocked!" Then the massed faces of the congregation came back to his eyes. A terrible weariness and sadness came upon him. He was too old, had made too many concessions to the world. He drew breath and preached from the first book of the Maccabees, "they fought with cheerfulness the battle of Israel." Not until the first sermon was over do we know that it was but a rapid thought through his mind, a possible sermon, but not the one he gave (Pargeter, pp. 186–91).

Chapter 17—Minor Figures

1. Puttenham, p. 260.
2. Empson, p. 102.
3. Nowottny, p. 154; see chap. 1, sect. 3, and chap. 5, sect. 15.
4. Empson, p. 148.
5. Ibid., p. 192.
6. Mitry, p. 45 ff; Burch, Chapter 1; John Katz, "An Integrated Approach to the Teaching of Film and Literature," *Screen* 11, nos. 4–5 (1970): 58–59.
7. The skill and sureness with which writer and director sustain the ambiguity through this film may be explored with profit by looking at the text: Robbe-Grillet.
8. Act l, sc. 7, line 59.
9. At this time the National Film Board of Canada did not print production credits in its films, nor could the board supply them.
10. Smith MR, p. 99.
11. Gray, "The Progress of Poesy," lines 17–19, p. 42.
12. Puttenham, p. 185.
13. *Henry the Fourth* part 2, act 3, sc. 2, lines 242–43.
14. Lanham, p. 67.
15. Antoine, p. 163.
16. Smith MR, p. 105; Joseph, p. 166.
17. Macbeth, pp. 282, 286.
18. Empson, p. 102.
19. Ruskin, p. 160. Eisenstein FF, p. 134, does not mention the pathetic fallacy as such, but after discussing synecdoche, he remarks that all the elements of a scene must sound in the same key, citing as an example, the storm that lashes Lear from without, which matches the storm within him.

If any demonstration is needed of the strength and elegance that figures add, *Brief Encounter* provides it. This is the title of two films made from Sir Noël Coward's play *Still Life,* one in color by Alan Bridges, strictly chronological, and one by David Lean in black and white, told in flashback. Lean's use of repetition, sound, anastrophe, anamnesis and the pathetic fallacy give his film a power and a poignancy lacking in the other.

20. Scott, p. 217, quotes I. A. Richards on the relation between personification and metaphor.
21. Donne, "The Sun Rising," vol. 1, pp. 12–13.
22. Gray, "The Bard," lines 73–74, p. 49.
23. Donne, "The Message," vol. 1, p. 43.
24. Aurelius, chap. 12, sect. 3, p. 182.

25. *Dream*, 24 May 1974.
26. As quoted in the *Oxford English Dictionary*, s.v. In Puttenham at p. 259, his comment is, "It is no small fault in a maker to use such wordes and termes as do diminish and abbase the matter he would seem to set forth, by imparing the dignitie of the cause he takes in hand."
27. Treble, p. 22, s.v. anticlimax.

Chapter 18—Fantasy—Allegory—Abstraction

1. For example, Kracauer TF, pp. 22–74, passim.
2. Forster, p. 105.
3. Lewis, chap. 2; MacNeice, passim.
4. Lewis, p. 44; MacNeice, pp. 104, 131.
5. MacNeice, pp. 67, 131.
6. Lewis, p. 60.
7. Tuve, pp. 10, 11.
8. Boccaccio, pp. 48–49.
9. Quoted from Thomas Lodge by Tuve, pp. 7, 9.
10. Wickham, p. 153.
11. MacNeice, p. 68.
12. Tuve, p. 15.
13. Ibid.
14. Fletcher discusses personification or simplification of character in chapter 1, the battle and the quest in chapter 3, and the magic and supernatural elements in chapter 4.
15. Frye, pp. 90–91; MacNeice, pp. 16–18.
16. Zoilus is said to have given the earliest known definition of a figure: "to pretend one thing and to say another" (Kennedy, p. 116).
17. In works of "literary art," Frye, p. 72, finds such a conclusion "inescapable," without exception.
18. The phrase "spine of allegory" is from MacNeice, who holds the view that in however slight a sense, every "realistic" tale must be a parable, pp. 138, 130. Boccaccio too held that every worthwhile narrative concealed a kernel of allegory (MacQueen, p. 47). Lewis, p. 44, thinks that allegory belongs to mind in general, it being in the nature of thought to find pictures by which to express the immaterial.
   It is some evidence for this that in films like *The Last Laugh*, *Pandora's Box*, *The Blue Angel*, and others made and seen in Germany of the 1920s, characters looked back in time of misery to days of power, prestige, or well-being, perhaps because makers and viewers, even if not in a fully conscious way, felt themselves to be in the same plight as members of a defeated nation on the skids of inflation. Kracauer CH has found in the "German collective soul" and allegorically echoed in the films of the time, a swinging to and fro between the chaos of "disorderly passions" and "unconditional submission to absolute authority" (pp. 86–87, 118) and other characteristics, but has been criticized by Manvell (pp. xiii, 15) for exaggerating, and by Barry Salt for ignoring large numbers of popular films that would not have supported his argument. See "From Caligari to Who?" *Sight and Sound* 48, no. 2 (Spring 1979): 122–23.
19. Boccaccio, p. 49.
20. Hayakawa, p. 127.
21. Ibid., pp. 165–72.
22. As T. S. Eliot has pointed out in "Hamlet," feeling must be expressed in art by means of things and events, chosen so aptly that when we sense them, the feeling intended is inevitably aroused, and he speaks of such things and events as the "objective correlatives" of the feelings (Eliot, p. 143).
23. Kuleshov stresses that a setting used merely to show place should be as sparse and unobtrusive as possible, for a viewer sees a shot for a brief time, during which his attention must be kept on what is essential, not caught by a plenitude of things (p. 74). He prefers in the foreground a large object, which, in itself, by metonymy, sufficiently suggests the whole setting of which it is part (p. 68).
   Lawren Harris's later paintings reduced landscapes to bold, austere patterns, void of detail, as may be seen by comparing his picture *Pic Island* with A. Y. Jackson's of the same name.
24. Korzybski, p. 290.
25. MacNeice, p. 15.
26. Nowottny, pp. 155–56, quoting from D. G. James where he speaks of the "muteness" to which poetry always aspires.
27. Korzybski, p. 22.
28. MacNeice, p. 95.
29. Bert Haanstra, *The Mirror of Holland*.
30. Boehme, p. 91.
31. Nock, p. xliii.
32. Grenfell, p. 38.

Glossary

To suggest what to look for in film, to talk about it when found, the viewer needs terms. For the viewer then, not for the filmmaker, who needs a larger number, the following terms have been chosen and explained. They are the smallest practicable number, for fluency with an esoteric vocabulary can take the place of sensitivity. Many of the words included are in fact familiar enough that the definitions are as much a prescription to myself as a help to the reader.

The meanings of the figures are given in the book itself and may be found by using the general index.

ANGLE. The direction the camera faces when shooting.

ANGLE, REVERSING THE. Changing the direction of the camera one hundred eighty degrees, often to show the face of someone of whom we saw the back in a former shot.

CUT. Where one shot follows another, with no bridging device like a wipe or dissolve.

DIEGESIS, DEIGETIC. The diegesis is the story the film is telling. A diegetic metaphor is one whose image is drawn from the setting or incidents of the story. A man's hat falls as he is killed, and its ceasing to move is a figure for its owner's death. The stone lions of Eisenstein were photographed some distance away from the scene of the action, as a commentary on it, and thus were nondiegetic. If, as we hear a siren, we see the blast of steam that is causing the sound, it is diegetic. If, like incidental music, it is not played by anyone seen in the film, it is nondiegetic.

DISSOLVE. A form of filmic punctuation in which a fade out that ends a shot is superimposed on a fade in that starts the next one. Two shots are seen at the same time.

FADE-OUT. A lessening in the clarity and brightness of a shot until the screen is black or otherwise blank.

FADE-IN. An oxymoronic expression, (by analogy to *fade-out*) for the growing in clarity and brightness of a shot, from a black or blank screen to full intensity.

FLASH. A piece of film so short as barely to be seen when projected. It may be as short as two frames. *An American Time Capsule* is said to use single frames.

FLASHBACK. The insertion in a narrative of an incident from a time anterior to it. Anamnesis.

FRAME. One of the series of pictures making up a shot. For the viewer this becomes the rectangular screen cut into the dark wall of the cinema, where, by persistence of vision, the individual frames lose their identity in giving the illusion of movement. In this book, therefore, the distinction between screen and frame is largely ignored.

FROZEN IMAGE. A metaphor for describing the effect of taking a single frame from a shot and repeating it. It is like isolating a cross section in time, and has the effect of a still photograph.

IMAGE. Used in this book only of a pattern projected on the screen. It is not used in the sense of trope or figure.

IRIS OUT. A kind of wipe that shrinks in from all sides of the frame in the shape of a circle. It usually stops before the frame is fully black to circle and emphasize a detail. After a pause long enough to focus our attention on it, the wipe is completed. Now, as a means of emphasis, it is largely replaced by approaching to a close-up.

IRIS IN. The reverse of IRIS OUT. A shot begins with a detail, seen through a disk that is cut in a black mask. After a pause the rim of the disk expands off the frame, to disclose the rest of the scene.

JUMP CUT. A cut from one shot to another, where, at the time, for a given viewer, there is no logical or narrative continuity.

MASK. A usually black wall or curtain concealing the image, with apertures of many shapes—disks, panels, keyholes—through which we observe part of a scene.

MULTIPLE FRAME OR IMAGE. A term used where more frames than one appear at the same time in the screen rectangle. The images are of necessity shrunk in size. The frames may be of any shape, and are usually cut in a mask. Where the size or shape of these frames changes during projection, this is called by Christopher Chapman "multiple dynamic image."

NEGATIVE IMAGE. As photographed on the negative, light things print dark and dark ones light. In the positive made from it, the original values return. For certain effects, the reversed negative light value is left unchanged in the final film.

PAN and STREAKING PAN. See Chapter 13, sections 9 and 14–20.

SHOT. A strip of film containing the frames for one continuous take of a scene.

Approaching, retreating shot—See Chapter 13, sections 9–12.

Down, up shot—Where the camera is directed at an angle, respectively below or above the horizontal.

Establishing shot—One taken from a sufficient distance to show the whole of a working area, of which other shots will show parts only.

Following, leading, sidling shots—See Chapter 13, sections 9 and 13.

Rising, sinking shot—Where the camera is moved vertically up or down while taking a shot.

NOTE: In terms of distance, the conventional filmmaker's terms, big close-up, close-up, medium, long, and so on, are vague for the viewer who wishes to describe or visualize a scene. In my own notes, I use numbers. For example 1 stands for a person exactly the height of a frame. In a 2 shot the person is twice the height of the frame, seen thus from the waist up or down. In a ½ shot the person is half the height of the frame, and so on. I have found that this allows precise description. To a director, however, a two-shot is one with two players, and a phrase that means two things would be confusing. If, as I had first intended, I had used the numbers in the book, it would have been one more set of terms for a reader to master. As I am resolved not to depart from plain English unless it is unavoidable, my 1-shot has therefore become a full-length, my 2-shot a half length, my 3-shot a head and shoulders shot, and my 4-shot, a close-up.

SIGNIFICANT OBJECT. *Image* or *symbol* may trail for some readers a net of theories or ambiguities (for some a symbol may require "motivated transcendance"). Things are sometimes used, besides being themselves, to carry a meaning, either by convention, as when a skull suggests death, or acquired in the course of a narrative, where a ring or a key, for example, seen early in the story, may be used later to convey someone's thoughts or a director's comments. These I prefer to call, not symbols but significant things.

SLOWED MOTION. When movement is recorded at more than twenty-four frames per second and projected at twenty-four, the effect is to slow the movement from what it actually was.

SPEEDED MOTION. When movement is recorded at fewer than twenty-four frames per second and projected at twenty-four, the effect is to speed the movement up from what it actually was.

SPLIT SCREEN. A form of multiple image, in which the screen is divided up between two or more shots, with no mask between them, the action in all continuing simultaneously.

SUPERIMPOSITION. The printing of a second transparent image on top of a first, which remains visible still through the second.

Index of Directors and Films

For certain identification of a film, title is not enough, since the same story may have have been filmed more than once. The director has therefore been given as well, for although the film is a collaborative art, a strong director, like Asquith or Eisenstein, Lang or Hitchcock, leaves a personal mark on many of the films he directs; and second, on the principle formerly applied in negligence cases, the director has the last chance to make or mar the content, and in many cases the editing, and thus must must be held finally responsible. To make finding a reference easy, directors' names are printed in roman capitals, and films in italics.

In this index the English title of the film is used, except in a few cases, where a film seems to be better known under its original one, perhaps because the film is little shown in English-speaking countries. Where a film is known by more than one title, the one used is either the original one (*Moscow Nights* instead of *I Stand Condemned*, or *Dangerous Moonlight* instead of *Suicide Squadron* or *Warsaw Concerto*), or the title that is better known (*Storm Over Asia* instead of *The Heir of Jenghiz Khan* or *Saps at Sea* instead of *Horn Hero*).

It is proper to express the gratitude of any writer on film to Kevin Brownlow, whose indefatigable searches have at last brought us a reasonably full reconstruction of *Napoleon*, and to the British Film Institute, which gave him the means of doing it. Before its recent release and the accompanying revival of other films of Gance, Brownlow's valuable biographical anthology, *Abel Gance: The Charm of Dynamite*, provided our only convenient access to Gance's work.

References to plates are printed in boldface.

The reader should bear in mind in looking up a page cited in the indexes, that in over a hundred instances there is more than one reference to the item he seeks on the page cited.

Index of Directors and Films

General Index

This index does not contain references to films discussed and the names of those who directed them, for which there is a separate index, nor to authors of books referred to, which may be found in the *Index of Books Cited*. However, references to directors, authors, or books which cannot be found by using the other indexes—a director's magazine writings, a poem whose author the reader may have forgotten, or the titles of plays—have been included. Important statements on film by a few writers such as Eisenstein, Arnheim, and Balazs have been indexed here by subject, even if the index of books might, though at some expense of time, lead the reader to them.

Magazine articles are indexed only by the publication in which they appeared, not by author or title, and a full list of the publications indexed will be found under the heading *Periodicals*.

Under the heading *Figures* will be found a full list of all the figures discussed, with brief reminders of their functions, and the placing of accents for those that may be unfamiliar.